AN INTRODUCTION TO
International
Relations

SECOND EDITION

Invaluable to students and those approaching the subject for the first time, *An Introduction to International Relations, Second Edition* provides a comprehensive and stimulating introduction to international relations, its traditions and its changing nature in an era of globalisation.

Thoroughly revised and updated, it features chapters written by a range of experts from around the world. It presents a global perspective on the theories, history, developments and debates that shape this dynamic discipline and contemporary world politics.

Now in full colour and accompanied by a password-protected companion website featuring additional chapters and case studies, this is the indispensible guide to the study of international relations.

- Includes contributions from leading experts and academics from across the globe, including Hidemi Suganami, Alex J. Bellamy, Peter Singer, J. Ann Tickner, Paul Sharp, Geoffrey Wiseman, Robyn Eckersley, David Kilcullen and Thomas G. Weiss.
- Features a companion website with additional chapters and case studies.
- Provides a wide-ranging, engaging and accessible introduction to International Relations.

Richard Devetak is Senior Lecturer in International Relations in the School of Political Science and International Studies at The University of Queensland.

Anthony Burke is Associate Professor in the School of Humanities and Social Sciences at the University of New South Wales, Canberra.

Jim George is Senior Lecturer in the School of Politics and International Relations at the Australian National University.

AN INTRODUCTION TO

International
Relations

SECOND EDITION

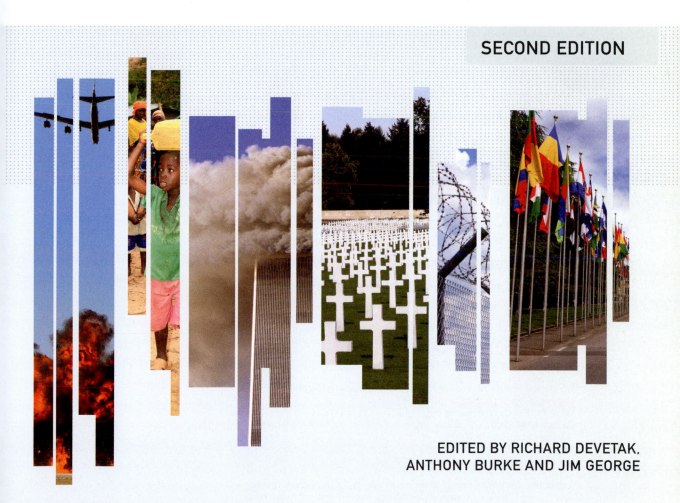

EDITED BY RICHARD DEVETAK,
ANTHONY BURKE AND JIM GEORGE

CAMBRIDGE
UNIVERSITY PRESS
www.cambridge.org

CAMBRIDGE UNIVERSITY PRESS
Cambridge, New York, Melbourne, Madrid, Cape Town,
Singapore, São Paulo, Delhi, Tokyo, Mexico City

Cambridge University Press
477 Williamstown Road, Port Melbourne, VIC 3207, Australia

Published in the United States of America by Cambridge University Press, New York

www.cambridge.org
Information on this title: www.cambridge.org/9781107600003

First published 2012

Cover and text design by Sardine Design
Typeset by Newgen Imaging Systems Pvt Ltd
Printed in Hong Kong by C&C Offset Printing Co.

A catalogue record for this publication is available from the British Library

National Library of Australia Cataloguing in Publication data
Devetak, Richard.
  An introduction to international relations / Richard Devetak, Anthony Burke, Jim George
  2nd ed.
  9781107600003 (pbk.)
  Includes bibliographical references and index.
  International relations.
  Australia—Foreign relations.
  Burke, Anthony, 1966–
  George, Jim, 1946–
  327.94

ISBN 978-1-107-60000-3 Paperback

Additional resources for this publication at www.cambridge.edu.au/academic/international

Reproduction and communication for educational purposes

The Australian *Copyright Act 1968* (the Act) allows a maximum of
one chapter or 10% of the pages of this work, whichever is the greater,
to be reproduced and/or communicated by any educational institution
for its educational purposes provided that the educational institution
(or the body that administers it) has given a remuneration notice to
Copyright Agency Limited (CAL) under the Act.

For details of the CAL licence for educational institutions contact:
Copyright Agency Limited
Level 15, 233 Castlereagh Street
Sydney NSW 2000
Telephone: (02) 9394 7600
Facsimile: (02) 9394 7601
E-mail: info@copyright.com.au

For Naomi, Chiara and Allegra

For Jenny, Nikos, Sophia

For Sara, Joanna and Pablo ... with love

FOREWORD

Gareth Evans

There is a certain piquancy in someone introducing a student textbook on international relations who has never formally studied the subject, and whose grasp of contemporary IR theory remains – as my academic colleagues gently tell me, and as my later comments may reveal – somewhat less than absolute. But after many years' immersion as a foreign minister, head of a major international conflict-prevention NGO, and participant in multiple global policy commissions and panels, I have learned something about the way the international relations world actually works. And let me tell you immediately: that world – of foreign minsters, diplomats, international organisations and conferences, civil society activism and think-tank policy debate – is important, fascinating, and intellectually stimulating, and you should plunge into the study of it with a real sense of excitement.

What is most exciting to me, and I hope will be to you, is appreciating that this is a world that can be very much influenced by good ideas, good policy, good understanding of the way organisations work, and – above all – by well-informed, energetic and creative professionals, of the kind that you will, hopefully, be helped to become by absorbing (and challenging where necessary!) the material in this admirably comprehensive book. We are not all prisoners of dark, inevitable forces that are bound to have their way whatever any of us try to do. Those of us who have spent most of our professional lives trying to rid the world of deadly conflict and weapons of mass destruction (what this book describes as the 'traditional agenda'), or to inch forward toward cooperative solutions to any of the globe's other most pressing problems (now recognised as the 'new agenda'), including environmental stress, poverty and inequality, drug and people trafficking, terrorism, gross and systematic human rights violations, and many more, are not all wasting our time.

There is some good evidence for this in the statistics that have accumulated since the end of the Cold War (mainly via the Human Security Report Project in Canada) about the dramatic decline – counter-intuitive though this may seem every time we watch or read a news bulletin – in both the number of wars and the casualties they generate. Over the last two decades, more old conflicts have ended than new ones have started. And major conflicts (those resulting in 1000 or more battle deaths a year) have declined by an extraordinary 80 per cent, as have the number of people being killed by them. There are a number of explanations, but the best is simply the huge upsurge in activity in mediation, negotiation, peacekeeping and post-conflict peace-building activity that has occurred, particularly since the mid 1990s, with significant roles being played by regional organisations, certain individual states, major NGOs and the UN itself – all involving deeply committed people doing tough jobs in tough situations.

If individuals matter, so do ideas. One should never lose sight of, or confidence in, their transformative power to change for the better the way the world both thinks and acts. One of the most important to emerge in recent years – in response to the orgies of hate-fed killing and maiming that destroyed the lives and futures of so many hundreds of thousands in the 1990s in Rwanda, Bosnia and elsewhere – is that of the international community's 'responsibility to protect' populations at risk from genocide and other mass atrocity crimes. Cutting across the centuries-old notion that state sovereignty was all about immunity from external scrutiny and interference was never going to be easy, and challenges still remain to translate rhetoric into effective action in every case where this becomes necessary. But since the UN General Assembly unanimously embraced the new principle in 2005, it has been steadily gaining traction, and does hold out the hope that never again will we have to say 'never again' to another Srbrenica, Cambodia or Holocaust. And that is just one of the many ideas discussed in this book currently impacting on international debate.

Much of the study of international relations involves trying to understand, intellectually, the currents that underlie and explain decision-making and action, and the mindsets and perspectives that policymakers and those who influence them bring to bear. Practitioners like me who have seen over the years, situation by situation, the variable impact of quite different factors – sometimes of ideas, ideals and norms; sometimes of genuine instinct to cooperate for the common good; sometimes of crude, hard-nosed *Realpolitik* – tend to find it difficult to identify wholeheartedly with realism, liberalism, constructivism, or any of the innumerable other particular theories that all have distinguished adherents. Perhaps we will just have to find solace in 'analytical eclecticism', that recently identified new approach which seems eminently capable of accommodating, no doubt among others more respectable, the intellectually undisciplined and disreputable.

Whether one is wrestling with the nuts and bolts of practical policymaking – across both the traditional and new agendas – or the higher abstractions of IR theory, the study of international relations is engaging and challenging. There is a whole smorgasbord of issues and approaches laid out here for you to sample in this book, all written by experts in their field, many of them world-renowned. You should find working through it fascinating and stimulating. And you should come away from it much better equipped than I ever was at the start of my career to make a contribution of your own to making this tumultuous world of ours a little safer and saner.

8 March 2011

Gareth Evans is Professorial Fellow at the University of Melbourne and Chancellor of the Australian National University, and President Emeritus of the International Crisis Group, the independent global conflict prevention and resolution organisation which he led from 2000 to 2009. He was Australia's Minister for Foreign Affairs from 1988 to 1996, and co-chair of the International Commission on Intervention and State Sovereignty, which published the *Responsibility to protect* report in 2004, and of the International Commission on Nuclear Non-Proliferation and Disarmament, whose report *Eliminating nuclear threats* was published in December 2009.

CONTENTS

Foreword   vii
Tables, figures and boxes   xix
Contributors   xxv
Preface and Acknowledgements   xxix

**An introduction to International Relations: the origins and changing
agendas of a discipline**   1
  Richard Devetak

Introduction   1
What is International Relations?   1
International Relations as a discipline: traditions, origins and evolution   4
Changing agendas: theory and practice   12
Conclusion   18
Questions   18
Further reading   18

Part 1: Theories of International Relations   21

1   International Relations Theory in an Age of Critical Diversity   22
  Jim George

Introduction   23
The necessity of theory   23
Ontology, epistemology and the science question in international relations
    theory   24
Mainstream international relations theory   26
The era of critical diversity   29
Conclusion   33
Questions   34
Further reading   34

2   Realism   35
  Michele Chiaruzzi

Introduction   36
Who are the realists? Genesis of a tradition of thought   37
What is realism? Synthesising theory and practice   43
Conclusion   46
Questions   47
Further reading   47

3   Liberalism   48
  James L. Richardson

Introduction   49
Liberalism   49
The historical–political context   49
Contemporary liberal IR theory   54

Conclusion   59
Questions   60
Further reading   60

4 Marxism and Critical Theory   62
Richard Devetak, Jim George and Martin Weber

Introduction   63
Historical and intellectual context: Marx and the critique of capitalism   63
Marxism as historical materialism   65
Marx and Marxism in IR   67
Critical Theories of IR   68
Conclusion   74
Questions   75
Further reading   75

5 Feminism   76
Katrina Lee-Koo

Introduction   77
International relations meets feminism   77
The feminist IR agenda   77
Tracing feminist international relations: challenging the masculine bias   79
Where are the women?   80
Reconstructing international relations: examining the differences between
    sex and gender   81
J. Ann Tickner: Progress towards gender equality in the academy and the
    policy world   82
Men have genders too!   84
Feminist theories of international relations   86
Conclusion: what does feminism add to our study of international relations?   89
Questions   90
Further reading   90

6 Postmodernism   91
Roland Bleiker

Introduction   92
Postmodernity as a new historical period   92
Postmodernism as a critical way of understanding modernity   93
The emergence of the third debate in IR scholarship   97
The polemical nature of debates about postmodernism   99
Conclusion   100
Questions   101
Further reading   102

7 Constructivism   103
Patrick Thaddeus Jackson and Joshua S. Jones

Introduction   104
What does constructivism do? Identity and international institutions   104
Neta C. Crawford: Norms and violence   109
Constructivism's understanding of change in the international system   111
Conclusion   118

Questions   118
Further reading   118

8 Theories of Global Justice   **119**
Richard Shapcott

Introduction   120
Justice and international relations   120
Why justice is global   121
What is a just global order?   126
Peter Singer: Global ethics   127
Conclusion   130
Questions   131
Further reading   131

Part 2: The Traditional Agenda: States, War and Law   **133**

9 The Modern State   **134**
Richard Devetak

Introduction   135
What is a state?   135
Origins of the modern state   137
The idea of the sovereign state   138
The triumph of the sovereign state: state-building as war making   142
Whither the sovereign state?   145
Conclusion   146
Questions   146
Further reading   147

10 Nations and Nationalism   **148**
Gavin Mount

Introduction   149
Terminological debates   149
How nationalism shaped modern states and international society   152
Understanding nations and nationalism in IR   155
Appeals to 'the people' in the New World Order   157
Conclusion   158
Questions   159
Further reading   159

11 Security   **160**
Anthony Burke

Introduction   161
Four crises   161
Defining security   163
Key theories and concepts   163
Conclusion   170
Questions   170
Further reading   170

12 Arms Control · 172
Marianne Hanson

Introduction	173
What is arms control?	173
Why do states engage in arms control practices?	174
Cold War arms control	174
Why is arms control still important in the post-Cold War period?	175
New initiatives in arms control: small arms and conventional weapons	179
Arms control and international relations theory	181
Nuclear weapons: a special case?	182
Sergio Duarte: Disarmament and international security	183
Initiatives to strengthen the nuclear non-proliferation regime	186
Conclusion	187
Questions	187
Further reading	187

13 The Causes of War · 189
Hidemi Suganami

Introduction	190
War, sovereignty and sociability	191
Necessary causes of war?	193
Regular causal paths to war?	194
Contributory causes of war	194
Conclusion	197
Questions	198
Further reading	198

14 The Changing Character of Warfare · 199
Robert Ayson

Introduction	200
The diversity of warfare	200
Sebastian Kaempf: Digital battlespaces and virtual media wars	202
War as *violence*	204
War as *organised* violence	206
War and *politics*	208
War as a case of *between*	210
War as *large-scale*	211
David Kilcullen: Contemporary war	212
Conclusion	215
Questions	215
Further reading	216

15 The Ethics and Laws of War · 218
Alex J. Bellamy

Introduction	219
When is it right to fight? (*jus ad bellum*)	219
How should war be waged? (*jus in bello*)	222
Jus ad bellum dilemma: preemptive self-defence	225

Jus in bello dilemma: cluster bombs 227
Conclusion 229
Questions 229
Further reading 230

16 International Law — 231
Donald R. Rothwell

Introduction 232
Contemporary development of international law 233
Institutions 233
Sources of international law 234
Major areas of international law 238
Contemporary controversies 240
Conclusion 241
Questions 241
Further reading 242

17 International Society and European Expansion — 243
Paul Keal

Introduction 244
International society 244
The nature of international society 246
The limits of international society 249
European expansion 250
Conclusion 254
Questions 255
Further reading 255

18 Diplomacy — 256
Geoffrey Wiseman and Paul Sharp

Introduction 257
Defining diplomacy: what is diplomacy and who are the diplomats? ... 257
The evolution of diplomacy 258
Trends 264
Diplomacy and the study of IR 265
Conclusion 266
Questions 267
Further reading 267

19 Great Powers — 268
Marco Cesa

Introduction 269
What is a great power? 269
The great powers in historical perspective 271
The great powers in the theory of international relations 273
The great powers after the Cold War 276
Conclusion 278
Questions 279
Further reading 279

20 The Cold War 281

Nick Bisley

Introduction	282
The beginnings of the Cold War: 1945–53	282
The Cold War spreads: 1953–69	286
Détente and the 'second' Cold War: 1969–85	287
The end of the Cold War: 1985–91	288
The Cold War and International Relations	290
Conclusion: echoes of the Cold War	291
Questions	293
Further reading	293

Part 3: The New Agenda: Globalisation and Global Governance 295

21 The United Nations 296

Ian Hurd

Introduction	297
The UN in the Charter	297
The UN's principal organs	299
The UN as actor, forum and resource	304
Conclusion	308
Questions	309
Further reading	309

22 Non-State Actors: Multinational Corporations and International Non-Governmental Organisations 310

James Goodman

Introduction	311
MNCs: transnationalised material power	311
INGOs: transnationalised normative power	316
Conclusion	320
Questions	321
Further reading	321

23 Religion and Secularism 322

Elizabeth Shakman Hurd

Introduction	323
Religion and international relations	323
History of a concept: secularism	325
Secularism and world politics	326
The politics of secularism in the Middle East and North Africa	329
Conclusion	333
Questions	334
Further reading	334

24 Global Economic Institutions 336

Marc Williams

Introduction	337
Global governance and the global economy	337

Global economic institutions and the management of the global economy   340
Legitimacy, democracy and global economic institutions   345
Conclusion   347
Questions   347
Further reading   347

25 Global Trade   348
Maryanne Kelton

Introduction   349
Free trade and the international trading system   350
An imperfect system   352
Preferential trade arrangements   354
Reform of the trading system?   355
The Global Financial Crisis and trade   356
Prospects for recovery   357
Conclusion: systemic recovery and reform   358
Questions   359
Further reading   359

26 Global Finance   360
Leonard Seabrooke

Introduction   361
Death of the last great financial globalisation, 1900–45   362
The rise and fall of the Bretton Woods system, 1946–71   363
Domestic stagflation and international over-lending, 1972–81   364
Debt crises at home and abroad, 1982–92   365
Talking about architecture, 1993–2000   366
Promises, promises: credit booms and liquidity busts, 2001 to the present   368
Conclusion: how should we study global finance?   369
Questions   370
Further reading   370

27 Global Poverty, Inequality and Development   372
Heloise Weber and Mark T. Berger

Introduction   373
Background to understanding poverty and inequality   373
A relational approach to global poverty, inequality and development   376
From the Washington Consensus to the Millennium Development Goals   379
Perspectives on the Millennium Development Goals and global poverty   381
Conclusion   384
Questions   384
Further reading   385

28 Globalisation and Its Critics   386
Steven Slaughter

Introduction   387
Understanding globalisation   387
The anti-capitalist movement   392
Scholarly critiques of globalisation   396
Conclusion   397

Questions 397
Further reading 397

29 Global Terrorism 398
David Wright-Neville

Introduction 399
What is terrorism? 399
Some secondary warnings for the unaware 401
Contemporary terrorism in context 403
The globalisation of terrorism 406
Some final misperceptions 409
Conclusion 410
Questions 412
Further reading 412

30 Post-Conflict State-Building 414
Beth K. Greener

Introduction 415
The rise of post-conflict state-building 415
The post-conflict state-building agenda 418
The politics of contemporary post-conflict state-building 419
Critics of the current agenda 420
Impacts of post-conflict state-building 422
The future of post-conflict state-building? 422
Conclusion 424
Questions 424
Further reading 425

31 Humanitarian Intervention 426
Thomas G. Weiss

Introduction 427
The origins of humanitarianism 427
A short history of humanitarian intervention 431
The responsibility to protect 433
Noel Morada: Responsibility to protect (R2P) and prevention of mass atrocities 435
Conclusion 438
Questions 438
Further reading 439

32 Human Rights 440
Anthony J. Langlois

Introduction 441
The historical development of an idea 442
The human rights idea today 444
The politics of liberal universalism 445
The future of human rights 447
Conclusion 449
Questions 449
Further reading 449

33 Migration and Refugees 450
Sara E. Davies

Introduction 451
States, refugees and immigrants 451
Controlling migration: a brief history 451
The origins and purposes of refugee law 453
The distribution of refugees around the world 455
The present situation 458
Conclusion 460
Questions 460
Further reading 461

34 Global Environmental Politics 462
Robyn Eckersley

Introduction 463
The rise of the environment as a global political problem 464
The post-Cold War context 466
Theories of global environmental politics 469
The US as the reluctant environmental state 471
Conclusion 473
Questions 473
Further reading 474

35 Climate Change 475
Peter Newell

Introduction 476
A brief history of climate change politics 477
Explaining the global politics of climate change 482
Conclusion 484
Questions 485
Further reading 485

Glossary of Terms 487
Bibliography 502
Index 542

TABLES, FIGURES AND BOXES

Tables

0.1	The 'Great Divide'	4
0.2	Realism and liberalism compared	7
1.1	Mainstream IR theories	29
1.2	Critical IR theories	33
4.1	Knowledge and interests	70
7.1	Three cultures of anarchy	107
12.1	Major arms agreements reached since 1990	178
19.1	The great powers in 2010	277
29.1	Recent trends in terrorist violence	412
33.1	Persons of concern to UNHCR – by region	457

Figures

0.1	*Graffiti*, Sarajevo 2005, by David Kozar	2
0.2	Anti-government demonstrations during the 2010–11 Tunisian uprising	17
3.1	Mary Wollstonecraft – engraving by James Heath from a painting by John Opie	51
3.2	Portrait of John Stuart Mill	52
4.1	Karl Marx, 1867	64
4.2	Antonio Gramsci in 1915	72
4.3	Cox's dialectic of hegemonic forces	74
5.1	The gendered politics of war: front cover image from *The Queenslander*'s Christmas supplement, 1915	85
5.2	*Coffin grief, Srebrenica*, by David Kozar	85
6.1	Friedrich Nietzsche, 1882, by Gustave Schultze	96
9.1	Frontispiece of Hobbes's *Leviathan*, 1651	140
12.1	Soviet General Secretary Gorbachev and US President Reagan signing the INF Treaty at the White House, December 1987	175
12.2	Estimated nuclear weapons stockpiles	177
12.3	Nuclear weapon test Romeo on Bikini Atoll, March 1954	186
14.1	The diversity of war – child soldier in the Congo, by Rivkah Larkin	201
14.2	An F-20 fighter aircraft firing an air-to-ground missile	201
14.3	Wars since 1990	217
15.1	*White house*, Omarska, by David Kozar	222
19.1	US President Obama in discussion aboard *Air Force One*, June 2009	278
20.1	Allied leaders Winston Churchill (UK), Franklin D. Roosevelt (US) and Joseph Stalin (USSR) at the Yalta Conference, February 1945	283
20.2	The Cold War: NATO and Warsaw Pact countries (1949–89)	285

25.1	The great trade collapses in historical perspective, 1965–2009	356
25.2	The volume of world trade, now vs then	357
27.1	Slums built on swamp land near a garbage dump in East Cipinang, Jakarta, Indonesia	374
29.1	Members of the National Guard at the World Trade Center, New York, 19 September 2001	408
30.1	US Defense Secretary Robert M. Gates boards a UH-60 Blackhawk on Camp Montieth, Kosovo, 7 October 2008	417
31.1	UN chopper	430
33.1	UN refugee tents	458

Boxes

0.1	Terminology: What are the differences between International Relations and international relations, and international politics and world politics?	3
0.2	Discussion points: A divided discipline?	5
0.3	Discussion points: Was Thucydides a realist?	9
1.1	Terminology: Key terms in the philosophy of science	24
1.2	Terminology: Positivism and scientific IR	25
2.1	Terminology: Hobbes's 'state of nature'	38
2.2	Discussion points: Hans J. Morgenthau's six principles of political realism	40
2.3	Terminology: Waltz's theory of international politics: key terms	41
2.4	Discussion points: Realism's political morality	45
2.5	Case study: Realism and the Iraq War	46
3.1	Discussion points: Early liberal thought	50
3.2	Discussion points: John Stuart Mill, from *On liberty* ([1859] 1983)	52
3.3	Discussion points: Liberal legacies?	55
3.4	Discussion points: Neoliberal institutionalism and neorealism: what's the difference?	55
4.1	Discussion points: Key features of Marx's theoretical framework	65
4.2	Terminology: Cox on critical and problem-solving theories	69
4.3	Discussion points: Kant, Habermas and Linklater on normative justification	71
5.1	Discussion points: The feminist international relations agenda	77
5.2	Discussion points: The goals of feminist international relations theory	79
5.3	Terminology: Feminist theories of international relations	86
6.1	Key figures: Friedrich Nietzsche: the 'postmodern' philosopher	95
6.2	Discussion points: The politics of representation I: René Magritte's 'This is not a pipe'	97
6.3	Discussion points: The politics of representation II: Remembering and forgetting	98

7.1	Case study: 'Anarchy is what states make of it'	106
7.2	Terminology: John R. Searle on facts and rules	112
8.1	Discussion points: John Rawls on justice	121
8.2	Discussion points: Charles Beitz on impartiality	123
8.3	Discussion points: Rawls's social contract: the original position	124
8.4	Discussion points: Pogge on how societies impact on outsiders	125
8.5	Discussion points: States as 'good international citizens'	129
9.1	Terminology: The state, the modern state, and sovereignty	135
9.2	Discussion points: When a state is not a state	136
9.3	Discussion points: Sovereignty versus international law	142
9.4	Discussion points: Declarations of independence: the birth of new states	144
10.1	Terminology: Nations and nationalism	150
10.2	Discussion points: The modernity of nations? Three schools of thought	152
10.3	Discussion points: American and French revolutions	153
11.1	Key texts: Preamble to the UN Charter	165
11.2	Discussion points: Global security and nuclear fears	166
11.3	Key texts: 'Sex and death in the rational world of defense intellectuals'	169
12.1	Terminology: Small arms and light weapons	180
13.1	Discussion points: Self-defence, preemptive strikes and preventive wars	192
13.2	Discussion points: Three kinds of contributory causes concerning war	195
14.1	Key figures: Carl von Clausewitz	205
14.2	Key figures: Martin van Creveld	207
14.3	Key figures: Thomas Schelling	210
15.1	Terminology: *Jus ad bellum* criteria	221
15.2	Key texts: International humanitarian law: some important documents	223
15.3	Case study: The *Caroline* affair	226
16.1	Key texts: Statute of the International Court of Justice	235
16.2	Terminology: Titles given to treaties	236
16.3	Discussion points: Non-legally binding international instruments	238
17.1	Discussion points: The English School	244
17.2	Discussion points: R. J. Vincent on egg boxes	246
17.3	Terminology: Hedley Bull on system and society	247
17.4	Discussion points: Racial hierarchy and dispossession of Australian Aboriginal peoples	251
17.5	Terminology: The 'standard of civilisation'	251
18.1	Terminology: Some definitions of diplomacy	257
18.2	Discussion points: George Kennan's view of the emerging bipolar Cold War	261

18.3	Discussion points: Proliferation of sovereign states	261
18.4	Key texts: The 1961 Vienna Convention: functions of a diplomatic mission	262
18.5	Key texts: The 1961 Vienna Convention: diplomatic immunity	262
19.1	Discussion points: Ranke on the rise of the great powers in Europe	272
19.2	Discussion points: Different views on the great powers in the Concert of Europe	273
20.1	Terminology: Cold War: meanings and temperature	282
20.2	Discussion points: Containment and George Kennan	283
20.3	Discussion points: The arms race	287
20.4	Key figures: Mikhail Sergeevich Gorbachev	289
20.5	Discussion points: A new European map	290
21.1	Key texts: UN Charter: ECOSOC	299
21.2	Key texts: UN Charter: the International Court of Justice	299
21.3	Key texts: UN Charter: the Trusteeship Council	300
21.4	Key texts: UN Charter: the Security Council	301
21.5	Key actors: The P5: permanent members of the UN Security Council	302
21.6	Key texts: UN Charter: the General Assembly	303
21.7	Key texts: UN Charter: the Secretariat	307
22.1	Discussion points: MNCs and tax avoidance	313
22.2	Discussion points: Investment protection and corporate–state litigation	315
22.3	Discussion points: UN – INGOs 'catalyse change'	318
23.1	Terminology: Key concepts	325
23.2	Discussion points: Religious – secular	327
23.3	Discussion points: Popular revolutions 2011	333
24.1	Terminology: The Washington Consensus	339
24.2	Terminology: Structural adjustment policies	342
24.3	Discussion points: The Millennium Development Goals	343
24.4	Key figures: Membership of the GEIs	345
25.1	Terminology: Key global trade terms	349
25.2	Discussion points: Agricultural trading reform and the Cairns Group	355
26.1	Key organisations: Key international regimes for global finance	361
26.2	Terminology: Disintermediation and securitisation	366
27.1	Terminology: Poverty	375
27.2	Terminology: Modernisation theory	376
27.3	Case study: Narmada Valley dam, India	377
27.4	Discussion points: Dimensions of poverty and inequality	378
27.5	Terminology: Dependency theory	379
28.1	Terminology: Three explanations of globalisation	387
28.2	Discussion points: Timeline of the 'G' system of forums	391
28.3	Discussion points: A brief timeline of the global anti-capitalist movement	393

28.4	Discussion points: World Social Forum attendance at a glance	394
29.1	Case study: The first terrorists?	402
29.2	Discussion points: Some recent terrorist plots	404
29.3	Discussion points: US President Barack Obama on the terrorist threat	411
30.1	Case study: Post-war state-building in Japan	415
30.2	Case study: Post-conflict state-building in Kosovo	416
30.3	Case study: Regional assistance to the Solomon Islands	419
30.4	Discussion points: *OECD Principles for Good International Engagement in Fragile States*	423
31.1	Key texts: Extracts from Henry Dunant's *Memory of Solferino* ([1862] 1986)	428
31.2	Key texts: The ICRC's Mission Statement	429
31.3	Key texts: Chapter VII of the UN Charter	432
31.4	Key texts: *The responsibility to protect: Report of the International Commission on Intervention and State Sovereignty* (2001)	433
32.1	Discussion points: Key human rights instruments of the UN	442
32.2	Discussion points: Three generations of rights	445
32.3	Discussion points: Asian values	447
32.4	Discussion points: Human rights promotion: difficult cases	448
33.1	Terminology: Migrants and refugees	452
33.2	Terminology: Definitions of a refugee according to international law	453
33.3	Key texts: Important articles in the 1951 Convention relating to the Status of Refugees	454
34.1	Key texts: Where can I find published research on global environmental politics?	464
35.1	Terminology: What is climate change?	476
35.2	Discussion points: The global governance of climate change: a short chronology	477
35.3	Key texts: The Kyoto Protocol in brief	479

CONTRIBUTORS

Robert Ayson is Professor in the Centre for Strategic Studies at Victoria University of Wellington.

Alex J. Bellamy is Professor of International Security in the Griffith Asia Institute and Centre for Governance and Public Policy at Griffith University.

Mark T. Berger is Professor in the Department of Defense Analysis at the Naval Postgraduate School, Monterey.

Nick Bisley is Professor in the Politics and International Relations Program at La Trobe University.

Roland Bleiker is Professor in the School of Political Science and International Studies at the University of Queensland.

Anthony Burke is Associate Professor in the School of Humanities and Social Sciences at the University of New South Wales, Canberra.

Marco Cesa is Professor of International Relations in the Paul H. Nitze School of Advanced International Studies at Johns Hopkins University, Bologna; and in the Dipartimento di Politica, Istituzioni, Storia at the University of Bologna.

Michele Chiaruzzi is Lecturer in International Relations in the Dipartimento di Politica, Istituzioni, Storia at the University of Bologna.

Neta C. Crawford is Professor of Political Science and African American Studies at Boston University.

Sara E. Davies is Senior Research Fellow in the Griffith Asia Institute and Centre for Governance and Public Policy at Griffith University.

Richard Devetak is Senior Lecturer in International Relations in the School of Political Science and International Studies at the University of Queensland.

Sergio Duarte is the United Nations High Representative for Disarmament.

Robyn Eckersley is Professor in the School of Social and Political Sciences at the University of Melbourne.

Gareth Evans is Professorial Fellow at the University of Melbourne and Chancellor of the Australian National University.

Jim George is Senior Lecturer in International Relations in the School of Politics and International Relations at the Australian National University.

James Goodman is Associate Professor in the Faculty of Arts and Social Sciences at the University of Technology, Sydney.

Beth K. Greener is Senior Lecturer in the Politics Programme at Massey University.

Marianne Hanson is Associate Professor in the School of Political Science and International Studies at the University of Queensland.

Elizabeth Shakman Hurd is Assistant Professor in the Department of Political Science at Northwestern University.

Ian Hurd is Associate Professor in the Department of Political Science at Northwestern University.

Patrick Thaddeus Jackson is Associate Professor in the School of International Service at the American University.

Joshua S. Jones is Adjunct Instructor in the School of International Service at the American University.

Sebastian Kaempf is Lecturer in Peace and Conflict Studies at the School of Political Science and International Studies at the University of Queensland.

Paul Keal is Adjunct Senior Fellow in the Department of International Relations, School of International, Political and Strategic Studies at the Australian National University.

Maryanne Kelton is Senior Lecturer in the School of International Studies at Flinders University.

David Kilcullen is an author and consultant on counter-insurgency and counter-terrorism and CEO of Caerus Associates.

Anthony J. Langlois is Associate Professor of International Relations in the School of International Studies at Flinders University.

Katrina Lee-Koo is Senior Lecturer in International Relations in the School of Politics and International Relations at the Australian National University.

Noel Morada is Executive Director of the Asia-Pacific Centre for the Responsibility to Protect at the University of Queensland.

Gavin Mount is Lecturer in Global Politics in the School of Humanities and Social Sciences at the Australian Defence Force Academy, University of New South Wales.

Peter Newell is Professor of International Relations at the University of Sussex.

James L. Richardson was Professor in the Department of International Relations at the Australian National University.

Donald R. Rothwell is Professor of International Law in the ANU College of Law at the Australian National University.

Leonard Seabrooke is Professor in the International Centre for Business and Politics at the Copenhagen Business School.

Paul Sharp is Professor in the Department of Political Science at the University of Minnesota Duluth.

Richard Shapcott is Senior Lecturer in the School of Political Science and International Studies at the University of Queensland.

Peter Singer is the Ira W. DeCamp Professor of Bioethics at Princeton University and Laureate Professor at the University of Melbourne.

Steven Slaughter is Senior Lecturer in International Relations in the School of International and Political Studies at Deakin University.

Hidemi Suganami is Professor of International Politics in the Department of International Politics at Aberystwyth University, Wales.

J. Ann Tickner is Professor of International Relations at the University of Southern California.

Heloise Weber is Senior Lecturer in the School of Political Science and International Studies at the University of Queensland.

Martin Weber is Senior Lecturer in the School of Political Science and International Studies at the University of Queensland.

Thomas G. Weiss is Presidential Professor of Political Science and Director of the Ralph Bunche Institute for International Studies at The City University of New York's Graduate Center.

Marc Williams is Professor in the School of Social Sciences and International Studies at the University of New South Wales.

Geoffrey Wiseman is Professor of the Practice of International Relations in the School of International Relations at the University of Southern California.

David Wright-Neville is Director of Domestic and International Risk Analysis at Globe Communications.

PREFACE AND ACKNOWLEDGEMENTS

This textbook is designed specifically for students studying Introduction to International Relations courses. The success of the first edition, followed by encouraging reviews and conversations with overseas colleagues, led us to prepare a second edition aimed specifically at an international audience. The text has been enlarged and substantially revised with this in mind, and includes new authors from the US and Europe. Where the first edition of this book drew largely upon scholars teaching and researching in Australia, or Australian scholars overseas, for this edition a broad range of new contributors has written on topics previously covered and on new topics, while previous contributors have made updates and revisions to all the remaining chapters. Much of the material excised from the first edition is now available on the new companion website – an important supplement to this book's second edition.

Like any good textbook, this one aims to introduce students to the study of International Relations (IR) by laying out its chief theories, main actors and institutions, and leading issues, in a manner that both excites interest and lucidly explains topics for students with no previous background in IR. Carving up the topics of a complex, dynamic, growing discipline like IR is no easy task. Decisions must inevitably be made about which topics to include, and which to exclude. Topics chosen no doubt reflect but one particular perspective of the discipline's present make-up, one account of what is important for students to learn, and what is not. Since there is no single correct way to present the material to undergraduate students, there is always a degree of arbitrariness involved in topic selection; and we do not pretend otherwise. However, we believe that the structure adopted here, developed over years of teaching undergraduate Introduction to IR courses in Australia and the UK, offers one useful way into the wide range of fascinating topics that fall under the heading International Relations.

The textbook is divided into three parts: Part 1 on theories of IR; Part 2 on what we call the 'traditional agenda' of IR, which focuses on states, war and law; and Part 3 on the 'new agenda' which focuses on globalisation and global governance. These are more fully explicated in the Introduction. But it is worth emphasising that the new agenda does not succeed the traditional agenda in either time or intellectual resourcefulness. The distinction between traditional and new agendas is a heuristic device meant to remind students that the discipline has evolved and changed, and to encourage reflection on the discipline's historical character. Quite often textbooks imply that our present conception of the discipline represents something like the endpoint in the discipline's ineluctable progression from primitive origins to full development. This conceit is easy to succumb to in the absence of historical-mindedness. We hope that a greater appreciation of the past, including the discipline's past, will enable students to gain a better understanding of how the discipline has come to assume its present historical form. This should also encourage students to reflect more deeply on the sources of the tensions, debates and disagreements that shape IR and make it one of the most intellectually exciting disciplines in the human and social sciences today.

There are a number of people we need to thank. A handful of people were directly and actively instrumental in the production of this textbook. First, we would like to thank the contributors who gave their time and effort to this textbook. A special thank you must go to the new contributors, some of whom came on board at late notice. All the new contributors are internationally recognised and greatly enhance the textbook's quality and global relevance.

Second, we owe a large debt of gratitude to Kim Armitage at Cambridge University Press, Melbourne, who has supported this second edition, just as she did the first, from its inception to its realisation, with great enthusiasm and sustained drive. She also diligently helped in conceiving the textbook's format and ensuring it would meet students' needs most effectively. We thank her for wholeheartedly embracing the second edition's ambition to reach students across the globe. Thank you also to Isabella Mead at the Press for her great assistance along the way. Many thanks must also go to Kath Harper whose great efficiency, precision and eye for detail helped to root out numerous discrepancies and omissions in the manuscript.

Third, we must also thank Katie Linnane for her tremendous assistance in preparing the manuscript. She worked promptly, efficiently, carefully and cheerfully on the entire manuscript, helping tidy and format chapters, compile the Bibliography, and construct the Table of Contents.

Fourth, we would like to thank Jelena Subotic of Georgia State University who provided very helpful feedback on our proposed changes for this second edition. Her suggestions helped us understand some of the differences between the ways IR is taught in Australia and the UK on the one hand, and the US on the other.

There is a collection of other people we would like to thank also. They may not have had a direct hand in the textbook, but indirectly they have contributed to it. First of all, our teachers, without whom we would not ourselves be teaching, let alone editing textbooks for future generations of students. Richard would like to acknowledge, once again, his enduring debt of gratitude to Andrew Linklater, Peter Lawler and Hidemi Suganami. They will, he hopes, see the mark their inspirational examples have left on him in the chapters he has contributed to the textbook. He would also like to thank his co-editors, Tony and Jim, for their readiness to take on this ambitious project and make it work so well, and for their good judgment and friendship. It was a pleasure to work with them once again. Anthony thanks Caroline Graham, Jim George, Mike McKinley, Jindy Pettman, Lorraine Elliott, Graeme Cheeseman, Greg Austin, Bill Tow, Greg McCarthy, Pal Ahluwalia, Paul Nursey-Bray, Carol Johnson and Christine Beasley, who taught him to understand and care about global politics, and who helped him immeasurably as he first began to teach it. Jim remembers with gratitude the inspiration offered both directly and indirectly by Ian Clark, Richard Higgott, Andrew Linklater and Jim Richardson.

We must also thank our students. Students of Introduction to International Relations courses at the Australian National University, Monash University, and the universities of Adelaide, New South Wales and Queensland, where we have taught in recent years, have all contributed to this textbook. It is they who make the teaching so enjoyable by their intellectual curiosity and thirst for learning.

Finally, we would like to thank friends and family who have had to suffer our distraction as we wrestled this textbook into submission. Richard would like to register the unpayable debt he owes to his wife Naomi and daughters Chiara and Allegra for their tolerance, patience and forgiveness, especially in the final stages of the manuscript's preparation. Anthony thanks his wife Jenny, who was ever supportive even as she chided him gently for taking on too much, and dedicates the book to her and his young twins, Nikos and Sophia, who hopefully will grow into a less troubled world than they were born into. Jim wants to thank Joanna, in particular, for her love and support when it was needed most.

Richard Devetak, Anthony Burke, Jim George

Brisbane and Canberra

March 2011

AN INTRODUCTION TO INTERNATIONAL RELATIONS: THE ORIGINS AND CHANGING AGENDAS OF A DISCIPLINE

Richard Devetak

Introduction

This Introduction begins by outlining what is meant by international relations. Second, it tells the story of how and why the study of international relations emerged when it did in the early twentieth century. Knowing something about the **discipline**'s origins does not tell us everything we need to know about international relations today, but it will help us to understand the legacy left by the discipline's original purpose and by older traditions of thought. Third, it sketches the contours of the changing agenda of international relations, a shift that some scholars describe as a transition from international relations to world politics or from the 'traditional' to the 'new' agenda. Although there can be little doubt that as political reality has changed new theoretical and conceptual tools have become necessary to grasp it, we should not assume that the myriad changes to our world have rendered the 'traditional' agenda and its theories obsolete. Far from it; the 'new' agenda, as we shall see, supplements but does not supplant the 'traditional' agenda. It is now more important than ever to consider the relationships between 'traditional' and 'new' theories and issues. This textbook is intended to help you think about these relationships.

What is International Relations?

Every day the global news media carry stories of events involving foreign governments and their populations. Usually featured under the heading of 'international affairs' or 'world news', these stories all too frequently tell of political violence, lives and livelihoods lost, **human rights** violated, infrastructure damaged, and hopes for the restoration of **peace** and prosperity dashed. **War** rather than peace makes the news headlines, and understandably so, because the violent conflict of war so visibly ravages human societies. 'If it bleeds, it leads', as the cynical media adage goes.

For over 2000 years of recorded history humans have been fascinated and frustrated by war and its consequences, so we should not be surprised by its continuing preeminence. But human societies are harmed by so much more than war. Chronic underdevelopment, poverty, human rights violations, environmental degradation and climate change are no less harmful, if less visible. Occasionally, however, the plight of the world's impoverished populations becomes headline news when famines occur or natural disasters such as droughts, earthquakes, floods, tsunamis or avalanches strike, compounding already fragile or impoverished political societies. Sympathies will be aroused in faraway places, and celebrities, **humanitarian** organisations, non-governmental organisations (NGOs), the **United Nations (UN)** and canny politicians will talk the talk of collective grief, human community and global responsibility. Excitement will die down after a flurry of activity and the poor souls will inevitably be cast back to the margins of international attention as developed countries return to more pressing domestic matters – tax

Figure 0.1   *Graffiti*, Sarajevo 2005 by David Kozar (with permission)

cuts, elections, salacious scandals, and so on. And so goes the daily round of international relations – war and peace, poverty and underdevelopment, global attention and global neglect.

This common-sense understanding of international relations only scratches the surface of all that the discipline of International Relations covers (see Box 0.1). So what precisely do we mean by 'international relations'? To answer this question, let us first say a few things about what it is not, before turning to an account of what it is.

First, the study of international relations is not to be equated with 'current affairs'. It is important not to reduce international relations to the lead stories of the global news media. News, by its nature, is ephemeral; each day brings a new story to tell. Moreover, news agencies make no attempt at drawing connections between stories. Their concern is not with showing how the stories 'hang together' or relate to each other but is solely with reporting the news, so each news item is reported independently of others. International Relations (IR), by contrast, seeks to go beyond the ephemeral and common-sense: to reflect more deeply on events, structures, processes and actors, and to offer explanations, interpretations and **normative** analyses. Second, the study of international relations is not reducible to what happens in particular countries, even though it may include this. Political machinations in other countries, especially powerful ones, always hold particular interest; Washington politics are never far from the headlines. But in IR, any interest in the politics of other countries will be determined by how these impact on or play out in the international sphere or how they are shaped by international forces. Third, IR is not reducible to foreign policy analysis, though once again it includes this within its scope (see Waltz 1979: 121–2 for one explanation).

Turning to a more positive definition of international relations, we can start by saying that it refers to *external relations among* **nations**, **states** *and peoples* – although, as

BOX 0.1: TERMINOLOGY

What are the differences between International Relations and international relations, and international politics and world politics?

It is conventional to differentiate the discipline of 'International Relations' from the subject matter of 'international relations' by the use of upper and lower case respectively. As Chris Brown (1997: 3) puts it, '"International Relations" (upper case) is the study of "international relations" (lower case)'.

International politics is used here as a synonym of international relations. It does, however, have the advantage of highlighting the political dimension of relations that are international.

World or global politics: Insofar as new actors, issues, structures and processes are thought to have emerged in recent decades as a result of **globalisation**, rendering the traditional state-focused agenda incomplete, some scholars prefer 'world' or 'global politics' to 'international relations'. This has prompted some scholars to talk of an historic shift from 'international relations' to 'world politics' or 'global society' (R. B. J. Walker 1995; Barnett and Sikkink 2008).

we explain below, this statement will need to be considerably qualified. The adjective 'international' was coined by the English political philosopher, Jeremy Bentham, in 1780. The neologism's purpose was to capture in a single word *relations among nations* (Suganami 1978). Although 'international' literally means relations among nations, it has for most of its existence referred to relations among **sovereign states**. In Bentham's time 'nation' and 'state' were often used interchangeably, so his meaning was closer to what we should probably call 'interstate' relations. In any case, *international* relations have been distinguished first and foremost from *domestic* politics. Ian Clark (1999) calls this the 'Great Divide' (see Table 0.1).

Leading scholars have for decades defined international relations by opposing the international and domestic realms as if they represented a 'Great Divide'. On what constitutes this 'Great Divide', the most influential realist IR theorist of the late twentieth century, Kenneth Waltz (1979: 103), remarks that '[t]he difference between national and international politics lies not in the use of force but in the different modes of organization for doing something about it'. What, then, are the possible modes of organisation? Waltz offers two, and only two, organising principles: **hierarchy** and **anarchy**. Relations between units (or actors) are either *hierarchical*, involving clear lines of authority and obedience, or they are *anarchical*, involving no such lines of authority and obedience (Waltz 1979: 88). There would appear to be no other possibilities. The key, according to Waltz, is

governance; is there a supreme authority with the right to lay down and enforce the law? If the answer is 'yes', then we must be in the hierarchical realm of domestic politics – politics *within* the state. If the answer is 'no', then we must be in the anarchical realm of international relations – politics *between* states. In any case, the presumed differences between domestic and international politics seem to vindicate Martin Wight's (1966b: 21) observation that '[i]t has become natural to think of international politics as the untidy fringe of domestic politics'. I shall suggest below that while it has indeed become natural to think in these terms, there may be good reasons for casting doubt over the 'Great Divide' as the point of departure for IR today.

According to the 'Great Divide', domestic politics is what takes place on the *inside* of states whereas international relations is what takes place on the *outside*, as if they were two mutually exclusive realms. Domestic politics is premised on the presence of a central authority or government that has monopoly control over the instruments of violence, that can lay down and enforce the law, that establishes and maintains **order**

Table 0.1 The 'Great Divide'

Domestic	International
Inside	Outside
Hierarchy	Anarchy
Monopoly over instruments of violence	Decentralised instruments of violence
Lawful authority	Self-help
Security	Insecurity/Security dilemma
Justice	Power
Community	Friends and enemies
Peace and order	War

and **security**, and that permits justice and peace to be delivered to the community of citizens. International relations is the negative image of domestic politics. By contrast with the domestic realm, the international is premised on the absence of an overarching authority or government that can lay down and enforce the law because the instruments of violence are dispersed and decentralised. This establishes ripe conditions for insecurity, where injustice and war are permanent potentials and regular actualities for states. It is a world of friends and enemies where **power** rather than justice will determine international outcomes, and where states cannot afford to put their trust or security in others. States are trapped in a '**security dilemma**' where measures taken to enhance their security lead others to take similar counter-measures and in the process generate further mistrust and insecurity.

Perhaps the term that distinguishes international relations more than any other is *anarchy*. Anarchy – meaning the absence of rule, but not necessarily disorder and chaos – has been the core presumption and **constitutive** principle for much of the discipline's history (Onuf 1989: 166; Schmidt 1998). Richard Ashley (1989) has called IR the 'anarchy problematique' – that is to say, a field of knowledge revolving around the organising principle of anarchy.

International Relations as a discipline: traditions, origins and evolution

Universities, as centres of research and learning, have long divided knowledge into different disciplines. This division is heuristic: that is to say, it is meant to help facilitate learning. A discipline comprises a distinctive focus, a set of institutions and traditions of thought. All three are crucial to the development and growth of a field or body of knowledge. But it is worth noting that 'discipline' has another, not altogether unrelated, meaning: to bring under control, train to obedience, maintain order. Disciplines thus help to maintain intellectual order by keeping a focus and keeping clear of distracting, extraneous issues.

First, a discipline carves out a branch of learning focused on a relatively distinct subject matter. I say 'relatively' because attempts to cordon off one subject from all others are bound to fail or to appear arbitrary. For example, where do we draw the boundaries between international politics, international morality, **international law** and international economics? Politics, morality, law and economics intersect and overlap in so many ways that efforts to draw final boundaries around them would be futile and possibly unhelpful, since understanding the politics of international relations cannot be separated from an understanding of the moral, legal and economic dimensions of these relations.

Nevertheless, if a discipline implies a subject matter relatively distinguishable from others, it must have questions and topics it calls its own. Though agreement will never be total, the questions and topics to be addressed should meet with broad agreement. Some disagreement about the scope of a discipline is to be expected, but there will always be dominant tendencies – questions and topics that occupy the thought and research of most students and scholars (see Box 0.2). These will define the discipline at any given moment, but there will always be other questions and topics that are neglected or ignored by the mainstream. I return to the question of subject matter in the final part of this Introduction where I sketch contending 'traditional' and 'new' agendas.

BOX 0.2: DISCUSSION POINTS

A divided discipline?

In the late 1980s International Relations undertook a self-examination. Eminent scholar K. J. Holsti (1985: 1) lamented that 'International theory is in a state of disarray'. The 'intellectual consensus' that guided research and learning for over three centuries had, in Holsti's opinion, 'broken down'. No longer was there 'a consensus on the subjects of inquiry and theorizing. The view that international theory should be organized around the structures and processes of the states system, the activities of the **great powers** and their decision makers, particularly as they relate to war and peace, is no longer accepted by a significant number of scholars' (Holsti 1985: 2). Holsti's concern was not so much that the dominant view of the discipline's focus and purpose had been abandoned – this was reasonable given the fundamental changes that had occurred in the twentieth century – but that the 'theoretical profusion' had made coherent dialogue and debate very difficult. His fear, in short, was that the discipline might never regain its focus and sense of purpose. Holsti was not alone. Mark Hoffman (1987) accepted Holsti's assessment of a discipline divided over purpose, focus or appropriate methodology, but advocated a 'next stage' in which Critical Theory (see Chapter 4) would reconstruct and reorient the discipline. Others, such as Yosef Lapid (1989a: 83) questioned whether establishing a 'new hegemonic orthodoxy' would be 'possible' or 'desirable', preferring to celebrate theoretical diversity (see also George and Campbell 1990). For fuller treatment of this approach, see Chapter 1.

Second, disciplines grow within institutions and grow their own institutions. Universities are the most obvious sites for the institutionalisation of the research and teaching of particular subjects, but they are not alone, as we shall see. Departments, schools or centres have been established in universities around the world to study international relations. The first was established in 1919 at the University of Wales, in the seaside town of Aberystwyth, when Welsh industrialist and philanthropist David Davies established the Woodrow Wilson Chair of International Politics. The London School of Economics and the University of Oxford followed shortly after, with the establishment of Chairs in 1923 and 1930 respectively. In the US, the institutionalised study of IR began with the establishment of Georgetown University's Edmund A. Walsh School of Foreign Service in 1919, which was followed by the University of Southern California's School of International Relations in 1924. The first university dedicated to the study of international relations was established at the Graduate Institute of International Studies in Geneva, Switzerland, in 1927.

The institutionalisation of academic areas of study is vital because it provides housing for teaching and research. Both teaching and research, the two preeminent tasks of university departments, are crucial to the accumulation, expansion and transmission of bodies of knowledge. Teaching passes on knowledge and modes of analysis from one generation to the next in the classroom. Research, of course, needs to be published, so that findings and analyses can be widely disseminated and tested, not only from one generation to the next but to contemporary teachers and students as well. Journals, periodicals, books, conferences and workshops are sites for debate, the exchange of ideas, and the sharpening of arguments, all of which reproduce and revise a discipline's body of knowledge.

Disciplines also grow their own institutions such as academic journals and professional associations. I have listed some of the relevant journals in the 'Further reading' section at the end of this chapter. Added to journals are professional bodies such as the British International Studies Association (BISA) and the American-based International Studies Association (ISA), which not only organise conferences but publish journals: the *Review of International Studies* (since 1975) and *International Studies Quarterly* (since 1957, although it was published under the name *Background on World Politics* until 1970) respectively. In Australia, the *Australian Journal of International Affairs* has been published since 1946 (originally under the title *Australian Outlook*). Think tanks have also made a long-standing contribution to the advancement of learning, and are an integral part of the discipline's landscape. The Carnegie Endowment for International Peace was established in 1910; the Royal Institute of International Affairs was established in 1920, and its antipodean offshoots, the Australian and New Zealand Institutes of International Affairs, in 1933 and 1934 respectively.

Third, a discipline draws upon traditions of thought that have developed and evolved around the subject matter. Although the first university department was not established until 1919 it would be a mistake to believe that the study of international relations began at that point. When departments were being established, scholars and students were not inventing a discipline out of thin air; they had over two millennia of recorded words, thoughts and actions to draw upon. Cognate departments such as Government, Law and History also provided useful resources (Schmidt 1998). But so too did thinkers subsequently drafted into the International Relations canon.

Thucydides (c. 460–406 BC), **Machiavelli** (1469–1527) and Grotius (1583–1645), for example, may not have taught in universities, but they wrote about the actors and events that shaped the 'international relations', as we now call it, of their day. Care must be taken here, however, because the actors and events they described and analysed are vastly different to the ones that now animate international relations. Moreover, none of these great thinkers limited himself to the external relations of actors, whether city-states, empires or sovereign states. Indeed, it is closer to the truth to say that they discussed what we would call IR either indirectly or only in occasional passages of their classic texts. So we need to be careful when discussing the past not to commit the sin of *anachronism* – discussing one historical epoch in terms of language, concepts and understandings borrowed from another. In other words, we risk anachronism when we speak of these great thinkers writing about 'international relations' because, in fact, they did not neatly distinguish international relations from domestic politics or international

Table 0.2 Realism and liberalism compared

	Realism	Liberalism
Main actor	States	Individuals
Contextual focus	Anarchy	Institutions
Fundamental value	Security	Liberty
Elemental behaviour	Conflict	Cooperation
Outlook	Pessimism	Optimism
View of history	Recurrence and repetition	Progressive change

law or morality in the way the discipline of IR has done since its inception. Neither the 'Great Divide' nor the 'anarchy problematique' underpinned their thinking.

Traditions of thought

What are the traditions of thought that have influenced the study of international relations? How one answers this question depends on which classificatory scheme one uses, and there are several such schemes. During the discipline's early years, the dominant classificatory scheme was of **idealism** or **liberalism** on the one hand and **realism** on the other (see Table 0.2); this was how E. H. Carr (1946) presented the field of study. Arguably this scheme still dominates the discipline today in the USA – albeit in revised form as a debate between **neoliberalism** and **neorealism** (see Baldwin 1993). It is vital to come to grips with these two dominant IR theories, as they have largely set the parameters of the discipline, shaping its core assumptions and key questions.

Realists argue that states exist in a condition of anarchy that compels them to seek and to balance power to ensure their survival and security (see Chapter 2). They paint international relations as a tragic realm of '**power politics**' where '**national interests**' clash and moral claims hold little sway. For realists, the character of international relations remains unchanged through history. Marked by what Kenneth Waltz (1979: 66) calls 'a dismaying persistence' of war, international relations is, in Wight's (1966b: 26) words, 'the realm of recurrence and repetition'. Thucydides, the great Athenian historian of *The Peloponnesian War*, brilliant Florentine diplomat and writer, Niccolò Machiavelli, and towering English political philosopher, Thomas Hobbes (intellectually and physically towering – he was almost six foot tall, well above average height in the seventeenth century) are canonical names in realism's hall of fame. They not only provided insights into their own times, but also offered wisdom and insight that realists believe transcend time. In the realist view, if Thucydides or Hobbes were transported to our own time they would observe nothing different other than the names of the actors (Waltz 1979: 66; Wight 1966b: 26).

Liberals take a more optimistic view. If realists see history as static or cyclical, liberals see it as progressive. They tend to emphasise humanity's capacity to improve: they are committed to ideals of technological and economic as well as moral, legal and political progress (see Chapter 3). That the world is anarchical and war-prone is as true for liberals as it is for realists, but the former believe it is possible and necessary for humankind to escape the **Hobbesian** 'state of war' – a condition in which states are insecure and constantly preparing for war. Strategies of 'peace through law' and 'peace through commerce' are the dominant liberal approaches. In international relations they see the gradual development and strengthening of international trade, international law and international organisations as the key to world order (Suganami 1989). Names in the liberal pantheon include great English political philosophers John Locke and John Stuart Mill, and the superlative philosopher of Königsberg (now called Kaliningrad), Immanuel **Kant**.

Others have posited a tripartite scheme. One of the most common is the tripartite scheme of realism, liberalism and **Marxism**, or variations thereof (Doyle 1997; Holsti 1985; Walt 1998). This extends and complicates the realism/liberalism debate by adding a Marxist tradition of thought. This tradition shifted emphasis away from states to the historical development of the capitalist system and the class conflict it generated (see Kubálková and Cruickshank 1985; Linklater 1990). It redirected the focus to an examination of how the twin logics of capitalist development and geopolitical rivalry interacted. It is worth noting here that Marxism played a vital role in stimulating the Critical Theory pioneered by Robert Cox (1981) and Andrew Linklater (1990), because Marx critically analysed the tensions between hopes of universal freedom and concrete realities of inequality and oppression (see Chapter 4).

In his famous lectures at the London School of Economics (LSE) in the 1950s, Martin Wight (1991) also distinguished three traditions of thought, but rather eccentrically called them realism, **rationalism** and **revolutionism** (also see Bull 1976). If realism was the tradition associated with power politics and 'the blood and iron and immorality men', as Wight called them (Bull 1976: 104), revolutionism was associated with the perpetual peace of liberal internationalism *and* the **revolutionary** internationalism of Marxism – 'the subversion and liberation and missionary men'. Rationalism was a 'middle way' that sought to avoid the extremes of realism and revolutionism. It is a tradition of thought most closely associated with seventeenth-century Dutch jurist Hugo Grotius (who, by contrast with Hobbes, was barely five feet tall!), and eighteenth-century Swiss lawyer, Emer de Vattel – 'the law and order and keep your word men', to use Wight's description (Bull 1976: 104). Rationalists accept the realist premise that states exist in a condition of anarchy (where no state has the authority to lay down and enforce the law), but deny that this condition is bereft of rules and **norms**. Rather, they argue that, to use the felicitous phrase of Wight's foremost protégé, Hedley Bull (1977), states exist in an 'anarchical society'. States tend to form international societies where order is maintained through mechanisms such as international law, diplomacy, balances of power, great power management and occasionally war (Bull 1977; see also Chapter 17). This 'middle way' continues today under the name of the **English School** (see Dunne 1998; Linklater and Suganami 2006), and has some affinities with neoliberal **institutionalism** (Hurrell 1995) (see Chapter 3).

In Wight's hands, the three traditions (the 'three Rs') were not meant to be water-tight containers, but more like 'streams, with eddies and cross-currents, sometimes interlacing' (Wight 1991: 260). To continue the metaphor: in practice, canonical thinkers tend to cross and sometimes straddle streams rather than soak their feet permanently in one. Wight's purpose was merely to present the traditions as historically embodied styles of thought handed down by scholars and practitioners alike.

Needless to say, there are various classificatory schemes, each as arbitrary as the next. What matters is not so much the historical veracity of the scheme as the analytical tools it serves up. Traditions of thought, whichever scheme we choose to employ, provide us with the premises, tenets and concepts without which we could not intelligibly discuss and analyse international relations. Traditions are the source of our lexicon, the common vocabulary we use to study our subject – even if, as Renée Jeffery (2005) contends, the very idea of a 'tradition of thought' is questionable.

We have to depart from somewhere (there is actually no point outside all tradition), so we start with what the competing traditions leave to us. But traditions are not given and homogeneous. They are 'invented', which is not to say that traditions are false or arbitrarily fabricated, only that the inheritance must be selected and interpreted before it can be received. Traditions are also heterogeneous, comprising multiple strands and legacies. What we believe they leave to us depends on how we sift through, select and interpret the tradition's inheritance (see Box 0.3). As Jim George (1994: 196) rightly points out, 'the "great texts" of International Relations can be read in ways entirely contrary to their ritualized disciplinary treatment'. Which is why IR has in recent years witnessed an 'historiographical turn' (Armitage 2004, Duncan Bell 2001, Keene 2005) – reflecting on the aims and methods of writing history, particularly intellectual history or the history of ideas. In keeping with this historiographical turn, this Introduction, and the textbook as a whole, aims to encourage and cultivate what Herbert Butterfield (1955: 17) called 'historical-mindedness'.

BOX 0.3: DISCUSSION POINTS

Was Thucydides a realist?

As an illustration of how traditions depend on interpretation, consider the tendency of realists and others to assign Thucydides uncritically to the realist tradition. Behind this assignation lies the supposition that the realist tradition is centred around the concept of material or military power and that Thucydides is a realist par excellence. The one episode in his account of the Peloponnesian War that is always invoked is 'The Melian Dialogue'. According to Thucydides' (1972: 402) narrative, the Athenian envoy says to his Melian counterpart, 'the strong do what they have the power to do and the weak accept what they have to accept'. Captured in this remark is one of the most powerful expressions of realism's emphasis on material power determining international outcomes – which is why it is realism's favourite hymn, and why Thucydides is viewed as the first great realist. It would be a mistake, however, to suppose that Thucydides subscribes to this realist view, since he is simply retelling the story. In fact, much else in his narrative suggests that Thucydides would be out of place in the realist tradition, not least because he places a good deal of emphasis on normative standards for assessing conduct and moral responsibility. Furthermore, the Athenian empire's reliance on military force and war proves insufficient to prevent eventual collapse. We can conclude, therefore, that how traditions are understood and who is included in them is indeed a matter of selection and interpretation.

To summarise, as Wight has suggested, and as R. B. J. Walker (1993: chapter 2) and Jim George (1994: 192–7) have amply demonstrated, traditions of thought are never as internally coherent or self-enclosed as they appear. Common though it may be to bundle Machiavelli and Hobbes together in the realist tradition, they actually differ considerably on many key points, especially on how they view time and change in politics, with the Florentine seeing politics as permanently in flux and the Englishman holding to a more static and spatial conception that is perhaps more consistent with some aspects of the 'Great Divide'.

Origins and evolution of the discipline

The origins of the discipline are to be found in one crucial historical moment: World War I (1914–18) as we know it now, but the 'Great War' as it was known before World War II. It was the most intense and mechanised war yet experienced, with new technologies, including the advent of air power, allowing for new heights of destruction to be reached. The unprecedented destructiveness prompted calls for the eradication of war; it was indeed often referred to as the 'War to End All Wars'. The traumatic experience of the Great War for Europeans was perhaps compounded by the fact that the years preceding it were relatively peaceful and stable, witnessing marked increases in 'the number of multilateral conferences, institutions, and organizations' (Reus-Smit 1999: 133). In particular, significant strides were taken regarding the laws of war with the Hague Conferences of 1899 and 1907, which seemed to vindicate liberal optimism for international reform.

After the war, an understandable tide of anti-war sentiment surged through Europe – the continent that had witnessed so many terrible wars over the centuries. It was not only war's destructiveness that fuelled anti-war sentiment, it was also its apparent futility. As an instrument of foreign policy, war appeared to many to be ineffective and counterproductive (see Angell 1912).

We might think such sentiments to be a natural reaction to war. But until the eighteenth century, while war had always been lamented, it was rarely viewed as eradicable. This is why English jurist Sir Henry Maine (cited in Howard 2001: 1) observed in the middle of the nineteenth century, 'War appears to be as old as mankind, but peace is a modern invention'. It was only with the initiation of 'plans for perpetual peace' in the eighteenth century, drafted most famously by the Abbé Saint Pierre and Immanuel Kant, that thinkers and scholars put their minds to determining how peace might permanently prevail over war in a system of states. But only after the Great War did a widespread 'peace movement' arise with the intention of eliminating war for all time.

To this sentiment were added practical, institutional measures, including the establishment of the League of Nations at Geneva in 1920 and, in accordance with the League's Covenant, the Permanent Court of International Justice at The Hague in 1922 (originally the Permanent Court of Arbitration, as established under the 1899 Hague Conference). According to Chris Reus-Smit (1999), a new *legislative* principle of procedural justice emerged at this time which found concrete expression in these new institutions. Two precepts informed this new legislative justice: 'first, that only those subject to the rules have the right to define them and, second, that the rules of society must apply equally to all' (Reus-Smit 1999: 129). Reus-Smit (1999: 123–54) traces the origins of these ideas back to the eighteenth century – to the **Enlightenment** and to the American and French revolutions; but it is arguable that it was only in the aftermath of the Great War that a new diplomatic and legal order took shape based on contractual international law and **multilateralism**. The war not only marked a break with the previous peace, it brought about a different kind of peace, one where permanent international institutions were designed 'to promote international co-operation and to achieve peace and security', as expressed in the League of Nations Covenant (printed in Claude 1964: 409).

This is the general context in which the discipline of International Relations was established. It was a period of progressive institutionalisation of liberal–constitutional principles as a reaction to war (see Chapter 3). This 'desire … to prevent future wars', says William Olson (1972: 12), 'must never be forgotten' when assessing the discipline's origins. More than just the study of the causes and conditions of war and peace, the study of international relations was, from the outset, guided by a purpose: to develop theories aimed at preventing or eliminating war. It would do so by focusing on states and their interactions in the states-system, but also by bringing liberal tenets to bear on the prevailing bellicose system. Liberals such as Sir Norman Angell and US President Woodrow Wilson believed that a lasting peace could only be achieved by overcoming the **balance of power** and secret diplomacy; they argued for developing a new diplomatic and legal order around international organisations based on practices of **collective security** and open diplomacy (see Ashworth 1999; Woodrow Wilson 1918). 'The distinctive characteristic of these writers', says Hedley Bull (1972: 34), was their belief in progress: 'the belief, in particular', he continues,

that the system of international relations that had given rise to the First World War was capable of being transformed into a fundamentally more peaceful and just world order; that under the impact of the awakening of democracy, the growth of 'the international mind', the development of the League of Nations, the good works of men of peace or the enlightenment spread by their own teachings, it was in fact being transformed.

Liberal–constitutional values and ideals thus set the agenda for the discipline in the inter-war years, the agenda against which E. H. Carr aimed his withering criticism. First published in 1939, Carr's *The twenty years' crisis, 1919–1939* (1946) has had a massive influence on the discipline of International Relations. Carr's book is a brilliant polemical attack on the liberal thinking associated with Angell, Wilson, Alfred Zimmern and others, which he characterised as a hollow sham (Carr 1946: 89). Carr believed **utopianism** (for which you can substitute liberalism) utterly failed to take account of power in its analysis of international relations; it ignored Machiavelli's injunction to deal with what *is* the case, rather than what *ought to be* the case (Carr 1946: 63). The structure of Carr's masterpiece revolves around the dichotomy between realism and liberalism. In fact, he helped create the impression that the newly established discipline was dominated by a debate between realism and liberalism. This subsequently became known as the 'first great debate', though – as Peter Wilson (1998) and Lucian Ashworth (1999) have shown – no debate actually occurred, if by that we mean that a series of exchanges took place between realists and liberals. Indeed, recent work suggests that the very idea of narrating the discipline's history as a series of 'great debates' is questionable. Even so, it is important for students to learn and appreciate the stories the discipline has told about itself, which is why I persist with the narrative.

Since the late 1960s and early 1970s when scholars began to reflect more on the origins and evolution of the discipline, it has become conventional to narrate the discipline's history through a recounting of 'great debates'. The 'second great debate' is said to have been a methodological quarrel in the 1960s and 1970s between 'behaviouralism' and 'traditionalism'; at stake was the question, 'what is the most appropriate way of pursuing and acquiring knowledge in international relations?' Bull (1966) frames the debate in terms of 'scientific versus classical' methods. He identifies two broad criticisms of the scientific approach, which wants to emulate the methods of the natural sciences in its attempts to explain international politics. First, that it cannot live up to its aspirations and must fall back on non-scientific (read 'classical') methods. Second, that it is an inappropriate method for studying many of the central issues in international relations, because even empirical questions are not susceptible to pure observation, but depend upon 'intuition or judgment' (Bull 1966: 367), and because many questions are in part normative. Essentially, Bull thinks the 'scientific' approach removes students and scholars too far from the stuff of international relations – 'as remote from the substance of international politics as the inmates of a Victorian nunnery were from the study of sex' (Bull 1966: 366). Bull defends the 'classical' approach which, he contends, is interpretive, more historical and better attuned to normative judgments.

Chris Brown (1997: 36–7) is probably right to describe the second debate as a 'minor skirmish' rather than a 'great debate', since it was in fact 'something of a non-event' at the time. Having said that, it was the first time the study of international relations opened itself up to theoretical self-reflection. Though little was resolved by the debate, it highlighted the importance of reflecting on inescapable questions related to how we acquire knowledge. Knowledge does not fall from the heavens fully formed, so clarifying how to pursue or acquire knowledge is essential – it helps us discriminate between competing descriptions or analyses of international relations. Indeed, this unresolved question feeds into the 'third great debate', which, according to Yosef Lapid (1989b), pits **positivism** against post-positivism. In this debate, the mainstream approaches of neorealism and neoliberalism defend themselves against a variety of 'critical' theories. Steve Smith (1996: 11, 13), in a most valuable account of what is at stake in the 'third debate', accuses positivism of restricting our understanding of 'what kinds of things [exist] in international relations' and of narrowly limiting ethical and practical possibilities. The theoretical profusion associated with the 'third debate' can be usefully linked to the changing agenda of international relations.

Changing agendas: theory and practice

Since its inception International Relations has continued to evolve, largely in reflection of changing political circumstances. In this final section I want to outline some of the ways that the study of international relations has changed over time. First, I set recent developments in international relations theory in the context of what has been referred to as the 'third debate'. My purpose is not to provide a comprehensive account of the theoretical scene (that is provided in Chapter 1), but merely to indicate how the theory chapters in Part 1 relate to the 'traditional' and 'new' agendas comprising Parts 2 and 3 respectively. Second, I sketch the 'traditional' and 'new' agendas of international relations. My argument is not that the 'new' agenda displaces or renders obsolete the 'traditional'; rather, the two agendas exist alongside one another, intersecting in complex ways that require further study.

The 'critical turn' against the 'Great Divide'

The mainstream approaches of realism and liberalism have been instrumental in shaping the 'traditional' agenda (see Chapters 2 and 3). This should come as no surprise given the discipline's liberal origins and realism's rise to prominence during the **Cold War** (see Chapter 20).

The first point to note is that both realism and liberalism tend to accept the terms of the 'Great Divide', and to naturalise the 'anarchy problematique'. They view the domestic and international realms as distinct and mutually exclusive. Both also tend to take the state for granted as a form of political community, even if liberals are more likely to acknowledge the threat states pose to their own citizens. Liberalism, after all, emerged as a critical intervention against the disturbing concentration of state power in the seventeenth and eighteenth centuries.

Liberalism and realism diverge, however, over questions of war and law. Realists and liberals both deplore war as a tragic and destructive phenomenon, but how they explain war varies. Realists see war as an inevitable and ineradicable part of international relations insofar as the condition of anarchy prevails (Waltz 1959). Liberals accept this description, but believe that change is possible. They argue that institutional change at the level of the state and the **international system** will release potentials for eradicating, or at the very least considerably limiting, war. In essence liberals argue that the key to achieving perpetual peace is to transform the international realm so that it comes to resemble the domestic realm. Realists reject this 'domestic analogy' (see Suganami 1989), being sceptical that international anarchy can be transformed into an international hierarchy where some kind of global sovereign exercises power *and* authority. Liberals, on the other hand, believe the spread of liberal **democracy** will result in the strengthening of international organisations and the rule of international law, which will mitigate the worst aspects of anarchy and contribute to the 'domestication' of the global system.

The 'critical turn' in international relations posed a challenge to both realism and liberalism for taking the world more or less as it is, 'with the prevailing social and power relationships and the institutions into which they are organised, as the given frame of action' (Cox 1981: 128). One of the pioneering scholars of Critical Theory, Robert Cox identified liberalism and realism (especially in their 'neo' versions) with 'problem-solving' theory. Problem-solving theories work within the present limits of the system to smooth over instabilities or problems (Cox 1981: 129); they tend to work in favour of stabilising prevailing structures of world order and their accompanying inequalities of wealth and power. Cox's main point is that problem-solving theories like realism and liberalism fail to reflect on the prior framework within which they theorise (see Box 4.2). The upshot is that they tend to be conservative, notwithstanding their claims to objective or value-free analysis.

By contrast, critical theories (including for the moment Marxism, **feminism**, postmodernism, Critical Theory and sometimes **constructivism**; see Chapters 4–7) start from the premise that 'theory is always *for* someone and *for* some purpose' (Cox 1981: 128). All knowledge, according to critical theorists, is coloured by social, cultural and ideological influence, and it is vital to reveal the effect of this conditioning. Critical theories of international relations, then, seek to bring to consciousness latent assumptions, interests or purposes that give rise to and orient thinking about international relations. Refusing to take the present system as normal or natural, they explore the possibilities of **emancipation** by forming more inclusionary political communities committed to principles of dialogue and procedural justice (see Linklater 1998 and 2007). To put the point slightly differently, critical theories are constructivist insofar as they take the prevailing structures of world order to be human creations sustained through patterned social practices. If they are constructed, then they can be transformed into less violent, more just structures of world order. Critical theories, with the possible exception of constructivism (see Shapcott 2000: 154), place emancipation at the centre of their approach. They are all, to that extent, children of the Enlightenment, as are theorists of global justice (see Chapter 8). The knowledge they seek makes no claims to being objective or value-free. Instead, they offer a politically and ethically charged account of international relations, one aimed at expanding human freedom and global justice by radically transforming the prevailing structures of world order (see Table 4.1).

In questioning taken-for-granted assumptions, critical theories compel us to reflect on the 'Great Divide'. There is broad agreement among Marxism, Critical Theory, feminism, constructivism, postmodernism and global justice theories that the distinction between inside and outside, hierarchy and anarchy is by no means natural or necessary. It is, rather, a socially and historically constructed device for organising political life in a particular way; one that, in empowering sovereign states to pursue self-interest through power politics, disempowers and renders invisible social classes, women and the excluded in general. The 'Great Divide' also functions to reproduce the logics of self-help and power politics in international relations. As Alexander Wendt (1992) has persuasively argued, however, 'anarchy is what states make of it' (see Box 7.1). His point is that anarchy (the absence of an overarching authority) does not occur naturally or independently of states and their practices. If anarchy resembles a self-help, power-political system it is because states choose policies that make it so.

From states, war and law to globalisation and global governance

The 'Great Divide' sets up the study of international relations in a particular way – it points us towards certain issues and assumptions, and away from others. In particular, it points us towards the 'traditional' agenda of 'high politics' where diplomatic and strategic issues take centre stage. States become the principal actors and focus is concentrated on issues pertaining to their external relations: issues of **nationalism**, security, **arms control**, war, **diplomacy** and great power relations (see Chapters 9–14 and 18–20). But law has always been an important part of the traditional agenda too. From the discipline's founding, realists and liberals have long studied the relationship of states to international law (see Chapter 16), with liberals tending to put their faith in law as a force for peace, and realists tending to be sceptical of the idea that a law not backed by force can make a difference. For realists, international law may lack coercive force, but it is important nonetheless because, as the great French thinker Jean-Jacques Rousseau ([c. 1756] 1917: 125) noted, 'on every side the strong [are] armed with the terrible powers of the Law against the weak'. In other words, law (domestic or international) serves political functions and can be manipulated in precisely this manner by powerful actors. The branch of international law concerned with war has also been a constant feature of the traditional agenda (see Chapter 15), and is even more important in the current context of the global 'war on terror' (see Chapter 29).

We should not conclude, therefore, that the subject matter of the 'traditional' agenda is in any way obsolete. It will only become obsolete when sovereign states disappear and when war is eradicated. So long as these conditions are not in prospect, we would do well to reflect on the continuing relevance of states, war and law. The key question, as prompted by the 'critical turn', is whether the traditional agenda contains all the necessary intellectual resources to make sense of the contemporary politics of states, war and law in international relations. Does the traditional agenda _wisuy_

pose all the right questions, or is it necessary to rethink and re-pose some of these questions, perhaps by drawing on intellectual resources afforded by the 'critical turn'?

In any case, what is excluded from the traditional agenda is everything associated with 'domestic' or 'low politics', everything that does not fit neatly into the agenda of states, war and law. Issues relegated to the margins include economics and the environment, morality and religion, and a range of **non-state actors** from refugees to terrorists, from multinational corporations (MNCs) to non-governmental organisations (NGOs). Incorporating such issues and actors into the traditional agenda would effectively collapse the 'Great Divide'; it would dissolve international relations into world politics. Critical Theorists and postmodernists have argued for just this move (R. B. J. Walker 1995); they tend to reject or at least cast doubt on the 'Great Divide'. From their perspective the task is not to maintain disciplinary insularity, but to reflect on whether it is tenable any longer to suppose a 'Great Divide'. Especially in the context of globalisation, it has become more urgent to ask if it is still adequate to conceive of international relations as a completely separate realm of politics from domestic politics (Clark 1999).

Part 3, The New Agenda: Globalisation and Global Governance, covers many topics that do not sit comfortably with the 'Great Divide'. These topics can be generally included under the heading 'globalisation and global governance'. Both these topics have spawned large industries of scholarly research, especially globalisation. An essentially contested term, globalisation has been defined by David Held, Anthony McGrew, David Goldblatt and Jonathon Perraton (1999: 15) as the 'widening, deepening and speeding up of global interconnectedness' made possible by new information, communication, and transportation technologies. As a multidimensional phenomenon, globalisation holds different, sometimes contradictory, implications for international relations (Devetak 2008). At the same time as it promises global interconnectedness, cosmopolitan community and secular modernity (see Chapter 23), it results in the fracturing of states and the rise of virulent forms of ethno-nationalism and religious **fundamentalism**. At the same time as it enables prosperous individuals to travel across the globe, it casts asylum seekers into a precarious 'frontierland' (Bauman 1998), sometimes even beyond the safety of international law (see Chapter 33). At the same time as it promises prosperity and peace, it also enables transnational terrorists to deploy violence to their own ends (see Chapter 29).

Globalisation has also given rise to actors and institutions concerned to regulate world politics through a combination of 'public' and 'private' organisations. Global governance is not the same as global government; it refers, as James Rosenau (1992: 4) says, to a global system of rule that rests on a blend of formal and informal authorities, officially sanctioned laws and tacit norms. On the formal side we have international organisations like the United Nations (UN) (see Chapter 21) and the **World Trade Organization**. On the informal side we have 'private' authorities (such as credit-rating agencies), which operate at the global level to monitor and regulate financial activities of states (see Chapter 26), and international **non-governmental organisations** (INGOs), which also operate at the global level in assisting states and international organisations in the provision of 'global public goods' (see Chapter 22).

Crucial elements in the contemporary architecture of global governance are global economic institutions (GEIs) like the **World Bank**, **International Monetary Fund (IMF)** and World Trade Organization, which generally lie outside the traditional parameters of realist theories of international relations because they are thought to be marginal to the 'high politics' issues of strategy and diplomacy. Yet GEIs continue to exercise, controversially, a great deal of influence over countries of the global South (see Chapters 24 and 27). Debate continues about the power of these institutions to regulate the global economy and in whose interests they do so. These debates feed into more general discontent with globalisation (Chapter 28).

If the traditional agenda focuses on the system of states, the new agenda recognises the growing influence of global or transnational actors, structures and processes. If the traditional agenda downgrades ideas and norms to material considerations of power, the new agenda frequently plays up the power of ideas and norms. This is clear in the rising prominence of religion, human rights, **refugees** and the environment on the agenda of global politics (see Chapters 23, 32–35); all are issues of global scope (transnational issues that cross state borders), all are irreducible to material sources of power. These issues also tend to raise moral considerations (what are our obligations?). It is on this basis that **humanitarianism** has flourished in recent decades. Organisations such as Oxfam, Amnesty International, Doctors without Borders (Médecins Sans Frontières) and the International Committee of the Red Cross make it their business to assist humans in need around the globe. Since the 1990s arguments have even been made that humanitarianism must be prepared to use force if suffering strangers are to be saved (see Chapter 31).

It is arguable that the 'critical turn' and the rise of a 'new' agenda have turned the world of international relations into a different place. It is not only that the 'furniture' of the world is different (state as well as a variety of non-state actors, the states-system as well as transnational networks populate this world); our understanding of these actors, networks, structures and processes also changes. They are no longer seen as clearly defined or fixed objects in an external world of material power relations; rather, they are seen as contested objects constructed by a range of material and non-material ('ideational') social, political, legal, economic and religious practices. The things of this world are imbued with meaning and value by humans and their social relations, and insofar as they are socially constructed, they are susceptible to modification and change (see Chapters 4 and 7). But change need not involve large-scale violence. The Cold War ended peacefully, and authoritarian regimes across Eastern Europe (Georgia's 2003 'Rose Revolution', Ukraine's 2004–2005 'Orange Revolution') and the Arab world (Tunisia and Egypt in early 2011) have been overthrown through largely peaceful popular uprisings.

Indeed, change itself has become a more prominent feature of International Relations. It is not just that change emanates from the new agenda, however; traditional agenda issues such as war are equally disposed to change as actors (other than states' armed forces) engage in organised violence, adopting tactics of **guerrilla warfare** and **terrorism**, and applying new technologies that can transform war. In the context of some **civil wars** in the 1990s scholars such as Mary Kaldor (1999) argued that 'new wars' had arisen in places like the former Yugoslavia, Rwanda and Sierra Leone which did not fit the usual understanding. In the context of the global 'war on terror' the US has argued for changes to international law and the laws of war in order to fight terrorism more effectively.

These examples suggest that the 'Great Divide' is not nearly as clear cut as formerly imagined. Domestic hierarchy and the state's monopoly over the instruments of violence

Figure 0.2   Anti-government demonstrations during the 2010–11 Tunisian uprising

have been undone, leaving citizens insecure and uncertain of who their friends are when wars of ethno-nationalism break out. In some respects, the domestic comes to acquire traits of the international realm. At the same time, the gradual development and consolidation of global governance suggests that international relations may be approximating the domestic realm in some important respects. In the final analysis, the rise of the new agenda and the critical turn suggest that the 'Great Divide' should not be taken for granted.

Conclusion

This Introduction has tried to show the fascinating history and the complex dynamics that continue to shape international relations, making it such an exciting area to study. Continuity and change, traditional and new agendas define International Relations today. It is important to note, however, that the 'new' agenda does not replace or supplant the 'traditional' agenda, it *supplements* it. The traditional agenda is necessary, if insufficient, to understanding or explaining international relations *or* world politics today. True, the prevention or elimination of war remains as urgent today as it was in 1919, but the character of war has changed dramatically since then and we must study these and other differences as well as the things that remain the same.

The two agendas (traditional and new) exist alongside each other; though not without tension. The task for IR students today is to come to a better understanding of how these agendas interact. This textbook is designed to introduce you to both agendas and to show you the continuing vitality of some dimensions of the traditional agenda and the emergence of novel features of the new agenda that demand different theoretical approaches. Coming to terms with the main features of both traditional and new agendas should enable you to attain a deeper understanding of the issues covered in the global news media. It should also alert you to the tremendous range of intellectually exciting and politically urgent questions that define the study of International Relations today.

QUESTIONS

1. What should be studied under the heading 'international relations'?
2. Should the discipline's founding premises and purposes still govern the study of international relations? What, if anything, should be the purpose of studying international relations?
3. Does what Ian Clark calls the 'Great Divide' still hold today?
4. Does the 'new' agenda adequately capture the changes in recent international relations?
5. Which theory or theories can provide most insight into past and present international relations?

FURTHER READING

Doyle, Michael 1997, *Ways of war and peace: realism, liberalism and socialism*, New York: W. W. Norton & Co. Impressive account of realism, liberalism and socialism's intellectual contributions to the study of international relations.

George, Jim 1994, *Discourses of global politics: a critical (re)introduction to international relations*, Boulder: Lynne Rienner Publishers. Most important book published in the context of the 'third great debate'; captures the complexity of the discipline.

Griffiths, Martin (ed.) 2005, *Encyclopedia of international relations and global politics*, London: Routledge. Indispensable resource with entries on all major and minor topics.

Reus-Smit, Christian and Snidal, Duncan (eds), 2008, *The Oxford handbook of international relations*, Oxford: Oxford University Press. Major reference book that provides an invaluable account of the 'state of the art' of IR.

Smith, Steve, Booth, Ken and Zalewski, Marysia (eds) 1996, *International theory: positivism and beyond*, Cambridge: Cambridge University Press. Still valuable overview of the discipline on the seventy-fifth anniversary of the Department of Politics at the University of Wales, Aberystwyth.

Journals

There are also a number of academic journals you should acquaint yourself with. I mention only a few of the most important ones here. *International Organization*, *International Studies Quarterly* and *World Politics* from the US; *Review of International Studies* and *International Affairs* from the UK; *European Journal of International Relations* based in Europe; *Australian Journal of International Affairs* from Australia. There are also some important theory journals that reflect the 'critical turn', including the London School of Economics-based *Millennium: Journal of International Studies* (UK), *Alternatives: Global, Local, Political* (Canada/India), and the new journal, *International Theory* (US).

Theories of International Relations

PART **1**

1 **International Relations Theory in an Age of Critical Diversity**   22
  Jim George

2 **Realism**   35
  Michele Chiaruzzi

3 **Liberalism**   48
  James L. Richardson

4 **Marxism and Critical Theory**   62
  Richard Devetak, Jim George and Martin Weber

5 **Feminism**   76
  Katrina Lee-Koo

6 **Postmodernism**   91
  Roland Bleiker

7 **Constructivism**   103
  Patrick Thaddeus Jackson and Joshua S. Jones

8 **Theories of Global Justice**   119
  Richard Shapcott

1

International Relations Theory in an Age of Critical Diversity

Jim George

Introduction	23
The necessity of theory	23
Ontology, epistemology and the science question in international relations theory	24
Mainstream international relations theory	26
The era of critical diversity	29
Conclusion	33
Questions	34
Further reading	34

Introduction

This chapter introduces students to the range of theoretical perspectives and issues that have animated the study of international relations down the years. First, it explains why theoretical reflection is indispensable to explaining and understanding international relations. Second, it addresses unavoidable ontological and epistemological issues in the quest for theoretical understanding. Third, it traces the growth of mainstream international relations theory. Finally, it analyses the rise of diverse critical approaches to the study of international relations.

The necessity of theory

Students in International Relations (IR) are often wary of 'doing' theory. Sometimes they are frightened of it, sometimes hostile to it. The reasons for these attitudes vary. Theory, it is often proclaimed, is too difficult, too abstract or irrelevant to the real world. Thankfully, these attitudes are changing as IR students become more aware of sophisticated debates about the nature and role of theory in understanding and explaining the real world they speak of and live in. These debates illustrate that theorising is not something one can choose to avoid; that in the process of giving meaning to the things, peoples, events and controversies in the world, we are engaged in a theoretical process, explicitly or otherwise.

In particular, we cannot simply observe the everyday world of international relations without giving theoretical meaning to what we are seeing. And in this process of observation, of course, we might well bestow different meanings on the same event, as we theorise these 'real world' things in different ways. For example, when we see an American president or British and Australian prime ministers enthusiastically advocating war in Iraq and Afghanistan what meaning are we to accord these actions? Are these actions – designed to bolster global security against terrorist threat – prudent and justifiable? Or are they political and strategic commitments likely to increase Islamist recruitment and fanaticism and make us more vulnerable in security terms?

Rarely are the questions of contemporary international relations as clear cut as this. More often than not we are concerned with multiple shades of grey when making judgments on complex foreign policy and security issues. But the point is clear enough: when one seeks to explain something in the real world of international relations, it is never enough to just 'look at the facts', because the facts – in this case concerning major policy decisions on Iraq and Afghanistan – can be accorded a range of different meanings, depending on how they are understood, processed and prioritised; depending, more precisely, on the theoretical frame of reference one brings to them.

We still, nevertheless, have to make judgments on such issues. Indeed, as members of the international community it is imperative that we do so. We have to be aware, however, that our judgments do not rest on some infallible foundation of absolute correctness, but on a process of theoretically framing the world which provides 'correct' cognitive and political meaning for us. This need not lead to either philosophical or political relativism. It is not good enough to conclude that because there might be no single, irreducible way of understanding the political world we need not bother thinking seriously about where we stand on important contemporary issues. On the contrary, because our thinking, social behaviour and political judgment is not determined by absolute categories of truth or reality, we must think ever more seriously about the theorised truths and reality which give us the political and ethical foundations on which we live our lives.

Our task as students of international relations is to become increasingly aware of the strengths and weaknesses of the theorised positions we take, to acknowledge that these positions are, by definition, never beyond question, never closed to greater knowledge as we experience a volatile, changing world. This chapter seeks to help in developing this awareness. It seeks to illustrate that studying international relations theory is an exciting and stimulating experience which engages a range of difficult but crucial questions about human knowledge, political power and possible global futures. Questions, traditionally, about 'man, the state and war' (Waltz 1959), but now re-articulated and refocused to include questions of community, religion, global poverty, terrorism, gender, refugees, justice and the environment in a complex contemporary world. Questions of who we are, what we stand for and how we should live and engage with others in the twenty-first century.

To begin to adequately address questions such as these one needs to go beyond a simple 'current affairs' approach to international relations in order both to understand the development of theory since the institutionalisation of the IR discipline in 1919 (see Introduction), and to understand those areas of intellectual and political contention that have helped accelerate the current era of critical diversity in international relations theory – particularly the contention concerning questions of scientific knowledge and international relations. Something, in particular, needs to be said about questions of **ontology** and **epistemology** in this context. This is necessary because since the early days of the IR discipline these have been issues integral to its major debates.

Ontology, epistemology and the science question in international relations theory

Ontology is, formally at least, the theory of 'being'. It is concerned with what one considers to be the fundamental elements of the world. Epistemology is the theory of 'knowing'; it is concerned with the question of how we come to know what we know about these fundamental elements. From this position we can make decisions about our methodological preferences – how we illustrate that our ontological premise is correct.

Kant's ontological position, for example, is that self-creating individuals are the fundamental elements of the social world. He 'knows' this, and seeks to illustrate it by reference to a progressivist history in which the rational and moral capacities of individuals are increasingly expressed in democratic social formations. Realists 'see' the world differently because their ontological and epistemological positions direct their image of

BOX 1.1: TERMINOLOGY

Key terms in the philosophy of science

Ontology: the branch of philosophy that studies the nature of being. It asks: What is there in the world? What is the character of the things that make up the 'furniture' of the world?

Epistemology: the branch of philosophy that studies how we produce and acquire knowledge. It asks: Are our knowledge claims valid? How do we justify our knowledge claims?

Method: a way or means of producing or attaining knowledge.

Methodology: the study of ways (methods) of producing or attaining knowledge. It asks: What are the best conceptual tools for producing knowledge about international relations?

Meta-theory: theory about theory.

reality in a different way. Their ontological position has, arguably, the same focus – individuals – but not of the **Kantian** variety. The realist individual instead is driven by a lust for power and the relentless pursuit of security. Realists 'know' this also by reference to history – this time the history of the anarchical states-system. Thus, epistemologically realists concentrate on states and a history of 'recurrence and repetition' rather than of developmental change.

It is via this 'meta-theoretical' (see Box 1.1) process that Kantian liberals and their realist counterparts make their theoretical claims for real knowledge. Both have coherent and cogent ways of illustrating their case, both point to 'history' as the vehicle for their knowledge of reality, and yet they are substantially different, holding different implications for understanding international relations and making foreign policy decisions. What then is the truth of the matter? And how is judgment to be made?

These were the kinds of questions which led to the search for a science of IR: for a process by which different knowledge claims could be transformed into a single scientifically established knowledge form, a body of objectively gleaned knowledge generated via methods of the natural sciences. This issue was integral to the early realist–**idealist** debate in the 1920s and 1930s (the so-called 'first great debate'), and in the 1950s and 1960s it was an issue of stark contention between the mainly American behaviouralists and their traditionalist critics (the so-called 'second great debate'). And it was at the core of the disputes between positivists and anti-positivists that characterised 'the third great debate' in IR during the 1990s.

It remains an ongoing issue of contention in the twenty-first century, particularly with regard to the US core of the discipline where a positivist form of scientific enquiry has held sway since the 1950s (Vasquez 1998). A section of the IR community became increasingly opposed to this positivist approach in the 1980s and 1990s. It is important to note that this was never an attack on science per se, but ironically, on the *anti-scientific* tendencies of positivism which, its critics argue, has misrepresented and/or ignored some of the most sophisticated dimensions of scientific thinking since the 1920s, in the field of quantum physics in particular (see Box 1.2).

The point here is that with the shift from seventeenth-century Newtonian physics to twentieth-century quantum physics came the shift from a science based on observable things to a science based on unobservable things – a science of sub-atomic particles as the new building blocks of existence, the new ontological foundations of 'being'. Because they are not directly available to the 'senses' these building blocks of existence cannot be 'observed' in any direct or objective manner; they thus defy the empiricist epistemology of positivism.

The significance of all this for contemporary IR is that it severely problematises positivist approaches to science, while maintaining a healthy respect for the scientific enterprise which, at its best, proposes that there are facts and truths and realities in the world – but that

BOX 1.2: TERMINOLOGY

Positivism and scientific IR

Positivism utilises empiricist epistemology. **Empiricism** maintains that only observable facts should form the basis of 'real' knowledge; facts that can be scientifically validated to create a knowledge base for IR analogous to the natural sciences. This strict empiricist line has been the norm in 'scientific' IR, but it has not been adopted by all positivists.

Outside the study of IR, German theoretical physicist Werner Heisenberg (1961: 20) has questioned the universal applicability of empiricism: 'In atomic physics observations can no longer be objectified … The science of nature does not deal with nature itself but in fact with the science of nature as man thinks it and describes it'.

facts are always contingent, and that the truths and realities are always infused with theoretical and interpretive dimensions. There is no room for intellectual closure in this scientific enterprise, no room for dogmatic insistence about single, universal truth and/ or unchangeable and unchallengeable reality. No room either for the notion that theory is divorced from, or irrelevant to, the 'real world'.

This kind of scientific insight has been rare in IR circles. For the most part the debate over science and IR has been carried out as a debate between positivism and its critics. This debate continues into the present with tensions within constructivist theory a particularly evident example of it (see Chapter 7). But the insights evident at the apex of scientific scholarship have had significant influence within a range of critical international relations theories, and we will touch on this influence shortly.

Mainstream international relations theory

For now suffice it to say that the debate over scientific knowledge underlay the more immediate concerns of early IR scholars in 1919 as they sought to explain the reasons for the carnage of World War I and find ways of avoiding such mayhem in the future. A liberal perspective dominated the early years of the discipline; a perspective exemplified in the neo-Kantianism of US President Woodrow Wilson (1856–1924), who urged a new world order based on individual liberty and the rule of law, capitalist free trade, scientific progress, and the establishment of liberal institutions of crisis management such as the League of Nations and the International Court of Justice.

But as the mood again darkened during the years of Depression and rising ideological extremism, realists attacked liberalism as dangerously **utopian** in the face of extreme danger. E. H Carr's *The twenty years' crisis, 1919–1939* (1946) is the literary exemplar in this regard. Carr was scathing about liberal idealism at a time of looming catastrophe and about liberal theory more generally in an international environment characterised, he argued, by the logics and strategies of traditional power politics.

A major problem of the inter-war years, Carr proposed, was that under liberal tutelage IR as a field of knowledge was in a 'pre-scientific' phase of its development, whereas under realism it could become scientifically advanced – dealing with reality as it actually 'is', rather than how idealists assume it 'ought' to be. This is not quite the simple positivism it might appear. Carr understood that crude dichotomies of 'is/ ought' and 'realism/idealism' are unsophisticated and inadequate explanatory devices. But for a variety of reasons – concerning the ambiguity of some of his arguments, and the pragmatic way in which his work was later read and appropriated by Cold War realists – this dichotomised frame of reference (realism v. idealism) arguably became Carr's major legacy to IR scholarship. A more appropriate legacy is one which acknowledges *The twenty years' crisis*: first, as an extraordinarily insightful commentary on inter-war international relations as **fascism** threatened; second, as an early attempt to deal with some complex theoretical issues that were not seriously revisited by the discipline of IR until fifty years later; and third, as a work which indicated something of what realism and liberalism represent, at their best and at their worst.

Realism, at its best, reminds us that the international environment is invariably dangerous and volatile and that in such an environment the use of violence is sometimes necessary to counter the violent intent of others; that sometimes rational debate is not enough to deter this violent intent. At its best realism reminds us of something else too: that the use of force should be sanctioned only as a last resort, when national security and/or fundamental values are threatened; that rules of proportionality be applied; that the safety and rights of non combatants be strictly observed. And at its best realism uses power as a 'means' to an ordered and relatively peaceful 'end' – not as an end in itself.

Liberalism, at its best, reminds us that even in a world of danger and violent intent there can be realistic alternatives to force projection as a means of maintaining international order. Liberalism reminds us that ideas – of freedom and democracy, and individual dignity and human rights – are not just abstractions but have real concrete significance in the changes that have shaped the modern world; inspiring progressive change for many millions of people over the past few centuries, and inspiring social **emancipation** in the face of seemingly overwhelming structures of violence and oppression. At its best liberalism does not ignore the fact of violent conflict but refuses to reduce the human condition to the perceived dictates of an anarchical system of states, insisting instead on the power and persuasiveness of international law (see Chapter 16) and of the humanitarian instinct (see Chapter 31).

After World War II, however, increasingly crude variants of realism (and liberalism) came to dominate the IR agenda. No sooner had the fascists been defeated than the USSR emerged as the major threat on the Western international relations agenda. Consequently, the intellectual and strategic focus of the discipline became the Cold War, with international relations theory increasingly focused on American Cold War interests and perspectives. During this period Hans Morgenthau (1904–1980) became the emblematic American realist, with his *Politics among nations* (1973), first published in 1948, largely framing the agenda for generations of students and policymakers during the Cold War.

Informed principally by Max Weber and Carl Schmitt, Morgenthau's ideas infused realism with a deep intellectual tension derived from the pessimism of much nineteenth-century European thought about 'human nature', and a commitment to the notion that a science of modern political life is possible and necessary. This had a number of implications for Morgenthau's conclusions about international relations in the early years of the Cold War – in particular, his conclusion that the struggle for power is the fundamental political fact which determines the foreign policy behaviour of all states (as they pursue their **national interest** defined as power') in an anarchical system. This leads to a second major proposition: that the pursuit of power by all states in the system is an 'objective law' of international relations. The superiority of realist theory, consequently, is that it is 'governed by objective laws that have their roots in human nature' (Morgenthau 1973: 5).

Elsewhere, Morgenthau makes clear the need for realist policymakers to take into account specific historical and political factors in making judgments on the workings of these 'objective laws'. As had happened with Carr's work, however, the ambiguity and inconsistency of Morgenthau's attempts to answer the 'big' questions of international relations at a time of political crisis resulted in a number of possible interpretations of his positions which were variously seized upon by the IR community, particularly in the US.

Indeed, Morgenthau articulated both classical and scientific realist influences (referred to as 'classical' and 'structural' realism in Chapter 2), and both strains of realism have claimed him as their own. The latter's influence helped accelerate the movement toward the 'scientific turn' and positivism in American realism in particular. It was also to be the catalyst for major critiques within realism and, beyond it, by those concerned about the nature of the positivist quest per se.

One internal critique is of special significance: Hedley Bull's (1932–1985) attack on the employment of scientific method in IR. Bull's (1966) intervention is important because it indicates that realism is a much more theoretically nuanced perspective than it is sometimes given credit for. Although Bull was an Australian his work increased the profile of the so-called 'English School' of IR, an approach which remains significant to the present day (Dunne 1998, 2007; Linklater and Suganami 2006).

There is contention surrounding precisely what the English School approach stands for (but see Box 17.1). In its early manifestations it appeared a kind of gentrified realism in comparison to the harder-edged American variant. It has developed into rather more than this and Bull's works indicated this potential (see his *The anarchical society*, 1977). It suggests that a rudimentary 'international society' operates in the realist 'anarchical' sphere, which sees states and other actors dealing with their clashes of interests not just by resort to war or aggressive **alliance**-building, but also by recourse to agreed-upon social norms and regulations and the processes of international law.

This does not add up to liberal internationalism. The English School approach repudiates the progressivism intrinsic to liberal IR thinking while positively engaging with some of its major concerns, such as human rights and questions of justice in the international system (Vincent 1986) – concerns, it stresses, which cannot be adequately addressed in value-free scientific terms. Nor, however, can they be answered without taking into consideration an abiding reality about 'international society' – that it exists because its members have very basic interests in common (what the Soviets used to call 'peaceful coexistence'), not because they share a common desire for cosmopolitan democracy.

The English School perspective, and its critique of orthodox realism, has continued to have influence in IR theory circles, primarily in the UK and Australia, though it has been much less influential at the core of the discipline in the US.

Since the 1970s the critiques of realism and of liberalism have gone well beyond English School perspectives. The Vietnam War (1964–1973) was the catalyst for much of this wider critique as US foreign policy and its way of thinking about international relations came under increasing scrutiny. The breakdown of the **Bretton Woods** system and the development of an unregulated global marketplace only enhanced the sense that neither realism nor liberalism had the capacity to deal with the changing nature of an international agenda where questions of poverty, justice and human rights were increasingly perceived as first order issues.

A second critical dimension became more evident at this time, which saw attention paid to the similarities between realism and liberalism – as effectively two sides of the same historical and cultural coin. So many peoples, cultures and interests, it was argued, are left out of the orthodox narratives. The traditional frame of reference, critics contended, was inadequate for understanding a world where ontological commitments to the sovereign state, or the sovereign individual, simply do not encompass the experiences of a multi-faceted, multi-ethnic, multi-religious world – a world where Western theory and practice might no longer be dominant in the future.

This critical pace increased in the 1980s and 1990s as a response to the emergence of **neorealism** and **neoliberalism** as the mainstream answers to post-Vietnam, post-

Table 1.1 Mainstream IR theories

Theories	Theorists
Realism	E. H. Carr, Hans J. Morgenthau
Liberalism	Michael Doyle, Richard Rosecrance
Neorealism	Kenneth Waltz, John Mearsheimer
Neoliberalism	Robert O. Keohane, Andrew Moravcsik
English School	Martin Wight, Hedley Bull

Bretton Woods critiques; answers which, on the one hand, reasserted realist notions about structural imperatives and unchangeable principles of anarchy, security and fear at the core of modern international relations (Waltz 1979; Mearsheimer 2007), and, on the other, which reasserted the individualistic free-trade mantras of liberalism as the universalistic basis for prosperity and peace in a new age of economic globalisation (Friedman 1999).

In both cases the self-interested, power hungry individual-cum-state is the primary ontological assumption; in both cases universalist and scientifically inclined epistemologies are retained; in both cases systemic order and efficient market performance is considered dependent upon US global hegemony. There are differences between the 'neos' (Lamy 2005), but it has been these similarities which have most concerned their critics, and it has been the resulting narrowness of the mainstream agenda that has been a catalyst for much of the critical diversity in international relations theory since the 1990s.

The era of critical diversity

Among radical liberals, for example, there are those who fear the static and militaristic orientations of neorealism but also reject neoliberal perspectives on globalisation and free market progress. The two dominant 'neos', they argue, are indeed two sides of the same coin and liberalism has dimensions that are not encompassed by the neo–neo exchange (see Chapter 3). Neoliberalism, it is proposed, is actually designed to enhance the power and prosperity of the global North, whatever its rhetoric about liberalisation and democratisation. In this context, and hand-in-hand with neorealism (e.g. the US iron fist in the velvet glove) it is producing a 'global apartheid' as privilege and poverty increase in the world (Falk 1999). Simultaneously it is provoking global dissent and 'blowback' terrorism aimed at the major western states (C. Johnson 2000).

From this particular variant of radical liberal internationalism, IR theory and practice should concentrate less on a zealous free market doctrine and more on issues of global justice, sustainable development, cultural pluralism, human rights and genuine democratisation (see Chapter 8). Much of the empirical analysis in this liberal critique centres on the question of global governance and how major economic and political institutions might be restructured to assist the world's 'have nots' (S. George 2004).

Marxists, of course, have been concentrating on the relationship between the global rich and poor for many years. And while Marxism (Chapter 4) was effectively silenced in mainstream IR during the Cold War, there is now a renewed interest in what Marx had to say about advanced capitalist societies, globalisation and the limitations of liberalism (and neoliberalism) in international relations (Colas and Saul 2006).

Critical challenges have come also from neo-Marxist perspectives, with the works of Italian Marxist Antonio Gramsci (1891–1937) particularly important in prompting a range of contemporary counter-hegemonic challenges to the mainstream in recent years. Central to this project, accordingly, are a range of works on critical social movements around the world seeking, in their different ways, to overcome the impact upon them of hegemonic power (see Rupert 2003, 2007).

Writing in the 1920s and 1930s in Fascist-ruled Italy, Gramsci reformulated Marxism in line with perceived weaknesses in its classical formulation. States no longer protected their ruling class interests by explicit or direct means, he argued, but now utilised more nuanced and insidious forms of cognitive and political persuasion to undermine emancipatory theory and practice. This process of ruling class 'hegemony' was so powerful, Gramsci proposed, because it didn't appear to be happening, and because it took place in seemingly neutral spaces – in schools, universities and churches – where ideas are infused into working people, naturalising capitalist relations of production, political passivity and nationalism, rather than cultivating critical reflection and internationalist sentiments. The task for those committed to radical change consequently was to engage in 'counter-hegemonic' projects designed to expose and undermine the processes by which ruling classes gained 'consent' for their rule from those most disadvantaged by it.

Since the 1980s neo-Gramscians in IR theory have been utilising these broad Gramscian themes to illustrate how an international 'ruling class' – of states, corporations, and a variety of global economic institutions such as the IMF, World Bank and the WTO (see Chapter 24) – acts to naturalise a system designed to enhance the power and prosperity of a small minority of the world's states and peoples. Central to this project too is a range of neo-Gramscian works on critical social movements and counter-hegemonic forces around the world seeking in their different ways to overcome the impact upon them of hegemonic power (Morton 2002; Butko 2006; Gill 2000).

Another dimension of this project has seen scholars such as Robert Cox critically analysing the process by which certain ideas and attitudes become hegemonic in international relations. Cox indicates this via his oft-quoted proposition that theory 'is always *for* someone and *for* some purpose' (Cox 1981: 128). His point here is to reiterate that there are no neutral vantage points in international relations theory, and to illustrate how neorealism seeks to present itself as an objective analysis of the world 'as it really is' (see Box 4.2). It is, Cox argues, a problem-solving theory which accepts the **status quo**, seeking only to make the present system work more efficiently. Critical Theory (Chapter 4), by contrast, locates current problems in a broader historical and intellectual context. This helps it question how the system came to be the way it is, how various social forces impacted upon its historical development, and how further change might be possible (Cox 1987; Linklater 1996).

These themes have been central to other works influenced by Gramsci (and by Kant) – those of Andrew Linklater, for example, whose work resonates with critical concerns about new forms of identity in the age of globalisation; about the possibilities for an ethics of human community; and about the relationship between knowledge and power in international relations (Linklater 1990, 1998). Two works by Linklater are particularly important in this context. The first, *Men and citizens in international relations* (1982) offered a philosophical critique of state sovereignty and defence of global ethical obligations. The second, *Beyond realism and Marxism: Critical Theory and international relations* (1990), sought to build upon realist insights into power and anarchy and upon Marxist concerns for 'universal emancipation' beyond state boundaries (1990: 4). A daunting analytical and normative ambition to be sure, but one which Linklater has confronted in sophisticated fashion and which has established some qualitative benchmarks for Critical Theory scholarship in the twenty-first century.

Linklater's concerns about community, ethics and difference have been intrinsic also to a range of other critical perspectives on the contemporary IR theory agenda – feminism, post-colonialism, postmodernism and constructivism among them. Intrinsic to these approaches also has been an explicit concern with the power–knowledge nexus in IR.

Postmodernism gleans its primary understanding of the relationship between knowledge and power from Friedrich Nietzsche (1844–1900), who proposed that all knowledge claims, particularly those invoking universalist stances on behalf of the truth, or the reality of human life, are actually driven by a 'will to power' on the part of the claimant, be they Platonic philosophers, theologians, or modern radicals and conservatives (see Chapter 6). This Nietzschean legacy was filtered through the works of a number of French intellectuals in the 1960s and 1970s (especially Michel Foucault and Jacques Derrida) as their disillusionment with the structuralism of Louis Althusser saw them developing post-structuralist critiques of both the radical enlightenment and contemporary liberal-capitalism.

As it was filtered into IR during the 1980s and 1990s, 'postmodernism' sought to re-locate the dominant IR narratives of reality as foundationalist discourses of power and to illustrate the dangers and limitations of such discourses (see Campbell 2007). **Foundationalism** in this sense represents a claim to knowledge perceived as beyond challenge, beyond change, beyond social reassessment and adaptation.

Postmodernists in IR have sought to challenge these claims since the 1980s, maintaining that, as the major foundationalist articulations of theoretical orthodoxy in the 1990s, neorealism and neoliberalism are incapable of the critical self-reflection needed in a changing, volatile post-Cold War world. In this regard an important political aim associated with exposing the silences and limitations of the dominant 'neos' is to create 'thinking space' for analytical and policy options previously excluded from the 'art of the possible' in traditional IR. This was a theme central to Richard Ashley's groundbreaking works (1988, 1989) and to a range of similarly focused studies that introduced postmodern perspectives to an IR audience (R. B. J. Walker 1987; Der Derian and Shapiro 1989).

It is a theme central to the second wave of postmodern IR literature which, building upon these earlier 'breakthrough' works, and no longer burdened by the need to argue at the level of discursive foundations, has used the clear analytical space to more directly engage some of the crucial international relations issues of the day. Works, for example, on US foreign policy (see Campbell 1992; Shapiro 1988); on the war in Bosnia (Campbell 1998); on the tensions on the Korean peninsula (Bleiker 2005); on questions of humanitarian intervention (Orford 1999; Edkins 2004); on the global political economy (de Goede 2006); and on security policy (A. Burke 2006) have helped broaden and deepen the postmodernist contribution to the critical turn in IR in recent years. Another theme constant within postmodernist writings has been its concern for those excluded from the dominant discourses of power politics and free-market individualism. In this sense postmodernism shares an ethical position with Critical Theorists like Linklater and Cox and with much feminist scholarship in IR theory, particularly in its first wave articulation in the 1980s and 1990s.

At the core of early feminist literature was the claim that women had been systematically excluded from the IR agenda (see Chapter 5). More precisely, that IR theory has never been gender neutral; that, on the contrary, its orthodox frame of reference – centred on notions of 'fallen man', endemic anarchy and/or aggressive, market-oriented individualism – rests on a deeply gendered caricature of humankind (Tickner 1992; Grant and Newland 1991). Since the 1990s a second wave of feminist literature has continued this theoretical assault on gendered theories and practices of international relations.

In so doing it has produced a broad and burgeoning literature which speaks in different ways of women's lives and experiences, which illustrate their struggles and achievements and their intrinsic contributions to the everyday world of international relations (see Tickner and Sjoberg 2007; also Chapter 6). Feminists have sought to add important extra dimensions to core IR themes. On security, for example, orthodox concerns have been supplemented with works on other kinds of security threats – concerning rape, poverty and sexual degradation (Lee-Koo 2008).

And on issues of global economics, feminist scholars have focused on the particular burdens placed on women and children as, for example, the main victims of decisions taken to impose sanctions (e.g. on Iraq in the 1990s), and/or to impose structural adjustment policies upon already impoverished societies (Tickner and Sjoberg 2007).

This flourishing feminist literature is very much an indication of the 'age of diversity' in IR – even more so, perhaps, in regard to post-colonial theory which, above all, insists that its voice now be heard on the IR agenda. The desire of the diverse peoples of Africa, Asia, the Arab world and elsewhere to speak in their own voice has particular resonance for post-colonial scholarship because of its central argument that the voices, cultures and histories of colonised peoples have been reformulated or caricatured or erased completely by the dominant Western powers in the modern era (Ashcroft et al. 1989; Darby 2000; Spivak 1987).

A powerful and influential dimension was added to this literature by Edward Said (1935–2003) via his notion of 'orientalism' (1979), a process, Said argued, which transformed the identities, cultures and religions of colonised peoples into simple caricatures of imperialist imagination, most often in terms which rendered them inferior to their colonial rulers and susceptible therefore to Western discipline and punishment. Post-colonialist literature thus rejects both culturally specific and imperialistic images of human society, and those liberal and radical alternatives which remain ignorant of cultural otherness, or patronising when it comes to the 'poor world' (see Chowdrey and Nair 2002). In all of these contexts post-colonialism argues for global inclusiveness and a toleration of difference as fundamental elements of any 'universalist' approach to international relations.

All these critical perspectives are currently making their contributions to a vibrant IR theory agenda in the twenty-first century, as is constructivism, which is arguably the most influential of the critically-inclined perspectives on the current theory agenda. This is primarily because it has been accepted, and in many ways appropriated, by the mainstream of IR in the US. It has used this opportunity to produce a body of theoretical and empirical work which has added insightful dimensions to the 'critical turn' in IR

Table 1.2 Critical IR theories

Theories	Theorists
Marxism	Immanuel Wallerstein, Fred Halliday
Critical Theory	R. W. Cox, Andrew Linklater
Feminism	Cynthia Enloe, J. Anne Tickner
Postmodernism	R. B. J. Walker, Richard Ashley
Constructivism	Nicholas Onuf, Alexander Wendt

theory (see Chapter 7). Importantly, this has allowed constructivists to refashion the lexicon of real meaning in American IR circles, in particular, on issues of power, identity and rationality and most famously on anarchy, which, as Alexander Wendt has put it, 'is what states make of it' (Wendt 1992).

This is not simply to wish anarchy away in idealist fashion, but to underline the point that nothing in international relations exists independently of the meanings and practices of social actors. This has significant implications for the way in which the behaviour of states, global organisations and individual actors might be understood, and constructivist writings have explored these possibilities in works on the ideas, norms, rules and meanings that constitute everyday theory and practice in international relations (Kratochwil 1989; Reus-Smit 2004a; Onuf 1998).

A good deal of this constructivism continues to utilise traditional positivist methodology; hence its popularity in the US. Some constructivism, however, has a more radical edge and pursues the 'social construction of reality' theme on issues of global peace and systemic transformation where it has, to some extent, overlapped with elements of the English School (see Reus-Smit 2002).

Conclusion

This chapter has provided an account of how one might understand not only the evolution of IR theory since its inception, but also how we might begin to think about the relationships between the diverse theoretical approaches. It has advanced two important propositions: first, that international relations cannot be understood independently of the theoretical frameworks which give meaning to the world; second, that the development of IR as a discipline has seen the progressive enlargement of the theoretical imagination as a diverse range of critical theories have challenged mainstream approaches.

None of this is to suggest that the realist and liberal mainstreams have been swept away on this tide of critical diversity. In policy communities and in many areas of the IR community in general the traditional agenda's vocabulary and lexicon of meaning still dominate. Indeed, in the post-September 11 era 'classical' realism has undergone something of a renaissance as attention has shifted back to traditional issues of power, war and international order. But, as a number of critical theorists have suggested, realism no longer has an analytical mortgage on the meaning of power in international relations, or on realistic understandings of its implications. Additionally, liberalism faces many challenges as it seeks to articulate a universal voice beyond the suspicion and cynicism widely held around the world as to its real meaning and intent in an age of globalisation and global governance.

As for the critical approaches touched on here – all of them have strengths and weaknesses. All deserve respectful attention, but none of them should be accepted or advocated without rigorous, scholarly inspection and contemplation. This chapter has sought to give you a frame of reference by which this process might usefully begin. You are invited now to continue this process in regard to the more comprehensive treatments of the traditional and critical theory agendas.

QUESTIONS

1. Why are questions of ontology and epistemology integral to the IR theory debate?

2. Why does the issue of 'scientific' IR theory continue to evoke major disagreement within the IR theory community?

3. Carr's *The twenty years' crisis*, Morgenthau's *Politics among nations* and Waltz's *Theory of international politics* are arguably the three major realist texts in IR theory. What does this tell us about the development of the IR discipline?

4. Are neorealism and neoliberalism 'two sides of the same coin'?

5. What, if anything, are the political and analytical themes which bind together Marxism, Critical Theory, postmodernism, feminism, post-colonialism and constructivism?

FURTHER READING

Burchill, Scott, Linklater, Andrew et al., 2009, *Theories of international relations*, 4th edition, London: Palgrave. Advanced introduction to IR theory.

Dunne, Tim, Kurki, Milja and Smith, Steve (eds) 2007, *International relations theories: discipline and diversity,* Oxford: Oxford University Press. Excellent introduction to IR theories.

George, Jim 1994, *Discourses of global politics: a critical (re)introduction to international relations*, Boulder: Lynne Rienner. Comprehensive account of both mainstream and critical theories of IR.

Jackson, Patrick Thaddeus 2010, *The conduct of inquiry in international relations: philosophy of science and its implications for the study of world politics*, London: Routledge. Lively, wide-ranging constructivist account of competing IR methods.

Waltz, Kenneth 1979, 'Laws and theories', in *Theory of international politics*, New York: Random House. Unsurpassed account of neorealism's positivist approach to IR.

2

Realism

Michele Chiaruzzi

Introduction   36

Who are the realists? Genesis of a tradition of thought   37

What is realism? Synthesising theory and practice   43

Conclusion   46

Questions   47

Further reading   47

Introduction

This chapter reflects on the tradition of political thought known as realism. Its main purpose is to identify who realists are, and to explain what realism is in the study of international relations. The first part of the chapter introduces students to some important thinkers, both ancient and modern, ascribed to the realist tradition of thought. It also identifies two broad strands of realist thought: 'classical' and 'structural' or 'neorealist'. The second part investigates attempts to conceive realism as a unified theory and practice of international relations. It highlights realism's central concepts of the state and anarchy before reflecting on realism's normative dimension.

Realism has historically been the dominant theory of International Relations and a point of reference for alternative theories, even if only critically. It aspires to be suprahistorical, explaining in all epochs the fundamental features of international politics: first and foremost, conflict and war. Emerging in the 1930s, realism's polemical target was the progressive, reformist optimism connected with **liberal** internationalists such as American president Woodrow Wilson. Against this optimism, realism comported a more pessimistic outlook which was felt to be necessary in the tragic realm of international politics.

Realists lay claim to a long tradition of political thought, including such eminent thinkers as Thucydides, Machiavelli and Hobbes, whose point of departure is the study of conflict and power politics. According to realists, conflict is inevitable, even necessary in international politics. When disputes cannot be resolved peacefully or diplomatically, force, and ultimately war, is a decisive means of settling matters. Insofar as order exists in international relations, it is the precarious product of the balance of power or **hegemony** (domination by a **great power** and its allies), say realists (Dehio 1962; J. Levy 1983). The pragmatic acceptance of conflict and power politics are essential to realism's outlook. But who are the realists? And what is realism? This chapter provides answers these two questions.

It will be suggested here that realism is best understood, first, as an eclectic and plural tradition of thought, rather than a theory as such; and second, as a practical guide to the politics of international relations. Realists are political theorists and practitioners who, since the interwar years (1918–1938), have self-consciously subscribed to this tradition of thought.

Despite the efforts of late twentieth-century neorealists such as Kenneth Waltz (1979), realism is not properly speaking a theory – an explicative coherent whole, clearly defined by an explicit set of axioms and propositions. Rather, realism is the name given by exponents and critics alike to a tradition of thought, signifying an approach to international relations which claims to avoid wishful thinking by dealing with international politics as they actually are, rather than as we would like them to be. It does not abandon morality altogether, but it does extol a morality specific to the state (***raison d'ètat*** or **reason of state**) and statesman (ethics of responsibility). So although realism rejects morality as the starting point for the theory and practice of international relations, it does not eschew morality altogether (A. Murray 1997: chapter 3; Hulsman and Lieven 2005).

Who are the realists? Genesis of a tradition of thought

The classical approach: realism

In one of his 1950s lectures, Martin Wight, a British professor, told his students: 'The initial pointer towards the Realists was that they are those who emphasize in international relations the element of **anarchy**, of **power politics**, and of warfare. Everyone is a Realist nowadays, and the term in this sense needs no argument' (Wight 1991: 15). Wight here is emphasising the distinctive importance and disciplinary dominance of realism as a tradition in the theory and practice of international politics. But he also alludes to some of realism's key tenets: the concept of anarchy and the historical supposition that international relations are unavoidably shaped by power politics and war. According to the realist construction of the tradition, the intellectual origins of these tenets may be traced back to the historical and political thought of arguably the first and the greatest political realists respectively, Athenian general (*strategos*) and historian, Thucydides (c. 460–406 BC) and Florentine diplomat and writer, Niccolò Machiavelli (1469–1527).

One of the reasons for realism's enduring relevance is its emphasis on history. Realism claims to speak about historical reality and takes its convictions, orientations and practice from history. Thus, it is not surprising that we can locate its roots in the Greek political and historical thought of the fifth century BC as embodied in Thucydides's *History of the Peloponnesian War* (1972) (see Box 0.3). Looking at the clash between the great powers of his time (Athens, Sparta and Persia), Thucydides searched for the fundamental causes of conflict, the profound logics behind political events, and the instruments of power which political actors deployed, either openly, secretly, or through dissimulation. He concentrated on war because war is the ultimate test for those who want to distinguish reality from appearance in international politics. As the name itself reveals, this resolute striving to engage with stubborn political realities, no matter how violent or tragic, is one of the principal claims of realism as a tradition of thought.

In the most controversial and powerful advice-book for rulers ever written, *The prince* ([1513] 1998), authored by Machiavelli during the critical age of the Italian city-states, we can detect a view of international politics partially inherited from Thucydides. We find, for example, a cyclical conception of history based on a recurrent nexus of necessity, chance and human decision. Using a modern expression, international relations are conceived as a 'realm of recurrence and repetition' where 'political action is most regularly necessitous' (Wight 1966b: 26). The essence of this recurrence and repetition lies in the historical fact that rulers are regularly called upon to suspend conventional moral and legal rules to deflect threats to the state. We can call this Machiavelli's doctrine of necessity, which is central to the logic of politics.

We see in Machiavelli's writings recognition of the autonomy of politics from other realms of human action, most especially its ultimate independence from morality and law. Politics has its own rules, and cannot be reduced to or contained by moral or legal rules since it must respond to the demands of necessity. We also see the primacy of the political, because conflict and competition for power are inevitable and irrepressible. Four centuries later, these notions of the autonomy and primacy of the political were rearticulated and reformulated by two influential German jurists, Hans J. Morgenthau (2010) and Carl Schmitt (1976), who identified the intense antagonism between friend and enemy as the crucial dimension of concrete historical politics.

Above all, it was through Machiavelli's analytical lens that it became possible to regard international politics free of ethical prescriptions. He insisted on attending to 'the effectual truth' of political matters, not **idealised** or **utopian** constructions (Machiavelli 1998: 52). In other words, he advocated a clear-eyed, pragmatic consideration of the amorality of power that St Augustine (AD354–430) acknowledged from a Christian perspective and that was to become so influential on many twentieth-century realists, including Reinhold Niebuhr and Herbert Butterfield. Significantly, Carr (1946: 63) considers Machiavelli 'the first important political realist'. From Machiavelli he deduces three essential realist tenets. First, 'history is a sequence of cause and effect, whose course can be analysed and understood by intellectual effort, but not … directed by "imagination"'. Second, 'theory does not create practice …, but practice theory'. Third, and most contentious of all, 'morality is the product of power' (Carr 1946: 63–64). Finally, Machiavelli, like Thucydides and St Augustine, draws our attention to certain anthropological and psychological features alleged to be constant. They discern the political dimension of human nature, and the role of fear, avarice and ambition in driving political action and generating conflict.

This combination corresponds to the causes of war indicated by the English philosopher Thomas Hobbes (1588–1679). His masterpiece *Leviathan* ([1651] 1968) has provided the realist tradition with perhaps its most fundamental idea, later taken up by the French thinker Jean-Jacques Rousseau (1712–1778): that international life is a miserable condition because it is actually a condition of war, whether latent or actual. Realists conceive the anarchical structure of international relations through an analogy with an imaginary and primordial condition called the state of nature. In this 'natural condition' conjectured by Hobbes in Chapter 13 of *Leviathan* ([1651] 1968: 185), individuals exist in a lawless or ungoverned environment, 'without a common Power to keep them all in awe'. Hobbes equates this state of nature, which exists prior to the establishment of a state, with a state of war (see Box 2.1). To escape this intolerable condition, individuals agree to enter a civil society and install a sovereign power. But though individuals may escape this state of war, the states they form do not, Hobbes suggests; international relations are thus a state of war.

This condition originates in the absence of an overarching sovereign power. Therefore domestic political life, where sovereignty is present, is essentially different from international life, where there is no world government. This latter condition is properly described in modern terms as international anarchy. This does not indicate a state of disorder or chaos, but rather captures the fact that **sovereign states** do not recognise any other higher authority above

BOX 2.1: TERMINOLOGY

Hobbes's 'state of nature'

In *Leviathan* ([1651] 1968) Hobbes portrays the state of nature as the antithesis of the civil society that forms when individuals agree to establish a state and sovereign authority. The state of nature, says Hobbes, is a state of war that pits 'every man, against every man' because there is no 'common Power to keep them all in awe' (p. 185). In such a condition there is no justice, no law, and no property, says Hobbes (p. 188); 'every man has a Right to every thing' (p. 190). This is why Hobbes famously described the life of individuals in this condition as 'solitary, poore, nasty, brutish, and short' (p. 186).

themselves. Two consequences derive from the absence of world government (or the presence of a state of nature) according to realists: first, nothing can impede the normal recurrence of war; and second, states are responsible for their own self-preservation.

A turning point: the 'international anarchy'

The expression 'international **anarchy**' made its first appearance during the Great War, and became a fundamental concept not just for realists but more generally for International Relations as a twentieth-century academic discipline. Ironically, G. Lowes Dickinson, who published books titled *The European anarchy* (1916) and *The international anarchy* (1926), was one of the authors whom British diplomat, newspaper editor and historian E. H. Carr discredited as a naïve idealist in his classic, *The twenty years' crisis*. This latter book, considered by one historian as 'the first coherent realist theory yet in print' (Haslam 2002: 187), has had an immense impact not just on realist thought but on the development of IR as a discipline.

Carr's seminal text has been perpetually discussed and debated since it was published on the brink of World War II. Originally proposed under the title *Utopia and reality*, it consists of a polemical attack in the name of realism against the so-called utopian approach. Carr considered this intellectual approach, basically consistent with nineteenth-century principles of liberalism (see Chapter 3), flawed and in many respects responsible for the disaster of World War I. The most important, and the most problematic, assumption was that of a natural harmony of interests in international relations, born of 'the almost total neglect of the factor of **power**' (Carr 1946: cv).

For Carr international relations have an oligarchical configuration, where a few states are more important than others. States are basically divided into two classes, which he called the 'haves' and the 'have-nots'. The inescapable disparity between the 'haves', states that possess wealth and influence and that are satisfied with the existing international **order** (**status quo** powers), and the 'have-nots', dissatisfied states or **revisionist** powers, explains recurrent tensions. Therefore, Carr rejects 'the utopian assumption that there is a world interest in peace which is identifiable with the interest of each individual **nation**' (Carr 1946: 51). This 'harmony of interests' assumption fulfils an ideological rather than analytical function, concealing 'the unpalatable fact of a fundamental divergence of interest between nations desirous of maintaining the status quo and nations desirous of changing it' (Carr 1946: 51).

At the end of World War II, Hans J. Morgenthau, a German-Jew who escaped from Nazi Germany to the United States, would again declare the end of liberal illusion and its **rationalist** faith in progress. Echoing Nietzschean sentiments, Morgenthau conceded 'the tragic presence of evil in all political action', and 'the lust for power [which] manifests itself as the desire to maintain the range of one's own person with regard to others, to increase it, or to demonstrate it' (Morgenthau 1946: 202–203, 192). Morgenthau, like US ambassador George Kennan (1951), was sceptical about human rationality in international politics and critical of the excessive American confidence in a 'legalistic-moralistic approach' to international relations (Morgenthau 1973: 11). These realists stress the corrupting and pervasive influence of power on human relations, including international relations. Morgenthau's seminal book, *Politics among nations* (1973), first published in 1948, places power at the centre of the political universe, declaring: 'International politics, like all politics, is a struggle for power' (Morgenthau

1973: 25). However, this struggle does not obstruct a search for a rational – as opposed to a 'rationalist' – understanding and conduct of international politics.

Morgenthau's commitment is summarised in six general principles of political realism, which are a concise formalisation of a more complex theory (Morgenthau 1973: 3–13). Here we can recognise some of the typical elements we have seen in other realists: a flawed human nature in which the laws of politics have their roots; politics as an autonomous field of human activity; moral principles with relative, rather than universal, value (see Box 2.2 for Morgenthau's full list of realist principles). Among these principles, one deserves particular attention. According to Morgenthau, there is a 'main signpost that helps political realism to find its way through the landscape of international politics': this is 'the concept of interest defined in terms of power', which he considers 'an objective category which is universally valid'. It is this concept that makes possible the distinction between political and non-political facts. It also provides the 'link between reason trying to understand international politics and the facts to be understood' (Morgenthau 1973: 5). The rationale behind this notion is linear: if we think in terms of interest defined as power, we think as statesmen and stateswomen think. Thus, we can understand, and perhaps foresee, their thought and actions. However, before any other purpose in foreign policy, these actions are, or should be, directed towards the defence of the **national interest**, what one's own nation needs and wants in order to reach its aims.

BOX 2.2: DISCUSSION POINTS

Hans J. Morgenthau's six principles of political realism

1. Politics are governed by 'objective laws that have their roots in human nature'.
2. The concept of 'national interest defined in terms of power' is the most important foreign policy goal.
3. While 'interest defined as power' remains unaffected by historical change, the exercise of power is permanent.
4. 'Universal moral principles' cannot be used to judge the actions of states in their abstract formulation. Prudence is the morality proper to politics.
5. 'Political realism refuses to identify the moral aspirations of a particular nation with the moral laws that govern the universe'.
6. Politics is an autonomous sphere, distinct from, and not subordinate to the standards of, economics, law, morality, and so on (Morgenthau, 1973: 3–13).

Notwithstanding the contested nature of the national interest, in the context of international anarchy **security** is one of the interests that Raymond Aron (1966: 72), following Hobbes, calls 'eternal'. As in the state of nature, self-help is the only certain means to the uncertain end of self-preservation or survival. Each state aspires to survive as independent, making major decisions on its own. But, in the last analysis, it can count only on itself. Since sovereign states do not recognise any other higher authority, nothing other than states themselves can prevent, or counter, the use of force in their relations. It is only through the **balance of power** that states, alone or through **alliances**, can check the power of other states. Most importantly, the balance of power can preserve a state's independent existence from threat, aggression and **hegemony** (the domination by a great power and its allies). It is for these reasons that realists see the balance of power as the only real means of achieving **common security**.

Diplomacy, the art of communication and negotiation between powers (see Chapter 18), is an essential part for the conscious preservation of political equilibrium among states. It is also for this reason that some realists (Aron 1966; Wight 1978), including former US Secretary of State and Nobel Peace Prize winner Henry Kissinger (1964) and George Kennan, have assigned a relevant role not just to power and its distribution among states, or to the motives and intentions of statesmen and stateswomen, but also to the nature of states and their internal characteristics. Cultural and ideological factors matter because states that belong to the same type and share common policy goals prefer resolving disputes through the work of a trusted diplomacy. Having considered the concepts and ideas of some authors of classical realism, we should now explore what is called structural realism or neorealism.

The structural approach: neorealism

The basis of **neorealism** is a scientific method that systematises core doctrines of realist thought into a structural model of international relations. Elaborated during the second half of the Cold War (see Chapter 20), it is based more on economic theory and philosophy of science than on historical reflection. In Waltz's (1959, 1979) parsimonious version, neorealism breaks the connection between the internal and external dimensions of politics, denying that the internal structure of states has any serious effect on inter-state relations. By defining the structure of the international system, neorealism seeks to establish the autonomy of international politics.

Waltz rejects the classical realist arguments that human nature or the domestic character of states are relevant factors in explaining fundamental aspects of international relations. War, alliances, the formation of a balance of power, and the precariousness of cooperation cannot be explained by focusing on the behaviour of the 'units' or states in themselves, an approach Waltz criticises as reductionist. States, or 'units', according to Waltz, must be treated as empty boxes because their domestic arrangements and characteristics do not really make a difference at the level of the international system, which is the concern of international relations theories. At the system level, it is the fundamental structure of anarchy that shapes the behaviour of states or units, not their internal make-up.

For a systemic analysis of structure, Waltz says, there are only three elements that matter: the differentiation of units, the organising principle, and the distribution of capabilities (see Box 2.3). However, with regard to the international system, the differentiation of units is irrelevant since states are undifferentiated in their primary function: to produce their own security. States are required to pursue their own security because no one else can

---

BOX 2.3: TERMINOLOGY

Waltz's theory of international politics: key terms

System = structure + interacting units.

Structure, Waltz says (1979, 79) is 'the system-wide component that makes it possible to think of the system as a whole'. It is made up of three components:

1. ordering principle, sometimes called 'deep structure' (either hierarchy or anarchy)
2. differentiation of units according to their function (in international relations the units (states) are functionally the same or *un*differentiated – performing the same range of functions and concerned primarily with security)
3. distribution of capabilities (how states stand in relation to one another, according to the power they can mobilise and the aggregation of power around one or more poles – unipolarity, bipolarity, multipolarity).

be counted on to do so. The reason is that the organising principle of the international system is anarchy, not hierarchy; and 'self-help is necessarily the principle of action in an anarchic order' (Waltz 1979: 111). This structural condition obliges each state constantly to guard its security and defend its relative position with regard to other states without relying on others.

Anarchy imposes mistrust and uncertainty on others' intentions, obstructing mutually advantageous cooperation even in 'soft' dimensions like economics and trade (Grieco 1990). States, like oligopolistic firms, must be concerned with the asymmetric distribution of advantage, worrying about relative gains ('Who will gain more'?) rather than absolute gains ('Will both of us make some gain?'). Further, cooperation under anarchy is limited because to be dependent on others who are free to cheat is risky. **Interdependence** thus produces not just amity, as liberals claim, but also, and more importantly, reciprocal vulnerability, according to neorealists.

Virtually all states 'at a minimum, seek their own preservation and, at a maximum, drive for universal domination' (Waltz 1979: 118). Hence the distribution of capabilities across states, especially in the military field, is the only fundamental changing element in the international system. As a result it can be **bipolar** (with two great powers) or **multipolar** (more than two). These systemic configurations are regularly produced by the balance of power, which counteracts excessive accumulation of power, even provoking war. Waltz (1979) thinks, like Rousseau ([1756] 1917: 138), that the balance of power works as an automatic mechanism. It is not the product of intentional diplomatic efforts made by states. On the contrary, it is an unintentional and inevitable outcome of their interactions under conditions of anarchy. Facing the unavoidable repercussions of balance of power constraints, great powers tend to adopt a defensive behaviour that upholds the status quo. For this reason the international system, like the market, always tends towards equilibrium, according to Waltz's theory of international politics.

Neorealists, however, present at least one other view. John Mearsheimer (2001: 29, 250), concentrating on war and strategy in his *Tragedy of great power politics*, suggests that great powers 'are always searching for opportunities to gain power over their rivals'. Here Mearsheimer diverges from both Waltz and Carr. Great powers, he argues, are rarely satisfied and, instead, seek to extend their hegemony. This implies that the ultimate concern for states is not simply for security, as Waltz asserted (1979), but for maximising power. Here Mearsheimer's offensive realism is closer to Morgenthau's classical realism than to Waltz's neorealism.

Mearsheimer has studied how offensively-oriented states could behave as **revisionist** powers in response to structural constraints. Thus he has considered one of the criticisms made of neorealism by contemporary realists. These realists, who have integrated into their thinking elements of the classical tradition (and thus earn the name 'neoclassical' realists), have contested neorealism's assumption that all states have an equal set of interests (Schweller 1998). Some have reaffirmed the relevance of domestic politics and human nature factors, like perceptions and motivations (Walt 1987); others have challenged the automaticity that neorealism attributes to the political process, primarily the balance of power (Schweller 2006). All this suggests that realism is a broad tradition of thought with an ongoing debate about the relative importance of power and security in grasping the interests of states under conditions of anarchy.

What is realism? Synthesising theory and practice

The previous section has shown that realists compose an eclectic and heterogeneous tradition of thought with at least two main approaches, classical and structural, named realism and neorealism. Despite their differences, however, the two varieties of realism share key concepts and doctrines, as explained above. In this section we are going to reconcile the two varieties of realism in a single scheme of thought. Two shared assumptions are analysed: the state as the main actor in world politics and the logic of anarchy as a dominant constraint in international relations. Finally we will consider realism as a practical guide to politics that, despite allegations to the contrary, affirms two moral values: prudence and responsibility.

The state

We have seen that realism, as a theory of international politics, is principally concerned with states as power- and security-maximising actors in a context of international anarchy. States are the fundamental units of organised, hierarchical power and their relations dominate world politics. We may identify three key features of the state as understood by realism. First, states possess **sovereignty**, the supreme authority to make and enforce laws. Second, states govern by exercising a monopoly over both internal and external instruments of legitimate violence (embodied in the police and armed forces respectively). Third, these sovereign organisations are territorial, partitioning the Earth by imposing both material and immaterial barriers between people (namely, borders and citizenship respectively).

Other existing organisations – international (e.g. United Nations), supranational (e.g. European Union), transnational (e.g. NGOs) – perform important roles but are always ultimately subordinate to states, or, at least, to the most powerful among them. **International law** occupies an analogous condition of subordination, being the product of the contingent will and actual practice of the states (see Chapter 16). Individuals and other non-state actors (e.g. activists, transnational corporations) without the state's support have reduced political space to conduct their transborder activities in international relations (see Chapter 22).

States perform essential political, social and economic functions for all other actors in world politics and no other organisation appears today as a possible competitor (Spruyt 1994). In particular, most powerful states make the rules and maintain the institutions that shape international life, including its economic and cultural dimensions, popularly known as 'globalisation' (Waltz 1999). That is why even today globalisation's core values are those championed by the United States and its liberal and capitalist allies, predominantly in the West. These values could change if another state with different values and interests, perhaps China, were to achieve hegemony in international relations; but the point for realism is that dominant global trends generally depend on the power and interests of hegemonic states.

For realism the international use of violence by civil factions, like terrorists, against a foreign enemy's territory is nothing new or unusual. There are historical precedents, such as the Egyptian-based *fedayeen* raid against Israel before the 1956 war. What is new are the ideological goals and the worldwide nature of Islamist terrorism, in particular its links across frontiers, as in the case of the September 11, 2001 attacks on the US (see Chapter 29). Among other things, these attacks represented a challenge to the claim that only states may legitimately employ violence. In response, a US-led coalition of states destroyed the Afghan-based terrorist headquarters of al-Qaeda and overthrew the ruling Taliban government. Shortly thereafter, 'September 11' was taken as an opportunity by the world's most powerful state and its allies to launch a war against Iraq, despite opposition from many states and by the UN. The US thus reasserted its legitimacy and power in the face of the terrorist challenge by attacking states alleged to be complicit with terrorism. Moreover, the US's actions are consistent with Mearsheimer's logic of offensive realism. Since opposition to the Iraq War did not generate a balancing coalition, US power was thus left unchecked. This may be considered a concrete sign of **unipolarity**, meaning the supremacy of the US in an international system bereft of any comparable power.

Anarchy

The logic of international anarchy conditions and constrains inter-state relations. For realism, conflict over power and insecurity can only be definitively superseded through a hierarchical structure of dominion based on command and obedience – in other words, when world government supersedes anarchy. In the absence of world government, however, security can only be obtained through self-help. For this reason survival in international relations is of paramount relevance and fear is a fundamental emotion because it is an indispensable emotion for survival.

The absence of an overarching authority to prevent and counter the use of force creates a crucial uncertainty about others' intentions. This lack of trust generates what in 1748 the French philosopher Montesquieu (2000: 224) called a 'disease' that has 'necessarily become contagious'. He was noting that 'as soon as one state increases what it calls its troops, the other suddenly increases theirs, so that nothing is gained thereby but the common ruin. Each monarch keeps ready all the armies … and this state in which all strain against all is called peace'. In modern terms this spiral of insecurity is called the **security dilemma** (Herz 1962). It means that providing for one's own security can, often inadvertently, increase the sense of insecurity in other states. Thus the military arrangements of one state, including 'defensive' ones, are likely to be matched by other states, thereby creating a dangerous spiral that, paradoxically, leaves every state feeling even more insecure.

International anarchy breeds not only fear but also hostility among states. When this hostility is mixed with scarcity of resources it makes peaceful and just solutions to political conflicts difficult to achieve. Indeed, without hostility an equal distribution of resources, or power, would be possible. Without scarcity, hostility could be neutralised. For realism this is not the case in international politics. Hostility and scarcity are structural conditions left unsettled by the absence of a common government. Hence conflict is inevitable and may always reach the point where **war** becomes a legitimate instrument for reaching a final decision.

Prudence and responsibility

Neorealism is more theoretically rigorous but less historically or normatively rich than classical realism. The scientific inspiration of the former reduces, or removes, the latter's normative interest in the tension between morality and politics; a tension that inevitably affects the conduct of statesmen and stateswomen in the realm of international relations. However, we can find, implicitly or explicitly, a common normative theme: the ethic of responsibility.

The logic of international politics grants supreme moral value to the survival of the state and its interests. This supreme moral value – which legitimates the infringement of 'secondary' values such as liberty and justice, because they depend on the state's survival first and foremost – yields the doctrine of reason of state (Meinecke 1962). Reason of state (from the original French, *raison d'état*) is a specifically political form of reasoning that responds to necessity. It is based on the idea that politics is both autonomous and primary; that political reasoning, especially when the state's vital interests or survival are at stake, obeys its own rules and logics, independently of morality or law.

But this is not to say that reason of state is completely free of normative intent (see Box 2.4). As already indicated, reason of state is a morality of and for states; it generates an 'ethic of responsibility', as opposed to an 'ethic of conviction', to use Max Weber's (1948) terms. The latter conceives politics as the realisation of morally pure 'ultimate ends'. The former, by contrast, is based on a sharp distinction between personal and political moral behaviour, and privileges consequences over intentions. Good intentions or convictions do not matter in international politics as much as the consequences of actions, which is why realists have often been outspoken critics of US foreign policy adventurism (see Box 2.5). The duty of statesmen and stateswomen is to accept the responsibility for these consequences on behalf of the nation. Justifying bad consequences in terms of good convictions is politically unacceptable. On the contrary, leaders must confront the reality that good political consequences often require morally questionable, or even evil, means. For Machiavelli (1998: 60), this meant rulers were often obliged to act against conventional ethics, and should be prepared 'to enter into evil when necessity commands'.

BOX 2.4: DISCUSSION POINTS

Realism's political morality

Morgenthau (1973: 3–4) on the 'lesser evil':

'This being inherently a world of opposing interests and of conflict among them, moral principles can never be fully realized … [Realism] appeals to historic precedent rather than to abstract principles, and aims at the realization of the lesser evil rather than of the absolute good'.

Kennan (1996: 270) on the amorality of reason of state:

'The interests of the national society for which government must concern itself are basically those of its military security, the integrity of its political life, and the well-being of its people. These needs have no moral quality. They arise from the very existence of the national state and from the status of national sovereignty it enjoys. They are the unavoidable necessities of a national existence and therefore not subject to classification as either "good" or "bad"'.

Morgenthau (1973: 12) on prudence:

'There can be no political morality without prudence; that is, without consideration of the political consequences of seemingly moral action. Realism, then, considers prudence … to be the supreme virtue in politics'.

For realists, IR theories built on an ethic of conviction cannot solve the dilemmas and paradoxes of international politics. Hence, the ethic of responsibility is the proper political ethic, and prudence, as the judging of consequences of different political actions, is the supreme moral virtue in politics. The distinction between an ethic of responsibility and an ethic of conviction, made by Max Weber, can be considered a lasting, albeit inconclusive, word from realism about the morality of states.

BOX 2.5: CASE STUDY

Realism and the Iraq War

It may seem curious, but realists have often been outspoken critics of war, especially 'unnecessary wars'. In early 2003, before the US launched its war against Iraq (19 March 2003), John Mearsheimer and Stephen Walt (2003), two prominent US realists, published a powerful critique of the neoconservative case for war. They rejected claims made by the Bush administration that Saddam Hussein's Iraq could not be managed through a policy of containment. Hussein's past behaviour, they argued, however deplorable, was not irrational. Though a brutal dictator with a history of aggression (the Iran-Iraq War, 1980–88 and Gulf War, 1990–91), Hussein would remain deterrable, even in the event of acquiring a chemical or nuclear weapons capability. 'Why? Because the United States and its regional allies are far stronger than Iraq' (2003: 59).

Mearsheimer also argued elsewhere (2005) that this critique of the Iraq War was consistent with Hans Morgenthau's critique of the Vietnam War. The neo-conservative case for war, built around Wilsonian idealism 'with teeth', failed to appreciate the historical tendency of states to balance against power (rather than bandwagon), and failed to recognise nationalism as a more powerful ideological force than democracy. Following Morgenthau, Mearsheimer emphasised the dangers of pursuing global crusades (whether against **communism** or for democracy). Mearsheimer concluded that Morgenthau 'would have opposed [the Iraq War] as well if he had been alive'.

Conclusion

In this chapter we have seen that, despite some differences among realists, realism offers a range of concepts and ideas to capture enduring, if tragic, aspects of international relations. But we have also understood that the barycentre of realism is historical continuity. This reveals a tendency to occlude a crucial dimension of international relations – change (Ruggie 1983). Theories influenced by the 'critical turn' (Marxism, Critical Theory, postmodernism feminism and constructivism) and liberalism are sceptical about realism's assumption of anarchy's historical permanence, and enquire into logics of transformation and potentials for change neglected by realism.

States continue to be the dominant political units in international relations and do not show much inclination to abandon their sovereign powers or to convert international anarchy into some kind of formal hierarchy. On the contrary, they seem to sustain the logic of international anarchy that realists describe. In international relations, power and its immediate expression, force, remain central preoccupations. Demands for justice are commonly outweighed by reasons of state, and human interests are often sacrificed for national interests. These are but some of the reasons why realism remains an indispensable tradition of thought for any student of international relations today.

QUESTIONS

1. What is international anarchy and why it is a fundamental element for realism?
2. According to realists, what was the most flawed assumption of so-called 'idealist' thinkers? Why?
3. Why do realists view international relations as a 'realm of recurrence and repetition'?
4. What are the main differences between classical realism and neorealism?
5. Realism is often accused of being immoral. Why? And do you agree with this accusation?

FURTHER READING

Aron, Raymond 1966, *Peace and war: a theory of international relations*, New York: Doubleday. Twentieth-century realist classic by leading French intellectual.

Bell, Duncan (ed.) 2009, *Political thought and international relations: variations on a realist theme*, Oxford: Oxford University Press. Excellent collection of essays interpreting and examining the complex and rich contribution of realism.

Buzan, Barry, Jones, Charles and Richard Little 1993, *The logic of anarchy: neorealism to structural realism,* New York: Columbia University Press. Attempt to make neorealism methodologically open and historically sensitive.

Haslam, Jonathan 2002, *No virtue like necessity: realist thought in international relations since Machiavelli*, New Haven: Yale University Press. Wide-ranging history of realist thought.

Keohane, Robert (ed.) 1986, *Neorealism and its critics*, New York: Columbia University Press. As the title suggests, a collection comprising some of the most important neorealist authors and their critics.

Smith, Michael J. 1986, *Realist thought from Weber to Kissinger*, Baton Rouge: Louisiana State University Press. Important account of political realism in the twentieth century.

Williams, Michael C. 2005, *The realist tradition and the limits of international relations*, Cambridge: Cambridge University Press. Thoughtful reading of Hobbes, Rousseau and Morgenthau.

3

Liberalism

James L. Richardson

Introduction	49
Liberalism	49
The historical–political context	49
Contemporary liberal IR theory	54
Conclusion	59
Questions	60
Further reading	60

Introduction

This chapter discusses a political theory, long present as one of the traditions of thought about international relations, which has come to the fore in the discipline since the end of the Cold War. Understanding **liberalism** requires acquaintance with the historical context in which the political arguments for freedom and toleration were first enunciated. After providing a brief survey of some key liberal tenets and the manifestation of these tenets in international institutions and foreign policies, the chapter considers the way that contemporary liberal theories of international relations (IR) have developed along empirical and normative trajectories.

Liberalism

Liberalism is often seen as the characteristic political philosophy of the modern West. Its central principles – freedom, (human) rights, reason, progress, toleration – and the norms of **constitutionalism** and **democracy** are deeply embedded in Western political culture. Nonetheless, liberal theories of IR were until recently disdained as **utopian**, by IR scholars no less than by diplomats. The two world wars and the **Cold War** seemed to bear out the realist thesis that the international milieu was inevitably subject to the harsh imperatives of **power politics**.

Since the end of the Cold War, however, the world has looked quite different. There is no hostile power threatening the liberal democracies, indeed major **war** has come to seem unthinkable, and the international economy is organised in accordance with the norms of the liberal market. Liberal internationalism has gained a new relevance. The predominant school of liberal IR theory, most strongly represented in the United States, focuses on the forces of change that are regarded as having brought about this transformation: democratisation, institutionalisation and economic **interdependence**. Liberal thinkers outside that school, dispersed internationally and across academic **disciplines**, are concerned with more troubling questions. Can liberalism, grounded in Western historical experience, sustain its universal claims in a world of many cultures? Can liberal ideals really be translated into practice in a world marked by today's extreme inequalities, and if so, how? These theorists are aware of the need to address tensions among the traditional liberal concepts that have become more acute in today's global setting, and perhaps even to rethink liberalism's fundamental principles.

The historical–political context

The term 'liberalism' dates only from the nineteenth century, but the distinctive liberal pattern of ideas crystallised much earlier, in the political struggle against monarchical absolutism in seventeenth-century England, and were formulated as a coherent political doctrine by the English philosopher, John Locke, whose *Two treatises of government* ([1690] 1988) ranks as the first great liberal text. For Locke the rights and freedoms of the individual were paramount; government should rest on consent, not monarchical or religious authority, its powers should be strictly limited, and it should practise religious toleration (see Box 3.1).

Liberalism developed as a full-fledged ideology in the ideas of the French **Enlightenment** *philosophes* and the American founding fathers. History, viewed as the advance of civilisation, had reached a stage where the oppressive absolutist **regimes** of the day lacked all rational justification. It was time to establish government anew, based on universal principles derived from reason. Liberal rights and freedoms were proclaimed in declarations such as the American Declaration of Independence (1776) and the French Declaration of the Rights of Man (1789), and manifestos such as Thomas Paine's *Rights of man* (1791–92) and Mary Wollstonecraft's *A vindication of the rights of woman* (1792). Liberal thought on political economy developed along similar lines. Adam Smith's *Wealth of nations* ([1776] 1998) with its themes of the division of labour, **free trade** and the beneficent 'invisible hand' of the market, remains the Bible of liberal economists, much revered but little read, its qualifications long forgotten (see Box 3.1).

BOX 3.1: DISCUSSION POINTS

Early liberal thought

Locke ([1690] 1988: 306) on liberty:

'*[T]he end of law* is not to abolish or restrain, but *to preserve and enlarge Freedom*: … *where there is no Law, there is no Freedom*. For *Liberty* is to be free from restraint and violence from others which cannot be, where there is no Law: But Freedom is not, as we are told, *A Liberty for every Man to do what he lists* [desires]: (For who could be free, when every other Man's Humour might domineer him?) But a *Liberty* to dispose, and order, as he lists, his Person, Actions, Possessions, and his whole Property, within the Allowance of those Laws under which he is; and therein not to be subject to the arbitrary Will of another, but freely follow his own' (Second Treatise, chapter VI, paragraph 57).

Smith ([1776] 1998: 289, 292) on the market's 'invisible hand':

'Every individual is continually exerting himself to find out the most advantageous employment for whatever capital he can command. It is his own advantage, indeed, and not that of the society, which he has in view'. … '[H]e intends only his own gain, and he is in this, as in many other cases, led by an invisible hand to promote an end which was no part of his intention. Nor is it always the worse for the society that it was no part of his intention. By pursuing his own interest he frequently promotes that of the society more effectually than when he really intends to promote it' (Book IV, chapter ii).

Liberal ideas on international relations also took shape in the later eighteenth century. Viewing war as irrational violence and attributing it to the unrestrained power, vanity and ambition of monarchs, liberals looked to the same remedy as for internal oppression: the removal of the old regime. The republics which were to replace it would have no reason to make war, but would be free to enjoy the benefits of peaceful commerce. There is no major theoretical statement of these ideas, but they were drawn together by the German philosopher Immanuel Kant in a brief essay, *Perpetual peace* ([1795] 1970).

Early liberal thought was not democratic. In line with Locke's emphasis on property rights, 'consent' meant election by property-holders, then a small minority. Kant's republics were not democracies. The violence of the French **Revolution** confirmed liberal fears of the 'tyranny of the majority' – or, more simply, 'the rule of the mob'. Liberal democracy dates only from the nineteenth century – relatively early in the US, much later in Europe, initially for men only. Women had to wait until the twentieth century.

Liberalism has always been a broad creed, permitting many variations. Liberal principles have been grounded in different philosophical systems; there are

Figure 3.1 Mary Wollstonecraft – engraving by James Heath (1757–1834), from a painting by John Opie (1761–1807)

remarkable contrasts in intellectual styles; and there are even major differences over the content of liberal principles. Space permits no more than a mention of philosophical differences: **utilitarianism** ('the greatest happiness of the greatest number'), popularised by Jeremy Bentham, flatly contradicted the natural rights philosophy of most earlier liberals, and the German **idealism** which inspired later nineteenth-century liberals qualified the traditional individualism by introducing a concern for the community.

The intellectual style of the Enlightenment was notable for its self-confidence: liberals appealed to Reason for unambiguous answers to all questions, and came under criticism for making light of serious problems, for assuming that there were simple solutions, evident to right reason, and that 'all good things go together' – that no truly difficult choices need to be made. A quite different style of theorising – reflective and critical, struggling with ethical dilemmas – may be dated from the time of John Stuart Mill's *On liberty* ([1859] 1983) (see Box 3.2). This became more characteristic in Europe, especially in the twentieth century, while American liberals remain closer to the Enlightenment tradition.

BOX 3.2: DISCUSSION POINTS

John Stuart Mill, from *On liberty* ([1859] 1983)

'The aim, therefore, of patriots was to set limits to the power which the ruler should be suffered to exercise over the community; and this limitation was what they meant by liberty. It was attempted in two ways. First, by obtaining a recognition of certain immunities, called political liberties or rights, which it was to be regarded as a breach of duty in the ruler to infringe, and which if he did infringe, specific resistance or general rebellion was held to be justifiable. A second, and generally a later, expedient was the establishment of constitutional checks by which the consent of the community, or of a body of some sort, supposed to represent its interests, was made a necessary condition to some of the more important acts of the governing power' (60).

'… the sole end for which mankind are warranted, individually or collectively, in interfering with the liberty of action of any of their number is self-protection … the only purpose for which power can be rightfully exercised over any member of a civilized community, against his will, is to prevent harm to others' (68).

'The only freedom which deserves the name is that of pursuing our own good in our own way, so long as we do not attempt to deprive others of theirs or impede their efforts to obtain it' (72).

A major difference over the content of liberal principles opened up in the later nineteenth century. While 'classical' liberals retained their faith in the wholly free market ('*laissez-faire*') and in limiting the powers of government to the minimum, a new school of thought was more responsive to the socialist critique of the inequities of the early industrial era. 'Social' liberals saw a positive role for the **state** – in preventing the abuse of economic power and in promoting basic services, for example in public

Figure 3.2   Portrait of John Stuart Mill

Source: *Popular Science Monthly*, vol. III, 1873.

health and education. For classical liberals, freedom meant freedom from control or interference by the state ('negative freedom'); for social liberals it meant, in addition, the opportunity for all members of society to develop their individual capacities ('positive freedom'). This division between two senses of freedom, originally articulated by Benjamin Constant ([1819] 1988), and made famous in the twentieth century by Sir Isaiah Berlin (1982), has proved extraordinarily persistent, reemerging in the cleavage between today's economic **neoliberalism** and the social or 'inclusive' liberalism of those who seek a more equitable ordering of the economy, at both the national and international levels.

The critique of **imperialism**, challenging the traditional liberal confidence in the virtues of the economic **order**, opened up a further division within liberalism. J. A. Hobson's *Imperialism: A study* ([1902] 1968) mounted an uncompromising critique of certain tendencies inherent in the liberal society of the day. His wide-ranging analysis of the economic and political sources of imperialism, which he saw as a deformation of liberal **capitalism**, had much in common with the Marxist critique. But whereas Marxists saw no remedy short of war or revolution, Hobson looked to democratic political processes to overcome the vested interests and prejudices which lay behind the phenomenon. Liberal imperialists, on the other hand, continued to support what the French called the civilising 'mission' of European colonial rule (Duncan Bell 2006; Hindess 2001; Pitts 2005).

With respect to international relations more generally, nineteenth-century liberalism remained in opposition to the realist assumptions of great-power diplomacy, maintaining the traditional Enlightenment critique but also bringing in realist arguments of the **national interest** to support liberal policies such as free trade, arms reduction, adherence to **international law** and support for liberal movements elsewhere. It became evident that liberal principles could lead to opposing policy choices: for example, with respect to intervention, support for nationalism or even involvement in war.

The creation of the League of Nations in 1919 briefly raised hopes for a new liberal international order, hopes that were dampened by the US refusal to join the League and extinguished by the aggression of the Axis powers in the 1930s. Nevertheless, the liberal vision of Woodrow Wilson, the chief sponsor of the League, and in particular his confidence in America's leading the way to a universal liberal future, the 'American mission', has remained an unquestioned premise of US foreign policy.

The mood associated with the founding of the **United Nations (UN)** in 1945 was more sober, and 'Cold War liberals' soon became reconciled to a protracted struggle against the Soviet Union. The preoccupation with the Cold War diverted attention from the principal post-war liberal achievement: the construction, under American auspices, of a dynamic liberal economic order in the Western world. The unexpected collapse of the Soviet Union opened the way to the world-wide extension of this system ('**globalisation**'), generating in some circles a mood of liberal triumphalism: there was now no alternative, it was proclaimed, to the market economy and liberal democracy (Fukuyama, 1989).

Although the various Western countries proclaim the same liberal values and share a common political culture, this finds quite different expression in their foreign policies, reflecting their different historical experience. In the US, as we have seen, it is the sense of an American mission to promote a liberal world order. In Britain, the leading liberal power in the nineteenth century, while there was genuine support for liberal causes, it was never at the expense of the Empire nor of the traditional principle of upholding the balance of power. In Australia, the primary concern was the potential threat from the unfamiliar, culturally alien and densely populated Asian continent, and the consequent need for a powerful ally/protector. This came to be complemented by support for the UN, especially on the part of ALP (Australian Labor Party) governments, but it is only recently that the idea of regional engagement has come to the fore.

Contemporary liberal IR theory

The contemporary social sciences draw a basic distinction between empirical and **normative** theory. The former is concerned with the factual: what is the case, what patterns of behaviour can be observed and explained? The latter examines what is desirable or obligatory: what goals should be pursued, what norms should be accepted as binding? The distinction is not as straightforward as is assumed, and indeed raises difficult philosophical issues. Moreover, most significant political questions raise both kinds of issue; the normative and the empirical are not separate worlds. However, since the two types of theory have been developed separately, it is convenient to consider them under these headings.

Empirical theory: an emerging liberal order?

As noted earlier, the three most prominent liberal empirical theories are concerned with democracy, international institutions and interdependence. In the forefront of the liberal challenge to **realism** is the **democratic peace theory**, first set out by Michael Doyle (1983, 1986). This holds that, contrary to the realist claim that peace depends on the **balance of power**, not on forms of government, the crucial factor is whether or not the governments of the major powers are democracies. In effect, so long as the balance of power favours the democracies, it ceases to be relevant; thus it is not of fundamental importance whether the present world is '**unipolar**' – a quasi-American empire – or **multipolar**. In either case there is no danger of major war.

The basis for this confidence is the convincing body of evidence that has been assembled in support of the liberal claim that democracies do not go to war against one another (Doyle, 1983, 1986; Russett, 1993) (Box 3.3). Theorists offer two principal explanations for this. First, democracies are committed to the principle of resolving political differences non-violently, and they adhere to this in their relations with other democracies no less than in internal politics. Second, the public, who would bear the cost, is unwilling to support war against another democracy. These explanations are plausible, but not conclusive. A realist can argue that the reason for the democratic peace in the twentieth century was that the democracies were allies against a common enemy, and that at present nuclear weapons are a more secure guarantor of peace than the ascendancy of democracy. A Marxist can argue that peace is to be expected so long as the international system is controlled by a transnational business class with an interest in preserving an economic order highly advantageous to it.

BOX 3.3: DISCUSSION POINTS

Liberal legacies?

Michael Doyle (1983, 1986) made a powerful and provocative argument in the mid-1980s that modern liberalism bore two main legacies. First, 'the pacification of foreign relations among liberal states'; and second, 'international "imprudence"' (Doyle 1986: 1156–7). The first legacy is based on the claim that stable liberal democratic **sovereign states** (comprising market economies, the rule of law and democratic representation) historically have never waged war against each other. By exercising restraint, liberal democracies have created a separate 'zone of peace'. The second legacy is that liberal democracies exercise this restraint, and form a separate zone of peace, only among themselves. Liberal democracies have 'discovered Liberal reasons for aggression' (Doyle 1997: 206), and continue to fight wars against 'non-liberal' and 'non-democratic' states. Afghanistan and Iraq are only the most recent examples where liberal democracies have waged such wars. Are they examples of 'liberal imprudence'?

Nevertheless, the thesis of the democratic peace has greatly influenced policy thinking in the US. Not always for the best: scholars of the democratic peace, who never envisaged war as the means of promoting democracy, were dismayed by the way in which their theories were put into practice by George W. Bush (Russett, 2005). Liberal political thinking outside the US, on the other hand, has not been so greatly influenced by the democratic peace thesis. While other Western countries generally support the establishment of democratic institutions, they do not share the US zeal for the promotion of democracy.

A second school of liberal theory, **institutionalism**, seeks to explain why, and how, international institutions have become so important with the rise of complex interdependence (Keohane and Nye [1977] 1989). It is concerned with questions such as: what are their principal functions, what determines their effectiveness, and how much do they 'matter' (i.e. are they more than just convenient vehicles for the exercise of power by their strongest members)? This last question shows that institutional theorists such as Robert Keohane (1984) and David Lake (1996) take realism very seriously, but argue that it needs to be supplemented (see Box 3.4). Although institutional theory no longer focuses directly on the goal of promoting peace, there is an assumption that institutions contribute indirectly to this goal by fostering habits of cooperation and a sense of shared interests. Institutionalists maintain that international cooperation is far more extensive than realist theory would lead one to expect, and indeed has become indispensable in many areas, such as economic relations. But it is not automatic: a shared interest in peace, for example, or in a clean environment, does not ensure cooperation to achieve it. Institutions can devise means to implement shared goals, to apportion costs, and to prevent cheating. Through showing how cooperation can be achieved in practice, institutions influence the perception of national interests and shape expectations. At the most general level of abstraction, institutional theorists focus on information, norms and conventions as fundamental aspects of international relations.

BOX 3.4: DISCUSSION POINTS

Neoliberal institutionalism and neorealism: what's the difference?

Neoliberal institutionalism, as the name suggests, identifies with the broad tradition of liberal political thought. However, it shares several key assumptions with neorealism (Nye 1988).

Indeed, one of the first major statements of neoliberal institutionalism, Robert Keohane's *After hegemony* (1984) explicitly and deliberately embraces neorealism's starting assumptions only to show how they can lead to altogether more 'liberal' and less pessimistic international outcomes if institutions are taken seriously. Keohane accepts not just neorealism's **positivist** method, but its substantive claims about the state as a self-interested 'rational egoist', and the international system as a structure of anarchy. Nonetheless, according to Keohane, states are capable of sustaining international cooperation under conditions of anarchy, especially when levels of interdependence are high. Institutions provide mutually beneficial contexts in which information is communicated, transaction costs are reduced, and expectations are stabilised (Keohane 1989: 166–7). For further reading on neoliberal institutionalism, see Stein (2008) and J. L. Richardson (2008).

Institutions are understood, in a broad sense, to include much more than formal organisations. The useful concept of an international regime has been introduced to include, as well, informal agreements and understandings, and also norms and practices that can decisively influence the effectiveness of organisations (see Krasner 1983). To take an example: the nuclear non-proliferation regime, centred on the Non-Proliferation Treaty and the organisation responsible for monitoring it, the International Atomic Energy Agency, includes informal agreements not to export sensitive technology and equipment, **security** assurances to many non-nuclear states, and more generally the concerting of incentives and disincentives to increase the cost of acquiring nuclear weapons; and all this rests on a broad consensus on the dangers of an unrestricted nuclear proliferation. Due to nuclear developments in Iran and North Korea, this regime is now under stress, but this is not for the first time, and thus far it has succeeded in keeping the number of nuclear-armed states far below the number technically capable of acquiring the weapons, and once widely expected to do so.

Western governments for the most part endorse liberal institutionalism, in the belief that the increasing recourse to international institutions makes for a more predictable, cooperative and thus peaceful environment. Even **great powers** appreciate the order institutions help maintain. G. John Ikenberry (2001) has shown how the liberal-constitutional postwar order built by the US and its allies has functioned to bind and restrain US **hegemonic** power. Nevertheless, major powers such as the US at times prefer 'unilateralism'. In many other countries, however, policymakers prefer a situation where important sectors of international activity are regulated through generally accepted rules rather than through ad hoc bargaining among the strongest actors. The active involvement of small and middle powers in the **World Trade Organization**, **arms control** regimes, UN **peacekeeping** and regional economic cooperation can be seen in these terms. And, in these and other liberal democracies, the continuing relevance of an earlier form of liberal institutionalism can be seen in the contrast between the consensus supporting the UN-sanctioned Gulf War (1991) as against the divisiveness of the Iraq War (2003), which lacked the endorsement of the UN.

The third theoretical school, commercial liberalism, has focused on the rise of the international trading system. It has sought to explain the shifting relationship between what Richard Rosecrance (1986) calls the 'two worlds of international relations': the 'military-political' world of the territorial states, and the increasingly interdependent world of trading states. This school has seen little innovation, but rather a refinement of the traditional liberal claim that commerce promotes peace. In the years before

1914 liberals were over-optimistic on this score, some going so far as to assert that the unprecedented interdependence of that era rendered major war impossible or, as Norman Angell (1912) put it, 'futile'. World War I totally discredited this idea, but commercial liberals now advance the plausible but unremarkable thesis that extensive economic links reduce the likelihood of war among those involved. Thus, for example, according to this view, increasing trade and investment in the Asia-Pacific region, through enhancing prosperity and welfare, strengthens the incentive on all sides to avoid actions that could lead to major war. Since the early nineteenth century free trade has amounted to an article of faith for liberal economists. IR scholars, though uneasy over the universality of the economists' claims, tend to defer to them, such that the political economy of trade remains underdeveloped. Studies of free trade and protection, for example, tend to see the issues through the lenses of orthodox economic theory.

An interesting exception is the concept of 'embedded liberalism', introduced in John Ruggie's analysis of the post-1945 international economic order (Ruggie 1982). What was notable about the reconstruction of the liberal system, in Ruggie's view, was that it did not give total priority to liberalising trade, but sought a balance with other goals such as full employment, social equity and political stability. He suggests that the success of the liberal reconstruction was due to this balanced approach. Since the 1980s, however, international economic relations have been reordered in accordance with the neoliberal doctrine which subordinates such political goals to achieving the maximum of liberalisation, not only in trade but in all aspects of economic life – notably deregulation, privatisation and the free movement of capital. This extended version of commercial liberalism, originating in the US and Britain under Reagan and Thatcher, has been wholeheartedly endorsed by policy communities and governments in many Western countries where they have dismantled tariff barriers and undertaken major economic restructuring in accordance with neoliberal doctrine.

Although this subordination of society and politics to the rule of the market was contested in many countries, Western governments remained committed to the neoliberal orthodoxy until the outbreak of the global financial crisis in 2008, which shook confidence in the virtues of deregulation. Long prior to this, however, there had been extensive theoretical debate on the issues raised by the neoliberal version of globalisation, but liberal IR theory was conspicuously absent. There was little theorising of a social liberal alternative to neoliberalism, although some IR scholars such as Richard Falk (1999) offered valuable critical studies of its consequences.

To conclude this part of the discussion, it may be said that empirical liberal theory and research have shown that in important respects the liberal understanding of current world politics is more illuminating than the realist. It cannot yet be said whether this represents a historical turning point or just another 'false dawn' for liberalism. And a number of questions and reservations suggest themselves. First, while IR theory in the US tends, like the foreign policy debate, to oscillate between realism and liberalism, these do not exhaust the theoretical universe. Second, is this liberal theory too close to the American political discourse, mirroring its emphases and silences? The tone of the theorising is always positive and occasionally celebratory, as when the president of the International Studies Association hailed the indications that the liberal vision of Woodrow Wilson was at last coming to fruition (Kegley 1993). In many ways empirical liberal theory offers the perspective of those comfortably located at the top of the global **hierarchy** (Falk's 'globalisation from above'), excluding the dark side of globalisation and the many ways in which the partially liberal order falls short of a more critical liberal vision. Some of these issues are taken up by normative liberal theorists.

Normative theory: dilemmas and aspirations

Liberal normative issues form part of the everyday foreign policy debate. For example: what priority should be accorded support for human rights (see Chapter 32)? At what cost, in terms of important relationships with emerging or great powers (see Chapter 19), such as China, Russia or Indonesia? Under what circumstances is humanitarian intervention justified (see Chapter 31)? Must it be approved by the UN (see Chapter 21)? Is there an obligation to assist the globally disadvantaged, many of them at the margins of subsistence (see Chapters 8 and 27)? Some of these debates remain inconclusive, others arrive at a practical compromise, but the reasoning behind differing ethical claims is never pressed very far. The task of normative theory is to pursue this reasoning in order to establish consistent ethical principles grounded in a coherent philosophy. Since philosophies differ over fundamentals, this cannot lead to a consensus; but the search for a philosophical grounding enhances the awareness of the complexity of ethical issues and the import of contending philosophical traditions.

Liberals are divided among several traditions, including the utilitarian, the pragmatist, the **Kantian**, and more recently followers of American theorist John Rawls, who shares much with the Kantians. Normative theory may seem remote from the everyday debate, but on reflection it is not difficult to see that familiar policy standpoints are associated with one or other liberal tradition: for example support for human rights with 'classical' **Lockean** liberalism, **foreign aid** with social liberalism, and the UN with liberal internationalism. Within each philosophical school it is possible to distinguish between 'ideal theory' (Rawls's term) – a normative vision based on first principles – and theorising which focuses on what is practicable and also on ethical dilemmas, when accepted principles come into conflict (see Chapter 8). Students of international relations tend to be drawn to the practicable, and even to disparage ideal theory as utopian. But there is a place for both kinds of theorising: ideal theory enlarges the awareness of what could become practicable, but meanwhile – as argued powerfully by Amartya Sen (2009) – there is an urgent need for theorising on practicable remedies for manifest evils and injustices.

It is not possible in this short survey to do justice to the range of issues addressed by liberal normative theorists. Two of the most prominent issues, human rights and humanitarian intervention, are the subject matter of later chapters (Chapters 31 and 32). A discussion of one major issue area, however – global distributive justice – may serve to illustrate the range of different liberal approaches and viewpoints.

Western development assistance dates from the 1950s, but the issue termed global distributive justice stemmed from third-world demands for a new international economic order in the 1970s, in the context of increasing awareness of international interdependence. The policy issues and the problems of effective implementation are highly complex, but for purposes of normative theory the relevant question is whether, as a matter of justice, not self-interest or a sense of a common humanity, the wealthy countries should make substantial resources available for the purpose of improving the conditions and opportunities of the less well off – many of them living in conditions unimaginable in the Western world.

At one pole of the debate are classical liberals such as Friedrich Hayek, for whom justice can refer only to the conduct of individuals, not the ordering of society (Hayek 1976). Thus, social justice is a meaningless concept: there can be no obligation to assist the disadvantaged. At the other extreme, the utilitarian principle of the greatest good of the greatest number can be interpreted to justify a transfer of resources on an almost unimaginable scale, since any additional resources made available to the poor will tend to increase their welfare by a greater amount than the loss of those resources will diminish the welfare of the well off.

The debate between Rawls and his followers shows that a common philosophical starting point can lead to quite different conclusions, depending on what further considerations are taken to be relevant. Rawlsian theorists start from the ethical principle that social inequalities can be justified only if their overall effect is to benefit the least well off (Rawls 1971). This is usually taken to require measures to enhance the well-being and opportunities of those socially disadvantaged. For Rawls himself, however, the principle is not relevant in international relations, since the world as a whole is not a political community as he understands it, but (still) a world of independent communities (Rawls 1999). Some Rawlsian theorists, on the other hand, hold that when globalisation is taken into account, and in particular the extent to which economic life in the poorer countries is subject to regulation by international institutions controlled by the Western states, the principle is indeed relevant (Pogge 2002). As in the case of utilitarian theory, this would lack credibility if it were taken to require near-limitless transfers of resources. But either principle would justify practicable transfers to meet urgent needs, well beyond present limits.

The separation between empirical and normative theory is disadvantageous to the study of international relations. The normative theorists are keenly aware of deficiencies in today's partially liberal order that empirical theory does not address. A closer engagement with normative theory would bring a critical dimension to empirical theory and could prompt research into ways in which that order falls short of liberal ideals, and how improvements might be brought about.

Conclusion

Liberalism developed in opposition to realism, a theory of constraint which sees the world of states as subject to the imperatives of **geopolitics**, with major war the final arbiter. Liberalism is a theory of choice: social and political evils are not just a given of the human condition, but can be remedied – if only after protracted struggles. One of the strengths of contemporary liberal theory is that it takes the realist constraints seriously, while denying that they are final imperatives. If traditional liberal thought underestimated the importance of power in international relations, recent theory incorporates realist understandings of power while insisting that they do not tell the whole story. But the major strength of liberal theory is its orientation to new trends in world politics. Most of the new agenda issues discussed in Part 3 can be related to one or other area of liberal theory. This does not mean that liberalism seeks to incorporate every new issue. To take the case of global **terrorism**: a liberal might well regard the issue as vastly over-sold as a 'war on terror' heralding a new era in world politics (see Chapter 29).

One criticism of liberalism which remains valid is that it tends to underestimate the strength of ethnicity, **nationalism** and religion in both internal and international politics. A typical liberal response is that while this may be true in the short run, the appeal of liberal values is such that they are bound to prevail in the longer run. As Francis Fukuyama expresses it, only liberal democracy can satisfy the material needs and the aspirations that are common to all mankind (Fukuyama 1989). But it is precisely this universalism which is increasingly under challenge. It would not be surprising if non-Western cultures such as the Chinese and the Islamic should remain resistant to the liberal model. But many liberals, lacking respect for non-liberal values, are ill-prepared for coexistence with such cultures.

Overall, liberalism, like most theories, is weak in self-criticism. Thus there is little liberal theorising on the dangers posed by the liberalism of the powerful – whether the militant liberalism of the Bush Administration or neoliberal ideology's enhancing of the power of the economically strong at the expense of the weak. Nor have liberal theorists devoted much time to the hollowing out of liberalism at home through misuse of executive power in the name of 'security'. At a time when the most familiar liberal theories can make for a certain complacency, it is important to become as aware as possible of liberalism's typical biases and blind spots.

QUESTIONS

1. What are the major historical and intellectual factors that shaped liberalism?
2. There are a number of distinct 'liberalisms' – which of these has most influenced the international relations agenda?
3. What did the neo-Kantian liberalism of Woodrow Wilson stand for in the years between the two world wars? Is Wilsonian liberalism still significant in the contemporary era?
4. What are the main characteristics of 'commercial' liberalism? Are these characteristics discernible in the neoliberal globalisation project?
5. What is Democratic Peace Theory?
6. How do countries other than the US embody liberalism in their foreign policy?

FURTHER READING

Gray, John 1995, *Liberalism*, 2nd edition, Minneapolis: University of Minnesota Press. Concise historical outline of liberal political thought.

Howard, Michael 1978, *War and the liberal conscience*, London: Temple Smith. Classic account of liberal thinking about war from the Renaissance to the twentieth century.

Kegley, Charles W. Jr (ed.) 1995, *Controversies in international relations theory: realism and the neoliberal challenge*, New York: St Martin's Press. Contains a number of very useful chapters on contemporary liberalism.

Keohane, Robert O. 1989, *International institutions and state power: essays in international relations theory*, Boulder: Westview. Collection of chapters by one of the leading theorists of neoliberal institutionalism.

Richardson, James L. 2001, *Contending liberalisms in world politics: ideology and power*, Boulder: Lynne Rienner Publishers. Extended set of reflections on the theory and practice of liberalism in international relations.

Russett, Bruce 1993, *Grasping the democratic peace: principles for a post-Cold War world*, Princeton: Princeton University Press. Presents an incomparable overview of liberal institutional theory on the democratic peace.

4

Marxism and Critical Theory

Richard Devetak, Jim George and Martin Weber

Introduction	63
Historical and intellectual context: Marx and the critique of capitalism	63
Marxism as historical materialism	65
Marx and Marxism in IR	67
Critical Theories of IR	68
Conclusion	74
Questions	75
Further reading	75

Introduction

This chapter introduces students to the rich and controversial legacy of Marxism and one of its major offshoots in the twentieth century, Critical Theory. The common thread linking the two theories is an interest in struggles to dismantle structures of oppression, exclusion and domination. The chapter is in two parts. The first focuses on Marxism and its contribution to IR, the second on an offshoot of Marxism that goes by the name Critical Theory. The part on Marxism provides a discussion of how Marx's ideas have been received in IR, an account of the historical and intellectual context that 'created' Marxism, and an account of Marx's method of historical materialism. The part on Critical Theory provides outlines of the two strands of Critical Theory that have emerged within IR: a strand derived from the so-called Frankfurt School, and a strand derived from Italian thinker Antonio Gramsci.

Historical and intellectual context: Marx and the critique of capitalism

During the nineteenth century, European societies underwent dramatic and sometimes traumatic changes internally, while expanding their colonial rule to almost every corner of the world. Importantly, this expansion of European **imperialism** and the global consolidation of what is often referred to as the 'Westphalian states-system' occurred simultaneously with the comprehensive shift to industrialised production (known as the Industrial Revolution), significant changes in the ownership and control of property and large-scale population transfers, both internally and externally towards parts of the colonised world. By the nineteenth century economic affairs were also changing significantly, with the gradual demise of **mercantilism** and the rise of **capitalism**. Victorian Britain (England, specifically) had emerged as the hotbed of these developments, with its extraordinary innovations in industrial production and technology and in the capitalist production processes. It also provided many of the conceptual principles for understanding and legitimising the socio-economic transformations inaugurated by capitalism.

Building on the works of earlier liberal thinkers, and on a generalised desire to advance Enlightenment 'reason' in line with scientific research into both the natural and social worlds, philosophers like Adam Smith (1723–1790) in the eighteenth century and David Ricardo (1772–1823) in the nineteenth century were involved in developing what became known as liberal 'political economy'. An outgrowth of moral philosophy, this field of inquiry was concerned primarily with the political and economic conditions of social change. It also became the basis for the discipline of (neo-classical) economics.

The new political economists advanced more stringent conceptions of 'efficiency' under capitalism. Arguing against the accumulated wealth and land ownership of the traditional aristocracy, they insisted wealth must be circulated and invested across the whole society. In this regard they were advocates of an 'entrepreneurial' shift from subsistence economies to industrial production, and of social progress guided by scientific reason.

The optimism and pragmatism of these liberal political economists, however, ran into some rather stark practical problems during the course of the nineteenth century. Rural displacement and unplanned urbanisation led to widespread urban poverty, destitution and social problems (including the rampant alcoholism of London's famous 'Gin Lane'), and industrial labour proved costly, not least in terms of human lives. What Adam Smith, and many other liberal advocates of the capitalist political economy, had envisaged as a pathway to widespread freedom and prosperity turned out to be much more ambiguous.

Forced to accept the terms of their employment, workers organised to contest their often meagre wages and workplace conditions. Industrial capitalists became increasingly involved in disputes and confrontations with their often hungry and desperate labourers. What the political economists had advanced in theory as a system of symmetrical contract relations between capital and labour thus turned out in practice to be a highly explosive mix of social unrest and oppression.

Into this situation came Karl Marx (1818–1883), a friend and collaborator of Friedrich Engels (1820–1895), whose father was a wealthy industrialist in Manchester. Like the liberal political economists whose work they would criticise quite fundamentally, Marx and Engels agreed that industrial development was necessary and desirable; 'because only with this universal development of productive forces is a universal intercourse between men established' (Marx 1977: 171). Where they disagreed with their liberal (or, as they preferred to call them, bourgeois) counterparts was in regard to the social and political relations which attended the modernisation process. They wanted to develop what might be called a 'critical social theory' that would overcome capitalism's intolerable excesses, yet harness modernity's progressive forces to the welfare of all. Capitalism – defined as a social system based on the accumulation of capital or the extraction of surplus value – therefore formed the central object of Marx's critique, while modernisation retained its potential to liberate humankind.

In late 1849 Marx arrived in England, convinced the contradictions of capitalist societies like England would explode into crisis and lead to the revolutionary overthrow of capitalist class rule and its replacement by more equitable and democratic political societies. While Marx realised the necessity of struggle and leadership in overturning capitalist social relations, he also seemed to think that, ironically, bourgeois capitalism, in its antagonistic augmentation of capital, was preparing its own demise: 'What the

Figure 4.1   Karl Marx, 1867

Source: Photograph by Friedrich Karl Wunder.

bourgeoisie, therefore, produces, above all, is its own grave-diggers', as he and Engels ([1848] 1977: 231) dramatically put it in the *Communist manifesto*.

With this brief snapshot we have introduced some key features of Marxism (see Box 4.1): first, an acknowledgement of the negative consequences of industrialised capitalism without completely dismissing its latent potential for an **emancipated**, post-capitalist society. Second, a critique of capitalism focused on the social relations established by its mode of production rather than the productive forces themselves. Marx's concern here was that capitalist economies generate unequal social relations of power that lead to domination, exploitation and oppression. Third, that the domination of the great majority by a small wealthy minority which owns and controls the means of production creates the sources of class conflict. Fourth, a critique of capitalism's ideology: liberalism – the argument being that liberalism is designed to legitimate, yet conceal, the true nature of capitalism's relations of domination, exploitation and alienation. Finally, an historical and materialist method capable of explaining the reproduction of capitalist society, understanding and criticising its exploitative social relations, and exploring potential sources of progressive social change; a method Marx called 'historical materialism'.

BOX 4.1: DISCUSSION POINTS

Key features of Marx's theoretical framework

1. Recognition of industrial modernity's emancipatory potential.
2. Critique of capitalism for generating unequal social relations which lead to domination, exploitation and oppression.
3. Explanation of class conflict as an outgrowth of power struggles between those who own and control the means of production (the bourgeoisie) and those who do not (the proletariat).
4. Critique of liberalism as an ideology that legitimises capitalism.
5. Exploration of potential sources of progressive social change.

Marxism as historical materialism

As the above section suggests, Marx had a good deal in common with liberal political economists even if, in the end, he offered devastating critiques of capitalism and its ideological accompaniment, liberalism. In this section we map out some of the common ground Marx shared with the liberal political economists before outlining their differences. Marx's progressivist but non-liberal account of political economy grew out of an historical materialist theory premised on a materialist method that identified conflict and struggle as the driving forces of history.

Both Marx and the liberals shared a commitment to a progressivist conception of history. On this view history is understood as a progressive unfolding of better and *more* rational social arrangements in which people could look forward to more fulfilled, more 'civilised' lives than previous generations. Capitalism was modernising society, generating progressive potentials for all societies, even the most primitive. As Marx and Engels pronounced ([1848] 1977: 225), capitalism's global expansion at the behest of the bourgeoisie 'draws all, even the most barbarian, nations into civilization'.

Some versions of Marxism speak as if this historical progress is inevitable – that it is somehow inherent in human relations. But to be fair to Marx, the emphasis in his works is only sometimes (and polemically) on inevitability; more often it is on the need for those who seek progressive change to understand the necessity of struggle. Those who have power, Marx argued, will not willingly cede it. The key to historical, political and economic change depends upon organised struggles for change at those historical moments when the defenders of the **status quo** are at their most vulnerable – at moments of great class antagonism and crisis. The point – well understood by the Russian revolutionary leader V. I. Lenin (1870–1924) and Italian **Communist** Party leader Antonio Gramsci (1891–1937) – was that active political leadership was necessary if struggles were to realise radical, progressive change; such transformations would not occur automatically, no matter how unequal or oppressive capitalist societies were.

To help make sense of Marx's theory of historical materialism it will be useful to note what makes this theory both materialist and historical. Marx famously proclaimed that Hegel's **idealist** philosophy needed to be turned on its head. To achieve this Marx developed his materialist method of analysis, which is premised on the production of physical life by individuals in society; the 'way in which men produce their means of subsistence', which involves, 'before everything else eating and drinking, a habitation, clothing', and so on (1977: 161, 165). While Marx does seem to accord primacy to this physical or material dimension of human social life – 'Life is not determined by consciousness', he says, 'but consciousness by life' (Marx 1977: 165) – he also recognises the vital importance of the ideational dimension. How individuals and societies intellectually conceive 'modes of life' is an activity integral to the human condition. 'As individuals express their life, so they are', says Marx (1977: 161). Humans are what they do; and what they do, and therefore what they are, is historically changing. As the material bases of the human condition change, history moves on and politics acquires new forms.

This suggests that states, markets and all other human institutions must be understood as historical products, not abstract unchanging entities. Indeed, as we shall see, Marxists insist on seeing these institutions as manifestations of an underlying social whole or totality. To this historical proposition must be added another, which posits the structural constraints, as well as freedoms, of history:

Men make their own history, but they do not make it just as they please; they do not make it under circumstances chosen by themselves, but under circumstances directly encountered, given, and transmitted from the past (Marx 1977: 300).

This proposition has affinities with constructivism (see Chapter 7), which also recognises that while the worlds of politics and international relations are social and historical productions, they cannot be changed at will.

The final, and perhaps central, historical proposition is that, as Marx and Engels put it in the *Communist manifesto* ([1848] 1977: 222), 'The history of all hitherto existing society is the history of class struggles'. This ongoing struggle is the driving force of history for Marx, shaping social relations and all the civil and political institutions that grow out of them, not least states, markets and the states-system – the political and economic manifestations of changing modes of production. Against liberal expectations of harmonious social progress under capitalism, Marx expected heightened class conflict. By placing class conflict and struggles between capital and labour at the centre of its analysis, and by redescribing politics (the state and states-system) as a product emanating from the social relations of global capitalism, Marx's theory of historical materialism offers a radically different understanding of the evolution of the international system.

Marx and Marxism in IR

Years before he penned his realist classic, *The twenty years' crisis, 1919–1939* (1946), renowned realist E. H. Carr wrote a study of a thinker generally thought to be the complete antithesis of realism. *Karl Marx: A study in fanaticism* (1934) was a respectful, if critical, engagement with Marx's life and thought. Of Marx's thinking, Carr (1934: 72–3) said: 'it is a tour de force of unparalleled dexterity and brilliance. It is fascinating to watch the disjointed fragments, marshalled by Marx's ingenious brain, fall into place like pieces of a well-made puzzle. Everything fits, and nothing is superfluous'. Carr's deep interest in Marx may come as a surprise to many, but it should be remembered that realism, like Marxism, is concerned with the material and historical dimensions of conflict and struggles for power. It may be that realism and Marxism take opposing views on the sources of these conflicts and struggles, but they nonetheless occupy some common ground.

Carr notwithstanding, the general view IR scholars have taken of Marxism is that it has little or nothing to say about international relations. Martin Wight (1966b: 25) famously asserted that 'Neither Marx, Lenin, nor Stalin made any systematic contribution to international theory'. Even Lenin's theory of imperialism, which Kenneth Waltz (1979: 19) concedes is 'elegant and powerful', is ultimately dismissed because it fails to deliver a systemic theory of international politics. The reasons are obvious: Marx's thinking did not take the state or states-system as its primary focus; it did not take questions of war and peace as its *raison d'être*; and it did not engage extensively with the canonical thinkers usually associated with IR. For these and other reasons, Marxism's focus was long considered extraneous to the traditional agenda of IR. This seemed to find confirmation with the Cold War's ending (see Chapter 20), and liberals and capitalists triumphantly claimed that Marxism had, like the Soviet Union, finally been tossed into the dustbin of history.

Refusing to go the way of purportedly communist states like the Soviet Union, Marxist IR scholars have continued to build upon the large and intellectually significant body of knowledge guided by the spirit of Marx and his interpreters. The main focus of Marxist theorists of IR has been on the nature of the state and states-system and their relationship to the capitalist world economy. While Marxists continue to debate the true nature of the state and states-system and the precise nature of their relationship to the capitalist mode of production, there is agreement that the global expansion of the modern state (see Chapter 9) is inseparable from the development of global capitalism.

Marxist theorists of the state and international relations, including world-systems theorists such as Immanuel Wallerstein (1974; 1996), have tended to regard the state and states-system as the political forms of the global capitalist system. For Wallerstein, it is best to conceive of a functionally integrated modern 'world-system' – composed of a states-system and a world economy – which is governed by a single logic and set of rules associated with the relentless accumulation of capital. Emerging out of the 'long sixteenth century' (1450–1640) crisis of feudalism, the world-system was, according to Wallerstein (1974: 19), 'from the beginning an affair of the world economy and not of **nation**-states'. Indeed, Wallerstein (1996: 89) argues that the states-system and world economy were born together:

> Capitalism and the modern state-system were not two separate historical inventions (or conceptions) that had to be fitted together or articulated with each other. They were obverse sides of a single coin. They were both part of a seamless whole. Neither is imaginable without the other.

Wallerstein's world-systems theory has been criticised by some Marxists for, among other things, economic determinism and failing to grasp the original geopolitical context in which capitalism arose. Marxist IR scholars composed counter-histories to achieve better understandings of the relationship between the states-system and capitalist world economy, and more nuanced understandings of the relative autonomy of politics and the state from capitalist logics. Two IR scholars stand out for their attempts to provide more subtle historical accounts of the relationship between the states-system and capitalism: Justin Rosenberg and Benno Teschke.

Rosenberg (1994) argues in his seminal Marxist account of international relations, *The empire of civil society*, that different historical states-systems (although this term is anachronistic) are governed by different modes of production, and therefore different social structures. He argues that 'geopolitical systems are not constituted independently of, and cannot be understood in isolation from, the wider structures of the production and reproduction of social life' (Rosenberg 1994: 6). He insists that if we remain attentive to structural change we will see that the eighteenth century gave rise to distinctive new institutional forms, namely, the sovereign state as the modern form of political rule specific to capitalism (Rosenberg 1994: 126–9).

Another important application of historical materialism to IR can be found in Teschke's (2004) historical studies of the transition from feudalism through absolutism to modern capitalism. He argues that historical changes in the modern state and states-system are a reflection of the changing ways in which societies organise their economic lives, especially the way property is conceptualised and distributed. Despite nuanced differences, both Rosenberg and Teschke hold the view that the particular form taken by the state at any moment in time is always an outward reflection or manifestation of capitalism's inner logic as it interacts with geopolitical logics. This is in keeping with the spirit of Marx's theory of historical materialism, that political and economic institutions are manifestations of changing modes of production.

Critical Theories of IR

Frankfurt School Critical Theory in IR

'**Frankfurt School** Critical Theory' is the name given to the kind of Marxist-inspired social and political philosophy that emerged out of the Institute of Social Research. Established in Frankfurt under the directorship of Max Horkheimer (1895–1973) in 1923, the Institute brought together a number of like-minded scholars and researchers, including such twentieth-century German luminaries as Theodor Adorno, Benjamin Walter and Herbert Marcuse (see Held 1980; Jay 1973). Though inspired by Marx,

BOX 4.2: TERMINOLOGY

Cox on critical and problem-solving theories

In his seminal 1981 *Millennium* article, Robert W. Cox proposed a distinction between what he called 'problem-solving theory' and 'critical theory'.

- *Problem-solving theory* is based on positivist methods and oriented to maintaining the prevailing structures of social power, or at least working within the constraints of the present system to smooth over any problems or crises. 'It takes the world as it finds it, with the prevailing social and power relationships and the institutions into which it is organised, as the given framework of action' (Cox 1981: 128).

- *Critical theory*, as Cox portrays it, is based on historical materialism and seeks more radical transformations that will enhance the global conditions for freedom and democracy. It does not take the prevailing order of social and power relationships and institutions as the given framework for action, but 'asks how that order came about', calls that order into question, and enquires 'whether [it] might be in the process of changing' (Cox 1981: 129).

Cox denied that knowledge of the social world could be neutral or objective in any genuine sense, despite mainstream theorists' claims to the contrary. As Cox put it in his oft-cited proposition: 'theory is always *for* someone and *for* some purpose' (1981: 128). In other words, all theory derives from a perspective or position in the social world, is embedded in social relations that characterise the political and ideological order at any given time, and thus cannot claim to be 'divorced from a standpoint in time and space' (Cox 1981: 128). Critical theories, including feminism, Marxism and postmodernism, are usually quite open and explicit about the position, perspective and interest of their theories.

Frankfurt School Critical Theorists were interested in analysing the multiple modes of domination afflicting the modern world, from psychological and cultural to political and economic modes.

From its inception Critical Theory questioned the impact upon social life of scientific-**rationalist** modes of inquiry. In particular, it believed that post-Enlightenment modernity had become colonised by a form of instrumental rationality interested only in calculating the efficient means to ends, not evaluating the moral legitimacy of those ends. Instead of assisting humankind's mastery over nature, instrumental rationality had arrested human freedoms and empowered various forms of social domination. For the Frankfurt School, one of the key tasks of the social philosophy they advocated was to recover alternative forms of rationality with emancipatory potentials. This can be illustrated by referring to a distinction made by Max Horkheimer.

Horkheimer distinguished between 'traditional' theory, which is based upon scientific principles of **positivism** and **empiricism** and designed to buttress the status quo, and 'Critical Theory', which is based on interpretive and self-reflective methods and designed not just to 'describe' the world, but to 'act as a force within it to stimulate change' (Horkheimer ([1937] 1972: 215). In this, Horkheimer was paying homage to Marx's *11th thesis on Feuerbach*: 'philosophers have only interpreted the world, in various ways; the point is to change it' (Marx 1977: 158). By privileging instrumental rationality, 'traditional' theory becomes the handmaiden of social domination (Jay 1973: 171–2). Rejecting the positivist separation of facts and values, subject and object of knowledge, Critical Theory examines and reflects on the theorist's immersion in a particular historical and socio-political context and seeks to remove forces and forms of domination. A very similar distinction has been proposed in IR by Robert W. Cox, although he has confessed to having no knowledge of Horkheimer or the Frankfurt School when he coined the distinction (see Box 4.2).

Jürgen Habermas (1929–) is the most famous of the second-generation Frankfurt School scholars who has continued the project of Critical Theory. He has remained committed to the idea that societies can undergo social learning or normative development; by which he means improving

Table 4.1 Knowledge and interests

Knowledge constitutive interest	Purpose	Method	IR theory
Instrumental or technical	Achieving technical control over natural and social environments	Positivist and empiricist	Neorealism, neoliberalism
Strategic or practical	Achieving a framework of mutual understanding and coordination for social interaction	**Hermeneutic** and interpretive	Classical realism, English School, constructivism
Emancipatory	Achieving freedom and autonomy from various forms of domination and exclusion	Self-reflective	Marxism, feminism, Critical Theory, postmodernism

the human capacity to devise social and political arrangements built on principles of justice, democracy and the rule of law. He has persistently argued that politics can always be analysed and evaluated from a 'moral point of view'. It is the recovery and clarification of this normative or moral perspective in politics that Critical Theories of IR have embraced.

In his early writings Habermas (1972) focused on how we acquire knowledge and how this knowledge is shaped by prior interests of which we are often unaware. He sought to illustrate how particular 'knowledge **constitutive** interests' shape and limit the way in which people think and act. Habermas differentiated three kinds of knowledge based on underlying interest or purpose:

- *instrumental* – referring to 'scientific' knowledge regarding human relations with nature
- *strategic* – referring to 'political' knowledge aimed at coordinating human action for particular social purposes, and
- *emancipatory* – referring to knowledge directed at overcoming coercive or oppressive social and political relations (see Table 4.1).

All these knowledge constitutive interests are crucial to a healthy, functioning society. Habermas does not deny the validity and great value of instrumental or strategic knowledge – we rely on instrumental rationality for achieving technical knowledge in fields such as medicine, engineering, aeronautics, and so on – only that they should not 'colonise' all spheres of knowledge, especially social and political spheres where the emancipatory interest should also guide the ways we think and act.

The first significant effort to introduce these ideas into IR was undertaken by Richard Ashley (1981). In this work Ashley used the 'knowledge constitutive interests' framework to argue for critical reflection on the guiding assumptions and interests of the two dominant IR theories, **neorealism** and **neoliberalism**. Both theories, argued Ashley, provide important explanations of the way the world works, at least from the viewpoint of the dominant states in the states-system and global economy – explanations they tend to represent as reality per se; and both underpin their explanations with an objectivist and 'scientific' **ontology** (see Chapter 1). What was missing from these dominant IR theories, Ashley insisted, was an 'emancipatory' interest in changing the system in order to remove the sources of domination and cultivate freedom and democracy. Ashley was subsequently to shift his thinking in line with **postmodern** perspectives (1984; also see Chapter 6) but his early engagement with Frankfurt School Critical Theory represented an important breakthrough in the development of a critical diversity in IR theory in the twenty-first century (see Chapter 1).

The influence of Habermas and Frankfurt School Critical Theory has been growing in IR since the 1980s, with many scholars engaging Frankfurt School themes and methods to analyse world politics (see Bohman 2010; Crawford 2009; Devetak 2009a; George 1994; Hoffman 1987; Hutchings 2005; Neufeld 1995; Roach 2010; Shapcott 2009; Martin Weber 2005). Its influence is most evident, however, in the writings of Andrew Linklater (1990, 1996, 1998, 2007).

BOX 4.3: DISCUSSION POINTS

Kant, Habermas and Linklater on normative justification

Kant's ([1785] 1987: 27, 58) categorical imperative: 'I am never to act otherwise than so that I could also will that my maxim should become a universal law'. He later presents an alternative formulation: '*So act as to treat humanity, whether in thine own person or in that of any other, in every case as an end withal, never as means only*'.

Habermas's (1998: 41) discourse ethics: 'Only those norms can claim validity that could meet with the acceptance of all concerned in practical discourse'.

Linklater's (1998: 96) dialogical ethics: 'The widening of the circle of those who have rights to participate in dialogue and the commitment that norms cannot be regarded as universally valid unless they have, or could command, the consent of all those who stand to be affected by them'.

Utilising themes drawn from Kant and Habermas, Linklater has pushed further the notion that in the post-Cold War era, and in an age of globalisation, the possibilities of democratic dialogue between peoples have improved significantly (see Box 4.3). Linklater's Critical Theory adopts a cosmopolitan ethic (see Chapter 8) that, while appealing to the principle of humanity, nonetheless reaffirms the multiple communities to which individuals belong; recognising subnational, national, regional and transnational identities. Essential to this cosmopolitan ethic is the desire to overcome the 'moral deficits' created by gendered, economic, cultural and political exclusions built into the modern state and states-system. The political goal is to enlarge the spheres of freedom and equality by creating appropriate constitutional arrangements for states in a reconstructed world order. Linklater (1998: ch. 6) sees the European Union's extraordinary experiment in cross-border cooperation and constitutionalism, for all its faults, as offering concrete hope that less exclusionary, less violent, more tolerant and diverse forms of political community might be realisable in a 'post-**Westphalian**' world order.

Gramscian Critical Theory in IR

There is an alternative version of Critical Theory that has emerged in IR, associated primarily with the writings of Robert W. Cox. In positing and defending critical theories against

Figure 4.2   Antonio Gramsci in 1915

Source: Photographer unknown: Wikimedia commons.

problem-solving theories (see Box 4.2), Cox shared a conception of theory's purpose with the Frankfurt School theorists. But Cox's main intellectual influence was an Italian Communist Party leader, Antonio Gramsci, and his reformulated historical materialism.

Sardinian by birth, Gramsci lived a short and dramatic life. He became a major Marxist intellectual and political activist in the period after the Great War when Italy became the violent site of the first **fascist** regime in history (1922–1944). Arrested in 1926 for his political activities, Gramsci was tortured and mistreated in jail, dying shortly after his release. But, remarkably, while in prison Gramsci wrote his influential *Prison notebooks* (1971) in which he reassessed and reformulated the works of Marx and effectively created another major strand of Critical Theory.

One of the keystones of Gramsci's reassessment of Marxism, and of the kind of Critical Theory that bears his name in much contemporary IR, is the notion of **hegemony**. The Gramscian concept of hegemony affords an understanding of the state as a distinctive mode of rule achieved through the consent the masses give to the social, political and legal ideas and institutions cultivated by the ruling classes. For Gramsci, modern rule was not secured by direct coercion alone, but indirectly through a range of compromises and concessions made to the populace. This is why Gramsci (1971: 170) invokes Machiavelli's image of Chiron the centaur (half man, half beast) to make his point that the state combines coercion with consent, violence with civilisation.

Gramsci showed that the full array of civil society institutions – such as the family, the church, the school, the media, the workplace, and so on – provide the state with vital assistance in helping to socialise citizens, cultivating a willingness to embrace the ruling class's economic, cultural, moral and political agenda even as it effectively disenfranchises them as democratic political participants. The state thus plays an 'educative and formative role', says Gramsci (1971: 242), in adapting the populace 'to the necessities of the continuous development of the economic apparatus of production'. It works to create and sustain 'a certain type of civilisation and citizen' (Gramsci 1971: 246).

Through his notion of hegemony Gramsci redirected Marxist theory to the role of culture and ideology in reproducing the state and capitalism. In focusing on the material (base) at the expense of the cultural and ideological (superstructure), dominant variations of Marxism neglected powerful ideational forces mobilised to sustain the state and capitalism; forces that could, with savvy leadership, perhaps serve to dismantle prevailing political structures through 'counter-hegemonic' political movements. For Gramsci it was important to broaden our understanding of the mode of production beyond the materialist focus – on the means of production (work and technology) and consumption (buying and selling goods and labour) – to include the cultural and ideological resources utilised to produce 'a certain type of civilization and citizen' through civil society's educational and formative processes.

In a number of works over more than two decades, Robert W. Cox has combined painstaking empirical analyses of states, social forces and world orders with insights drawn primarily from Gramsci to illustrate the problems of contemporary global life and the potential sites of counter-hegemonic struggle. By deploying Gramsci's notion of hegemony in IR, he thus adopts Gramsci's dual focus: on the role of ideas and culture in producing and reproducing the prevailing world order, and on counter-hegemonic potentials latent within it.

Cox provides an approach to international relations that focuses on the interplay of ideas, institutions and material capabilities (see Figure 4.3); its aim is to explain 'the relative stability of successive world orders' by utilising Gramsci's notion of hegemony (Cox 1981: 139). Neorealist and neoliberal accounts of hegemony, premised on the dominant state's material capabilities, fail to recognise the political importance of ideas. Recalling Gramsci's Machiavellian allusion to Chiron the centaur, Cox (1983: 164) insists that hegemony is not achieved purely with instruments of material power. Explaining how hegemony produces and maintains a particular world order configuration requires an account of how ideas and ideologies socialise states and institutions into adopting certain policies and practices, cultivating certain conceptions of the state's role and purpose, and consenting to certain world order arrangements. Hegemony, as Cox (1987: 7) understands it, is a form of dominance where the preeminent state in the international system creates a world order consistent with its ideology and values and serving to maintain the pre-eminence of that state and its ruling classes, yet able to secure some degree of consent from other states and classes by offering 'some measure or prospect of satisfaction to the less powerful'.

Some of the most influential neo-Gramscian work has explored contemporary hegemonic formations of world order, focusing particularly on the crisis and transformation of *pax americana* triggered by globalisation and the rise of neoliberal economics (see Cox 1987; Gill 1990, 1993a, 1995; Bieler and Morton 2004; Rupert 1995). The central proposition here is that a global 'common sense' has been constructed around the deregulation of trade and finance – what Gill (1995) refers to as 'market civilization' – which, while claiming to serve global interests, in fact serves to consolidate and enhance the power and prosperity of the major states and global corporations. At the apex of this process is the US, which, alongside its unrivalled military and economic power, utilises its extensive reserves of '**soft power**' (from political and diplomatic influence to the cultural power exercised through its music and film industries) to embed its ideology and ideas in global economic institutions (GEIs) (see Chapter 24) which support world order arrangements favourable to its hegemony.

Since the 1980s, and for a range of reasons, Cox has suggested that this dimension of hegemonic rule is becoming increasingly problematic for the US as it faces a 'legitimation crisis' concerning both its strategic and its economic behaviour around the world. After the Cold War this difficulty has arguably increased as, via neoconservative belligerence in recent years, it has sought to shore up its power and status – in the Middle East and

Figure 4.3   Cox's dialectic of hegemonic forces

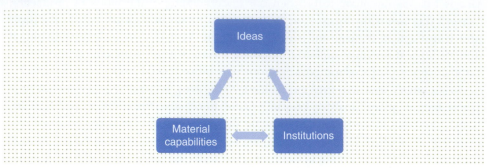

in Central Asia – and as the 'market civilization' it champions provokes widespread discontent and resistance (see Chapter 28). The rise of these 'counter-hegemonic' forces (e.g. global labour movements, social movements, women's movements, indigenous movements and environmental movements) has heightened the legitimation crisis facing the prevailing US-led world order.

Neo-Gramscian Critical Theory offers a different way of thinking about the realities of IR than do mainstream perspectives that focus on the material dimensions of great-power politics or global economic hierarchy. Consistent with the Frankfurt School, it asks: how was it that the powerful became so dominant and what is the price to be paid for this dominance? It examines successive world orders and finds not just triumphant 'winners', but disenfranchised 'losers' (see Chapter 27). However, it is also interested in identifying vulnerabilities in the prevailing world orders that may open up alternative, less exclusionary, more democratic futures.

The cautious dialectics of this approach are well articulated by Mark Rupert and Scott Solomon (2006: 2) on the issue of neoliberal globalisation. Pursuing an inquiry originated by Marx and continued by Gramsci and the Frankfurt School in different ways, they ask: in a world of massive corporate profits and unimaginable wealth for relatively few, and a world of 'sweatshops, domestic servitude and toxic waste dumps' for so many others, how can we construct alternative futures? How, more precisely, might we construct 'a transnational culture of solidarity, mutual respect and reciprocal responsibility' as the basis for a progressive global future? Their answer invokes the Marxist theory of historical materialism, but bereft of any sense of imminence or inevitability; it acknowledges that, as 'a complex and contradictory phenomenon', globalisation harbours both progressive and regressive tendencies. Which tendencies will prevail depends on the outcome of multiple, cross-cutting struggles within civil society (Rupert and Solomon 2006: 2). But they, along with Cox (1999), see in national and transnational civil societies progressive, counter-hegemonic potentials to eliminate inequalities between rich and poor, powerful and powerless, and to create new democratic spaces, new forms of **self-determination**.

Conclusion

For most of the Cold War era Marxism occupied the fringes of IR (Kubálkova and Cruickshank 1985). More recently, however, there has been a resurgence of interest in Marx's works, particularly his detailed critiques of capitalism which, for many, contain valuable insights into globalisation, and offer pointers to a Critical Theory of IR. In this chapter we have introduced the chief elements of the Marxist approaches to IR, and showed how the Marxist legacy has been carried forward and modified by Frankfurt School and neo-Gramscian versions of Critical Theory. In an era of increasing global poverty and multiplying crises throughout the capitalist world economy, Marxism and Critical Theory offer valuable conceptual resources for thinking about IR in radically different ways. Most importantly, they encourage explanations and understandings guided by an interest in eliminating various kinds of domination, inequality and exclusion that characterise the present world order.

QUESTIONS

1. What is capitalism and why are Marxists so critical of it?
2. How do Marxists understand the relationship between the capitalist world economy and the states-system?
3. What assumptions, if any, are shared by realism, liberalism and Marxism? How does Marxism differ from these mainstream theories?
4. What are the distinct characteristics of historical materialism?
5. Why do Critical Theorists focus on the interests underlying theories?
6. What are the major problems of the Westphalian world order as identified by Linklater and Cox?

FURTHER READING

Anievas, Alexander (ed.), 2010, *Marxism and world politics: contesting global capitalism*, London: Routledge. Very useful and accessible collection of essays on the Marxist contribution to IR.

Cox, Robert W. and Sinclair, Timothy 1995, *Approaches to world order*, Cambridge University Press. Extremely readable and useful volume of Cox's essays; useful for his explication of neo-Gramscian critical theory.

Held, David 1980, *Introduction to Critical Theory*, Berkeley: University of California Press. Good book-length introduction to Frankfurt School Critical Theory.

Linklater, Andrew 1990, *Beyond realism and Marxism: Critical Theory and international relations*, London: Macmillan. Pioneering contribution to Critical Theory of IR which is also very useful in surveying Marxist literature and linking it to IR.

Linklater, Andrew 2007, *Critical Theory and world politics: citizenship, sovereignty and humanity*, London: Routledge. Collection of essays on a range of themes central to IR and Critical Theory.

Roach, Steven C. (ed.) 2008, *Critical theory and international relations: a reader*, London: Routledge. Comprehensive range of articles and chapters from Kant, Hegel and Marx, through the Frankfurt School to Critical Theorists of IR.

Rosenberg, Justin 1994, *The empire of civil society: a critique of realist theory of international relations*, London: Verso. Excellent Marxist engagement with dominant IR theories and key concepts such as sovereignty.

5

Feminism

Katrina Lee-Koo

Introduction	77
International relations meets feminism	77
The feminist IR agenda	77
Tracing feminist international relations: challenging the masculine bias	79
Where are the women?	80
Reconstructing international relations: examining the differences between sex and gender	81
J. Ann Tickner: Progress towards gender equality in the academy and the policy world	82
Men have genders too!	84
Feminist theories of international relations	86
Conclusion: what does feminism add to our study of international relations?	89
Questions	90
Further reading	90

Introduction

This chapter examines different feminist approaches to the study and practice of international relations. It highlights the similarities between these approaches, but also the differences. It does this first by tracing the interventions made by feminists into international relations and the creation of a distinctly feminist agenda. Second, it uses the 'gender lens' to demonstrate and analyse how experiences and understandings in international relations can be 'gendered'. Finally, it explains and criticises the different feminist approaches to international relations.

International relations meets feminism

With evidence of continued inequality between women and men in key areas of international politics, the goal of feminist IR is to highlight, understand and address this inequality, and to encourage the discipline to recognise the importance of gender politics. Consequently, like international relations generally, feminist IR is a broad and diverse field of study. It is a field rich with debate, controversy, cutting-edge research and challenging new **methodological** approaches. Feminist IR scholars are often necessarily interdisciplinary, synthesising international relations with gender, cultural, post-colonial, environmental and other studies while also drawing heavily from more traditional **disciplines**. Feminist scholars have made important contributions to international relations **theory**, security studies, international political economy, development studies, international law and questions of global governance, among other fields.

While feminist international relations encompasses numerous **feminisms** which are based on distinct theoretical approaches, feminist IR scholars have a common commitment to highlighting and addressing the discrimination and disadvantage that women in particular suffer in international politics. Feminist IR scholars are concerned primarily with the ways in which the study and practice of international politics discriminates against women. This discrimination can lead to disadvantage which results in, for example, the lack of access that women have to political **power** and to economic resources. These issues of discrimination and disadvantage set much of the agenda for feminists working in international relations (see Box 5.1).

BOX 5.1: DISCUSSION POINTS

The feminist international relations agenda

Feminists contribute to a broader international relations analysis in two ways:

1. By offering a broader set of issues to consider.
2. By offering new insights into existing international relations concerns.

The feminist IR agenda

Feminist IR examines a vast range of issues covering women (and men) from different social, political and economic backgrounds. Its agenda includes at least three key issues: first it highlights and examines cases of gender inequality between men and women (such as the disparities in political representation); second, it looks at issues that disproportionately affect women but have remained largely neglected by IR scholars (such as the human trafficking of women for the purposes of sexual slavery); third, it explores the ways that key issues in IR (such as conflict) differently affect men and women. In doing so it examines men and women's experiences of **war**, **peace**, **democracy**, governance, economics, development, justice, **security** and health. A focus on these topics, with gender in mind, promotes a rich agenda of important issues that are often neglected by more mainstream approaches to IR.

For example, by considering gender equality in global politics we can reveal the extent to which women are often disadvantaged. The UN's Commission on the Status of Women reported in 2010 that in the preceding year women held only 18.8 per cent of parliamentary seats while only fifteen women were heads of states or governments (UNESC 2010: 45–6). In the developing world women do the majority of unpaid work (such as caring, subsistence farming and agricultural work) and in the developed world women still earn less than men for the same work. This discrimination is also reflected in access to education, health care, land ownership and legal rights. Feminists argue that the causes of this discrimination are structural and institutional. For instance, there are many reasons why women are less likely to be landowners. These reasons could include discriminatory laws relating to land ownership, lack of access to credit, inheritance or divorce settlements, or there could be social and cultural practices which inihibit women's abilities to access land rights. The feminist IR agenda therefore involves identifying patterns of discrimination and seeking to explain their causes.

Second, the feminist agenda includes a consideration of issues that disproportionately affect women. An example of this is the global campaign to stop violence, including sexual violence, against women, particularly during times of conflict. Feminist scholars have spent decades documenting the violence committed against civilian women during conflict. The reason it is considered to be gender-based violence is that it specifically targets women because they are women. Feminists have argued that violence against women is often a deliberate strategy of war which can be used to achieve a range of political or military goals. These might be to humiliate a **nation**, to enact policies of **ethnic cleansing** and genocide, to punish communities for supporting an enemy, to gather intelligence, or to ensure the compliance of a community. Research by feminist IR scholars on this topic has raised awareness and increased understanding of the experiences of women in conflict which, in turn, also contributes to our overall understanding of conflict. For example, these arguments have been accepted by the international community and have led to the prosecution of war rape as a crime against humanity and a crime of **genocide** at the international criminal tribunals for the former Yugoslavia (established in 1993) and Rwanda (established in 1994).

Finally, feminist IR scholars are interested in how the same global challenges affect men and women in different ways. For example, pandemics, climate change and natural disasters will affect men and women differently. This is usually because of their different levels of social, political and economic power as well as the social expectations of their behaviour. For instance, while HIV/AIDS affects both men and women, women are two to four times more vulnerable to infection than men. This is because they often have less social, cultural and political power to negotiate safe sex and to access redress for rape and sexual abuse (UNIFEM 2009). Similarly, while the 2010 Pakistan floods devastated the lives of men and women throughout the country, it affected them differently. In some cases women had less mobility to evacuate from floods as they were caring for the young and elderly, were unaccustomed to travelling independently, had not been taught to swim, and had less access to public communication announcements about flood warnings. It is also the case that the aid efforts were 'gendered'. NGOs on the ground found that aid was often delivered to men, because men traditionally occupy public spaces, without ensuring that women had appropriate access to it. In other cases the specific needs of women's health (such as maternal health) and women's safety (such as protection from violence in the displaced persons camps) were not adequately addressed (see UNIFEM 2010). Feminists are interested in studying these differences to ensure that the needs of both women and men are met (see Box 5.2).

BOX 5.2: DISCUSSION POINTS

The goals of feminist international relations theory

1. To highlight and challenge the way international relations privileges certain masculine identities and ways of knowing.
2. To examine the roles and experiences of women in international politics.
3. To analyse how gender is constructed and the consequences this has for men and women in international politics.
4. To examine the relationships within and between masculinity, femininity, men and women.

Tracing feminist international relations: challenging the masculine bias

In the early 1990s feminists began to make their mark in international relations. One of the first goals of these scholars was to highlight what they saw as the masculine bias of the core assumptions and concepts of the discipline. Important contributions like Jan Jindy Pettman's *Worlding women* (1996) and J. Ann Tickner's *Gender in international relations* (1992) demonstrated how the theories and practices of international relations reflect and respect the experiences of certain men and certain masculine qualities. For example, one of the first achievements of feminist engagement in international relations was its questioning of **realism**'s 'rational man' as the basis of international life. It argued that the 'rational man' model of human nature (which is self-serving, aggressive, competitive and warlike) does not speak for many women, or indeed many men (Tickner 1992: ch. 2). Similarly, these feminists argue that the 'important concerns' of international politics such as **states**, **sovereignty**, **anarchy** and military power all reflect, to the neglect of alternatives, masculine ways of knowing and masculine traits. Moreover, they reflect a particular kind of masculinity, a **hegemonic** masculinity, that prefers aggressive and liberal/realist ways of thinking about the world. Feminist IR scholars argue that this is why mainstream accounts of international relations typically feature elite men and their experiences in war, statecraft and diplomacy.

For feminist IR scholars, however, this only accounts for part of the story of international relations. After all, there are far more examples of states peacefully negotiating potential disputes than there are of war. Similarly, global relations are not confined to Europe and North America, as is sometimes implied by the discipline's grand narratives. A key goal of feminist theorising, therefore, is to demonstrate, firstly, how this masculine bias operates in such a way that it often privileges and promotes certain actors and experiences and, secondly, to reject the claim that these are universal experiences. Consequently, much feminist international relations scholarship is directed towards uncovering the experiences of people who are hidden by this masculine bias.

Where are the women?

A key goal of feminist research is to correct the male-centric bias in international relations by asking 'where are the women?' and then redressing this imbalance by incorporating women's experiences into any analysis of international relations. Groundbreaking works like Cynthia Enloe's *Bananas, beaches and bases* (1990) reveal that women play important roles in international relations. In addition to the popularly known stories of Western women as nurses and factory workers during wartime, feminists point out that women, in their everyday lives, are also agents and activists in war, in the international political economy, and in the search for peace, security and reconciliation. Enloe argues that the lives of ordinary women can provide useful insights into how international relations operates. For instance, a young Mexican woman working as a cleaner in a New York hotel may not appear to be a major actor in international relations. However, an analysis of her life can tell us a great deal about the workings of state relations, the international political economy, migration, globalisation, the politics of labour and gender relations. In this sense she is an important agent of international politics.

Consequently, asking 'where are the women?' offers a fount of empirical knowledge which can be used to analyse and understand international relations. In compiling this catalogue of women's experiences, however, feminists have had to employ new kinds of methodologies. First, in order to uncover many of these experiences it has been necessary to move away from some of the more established ways of research used in mainstream international relations. Feminist IR scholars, therefore, sometimes rely upon sources of knowledge that are unashamedly subjective, including personal interviews, diaries, letters and memoirs. Furthermore, they use as sources of knowledge people who do not claim to be prominent decision-makers in international relations, but who nonetheless significantly contribute to the practice of international relations and whose lives international relations can profoundly affect. Second, therefore, feminists often employ a bottom-up, rather than top-down, approach to studying IR. Rather than describing international relations through a grand narrative that analyses the actions and behaviours of whole nation-states in a geopolitical context, these feminists prefer to offer micro-narratives by explaining how individual people, because of their gender, affect, or are affected by, the behaviours and actions of nation-states in different ways.

Reconstructing international relations: examining the differences between sex and gender

For feminists working in international relations, the question then becomes 'how can we reconstruct the ways in which we study and practise international relations so that the experiences of all people are accounted for and there is no gendered discrimination?' It is perhaps this project that causes much of the controversy between feminist scholars. For some feminists it is simply a case of adding women to areas where they are absent, such as in parliaments, militaries, boardrooms, peace negotiations, and in other positions of power. For other feminists, however, this cannot be done without first addressing the **patriarchal** culture that exists in international relations and that enables the discrimination in the first place. This controversy surrounds the politics of moving from 'adding sex empirically' to 'analysing gender critically'.

Feminist theories rely upon an understanding of the differences between biological sex and socially constructed gender. These terms are politically loaded and remain contested. The term 'sex' is usually used by social scientists to refer to the biological characteristics which define a person as being male or female. However, gender, most feminists argue, is an identity which is not biologically determined but is instead socially constructed. It is a construction that dichotomises identities, behaviours, responsibilities and expectations in society as being not male or female but, rather, masculine or feminine.

For example, some may argue that many Western societies continue to be gendered. This implies that men and women are socially expected to adopt the gendered roles of masculine and feminine respectively and behave in ways that are supposedly appropriate to those roles. This might mean that men are the members of parliament while women are their supportive wives. In this sense, gender is not a biological imperative but a social expectation. Consequently, when a man or woman steps out of their traditionally defined gendered identities they appear peculiar or are thought to lack credibility. For instance, in 2010 Australia elected its first female Prime Minister, Julia Gillard. Throughout her career she has often been questioned about the fact that she does not have a husband and is not a mother (the traditionally defined social expectations of her gender). Frequently, there is also public comment on her choice of clothing, her fashion sense and her hairstyle. These comments are dwelt upon in a way that is not usually the case for male politicians. The gendered expectation that 'women should dress nicely' was summed up by one commentator who told Gillard, 'If you can't put an outfit together, how can we trust you to put the Labor Party back together?' (Quigley 2006).

Feminist scholars use examples like this to demonstrate that politics still operates on powerfully gendered ideas and social expectations of behaviour. Yet for feminists it is not simply the case that there is a difference between the social constructions of masculinity and femininity. They argue that there is an unequal relationship between masculinity (and its associated characteristics of being strong, decisive, aggressive and dominating the public realm) and feminine characteristics (which are seen as weak, irrational, peaceable, conciliatory and restricted to the private realm). This unequal relationship sees femininity as politically, economically and socially devalued while masculinity is valorised.

Progress towards gender equality in the academy and the policy world
J. Ann Tickner

As the second decade of the new millennium begins, indicators of vast gender inequality in global economic, social and political life remain. Women are still the majority of the world's poor, and underpaid relative to men; the majority of civilian victims in war are women and women are less than 20 per cent of elected political leaders worldwide. Since it entered the discipline, just over twenty years ago, feminist International Relations (IR) theory has been concerned with bringing these inequities to light, helping us to understand what causes them, and thinking about ways to end them. Many of the IR scholars, myself included, who write about gender and women in global politics were first motivated to do so when we began to notice how few IR books were written by women scholars. We also began to see that the subject matter of the discipline rarely included anything about women's lives.

For those of us who began this work in the late 1980s, it was remarkable that similar ideas seemed to be emerging in different geographical locations at the same time. Feminist scholars in Europe, the Asia-Pacific and North America began to express similar ideas about how the IR discipline was gendered – and gendered masculine – and how few women were visible in international policymaking. In most societies, this did not appear to be due to legal barriers alone, so we had to look elsewhere for explanations. Consequently, IR feminists began to examine the *language* of international politics, noting that concepts such as autonomy, power, independence and rationality – characteristics so often described as masculine by men and women alike – were preferred ways for states to behave also. It appeared that the language of international politics and its subject matter – national security and **war** being the most important – were subjects about which women were presumed to have little of importance to say.

It has been gratifying to those of us who embarked on this journey twenty years ago to watch how feminist IR has grown and flourished. Courses about gender and international relations are regularly taught at universities around the world. Books and scholarly articles have multiplied; new ways of thinking about international relations have been introduced and feminists have helped to broaden the subject matter that is now included in the discipline. Feminists are thinking about security in new ways – about what goes on in war, as well as how wars begin and end. Feminists have drawn attention to the increasing number of civilian casualties in recent wars – many of them women and children. Rape in war is now recognised as part of military strategy rather than an unavoidable consequence of conflict. Feminists have introduced trafficking and forced prostitution onto the security agenda. They have pointed out that the majority of the world's **refugees** are women and children and they have written about women who are crossing state boundaries to seek work as domestic servants and nannies in order to provide income for their families back home. All of these issues have important consequences for how we analyse security and the global economy and it has been exciting for me to see how these issues are now considered part of the subject matter of our discipline.

We usually find that what is included in the discipline reflects broader concerns of the policy world, and it is indeed the case that women and gender have received much greater attention from the policy community over the past forty years. Gender issues in development were first introduced onto the international policy agenda in the 1970s. Before that time, aid agencies and development experts had not considered whether programs aimed at improving people's material lives might have differential effects on women and men. That such considerations are now routinely included on the policy agendas of intergovernmental organisations is largely due to the efforts of women themselves, organising at the national and international levels.

Under pressure from women's **non-governmental organisations (NGOs)**, and aiming to focus attention on the status of women, both within the **UN** and in its member states, the UN General Assembly declared 1975 as International Women's Year. This year marked the beginning of the United Nations Decade for Women; three UN Conferences on Women were held during the decade (in 1975, 1980, and 1985). A fourth, the largest, was held ten years later, in Beijing (1995). Parallel NGO conferences were held at each of the official conferences. Attendance at these conferences increased from 5000 in Mexico City in 1975 to an estimated 25 000 in Beijing.

Pressure from women's groups was important in getting the UN to disaggregate its data – such as its quality of life indicators – by sex. Adoption of the Gender Development Index (GDI) by the UN Human Development Programme in 1995 was an important step in helping to formulate policies to improve women's well-being. The GDI has helped policy-makers to see that countries that score low on gender equality tend to be the same countries that score low on development more generally. This shows that ignoring gender comes at great cost, not only to women but also to men and to development more generally. In response to this concern, in 1997 the UN Economic and Social Council (ECOSOC) articulated its Agreed Conclusion on Gender Mainstreaming, a strategy for making women's as well as men's concerns and experiences an integral dimension of the design, implementation, monitoring and evaluation of all UN policies and programs. Now all UN agencies are required, in theory at least, to operate under its mandate.

Again, due to pressure by women's groups, in 2000, the UN Security Council (UNSC) passed a milestone resolution 1325. UNSC 1325 was the first resolution ever passed by the Security Council to specifically address the impact of war on women, and women's contributions to conflict resolution and sustainable peace. It was the first in a series of Security Council resolutions recognising women's vulnerabilities and also women's right to participate in **peace-building** processes. Within the next ten years, the Security Council built on 1325 with additional resolutions. In 2008, UNSC 1820 recognised sexual violence as a tactic of war, and in 2009, UNSC 1888 was passed to advance its implementation.

There is still a long way to go before the practices of international policy-making live up to the lofty goals that these resolutions have articulated. Since academic feminism was born out of a political movement, those of us who work in the academy believe that we cannot and should not separate our intellectual work from politics and activism. Knowledge is an important first step to building a more equitable, just and peaceful world. I hope learning about how our discipline has expanded over the past twenty years to include the lives of those who had not previously been part of what we call IR will inspire you to think about further steps we can all take towards building a discipline and a world that includes us all.

J. Ann Tickner is Professor of International Relations at the University of Southern California, and one of the discipline's leading feminist thinkers. A TRIP survey ranked her twenty-first of academics with most impact on the field, and she was included in Routledge's *Fifty key thinkers in international relations.* Her books include *Gender in international relations: feminist perspectives on achieving global security, Gendering world politics: Issues and approaches in the post-cold war era;* and (with Laura Sjoberg) *Conversations in feminist international relations: Past, present and future?*

Men have genders too!

Feminist international relations can never be *only* about women. While the focus may be on the discrimination and disadvantage that women face in international politics, it can only be understood within the context of the relationship between men and women and the relationship between the masculine and the feminine. For instance, feminists are interested in how some men can be 'feminised' while some women are 'masculinised'. Western militaries, for example, are sites where gay men are often feminised and women are expected to be masculine. Consequently, until 2011 the 'don't ask, don't tell' policy prohibited gay men and lesbians from serving openly in the US military (see Belkin and Bateman 2003), while films like *GI Jane* (1997) portray successful women in the military as being necessarily masculine and aggressive. However, it is important to recognise that these cultures do change and feminists are interested in mapping these changes and directing them towards outcomes of equality. Useful discussions of the relationships between gendered roles and between men and women can be found in Zalewski and Parpart's *Rethinking the 'man question' in international relations* (2008) and Kathy Ferguson's *The man question* (1993) as well as contributions by male scholars like Terrell Carver (2003, 2004), Joshua Goldstein (2001), Fred Halliday (1988) and Steve Smith (2005).

It is a common misconception that feminism is only interested in women. It's important to remember that men are also affected by gender politics. While feminists often describe the international relations field as male-dominated, it is worth noting that it is often dominated by certain groups of elite men. Furthermore, it is important to identify areas and issues where certain groups of men may be discriminated against or disadvantaged by international politics. For instance, R. Charli Carpenter (2006) has argued that in conflict able-bodied men of combat age are frequently the targets of wartime violence as both combatants and civilians. This is because men are assumed to be natural combatants and therefore are seen to pose an immediate threat, even if they are civilians. Similarly, even though there has been growing awareness of sexual

Figure 5.1   The gendered politics of war: front cover image from *The Queenslander*'s Christmas supplement, 1915. During World War I it was expected that men would take part in the war-fighting to protect the women and children at home. These expectations of gendered roles and responsibilities were repeated during the Bosnian War where, in 1995 in Srebrenica, 8000 civilian men and boys were killed while the women of the village were left as mourners (Figure 5.2).

Figure 5.2   *Coffin grief, Srebrenica*, by David Kozar (with permission).

violence committed against women in war, there has been less attention given to such violence against men.

However, while feminists generally agree on the importance of understanding and addressing gender-based discrimination and disadvantage, they can (and do) disagree in a number of important areas. It is from these sites of contention that different feminist international relations theories (and practices) arise.

Feminist theories of international relations

Like all political theories, feminist international relations has many strands, some of which contradict each other. While two people may each call themselves a feminist, they can still find themselves disagreeing on basic ideas about women, men and the **international system**. Feminisms such as liberal, radical, Marxist, cultural, post-colonial, constructivist, critical and postmodern feminisms all reflect the different ways in which feminists interpret the information before them (see Box 5.3). In this context, the various feminisms look in different ways at: the nature of international relations and how we should study it; the nature(s) of men and women; the power relationships that men and women (and masculinity and femininity) have both with each other and the international system; the idea of what constitutes the good life; and strategies of how to attain it. While this means that the strands of feminism can be quite distinct, they can be broadly divided into positivist and post-positivist approaches (Tickner 2005). Examples of positivist approaches are liberal, radical, Marxist, cultural and some constructivist feminisms, while post-positivist approaches include critical, postmodern, some constructivist and most post-colonial feminisms.

Liberal feminism

Liberal feminism is centrally concerned with equal rights between men and women (Steans 2006: ch. 2). As its name suggests, it is broadly derived from the political theory of **liberalism**. Liberal feminists, like liberals, support the rights of individuals to seek fulfilment, to pursue their own interests, and to be equal before the law. Liberal feminism has a long political tradition. British feminist Mary Wollstonecraft's *Vindication of the rights of woman* in 1792 was perhaps the first attempt to make the liberal case for women's rights. She argued that discriminatory practices, such as denying women education and full citizenship, did not give women the opportunity to fulfil their potential as human beings. Today, liberal

---

BOX 5.3: TERMINOLOGY

Feminist theories of international relations

Below are some of the theories developed by feminist scholars:

- *Liberal feminism* is based on liberal ideas of equality between men and women.
- *Marxist feminism* argues that the liberation of women can be achieved through the dismantling of **capitalism** and oppressive class relations.
- *Black feminism* examines the relationship between gender and race-based discrimination.
- *Cultural and maternal feminism* argues that women's peaceful natures can contribute to a politics of global peace.
- *Post-colonial feminism* seeks to examine the different forms of oppression facing women in colonial and post-colonial societies that are often neglected by Western-based feminisms.
- *Critical and postmodern feminisms* seek to ask fundamental questions about women's and men's identities, the gendered nature of the international system and possibilities of **emancipation** for women.

feminists continue to argue that sex-based discrimination deprives women of equal rights and the right to pursue their political, economic and social self-interest. They argue that this can be eliminated by the removal of legal and other obstacles that have denied them the same rights and opportunities as men. Consequently, most liberal feminists agree that the state is the proper authority for lobbying for, and enforcing, women's rights. It is believed that even though the state may itself engage in discriminatory practices, it is nonetheless capable of becoming the neutral and objective arbiter of gender equality.

In Western nations, liberal feminism remains powerful in policy-making circles and political lobbying. Throughout the centuries many prominent women's organisations have argued their cases from a liberal feminist perspective. These campaigns are often rights-based, making reference to equal rights and the rule of law. These have included the suffragette movements in the nineteenth and twentieth centuries which championed the 'right to vote' campaigns for women, the ongoing 'equal pay for equal work' campaigns, the 'right to choose/pro-choice' campaigns around issues of women and sexual health, and the 'right to fight' campaign for women in the military.

The success of liberal feminism can be attributed in part to its reliance upon a positivist form of understanding knowledge that is familiar to international relations as a discipline (Tickner 2001: 12–13). Liberal feminists are concerned only with women's exclusion from, and inequality in, areas of public life. They are *not*, however, concerned with the nature of that public life (be it in the military, the state, the workplace or the economy). It is on this point that a number of feminists have criticised liberal feminism.

Critiques of liberal feminism

Critiques of liberal feminism parallel many of the critiques of liberalism generally. First, liberal feminism's claim to universality is problematised. Just as liberalism speaks of the rights of 'man', so too does liberal feminism speak of the rights of 'woman'. It is accused, particularly, of representing the interests of white women in Western societies as if they were the interests of all women. In this sense it is often charged with claiming objective knowledge for all women and being ignorant of subjective concerns and issues based on other identities such as race, ethnicity, religion or socio-economic background.

It is from this particular criticism that we see the rise of specific issue/identity-based feminisms such as black, Third World and post-colonial feminisms. This array of feminisms points out that liberal feminism's agenda may not always be relevant to non-white women and that, in some cases, liberal feminist discourse excludes them and their needs. For instance, bell hooks' text *Ain't I A Woman?* criticised American liberal feminists for excluding the needs and interests of African-American women (hooks 1981). Five years later Chandra Mohanty's famous essay 'Under Western eyes: feminist scholarship and colonial discourses' (1984) critiqued Western feminists for treating women from the developing world as a homogeneous group rather than understanding the differences between these women and the challenges they faced. These critiques do not mean that these scholars are not feminists, but rather that their goals and ambitions as feminists are different and not necessarily based on a liberal model.

This leads to the second major criticism of liberal feminism: its claim to know 'the real world' objectively. Liberal feminism by and large accepts current mainstream articulations of the world 'as the way it is'. It accepts the idea that the world is necessarily a conflictual place made of states vying for power in an international anarchical realm. It doesn't seek to *change* the nature of the world, but only to change women's roles and opportunities in it. In this sense, a woman like former US Secretary of State Condoleezza Rice is an important role model. Rice is proof that a woman is as capable as a man of running the State Department and coordinating the wars in Afghanistan and Iraq. This approach does not, however, question the utility or efficacy of war as a key feature in international relations.

Maternal and cultural feminism

Liberal feminists reject the idea that women are more nurturing and peaceable than men; maternal and cultural feminists, on the other hand, argue that there *is* a connection between women and peace and that this connection should be exploited and emphasised to create a better world. This kind of feminism includes, first, those who believe that women are 'biologically' more peaceful than men and, second, those who argue that women are socialised into being more peaceful than men. These feminists argue that women's roles in the private sphere as mothers, carers, moral guardians and nurturers link them to peace. Such arguments have been put forward by Sara Ruddick (1989) and Jean Bethke Elshtain (1982) and have been a powerful organising tool in women's peace activism. For instance, throughout the Pacific Islands women use their roles and experiences as mothers to give them legitimacy as activisists on a range of social causes from domestic violence to peace building (see N. George 2010). Similarly, American Cindy Sheehan founded the organisation Gold Star Families for Peace after her son was killed serving in Iraq. She too draws upon her identity as a mother and what she calls 'matriotism' (a maternal patriotism), claiming that mothers (and those who have been mothered) have unique insights into peace (Sheehan 2006). While these ideas have a high profile in public debates, some feminist theorists are troubled by these essentialist claims.

Critical and postmodern feminisms

For critical and postmodern feminists, essentialist and universal claims about women's and men's natures and needs are problematic. Consequently, critical and postmodern feminists are distinct from liberal, maternal and cultural feminists in a number of ways. The first key distinction is that the former problematise and investigate the category of 'woman'. They reject the idea that 'woman' is a universal category and that women have a specific, shared way of knowing and being. Instead, they not only acknowledge the differences between women, they also embrace them. Critical and postmodern feminists argue that, like all identities, being 'a woman' is a subjective experience. They suggest that different women may suffer different forms of oppression and have different needs or ways of addressing these issues. Therefore, individual feminists should not assume that their own needs are the same as every other woman's, and should accept the possibility that different feminists may think differently about important issues. Feminists, for example, may disagree about whether Islamic headscarves for women are a source of oppression or a source of personal empowerment. Critical and postmodern feminists argue that knowledge about this is subjective, therefore it is up to individual women to make the decision for themselves, rather than rely upon a universal decision imposed on all women.

The second key feature of critical and postmodern feminisms is their claim that gendered constructions pervade not just individuals' but also institutions' knowledge and political discourse. Consequently, these feminisms attempt to challenge women's disadvantage and discrimination through an investigation and critique of the gendered nature of broader political structures and institutions. Critical and postmodern feminists do not accept any institution or claim to knowledge in international relations as unproblematic and neutral, or free of gendered construction. They argue that institutions like the state, the economy, the military and the academic discipline of IR are all gendered in specific ways that promote masculine values and subordinate feminine ones (Pettman 1996).

Consequently, critical and postmodern feminists argue that knowledge about what should constitute the study of international relations is gendered to promote masculine characteristics. Particularly, they argue that realist international relations is not objective but, rather, privileges masculine values (Tickner 1992). Because it values states, anarchy, power, aggression and rationality and devalues notions of cooperation, conciliation, self-sacrifice, peace, physical weakness and emotion, it is considered a masculine practice that often privileges elite men. As a result, it is these men who have dominated international relations. Even though women such as Condoleezza Rice, Madeline Albright (the first woman Secretary of State in the US) and Margaret Thatcher (Britain's first woman Prime Minister) have all been successful Western state leaders, critical and postmodern feminists argue that their success can perhaps be accounted for because they conformed to the masculine culture which dominates international relations. In the 2003 conflict in Iraq, the war in the former Yugoslavia, and the Falklands War, each of these women was able to demonstrate masculine qualities that earned respect.

Finally, critical and postmodern feminists argue that because they can demonstrate the ways in which gendered relations are constructed in international life, international life is not immutable. This means that international relations, and the ways in which we think about and study it, can change. International relations can be thought about and practised differently, perhaps towards ways that are more emancipatory for women and men (Lee-Koo 2007). For critical and postmodern feminists, then, international politics does not need to be predicated on war, power, violence or oppression but can (and perhaps should) be understood and valued in terms of its potential for peace, emancipation, cooperation and equality. Tickner (2001: 47) argues that a critical feminism should work towards an emancipatory politics of international life that is inclusive of all identities and committed to 'improving the lives of the whole of humankind'.

Conclusion: what does feminism add to our study of international relations?

For many feminists the role of gender in international relations is not a subset of the discipline, but something that is intrinsic to every aspect of it. Feminist international relations implies that there are other legitimate ways of seeing, knowing and being in the world. This gender-sensitive lens offers international relations scholars a broader series of issues which should be studied as part of the discipline, and a guide to how to address areas of gender-based discrimination. Its bottom-up approach brings the lives of ordinary people into focus, and works towards understanding international relations not as an abstract practice, but as something that affects, and is affected by, the lives of people.

QUESTIONS

1. Why should international relations consider gender issues?
2. Why do most countries have more men than women in political leadership roles?
3. Why was international relations resistant to feminist theories for so long?
4. Feminists often investigate the ways in which women's experiences in the international labour market, development projects, diplomacy and post-conflict societies are different from those of men. What might some of these differences be?
5. What does a study of the experiences of women and men add to our understanding of international relations?

FURTHER READING

Enloe, Cynthia 1990, *Bananas, beaches and bases: making feminist sense of international politics*, Berkeley: University of California Press. Modern classic that answers the question, 'where are the women in international relations?'

Pettman, Jan Jindy 1996, *Worlding women: a feminist international politics*, Sydney: Allen & Unwin. Pioneering feminist analysis of international relations.

Shepherd, Laura (ed.) 2010, *Gender matters in global politics: a feminist introduction to international relations*, London: Routledge. A broad-ranging collection of feminist insights into a number of IR's key issues by some of the world's leading feminist IR scholars.

Steans, Jill 2006, *Gender and international relations: issues, debates and future directions*, 2nd edition, Cambridge: Polity Press. Excellent introductory study of the various dimensions of gender in international relations.

6

Postmodernism

Roland Bleiker

Introduction	92
Postmodernity as a new historical period	92
Postmodernism as a critical way of understanding modernity	93
The emergence of the third debate in IR scholarship	97
The polemical nature of debates about postmodernism	99
Conclusion	100
Questions	101
Further reading	102

Introduction

This chapter offers an account of postmodernism. It begins by drawing a distinction between two broad approaches to the postmodern: one that outlines the contours of a new historical period (postmodernity), and another that places emphasis on finding new ways of understanding modern practices of knowledge and politics (postmodernism). The second part of the chapter examines how postmodern ideas entered international relations scholarship, and how the ensuing debates often had a strong polemical tone. Given the complexity of these debates and the limited space available here, my engagement in no way claims to be comprehensive. My objective is limited to identifying some of the key themes in postmodern thought so that interested readers can then explore the issues at stake if they wish to do so.

Before starting off it is useful to acknowledge that defining **postmodernism** is no easy task. Postmodern scholarship is characterised more by diversity than by a common set of beliefs. Add to this that the postmodern has become a very contentious label which is used less by its advocates and more by polemical critics who fear that embracing postmodern values would throw us into a dangerous nihilist void. But while the contours of the postmodern will always remain elusive and contested, the substantial issues that the respective debates have brought to the fore are important enough to warrant attention.

Postmodernity as a new historical period

The postmodern has become a stretched, widely used and highly controversial term. It first achieved prominence in literary criticism and architecture, but eventually spread into virtually all realms, including international relations. What the postmodern actually means is highly disputed. The increasing sense of confusion in the proliferation of the postmodern led Gianni Vattimo (1992: 1) to note that this term is so omnipresent and faddish that it has become almost obligatory to distance oneself from it. But Vattimo, and many others, nevertheless held on. He, alongside such diverse authors as Jean-François Lyotard (1979), Jean Baudrillard (1983), David Harvey (1989), and Fredric Jameson (1984), viewed the postmodern as both a changing attitude and a fundamentally novel historical condition. They focused on cultural transformations that have taken place in the Western world and assumed, as Andreas Huyssen (1984: 8) summarises, that we are witnessing 'a noticeable shift in sensibility, practices and discourse formations which distinguishes a postmodern set of assumptions, experiences and propositions from that of a preceding period'. Such shifts are recognised in various globalising tendencies, such as the rapid evolution and global reach of mass media and other information and communication tools.

There are two broad ways of conceptualising inquiries into the postmodern. The first one revolves around attempts to demonstrate that we have entered a fundamentally new historical epoch. Some scholars believe that the all-encompassing historical period called modernity has given way to something else, a postmodernity (Vattimo 1988). To understand postmodern approaches one must thus first investigate the modern elements from which they try to distinguish themselves. No easy task, for modernity is a highly ambiguous concept, an elusive set of complexities that defy single meanings.

Modernity is generally understood to be the historical period that followed the Middle Ages. It emerged with the onset of the Renaissance in fifteenth-century Italy and spanned the centuries that followed. The past 500 years have brought about changes that are more radical and far-reaching than virtually anything that had happened in previous human history. Countless dynamics started to unfold during the modern period. They are linked to such features as industrialisation, advances in science and technology and the spread of **weapons of mass destruction**. The **nation**-state, with all its disciplinary practices, emerged as the dominant political actor.

Postmodern approaches assume that changes over the past few decades have been significant enough to suggest that we have entered a period that is fundamentally different from the preceding modern one. The key features of this new postmodernity are associated with processes of **globalisation**, such as the rapid evolution and spread of mass media, computers and other communicative features. These processes, it is said, have led to a 'transparent society' (Vattimo 1992); to an 'ecstasy of communication' (Baudrillard 1985); to a post-industrial phase whose main feature is knowledge production (Lyotard 1984); or to the advance of new technologies and a consumer **democracy** which provides **capitalism** with an inherently new cultural logic (Jameson 1984). Paul Virilio believes that these developments have fundamentally altered the relationship between time and space. The centrality of the latter, he stresses, has decreased and time has taken over as the criterion around which many global dynamics revolve. The instantaneous character of communication and mass media has reduced the importance of duration and locality. The 'now' of the emission is privileged to the detriment of the 'here', the space where things take place (Virilio 1986; see also Harvey 1989).

Some commentators portray this new postmodern period in rather gloomy terms, stressing that our ability to influence political affairs is becoming increasingly elusive in a world that is too complex and interdependent to be shaped by the will of people. We hear of a nation-state that is no longer able to uphold its **sovereignty** and the spheres of justice and civility that the corresponding boundaries were supposed to protect. Disempowerment and disentitlement have become key features of globalisation. We hear of a **neoliberal** world **order** that is increasingly run by a few powerful multilateral institutions and **multinational corporations**. Jean Baudrillard even believes that we have lost the ability to distinguish between reality and virtuality. Our media culture, he says, has conditioned our minds such that we have lost the ability to penetrate beneath the manifest levels of surface (Baudrillard 1983). Others view the postmodern period more optimistically. They point out that increased trade opportunities have brought prosperity to many parts of the world. Or they stress that new communicative tools open up a range of positive opportunities, from better cross-cultural communication to the possibilities of articulating cosmopolitan notions of democracy (see Connolly 2002: 178).

Postmodernism as a critical way of understanding modernity

A second postmodern approach does not seek to identify the contours of a new historical epoch. Instead, it searches for means by which we can understand and live modernity in more reflective and inclusive ways. David Campbell (1998: 212–13) and Jean-François Lyotard (1991: 24–35) are examples of presumably postmodern authors who remind us that as modernity is already such an elusive phenomenon, the concept of postmodernity becomes nothing but a parody of the phantom it seeks to distance itself from. Instead of looking at modernity as a historical period or a set of institutions, these authors follow Michel Foucault's (1984: 39) advice and treat it primarily as an attitude, 'a way of thinking and feeling', 'a mode of relating to contemporary reality'. Modernity, then, is the broad common theme that runs through a set of diverse practices which, superseding and intersecting with each other, have come to constitute our contemporary consciousness.

Here too, the key task is to distinguish a modern set of assumptions about the world from a superseding, postmodern way of conceptualising socio-political issues. One could say that the modern political consciousness issued to a considerable extent from the tension between Romanticism and the **Enlightenment**. What has been retained from the romantic ideal is the autonomy of the self, the quest for independence and **self-determination**, the belief that people can shape history. This form of modern **idealism** was then supplemented with the scientific heritage of the Enlightenment, with the desire to systematise, to search for rational foundations and certainty in a world of turmoil and constant flux.

The romantic element of our contemporary consciousness is epitomised in Hegel. What makes modernity different, in Hegel's view, is its attempt at self-understanding, the desire to establish **norms** and values on their own terms, rather than by way of borrowing from or rejecting the ideas of a surpassed epoch. The keystone of this process of self-grounding is the principle of subjectivity, which – at least in Habermas's reading of Hegel – is linked to a perception of freedom that recognises an individual's autonomy and responsibility in the realms of action and reflection (Habermas 1987: 16–44). The legacy of the Enlightenment then provides this subjectivity-oriented approach with stable and scientific foundations. Charles Baudelaire (1961: 1163), in a much-cited passage, draws attention to the recurring quest for certainty in a world of turbulence and chaos. While describing modernity as 'the transient, the fleeting, the contingent', Baudelaire points towards the constant attempts to discover underlying patterns behind these ephemeral features. He describes the recurring quest for essences as a desire to 'extract the eternal out of the transient'.

Within such modern attempts to fuse subjectivity and science there is ample room for discussion and diversity, more than in any preceding period. Indeed, Hegel considers the right to criticism precisely as one of modernity's key characteristics (Habermas 1987: 17). The breathing space necessary for criticism was provided by the emergence of a public sphere in eighteenth- and nineteenth-century Europe. Passionate debates were waged about all aspects of modern life. Virtually every opinion, every thought, every **theory** was attacked, refuted or at least submitted to intense and sustained scrutiny.

While the waging of fierce intellectual debates emerged as a key feature of modernity, the range of these debates was not as boundless as it appears at first sight. William Connolly (1993) emphasises that modern debates all have a distinctive character: they are all well framed. The contours of the modern framing process have to a large extent been drawn by the recurring unwillingness to deal with what Nietzsche (see Box 6.1) called the death of God: the disappearance, at the end of the medieval period, of a generally accepted worldview that provided a stable ground from which it was possible to assess nature, knowledge, common values, truth, politics – in short, life itself. When the old theocentric world crumbled, when the one and only commonly accepted point of reference vanished, the death of God became the key dilemma around which modern debates were waged. Yet, instead of accepting the absence of stable foundations and dealing with the ensuing responsibilities, many prominent modern approaches embarked on attempts to find replacements for the fallen God. They desperately searched for stable foundations that could offer the type of order and certainty that was once provided by the Catholic Church. This is how Nietzsche famously put it:

God is dead; but given the way people are there may still be caves for thousands of years in which his shadow will be shown. – And we – we still have to vanquish his shadow, too. (Nietzsche, 1974: 167. Translation altered).

The quest to replace God and search for new ultimate foundations has taken different shapes in various stages of the modern project. For Renaissance humanists it centred around a sceptical and rhetorical belief in human agency and the virtue of 'men'. During the Enlightenment it was trust in science and universal reason. For Romantics it was the belief in aesthetics and a deified self. For **Marxists** it consisted of faith in history's teleological dimension.

BOX 6.1: KEY FIGURES

Friedrich Nietzsche: the 'postmodern' philosopher

The German philosopher Friedrich Nietzsche (1844–1900) is often said to have influenced postmodern thought. He held many views on numerous topics, but his most influential legacy might relate to the manner in which he approached fundamental questions of knowledge. Nietzsche questioned the deeply entrenched modern search for universal forms of truth, whether they be based in Christian morals or on scientific foundations. He believed that the search for truth always contained a will to power. This is why critics accused him of nihilism: that is, of advocating a world in which we no longer have moral values. Postmodern proponents of Nietzsche strongly disagree with such a view. They believe Nietzsche can provide us with crucial insights into political dynamics: he makes us realise why we need to pay attention to processes of inclusion and exclusion, and to how knowledge and power are always intertwined.

The well-bounded nature of modern debates is perfectly epitomised in international relations scholarship. Here, too, everything has been debated fiercely. Seemingly nothing was spared criticism. And yet these debates have all been well framed. They have been framed by the urge to impose order upon a complex and elusive modern world. Steve Smith has drawn attention to this framing process. For him, **positivism** is the common theme that runs through a diverse set of mainstream approaches to international relations. At its most elementary level, positivism is based on an attempt to separate subject and object. It implies that the social scientist, as detached observer (subject), can produce value-free knowledge of an independent reality (object); that our comprehension of facts can be separated from our relationship with them (S. Smith 1996: 11–44; see also 2004: 499–515; see Chapter 1).

For a postmodern scholar the key task is thus to accept the death of God: to recognise that there are no underlying foundations that can absolve us of taking

Figure 6.1   Friedrich Nietzsche, 1882, by Gustave Schultze

Source: Wikimedia commons.

responsibility for political decisions. Thinking and acting inevitably express a 'will to truth', a desire to control and impose order upon random and idiosyncratic events. 'To think', Adorno (1992: 17) says, 'is to identify'. When we think we identify choices, privilege one interpretation over others and, often without knowing it, exclude what does not fit into the way we want to see things. There is no escape from this process, no possibility of extracting pure facts from observation. To disrespect these limits to cognition is to endow one particular and necessarily subjective form of knowledge with the **power** to determine the nature of factual evidence. It is from such a theoretical vantage point that scholars like Jim George (1994) or Richard Ashley (1984) have tried to show how positivist approaches have transformed one specific interpretation of world political realities, the dominant realist one, into reality per se. As a result, realist perceptions of the international have gradually become accepted as 'common sense', to the point that any critique against them has to be evaluated in terms of an already existing and largely naturalised (realist) worldview. Smith detects powerful mechanisms of control precisely in this ability to determine meaning and rationality, to decide which issues are or are not legitimate concerns for international theorists. 'Defining common sense', he argues, 'is the ultimate act of political power' (Smith 1996: 13). It separates the possible from the impossible and directs the theory and practice of world politics on a particular path.

BOX 6.2: DISCUSSION POINTS

The politics of representation I: René Magritte's 'This is not a pipe'

We have seen in this chapter that postmodern authors believe that interpretation and representation are inevitable aspects of politics; that facts are not pre-given but depend on how we view and intellectualise them.

Nowhere do we find a more compelling illustration of this position than in a famous painting by the surrealist René Magritte (1898–1967). The painting features a carefully drawn pipe placed above an equally carefully hand-written line that reads '*Ceci n'est pas une pipe*' ('This is not a pipe'). On the one hand, this statement seems silly: of course this is a pipe. But at a closer look we realise that Magritte is right. This is not a pipe but only a drawing of a pipe, a representation. In everyday life we use such representations and others to make sense of the world around us. In this painting Magritte playfully highlights the complex relationship between representations and objects, words and things.

Michel Foucault wrote a little book on the subject called *This is not a pipe* ([1973] 1983).

The emergence of the third debate in IR scholarship

Postmodern approaches entered IR scholarship during the mid to late 1980s in the context of what is usually called the 'third debate' (see Chapter 1). The first great debate is said to have taken place during the inter-war period, when **liberalism** and **realism** (see Chapters 2 and 3) disagreed fundamentally about how to oppose the spectre of Nazi Germany. The second great debate was followed by post-war **methodological** disputes between behaviouralism and traditionalism. Various versions of these debates have emerged since, and so have disputes about the adequacy of representing IR scholarship as a series of great debates (see Introduction).

The third debate was waged around so-called **epistemological** questions, that is, questions about how we can know the realities of world politics. An increasing number of scholars identified themselves as 'dissidents'. They expressed a growing dissatisfaction with prevailing realist, positivist, **state-centric** and masculine approaches to the study of international relations (Ashley and Walker 1990: 263). Common to these dissident approaches was a strong opposition to what Lyotard (1979: 7–9) famously described as a modern tendency to ground and legitimise knowledge in reference to a grand narrative, that is, a universalising framework which seeks to **emancipate** the individual by mastering the conditions of life. Postmodern approaches, by contrast, try to understand processes of exclusion and inclusion that are inevitably entailed in the articulation of knowledge and political positions. They seek to challenge and uproot entrenched thinking patterns, such that we can see the world from more than one perspective and marginalised voices can be brought into the realm of dialogue.

Important early contributions to postmodern international relations scholarship can be found in the work of such authors as Richard Ashley, David Campbell (1992; 1998), William Connolly, Costas Constantinou, Simon Dalby, James Der Derian, Jenny Edkins, Jim George (1994), Michael Shapiro, R. B. J. Walker and Cynthia Weber (see Ashley and Walker 1990; Constantinou, 1996b; Der Derian and Shapiro 1989; Edkins, 1999; R. B. J. Walker 1993; Cynthia Weber 1995).

BOX 6.3: DISCUSSION POINTS

The politics of representation II: Remembering and forgetting

Here is a little political experiment you can do yourself to see why questions of representation are both inevitable and political:

Next time you sit in a restaurant, try to remember one minute of what you read, see, sense, smell, feel and rationalise during this short time span: everything, from all the items on the menu and their prices to the size, shape and colour of the objects you see, or the way they project shadows onto other objects. Remember all the details about all the people, how they look, the way they move, what they say, in all their different accents and languages. Remember all the smells and sounds, all your emotional and rational reactions to these impressions, and how you compared them, directly or subconsciously, to impressions from previous experiences.

Try to remember all the 'facts' during this one minute of your life. Of course, it is impossible to remember all of this. The only way to remember anything about these sixty seconds is to forget at least 99.99 per cent of what you have experienced.

If we cannot retrace a single minute of our mundane life, how could we possibly remember something as monumental as, say, World War I, the Cuban missile crisis, the collapse of the Berlin Wall or any other event in world politics? Again, the only way is to forget virtually everything about it, except for the few facts, impressions and interpretations that have been deemed memorable.

That is precisely what IR scholarship is doing: selecting what is to be remembered and separating it from the overwhelming rest. This is a process of representation and it is both selective, subjective and highly political.

Next time you read an account of a political event ask yourself: what kind of politics of representation is involved here? Which facts are remembered and which are forgotten? Why is this the case? What are the political consequences?

There are, meanwhile, several concise and highly convincing summaries of postmodern approaches to international relations. Three stand out. The first such study is by Richard Devetak (2009b). He identifies four common features: 1) a key concern with the relationship between power and knowledge; 2) the employment of post-positivist methodologies, such as **deconstruction** and **genealogy**; 3) a critical engagement with the role of the **state** and related questions of boundaries, violence and identity; and 4) the resulting need to fundamentally rethink the relationship between politics and ethics. A second study is an equally compelling chapter by David Campbell (2007: 203–28). He prefers the term poststructuralism over postmodernism. He speaks not of a paradigm or a theory, but of a critical attitude to understanding how certain forms of politics become possible and are seen as legitimate and rational. While conventional scholarly inquiries often take such factors as pre-given, poststructural approaches consider processes of interpretation and representation as both inevitable and as inherently political in nature. The respective scholars study the power relationships involved and help us understand how global politics is produced, conducted and understood. Finally, the most recent summary of postmodern approaches to international relations is authored by Anthony Burke (2008: 359–77). He too does an excellent job in crystallising the key issues at stake, focusing on the need to expose how prevailing approaches have imposed one particular version of 'reality' upon a far more diverse, complex world. Burke reveals how postmodern attempts to break free of such constraints are not only sophisticated and complex, but also of direct practical relevance.

These summaries already make clear that postmodern approaches are highly diverse. They also employ a range of different methods to study political phenomena. Among the most prominent ones are, as Devetak has pointed out, genealogy and deconstruction. The former is associated with Nietzsche and the French philosopher Michel Foucault. The latter is linked to Jacques Derrida and poststructuralism. Both genealogy and deconstruction recognise that we cannot represent the world as it is. Our understanding of political and social phenomena is intrinsically linked to the cultural environment we are embedded in, the values we hold and the language we use to express them. The term 'discourse' is often used to express how this intertwinement of political practices, cultural values and linguistic representations makes up the world as we know it.

The key objective for postmodern scholars is not to arrive at some objective truth about political events or phenomena. Such an endeavour would be as problematic as it is futile. The point, rather, is to increase understanding of how power and knowledge are intertwined in all representations of politics. Genealogy is an alternative form of history: an effort to illuminate how particular historical evolutions created the type of world we live in today. Deconstruction, by contrast, is a scholarly method designed to expose values and power relations that are entailed – either explicitly or implicitly – in particular texts, ranging anywhere from political speeches to legal documents and popular magazines. Both of these methods are an integral part of postmodern inquiries into the modern practices that make up our contemporary world.

The polemical nature of debates about postmodernism

Postmodern contributions to international relations soon became highly controversial. They triggered a number of heated debates and often very polemical attacks. Defenders of the postmodern presented it as a necessary critique of modern thought-forms and their problematic impact on political practices. Opponents justified the modern project at all cost, for they feared that postmodern alternatives would induce an endless fall into a relativist abyss. Many established scholars believed that a postmodern celebration of difference would undermine the search for coherent visions of world politics. And such visions, the argument went, were badly needed at a time when violent conflicts and economic insecurities haunted the post-**Cold War** system. Some went as far as fearing that heeding postmodern approaches would open up the floodgates to relativistic ravings according to which 'anything goes' and 'any narrative is as valid as another' (Østerud 1996: 386).

The polemical nature of the debate about the potentials and problems of postmodernism is well epitomised by the contribution of Darryl Jarvis. He edited one of the few collections that explicitly engage postmodern approaches to international relations (Jarvis 2002). The volume contains summaries of postmodern approaches followed by critical engagements with them. Jarvis himself is particularly sceptical of postmodernism. Taking on scholars such as Richard Ashley, James Der Derian and Cynthia Enloe, Jarvis (2000: xi) believes that postmodern approaches are 'taking the discipline down an ideologically destructive road'. He writes of postmodernism's 'radical rejectionism' and of 'a compendium of the visual arts, science fiction, identities, personal stories, and research whims whose intellectual agendas are so disparate as to be meaningless'. Without clear disciplinary boundaries, Jarvis believes, we 'lose sight of the subject we once used to study' and thus end up in a 'vacuous activity, facile and devoid of meaning' (Jarvis 2000: xi, 5, 7).

At stake is nothing less than the practical relevance of IR scholarship. Postmodernism is seen by its critics as a mere **meta-theory**: a scholarly endeavour that is concerned only with theory, thus lacking any meaning in the real world (Jarvis 2000: 21, 170, 197). This is not the point at which to engage and evaluate the debates between proponents and opponents of postmodernism. Nor is it the place to summarise, in detail, all postmodern contributions to international relations scholarship. Quite a few of them, including the present author, would refuse labelling practices altogether. Indeed, labelling and surveying, a postmodernist would say, is a typically modern attempt to bring order and certainty into a world of chaos and flux. It is a desire to squeeze freely floating and thus somewhat worrisome ideas into surveyable categories, to cut off and smooth the various overlapping edges so that each piece neatly fits into its assigned place. This is why the positive potential of postmodern approaches can be appreciated and realised in practice only once we move beyond the current polemic that surrounds the term postmodernism.

Conclusion

By challenging the modern assumptions of dominant approaches to international relations, postmodernists have tried to open up various possibilities for rethinking not only the relationship between theory and evidence, fact and value, but also the very nature of the dilemmas that have haunted world politics for decades.

Summarising the nature of postmodern approaches is not easy, for if they have a unifying point it is precisely the acceptance of difference, the refusal to uphold one position as the correct and desirable one. 'The postmodern begins', Wolfgang Welsch (1988: 29–30) says, 'where totality ends'. Its vision is the vision of plurality, a positive attempt to secure and explore multiple dimensions of the processes that legitimise and ground social and political practices. Once the end of totalising thought is accepted, it becomes, of course, very difficult to talk about the postmodern without descending into clichés or doing grave injustice to individual authors who explore various terrains of difference. Jane Flax (1990: 188) recognised this difficulty and admits that by speaking about postmodernism one already runs 'the risk of violating some of its central values – heterogeneity, multiplicity, and difference'.

This diversity is evident when we look at the postmodern approaches to international relations. Related authors have embarked on a great variety of projects. They have exposed numerous problematic features, including the state-centrism of realist and liberal approaches to international relations, as well as their narrow perceptions of what the international is and where its relations take place. They have challenged the masculine and Eurocentric values of existing approaches or re-examined such notions as **security**, identity, agency, sovereignty, diplomacy, **geopolitics** and ethics. And they have used a multitude of post-positivist methodologies to do so: genealogies and deconstruction, for instance.

Postmodern scholars express a deep scepticism towards totalising and universalising forms of knowledge. Although this form of scepticism is characterised more by the search for tolerance and diversity than by a common political agenda, one can still identify several broad postmodern features that are of direct practical relevance to both the theory and practice of world politics. Of particular political importance are the following three interrelated features.

First, postmodern approaches stress that order, security, **peace** and justice cannot be imposed by a preconceived universal model, be it of a **communist**, neoliberal or any other nature. There is no inherent model for peace, no grand plan that could free us of violence and deliver perpetual peace. Every political model, no matter how sensitive, is based on a system of exclusion. Such exclusion is as desirable as it is necessary. But in order to stay valid and fair, political foundations need to be submitted to periodic scrutiny. Extending William Connolly's approach, the search for peace should thus be linked to a certain attitude, an 'ethos', which is based not on a set of fundamental principles but on the very need to periodically disturb such principles (Connolly 1995).

Second, the search for peace, security and justice must pay key attention to questions of inclusion and exclusion, which lie at the heart of violence. No order can be just and promote peace unless it is sensitive to the power relations it upholds. Maintaining sensitivity to this process entails, as with the first factor outlined above, an ongoing self-critical engagement with the type of political project that is being advanced in the name of peace. Expressed in other words, the task is to expose the power–knowledge nexus entailed in all political projects, thereby opening up opportunities for marginalised voices to be heard and brought into the realm of dialogue.

Third, peace, security and justice can only be established and maintained through an empathetic engagement with and respect for difference, be it related to sexual, cultural, racial, ethnic, religious, political or any other form of identity. The challenge then consists of not letting difference deteriorate into violence, but making it part of a worldview that is tolerant of multiple political and moral sources.

QUESTIONS

1. Postmodern approaches to knowledge are said to be different from modern ones. How exactly are they different? What are the key components of each tradition of thought? And what are the concrete political consequences of these different ways of knowing world politics?

2. Postmodern approaches are said to display an inherent scepticism towards so-called grand narratives: forms of knowledge that proclaim 'true' insight into the world and then universalise the ensuing political positions. What are the reasons for this scepticism? Is it justified?

3. Postmodern approaches are often associated with pessimism and relativism, with positions that can no longer separate right from wrong, good from evil. Do you believe that this accusation is warranted? Defend your conclusion by juxtaposing arguments advanced by proponents and opponents of postmodernism.

FURTHER READING

Campbell, David 2007, 'Poststructuralism,' in Tim Dunne, Milja Kurki and Steve Smith (eds), *International relations theories: discipline and diversity*, Oxford: Oxford University Press, 2007. Excellent summary chapter stressing the need to view poststructuralism not as a theory, but as a critical attitude to understanding issues such as power, knowledge and identity in world politics.

Der Derian, James and Shapiro, Michael J. (eds) 1989, *International/intertextual relations: postmodern readings of world politics*, Lexington: Lexington Books. One of the first comprehensive collections to deal with postmodern contributions to international relations scholarship.

Devetak, Richard 2009b, 'Postmodernism', in Scott Burchill, Andrew Linklater, Richard Devetak, Terry Nardin, Jack Donnelly, Matthew Paterson, Christian Reus-Smit and Jacqui True (eds), *Theories of international relations*, 3rd edition, London: Macmillan. The most concise – and compelling – analysis of postmodern contributions to international relations.

George, Jim 1994, *Discourses of global politics: a critical (re)introduction to international relations*, Boulder: Lynne Rienner Publishers. An early contribution to postmodern debates, written by an Australian scholar, but still one of the most interesting single-authored treatments of postmodernism.

Lyotard, Jean-François 1984, *The postmodern condition: a report on knowledge*, trans. Geoffrey Bennington and Brian Massumi, Minneapolis: University of Minnesota Press. Perhaps the most influential and authoritative statement on postmodernism.

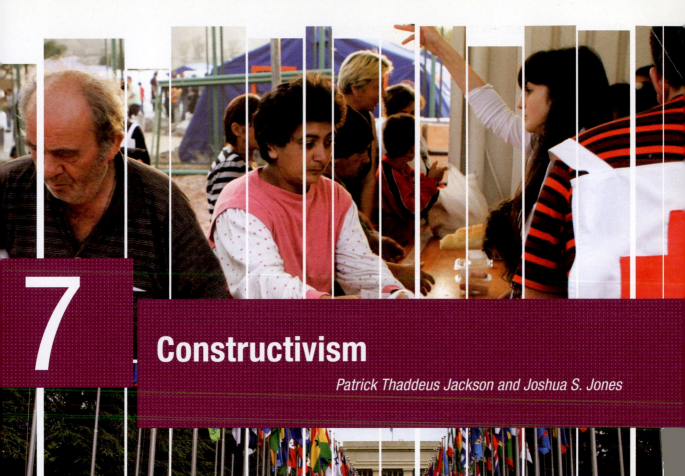

7

Constructivism

Patrick Thaddeus Jackson and Joshua S. Jones

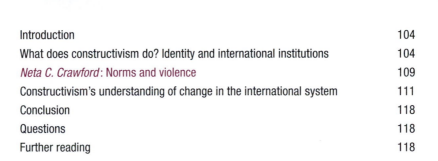

Introduction	104
What does constructivism do? Identity and international institutions	104
Neta C. Crawford: Norms and violence	109
Constructivism's understanding of change in the international system	111
Conclusion	118
Questions	118
Further reading	118

Introduction

This chapter presents a constructivist understanding of world politics. We begin with a discussion of state identity, a fundamental concept of constructivism, and explore the way that identity defines and bounds state actions. To illustrate this concept, we address a number of issues central to the study of world politics: change, governance, and security. Overall, our goal is to present a thickly textured, layered understanding of the international realm based on a notion taken for granted in much of IR theory, *meaning*.

Constructivism is the newest but perhaps the most dynamic of the main theories of international relations. The seminal works inaugurating the constructivist approach to the study of global politics – articles by Alexander Wendt (1987; 1992) and books by Nicholas Onuf (1989) and Friedrich Kratochwil (1989) – are only about two and a half decades old, even though the intellectual traditions on which they draw have long histories in other academic fields. Unlike **liberalism** and **realism** (see Chapters 2 and 3), which have taken their bearings from developments in economic and political theory, constructivism, like Critical Theory (see Chapter 4), is rooted in insights from social theory (e.g. P. Berger and Luckmann 1967; Giddens 1984) and the philosophy of knowledge (Searle 1995; Hacking 1999; Golinski 2005). Perhaps in consequence, constructivism does not predict events, or offer definitive advice on how a state should act in the international arena. Instead, constructivism is best understood as a set of wagers about the way that social life is put together, wagers that centrally revolve around the fundamental importance of meaning to social action: 'people act toward objects, including each other, on the basis of the meanings those objects have for them' (Wendt 1999: 140). Constructivist IR theory is an application of that basic analytical commitment to the study of global politics.

What does constructivism do? Identity and international institutions

So what exactly does constructivist IR theory hold? What are the basic tenets of constructivist IR? This is a very hard question to answer because, as a relatively new theory, there has not been as much time for people to work out in detail what the most central propositions of the constructivist way of doing things are. Important debates about **methodology** remain active among constructivists, and these debates have important implications for precisely *how* one should study the meaningful aspects of global politics (see P. T. Jackson 2010). But there are some substantive points on which most constructivist IR scholars would agree, and those points make for a nice contrast with realism and liberalism.

A core concern of constructivists is **identity**. Contrary to both realists and liberals, constructivists argue that the kinds of goals held by a state or other actor in world politics emerge from the actor's identity, so much constructivist research deals with the way in which states, state leaders and other actors conceptualise themselves and the roles they play and purposes they serve in the world. These public conceptions in turn translate into the sorts of goals and interests that those actors pursue in their foreign policy. Whereas realists look to the objective situation formed by the **balance of power** (or material capabilities) between actors, and liberals look to the subjective calculations of rational strategy by those actors' leaders, constructivists suggest that processes of meaning-making and identity-shaping necessarily intervene between material factors and strategic decisions.

Another way of saying this is that identity in a constructivist account is **intersubjective**: it doesn't exist 'out there' in the physical world and it doesn't just exist 'in here' inside our heads, but instead exists 'between us,' in the social transactions that people have with each other. A scholar knows that there is an identity in play by noticing that when people deal with each other they do so on the basis of categorical distinctions. Thus, for example, we know there is a Kurdish identity operative in the world because we see Kurds interacting with Kurds and non-Kurds and treating them differently. Intersubjective identity is public, and exercises its effects in observable transactions; at issue here is not belief, but the contours of acceptable action (Laffey and Weldes 1997).

One implication of this notion of identity is that for constructivists identity comes before and forms the basis of interests (Wendt 1992: 398; Ringmar 1996). Because we are a certain kind of people, forming a certain kind of community and holding certain values and ideals, therefore we can and should engage in some courses of action and not others. For instance, take the so-called 'isolationist' US foreign policy discourse that claims 'because we are the paragon of liberty, we should not interfere in the political affairs of the world but should preserve our democratic purity so we can lead by example'. Alternatively, there is the competing claim that 'because we are the most powerful country in the world, we have an obligation to send our troops into different parts of the world where people are experiencing hardship and use our great strength to support them in their struggles for freedom'. These rival narratives, which issue from different self-understandings of US identity, point in very different policy directions, and support different conceptions of US interests. Both these discourses are expressed in US presidential speeches and congressional speeches all the time; they are identity claims, all taking the form, 'because we are x, we can or should do y.' World politics for a constructivist is all about those kinds of claims, and about struggles between people making different and competing kinds of identity claims.

This is particularly important to the study of IR because identity is not just about Selves; identity is also about Others who are 'not Self', who are outside somewhere, beyond the borders – sometimes quite literally beyond the borders of a state, and sometimes more metaphorically excluded or disenfranchised from a community even though they physically live in its midst. So to say *we* are a certain kind of people is at the same time to say quite immediately that *they* are not, whoever *they* happen to be. A statement like 'because we are x' (where 'x' might be 'free,' 'democratic,' 'capitalist,' etc.) always implies the existence of another group who is not-x, and by virtue of not being x they have to be treated differently. This quickly becomes politically salient, because particular Others have to be treated differently by particular kinds of Selves. The categorical distinction between Selves and Others affects how interactions between the two groups will unfold.

For example, imagine that there is a group of people who practise a religion that we are not familiar with, and they engage in ritual acts that we find strange – and some adherents of that religion commit an act of political violence. It makes a difference whether we consider those people to be 'heretics', or 'terrorists', or 'primitives', or something else. Characterising them in any particular way raises different kinds of social and political implications. What do you do with heretics? Well, you either burn them or try to convert them. What do you do with terrorists? Well, you don't really convert them. You don't really burn them for their heresy. In the present day and age you go after them and kill them, or you try to prosecute them as criminals – which is a very different set of options to those available when dealing with heretics. Primitives, what do you do with them? Well, they're primitive; you either cordon them off and let them live in their pristine state of non-modernity, or you help to 'modernise', 'develop', or 'civilise' them. But you wouldn't help to develop terrorists or heretics. How that self–other relationship is configured has certain kinds of implications for action. So when constructivists want to try and understand what's going on in world politics, they first look to the kind of self–other relationships that are in force.

Some of these self–other relationships are relatively durable, because they are codified into rules and **norms** that govern interactions between entities in world politics. Realists and liberals also acknowledge the existence and importance of rules and norms, but treat them very differently: for realists (see Chapter 2), rules and norms reflect the underlying distribution of power at the time that they were instituted, while for liberals (see Chapter 3), rules and norms are instrumental means for various political actors to coordinate their actions for mutual benefit. Rules and norms for both of these perspectives are **regulative** and pertain to behaviour (what is permitted, what is prohibited), whereas for constructivists, rules and norms are also **constitutive** in that they specify not just what an actor can do but, more fundamentally, what kind of actor that actor actually *is* (see Box 7.2). Thus, sovereignty is a constitutive rule of the contemporary global political system that defines who are the legitimate players on the international stage (Reus-Smit 1999; R. Hall 1999). Because constructivists treat rules and norms as codified identity claims and self–other relationships, following rules and adhering to norms – or challenging rules and defying norms – necessarily involves shifts in identity, and these shifts and changes give rise to different courses of action.

BOX 7.1: CASE STUDY

'Anarchy is what states make of it'

Constructivists agree with the general realist picture of international relations as a condition of anarchy (defined in terms of the lack of a **hierarchical** world government), but introduce a conception of anarchy no longer 'emptied of content', as Nicholas Onuf (1989: 185) put it. Instead, they proffer a conception of *thick* anarchy comprising rules, norms and institutions of the kind studied by the English School (see Chapter 17). Onuf (1998: 62–3) argued that, despite appearances, international anarchy is not devoid of rules, norms and institutions; that, in fact, it forms a social arrangement with stable patterns of relations. It is just that this pattern of relations creates a condition where 'no one state or group of states rules over the rest'.

In a path-breaking article, Alexander Wendt (1992) further elaborated this argument by showing how international anarchy is socially constructed through the actions, interactions and self-understandings of states. Anarchy is not some pre-given structure, it is the result of social processes and practices, and is therefore intimately related to an intersubjective worldview held by states about the nature of the international environment (that it is a power-political system of self-help) and of states (that they are egoistic and self-regarding). It is because states internalise these understandings, socialising themselves into modes of behaviour consistent with a power-politics worldview, that anarchy takes the form it does. The key point for constructivists is that 'Self-help and power politics are institutions, not essential features of anarchy. *Anarchy is what states make of it*' (Wendt 1992: 395).

In a later work, Wendt (1999: ch. 6) elaborated three different logics or cultures of anarchy which he named Hobbesian, **Lockean** and **Kantian**. Each produces a different worldview and different conception of self–other relations (see Table 7.1).

When it comes to the contemporary international system, constructivists agree with realists and liberals that the present order of things is largely, although not exclusively, dominated by sovereign states interacting under conditions of **anarchy**. But anarchy as conceived by constructivists is a different kind of anarchy, because in the social space between states you have international law, state identities, and many other self–other relationships – it is a very complex, busy space (see Box 7.1 and Table 7.1). Constructivist anarchy, therefore, is *thick* anarchy; it is not thin anarchy as in realism, where the absence of a superior government requires states to take care of their own security and balance against each other by building up forces, which can inadvertently lead to conflict spirals, to arms races, and so on. It is not even the liberal notion of anarchy, in which states have the opportunity to strike mutually beneficial deals with each other, busily comparing their utility functions and saying, 'if I ally with you and we make a deal that will make us all richer, that will make us all better off, good!'

The constructivist notion of anarchy is a lot thicker; floating around out there in that intersubjective space there are rules and norms and other things, which states must

Table 7.1 Three cultures of anarchy

Culture of anarchy	Worldview	Self–Other relations	Corresponding IR theories
Hobbesian	Self-help; 'war of all against all'; zero-sum security; survival depends on military power	Enmity Violence between enemies has no limits	Realism
Lockean	Mutual respect of sovereign rights; rules, norms and institutions create social expectations and regulate state behaviour; 'live and let live' system	Rivalry Violence between rivals is self-limiting	English School, liberalism, constructivism
Kantian	Pluralistic security communities; 'thinking like a team'; mutual commitment to peaceful relations; subordination of military power to the rule of law and reasoned argument	Friendship Violence between friends is ruled out	Liberalism, Critical Theory, feminism, theories of global justice, cosmopolitan democracy

internalise in order to make their identity claims stick. Some of these rules and norms are so well-established that constructivists call them 'international institutions', by which they do not necessarily mean formal organisations. Instead, constructivists use the word 'institution' in a more sociological sense, approximately the same way that one might speak of the 'institution' of marriage – a set of socially established expectations for how a particular relationship ought to work. Constructivists claim that one can see such institutions operating at the level of international society as well. One of the prime institutions that constructivists like to point to is the institution of the balance of power, which for a constructivist is a management strategy, or a mechanism by which **great powers** manage the international system (see Chapter 19). It is something for which states and their representatives consciously and deliberately strive. In realism the balance of power is not necessarily a deliberately intended product, it is more of an inevitable consequence of states looking to take care of their own security needs. In constructivism, by contrast, the balance of power is a means or procedure for dealing with various shifts of capabilities: over time, countries get rich, countries get poor, countries develop bigger armies, countries develop smaller armies, so the capacities of states are often in flux. The balance of power is one important way of dealing with this flux.

Balance of power, for constructivists, does not just mean that states should be made roughly equal to each other in terms of their capabilities; it also means that if one state does something and it is somehow going to be infringing another state's power, then that infringed state needs to get some compensation for standing back and allowing another state's power to be augmented. European states have long engaged in this kind of balance of power politics among themselves, and during the eighteenth and nineteenth centuries one of the main things that happened was that various great powers would partition states and annex territories as compensation for events elsewhere in the world, particularly to offset great power expansion through colonisation. Consultation was built into this process too: the idea that great powers need to be consulted before anyone embarks on a course of action likely to unsettle the **status quo** or drastically alter the distribution of material capabilities. The point is that the institution of the balance of power is, for a constructivist, very closely linked to the identity of being a 'great power'. So, for constructivism, great powers have conferred on them certain rights and privileges, including consultation and compensation, which makes them active managers of the international system.

Another international institution in which constructivists are particularly interested is **war**. Realists and liberals are also interested in war, of course, but constructivists approach the topic rather differently. War, if you are a constructivist, is not just the use of deadly force; it is a social institution and, as such, comprises rules, laws and norms. Constructivists would first point to the fact that we have laws that govern war (for example, the Geneva Conventions); we have practices, protocols and codes about how war is supposed to be prosecuted (embodied in national military codes). We also have norms: binding sets of expectations such as, 'do not deliberately target or kill civilians' (see Chapter 15). While these expectations are not always perfectly reflected in political practice, violators of these norms do come in for criticism, and generally provide excuses and rationales for their deviation from the accepted rules of normal behaviour – something they would probably not do if the norm were not well established.

Norms and violence   Neta C. Crawford

Discourse about norms usually refers to the relationship between dominant behaviours ('the norm') and normative beliefs. From that perspective, the question is: what is the relationship between normative beliefs (ideas of what is good and for what reason) and the ways humans behave and structure their world? This is the analytical question – the positive social science question – which I consider first.

The ancient Roman scholar Cicero said that 'in time of war law is silent'. But when I think about war, I think about all the ways we limit the practice. War rarely goes to the most awful extremes. In every culture, it is almost always the case that the resort to war and the conduct of battle follows rules that limit violence. The question is, why?

There are three possible reasons why wars are limited. The first is the hope for reciprocity: if we restrain ourselves, we hope you will too. If you don't, we won't. We fear reprisal and so should you. The second reason is efficiency and expediency: if we restrain ourselves, we will not waste our energy and multiply our enemies. Absolute destruction vitiates victory in many cases. So, one of Gandhi's arguments for non-violence is expediency: 'Power based on love is a thousand times more effective and permanent than power derived from fear of punishment'. The third reason for restraint in war is the simple belief that to behave in certain ways – killing unarmed persons, poisoning, torturing – is simply morally wrong. When others sanction us because we have violated a norm, they do so because of their belief about what behaviours are right and what are beyond the pale. And so, when we make a calculation that it is to our advantage to use force, we might argue that force is necessary, and that certain limits may be disregarded. This is the reasoning behind **international humanitarian law**, also known as the law of war. The norm of military necessity thus trumps the norms of non-combatant immunity. Thus, for instance the Additional Protocol I of the **Geneva Convention** (1977), Article 57, says civilians should be protected but that protection is subject to military advantage. Parties to the treaty should 'refrain from deciding to launch any attack which may be expected to cause incidental loss of civilian life, injury to civilians, damage to civilian objects, or a combination thereof, which would be excessive in relation to the concrete and direct military advantage anticipated'. Further, 'an attack shall be cancelled or suspended if it becomes apparent that the objective is not a military one or is subject to special protection or that the attack may be expected to cause incidental loss of civilian life, injury to civilians, damage to civilian objects, or a combination thereof, which would be excessive in relation to the concrete and direct military advantage anticipated'.

These Geneva Protocols are an embodiment of the dominant normative beliefs about war and restraint in war. They are deeply ambivalent, reflecting the principled respect for human rights and the idea that war must be limited while at the same time embodying a form of **utilitarian** reasoning that stresses military necessity. The 'humanitarian' law thus sanctions violence. The belief that certain uses of force are wrong is a principled position that should not yield to the utilitarian calculus of military necessity so easily. Limiting the occasions and conduct of war because we desire that others do so, or because we fear reprisal, or because we desire to be more efficient, is not a principled limit on the use of force. In such a view 'respect' for the other is simply a healthy regard for how the other might now, or in the future, hurt us. The idea of the normality of violence is not challenged or destabilised.

Which brings me to the normative question: What should be the relationship between norms of violence and democratic norms? This is connected to something else Gandhi said about war: 'The science of war leads one to dictatorship, pure and simple. The science of non-violence alone can lead one to pure democracy.' By 'pure democracy', I take Gandhi to mean respectful deliberation and participation by all. It is the opposite of coercion. This is deep democracy, not the Freedom House version of democracy, which is simply the freedom to vote in order choose representatives who then, it is hoped, deliberate and negotiate on your behalf.

So as Gandhi was implying, and as Randall Forsberg stated explicitly in her work on the end of war as an institution, democracy is not simply the sum of the political right to vote and freedoms to associate and speak freely. Democracy is an institutional arrangement and a set of attitudes and beliefs that create the opportunity to deliberate, to argue. And if we are to argue fairly, with some hope of coming to an un-coerced understanding with another, we must renounce violence and the threat of violence. We must listen and be willing to be persuaded. This is what human rights and political rights share – the renunciation of violent means to resolve disputes. Forsberg believed that 'democratic institutions have prompted, or paralleled, a growing rejection of violence as a means of achieving political or economic ends within and between nations'. For Forsberg, it is not an exaggeration to say that democracy and a commitment to non-violence are synonymous: 'commitment to non-violence lies at the core of democratic institutions'. She continues:

Though little recognized, the renunciation of violence as a means to any ends except defense is as much a cornerstone of democratic institutions as its widely recognized counterpart, freedom of expression and other civil liberties. Commitment to non-violence protects and preserves freedom of expression and other civil liberties by precluding intimidation or coercion by violence or the threat of violence. Within democracies, wherever nonviolence is not the rule … other democratic rights and freedoms are lost or severely compromised (cited in Crawford 2009: 117).

The renunciation of a decision to use force is the first step to deep democracy. And deliberative democracy brings to politics a quality that Aristotle (2009: 142), in *The Nicomachean ethics*, called friendship:

Friendship seems too to hold states together, and lawgivers to care more for it than for justice; for concord seems to be something like friendship, and this they aim at most of all, … and when men are friends they have no need of justice; while when they are just they need friendship as well, and the truest form of justice is thought to be a friendly quality.

Neta C. Crawford is Professor of Political Science and African American Studies at Boston University. She is the author of *Argument and change in world politics: ethics, decolonization, humanitarian intervention* and co-editor of *How sanctions work: lessons from South Africa*. She serves on the board of the Academic Council of the United Nations System, and has appeared on radio and TV and written for newspapers including the *Boston Globe, The Christian Science Monitor* and the *Los Angeles Times*.

We also have various kinds of institutions like the ICRC (International Committee of the Red Cross/Crescent), which has the very odd right and ability to drive onto active battlefields and tend the wounded – this is strange because most countries respect the ICRC and permit them to do this, and to inspect prisoner-of-war camps and the like. So the institution of war includes this **humanitarian** practice to which many states adhere, that you can actually let the ICRC into the middle of a war zone, where they cannot be harmed or targeted by belligerents. Further, each side lets the ICRC tend to the enemy's wounded soldiers, not just their own. This may not make a lot of sense to a realist or to a liberal; but a constructivist would say this *does* make sense precisely because war is a social institution, it is not just something people engage in with no limits. War itself is regulated and has social meaning attached to it. Of course, the fact we have war crimes and courts for prosecuting such crimes is evidence of the ethical and normative boundaries within which war is supposed to be conducted, and reflects the social character of this international institution.

These points about war and the balance of power all add up to the idea that the international institutions that exist 'out there' in world politics provide sets of standards to which states can be held accountable. Think for a moment about an example closer to home, the speed limit on a major highway. On most highways in the US, for example, the speed limit is 65 miles per hour. While this does not guarantee that everybody drives under the speed limit, it does give the police the authority to penalise drivers who come breezing through at 90 miles per hour. Likewise, international institutions provide standards and expectations, not guarantees of specific rule-governed behaviour. Realist sceptics will sometimes say an international law is not really worth much, because in the absence of anyone enforcing it hierarchically, states can violate it any time they choose. International lawyers, most of whom are constructivists in practice, would say that is equivalent to saying there is no such thing as a law against murder because murders are still committed. Of course murders are still committed; that is not the point. The point is that the law establishes a certain set of expectations and standards by prohibiting murder. So when people do violate laws, they risk prosecution. The sceptic may ask: who punishes states when they violate international laws and norms? International lawyers and constructivists would retort by saying that often states mete out punishment to violators of international law among themselves. States, sometimes multilaterally, sometimes unilaterally, decide to intervene in order to provide some redress. In other cases, the enforcement mechanism may be a transnational social movement, which is able to use the socially established expectation of correct conduct as a way to shame a state and its leaders into changing their course of action (Keck and Sikkink 1998). The chief point in all this, for constructivists, is that international anarchy is a thickly textured social environment comprising normative principles, standards and expectations, the purposes ascribed to state identities, and the cultural components of legitimacy.

Constructivism's understanding of change in the international system

One of the principal implications of this constructivist account of global politics involves the way that we understand *change*. For constructivists, stability is not presumed in a way that it tends to be for either realist or liberals. An international system – indeed, any relatively stable system of social action – requires effort to sustain, effort that is *joint* inasmuch as it relies on the coordinated activity of multiple actors. Instead of starting out by taking for granted that there just is this given, naturally-existing thing called the international system, and that our primary task is to figure out how it works and how we should live in it (as explanatory and normative theorists do respectively), constructivists emphasise the social effort that goes into making and maintaining the present international system. On the one hand this means things could have been different, it means we did not have to have the kind of organisation of world politics that we have right now; but it also means that things still could be different in the future because there is nothing natural or necessary about the way in which we presently organise world politics. World politics could actually be organised in a radically different way in the future. There is a lot at stake in this idea that these social arrangements (including international systems) are produced by social action rather than being natural or brute facts (see Box 7.2).

Constructivists argue that stability in social systems is produced by everyday practices, everyday behaviours, and everyday ways of acting and interacting (Adler and Pouliot 2011). So a constructivist, thinking about a university, for instance, might say that universities are not natural or brute facts, that they are not given in the nature of things. The fact that there continues to be a university in a particular place day after day is a social or institutional fact, and that takes work to sustain. There are many things that people do to maintain the university, not just in the physical sense of disposing of waste and maintaining buildings and facilities, but in the cultural or social sense: there have to be ways of administering people using the categories of 'student,' 'professor' and 'staff'; there have to be organisational means of dividing bodies of knowledge into distinct disciplines; in fact, there have to be all kinds of little ways in which in the daily life of you and everyone else at the university ends up reproducing its existence in this particular social arrangement, because there is nothing natural about it. If all the people were to disappear, there would be no university. The university, as an institutional fact, would not exist independently of social actions and intersubjective understandings. For instance, you cannot just walk into the library and take home a book; you have to show your ID card and check it out. That is one of those everyday practices that re-inscribes the university, that reproduces the university's organisational existence at the same time as it reproduces your identity as a student. There are also joint understandings and formal rules about borrowing and returning books. Those are the sorts of everyday practices and activities that create the effect of a stable university.

BOX 7.2: TERMINOLOGY

John R. Searle on facts and rules

Brute and institutional facts:

'[W]e need to distinguish between *brute facts* such as the fact that the sun is ninety-three million miles from the earth and *institutional* facts such as the fact that Clinton is president. Brute facts exist independently of any human institutions; institutional facts can exist only within human institutions. Brute facts require the institution of language in order that we can state the facts, but the brute facts themselves exist quite independently of language or of any other human institution' (1995: 27).

Regulative and constitutive rules:

'Some rules regulate antecedently existing activities. For example, the rule "drive on the right-hand side of the road" regulates driving; but driving can exist prior to the existence of that rule. However, some rules do not merely regulate, they also create the very possibility of certain activities. Thus the rules of chess do not regulate an antecedently existing activity ... Rather, the rules of chess create the very possibility of playing chess' (1995: 27–8).

Constructivists would say the same thing happens in world politics writ large. A case from a few years ago illustrates the point: Augusto Pinochet (1915–2006) was a dictator in Chile who, like many dictators, managed to secure for himself sovereign immunity before leaving office in 1990. This immunity meant he was not prosecutable within Chile for any of his alleged crimes against the people, many of which were extremely well-documented. Since he gave himself immunity he did not have to worry about these things. In 1998 Pinochet travelled to Britain for a medical procedure, whereupon he was arrested. Spain – which often likes to think of itself as having certain special responsibilities for Latin American affairs, as part of a general identity-claim recurrent in Spanish foreign policy – had asked Britain to extradite Pinochet to Spain so it could put him on trial for numerous violations of domestic law and international law and crimes against humanity (Roht-Arriaza 2006). Spain's extradition request raised the question of what **sovereignty** means, because if the principle of sovereignty grants sovereigns the right to exercise authority and power without external interference, and to confer immunity on former heads of state, then Pinochet should not have been subject to prosecution, in Chile at least. But here we have a situation in which people were challenging this understanding of sovereignty, advancing a contrary identity-claim with different implications for social action. Essentially, the Spanish claim was that human rights law trumps sovereign immunity, because people are human beings before they are citizens and heads of states (see Chapter 32). Thus we have an identity contest: which set of expectations, and which set of identities, should dominate? To whom are obligations owed: sovereign states, or 'humanity'?

In the end, Britain's courts concluded that while they had the right to extradite Pinochet, they would decline extradition because Pinochet was a frail, sick old man; they extended mercy to the accused war criminal. What is interesting about this decision is that it re-inscribed certain understandings about international politics in everyday practice. By claiming it had the right to extradite Pinochet, Britain was affecting a small but important shift in the limits of sovereignty or the capacity of sovereign actors to do things: because if Britain does possess that right, as it claimed, then sovereign states do not have the ability to immunise former dictators from indictment under international law. But even if the British court had decided something else – for example, if it had judged that Britain had no right to extradite Pinochet – it *also* would have re-inscribed a certain understanding of sovereignty in everyday practice. Either way, state identities are being reproduced or re-inscribed.

Constructivists would argue that it is exactly these kinds of moments, these kinds of everyday decisions, that produce the greater social aggregates that we actually end up seeing in the world. Thus we have to investigate how those things happen in order to figure out what is going on in world politics. One of the ways constructivists like to do this is by pointing out that if you take these kinds of everyday practices seriously, you very quickly run into state and national identity as an important source of the reasons why states do things. Group identity pertains to who and what a people are, but also therefore what kinds of actions they can legitimately perform that are consistent with their identity. The logic goes like this: because we are a *certain* kind of people we will do *certain* kinds of things. For constructivists, this is not just a result of material factors, certainly not just the result of genetic factors or any other supposedly natural traits. A group of people will not act in a particular way just because they possess some set of common ethnic characteristics, and not just because they happen to live together.

Rather, what is of interest is how notions of commonality are deployed in practice, and what kinds of political effects they produce (Neumann 1999).

States, their populations, and their leaders can also be socialised; they can be taught, in effect, to adhere to certain kinds of norms. They can be placed in particular positions from which they conclude certain things and act accordingly. Constructivists suggest that it is sometimes possible to '**alter-cast**' another actor by starting to treat that actor the way that you would actually like them to be, whereupon the actor starts responding accordingly because you haven't given them many other choices. For example, treating the Soviet Union as if it were no longer the evil **Communist** empire but in fact an insolvent country looking for friendship and financial assistance might actually help to *produce* that situation because it structures certain types of behaviour around that new notion. Constructivists see this kind of socialisation operating throughout world politics, sometimes informally through **alter-casting**, sometimes through more formalised procedures. For example, when a country joins the European Union (EU), it has to take on a whole series of regulations called the *acqui communitaire*, which is a thick document of all the European Union laws and regulations which must be incorporated into their domestic legal structure. That is a relatively formal kind of process where, by virtue of signing up to rules which they are compelled to follow, states are socialised into new self-understandings and behaviours. In either case, the same basic process is at work, which is that actors take on and internalise various expectations that they find floating around in the intersubjective social environment, and incorporate them into their own senses of self, redefining their purposes and relations to other states accordingly.

Constructivists also argue that identity can change from the inside, after certain shifts in domestic political balances. This is not just about domestic pressure groups, and not just about the interests that they have; it is about how different domestic groups within a political entity like a state have very different visions about what the state's identity actually *is*. Because, to reiterate, state identity is not naturally given, it takes sustained work, joint effort and social practice in order to continue to exist. When new governments are formed, they may appeal to different identity narratives and envision different interests while implementing their foreign and domestic policies; this inevitably leads to the articulation of different conceptions of the state's 'moral purpose' (Reus-Smit 1999; Devetak and True 2006). This suggests not only that domestic political change can have an impact on fundamental self-images and self-understandings about a state's identity and role in international relations, but that such self-images and self-understandings are perennially open to contestation and challenge. It is not simply the state's preferences that are in flux during a change in domestic political rule, but the very meaning of what the state is and how it should behave.

Identity and governance

Identity change is particularly important to constructivists because a lot of things are anchored in how an actor thinks of itself. In some instances, identity change can produce global governance. This is the notion that states involved in international arrangements are not simply participating in instrumental bargaining, but that successful international organisations actually rest on shared principles and norms that states have incorporated into their own identities. The end result is what some have called 'governance without government' (Rosenau and Czempiel 1992): international organisations like the World

Bank and the World Trade Organization actually have authority, not just control. They're not just ways of coordinating actions between states, but they actually have their own authority as a result of the fact that the shared norms on which they rest are incorporated into the self-conceptions of all the various participating parties.

For instance, think about the United Nations (UN), which has the ability to create something as a **peacekeeping** mission that was not a peacekeeping mission before. Yesterday they were just armed forces in a foreign country, today they form part of a UN mission because a vote was taken and all of a sudden the situation changes dramatically; the armed forces now wear blue helmets, fly the UN flag, requisition UN vehicles and uphold UN resolutions. Less symbolically, the kinds of things that you can legitimately do in that combat zone are now different, because the *status* of a UN peacekeeping mission is different to the status of armed forces in a foreign country. Constructivists would say that this change is possible because it is accepted that the UN has the authority to change the status of armed forces from belligerents to peacekeepers.

Consider, as another example, the International Monetary Fund (IMF). One of the things the IMF is authorised to do is decide which countries are credit-worthy and how credit-worthy they are. Constructivists would say that is not just a technical decision, but a political and perhaps a cultural decision. Declaring that a state has strong economic health, and is a place one can lend money to (or not), is a shift in that state's public identity – a shift with real consequences in terms of the flow of capital. There is always room for discretion, so these calculations are never simple technical calculations; they always involve, at least implicitly, inferences about future action based on a putative grasp of what kind of state actor is being evaluated. Such inferences may shape judgments about whether a particular potential loan recipient is 'trustworthy' or is 'genuinely committed' to a program of privatisation and will not simply abandon it as soon as it gets an IMF loan. Such determinations and declarations are not made by other sovereign states, but by global economic institutions (GEIs) that command the authority to make those determinations (see Chapter 24).

If you want to go one step further in terms of what GEIs are actually capable of, consider Special Drawing Rights (SDRs). An SDR is effectively an IOU that the IMF writes to a particular country. So, when a country comes to the IMF and says, 'we have problems, we can't pay back our debts,' the IMF might elect to extend to that country SDRs instead of money. The country might then use the SDRs as a way of paying back their debt to other countries. In effect, the IMF is inventing its own currency. Despite the fact we live in a 'world of states', the expanding complex of rules is giving rise to a system of governance without government, where international organisations are actually tremendously important actors with power derived from their normative underpinnings. So powerful are these global economic institutions that they are now capable of launching the equivalent of a new currency.

Global governance is not limited to inter-state organisations, but also encompasses numerous **non-state actors** of various kinds (see Chapter 22). For example, global movements like Amnesty International (AI) form part of the overall system of global governance to the extent that AI is able to issue reports on human rights abuses that the global public is as attentive to as anxious state leaders are; thus non-governmental organisations (NGOs) help to regulate what countries can and cannot legitimately do. That, say constructivists, is only possible because those NGOs have actually acquired some authority or have succeeded in embedding the ideals and norms they champion in that intersubjective space between states. In this specific case AI's authority to make certain claims about human rights has helped to set the standard for what good human rights practice actually is, regardless of the fact that it commands almost no military, financial or other more traditional instruments of power. State leaders may make excuses, they may deny the charges, but the authority of AI is such that there are very few complete rejections of its reports or its standards, and international public opinion looks to AI as authoritative and trustworthy. This in turn rests on issues of identity, and the way that AI (aligned and allied with other non-governmental organisations) has managed to become an important voice in the general process whereby state identities are articulated, and state leaders are held accountable for their actions in terms of those identities.

International conflict and security communities

One especially noteworthy development that constructivists think happens sometimes in international politics is that a number of states identify with each other so strongly that they no longer seriously consider war among themselves as a real possibility (Wæver 1998). Constructivists think that under certain circumstances states can form a **security community** in which individual states have an extremely positive identification with each other – a very specific kind of self–other relationship in which the former Other becomes an extension of the Self. States in a security community regard all of the other states in the community as Selves rather than Others, sharing deeply-held common values, interests and commitments. Disputes within such security communities are resolved peacefully. In fact, states are expected to work together to ensure that vital interests are secured as smoothly and efficiently as possible through close coordination of activities, whether these activities relate to international trade and commerce, international development, or some other sort of collaboration to solve a persistent problem such as the proper management of fish populations that continually migrate between various states' territorial waters. These matters should be resolved peacefully inside the security community, because the states involved share common interests and commitments which in time may come to constitute a common identity (for example, the EU).

Part of the reason that constructivists are so interested in the formation of security communities is because they can dramatically change the context in which states interact. In other words, they can modify and ameliorate the condition of interstate anarchy. When a friend says something that annoys you, you are more likely to give them the benefit of the doubt and think they probably had a bad day and ask them for an explanation. But if a total stranger says exactly the same thing your reaction is likely to be quite different, perhaps provoking an angry or even aggressive response. Being in a community with someone changes how you react to their behaviour. You treat your friends differently than you treat other people, because human beings work and think in bounded categories as we try to figure out what is going on in the world and react appropriately. The key point here is that being in a security community changes the context of interstate interaction: disputes are likely to be resolved peacefully when they arise. Outside such security communities, however, there is always a risk that, in the absence of friendly understanding, the dispute may intensify into something not containable by peaceful methods.

Constructivists, like Critical Theorists (see Chapter 4), have argued for many years that one way to create community at the international level is to increase transactions between private citizens and commercial actors, and to establish other cross-cultural networks and exchanges between peoples. If you think about the Fulbright program or the Rotary Scholarships program or any other kind of study abroad experience, one of their functions, say constructivists, is simply to have more interaction between private citizens so people know more about each other and therefore they can help to form a community. Some states also directly and publicly address the issue of conflict and the reduction thereof through material and moral support for sub-national and international **peacebuilding** and conflict resolution organisations. To name just a few, the US Institute of Peace (United States), the Stockholm International Peace Research Institute (Sweden) and the West Africa Network for Peacebuilding (Ghana) all seek to develop, share and normalise peace and conflict resolution practices while supporting conflict resolution communities throughout the world. By shifting state identities, such peacebuilding efforts may contribute to the formation and reinforcement of security communities.

One other necessary condition for the formation of a security community is some sort of shared narrative of commonality, some notion that the members of a group belong together, share common values or ideals, and are willing to share a common future. One cannot just make that up out of whole cloth; rather, one has to use existing cultural resources to start building community and its supporting narratives. 'Europe' is a great example of this: constructivists note that the idea of Europe as a community has been around for hundreds of years. People (especially intellectuals) have been talking about it since the Crusades, and circulating the idea that countries in that particular part of the globe *belong together* and form some sort of natural unity. Not only was there a lot of interaction between this group of countries, but there was also a shared story of belonging to a common enterprise. This shared story made possible a '**nesting**' strategy (P. T. Jackson 2005) whereby a group of actors was collectively subsumed under a single larger identity. A nesting strategy, like a strategy of alter-casting, can produce actor-level identity change, but the direction of influence is different: where alter-casting involves one actor shifting another's identity by cajoling it into certain attitudes and behaviours, nesting involves a group of actors using a common narrative to reframe all of their interactions, changing them from contacts between separate states to transactions between the members of a larger cultural and political entity.

Along these lines, after World War II, there was a very deliberate attempt to eliminate the possibility of war between some of the primary belligerents, and particularly between France and Germany. These two countries were at war more often than not for large portions of European history, and a lot of major wars involved the French and the Germans on either side of the battle-lines. After World War II, there was a very deliberate effort to say no, we should re-frame this because we are all part of the same community and we do not resolve our disputes with military force (Parsons 2006). So the EU was born as states were nested within it – originally it was the European Economic Community, and then it transformed into the European Community and ultimately the EU. For a constructivist, this process was not just about militarily balancing against the Russians or anybody else, and not just about gains in trade; it was about change in the identities of states and their populations. The common story of Europe, incorporated into the identities of a group of states via a nesting strategy, helped to construct a community where war between its members has been rendered unthinkable.

Conclusion

The constructivist approach enriches, at the cost of complexifying, the study of world politics. When *meaning* becomes a component to explaining state action, issues such as anarchy and power become much more contingent and case-specific. At the same time, a treatment of identity based on meaning opens up wide opportunities concerning what may be possible when those identities begin to shift and change. Though constructivists are hesitant to predict the future, they are never limited in exploring the possibilities; change, as always, is the only thing that stays the same.

QUESTIONS

1. What is state identity and how does it influence world politics?
2. How is a constructivist understanding of change different from a liberal or a realist one?
3. How does a constructivist understanding of institutions explain state actions?
4. How might a constructivist approach to world politics inform an understanding of the causes and ways of ending inter-state war?
5. What are the strengths of the constructivist approach to world politics compared to other IR theories? What are its weaknesses?

FURTHER READING

Barkin, J. Samuel 2010, *Realist constructivism: rethinking international relations theory*, Cambridge: Cambridge University Press. An attempt to synthesise realism's insights into power and constructivism's understanding of method.

Katzenstein, Peter (ed.) 1996, *The culture of national security: norms and identity in world politics*, New York: Columbia University Press. Important early collection of essays by leading constructivists on a range of different security issues.

Ruggie, John Gerard 1998, *Constructing the world polity: essays on international institutionalization*, London: Routledge. Insightful collection of essays on multilateralism and the historical transition to the modern states-system from a constructivist perspective.

Wendt, Alexander 1999, *Social theory of international politics*, Cambridge: Cambridge University Press. Seminal account of a constructivist theory of international relations.

8

Theories of Global Justice

Richard Shapcott

Introduction	120
Justice and international relations	120
Why justice is global	121
What is a just global order?	126
Peter Singer: Global ethics	127
Conclusion	130
Questions	131
Further reading	131

Introduction

This chapter discusses the theories of international relations which have as their principal goal the transformation of the global international order so that it better meets the objectives of global justice. It begins with a discussion of the nature of justice as it is understood in the political context. It then addresses the **cosmopolitan** argument that principles of justice ought to apply to the world as a whole and not just within or between individual **states**. Next, it discusses the secondary argument that this requires significant reform of the relations between states and the democratising of the international realm. Finally, it examines the principal accounts of global justice including Rawlsian liberalism (see Boxes 8.1 and 8.3) and cosmopolitan **democracy**.

Unlike other theories of international relations, theories of global justice are explicitly evaluative theories. They seek to discuss and identify the proper rules for ordering society and the relationships between its constituent parts. In particular they assess the values which ought to guide social and political life and how they are embodied in institutions and practices. In the language of political **theory** they discuss 'the right and the good'. They do not merely explain or understand politics but assess it **normatively**, on the basis of ethical and moral grounds. The core concerns of these types of theories are the meaning of justice, equality, freedom and rights, and their relationship to **power**, violence and interests. Until relatively recently theories of this type have been rare in the **discipline**. Normative or evaluative thought in international relations has mostly been concerned with the meaning of **sovereignty** and the norm of non-intervention rather than with justice. Cosmopolitan theorists, however, argue that the vocabularies of justice and democracy *do* apply to the relations between states and, furthermore, that there is a moral imperative to transform the international realm into one that better conforms to these values.

Justice and international relations

Justice is a term that has many meanings and can be used in many ways. Hedley Bull, in his much discussed Hagey lectures on justice in international relations, used it to refer to what is more commonly known as international ethics (Bull 1983). Lawyers use the term to denote conformity with legal rulings and process, in the sense that justice has been done when the law has been followed and upheld. However, for political philosophers, justice is associated with the values of fairness and equality. Justice as a general concept means to treat like cases alike and to treat people according to fair rules. Fairness of this sort is embodied in the value of equality because to treat people equally means to treat them in a like fashion. Therefore, for political philosophers, justice is usually related to the value of equality of all human beings. Justice occurs when people are treated equally by political, economic and social institutions and laws. Much of contemporary political philosophy has been concerned with discussing how people are equal and how this equality should be recognised in law and society.

Justice can also be discussed in terms of substantive and procedural justice. Substantive justice refers to the equality of outcomes and the distribution of wealth or power; that is, distributive justice. Procedural justice refers to a fair process or mechanism for deciding who should get what. For example, a world in which there was no poverty might be considered substantively just, but if that situation was arrived at by discriminating against certain categories of people, like women, then we might think it was unjust in a procedural sense. Democracy is considered just because it treats all people as equal by giving them the vote, but it is unjust when, for instance, women are denied the vote. For instance, even if all women were wealthy, or financially equal to men, it would still be considered *procedurally* unjust if they were not entitled to vote.

Arguably the most important recent political formulation of justice has come from the liberal philosopher John Rawls (1971). Rawls argued that justice begins with the 'basic structure' of society, by which he meant 'the way in which the major social institutions distribute fundamental rights and duties and determine the division of advantages from social cooperation' (Rawls 1971: 7). In other words, to be just, society must examine its basic assumptions about who has rights, or equal moral standing, and duties, and who benefits materially from the production of goods and services. Rawls's theory of justice is both a procedural account of justice and a substantive one, concerned with distribution of wealth and advantage.

While Rawls's particular conclusion as to the content of justice is often contested (see Box 8.1), his general understanding of the focus of justice is accepted implicitly or explicitly by most cosmopolitan writers. Cosmopolitans concerned with global justice are predominantly, but not exclusively, concerned with the basic structure of global society, that is, with the ways in which the rules of global order distribute rights, duties and the benefits of social cooperation (that is, economic activity). Many cosmopolitans directly apply Rawls's theory to the international realm (a move which he resisted). These writers are often primarily concerned with distributive and substantive justice, and in particular the problems of global inequality and poverty (see Chapter 27). However, others place more emphasis on developing procedural accounts of global justice, and it is these arguments which are mostly associated with the idea of global democracy. For procedural accounts, justice requires not only an end to world poverty, but a legitimate and democratic means for negotiating different interests and identities. However, despite important differences, both accounts are loosely concerned with making the basic global structure of society just or equal.

BOX 8.1: DISCUSSION POINTS

John Rawls on justice

'Justice is the first virtue of social institutions, as truth is of systems of thought. … [L]aws and institutions no matter how efficient and well arranged must be reformed or abolished if they are unjust' (1971: 3).

'[T]he justice of a social scheme depends essentially on how fundamental rights and duties are assigned and on the economic opportunities and social conditions in the various sectors of society' (1971: 7).

'[S]ociety is a cooperative venture for mutual advantage' (1971: 4).

Why justice is global

The question of global justice is an extension of a broader, more general issue: the nature of any duties we may have to humanity. Western ethical thought has been torn by a tension between the duties we have to each other as citizens of the same state or community, and the duties we have to each other simply by virtue of our humanity – the duties we have not just to fellow nationals but to everyone else (Linklater 1990;

Nussbaum 1996). Therefore, before any cosmopolitan principles of justice can be delivered, the case has to be made for why justice and morality in general should be global, rather than merely national.

In contemporary times the major alternative to cosmopolitanism is characterised as **nationalism** (in academic debates this is sometimes conflated with **communitarianism**). Nationalists perceive an ethical demarcation between fellow nationals and the rest of humanity. While in the past this position has often presented a very stark choice involving indifference to the suffering of outsiders, most contemporary arguments of this type are less severe.

Contemporary critics of the idea of global distributive justice such as Michael Walzer and David Miller do not argue that we should be morally indifferent to foreigners, but only that the conditions for extending substantial moral obligations beyond the state do not exist. For these critics, justice requires a state and/or a shared culture which provide the basic values from which principles of justice are determined. Thus, for instance, Rawls's theory of justice relies on a presupposition of the existence of a basic core of liberal society. For the critics of global justice these conditions simply do not apply globally. Indeed, they are exacerbated by the sheer diversity of different conceptions of the 'good' present in the world.

Against this position cosmopolitans argue that either sufficient conditions do exist, or, even if they do not, we are not relieved of global obligations. If we think that all humans are equal then there are no good reasons for limiting our conception of morality to our own community; we must instead treat everybody according to the same principles. Many people think and act out their lives assuming that the national community, and the people they see on a daily basis, like family, are their primary moral realm of concern. This means that they do not consider themselves obliged to help people in distant countries, nor do they believe it is morally wrong to think this way. Cosmopolitans, however, argue that distance, difference and membership of a particular community should not inhibit or obstruct our moral responsibilities to the wider community of humankind. We should not let our sense of personal connection to some people prevent us from having a sense of obligation and duty to all people. For most cosmopolitans this means not merely that we should consider outsiders as equals, but that it is immoral not to.

As Martha Nussbaum argues:

If we really do believe that all human beings are created equal and endowed with certain inalienable rights, we are morally required to think about what that conception requires us to do with and for the rest of the world (1996: 13).

The burden of argument thus falls to those who seek to defend exclusionary moral communities and practices, not the other way round.

Equality and the categorical imperative

While not all cosmopolitan approaches are strictly **Kantian**, most are nonetheless consistent with his central premise of moral universality. This is expressed in the principle of the categorical imperative which states: 'Act only on that maxim through which you can at the same time will that it shall become a universal law' (quoted in Linklater 1990: 100). We must always ask first whether we are conforming, not with a national or particularistic law, but a universal, or universalisable, law. This means that 'if a person acts on a principle, which he could not wish another person to employ in his action towards him, that principle is not a moral one' (Linklater 1990: 100).

For Kant the most important expression of this imperative was the idea that humans should 'act in such a way that you always treat humanity, whether in your own person or in the person of any other, never simply as a means, but always at the same time as an end' (quoted in Linklater 1990: 101).

Acceptance of the categorical imperative means a number of things, but most importantly it leads to a critique of state sovereignty and nationalism, not only as practical obstacles, but as immoral institutions. The states-system is immoral because it is impossible to treat others as ends in themselves in a system that is ruled, not by law and collective will, but by necessity and force. As a result of this critique the major tasks of cosmopolitan theory are to defend moral universalism, to develop an account of an alternative political order based on it, and to explore what it might mean to follow Kant's imperative in a world divided into separate communities.

The requirements of justice

The first of these tasks has been developed in at least two different ways by **liberals** like Charles Beitz, Darrel Moellendorf and Thomas Pogge, and by **critical theorists** like Andrew Linklater. This section begins with the more dominant, but not necessarily more persuasive, account of the liberals.

Following Pogge (1994: 89) we can characterise liberal cosmopolitanism as individualistic, impartial and universalistic:

First, individualism: ultimate units are human beings, or persons … Second, universality: the status of ultimate unit of concern attaches to every living human being equally, not merely to some subset … Third, generality (impartiality): persons are the ultimate unit of concern for everyone – not only for their compatriots, fellow religionists, or such like.

For Beitz (1994: 124) (see Box 8.2), 'two essential elements define a point of view as cosmopolitan: it is inclusive and non-perspectival'. In other words, because there are no morally significant differences between people as people, the scope of morality is universal. In addition, equality requires impartiality between competing interests. If we are to treat everyone as equal then we need 'impartial … consideration of the claims of each person who would be affected by our choices' (Beitz 1994: 125). The only way to do this is to adopt a position which stands above all differences of culture, interest, class and most importantly nationality: to be impartial towards all particular affiliations, associations and contexts is to take account of the good of the whole (Beitz 1991). From an impartial perspective, national boundaries are morally irrelevant, or at best of secondary significance. These arguments all amount to the necessity of thinking globally, rather than nationally, when it comes to questions of justice.

BOX 8.2: DISCUSSION POINTS

Charles Beitz on impartiality

By 'inclusive' I mean that a cosmopolitan view encompasses all local points of view. It seeks to see the whole of which there are the parts. By 'non-perspectival' I mean that a cosmopolitan view seeks to see each part of the whole in its true relative size … the proportions of things are accurately presented so that they can be faithfully compared. If local viewpoints can be said to be partial, then a cosmopolitan viewpoint is impartial (Beitz 1991: 124).

The commitment to impartiality is also shared by **utilitarian** cosmopolitans like Peter Singer. Singer argues that in the face of persistent global hunger and dire poverty, which leads to the avoidable death of millions every year, people in affluent countries are in a comparable position to someone watching a child drown in a pond for fear of getting their trousers wet. If we think it wrong to let the child die then we ought also think it wrong to let millions die from preventable hunger and poverty. If we have the capacity to help, then we have the obligation to help. Thus, knowing as we do that many people starve, we ought to consider ourselves morally obligated to help those distant foreigners before we help less needy fellow nationals (Singer 2002). This is simply required by an impartial and universalist understanding of morality.

Interdependence and globalisation

However, perhaps the most persuasive characteristic of many cosmopolitan arguments is an emphasis on economic **interdependence**. Rawls argued that justice is only possible in the presence of a 'system of social cooperation for mutual gain' (see Box 8.3) which produces a surplus product. He argued that the international realm does not resemble a system for mutual advantage, therefore justice is inapplicable. However, most critics believe that Rawls's conclusion does not follow from his argument, and that he is open to further cosmopolitan interpretation (Caney 2001). Beitz and Pogge, among others, argue that it is no longer possible to justify treating states as self-enclosed, isolated systems. Instead there is a single global economic network of interdependence. States are intricately interconnected and very few, if any, can claim to be entirely outside of the global economic order. As a result we can claim that the equivalent of a scheme for mutual gain exists: 'All that is required [for justice] is that interdependence produce benefits and burdens; the role of a principle of distributive justice, then … would be to specify what a fair distribution of those benefits and burdens would be like' (Beitz 1979: 153).

BOX 8.3: DISCUSSION POINTS

Rawls's social contract: the original position

Rawls's social contract is the result of a thought experiment in which members of a closed society have been told they must design its basic rules. The catch is no individual can know where they may end up within this society. They may be wealthy, poor, black, white, male, female, talented, intelligent, etc. All they know about themselves is that they have a capacity to conceive of 'the good', to think rationally about ends and that they possess certain basic physical needs. Rawls describes this as decision-making behind a veil of ignorance.

Rawls thinks rational contractors constrained like this would choose a society in which each person would have 'an equal right to the most extensive scheme of equal basic liberties compatible with a similar scheme of liberties for others' (1971: 52).

He also thinks there would be a form of equality of outcome as well as opportunity. This he refers to as the difference principle, where 'inequality is unjust except insofar as it is a necessary means to improving the position of the worst-off members of society' (1971). In other words, some inequalities are acceptable but only if they increase the absolute position of the poorest.

For the international realm, a second contracting session takes place between the representatives of peoples. The conclusion of this round is a contract that resembles the traditional rules of **international society: self-determination, just war**, mutual recognition and non-intervention. In other words, rules of coexistence, not justice (1971).

The second part of this argument goes further and suggests not only that the interdependence *exists* but that the *content* of that interdependence requires justice. According to Pogge the wealthiest states in the world have imposed an economic order which disadvantages the poorest. In that context, he argues, we do have duties not to harm, or not to impose unjust institutions upon others:

There is an injustice in the economic scheme, which it would be wrong for more affluent participants to perpetuate. And that is so quite independently of whether we and the starving are united by a communal bond or committed to sharing resources with one another (1994: 97).

In other words, regardless of the lack of a common culture or 'global society', there are relationships of dominance, dependence and inequality which are unjust to perpetuate. Even if we disagree upon what a just world order would look like, we can agree that the present international order is unjust, and that there is a responsibility to make it more just. Nevertheless, the main point is that we have duties to others regardless of whether we are engaged in an activity of mutual advantage: these are general negative duties not to impose harms and to redress the harms we have inflicted.

This leads to a final and related point in favour of cross-border obligations and global justice. According to cosmopolitans, most versions of social contract theory never ask about the effects, positive or negative, of the contract on those outside it (see Box 8.4). As Henry Shue argues, 'it is impossible to settle the magnitude of one's duties in justice (if any) toward the fellow members of one's **nation**-state – or whatever one's domestic society is – prior to and independent of settling the magnitude of one's duties in justice (if any) toward non-members' (1983: 603).

BOX 8.4: DISCUSSION POINTS

Pogge on how societies impact on outsiders

'In assessing the institutional structure of a society by looking merely at how it affects its members we fail to come to terms with how our society affects the lives of foreigners (and how our lives are affected by how other societies are organised) – we disregard the (negative) externalities a national social contract may impose upon those who are not parties to it' (Pogge 1989: 256).

For instance, we can imagine a principle of domestic justice which does so only at the cost of a deeply exploitative relationship with another society. If this relationship is a necessary one for the realisation of justice in the first state, then from a cosmopolitan position the contract is not just. Alternatively, we could argue that if domestic justice requires the exporting of environmental hazards or is reliant upon a steady stream of raw materials from another country, subsequently denying the members of that country a measure of domestic justice, then the domestic contract is unjust from a global position.

This argument is very similar to, and draws upon the same premises as, the Kantian position of Andrew Linklater and Jürgen Habermas. These authors argue the international order, a world divided into separate **sovereign states**, cannot be considered just because it does not rest upon the consent of all those affected by it. This goes both for the institutions of the sovereign state and the institutions of global governance such as the **World Trade Organization** (WTO). To be just, any social arrangement must be consented to by all those affected, including those formally excluded from or outside it.

What is a just global order?

In addition to defending moral universalism, theorists of global justice also offer models of what a just, or more just, world order might look like, and suggestions as to how foreign policy can incorporate cosmopolitan principles. As already noted, a common argument is that everybody affected by an action, institution or norm should be able to consent to or participate in its construction. It follows that all political institutions, and the **norms** that govern them, ought to be at least minimally just: they must take into account the interests of everybody affected by them. This in turn means that there is an obligation upon states and citizens to develop globally, and not just nationally, just institutions.

Liberal justice

For liberals, the requirement to develop global institutions is met by the account of justice developed by John Rawls, and the most common approaches to global justice have, until very recently, been applications of Rawls's theory of justice (see Box 8.1). For Beitz, Moellendorf and Pogge, Rawls's substantive account of justice, as well as his mechanism for arriving at it, can provide the criteria for justice globally. Because justice is universal, the 'difference principle' must apply globally to individuals and not states. Justice involves 'a just and stable institutional scheme preserving a distribution of basic rights, opportunities and … goods that is fair both globally and within each nation' (Pogge 1989: 256). They come to this conclusion by arguing that we must begin with a cosmopolitan original position, not just a national one. There is no need for a second contract between the representatives of peoples because the original one will necessarily be universally inclusive. The basic structure of international relations should be governed, not by interstate principles, but by cosmopolitan ones that address the inequalities between individuals rather than states. What ultimately matters is how poor or badly-off you are *in the world*, and not just in your own country. While Beitz, Pogge and Moellendorf have some differences over the exact mechanisms for addressing inequalities, they nonetheless agree that the rules must meet goals of the difference principle to improve the conditions of the least well-off members of the human race: 'The terms of international cooperation … should … be designed so that the social inequalities they allow to arise from natural contingencies … tend to optimise the worst representative individual share' (Pogge 1989: 250). In other words, the structure of international trade and economic interdependence should ensure that, despite an unequal distribution of material resources worldwide, no one should be unable to meet their basic requirements, nor should they suffer disproportionately from the lack of material resources. To this Pogge also adds that the rules of the current system actively damage or disadvantage certain sectors of the economy, thus directly contradicting Rawlsian principles of justice. He argues that:

the citizens and governments of the wealthy societies, by imposing the present global economic order, significantly contribute to the persistence of severe poverty and thus share institutional moral responsibility for it (Pogge 2002: 57).

Therefore we, who gain most from the current order, have an obligation to change it in such a way that the most needy benefit.

Global ethics   Peter Singer

Primates typically live in small groups, not more than a couple of hundred animals. They all know each other as individuals, and the attitudes they have to members of their own group are different from the attitudes they have to strangers. Human beings are primates, and for most of our evolutionary history, after we separated from other primate species, we also lived in face-to-face societies, typically numbering around 100 or 150 individuals. Since our ethical beliefs, and the emotional attitudes that support them, are influenced by our evolved nature, it is not surprising that we have developed ethical views that are generally well-suited for living in such small groups.

During the last 10 000 years, in some parts of the world, humans began to form into larger communities – city-states, and then nations. They reflected about how they ought to live, and to write down their thoughts on ethical questions. The idea that ethics transcends our own small group, and even our nation, began to emerge with the first written philosophical traditions. In the fifth century before the Christian era, the Chinese philosopher Mozi, appalled at the damage caused by war, said that we should, out of love and also for our mutual benefit, regard other people's countries as if they were our own. Similarly, the ancient Greek iconoclast Diogenes, when asked what country he was from, is said to have replied: 'I am a citizen of the world.' Nevertheless, it is only in the twentieth century that we could really begin to speak in practical terms of the possibility of a truly global ethics. For until then, we had neither the capacity nor the knowledge to deal with global ethical issues.

Consider some of the distinctively global ethical issues we face today:

- More than a billion people live on less than the purchasing power equivalent of $US1.25 per day, while another billion have so much wealth that, without a moment's thought, they spend more than this on a bottle of water – despite having easy access to safe tap water at no cost.
- Although international law recognises that gross and widespread violations of human rights can amount to a 'crime against humanity', there is still no international regime that can effectively exercise sufficient force to prevent people committing such crimes, and ensure that those who do commit crimes against humanity are prosecuted before an international court.
- Some countries possess nuclear armaments powerful enough to kill tens of millions of people. If enough of these weapons were to be used, they would release radioactivity that would kill most living things on our planet, human beings included.
- By using fossil fuel, and raising unprecedented numbers of ruminant animals – mostly cattle – we are changing the climate of our planet. The first decade of the twenty-first century was the warmest since global weather records began to be kept in 1880, and extreme weather events, such as heatwaves, blizzards, storms, floods and droughts, are increasing. Sea levels are also rising, as ice melts. Yet the quantity of greenhouse gases emitted continues to rise.

The difference between rich and poor has existed for a long time, and so has the question of the moral obligations of the rich to aid the poor, but until recently the rich could only aid the poor in their own community, or close to it. The problem became a global issue only in the twentieth century, when the development of instant communications and rapid transport made it possible for the wealthy in developed nations to know of a famine in another country, while it was still happening, and to do something effective about it. Moreover, even though there have always been some people so poor that they die from poverty-related causes, never before have there been so many people living in such abundance that they could give away a significant part of their wealth and still be able to meet their basic needs, provide for their children's future and have a considerable degree of comfort as well. That gives an ancient issue a new sharpness.

The idea of global justice is also not really new, for the thought that a cruel tyrant deserves to be punished for his crimes is an inescapable extrapolation from the sense of justice that almost all human societies possess. But the feasibility of carrying it out, and the existence of an International Criminal Court, are important new developments in international law that also have consequences for global ethics.

The danger that nuclear weapons could wipe out our species did not even exist until the nuclear arms race began, in the decades after 1945 when the first atom bomb was dropped on Hiroshima and the ability to make nuclear weapons spread beyond the US. The science showing that emitting carbon dioxide and other greenhouse gases is changing the planet's climate was not sufficiently developed to be given much weight until the 1960s. Thus these are completely new global issues that have no real precedent.

All four of these ethical issues are critical for our future. The problem is that, as I mentioned at the beginning of this essay, we have not evolved to see them as critical ethical issues. We have evolved to be concerned about our kin and others close to us, not about strangers we cannot even see face-to-face. Hence we continue to spend money on things we don't need and that don't even really add to our happiness, when we could use that money to save the lives of children who otherwise will die from easily preventable or treatable diseases like diarrhoea, measles and malaria.

The difficulty is even greater when we turn to climate change because, unlike poverty, there is no near analogue in our more local experience of the wrong we are doing on a global scale. We struggle to see that emitting more greenhouse gases than we need is an ethical issue. It just doesn't feel like one to us, because for all of our evolutionary history there has never been a problem about greenhouse gas emissions. Yet climate change is the greatest ethical challenge of our generation. By any defensible ethical standard, the industrialised nations, the ones responsible for creating the problem, are continuing to use several times their fair share of the capacity of the atmosphere safely to absorb our waste gases. Unless there is, very soon, a dramatic drop in greenhouse gas emissions, hundreds of millions of people are likely to become refugees or to die because of extreme droughts and floods, rising sea levels and the spread of tropical diseases.

Since, like it or not, effective power currently rests at the level of countries rather than with some global body like the United Nations, all the world's countries need to agree on ethical standards that guide them as to the quantity of greenhouse gases they can emit. It is hard to see how there could be an ethical solution to this problem that will not involve significant increases in the cost of producing energy in the developed nations, and also eventually in other large countries like China, India and Brazil. It may also require a change in diet, especially less beef. That is why climate change is a unique test of the ability of our species to come together and solve a completely new global ethical problem.

Peter Singer is the Ira W. DeCamp Professor of Bioethics at Princeton University and Laureate Professor at the University of Melbourne. He is one of the world's leading ethical thinkers, and his books include *One world*, *Practical ethics*, and *The life you can save: how to do your part to end world poverty*.

Global justice in practice

From this account of the nature of justice a number of things follow for the practical realm of foreign policy and global governance. First and foremost, given its inequalities, there is a duty to reform the existing rules of international order. The current rules of international trade discriminate against the poor by subsidising the rich and blocking access to imports from the poorest countries. Global justice demands that rich countries should open their markets to the poorer countries. Pogge also argues that they can do so without causing disproportionate harm to the rich. Such reforms are no longer a matter for individual states but must take place in global forums such as the WTO. Rawlsians agree that a duty exists to create a just international order that does not systematically disadvantage or harm anyone, especially the poorest people. This is a duty both of international society collectively and of individual states: to change their practices and the multilateral agreements to which they are a party (see Box 8.5).

BOX 8.5: DISCUSSION POINTS

States as 'good international citizens'

All states, including middle-sized and small powers like Australia or Canada, have significant capacities to influence global policies along cosmopolitan lines. They have the opportunity to act, in Hedley Bull's words, as 'local agents of the world common good' or as 'good international citizens'. Peter Singer and Tom Gregg argue that a good global citizen 'seeks global solutions for global problems … [and] will not bargain too hard in order to extract the maximum benefit for its own citizens' (Singer and Gregg 2004: 80). Singer and Gregg argue that such states can effect change in five key areas of **foreign aid**, UN cooperation, trade, global environment, asylum seekers and **refugees**. In recent years many states' standing as good international citizens has diminished due to a decline in **multilateralism**.

Cosmopolitan democracy

While few cosmopolitans would dispute the account given above, for many the reforms suggested by Pogge and others do not go far enough. In particular, insofar as they leave state sovereignty in place, they remain constitutionally unjust. Instead cosmopolitans such as Daniele Archibugi (2004), David Held (1995, 1997) and Andrew Linklater (1998) argue that reforming the practices of states and international institutions is only the beginning of the necessary cosmopolitan transformation. Taking their lead from Kant and German Critical Theorist Jürgen Habermas (see Chapter 4) they argue that the categorical imperative requires a full democratisation of the international realm, as well as the implementation of distributive justice.

Cosmopolitan democrats tend to be social contract theorists of a different sort to Rawlsians. They begin by arguing that we cannot simply or fairly imagine what **idealised** agents might choose, in the way that Rawls claims. Human beings are too diverse for any theorist to be able to anticipate what they might agree to. In addition, the Rawlsian solution is vulnerable to the criticism that it is insensitive to cultural differences in varieties of justice because it imposes a liberal view on others.

Instead of beginning with a hypothetical social experiment, cosmopolitan democrats argue that, in order to be legitimate, the principles of global justice ought to be derived from a real dialogue between real people. They argue that the idea that people should be able to consent to actions which affect them should be taken literally. This principle has been embodied in democratic societies in the form of representative elections and institutional accountability. The same practices should also apply in the international realm. They argue that there is a duty to create institutional structures that allow participation in decision-making on matters that affect everybody, such as rules of global trade and finance. What is needed to make the international order both more just and more legitimate is the democratisation of its core institutions and practices. International institutions such as the UN, the WTO and the **World Bank**, as well as regional institutions, ought to be made representative of people and not just states. This would involve forms of direct representation and election and the creation of a third directly elected chamber in the UN (Held 1997).

The advantage of this approach to global justice is that it is a means for preventing the imposition of a single distributive scheme on anyone. The principles of distributive justice would not be worked out by politicians or philosophers alone and then imposed on the world; rather they would, at the very least, have to be consented to by the directly elected representatives of all the world's people. In addition, a degree of redistribution would be necessary to enable effective participation in any such assemblies. To participate in democratic practices requires that one not only be physically capable, but also be able to access relevant knowledge and information. Therefore cosmopolitan democracy requires global justice even as it seeks to legitimise the decision-making process.

It is important to note that it is not being argued that global justice requires either a world state or the destruction or homogenisation of other cultures. The main argument is that when people are affected by a rule or a practice of an institution (or other actors) then they ought to be able to participate in the decision-making process or have direct representation in the bodies most involved.

Conclusion

Theorists of global justice begin with the assumption that justice, understood broadly, is the first virtue of social institutions. In other words, the very purpose of the state or political community is to provide justice for its members. Cosmopolitanism also begins with the argument that the equality of the human species requires universal principles of justice. This argument is buttressed by the profound degree to which international institutions such as the WTO now affect people across the world. Interdependence and **globalisation** mean that even 'national' justice is in part dependent upon global factors. Under these circumstances justice necessarily requires global solutions, including the democratising of the international realm.

QUESTIONS

1. Why do Rawlsian cosmopolitans criticise Rawls's solution to global justice?
2. What is justice and should it be global?
3. Should the global order be more democratic?
4. Should democracy be cosmopolitan?
5. What are the arguments in favour of cosmopolitan reconstruction of international relations? What are the arguments against it?

FURTHER READING

Beitz, Charles 1979, *Political theory and international relations*, Princeton: Princeton University Press. Early attempt to apply Rawls's insights to international relations.

Linklater, Andrew 1998, *The transformation of political community: ethical foundations of the post-Westphalian era*, Cambridge: Polity Press. Important attempt to outline a cosmopolitan theory of international relations.

Pogge, Thomas 2002, *World poverty and human rights: cosmopolitan responsibilities and reforms*, Cambridge: Polity Press. Impressive philosophical account of universal obligations to alleviate poverty.

Shapcott, Richard 2010, *International ethics: a critical introduction*, Cambridge: Polity Press. Introduction to a range of ethical issues in IR.

Singer, Peter 2002, *One world: the ethics of globalisation*, Text Publishing: Melbourne. World's leading utilitarian philosopher examines some of the ethical implications of globalisation.

The Traditional Agenda

STATES, WAR AND LAW

PART 2

9 The Modern State   134
   Richard Devetak

10 Nations and Nationalism   148
   Gavin Mount

11 Security   160
   Anthony Burke

12 Arms Control   172
   Marianne Hanson

13 The Causes of War   189
   Hidemi Suganami

14 The Changing Character of Warfare   199
   Robert Ayson

15 The Ethics and Laws of War   218
   Alex J. Bellamy

16 International Law   231
   Donald R. Rothwell

17 International Society and European Expansion   243
   Paul Keal

18 Diplomacy   256
   Geoffrey Wiseman and Paul Sharp

19 Great Powers   268
   Marco Cesa

20 The Cold War   281
   Nick Bisley

9

The Modern State

Richard Devetak

Introduction	135
What is a state?	135
Origins of the modern state	137
The idea of the sovereign state	138
The triumph of the sovereign state: state-building as war making	142
Whither the sovereign state?	145
Conclusion	146
Questions	146
Further reading	147

Introduction

This chapter introduces the principal actor in international relations: the **sovereign state**. It begins by defining the **state**. Second, it explores the origins of the state in the transition from the medieval to the modern world. Third, it examines the concept of **sovereignty**, especially as it was enunciated in early modern political thought. Fourth, it surveys different historical explanations of how the sovereign state triumphed over alternative forms of political society. Finally, it surveys some of the continuing debates about the morality and utility of the modern state.

What is a state?

The state may not be the only actor in world politics (see Chapter 22), but it is widely recognised as the one that has the greatest impact on people's lives. It is, as John Dunn (2000: 66) says, 'the principal institutional site of political experience'. This is why the title of J. D. B. Miller's book, *A world of states* (1981), seems like such an apt description of international relations. But although we live in a world of states today, it was not always thus. At various moments in time, city-states, empires, feudal states, absolutist states or **nation**-states have been the dominant institutional form. So although humanity has always been divided into separate political societies, the character of these societies has varied historically and geographically. Sovereign states are distinctly modern inventions, and how long they will remain the principal institutional site of politics is a contentious issue, with some scholars suggesting that **globalisation** may be eclipsing the sovereign state (see Chapter 28). Whether or not they are declining in importance, moral doubts about the sovereign state continue to find expression. The state is, in many respects, a perpetually controversial subject precisely because it has been so central to domestic and international political life since the sixteenth century.

It is worth noting at the outset that a state, in its simplest sense, refers to an abstract entity comprising a government, a population and a territory (see Box 9.1). Much more needs to be said about this abstract entity, but for the moment it is enough to note that it possesses 'a collective personality which makes it immortal' (van Creveld 1999: 258). Governments come and go, populations are born and die, territorial borders may shift, but the state – as 'a continuing structure of government, decision-making, legal interpretation and enforcement' (Dunn 2000: 80) – remains.

One of the most incisive and influential definitions of the state was offered by the great German sociologist, Max Weber (1864–1920) at the beginning of the twentieh century. He defined the state as a 'human community that (successfully) claims the monopoly of the legitimate use of physical force within a given territory' (Max Weber 1948: 78). While this is consistent with the above definition of the modern state, it places the emphasis firmly on what the state does,

---

BOX 9.1: TERMINOLOGY

The state, the modern state, and sovereignty

State = government + population + territory

Modern state = state + sovereignty + nation

Sovereignty denotes a single, supreme decision-making authority

Article 1 of the 1933 *Montevideo Convention on the Rights and Duties of States* (1933) lists four criteria of statehood:

1. Population
2. Territory
3. Government
4. Recognition by other states.

rather than what it aspires to be or achieve. States are indeed political associations where governmental apparatuses, composed of politicians and administrative officials, establish and implement laws regulating social life within a particular territory in pursuit of various political doctrines. But the key to understanding the state, for Weber, lies neither in the laws nor the political doctrines, but in the *means* by which governmental rule is sustained: namely, through coercion.

For Weber and historical sociologists, such as Anthony Giddens, Michael Mann, Theda Skocpol and Charles Tilly, the state is best defined in terms of means specific to its functions: namely, the control and organisation of the force that underpins its rule. Tilly (1985: 170) defines states as 'relatively centralised, differentiated organisations the officials of which more or less successfully claim control over the chief concentrated means of violence within a population inhabiting a large, contiguous territory'. His definition includes reference to territory and population, but the key issue for him is control over the coercive means. This may seem counter-intuitive given that the state is commonly understood to be concerned with **order** and **peace**, but order and peace require *enforcement* through courts of law and the police. States claim a monopoly over the right to enforce the law internally and provide **security** against external threats through the establishment of police and military forces. So, force and the threat of force have never been far from states, either in their formation or in their maintenance, internally or externally.

One further important point to note hinges on Weber's word 'legitimate'. While states may exercise **power** and seek control, it is *authority* rather than power or control that defines the modern state's sovereignty and legitimacy. Although none can fully control its territory, states nonetheless claim the legitimate right or authority to make and enforce laws of their own choosing. This is an important mark of sovereignty.

The modern assumption, now taken for granted, is that a sovereign power claims *supreme* and *exclusive* authority to rule over a clearly bordered territory, and that the population residing there constitutes a nation (see Chapter 10). A modern state therefore is a particular model of political society; it is, most importantly, a state conceptualised as sovereign (see Box 9.2). It possesses 'the right to be obeyed without challenge' (Dunn 2000: 80). Later, we shall sketch the historical process through which the modern state achieved this supreme and exclusive authority; but first, it is important to identify the origins of the modern state's central ideas.

BOX 9.2: DISCUSSION POINTS

When a state is not a state

It should be noted that in countries with federal systems, like the US and Australia, the constituent parts are also called states. But California and Texas, Victoria and New South Wales, as large and wealthy and internationally active as they may now be, are not the states generally referred to in the study of international relations. Primarily, when the word 'state' is used, what is meant is the political unit or 'country' that claims, and is internationally recognised as possessing, sovereignty. These are the states represented in atlases of the world and with seats at the **UN**.

Origins of the modern state

The concept of state is not as ancient as may at first be thought. As Quentin Skinner (1989) has demonstrated, it was only in the sixteenth century that the word 'state' acquired a meaning close to the modern sense, referring to an abstract, impersonal entity, separate from the person of the prince. It was also around this time that, in the English-speaking world at least, discussions about the state, its purpose and powers became widespread (Skinner 2009: 326). This part of the chapter sketches some of the features that marked medieval Europe, contrasting it with the modern system that was eventually to follow.

Prior to the birth of state sovereignty, Europe looked like a patchwork quilt of overlapping and intersecting layers of power, authority and allegiance. Power, authority and allegiance were not monopolised by a central government, but shared among different actors – not just prince and parliament, but also the Pope, the Holy Roman Emperor, and jealous dukes and counts, many of whom were related by blood (note that the term 'prince' was often used to refer to the king). Quite often territory was partitioned, splintered, non-contiguous, and there existed no effective centre or capital capable of exerting its will exclusively and effectively over its disparate territories.

Medieval Europe thus presented a markedly different political map to the modern one with which we are familiar. This is not to say that the medieval world was sheer chaos and disorder. A powerful sense of order and social identity was provided by an overarching Christianity. The many fragments of the European patchwork saw themselves as local embodiments of a much larger universal community under the power of God and His earthly representatives in the Church. Indeed, in many ways it was Christendom that provided the only source of unity and identity in a fractured Europe. However, the Catholic papacy always struggled to exert its authority across all of Christian Europe; it constantly ran up against the earthly power, authority and will of princes, including the Holy Roman Emperor, not to mention the clergy and faithful of Protestant confessions. Ultimately, none of the pretenders to universal domination could overcome the 'feudal' character of European society.

The fragmented, decentralised system of government that dominated the medieval period (roughly from AD 500 to 1500) is now known as feudalism. Joseph Strayer (1965: 12–13) identifies three characteristic features of feudalism: the fragmentation of political power, public power in private possession, and armed forces secured through private agreements. Benno Teschke, drawing more from a Marxist perspective (see Chapter 4), offers a similar account, also emphasising the geographic decentralisation, institutionally personalised government and equally personalised, if divided, control over the instruments of violence. The feudal state, he says, was essentially 'an ensemble of lordships' (Teschke 2004: 31), with each lord claiming control over a share of the instruments of violence and, importantly for Teschke (2004: 31–2), a share of the land and labour. Political rather than economic accumulation, he says, was the driving force, pushing forward military innovation while the economy remained stagnant. However, he adds, eventually 'the systematic build-up of military power was also the precondition for, as well as the consequence of, intensifying the exploitation of labour' (Teschke 2004: 32).

Because the king lacked the administrative and financial capacity to extend his authority across the whole divided kingdom, he would appoint representatives, usually a count or duke, to administer justice at the local levels. Strayer (1965: 30) tells us that these local counts exercised 'full military, judicial and financial power' at the king's behest. The danger was that as counts and dukes consolidated their power by fighting wars, administering law and justice, and raising revenue through taxation, they became increasingly proprietorial; as Strayer (1965: 30) puts it, 'they became virtually independent rulers'. In time, the local power bases of counts and dukes grew to the point where they could challenge the capacity of royal power to impose its will.

Centripetal forces were thus constantly balanced by centrifugal ones in the medieval world. Tangled webs of dynastic power and splintered authority were spread unevenly across a fragmented European geography. Popes and princes had competing and crosscutting interests that were often complicated by inter-marriage, papal decrees, competing or overlapping territorial claims, conflicting religious beliefs, and general diplomatic intrigue and deception. Power and authority were thus shared or partitioned among a variety of actors. As a consequence, as Teschke (2004: 31) notes, there was 'no distinct sphere of anarchical "international" relations', because a clear distinction between the interior and exterior of states could not be drawn.

The important point for us about this medieval mosaic is that political space (territory) and authority (government) rarely, if ever, coincided with homogeneous communities (nations) to produce integrated political units. It was only with the rise of sovereign states that international relations properly speaking emerged.

The idea of the sovereign state

This section introduces and outlines two of the most central, if controversial, concepts in the study of politics and international relations – *sovereignty* and *the state*. It asks two questions: first, what does sovereignty mean? Second, how and why did the idea of the sovereign state arise? To help explain what sovereignty means it will be helpful to understand three eminent attempts to characterise sovereignty in early modern Europe – Jean Bodin and Thomas Hobbes's absolutist accounts, and Emer de Vattel's law of nations account. Their accounts will help convey the two interrelated dimensions of sovereignty: internal supremacy and external independence.

The meaning of state sovereignty

The principle of sovereignty found its first systematic presentation in Frenchman Jean Bodin's (1530–1596) *Six books of the republic*, published in 1576 (Bodin [1576] 1992). This was a time of tremendous political violence and instability in France, driven by religious conflict. In 1572 tens of thousands of Huguenots (French Protestants) were killed in what is known as the St Bartholomew's Day Massacre. Since the mid-sixteenth century the Huguenots had been agitating for greater religious toleration in France, struggling to resist occasional attempts by the Catholic crown to impose religious uniformity by force. Although Bodin agreed that the Catholic kings had adopted tyrannical policies against the Protestants, he denied that Huguenots had a right to resist the king. To allow this right would be to unleash **anarchy** and **civil war**, destroying any prospect of political stability.

Bodin's central innovation in the *Republic* was to argue that power and authority should be concentrated in a single decision-maker, preferably the king. He believed that a well-ordered society required an 'absolute and perpetual power', namely the sovereign, who would hold the 'highest power of command' (Bodin [1576] 1992: 1). One of the key aspects of sovereignty, as presented by the Frenchman, was that law and order could only be maintained within a society if one power alone possessed a distinct prerogative across the territorial jurisdiction. To make good on this idea, rules had to consolidate and unify previously detached territorial segments and populations. Most importantly, they had to monopolise the right to use instruments of force. The end result was a sovereign state characterised by a single, supreme legal and political power exercised over a society and territory.

Hobbes's (1588–1679) *Leviathan* – published in 1651 in the context of English civil strife – advances a powerful argument for establishing state sovereignty around a **theory** of political obligation. He argued that in the condition before a state is formed, individuals live in what he calls a 'state of nature' (see Box 2.1) where there is no 'common Power to keep them all in awe' ([1651] 1968: 185). In the absence of an overarching authority, there can be no peace or security because there is nothing to stop individuals harming one another. The state of nature is a condition lacking any rules and therefore any justice; mutual fear and insecurity are its defining features. According to Hobbes, only the establishment of a sovereign state – through a 'social contract' where the sovereign promises to protect and subjects promise to obey – can create the conditions of security and order necessary for society to develop freedom and industry. Like Bodin, Hobbes pressed the case for a single central authority with the power to enforce decisions. Sovereignty, therefore, implies authority to prevail over a jurisdiction.

The original frontispiece to Hobbes's *Leviathan* provides a brilliant image of the sovereign as conceived by absolutist thinkers (see Figure 9.1). It contains the image of a crowned prince standing majestically over his land and people, sword in one hand, crozier (bishop's staff) in the other; keeping watch over an orderly and peaceful city and surrounding countryside. A careful look at the image reveals that the prince's body is made up of tiny people all looking up to the prince. The image is a wonderful representation that captures several influential ideas about the state.

- First, and foremost, the sovereign is supreme and absolute, standing over and above a loyal people and territory. This absolutist idea is supported by the Latin inscription at the top of the page. It is a fragment which translates as: 'There is no power on earth that can be compared with him … '. Incidentally, Hobbes found this fragment and the very image of leviathan in the old testament Book of Job.
- Second, the instruments of coercion (represented by the sword) and religion (the crozier) are firmly in the grip of the prince. Two points are conveyed simultaneously here: that sovereign power monopolises law through its enforcement capacity, and that there is no higher earthly power than the state, including the Church.
- Third, the state is like a natural human body. Indeed, it was commonplace then, as now, to speak of the 'body politic' (Skinner 2009). Hobbes's Introduction to the *Leviathan* explicitly says that the state 'is but an Artificiall Man' ([1651] 1968: 81), from which we can infer a head (of state) with its unique rationality (**reason of state**), and a unified body with protective skin (borders) to keep out foreign bodies.

Figure 9.1   The frontispiece of Hobbes's *Leviathan*, 1651

Source: Rare Books and Special Collections, University of Sydney Library.

Hobbes saw with great clarity that achieving peace *within* states did nothing to diminish insecurity and violence *among* them; sovereign states were themselves plunged into a state of nature or 'state of war', which in contemporary parlance is called international anarchy. States became 'masterlesse men', in Hobbes's ([1651] 1968: 238) evocative words, adopting 'the posture of Gladiators; having their weapons pointing, and their eyes fixed on one another; that is, their Forts, Garrisons, and Guns upon the Frontiers of their Kingdoms; and continuall Spyes upon their neighbours; which is a posture of war' (Hobbes [1651] 1968: 187–8). Not only does this point to the state's need constantly to prepare for war if it is to be secure (see Chapter 11), but also to the external independence (or 'masterlessness') of sovereign states.

This claim to independence or 'masterlessness' is vital to the idea of the modern state. States claim to be 'constitutionally insular', Alan James (1986: 25) says; that is, they deny being subject to any superior authority and object to external interference. This notion of constitutional insularity was given its clearest modern formulation by Swiss lawyer and diplomat Emer de Vattel (1714–1767), who said states are 'free, independent and equal' (Vattel [1758] 2008: 74–5). As free and independent entities, states have a right to determine their own interests and policies, and to enjoy this liberty free of external interference. Vattel adds another qualification that remains central to modern conceptions of international society (see Chapter 17): all states, irrespective of strength or weakness, are formally equal and possess the same rights and duties. 'A dwarf', he said by way of analogy, 'is as much a man as a giant' (Vattel [1758] 2008: 75).

Historical origins of the idea of state sovereignty

Next let us consider how and why the sovereign state emerged as the resolution to sixteenth- and seventeenth-century political problems. The idea of the sovereign state proposed by Bodin and Hobbes was meant to be a solution to the religious conflict that was tearing apart European societies. Fiercely intolerant religious factions had, since the sixteenth century, generated a crisis of authority that was a clash not only between Christianities, but between civil and religious authority. Did ultimate authority lie with the Church or with civil government? Should governments foster the spiritual salvation of individuals in the afterlife or ensure peace and security here on Earth? If religious zealots wanted to subordinate politics to religion, Bodin and Hobbes wanted to 'de-theologise' politics by erecting a state that would stand outside theological disputes and eschew the moral absolutes that fuelled confessional conflict. Its purpose was not to secure everlasting life for its citizens' souls, but to ensure civil peace and security.

The principle of sovereignty established a new basis on which to conduct politics, displacing the medieval mosaic of fractured lines of power, authority and allegiance. Politics was now organised along exclusionary lines; the sovereign state came to embody the modern conception of politics, where authority, society and territory were coterminous. The jurisdiction of a political authority, and its related claim to the legitimate instruments of violence, was coextensive with the geographical limits of a society. The notion of sovereignty thus concentrated social, military, economic, political and legal life around a single site of governance, whether this was the power and authority vested in a prince or in parliament – that is, whether dynastic or popular sovereignty.

Even though sovereignty was expressed with such precision by Bodin and Hobbes, it remains a contentious concept to this day. Precisely which rights or prerogatives flow from sovereignty is not just historically variable but also politically contested. Rulers may give the impression that sovereignty is a licence to do anything they please, but this is far from the truth. Not only are rulers subject to national constitutions, but state sovereignty has always been governed by international rules and **norms** and conditional upon international recognition (see Box 9.3) (Bull 1977; Reus-Smit 1999). This means that sovereignty's meaning is historically and socially constituted, and inseparable from shared understandings, as **constructivists** insist (see Chapter 7).

BOX 9.3: DISCUSSION POINTS

Sovereignty versus international law

Does state sovereignty imply a rejection of **international law**? The answer is no; sovereign states acquire their rights in relation to evolving international rules and norms. States may sometimes ignore and indeed breach international law, but international law has been built up around states. It is historically a law of and for sovereign states; one which elaborates their rights and obligations (see Chapter 16).

The triumph of the sovereign state: state-building as war making

The rise of the modern state

The purpose of this section is to outline briefly the historical process by which the modern state emerged. It is important to recall the political and military context. The late sixteenth and seventeenth centuries were ravaged by pan-European civil and religious wars, trade wars on the high seas, and wars of conquest and assimilation in the New World. **War** was endemic during this period of European history. For example, in the years between 1555 (the Treaty of Augsburg) and 1648 (the **Peace of Westphalia**) there were 112 wars in Europe, working out at an average of 1.25 per year (Luard 1986: 35). This violence was intensified by the 'military **revolution**' underway in Europe at the time. Armies grew considerably in size, as did the cost of weaponry and equipment. The increasing length and intensity of armed conflict, as siege warfare evolved, also added to the costs of war, dramatically increasing the financial burden placed on states.

European rulers could not avoid war; they were, it seems, drawn inexorably into it. Consequently, states were increasingly being fashioned as 'war machines' in order to respond more effectively to the geopolitical situation that prevailed at the time. As we shall see, an effective response required an overhaul of the state's administrative, financial and political organisation in order to monopolise (and pay for) the instruments of violence under a single unrivalled authority.

Historical sociologists have drawn attention to the close connection between state-building and organised violence. Tilly's (1975: 42) pithy statement that '[w]ar made the state, and the state made war' captures the point nicely. The shift from feudal and other forms of pre-modern state grew out of the heightening demands of warfare, which in turn consolidated the state. The more centralised absolutist state, which replaced the feudal one, had the capacity not just to raise sufficient finance for growing military expenditure, but also to reorganise and manage the military more efficiently.

In the sixteenth century new methods of bookkeeping and collecting statistics were invented, allowing states to monitor and intrude in the lives of their populations much more intensively and extensively. Such knowledge was to prove crucial in the state-building process; it laid the basis for absolutist states to develop and maintain formal systems of regular taxation, and provided state rulers with information about the economic productivity of their populations. Previously, taxes were raised in an ad hoc manner only when required, often after war had already commenced. With the establishment of regular taxation, states were able to ensure a steady supply of funds to fuel military expenditure in times of war and peace. From the seventeenth century on, states needed a constant supply of finance to prepare for endless wars (Mann 1986: 453). Tilly (1985: 180) refers to the continuous increase in levels of finance as the 'ratchet effect', whereby public revenue and expenditure levels rose abruptly during wars, setting progressively higher floors beneath which peacetime levels of military financing never dropped.

A significant factor in the rising costs was the 'military revolution' of the seventeenth century. Advances in technology and weaponry, innovations in military tactics and strategy, heightened organisation of military forces, the introduction of standing armed forces, the growth in size of the armed forces relative to the population, and the escalating costs of maintaining maritime forces, all ensured that military expenditure would remain just as high in times of peace as in war (Mann 1986: 455). The management of relevant fiscal resources thus became crucial to the rise of the absolutist state and its successor, the modern state. There are two points to note here. First, that systematic revenue raising depended on developing administrative capabilities at the centre of the state. Second, that development of the absolutist state's revenue-raising and administrative capabilities was crucial to its monopolisation of coercive means. The upshot was that states became better able to extend their capacity to 'monitor, control and monopolise the effective means of violence' (Tilly 1992: 68), and thereby intensify their rule.

But what drove this monopolisation process? Historical sociologists are largely in agreement here with realists and with Teschke's **Marxism**. They all agree that the principal cause of this process lies in geopolitical pressures generated by war. In order to protect themselves against external aggression, states had constantly to prepare for war. The **balance of power**, **alliance** formation, **diplomacy** and military build-ups were therefore essential conditions in the rise of the absolutist state. As Skocpol (1979: 30) explains, 'geopolitical environments create tasks and opportunities for states and place limits on their capacities to cope with either external or internal crises'. The primacy accorded to the external dimension finds agreement in Mann (1986: 490), who argues, 'The growth of the modern state … is explained primarily not in domestic terms but in terms of geopolitical relations of violence'.

Disarming competing powers

Notwithstanding the growth of global terrorism in the twenty-first century we still tend to think of sovereign states as the exclusive holders of the legitimate instruments of force. But as Janice Thomson points out, this was not always the case. It was the result of long historical processes that eventually disarmed **non-state actors** so that control over the domestic and international employment of force would be concentrated in the sovereign state. This meant that privateers and merchant shipping companies who operated private seafaring vessels charged with the right to wage war; pirates, who used force without any official sanction; and mercenaries, who traipsed from war to war for a pay cheque, would no longer be tolerated as legitimate bearers of arms. Instead, the sovereign state became the exclusive bearer of the instruments of force as privateers, merchant companies, pirates and mercenaries were stripped of their right to bear arms against, or in competition with, states (Thomson 1994). The modern state was therefore the end product of the 'long and bloody struggle by state-builders to extract coercive capabilities from other individuals, groups, and organisations within their territory' (Thomson 1994: 3).

An argument that complements the history narrated by Thomson is to be found in the work of Hendrik Spruyt (1994). He explains how the sovereign state became the **constitutive** organising principle of the **international system** by displacing and excluding alternative forms of state. He explains why alternatives to the sovereign state, such as feudal, city-league and city-state systems, failed to become the dominant forms of political organisation as Europe shifted from the medieval to the modern system of states.

Spruyt concurs with Thomson that the principle of sovereignty 'altered the structure of the international system by basing political authority on the principle of territorial exclusivity' (Spruyt 1994: 3). The triumph of state sovereignty as a constitutive principle was the result, says Spruyt, of three things: first, its scale afforded greater administrative and organisational efficiency than small city-states and loosely integrated empires; second, it offered a more effective means of organising the external relations of states; and third, it successfully eliminated non-territorial, feudal systems of governance.

The sovereign state is a distinctively modern resolution of political life that emerged after long and bloody battles over power and authority, and that has now been globalised as a political form. One of the most important aspects of the modern state is its spatial configuration. Compared to the fragmented political order of the medieval world, the modern world is based on integrated, homogeneous political spaces ruled by a single and exclusive authority in the interests of a unified national society. By virtue of the role played by war and the monopolisation of legitimate violence, the rise of the modern state is inseparable from violence, including the violence exacted through Europe's colonial expansion (Keal 2003; Keene 2002). To this day, struggles to achieve statehood continue to involve some measure of violence, but that is the political risk of declaring independence from foreign or imperial rule (see Box 9.4).

BOX 9.4: DISCUSSION POINTS

Declarations of independence: the birth of new states

Declarations of independence are, as David Armitage (2007: 17) reminds us, documents of 'state-making'. They announce 'the emergence of new states … [marking] the transition from subordination within an empire to independence alongside other states' (Armitage 2007: 104).

Since the US Declaration of Independence (1776), there have been several 'waves' of what we might call 'state natality' (the birth of states):

- the early nineteenth-century declarations of independence in Central and South America (including Haiti 1804, Colombia 1810, Venezuela 1811, Mexico 1813, Argentina 1816)
- the collapse of major Eurasian land empires (Ottoman, Habsburg and Russian) after the Great War
- decolonisation after Word War II, especially as the British, French, Dutch and Portuguese empires retreated from Asia and Africa in the face of anticolonial struggles and the emerging norm of **self-determination**

- post-**Cold War** dissolution of multinational empires and states (the breakup of the Soviet Union, Czechoslovakia and Yugoslavia).

There are a handful of new states, including Eritrea (1993), Palau (1994) and East Timor (2002), and a number of 'aspiring' or 'yet-to-be-born' states, including Palestine, Kosovo and Abkhazia, among others.

Whither the sovereign state?

This final section briefly surveys arguments about the future of the sovereign state. In particular it focuses on debates surrounding globalisation's impact on and **normative** critiques of the sovereign state. First, however, it elaborates on the various monopoly powers claimed by modern states, since many of the debates revolve around the viability and moral defensibility of these monopolies.

The modern state is built on a series of monopolies. Aside from coercion, within their jurisdictions modern states claim a monopoly right to:

- national economic management
- law making
- international representation
- border control, and
- political loyalty.

It is important to recall here the distinction between authority and control. Although they may aspire to exercise full control over these issue areas, states will never entirely succeed. They will, however, retain the authority to decide matters in these areas.

Ever since globalisation became a hot topic, claims have been made about the demise of the sovereign state (see Chapter 28). 'Hyperglobalisationists' tend to see globalisation as a powerful economic and technological force hollowing out the state, depriving it of power over these monopolies. This is almost certainly an exaggeration since the state retains power and, more importantly, authority, over many vital issues, including aspects of globalisation itself, as both 'sceptics' and 'transformationalists' agree. But whereas sceptics tend to see globalisation as little more than a myth concocted primarily by Western states to promote **neoliberal** policy agendas, transformationalists tend to accept that some human activities have been 'deterritorialised'; that is to say, they increasingly take place on a global social plane unmoored from territoriality. The state is not a powerless victim of globalisation so much as one of its vehicles. But no matter how real or powerful globalisation is, the modern state still retains authority (if not control) over how global processes affect its monopoly powers.

Globalisation affects different states in different ways. For example, developing countries are not able to capitalise on all of globalisation's purported benefits in the same way as are developed ones. Moreover, some scholars argue that globalisation adversely affects many developing countries by disempowering them or compelling them to adopt harsh austerity measures favoured by the West (see Chapters 27 and 28). In some instances this may have contributed to the proliferation of what many refer to as '**failed states**' (see Chapter 30). Such states no longer successfully claim the various monopolies over their jurisdiction, as warlords, organised criminal networks or insurgents exert control, and sometimes authority, against the legitimate government.

Cosmopolitans like Andrew Linklater argue that the sovereign form of state fosters domination and exclusion. In monopolising so many dimensions of politics, the modern state has, through its coercive instruments, participated in the reproduction of violent practices and unjust structures. Other scholars such as R. B. J. Walker (1993) and David Campbell (1998) have delivered powerful critiques of sovereign practices with **postmodern** theories (see Chapter 6). The purpose of these critical accounts of the modern state is to challenge the supposition that authority, territory and community must be coterminous. The hope is that this will allow for freer, less exclusivist, more democratic forms of political society.

Cosmopolitans have explored forms of citizenship and 'post-sovereign' statehood that widen moral and political community beyond national–territorial borders. Linklater (1998) and David Held (1998), for example, have considered the potential of globalisation to strengthen **democracy** within and extend it between states. This, they believe, would give voice to minorities traditionally marginalised within sovereign states, and also compel states to give greater consideration to how their decisions impact on outsiders. In Linklater's view, modern states have consistently de-emphasised duties to the community of humankind. But he also believes there are progressive tendencies built into states that may promote normative commitments by refusing to see territorial boundaries as morally and politically decisive. His normative vision questions the monopolising tendencies of the modern state, while exploring potentials to share power and authority among different levels of governance: local, national, regional and global. This would necessarily de-emphasise the modern state's persistent distinction between insiders (citizens) and outsiders (foreigners), allowing for a politics that takes seriously moral and political responsibilities to all human beings.

Conclusion

As the final section shows, there are material and normative reasons for questioning the suitability of the sovereign state in contemporary international relations. This should not be surprising given that the sovereign state emerged as a response to a particular set of issues in the aftermath of medieval Europe. Insofar as the social, political and economic context has changed over the last four centuries, the sovereign form of state, a product of the seventeenth and eighteenth centuries, may have outlived its usefulness. In truth, it is too early to say, not least because the state has shown remarkable adaptability in the face of changing circumstances, and continues to attract aspirants. What we can say is that vigorous debates will continue about the modern state's purpose and effectiveness in a changing world.

QUESTIONS

1. What makes a state sovereign?
2. Why did the modern state triumph over other forms of political organisation?
3. Compare and contrast the modern world of states with its medieval predecessor.
4. How, if at all, is state sovereignty affected by globalisation?
5. What are the moral and political advantages and disadvantages of the modern state?
6. According to what set of criteria should new states be admitted into international society?

FURTHER READING

Armitage, David 2007, *The Declaration of Independence: a global history*, Cambridge, Mass.: Harvard University Press. Brilliant historical and theoretical account of how declarations of independence have shaped modern international order.

Creveld, Martin van 1999, *The rise and decline of the state*, Cambridge: Cambridge University Press. Excellent historical account of the rise and evolution of the modern state.

Hall, John and Ikenberry, G. John 1989, *The state*, Milton Keynes: Open University Press. Very useful introduction and overview.

Hinsley, F. H. 1986, *Sovereignty*, Cambridge: Cambridge University Press. Indispensable, classic account of the sovereign state's origins and evolution.

Krasner, Stephen 1999, *Sovereignty: organized hypocrisy*, Princeton: Princeton University Press. Stimulating and engaging analysis of sovereignty from a realist perspective.

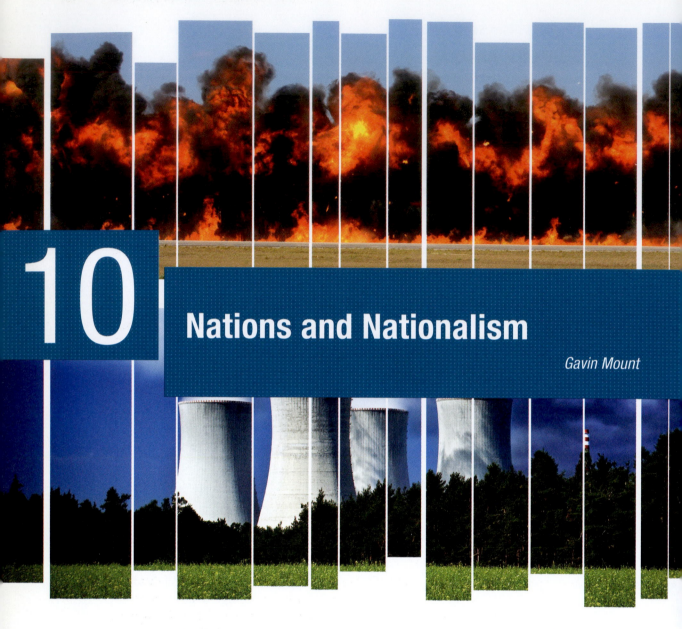

10

Nations and Nationalism

Gavin Mount

Introduction	149
Terminological debates	149
How nationalism shaped modern states and international society	152
Understanding nations and nationalism in IR	155
Appeals to 'the people' in the New World Order	157
Conclusion	158
Questions	159
Further reading	159

Introduction

In this chapter we will see that understanding the meaning and political importance of **nations** and **nationalism** in world politics is a challenging task. One recent survey of concepts in International Relations (IR) said of the term '**national interest**' that it was 'the most vague and therefore easily used and abused'; of nationalism it said that 'there is a lack of consensus about what it is and why it has maintained such a firm hold over so much of the world's population'; and that 'Nations and states seem identical but they are not' (Griffiths and O'Callaghan 2002: 202–13). The following discussion will survey debates on nation and nationalism around three broad questions. The first concerns debates around terminology and their contemporary relevance for the study of IR. The second relates to questions of nation formation and the origins of nationalism, particularly in terms of how it came to shape modern states and **international society**. The third illustrates how the ideas of nations and nationalism have been important in IR theory and practice.

The focus here will be on how interdisciplinary debates on nationalism have informed our understanding of this complex issue in IR. As a **discipline**, the field itself has made a surprisingly modest contribution to this scholarship (see Carr 1945; Hinsley 1973; and Mayall 1990). Nationalism is often not addressed explicitly but it has a significant tacit presence in all of the major schools of thought in the discipline. However, mainstream IR theories have compounded some of the analytical problems associated with understanding nationalism. For example, classical **realists** have tended to conflate nation and state into the concept of 'national interest', while **liberal** and **Marxist** theorists have been internally conflicted over the merits of nationalism versus its potential to undermine ideals of internationalism. The study of nationalism should be a central consideration for any analysis of the major issues in contemporary global politics because taking questions of national interest, values and identity seriously is one way of invoking the idea that culture and 'people' matter.

Terminological debates

The terms 'nation', 'nationality' and 'nationalism' are all notoriously difficult to define. Scholars disagree on whether the most important characteristic of a nation should be its physical, spiritual or social characteristics, whether it is old or new, whether it is imagined or real, whether it is separate from the **state** or not, and so forth (see Box 10.1). As political ideologies, nationalisms have been characterised as democratic or authoritarian, imperial or anti-imperial, forward looking or backward looking, state-led or state-seeking, and pre-modern or **postmodern**. In fact, the only thing that scholars on nations and nationalism seem to agree upon is that the concepts are 'impossibly fuzzy' (Kamenka 1975: 3) and that attempts to arrive at a coherent universal definition of these words are at best 'foolish' or at worst, 'a bootless exercise of definitional imperialism' (Nash 1989: 125; also see Seton-Watson 1977 and Connor 1994).

Regardless of whether academics can define the terms, nationalism is a real force in the sense that it has had, and continues to have, a very real impact on the lives of millions of people throughout the world. There are at least four main reasons why the concept seems to be so resistant to definition.

The first point of confusion is the conflation of the terms 'state' and 'nation'. As a legal entity, a state refers to the internationally recognised political institution comprised of a population, a territory and a government capable of entering into relations with other states (see Chapter 9). A nation can be broadly defined as 'a named human community connected to a homeland, and having common myths and a shared history, a distinct public culture, and common laws and customs for all members' (A. D. Smith 2010: 13). While there are similarities between these two entities – both refer to human groups, have a geography and a set of binding institutions – it is the subtleties that separate them.

Defining human groups as 'populations' versus 'communities' implies a distinction in terms of the formal categorisation of the collectivity as an empirically known and legally constituted entity. While the term 'peoples' is often used in international law, it is a very malleable concept. Distinctions between formally recognised 'territory' and a more symbolic concept of 'homeland' refer to different types of relationships between people and place. One is a notion of formal borders and control; the other is one of attachment and belonging. State archives, libraries, museums and memorials express different means of forging memory from the myths, folklore, art and traditions transmitted through culture. State institutions which facilitate a formal government that is recognised by others are different from the customs and laws of a nation, which tend to be more introspectively binding to the community.

A second reason for the confusion is that nationalism is a mass phenomenon but its formal expression is defined and refined by elites such as lawyers, politicians, historians, novelists, artists, sportspeople and others. Vernacular understandings of what it means to belong to a national identity draw upon a range of cultural ideas and practices. They are dynamic, contested, changeable and difficult to define. However, in formal terms, nationality is presented in more tangible ways through its associations with criteria for citizenship, the dominant symbols such as anthems, flags, currency, public holidays or monuments and the narratives of national memory. On this issue of elite versus mass

BOX 10.1: TERMINOLOGY

Nations and nationalism

'A nation is a soul, a spiritual principle. Two things, which in truth are but one, constitute this soul or spiritual principle. One lies in the past, one in the present' (Renan [1882] 1996: 52).

'A nation is a community of people, whose members are bound together by a sense of solidarity, a common culture, a national consciousness' (Seton-Watson 1977: 1).

'[A nation] is an imagined political community ... because the members of even the smallest nation will never know most of their fellow-members, meet them, or even hear of them, yet in the minds of each lives the image of their communion' (B. Anderson 1991: 6).

'A nation can therefore be defined as a named human population sharing an historic territory, common myths and historical memories, a mass public culture, a common economy and common legal rights and duties for all members' (A. D. Smith 1991: 14).

'[Nationalism] is a very distinctive species of patriotism, and one which becomes pervasive and dominant only under certain social conditions which in fact prevail in the modern world, and nowhere else' (Gellner 1983: 183).

'Nationalism has been both cause and effect of the great reorganizations of political space that framed the "short twentieth century"' (Brubaker 1996: 4).

'Nationalism is a political expression of group identity often coupled with a country or state. It is an intense, subjective feeling reflecting elemental ties of individuals to groups. This bonding has existed in many forms long before the group to which such passionate loyalty is given became the nation-state' (Hough 2003: 48).

views of nationalism, a seasoned scholar such as Eric Hobsbawm (1997: 11) concluded that 'official ideologies of states and movements are not guides to what it is in the minds of even the most loyal citizens or supporters'.

Third, nationalist ideology seeks to be simultaneously exceptionalist and universalist. As Tzvetan Todorov (1993: 93) notes, nationalism is 'paradoxical because while it is a perspective inherently based upon the centrality of one cultural perspective, it espouses a universal doctrine of humanity'. State-seeking national movements in particular seek recognition by the international community as having a legitimate claim for **self-determination**: 'the right for peoples to freely determine their political status and freely pursue their economic, social and cultural development' (*International Covenant on Economic, Social and Cultural Rights*, Art. 1.1). A good example of this is the case of the East Timorese who, for twenty-five years, sought recognition for their claim of self-determination until it was finally recognised, through the **UN**, by the former colonial powers of Indonesia and Portugal in 1999. More recently, the longstanding and extremely violent struggle in Sudan underwent a surprisingly peaceful referendum process, creating the world's newest nation-state.

Fourth, while nations claim to have objective geographical, historical and social ties, it appears that the subjective or imagined qualities are the most important. Empirical social science research must grapple with the paradox that while objective evidence of national and ethnic identity may be difficult to document, the members of these groups have very real perceptions that these ties are part of their physical, psychological, sociological or political experience in everyday life. Max Weber expressed this paradox when he observed that even though the idea of nation was an 'entirely ambiguous' empirical category it was 'a community of sentiment that would most adequately manifest itself in a state' (in A. D. Smith 1983: 25, 32).

What the above observations suggest is that just because an idea is vague and difficult to define doesn't mean that it lacks any substantial force as a concept. On the contrary, the invented character of national symbols and arguments on the national interest can increase the enthusiasm of patriots for sacrificing their lives 'with the satisfaction of serving eternal truth' because 'Men don't allow themselves to be killed for their interests; they allow themselves to be killed for their passions' (Connor 2004: 32, 206). Even faced with rational counter-arguments, the default nationalist position is invoked in the form of 'my country right or wrong'. As George Orwell (1945) reflected: 'Every nationalist is capable of the most flagrant dishonesty, but he is also – since he is conscious of serving something bigger than himself – unshakeably certain of being in the right'. The problem is that nationalists on both sides of a dispute or a war believe passionately not just in being 'right', but in giving authentic voice to the nation.

Analytically, the terminological confusion associated with the terms 'nation' and 'nationalism' should not be dismissed but needs to be understood as part of the complexity, character and allure of the phenomenon. Whenever the idea of 'nation' is deployed, consider how the term might be being used in a conflated sense; ask 'who is claiming to represent the idea and for whom are they speaking?' Consider how these claims might be translating corporate or elite interests into broader **normative** statements that appear to reflect the core values of a people. Are these claims inclusionary or exclusionary in nature?

How nationalism shaped modern states and international society

The idea of *nation* has a long lineage in Western political thought. The Ancient Greeks referred to the deep relationship between people and place as *patras*, much as we would use the term 'patriotism' today; the Romans used *natio* to describe peoples such as the Germans and the Britons who inhabited the outer provinces of the empire, and there are several references to the term in the Bible as God's chosen people – *And I will make of thee a great nation* (Tonkin et al. 1989; Genesis 12: 2). The contemporary uses of 'nation', 'nationality' and 'nationalism' have a different meaning associated with state authority in the conjoined term 'nation-state'. All of the terms prevail in modern political thought. A nation can be simultaneously understood to be a deep ancient cultural community connected to a homeland, a problematic regional identity and a spiritual or sanctified political community. From an IR perspective, we must add one more important meaning. To manage relations with frontier peoples, the Romans developed a set of principles called *jus gentium* (law of nations) which would leave an important legacy in international law. These principles regulated the rules of **peace** and **war** and negotiated territorial boundaries.

The greatest debate in nationalism studies concerns the relationship between nationalism and modernity (see Box 10.2). Arguably the strongest appeal of national identity is that it provides its members with a profound sense of continuity to the past, but nationalism is also understood to be a distinctly modern phenomenon. The so-called 'primordialist' school argues that national identity draws upon these deep affective ties through symbols and traditions which give national and ethnic identity its pre-given character; the attachment seems to 'flow from a sensual or natural – some would say spiritual – affinity' (Geertz 1963; Connor 1994). The 'perennialists' acknowledge the deep ethnosymbolic character of national identity but argue that it acquires different characteristics in the modern context (A. D. Smith 1986). 'Modernists' argue that nationalism is a 'functional component' of modernisation or even 'the blueprint' of a distinctly modern consciousness (Greenfeld 2006: 204). Some modernists argue that this identity was formed as early as the sixteenth century as the Reformation movements in Protestant countries began to challenge the political supremacy of the Catholic Church (Greenfeld 1992; Hastings 1997). For others, the process occurred later in the eighteenth century and was brought about by the demands of the Industrial Revolution (Gellner 1983; Hobsbawm 1997).

BOX 10.2 DISCUSSION POINTS

The modernity of nations? Three schools of thought

Primordialists, such as Clifford Geertz and Walker Connor, argue that national identity draws upon deep affective ties through symbols and traditions which give national and ethnic identity its pre-given, organic character. The attachment seems to 'flow from a sensual or natural – some would say spiritual – affinity' (Geertz 1963; Connor 1994).

Perennialists, such as Anthony Smith, acknowledge the deep ethnosymbolic character of national identity but argue that it acquires different characteristics in the modern context (A. D. Smith 1986).

Modernists, such as Ernest Gellner and Liah Greenfeld, argue that nationalism is a 'functional component' of modernisation or even 'the blueprint' of a distinctly modern consciousness (Greenfeld 2006: 204). While some modernists believe this identity was formed as early as the sixteenth-century Reformation (Greenfeld 1992; Hastings 1997), others believe the process occurred in the eighteenth century and was brought about by the demands of the Industrial Revolution (Gellner 1983; Hobsbawm 1997).

Notwithstanding these important theoretical debates, there is a broad consensus among nationalism scholars that the events of the American and French revolutions formalised the idea of national or popular **sovereignty** in the late eighteenth century. Both the American Declaration of Independence and the French Declaration of the Rights of Man and Citizen leave no doubt that 'the people' are the only legitimate foundation for sovereign statehood (see Box 10.3). National consciousness may claim a heritage that extends before this revolutionary period in the late eighteenth century but the formal normative shift from dynastic to popular sovereignty is widely regarded as having occurred in this period (Wight 1977: ch. 6; Hinsley 1973; Mayall 1990).

BOX 10.3 DISCUSSION POINTS

American and French revolutions

'Governments are instituted among Men, deriving their just Powers from the Consent of the Governed, that whenever any Form of Government becomes destructive of these Ends, it is the Right of the People to alter or to abolish it …' (Declaration of Independence, United States of America, 1776).

'The nation is essentially the source of all sovereignty; nor can any individual, or any body of men, be entitled to any authority which is not expressly derived from it' (Article 3 of the Declaration of the Rights of Man and Citizen, National Assembly of France, 1789).

Some of the most interesting research on nation formation has examined the way that the ideas of nation have been disseminated and constructed into a national consciousness. Two aspects that deserve mention here are the way that nationalism came to replace religion as the dominant form of political culture, and the special role that language has played in constructing this identity.

The concept of civil religion as a foundation for national identity has a long history in social and political thought. Drawing upon early work by Rousseau, Comte, Durkheim and Max Weber, contemporary scholars (Hayes 1960; Daniel Bell 1960; Bellah 1970; and Chatterjee 1993) have all examined the proposition that in replacing religion as the dominant means of defining political culture, nationalism reproduces, and is infused by, many of the characteristics of religious order (A. D. Smith 2000). As Robert Bellah puts it, nationalism underwent a process of 'sanctification'. Even if a civil religion is not aligned to a particular church or to a particular supernatural being, but it is a collection of beliefs, symbols and rituals that sanctifies the national community and confers a transcendental purpose on the political process (see Santiago 2009).

In his book *Imagined communities* (1991), Benedict Anderson argued that nationalism emerged as a result of the link between print technology and the emergence of a modern consumer class. Together these processes created a phenomenon called print capitalism which enabled a common, or vernacular, language to disseminate through the masses. The printing press enabled the mass consumption of pamphlets, newspapers and novels in a way that literally enforced a common vernacular on the people. Through this process, smaller groups previously separated by differences in dialect, religion or region were bound together into what Anderson described as 'imagined communities'. Print capitalism may have been a primary medium, but the message that was being distributed was one concerned with the rights of nations.

National languages are also essential for the creation and functioning of public institutions, which in turn play an important role in reinforcing national identity. In his seminal work, *Peasants into Frenchmen* (1976), Eugen Weber demonstrated how national cohesion, and indeed the prevalence of the French language, was quite weak among the French peasantry throughout much of the nineteenth century. It was not until the 1880s that the state more effectively integrated language and identity through the public 'agencies of change' such as the transport infrastructure, the military, schools and the church. Control of languages remains a fundamentally important mechanism and symbol of state authority. It is manifested in constitutional decrees and public services such as health and education systems. It is also worth noting that the establishment and spread of national language can be intensely destructive of minority ethnic identity. By one estimation, the spread of global languages and vigorous defence of national languages is causing the 'language death' of as many as half of the world's six thousand languages (Crystal 2000).

In the realm of international diplomacy, the idea of nationalism spread throughout Europe such that, with the defeat of Napoleon and the Congress of Vienna in 1815, the sixteenth-century doctrine of *cuius regio eius religio* (whose region, his religion) was adapted to the norm of *cuius regio eius natio* (whose region, his nation). Sovereignty now rested neither with popes nor with princes, but with the people. In this sense, nationalism formalised a *humanist* premise in international society by insisting that the source of real power and justice of states can only be built upon the representation and protection of peoples imbued with individual **human rights** and responsibilities.

Significantly, these ideas were also forged in the context of revolutionary warfare (in America and Europe). In the following centuries nationalism continued to be deeply implicated in the deaths and forced displacement of millions. Both state-led and state-seeking nationalists have been prepared to kill others and sacrifice themselves for the ideal of protecting or acquiring political independence for their people. While Western Europe experienced an 'age of nationalism' during the nineteenth century, it would be another century before the norm of self-determination began to be accepted as a universal right for all peoples across the globe.

In the early twentieth century, the inherent assumption in international legal and political instruments such as Woodrow Wilson's 14 Points and the League of Nations was that a politically demarcated territory should contain peoples who were racially, linguistically or culturally homogeneous, but even these ideals resulted in the mass relocation of peoples (Preece 1997). With the advent of the UN, self-determination of colonial peoples became a more developed norm, propelling a process of **decolonisation** which brought about the **emancipation** of millions of non-European peoples and allowed for a fundamental expansion of international society (Bull and Watson 1984; see also Chapter 17). But this process came at a great cost in human life. Independence struggles and post-independence repression caused many millions of deaths throughout the **Cold War** period.

Nationalist struggles continued to be highly significant in the post-Cold War period. Indeed, the last decade of the twentieth century witnessed widespread *ethnonationalist* struggles, particularly in the Balkans and sub Saharan Africa

(Connor 1994). Much of the commentary on ethnonational struggle in the post-Cold War period was alarmist, characterising the phenomenon as a threat to regional and international stability. In an age of globalisation, ethnic conflict came to be viewed as the dominant symbol of the counter forces of fragmentation (Mount 2000; 2010). While the international community failed to prevent tragic genocides such as those in Rwanda and Srebrenica, the longer term response of international society has been to develop norms for protecting minority peoples (Preece 2005). Even the norms relating to indigenous peoples, whose status as nations had always been questioned on the ground that they had not developed their political identities in adherence to European steps of nation-building, were addressed in a formal sense in the newly formed Declaration on the Rights of Indigenous Peoples (Keal 2003). The progressive ideal of self-determination remains one of the most important principles in contemporary international society.

Understanding nations and nationalism in IR

Inquiries into the nature of nations and nationalism have been a traditional area of study in IR, but the modern discipline has tended to treat the subject tacitly rather than explicitly. Most contemporary scholarship on the subject occurs in the disciplines of sociology, history, political theory and anthropology. Moreover, especially since the end of World War II, the field of IR has been engaged in an act of collective wishful thinking, anticipating the demise of nationalism. This was not always the case.

A century ago, a student of international affairs could expect their curriculum to begin with the study of nations; their role in shaping international society, their potential to cause war, and the significance of their main components – descent, geography, language and religion (see Moon 1925). For the first half of the twentieth century, it would continue to be normal for the study of our discipline to begin this way. A popular theme found in early IR textbooks was the 'Family', 'Society' or 'World' of Nations (see Burns 1915; Lawrence 1919; Newfang 1924; Potter 1929; Bailey 1932). The study of nations was part of an imperial mindset which required diplomats and colonial administrators to have an understanding of cultural differences between 'tribal' peoples and 'civilised' society. The focus was also typically very legalistic; but even so there was a conscious effort to understand the politics of cultural dynamics. For example, IR scholars in the 1930s examining the 'domestic, religious and national problems' in Iraq were interested in and aware of the 'unceasing conflict between the Sunnis and the Shiah' (B. Carpenter 1933: 375).

In the aftermath of the Great Depression, and on the eve of World War II, the family of nations was breaking up, and the civilised ideals of an international society were not being upheld or enforced. Emblematically, as the League of Nations appeared doomed to collapse, a more despairing tone began to emerge. The noble and *civilised* idea that nationalism 'should claim not its own aggrandisement, but its right to serve humanity as a distinct group' (Mazzini, cited in Burns 1915: 11) seemed to be losing traction. Liberals such as Norman Angell observed that the idea of nationalism was being distorted into narrow-spirited and parochial forms of militarism, Hitlerism and balkanisation (the breakup of a region or state into smaller, often hostile, ethnic or national groupings). Even newly formed nations in Europe had 'repudiated the principle of nationality' (Angell 1932: 255). The rise of this un-international nationalism was held to account as the root cause of the international order's collapse (Keeton 1939).

Hans Kohn's 1944 study, *The idea of nationalism*, explained the problem in terms of a conflict between 'civic' and 'ethnic' nationalisms. He argued that countries that defined national membership on the basis of 'blood' were more conflict-prone than those based on 'soil'. Improving citizenship laws would encourage greater loyalty to political instutions rather than one's ethnic community. Kohn's analysis is still regarded as highly pertinent in contemporary IR. In particular, it has been used to propose democratic solutions to avoid problems such as **ethnic cleansing** (Brubaker 1996 and Snyder 2000).

Another important contribution to current understandings of nationalism was made by E. H. Carr in his 1945 publication, *Nationalism and after*, which celebrated the achievements of the welfare state while repudiating pernicious nationalism for its exclusionary treatment of racial and ethnic minorities and as a cause of war. Carr's hope was that following the devastation of two world wars, a world *after* nationalism could be constructed; one where more open forms of political community would suppress the inward looking and exclusionary politics of nationalism. This analysis was recently revisited by **Critical Theorist** Andrew Linklater, who described Carr's work on nationalism as a significant contribution to resolving the political and moral questions of our epoch (Linklater 1997: 321).

For our purposes, it is important to recognise that prior to the end of World War II the study of nations and nationalism was considered as both the foundation and the most critically topical subject of study in the field. After World War II there appears to have been a strong desire to understand international politics through a state-centric lens. The postwar period did not culminate in the demise of nationalism, but IR became consolidated into a profoundly state-centric discipline with a marked 'lack of curiosity about different political identities, including nationalism' (Pettman 1998: 149).

The neglect of nationalism as an analytical category has meant that it is quite routine in world politics for the terms 'nation' and 'national' to be used as synonyms for the 'state'. We can observe this in the discipline of IR itself, global institutions such as the United Nations (UN), policy doctrines that appeal to the national interest, armed struggles for recognition of statehood characterised in terms of national independence and even the designation of an individual's legal citizenship status on passports as their nationality. In each of these cases, the term 'nation' refers predominantly to state agency. For instance, the UN is comprised of 192 legally recognised member states, not the estimated 5000 or so distinguishable ethnic groups in the world (Eller 1990: 4). Likewise, governmental policies that are rationalised as being in the national interest are generally informed by an overt set of material interests and legal entitlements rather than the more vague symbolic values of a cultural identity.

IR scholars can become very frustrated with this slippage between nation and state, in which the distinction between legal and cultural conceptions of bounded human communities is blurred. And yet it is possible that the uses of 'nation' in these instances are at least partially intentional. After all, the overarching aspiration of the UN goes beyond the idea that it is simply 'a club of states' when the preamble to its Charter, echoing the American Declaration of Independence, begins with the phrase, 'We the people of the United Nations'. Similarly, governments and political leaders are astutely aware that references to the nation and national interest are ways of summoning the power of the concept to speak of, and to, the deep cultural attachments of human communities. Internally, citizens can be reassured by justifications of a national security policy which is framed in terms of defending traditions and a 'way of life'. Externally, a diplomatic statement referring to another nation intuitively reaches out to the people of a country, not just the political institutions of government.

Appeals to 'the people' in the New World Order

We can observe this rhetorical device of invoking the 'people' as a required component in political addresses to the nation prior to the onset of war. Consider the following excerpt from a televised address to the American people made by President George H. Bush on 16 January 1991, delivered as the first phases of Operation Desert Storm were beginning:

We have no argument with the people of Iraq. Indeed, for the innocents caught in this conflict, I pray for their safety. Our goal is not the conquest of Iraq. It is the liberation of Kuwait. It is my hope that somehow the Iraqi people can, even now, convince their dictator that he must lay down his arms, leave Kuwait, and let Iraq itself rejoin the family of peace-loving nations.

The above appeal involves an intentional separation of nation and state in order to express solidarity with a people while politically isolating a belligerent political elite. Notice how the innocents are protected and 'prayed for' and that the justification for the war is in terms of repelling an aggressor not the conquest of a nation. The US president appears to be speaking directly to the Iraqi people, *bypassing* the state. Even if the loyalty (or fear) of Iraqi peoples proved too strong to be convinced by such an appeal, the other target audience is, of course, the American people and 'the family of peace-loving nations'.

President Bush's justification for the Gulf War was framed in liberal terms. Indeed it was emblematic of his New World Order doctrine that espoused a world of open borders and free markets; a world where the rule of law not the law of the jungle would prevail. It illustrates how the liberal tradition, though suspicious of the dangers of extreme nationalism, depends heavily on the idea that a nation embodies the inalienable right for peoples to be liberated from tyranny. Democratic constituencies demand this kind of justification from their leaders if they are to support acts of war. They will tolerate, and sometimes enthusiastically support, war against tyrannical governments, but 'people' are presumed innocent friends, not enemies. The problem for liberal nationalism and its support for self-determination is that it is all too often conditional on helping 'people who believe the way we do' (Dean Acheson, cited in W. A. Williams 1962: 10). Liberal internationalism places similar conditions on this so-called universal right when peoples pursue their freedom in ways that are insufficiently deferential to higher ideals such as universal human rights, or are simply anti-Western.

It would be remiss not to briefly mention the counter-arguments that IR scholars have made on this issue of justifying war in terms of its benefit to a 'people'. A realist analysis of Bush's New World Order doctrine might question its lack of reference to the material strategic interests of the US and its allies. While realists have always understood that political rhetoric may be necessary, the test of success lies firmly with an impartial analysis of material interests. In this sense, most realist analyses evaluated the 1991 Gulf War positively, not because the people of Kuwait were liberated, and only nominally because American values were upheld, but because the US adhered to a coherent and decisive strategy: US national interests were clearly defined and effectively defended (see Gelb 2009).

In contrast, a Marxist analysis of the above justification would highlight that the political economy of oil was critically important for a corporate elite and that the 'liberation' was not of an oppressed people but of a highly autocratic Kuwaiti monarchy. The war did not uphold 'any high principle in the Gulf' and, contrary to the rhetoric, **diplomacy** was obstructed and the 'people' of Iraq abandoned. The real, albeit disguised, goals – protecting 'incomparable energy resources' and reinforcing a dominant superpower position in the region – were achieved (see Chomsky 2003: 60–7). That the popular uprisings of Shi'ites in the South and Kurds in the North were unsupported by the coalition and abandoned to brutal suppression by a dictator left in power yields further evidence for Marxists and others who remain sceptical of the liberal rhetoric.

Postmodern IR theorists have focused on the politics of representation. Here the analysis of nation or people is either treated reflexively or rendered invisible. Some commentators characterised the Gulf War as a 'virtual war' because it all seemed (to Western audiences) to be occurring on CNN (Baudrillard 1995). So much of this coverage was focused on new military technologies that it became difficult to contemplate these events in terms of real people: the lead actors on stage were the superpower's hi-tech weapons. Viewed from this perspective, the broader strategic goal of the Gulf War was to project an image of the omnipresent and infallible character of US weapons as a means of discouraging dissent, reassuring allies and impressing an electorate. The overarching message was not the liberation of an unseen people, but the articulation of the US nation as *liberator* (Campbell 1992).

By asking how the concept of 'nation' is being used to justify policies or practices, we can understand a great deal about the way that the 'people' are conceptualised. Doing so also illuminates the way that significant markers of identity become sites of struggle in international politics. Some analysts of IR have discovered the importance of language as they looked more carefully into their subjects. For example, in his wide-ranging study of post-Cold War ethnic conflicts, Michael Ignatieff (1994: 7) concluded that the politics of language was more important than land or history in cultivating national belonging: 'To belong is to understand the tacit codes of the people you live with … People in short, "speak your language".' Earlier IR scholars would also have understood the political significance of language to nationalism.

Conclusion

Nations are the dominant means of expressing and defining political culture in modern states and international society. Alternative forms of political culture such as empire, monarchy, religion, principality or city have been dominant in the past; and over the past two centuries, nationalism has withstood rival appeals for loyalty orientated around international class, political regions or cosmopolitan ideals. Sub-national tribal and ethnic loyalties have also challenged national authority and loyalty, and in a globally networked information age we may speculate that new digital communities may supersede the appeal of national identity. In spite of these alternatives, nationalism has endured and thrived as the most distinctive means of organising human communities into culturally defined, politically discrete, units.

In broad terms, nationalism does not seem to be disappearing in our late modern context. Interdisciplinary studies in the field have observed that while globalisation is having a significant impact on national and ethnic identity, the effect of these changes is a strengthening of cultural identity and a weakening of the relationship between the citizen and the state (Young et al. 2007). Nationalism will adapt to the challenges of the coming century, and political struggles associated with stateless nations (a form of civil war) or nationless states (a form of tyranny) will continue. While these conflicts will be viewed as a source of fragmentation of the **international system**; they will also reflect the principle that peoples have a right to freely determine their political status and pursue their own form of economic, social and cultural development; a principle that has been extremely important in shaping and defining international society.

QUESTIONS

1. What is a nation and how does it differ from a state?
2. How did nationalism shape international society?
3. Why have language and print capitalism been regarded as important in nation formation?
4. Are nations secular or sacred?
5. Do you think nationalism is a progressive or regressive force in international relations?
6. Why do political leaders need to speak to the 'nation'?
7. How do international theories conceptualise 'the people' as analytical categories?
8. Will nationalism thrive or decline in the future?

FURTHER READING

Gurr, Ted R. 2000, *Peoples versus states: minorities at risk in the new century*, Washington DC: United States Institute of Peace Press. Wide-ranging analysis of ethnic and nationalist conflicts since the 1990s.

Hutchinson, John and Smith, Anthony (eds) 1994, *Nationalism*, Oxford: Oxford University Press. Valuable collection that includes some classics in the field.

Mayall, James 1990, *Nationalism and international society*, Cambridge: Cambridge University Press. Important book on the role of nationalism from an IR perspective.

Preece, Jennifer Jackson, 2005, *Minority rights: between diversity and community*, Cambridge: Polity. Excellent survey of the international politics of racial, religious and linguistic minority rights.

Websites

The Avalon Project: http://avalon.law.yale.edu/20th_century/default.asp. Provides a comprehensive archive of significant documents in international law such as the Covenent of the League of Nations and the United Nations Charter.

The Nationalism Project: www.nationalismproject.org. The most comprehensive online collection of summaries and anlaysis of nationalism studies.

Unrepresented Nations and Peoples Organization: www.unpo.org. A body that was established in 1991 to address the concerns of a wide range of stateless nations and peoples that have many different characteristics but share in common a lack of formal representation at the United Nations.

11

Security

Anthony Burke

Introduction	161
Four crises	161
Defining security	163
Key theories and concepts	163
Conclusion	170
Questions	170
Further reading	170

Introduction

This chapter introduces the concept and practice of security in international relations. It explores the dilemmas faced by states, individuals and the global community by, first, looking at contemporary crises and disagreements about security; second, examining how security has been differently defined and focused; and third, surveying how different theoretical approaches have understood and analysed security.

Four crises

In October 1962 a US U-2 reconnaissance aircraft returned from a routine overflight of Cuba with photographs of Soviet personnel and machinery installing nuclear missiles aimed at the US – precipitating a crisis that almost led to global nuclear war (Blight and Lang 2005). In July 1997 the government of Thailand floated its currency, the baht, on international markets after losing US$23 billion trying to defend its value from attack by traders. It lost 15 per cent of its value in one day, provoking a contagion effect across East Asia that resulted in widespread corporate bankruptcies, massive falls in economic growth and employment, the fall of governments, and protests, riots and civil violence that took thousands of lives (Robison, Beeson et al. 2000).

Two years later, in September 1999, the people of East Timor voted in a referendum on independence from Indonesia, only to fall victim to a campaign of murder and destruction by Indonesian-backed militias. After many days of carnage and intense international diplomacy, the **United Nations** Security Council authorised a military intervention led by Australia to stop the violence (H. McDonald et al. 2002). And on 11 September 2001, a group of twelve men boarded four aircraft in Boston, Newark and Washington. A few minutes after takeoff they hijacked the planes and directed them towards New York and Washington. Two of the aircraft were flown into the twin towers of the World Trade Center, the other into the Pentagon, and the last crashed into a Pennsylvania field. The towers caught fire and later collapsed. The attacks killed nearly 3000 people and wounded thousands more, and provoked a response that changed the strategic landscape of the world forever (National Commission 2004).

These are just four examples of many global events and problems that are understood and addressed under the name of **security**. Yet they constitute very different kinds of crisis and all – apart from the first – constitute a challenge to traditional ways of thinking about security. They thus illustrate two important facts about security issues and security studies. First, they refer to complex and profoundly important problems of survival, prosperity and social cohesion. And second, there is no agreement among scholars and policymakers about how to make security policy, the problems upon which it should be focused, or how security should be conceptualised and studied. Security is, as it is now commonplace to say, a 'contested concept', *and* a contested practice (Dalby 1997).

Consider the examples above. According to the dominant security paradigm in Southeast Asia, 'comprehensive security', the East Timorese independence movement was considered a threat to Indonesia's 'national unity' and 'territorial integrity', and Indonesia's Southeast Asian neighbours recognised its claim to the territory and largely turned a blind eye to its brutal repression of the population. Here the focus of security is the territorial state, and coercive and violent means are seen as acceptable ways of ensuring it. However, under a very different security paradigm, that of 'human security', it is the security of the East Timorese people that is most important and the state of Indonesia is seen as the primary threat – this doctrine would have generated efforts to promote **human rights**, demilitarise the territory, and use dialogue to achieve a lasting solution to East Timor's political status. A 'human security' approach also underpinned the obligations felt by members of the UN Security Council to intervene to stop the violence, and hence the 1999 crisis symbolised a profound clash of two paradigms, each of which laid claim to an authoritative understanding of security.

The East Asian crisis of 1997–8 simply did not register on the radar of regional security officials until after it occurred, wherein it was thought of (conventionally) in terms of the 'economic security' and 'regional resilience' of Asia, or, more radically, in terms of the way in which complex political and economic processes combined to gravely affect the human security of millions (A. Burke 2008; Acharya 2001; Collins 2003). The **Cuban missile crisis** represented a classical security problem – what the realist scholar Stephen Walt (1991) insists is the proper focus of security studies, that of the threat and use of military force – except that again it exemplified the impact of clashing paradigms. By 1962 the US and USSR were in a very unstable relationship of mutual nuclear '**deterrence**', which in classical strategic theory is meant to ensure that the weapons will not be used in anger. However the crisis highlighted the failure of this fragile 'balance of terror' to safeguard humanity should deterrence fail. Powerful forces in the US government prepared *and urged* a military invasion of Cuba to remove Castro's regime and deal with the weapons, while Kennedy and his advisors like Secretary of Defense Robert McNamara understood that such action could quickly escalate into a global holocaust. They successfully negotiated a deal that exchanged a Soviet withdrawal of the missiles for a later withdrawal of US weapons from Turkey and a guarantee not to invade Cuba, and the experience led to McNamara later becoming a vocal advocate of nuclear disarmament (Blight and Lang 2005: 60–85). Yet nuclear 'deterrence' remains a cornerstone of the security policies of many states,' including the US.

The 11 September attacks, like few events in US history, undermined many assumptions about the utility of military power to ensure national security. The lesson the Bush administration took from the events was that deterrence no longer held against **terrorists** and **rogue states**, and that threats must be met – with military force – before they could emerge. This doctrine was so revolutionary as to put the important security 'regimes' and '**norms**' that the global community has been developing since 1945 under great pressure.

In the wake of September 11 and the 2003 invasion of Iraq, the UN commissioned a major report by a group of statespersons – the High Level Panel on Threats, Challenges and Change – on the international security agenda. It called for a 'new security consensus' based around 'six clusters of threats', including economic instability and poverty, state conflict, internal conflict and large-scale human rights abuse, transnational organised crime, weapons of mass destruction and environmental crisis. It emphasised, in a way reflected in the UK National Security Strategy (UK Cabinet Office 2008), that 'today's threats recognize no national boundaries, are connected, and must be addressed at the global and regional as well as national levels'. Most significantly, it also noted a disturbing lack of consensus globally about what threats mattered, and to whom:

Differences of power, wealth and geography do determine what we perceive as the gravest threats to our survival and well-being ... Many people believe that what passes for collective security today is simply a system for protecting the rich and powerful ... What is needed today is nothing less than a new consensus between alliances that are frayed, between wealthy nations and poor, and among peoples mired in mistrust across an apparently widening cultural abyss. The essence of that consensus is simple: we all share responsibility for each other's security (High Level Panel 2004: 10).

Defining security

Given such disagreement, defining security becomes a highly political matter. Different paradigms define security differently and their definitions incorporate biases about who is to be secured and how. The classical (**realist**) definition, advanced by writers such as Walter Lippman and Arnold Wolfers, argues that a nation's security is determined by its ability to defend itself against threats to 'core' or 'acquired values', in war if necessary (Baylis 2001: 255). Hans Morgenthau defined **national security** as 'the integrity of the national territory and its institutions' and said that it was 'the irreducible minimum that diplomacy must defend without compromise'. He did gesture towards an understanding of 'international' security dynamics, one taken up by **liberals**, when he argued that statesmen must try to see problems from the point of view of other nations and diplomacy must seek to make all nations equally secure (Morgenthau 1973: 553–5). This contrasts with the views of some realists that security is a zero-sum game, that a nation is secure to the extent that others are not. Barry Buzan and his colleagues in the 'Copenhagen School' offer a revealing 'extended realist' definition when they say that

security is about survival ... when an issue is posed as constituting an existential threat to a designated referent object [the state] ... The special nature of security threats justifies the use of extraordinary measures to handle them (Buzan et al. 1998: 21).

Critical writers, on the other hand, define security very differently. They argue that security should be holistic and not focused primarily on the state or military conflict. Ken Booth, of the 'Welsh School' of critical security studies, argues that security should be about the 'emancipation ... of individuals and groups from those physical and human constraints which stop them from carrying out what they would freely choose to do' (Booth 1991: 319). The feminist scholar J. Ann Tickner defines security as 'the elimination of unjust social relations, including unequal gender relations' (Tickner 1992: 127–44). This shifts the referent to individuals and communities and is biased towards a politics of social transformation. Other critical scholars argue that if we want to understand the (often negative) impacts of security discourse and policy it is helpful to shift from analysing what security 'is' to what it 'does', to see it as a set of practices and techniques. Such scholars argue that just the use of the term 'security' grants governments enormous power. Security is less an end state than a process: it is a form of *power*, a 'political technology' that operates on individuals and populations at the same time. It thus must be 'deconstructed' and placed under suspicion (A. Burke 2001 and 2006; McDonald 2005). Rethinking security in more human-centred ways can follow such critique.

Key theories and concepts

There are a bewildering diversity of approaches to security policy and analysis. However, they can be usefully boiled down to the following broad categories:

- realist (incorporating 'classical' realist, **neorealist** and 'extended' realist approaches)

- liberal (incorporating 'collective', 'common', 'cooperative' and 'human' security approaches)
- **constructivist** (incorporating elements of realist and liberal approaches)
- critical and feminist approaches.

Realist approaches

As we saw with Hans Morgenthau's definition above, the realist paradigm focuses upon national security. Realist approaches privilege the state as the object of security and see threats primarily emerging from the military and economic competition between states. Because they discount the possibility of international cooperation or the development of peaceful norms of behaviour, they emphasise what they call the 'self-help' capacities of states in developing strong military forces and strategic **alliances** with other states. They are sceptical of the value of **international law** or 'collective security', although they do occasionally endorse the creation of coalitions of powers (such in the Gulf War of 1990–91) to punish or discipline a state that has acted in ways detrimental to their **national interests** or security. They regard **war** as a perennial tendency in human nature and argue that it cannot be abolished or controlled through law or moral suasion. Instead, they believe that the *fear* of unacceptable punishment (the core idea of 'deterrence'), or *prudence* in the face of unacceptable costs or a chaotic result, will restrain statesmen from acting aggressively.

Realists thus think of the threat and use of armed force, after the theorist of war Carl von Clausewitz (1989), as dictated by national interests and cost-benefit analysis. They utilise an instrumental, *strategic* perspective that seeks to link violent means with political ends. However, in this arena interesting debates among realists have arisen. On the use of force, realists have divided into two groups. A more hawkish group, associated with strategic studies and exemplified by thinkers such as Edward Luttwak (1987) and Colin Gray (1998, 1999), endorses violence as a tool of statecraft and is more concerned with technical issues of weapons systems, military preparedness, and military tactics and strategy. A second group argues that the use of force should always be a last resort and often has chaotic and costly effects that can't be anticipated (see A. Burke 2006; S. Brown 2003; Lebow 2003). The actions of Robert McNamara and his colleagues during the Cuban missile crisis sit within this camp, and the opposition of Stephen Walt and John Mearsheimer to the invasion of Iraq is another example (Blight and Lang 2005; Mearsheimer and Walt 2003).

Deterrence, which is defined as 'manipulating another's behaviour through threats', has also generated complex debates (Freedman 2004: 6; Jervis 1979). It developed after 1945 when US planners sought to grapple with the changes wrought by nuclear weapons. The strategist Bernard Brodie is famous for arguing that 'thus far the chief purpose of a military establishment has been to win wars. From now on its chief purpose must be to avert them' (Brodie 1946: 67). Nuclear and conventional strategy henceforth was framed around the problem of developing doctrines and weapons systems that would deter Soviet or other enemy attack. Such approaches still underpin military strategies around the world, especially in Northeast Asia where the US confronts China and North Korea with nuclear and conventional weapons. Yet realists also identified serious problems with the practice. John Herz (1950) described what he called the '**security dilemma**', which occurred as defensive measures by one state were perceived as aggressive or threatening by another, who in turn took new measures to secure themselves, leading to a spiral of arms acquisition and mistrust (Booth and Wheeler 2008). This could lead to crises such as those over Berlin (1961) or Cuba (1962), leading some analysts to point out that once deterrence failed, the doctrine lost all value.

What Alan Dupont calls 'extended' security approaches do not depart from traditional realist understandings of military security dilemmas but, especially since the end of the **Cold War**, have pointed to a wider range of security threats and challenges for states, such as terrorism, unregulated people movements, transnational crime, disease, or environmental degradation (Dupont 2001). These threats do not emerge from states or by armed violence, but, it is argued, can still affect the basic values and well-being of national communities. Some scholars and not a few policymakers have also characterised such threats (especially from migration) as threats to the *identity* of receiving states, directly making **identity** a security issue – something critical scholars strongly question (Chalk 2000; Buzan, Wæver and de Wilde 1998).

Liberal approaches

Liberals argue that it is inadequate for security to be based on the power balancing and deterrence calculations of individual states, believing that the carnage of the two world wars and the dangers of nuclear holocaust require the development of international rules and cooperative institutions to govern state behaviour and punish wrongdoers. This attitude has influenced the development of an important body of international law and a number of global and regional institutions relating to security. The most important of these are the UN and its Charter, which outlaws armed aggression and will only authorise the use of force in defence against attack with the concurrence of the fifteen-member Security Council (see Box 11.1). Key treaties, which have the moral force of international law, include those on the Non-Proliferation of Nuclear Weapons (NPT), the Chemical Weapons Convention, the Comprehensive (Nuclear) Test Ban Treaty, and the Ottawa Convention banning land mines. Not only does the UN seek to control when states go to war (*jus ad bellum*), it also seeks to control how states may conduct wars (*jus in bello*) through the Geneva Conventions regulating war. These operate against the background of a long list of other conventions protecting fundamental freedoms and human rights (see Chapter 15).

BOX 11.1: KEY TEXTS

Preamble to the UN Charter

WE THE PEOPLES OF THE UNITED NATIONS DETERMINED:

to save succeeding generations from the scourge of war, which twice in our lifetime has brought untold sorrow to mankind, and

to reaffirm faith in fundamental human rights, in the dignity and worth of the human person, in the equal rights of men and women and of nations large and small, and

to establish conditions under which justice and respect for the obligations arising from treaties and other sources of international law can be maintained, and

to promote social progress and better standards of life in larger freedom,

AND FOR THESE ENDS

> to practice tolerance and live together in peace with one another as good neighbours, and
> to unite our strength to maintain international peace and security, and
> to ensure, by the acceptance of principles and the institution of methods, that armed force shall not be used, save in the common interest.

The NPT is a particularly important treaty, because it has seen 182 countries agree both *not to develop* nuclear weapons and (in the case of six existing 'nuclear weapons states') to *disarm* themselves of their arsenals. The treaty also has provisions for long-term efforts at *general disarmament*, because states recognise that the processes of conventional and nuclear weapons proliferation are linked. Hence **disarmament** is an important element of liberal thinking about security, even if they acknowledge that it is difficult to achieve in a world where many states find themselves in dangerous security dilemmas, and that disarmament requires cooperation and agreement to be effective. Liberals emphasise the importance of disarmament because they believe deterrence to be dangerously flawed and unstable; hence disarmament is the only effective way to prevent escalation to major war or disasters during a crisis (see McNamara and Blight 2003; Schell 2001; ICNND 2009) (see Box 11.2).

BOX 11.2: DISCUSSION POINTS

Global security and nuclear fears

The years since September 11 have stimulated profound new fears about the dangers of nuclear weapons, and renewed efforts to begin a global process of strengthening nuclear security and achieving disarmament (A. Burke 2009). Consistent with its hawkish approach to the use of force, the Bush administration adopted a nuclear doctrine in 2001 that rejected its disarmament obligations under Article VI of the NPT, and adopted new uses for nuclear weapons including in conventional war or against WMD (weapons of mass destruction) facilities in enemy states, which had very destabilising effects (McDonough 2006). However, by 2007 a group of former US secretaries of defense and state (including a former advocate of limited nuclear war and negotiator of arms control agreements with the USSR, Henry Kissinger) were arguing for the US to support total nuclear disarmament as a key to US and international security (Shultz et al. 2007). They were especially concerned that non-state actors may gain access to nuclear weapons or radiological materials, as al-Qaeda leaders had stated they would use WMDs if they could obtain them. The proliferation of weapons technology to North Korea and Iran further raised fears of a nuclear 'tipping point' where the NPT would collapse in a cascade of proliferation. Stalemate at the 2005 review conference on the NPT – which could not agree on a final communiqué – worsened such fears.

In 2009 new US president Barack Obama announced he would pursue the goal of a world without nuclear weapons, although he cautioned that the goal would not be reached in his lifetime. He committed his administration to negotiating a new strategic arms reduction treaty with Russia, and to **ratify** new conventions banning nuclear tests and fissile material production. His administration also hosted a nuclear security summit, published a new nuclear posture review, and supported a successful 2010 NPT review conference. At this point the world faced three dilemmas: managing or reversing proliferation in North Korea, Iran and between Pakistan and India so as to hold the system together; beginning cooperative reductions to trigger disarmament momentum; and, over the long term, managing the security complexities of a world with few or no nuclear weapons. These problems were the subject of academic research (Ruzicka & Wheeler 2010; A. Burke 2009; Hanson 2010) and of a major report published by the International Commission on Nuclear Non-proliferation and Disarmament (ICNND 2009).

Regional cooperative security institutions include the Organization for Security and Co-operation in Europe (OSCE), which was established in 1973 to moderate Cold War tensions (and now includes initiatives on human rights and the environment), and the **ASEAN** Regional Forum (ARF), which is an Asia-Pacific grouping of states that seeks to promote greater transparency and dialogue on regional security problems. Southeast Asia is an interesting case where liberal norms of conduct that preclude the acquisition of nuclear weapons and the use of force to settle disputes *between* regional states coexist with extended realist norms *within* regional countries about the need to respond violently to internal threats to national unity and stability. This tangle of ideas is expressed in the Southeast Asian notion of comprehensive security – which expands security beyond the military dimension to incorporate political, economic and societal dimensions, but is still focused upon the 'stability' and 'integrity' of regional states (see Alagappa 1998: 624–5; Acharya 2001; Burke and McDonald 2007).

Liberals thus define their thinking and policy around three key concepts:

Collective security generally refers to efforts to build rules and laws at the international level, to create regional or global decision-making bodies and institutions, and to act in concert to enforce those rules. This is the paradigm at work when the UN Security Council deliberates or authorises military interventions, for example. In theory its decisions are meant to express a collective – even universal – consensus, but they can sometimes express the influence of more powerful states.

Common security was a concept developed by the 1982 Palme Commission to replace the doctrine of mutual deterrence. Its chairman, former Swedish prime minister Olaf Palme, argued that in the nuclear era we must 'achieve security not against the adversary but together with him. International security must rest on a commitment to joint survival rather than on a threat of mutual destruction' (Palme Commission 1982).

Cooperative security is an idea promoted by former Australian foreign minister Gareth Evans in the context of the formation of the ARF, one that he claimed could fold collective, common and comprehensive security into a conceptual whole (Evans and Grant 1995: 75–7). This idea he also used to promote more attention to the potential role of the UN in preventing genocide or crimes against humanity through diplomatic and military intervention; his and other efforts culminated in a report commissioned by the UN Secretary-General entitled *The responsibility to protect* (ICISS 2001).

However, a fourth concept – human security – challenges Evans's confidence in the coherence of the cooperative security concept, especially as it incorporates the idea of comprehensive security. Human security, which straddles the liberal and critical approaches, shifts the referent of security from the state to the individual human being, and incorporates a range of possible threats or processes that could negatively affect their basic welfare. While there has been much debate about the legitimate scope of human security, the most authoritative definition came from the United Nations Development Program (UNDP), which described it as 'safety from chronic threats such as hunger, disease and repression, as well as safety from sudden and harmful disruptions in the patterns of daily life' (Roesad 2000).

Human security allows us to conceive of states as threats to their citizens, and to see insecurity arising from complex social, political and economic processes (including those arising from widely accepted paradigms of development or political authority) rather than just military aggression or violence. However, human security is not without its critics – in Southeast Asia it challenges existing structures of power and many realist scholars believe that it complicates efforts to tightly define and focus upon security priorities (A. Burke 2001; Thomas and Tow 2002; Bellamy and McDonald 2002).

Constructivist approaches

Constructivist approaches to security develop and refine both liberal and realist analyses, although they tend to support liberal approaches in **normative** terms. They seek to understand the way *ideas* and *norms* affect international security and combine with national interests or military competition. As Peter Katzenstein and Rudra Sil (2004: 9) argue, 'constructivism is based on the fundamental view that ideational structures mediate how actors perceive, construct, and reproduce the institutional and material structures they inhabit as well as their own roles and identities within them'. Constructivists especially emphasise the way in which norms (broad inter-subjective agreements about what kind of policy or behaviour is legitimate, appropriate or effective) have the effect of controlling international politics (Reus-Smit 2004a: 40–68). Particular actions are then shaped or limited either *voluntarily* because an actor has internationalised a norm into their own identity or basic convictions, or because an actor feels *pressure* from other parts of their own or the international community.

A significant contribution of constructivist writers to security analysis is their development of Karl Deutsch's concept of the **security community**. As Emmanuel Adler and Michael Barnett state, this is to assert that 'community exists at the international level, that security politics is profoundly shaped by it, and that those states dwelling within an international community might develop a pacific disposition [and] settle their differences short of war'. Security communities emerge where there is 'a development of shared understandings, transnational values and transaction flows [such as trade]' (Adler and Barnett 1998: 3–4). Amitav Acharya (2001) and Alex Bellamy (2004) have both argued that features of security community exist in East Asia (especially among the ASEAN countries) who have agreed norms that prevent them settling inter-state disputes by force, that limit the role of great powers and prevent the acquisition of weapons of mass destruction. While some critical writers acknowledge the value of this, they have also questioned how ASEAN combines liberal values at the inter-state level with very coercive and authoritarian norms *inside* their countries (Burke and McDonald 2007). Others have questioned the way security communities can shift the antagonism to those *outside* the security community, potentially creating 'regional fortresses preparing for the kind of civilisational conflict envisaged by Samuel Huntington' (Bellamy 2004: 10–11).

Critical and feminist approaches

Critical and feminist approaches to security are diverse, but they have in common a continuation of the basic normative orientation to human security. This is admirably expressed by the 'critical security studies' thinker Ken Booth as a commitment to security as **emancipation**, in the form of 'a more just society' that 'progressively limits the repressive structure of powers and processes, steadily squeezing the space for violent behaviour in all its direct and indirect manifestations', and by J. Ann Tickner's vision of a security based upon 'the elimination of unjust social relations, including unequal gender relations' and for a reformulation of international relations in terms of the 'multiple insecurities' represented by ecological destruction, poverty and (gendered) structural violence. Booth argues that security needs to be 'holistic and non-statist', because 'the smaller units of universal human society … will not be secure until the whole is secured' (Booth 1991, 2005: 263; Tickner 1992: 127–44).

These are what Matt McDonald has called 'reconstructive' critical perspectives, 'aimed at advancing alternative claims about what security is or should mean'. Another set of critical approaches (although they often converge) is termed 'deconstructive': they aim to put the meaning and operation of security as a *concept* and *politics* into question (Burke and McDonald 2007). These approaches do not reject the desire to rethink security in better ways, but they also show how it has worked historically as a system of power and how this creates a barrier to defining it in ways that support human dignity. They are especially interested in how images of security and threat work to divide the world between 'us' and 'them', to construct identity in opposition to some 'Other' – a nation, group, religion or way of living – which must be contained, destroyed or expelled (Burke 2007a).

Critical scholars are also interested in how antagonistic constructions of identity are a factor in conflict. They point to the conflicts between North and South Korea, China and Taiwan, India and Pakistan, Indonesia and Papua, and Israel and Palestine, as particularly dangerous examples. Their argument is that even as there are significant military security dilemmas and other material interests at work, the roots of the conflicts lie in the ways identities have been constructed so as to deny the deep historical interconnections between societies, suppress or exaggerate claims to autonomy and difference, or deny the legitimacy and humanity of the other side. (Bleiker 2001; 2005; Burke 2001; 2007b) Hence critical and feminist writers seek to positively support *difference*, so as to show how inequality and violence are differentially distributed (the effects of the global economy or militarised violence affect men and women differently, for example) (Sylvester 2002; Lee-Koo 2002; J. J. Pettman 1996). (See Box 11.3.)

BOX 11.3: KEY TEXTS

'Sex and death in the rational world of defense intellectuals'

Feminist scholars rethink security in two ways: by alerting us to the distinctive effects of economic processes, war and conflict on women's lives, and by analysing how constructions of gender are central to dominant ways of thinking about security and defence (Tickner 1992: 6). An example was set out in a famous essay by Carol Cohn, who wrote about her experiences studying at a centre for strategic studies. Her essay analysed the very abstract and gendered language through which strategists made nuclear deterrence and war thinkable, acceptable and rational. The very destructive effects of nuclear weapons were sanitised by terms such as 'clean bombs' and 'counter-value attacks', and associated with masculine images of force, power and sexual domination through terms such as 'penetration aids' and arguments that US dependence on nuclear weapons for security was 'irresistible, because you get more bang for the buck', or that 'to disarm is to get rid of all your stuff'. Debates over the virtues of 'protracted' versus 'spasm' attacks were resolved by describing the latter as 'releasing 70 to 80 per cent of your megatonnage in one orgasmic whump'. Cohn suggests that this was both 'a deadly serious display of the connections between masculine sexuality and the arms race' and 'a way of minimizing the seriousness of militarist endeavours, of denying their deadly consequences' (Cohn 1987: 693, 696).

A further contribution of critical writers is to show the role of *representation* in threat analysis and security policy, and to highlight the increasingly politicised nature of security discourse. They argue that security threats are not objective (and that some threats are not threats at all), but are the product of representation through language and metaphor. They argue that the politics of fear (or security politics) is an increasingly common feature of modern democracies and that it is used to demonise particular groups, to gather votes, and to exert power over minorities or the left (McDonald 2005). Some critical writers, indeed, argue that such a politics is central to the way in which sovereign states and political communities have been conceived within modernity, and that it involves forms of 'biopolitical' power that takes hold of ordinary citizens' bodies and selves as a way of entrenching forms of economic **hegemony** and injustice, and violent ways of being (Burke 2007a; Agamben 1998; Dauphinée and Masters 2007). In such a circumstance, emancipation is a difficult task indeed, even if it is important to struggle for.

Conclusion

Security is currently the major preoccupation of modern world politics. It both expresses important concerns about human survival, values and community, and is liable to abuse by the unscrupulous in their struggle for political power and privilege. It forms a complex, interconnected set of global problems – encompassing war and civil conflict, nuclear weapons, faith, terrorism, environmental change and inequality – where the interests and dignity of individuals vie with the machinations of violent and powerful actors. We may have high hopes for a new spirit of consensus and cooperation to solve global security problems, but achieving it will be a major task in itself.

QUESTIONS

1. Why is the concept of security 'contested'?
2. Why is there global disagreement about what security problems matter? What should be done about it?
3. Does the use or threat of force lead to security?
4. What are the benefits and flaws of constructivist theories of security?
5. What is 'critical' about critical security approaches? Are they practical?
6. How might we begin to realise security for all human beings?

FURTHER READING

Acharya, A. 2001, *Constructing a security community in Southeast Asia: ASEAN and the problem of regional order*, London & New York: Routledge. An important work of constructivist security theory focused on Asia-Pacific politics and institutions.

Booth, K. (ed.) 2005, *Critical security studies and world politics*, Boulder: Lynne Rienner. A comprehensive statement of the 'Welsh School' of emancipatory critical security studies.

Booth, K. and Wheeler, N. J. 2008, *The security dilemma: fear, cooperation and trust in world politics*, Basingstoke: Palgrave. A major refinement of realist theories of deterrence and inter-state security, utilising liberal and critical perspectives.

Burgess, J. P. (ed.) 2010, *The Routledge handbook of new security studies*, London and New York: Routledge. A wide-ranging treatment of new security concepts, issues and practices, by leading scholars.

Buzan, B. and Hansen, L. 2009, *The evolution of international security studies*, Cambridge: Cambridge University Press. The first history of security studies as a global field.

Fierke, K. 2007, *Critical approaches to international security*, Oxford: Polity. An excellent guide to the range of critical approaches.

Tickner, J. A. 1992, *Gender in international relations: feminist perspectives on achieving global security*, New York: Columbia University Press. A landmark feminist work on global and human security.

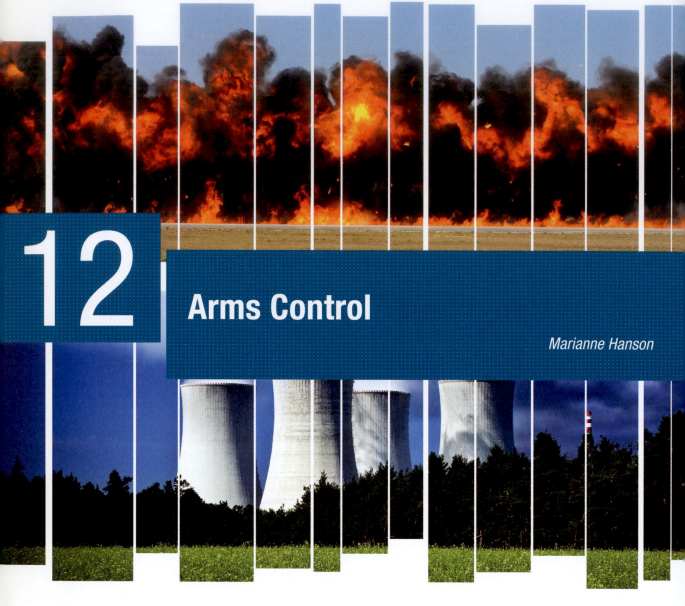

12

Arms Control

Marianne Hanson

Introduction	173
What is arms control?	173
Why do states engage in arms control practices?	174
Cold War arms control	174
Why is arms control still important in the post-Cold War period?	175
New initiatives in arms control: small arms and conventional weapons	179
Arms control and international relations theory	181
Nuclear weapons: a special case?	182
Sergio Duarte: Disarmament and international security	183
Initiatives to strengthen the nuclear non-proliferation regime	186
Conclusion	187
Questions	187
Further reading	187

Introduction

This chapter examines the evolution and practices of **arms control** in international relations. It begins by discussing what arms control is and why it has featured so prominently in world politics, even after the ending of the **Cold War**, the period during which arms control can be said to have developed extensively. After a discussion of the various weapons that are covered by arms control processes, and the legal **regimes** that accompany these, the chapter proceeds to outline some of the ways in which arms control can be conceptualised and how various schools of thought in international relations can be related to arms control practices. We then look at the specific case of the nuclear weapons regime, as more **states** acquire nuclear weapons, and as calls increase for the elimination of these particular **weapons of mass destruction (WMDs)**. The chapter also examines how a number of key states have been involved in upholding various arms control and **disarmament** regimes in the contemporary period.

What is arms control?

Arms control can be described simply as any arrangement made directly between adversaries or **multilaterally** by the broader international community to limit the weapons that might be used in warfare. A more formal, or classical, definition of arms control is provided by Hedley Bull: 'Arms control is restraint internationally exercised upon armaments policy, whether in respect of the level of armaments, their character, deployment or use' (Bull 1961: vii). Arms control can be conducted as a formal process involving treaties and other binding arrangements, or as an informal practice between states. These processes or steps can be **unilateral**, **bilateral** or multilateral; the most essential element is a willingness to cooperate with other states to achieve **security** interests. These interests could be 'exclusively those of the cooperating states themselves' or interests that are 'more widely shared' in the international community (Bull 1961: 2).

Arms control has been applied to both weapons of mass destruction (WMDs) and to conventional weapons, although it has been applied most heavily to WMDs. These are nuclear, radiological, chemical and biological weapons, and are categorised as WMDs because of their enormous potential for causing mass casualties. (These are nevertheless very different types of weapon systems, and their lethality and damage potential vary greatly. By way of example, consider that the large-scale use of nuclear weapons could result in between sixty and 300 million deaths; biological weapons, from thousands to perhaps 20 million deaths; and chemical weapons the much lower figure of several thousand dead (Butfoy 2005: 22–3). Equally, the ability to produce each of these types of weapon and maintain and deploy them successfully varies greatly.) Despite the heavy focus on this kind of weapon, there is no reason to limit arms control to WMDs only. While WMDs are rightly abhorred for their capacity for destruction, so-called conventional weapons – that is, weapons that are *not* WMD – have received much less attention from arms controllers, largely because of the implied right of **sovereign states** to possess a normal or 'conventional' weapons capability. This is changing, however, and although the focus for arms control continues to be on WMDs, certain kinds of conventional weapons are also now being considered as appropriate for restriction or elimination.

Why do states engage in arms control practices?

There are various compelling reasons why states might wish to conduct arms control arrangements. In a landmark study, Thomas Schelling and Morton Halperin ([1961] 1985) explored the motivations that compel states to agree to cooperate. First, mutually agreeing to limit the kinds or numbers of weapons states may hold can help to prevent the outbreak of **war** between them. In this sense, arms control can be seen as a means of lessening, if not overcoming, the negative effects of the '**security dilemma**'. A security dilemma is said to exist when states are uncertain of the intentions of their adversaries, and fear an attack; this uncertainty can propel a state to protect itself against any possible attack by arming itself. This very measure, however, can stimulate fear for its own safety in the other state, which thinks that the original state is undertaking military preparedness, and interprets this as a possible prelude to attack. This fear impels the other state also to undertake militarisation measures, which in turn reinforces the original state's fear, thus leading to a spiral of arms acquisition and increasing suspicion of the other's intent. Given that wars can occur because of the fear of the military **power** of one's adversary, any mutual agreement to limit arms can open up communication between states, and lead to greater transparency and a better understanding of a state's intentions. This process is also referred to as a 'confidence building measure'.

Arms control can also reduce greatly the military and economic costs of preparing for war; knowing that an adversary will not acquire a type or particular numbers of weapons is of benefit to states when making their own calculations about military preparedness. There is also, of course, a very compelling humanitarian reason for engaging in arms control: limiting the type and numbers of weapons can mean that if war does break out, deaths and casualties will likely be limited because of undertakings previously made to restrict weapons held by all warring parties. It is this humanitarian consideration which is now, arguably, the most prominent driver of contemporary arms control and disarmament efforts.

Cold War arms control

Arms control found particular resonance during the Cold War, when the world was faced with the very real possibility of war – especially nuclear war – occurring between the major antagonists in that conflict, the US and USSR and their respective allies. The US had exploded the world's first atomic bombs over Japan in 1945; the USSR acquired its nuclear capability in 1949 and an upward spiral of nuclear arms acquisition quickly followed. The intensification of what is sometimes called the 'first nuclear age' was, by the 1960s, seen as causing the need for formal and binding agreements between these states. Because of the hugely destructive nature of nuclear weapons, the US and USSR determined that various agreements must be reached if these states were to prevent a catastrophic war engulfing humankind. The concept of 'mutually assured destruction' – a situation which would occur if nuclear **deterrence** did not work and nuclear war was launched – was unacceptable to those who advocated an urgent reduction in weapons and therefore the likelihood of war.

Notable products of this effort at arms control by the **superpowers** included the Partial Nuclear Test Ban Treaty (1963), the SALT agreements (Strategic Arms Limitation Talks) of 1972 and 1979, the Anti-Ballistic Missile Treaty of 1972, the Intermediate Nuclear Forces (INF) Treaty of 1987 and the START agreements (Strategic Arms Reduction

Figure 12.1   Soviet General Secretary Gorbachev and US President Reagan signing the INF Treaty at the White House, December 1987

Source: US National Archives and Records Administration, Id. 198588, courtesy Ronald Reagan Presidental Library.

Treaties between the US and Soviet Union/Russia), begun in 1991. The earlier treaties did little except to enshrine a balance of terror between the superpowers, rather than bring about any meaningful reductions in the numbers of nuclear weapons. It was only towards the end of the Cold War, and especially with the emphasis put on arms control by the new Soviet leader, Mikhail Gorbachev, that substantial reductions began to occur, under the START process.

These were all bilateral treaties; there was little or no mechanism for states other than the superpowers to have any substantial impact on arms control during the Cold War. There were three notable exceptions to this series of bilateral arrangements. Even though it was an initiative of the two superpowers (and by this time Britain, France and China had also joined the nuclear club) the 1968 Nuclear Non-Proliferation Treaty (NPT) was clearly designed to operate at a global level. It was followed in 1972 by the Biological and Toxin Weapons Convention (BWC), also a multilateral treaty, albeit one that still lacks any effective monitoring and verification abilities. An important arms control achievement relating to conventional weapons, and again a multilateral agreement, the Conventional Forces in Europe (CFE) Treaty emerged in 1990 and was crucial to the winding down of conventional weapons held by the superpowers and their allies in the European arena at the end of the Cold War.

Why is arms control still important in the post-Cold War period?

The ending of the Cold War did not lessen the need for arms control, despite the thaw in relations between the US and Russia. If anything, it highlighted the need to continue to limit or proscribe certain kinds of weapons. It also freed up processes of arms control to include initiatives and participation from a much broader range of states than was possible during the more rigid structure of the Cold War order. The need to continue with arms control is not surprising when we consider that although the superpowers have made dramatic reductions in their nuclear arsenals, there still remain over 22 000 nuclear weapons in the world today (SIPRI 2010), many of them on hair-trigger alert. The vast majority of these weapons are held by the US and Russia. (See Figure 12.2 for details.)

If the continued existence of many thousands of nuclear weapons has been an incentive to continue with arms control measures after the end of the Cold War, so too is the view that certain other kinds of weapons should also be controlled. Thus, we have seen arms control processes extended to other WMDs (chemical weapons), and to certain kinds of conventional weapons such as landmines and cluster munitions, because of their highly destructive and/or indiscriminate nature, as well as to the spread of ballistic missiles and materials and technology that can be used for illicit weapons purposes. The most prominent arms control and disarmament agreements reached since 1990 are listed in Table 12.1.

In addition to these treaties, the post-Cold War era has seen the strengthening of various export-control measures vital to non-proliferation efforts, some of which had been established during the Cold War. These measures include:

- The Zangger Committee, 1974 – Thirty-seven members maintain a list of nuclear-related equipment that may only be exported if International Atomic Energy Agency (IAEA) safeguards are applied to the receiving state or facility.
- The Nuclear Suppliers Group, 1975 – An agreement among forty-six nuclear supplying states to ensure that exports of nuclear materials or technology for peaceful purposes cannot be used for weapons purposes.
- The Australia Group, 1985 – An informal arrangement among forty-one states to restrict the export of materials that might be diverted to the production of chemical or biological weapons.
- The Wassenaar Arrangement on Export Controls for Conventional Arms and Dual-Use Goods, 1996 – The successor to the Coordinating Committee for Multilateral Export Controls (CoCom) arrangement, this forty-member group attempts to regulate materials pertaining to conventional arms.
- The Missile Technology Control Regime, 1987 – An informal agreement between thirty-four states to prevent the proliferation of missile technology; it was supplemented in 2002 by the International Code of Conduct against Missile Proliferation (ICOC) and its membership of 119 states.

One fact becomes evident when we look at the range of agreements reached. Included among them are explicit programs of disarmament. Although arms control and disarmament have in the past been seen as distinct processes – with 'arms control' implying the continued, albeit limited, existence of particular weapons, and 'disarmament' specifying the complete abolition of a particular weapon – it is possible to argue that we are seeing a greater degree of convergence in these ideas. Where arms control was considered to be a discrete process, and one which aims essentially to confirm and, importantly, to *balance* weapons possession between participating states, disarmament was seen as both a process and an end state, the end state being the complete elimination of a type of weapon. Although disarmament acquired something of a bad name during the era of the League of Nations (it clearly was not able to disarm Germany effectively, let alone move the world towards even a vaguely defined sense of general disarmament), more recent attempts at the

Figure 12.2 Estimated nuclear weapons stockpiles

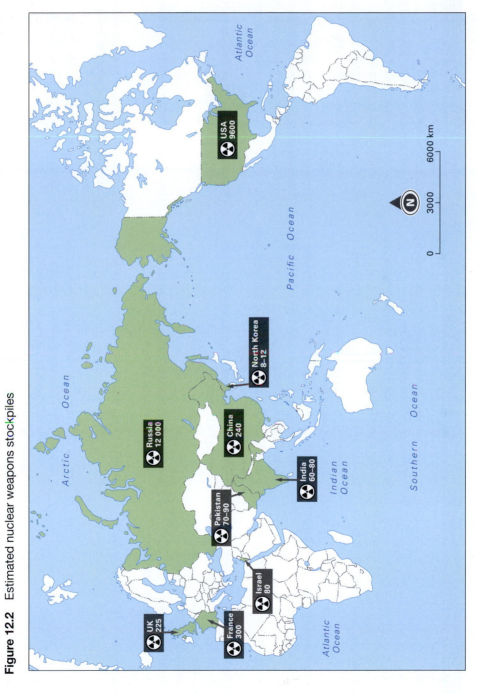

Source: This data is drawn from the *Bulletin of the Atomic Scientists, Global Nuclear Weapon Inventories* and SIPRI 2010. All figures are estimates only.

Table 12.1 Major arms agreements reached since 1990

Name of treaty/convention	Purposes	Relevant difficulties
START (Strategic Arms Reduction Treaty) 1, 1991 START 2, 1993	Restricted the US and Russia to no more than 6000 strategic nuclear warheads each and incorporated unprecedented verification and monitoring controls. To achieve further deep cuts in the strategic nuclear arsenals of the US and Russia.	Represented complex negotiations but resulted in a drastic reduction of Cold War nuclear arsenals. Not ratified by Russia until 2000; Russia then dismissed the treaty in response to US abrogation of the Anti-Ballistic Missile Treaty in 2002. Eventually overtaken by the SORT treaty.
The Chemical Weapons Convention (CWC), 1993	Banned the production, stockpiling and use of chemical weapons; global in scope; included well-developed monitoring and verification procedures.	Signed and ratified by most states, including all large states in the international system; the destruction of stockpiles is slower than envisaged.
The Nuclear Non-Proliferation Treaty (NPT) Review and Extension Conference, 1995	Five-yearly reviews of progress made in non-proliferation and disarmament efforts are routine; this review noted for extending the treaty indefinitely.	Marked by tension between the nuclear weapon states pushing for extension, and some non-nuclear weapon states who preferred extension to be conditional on disarmament by those states with nuclear weapons.
The Comprehensive Test Ban Treaty (CTBT), 1996	To ban the testing of nuclear weapons; part of the agreement to extend the NPT (note above).	Cannot enter into force until ratified by key states, among them the US, China, India and Pakistan.
The Convention on the Prohibition of the Use, Stockpiling, Production and Transfer of Anti-Personnel Mines and on Their Destruction (The Ottawa Landmines Convention), 1997	To ban the production, stockpiling and deployment of anti-personnel landmines.	Initiated by civil society groups and supported by Canada; US, China, Russia have resisted signing.
The SORT Treaty (Strategic Offensive Reductions Treaty, also known as the Moscow Treaty), 2002	To limit the US and Russia to 1700–2200 deployed strategic nuclear weapons each by 2012.	Critics argue that it allowed unlimited numbers of nuclear weapons to be held as non-deployed.
The Convention on Cluster Munitions (Oslo Treaty), 2008	To prohibit the use, transfer and stockpile of cluster bombs.	Led by civil society groups and the state of Norway, but resisted by key states who produce and use cluster bombs (including US, Russia, China, Pakistan and Israel).
New START, 2010.	Replaced the expired START1 Treaty. Limits the US and Russia to no more than 1550 deployed strategic warheads and a maximum of 800 launchers and heavy bombers. It also restores the monitoring and verification provisions that had lapsed with the expiration of START1.	Faced considerable ratification difficulties in the US, but is seen as a key victory in President Obama's campaign to eliminate nuclear weapons.

disarmament of specific kinds of weapons have been successful. We have seen the banning of biological weapons via the BWC, the destruction of a particular kind of weapon – intermediate-range nuclear forces – in the INF Treaty, the banning of chemical weapons with the CWC and, in terms of conventional weapons, the Ottawa Convention banning landmines and the 2008 Convention on Cluster Munitions. These latter treaties were the result of intense lobbying by non-government organisations concerned with the humanitarian effects of landmines. This element – of non-state drivers of arms control and disarmament processes, for humanitarian, rather than strategic, motives – is a noteworthy feature of contemporary international politics and will be examined further in this chapter.

While this growth in the limiting of weapons does not mean that we are inevitably moving towards disarmament at a broad level it does reveal that any differences between arms control and disarmament processes are now arguably more blurred than they once were. No agreement these days attempts to enshrine indefinitely the possession of particular weapons by states. Indeed it is possible to see, at least in some cases, arms control processes as being part of a desired move towards disarmament. The Strategic Offensive Reductions Treaty (SORT, between the US and Russia, 2002) or NewSTART (US–Russia, signed 2010) agreements respectively reduced deployed warheads to 1700–2200 and 1550 each; one can argue that these reductions are an essential step towards the goal of the eventual elimination of nuclear weapons – something the five 'legitimate' nuclear weapon states are obliged to achieve under Article VI of the Non-Proliferation Treaty (NPT). Sometimes, therefore, the terms 'arms control' and 'disarmament' are used interchangeably, even though the degree of overlap between these processes will vary according to the weapon under consideration.

New initiatives in arms control: small arms and conventional weapons

As noted at the opening of this chapter, arms control need not be limited to weapons of mass destruction only, although it is indeed WMDs which have received greatest attention from the international community. One important development in the area of arms control study is that conventional weapons, or rather, limited types of conventional weapons, are also now becoming objects of keen attention. This development should not be overstated; conventional weapons, as their name implies, are seen as 'normal' and it should not be interpreted here that the sovereign right of **nation**-states to possess (and indeed to manufacture and export) arsenals of various (non-WMD) weapons is coming under serious threat at the moment. We have also noted, however, that two very important agreements – the 1997 Ottawa Landmines Convention and the 2008 Convention on Cluster Munitions – banned widely used conventional weapons, a development that would have been considered highly unlikely even as recently as twenty years ago.

This could be considered as the beginning of a trend to scrutinise conventional weapons more closely. Since 1995 we have seen increasing concern about the spread and devastating impact of what are called small arms and light weapons (SALW), weapons which are commonly possessed by all states (see Box 12.1).

The spread of SALW has now come to be recognised as posing a substantial threat to international and domestic security, resulting as it does in the deaths of approximately 300 000 people in conflict zones every year, up to 80 per cent of them women and children. This is evident from numerous studies; see for example the report published by the International Physicians for the Prevention of Nuclear War, in their international campaign to prevent small arms violence (IPPNW 2005).

Perhaps it is SALW which we should consider as being the real weapons of mass destruction, as these are used on a daily basis and with devastating results. They are relatively cheap to purchase, easy to handle and have come to be the weapon of choice in numerous deadly internal conflicts around the world. There are estimated to be around 900 million SALW in circulation at present, serving to fuel and prolong conflict, and to make the processes of conflict-ending and development and reconstruction immensely difficult (Small Arms Survey 2010). The **UN** initiated a Conference on the Illicit Traffic in SALW in 2001, which resulted in a Program of Action to Prevent, Combat, and Eradicate the Illicit Trade in Small Arms and Light Weapons, a process which might be seen as the start of a more concerted restrictive process.

> ## BOX 12.1: TERMINOLOGY
>
> ### Small arms and light weapons
> Small arms are weapons designed for individual use, such as pistols, sub-machine guns, assault rifles and light machine guns. Light weapons are designed to be deployed and used by a crew of two or more, and include grenade launchers, portable anti-aircraft and anti-tank and missile launchers, recoilless rifles and mortars of less than 100 mm calibre. This working definition is taken from the website of the United Kingdom's Foreign and Commonwealth Office, www.fco.gov.uk.

It must be noted, however, that substantial barriers exist to any attempt to regulate conventional weapons generally. These include the fact that a vast global arms trade is perpetuated legally by the most powerful states in the **international system** – including China, France, Germany, Italy, Japan, Russia, the UK and the US – which account for the production of the majority of conventional weapons. The difficulties associated with restricting conventional weapons and sovereign rights were evident at the UN's SALW Conference; it was not able to address the licensed arms trade of these weapons in any form. Still, these attempts are being made. In October 2006, the vast majority of states at the UN voted in favour of a resolution to establish an International Arms Trade Treaty (ATT) that would establish common international standards for the import, export and transfer of conventional weapons – a limited, but nevertheless historic development; 139 states voted in favour of the proposal. The US was alone in voting against it, but the Obama administration has subsequently indicated that it will support negotiations for such a treaty (Amnesty International 2009).

Impediments to progress will remain for some time, but there is no doubt that the issue of arms control has evolved over time to the point where we are now beginning to see questions raised even about the (legal) arms trade and the extent to which the world can continue to tolerate the almost unfettered manufacture and distribution of conventional arms by sovereign states.

One of the reasons for this is that **human rights** and humanitarian issues have come to prominence in international relations in the past two decades and have affected the traditional agendas of politics, security and 'business as usual'. So while the 'human cost' element was raised even in early studies of arms control, we might argue that this issue is only now gaining significant attention in debates on how states may conduct themselves in warfare. The Ottawa Landmines Treaty, one of the first to focus on non-WMDs, was propelled by humanitarian concerns. For the first time, the report of the 2010 Review Conference of the NPT mentioned the link between nuclear weapons and **international humanitarian law** (the law of war). The SALW program of action, together with the proposed new Arms Trade Treaty, attempts to stop arms transfers if they are likely to be used for violations of international human rights or humanitarian law, or if they will negatively affect sustainable development. All this means that we are beginning to see even the normal sovereign 'rights' of states to produce and export conventional weapons coming under an unprecedented level of scrutiny.

Arms control and international relations theory

How might we view the ideas and processes of arms control at a conceptual level? Which theories of international relations can help us to understand the motivations and objectives of those state leaders and, increasingly, civil society groups, who participate in such processes?

Arms control, as noted at the outset of this chapter, is intrinsically tied up with conceptions of international and domestic security and how these might best be achieved. Typically, since 1945, security issues have been dominated by the **realist** school of thought in international relations. With its emphasis on self-help in an anarchical world, the need for military preparedness, and its contention that ongoing security dilemmas will always affect strategic calculations, we might conclude that for realists, arms control and disarmament matter very little. Cooperation with an adversary can never be as effective as unilateral, independent and unfettered action.

We can also see, however, that even for realists, the need to cooperate with an adversary can be overwhelming and can bring security benefits, in terms of stability, transparency and at least an element of predictability. Most early writers on arms control approached the subject from a hawkish perspective, but nevertheless understood the benefits, especially in the nuclear age, of exercising restraint (Bull 1961; Schelling and Halperin 1961). In this sense, we might even argue that such cooperation was an early variant of what has subsequently come to be known as '**common security**', a condition in which states recognise that achieving their own security requires consideration of an adversary's security concerns also (see Palme Commission Report 1982). It can be argued, then, that the practice of arms control and disarmament is actually an area where realists and liberal **institutionalists** can agree. Against such an interpretation, we do have to note the continuing relevance of assertions of independence of action, and the risk of defections from arms control regimes. The approach to arms control taken by the US from the late 1990s up to 2008 reminds us that, ultimately, sovereign rights cannot easily be dismissed in the search for compliance. The US, in this period, withdrew from a major arms control treaty (the 1972 ABM Treaty) and refused to sign or **ratify** various other significant treaties. Other large states occasionally act in a similar way (China, for instance, has not ratified the CTBT) but it has been the US which has been the most visible actor resisting the growing momentum for controlling weapons.

Yet while these independent or rejectionist approaches might remind us of the anarchical structure of our world, it is also important to note that the vast majority of states have indeed signed up to, and abide by, a wide range of arms control agreements. Here we might apply a **liberal**, and especially a liberal-institutional, conception of world politics, whereby there is a recognition that while conflict might be a permanent feature of our landscape, nevertheless it can be managed by confidence-building measures, recognition of human rights, cooperative agreements, and the institutionalisation of these through **international law** and organisations. Related here is the **English School** of international relations **theory** that posits an **international society** bound together by a raft of rules and **norms** that together make for a functioning and orderly international system. The co-chair of the International Commission on Nuclear Nonproliferation and Disarmament has aligned himself with such a perspective, even going so far as to label the contribution of states such as Australia to disarmament treaties as 'good international citizenship' (Hanson 2005). Of further interest are the questions posed by **constructivists**, who explore the origins and development of ideas and norms in international relations. They might well ask questions such as: how has the nuclear taboo arisen? (Tannenwald 1999); or, why is it that humanitarian issues and legal norms are increasingly imposing themselves onto strategic calculations? Importantly here, we can see that ideas about legitimacy, the moral responsibility of the state and duties to **humanitarianism** are changing and that there is no longer an *a priori* 'right' of states to arm themselves with particular weapons or to engage in unrestricted warfare.

Nuclear weapons: a special case?

Of all the arms control regimes discussed here, the most prominent (and arguably the most shaky) in international relations is that of nuclear weapons. This regime has as its cornerstone the Nuclear Non-Proliferation Treaty of 1968 (NPT). This treaty is reinforced by a number of related mechanisms and arms control measures, particularly the International Atomic Energy Agency (IAEA). The IAEA oversees monitoring and verification of compliance with the NPT, especially through its enhanced safeguards or 'Additional Protocol' programs (although it is unable to monitor or verify activities of the five established nuclear weapon states), the various mechanisms listed above designed to curb the illicit transfer of nuclear materials and technology, and the creation of nuclear weapon-free zones in various parts of the world.

While the world has not seen the military use of nuclear weapons since they were first used in 1945, there is a fear that they will be used in the future, either deliberately or inadvertently by states which possess them, or, in line with recent concerns, by **terrorists** or other sub-state groups. The overwhelming concern that is commonly portrayed is the need to prevent further states and terrorist groups from acquiring these weapons. In other words, the focus is very much on non-proliferation. For others, however, while remaining concerned about proliferation, a concomitant need is to hasten the elimination of nuclear weapons altogether – that is, to move towards full nuclear disarmament.

The NPT was essentially a bargain between the nuclear weapon states (NWS) and the non-nuclear weapon states (NNWS): in exchange for the latter promising not to develop or acquire nuclear weapons, the former – the 'acknowledged' nuclear weapon states of the US, Russia, Britain, France and China – have promised to eliminate their nuclear arsenals (although there is no date specified for this) and to assist the NNWS with the transfer and use of nuclear materials and technology for peaceful purposes. These three elements: non-proliferation, disarmament, and the peaceful use of nuclear technology, make up what are known as the three 'pillars' of the NPT.

All three pillars are now under unprecedented levels of stress. Non-proliferation, while it has been largely successful in that some 183 states have chosen not to acquire nuclear weapons, is now seen to be insufficiently strong against the desire of some states to acquire nuclear weapons. In addition to the fact that India, Pakistan and Israel hold nuclear weapons (and refuse to sign up to the NPT regime) there has been: the discovery in 1991 of the beginnings of a nuclear weapon program in Iraq; a similar program in Libya, now given up by the Gaddafi regime; the detection in 2004 of the **A. Q. Khan network** which had illegally provided nuclear assistance to various states; the testing in 2006 and again in 2009 of a nuclear device by North Korea, together with the seemingly intractable tensions on the Korean peninsula; and ongoing grave suspicions about the nuclear intentions of Iran which, while it has not rejected the NPT, has nevertheless enriched uranium in a covert manner.

Disarmament remains a slow and tenuous process, as the NWS resist implementing the promise of elimination made by them under Article VI of the NPT and which they reiterated 'unequivocally' at the 2000 NPT Review Conference. While the numbers of nuclear weapons have dropped considerably from the height of the Cold War, and the New START agreement pursued by US president Obama advances this even more, it seems clear that these privileged five states will not move quickly towards the full elimination of their nuclear weapons. The problem here, as many observe (Canberra Commission 1996), is that as long as some states hold nuclear weapons, this will inevitably be an incentive for others to acquire them.

Disarmament and international security   Sergio Duarte

On 5 April 2009, US President Barack Obama addressed a large crowd in Prague and declared: 'I state clearly and with conviction America's commitment to seek the peace and security of a world without nuclear weapons.' Six months later, the Norwegian Nobel Committee announced that he had won the 2009 Nobel Peace Prize. Its news release explained: 'The Committee has attached special importance to Obama's vision of and work for a world without nuclear weapons.'

Notice that President Obama did not say that he was seeking to establish international peace and security *so that* nuclear disarmament might occur. He was instead making the point that there were concrete security benefits to be obtained from the achievement of disarmament. This difference is significant, because progress in nuclear disarmament has long been frustrated by various conditions that have been prescribed by national leaders or arms control experts from states that possess such weapons or that belong to nuclear alliances.

I have worked on disarmament for almost half a century and must say that Alva Myrdal got it right in 1976 when she wrote *The game of disarmament*, which described how nuclear disarmament has been postponed indefinitely through this very old game of linkage politics. This result has followed from an insistence on various preconditions that must be achieved to make disarmament possible. Some commentators say: we must first achieve world peace. Others say: we must first solve the problem of war. Indeed, an entire cascade of such arguments is easy to observe: we must first eliminate all proliferation risks from all types of weapons of mass destruction; we must first reduce to zero all risks of terrorism involving such weapons; we must first settle all regional disputes; and we must first solve even the wider problem of armed conflict itself. And the conditions go on and on, *ad infinitum*.

Not surprisingly, in light of this game, more than 20 000 nuclear weapons still reportedly exist, fully forty years after the Nuclear Non-Proliferation Treaty (NPT) committed its parties to 'negotiations in good faith' on nuclear disarmament. Such negotiations have not occurred, and not one nuclear warhead has been physically destroyed as a result of a treaty commitment. So the weapons persist, along with the endlessly proliferating preconditions for disarmament.

Some of these conditions are identified more clearly than others. On 31 January 1992, at its first summit meeting ever, the UN Security Council reaffirmed 'the crucial contribution which progress in these areas [disarmament, arms control and non-proliferation] can make to the maintenance of international peace and security'. Yet on 24 September 2009, the Security Council held its first summit meeting specifically on disarmament issues and adopted Resolution 1887; its preamble stated that the Council was '*resolving* to seek a safer world for all and to create the conditions for a world without nuclear weapons'. In short, the 1992 statement recognised that security was a beneficiary of disarmament, not a precondition for it to occur, as suggested in the 2009 resolution.

For its part, the General Assembly has long emphasised the contributions of nuclear disarmament to international peace and security. The preamble to the Final Document of the General Assembly's first Special Session on disarmament stated in 1978 that the General Assembly was '*convinced* that disarmament and arms limitation, particularly in the nuclear field, are essential for the prevention of the danger of nuclear war and the strengthening of international peace and security and for the economic and social advancement of all peoples'.

On 26 October 2010, the First Committee adopted a resolution on 'united action towards the total elimination of nuclear weapons', with its preamble '*recalling* the need for all States to take further practical steps and effective measures towards the total elimination of nuclear weapons, with a view to achieving a peaceful and secure world free of nuclear weapons, and in this regard confirming the determination of Member States to take united action'. This was approved by an overwhelming majority, with the DPRK (North Korea) as the only dissenting vote.

The case for nuclear disarmament relates largely to its benefits in preventing the use of such weapons. This was emphasised in the consensus Final Document of the 2000 NPT Review Conference, which stated that the Conference '*reaffirms* that the total elimination of nuclear weapons is the only absolute guarantee against the use or threat of use of nuclear weapons'.

The alternative ways of 'preventing use' – such as by nuclear deterrence, the balance of power, threats of preemption or first-use, missile defence, and other such measures – have long been viewed with great scepticism in the world community, especially at the UN, because of the risks associated with each approach and the lack of any guarantees of their effectiveness. Accidents, miscalculations and wilful use remain real threats with each of these alternatives – and the mere absence of a nuclear war does not prove that they have worked.

Instead, the world is not only united on the basic goal of eliminating nuclear weapons, but has also agreed on certain multilateral criteria that must be satisfied in achieving it. These include: *transparency* of warheads, fissile material and delivery systems records; the *verification* and *irreversibility* of disarmament commitments; the *binding* nature of those commitments; and the need for *universal* adherence. These are not conditions, but standards to use in identifying genuine progress in achieving disarmament.

Thus, the world has come to support nuclear disarmament not as a mere hope or dream. By satisfying these rigorous standards, disarmament has enormous contributions to make in strengthening international peace and security. It has received this support not simply because it is morally correct, but also because it is more effective in eliminating nuclear-weapon risks than any other option. In short, it is the right thing to do, and it works.

Sergio Duarte is the United Nations High Representative for Disarmament. He is a career diplomat and holds the rank of Ambassador in the Brazilian Foreign Service, where he has served for 48 years, including appointments as Ambassador to Nicaragua, Canada, China and Austria. He has served as Chairman of the Board of Governors of the IAEA, and was President of the Seventh Review Conference of the Parties to the Treaty on the Non-Proliferation of Nuclear Weapons in 2005.

The third pillar of the NPT, the use of nuclear technology for peaceful purposes, is also undergoing stress as current and widespread concerns about energy resources propel more states to contemplate the use of nuclear energy. Apart from concerns about the safety of such energy programs, there are fears that recourse to this third pillar – which lacks adequate international safeguards and controls – will make nuclear weapons proliferation easier for a growing number of states.

The relatively weak nature of the NPT is a primary concern for advocates of arms control and disarmament. Moreover, the conflation, after 11 September 2001, of the 'war on terror' with an aggressive counterproliferation policy by the US, and that state's allegations of WMDs in Iraq as a reason for invading and occupying that country in 2003, have complicated and made an already difficult task – that of upholding non-proliferation and moving towards disarmament – harder than ever before.

All this sits against a background of long-standing calls for the nuclear weapon states to eliminate their arsenals (Blackaby and Milne 2000; Canberra Commission 1996). The reasoning here is compelling: nuclear weapons have little or no utility in resolving modern conflicts, and unless the NWS are seen to be practising the nuclear abstinence that they insist others adopt, it is hard to persuade would-be nuclear proliferators to desist (Hanson 2002). Additionally, the reasoning goes, if chemical and biological weapons have been banned – a ban accepted by all the NWS – why is it that the third kind of WMDs, nuclear weapons, remain permitted under international law, and then only to a select group of states? To complicate matters further, even those states once condemned for joining the nuclear 'club' in 1998, India and Pakistan, are now cultivated as strong allies by the US in its war against terrorism. This has been compounded recently by the US, which now assists India's civilian nuclear program, despite the fact that India has never signed the NPT. Thus an environment of deep inequality in international security continues (Perkovich 2005).

Figure 12.3   Nuclear weapon test Romeo on Bikini Atoll, March 1954

Source: US Department of Energy/NNSA Photolibrary.

Initiatives to strengthen the nuclear non-proliferation regime

Most states, however, are not ready to give up on the nuclear non-proliferation regime. Among these are many small states and 'middle powers' such as Australia, Japan, Norway and New Zealand, which have developed strong records in promoting arms control and disarmament, and which can be termed 'advocacy states' (Hanson 2010). This is notwithstanding any close association with their main ally, the US, which, at least during the George W. Bush years, moved away from cooperative arms control and disarmament measures.

A key initiative to promote disarmament was the Australian government's convening of the Canberra Commission to consider the utility of nuclear weapons and to propose a program for the elimination of these weapons. The Commission released its report in 1996, and remains a key reference point in the ongoing campaign for elimination. Importantly, the Commission included prominent military and political leaders, all of whom lent their weight to calls for a phased and balanced program of disarmament by the nuclear weapon states. Such calls remain strong today and have been recently echoed even by notable conservatives within the US such as Henry Kissinger (Shultz et al. 2007). Recent initiatives reiterate these calls, especially the International Commission on Nuclear Nonproliferation and Disarmament (ICNND), co-chaired by Australia and Japan, and the Norwegian government's Seven Nation Initiative, which aims to foster practical action towards a nuclear weapon-free world. All these 'advocacy states' were active in the landmark Review Conference of the NPT in May 2010, at which small but significant progress was made towards the long-term goal of elimination of nuclear weapons. Additionally, most states have readily embraced UN Security Council Resolution 1540, which tightens the controls on exports related to WMD manufacture.

Conclusion

This chapter has provided a general overview of arms control and disarmament practices and the ideas that inform these, and has focused on the problems facing the nuclear non-proliferation regime in particular. It noted that arms control, which during the Cold War primarily involved only two states and focused on WMD issues, has broadened out subsequently to involve a much larger number of actors, including on occasion **non-government organisations**, and has also moved to regulate certain conventional weapons.

This conclusion suggests that while there remain some substantial obstacles to further advancing arms control and disarmament, much is continuing in this field and the majority of states are taking their obligations seriously and accepting new controls on weapons proliferation, such as the program on small arms and light weapons, UN Resolution 1540, and the Arms Trade Treaty. While much will depend on the activities of the nuclear weapon states, when we calculate the probabilities of disarmament or further nuclear proliferation we can take some heart from the fact that the majority of states in our **international society** readily embrace existing and new measures designed to reduce the likelihood of war and to protect human life. This broad and habit-forming culture of compliance cannot guarantee an absence of defections, but neither should its **normative** and cumulative power be underestimated.

QUESTIONS

1. How important is the process of arms control for mitigating the security dilemma?
2. In what ways do contemporary arms control and disarmament efforts differ from the processes witnessed during the Cold War era?
3. If the possession and use of chemical and biological weapons have been legally banned, why hasn't such a ban extended to nuclear weapons?
4. Can the nuclear non-proliferation regime survive intact if Article VI, requiring the nuclear weapon states to disarm, remains unfulfilled?
5. Is it correct to say that humanitarian and legal factors are overtaking factors of strategy in the contemporary process of controlling arms?

FURTHER READING

Burns, Richard Dean 2009, *The evolution of arms control: from antiquity to the nuclear age*, Praeger. Useful overview of the historical antecedents which inform current thinking on arms control; also examines many oft-neglected background issues such as processes of demilitarisation, attempts to outlaw war and the regulation of arms manufacturing industries.

Cirincione, Joseph, John B. Wolfsthal and Miriam Rajkumar 2005, *Deadly arsenals: nuclear, biological and chemical threats*, 2nd edn, Washington DC: Carnegie Endowment for International Peace. Concise and useful overview of WMDs, including state possessors, examples of successes in non-proliferation, and challenges still facing the non-proliferation regime.

International Commission on Nuclear Non-Proliferation and Disarmament 2009, *Eliminating nuclear threats: a practical agenda for global policymakers*, Report of the International Commission on Nuclear Nonproliferation and Disarmament, www.icnnd.org/Reference/reports/ent/default.htm. Assesses the threat of nuclear catastrophe and proposes a number of short- and medium-term practical steps governments can take to reduce the dangers of accidental or deliberate nuclear weapon use.

Larsen, Jeffrey A. and Wirtz, James J. (eds) 2009, *Arms control and cooperative security*, Boulder: Lynne Rienner Publishers. Edited collection examining arms control in all its aspects, including useful chapters on conventional weapons.

Stockholm International Peace Research Institute (SIPRI) 2006, *The SIPRI yearbook: armaments, disarmaments and international security*, Oxford: Oxford University Press. Excellent resource, updated annually, reviewing global and regional security developments and listing armaments holdings of key states.

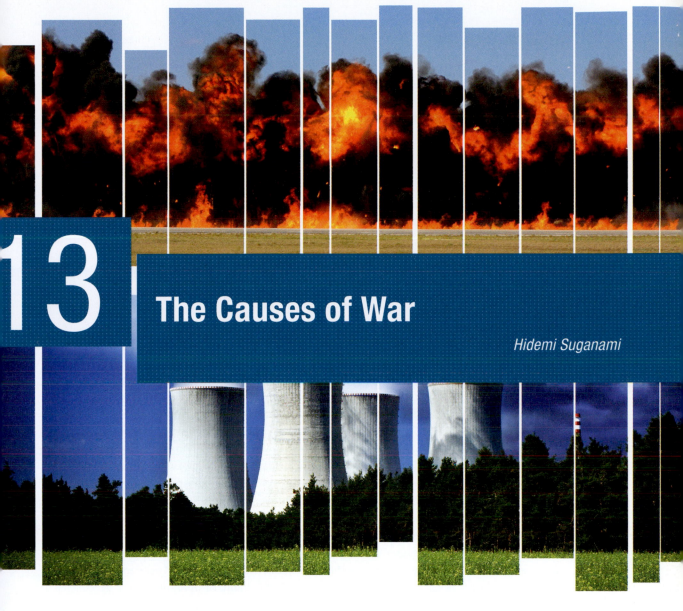

13

The Causes of War

Hidemi Suganami

Introduction	190
War, sovereignty and sociability	191
Necessary causes of war?	193
Regular causal paths to war?	194
Contributory causes of war	194
Conclusion	197
Questions	198
Further reading	198

Introduction

This chapter examines what causes **war**, focusing on war, or armed conflict, between **sovereign states**. The main part of this chapter is divided into the following four sections: 'War, sovereignty and sociability', 'Necessary causes of war?', 'Regular causal paths to war?', and 'Contributory causes of war'. The last of these sections comprises three subsections, dealing with 'Chance occurrences', 'War-conducive mechanisms' and 'Key actions and inactions', which are three key ingredients of war-causation, combining in a variety of ways to produce concrete instances of war.

It should be noted at the outset that war has not always been regarded as a problem requiring serious scholarly attention to its causes. Strange or outrageous though it may seem, some people have held a benign, or positive, view of war. But especially through the experience of World War I, a contrary view which sees war in a negative way has become more dominant. Our interest in the causes of war, and the conditions of peace, is a reflection of this broad shift in our attitude towards war (Suganami 1996: 189–90). Since this shift was also a key factor in the formation of International Relations (IR) as an academic **discipline**, it is unsurprising to find that inquiry into the causes of war has been a traditional concern of that subject (see Introduction).

Perhaps contrary to a general impression, however, war is relatively uncommon. Most states live in peace, or are not at war, with most other states most of the time. Still, when a war comes, its impact is massive in practically all cases. It is the intensely negative and often long-lasting consequences of war in the contemporary world that sustains our interest in the search for its causes (Levy and Thompson 2010: 56).

Scholarly inquiries into the causes of war, however, have not produced a straightforward answer. This is partly because resort to war involves human decisions; people react in different ways to similar circumstances and in similar ways to different circumstances. Given two similar and seemingly war-prone circumstances, war may follow from both, from one but not the other, or from neither.

Some researchers therefore suppose that there will not be any regular causal paths to war but only many different ones, and specialise in the study of the origins of particular wars. But others disagree and continue to explore regular patterns in the ways war comes about. Either way, some ingredients of particular paths to war may, under some general descriptions, reappear here and there, individually or in combination, in this order or that. Such items may be called war's contributory causes, some perhaps more common than others. There is also a possibility, though perhaps only a remote possibility, that one or more of these reappearing factors are contributory in a very strong sense – that is, indispensable. Such factors, if they were to be found, would count as war's necessary causes. It is against this background of diverse scholarly efforts that this chapter examines, in turn, war's necessary causes, regular causal paths, and contributory causes.

Before that, however, it is necessary to examine one very common line of thinking about what causes war. This is the oft-heard claim that the causes of war are not far to seek; we already know, or it is quite obvious that given state **sovereignty** and/or the selfish and aggressive nature of human beings war is bound to happen, inevitable, or not possible to rule out. According to this way of thinking, the causes of actual wars, whether case by case or in relation to some overall patterns, will require detailed historical or comparative investigations, but such 'obvious' linkages as exist between the nature of the state or the nature of 'man' on the one hand, and war on the other, are graspable straight away. However, it is this apparent graspability that gets in the way of more clear-headed thinking about the conditions under which war is 'not possible to rule out'.

War, sovereignty and sociability

Contrary to a popular view, a 'sovereign' state is not one that towers above other 'less sovereign' states in the world, like the US in the post-**Cold War** era; it is one of more than 190 equally sovereign political communities. By this is meant that there are so many 'constitutionally independent' political communities in the world which are not part of any other such political communities (A. James 1986) (see Chapter 9). Some thinkers suggest that a sovereign state has an inherent right to resort to war at will, that being a sovereign state in part means it has such a right. Clearly, however, there is no necessary connection between 'being a constitutionally independent state' and 'having a right to resort to war at will' in the way in which, for example, the idea of 'being a parent' contains that of 'having a child'.

Of course, 'state sovereignty' could be understood to imply a supreme authority to decide – without being subjected to any other authorities – what course of action to take. If so, a freedom to resort to war at will would seem to be a necessary ingredient of 'state sovereignty'. Such a freedom was indeed what European sovereign states considered themselves to enjoy by their very nature and standing until about the time of World War I. However, we no longer live in a world where sovereign states have an unconstrained freedom to resort to arms. Such a once supposedly inalienable freedom has been quite substantially curtailed by the development of **international law** through the establishment of the League of Nations and, subsequently, the **United Nations (UN)**.

Nevertheless, most of us, other than absolute pacifists, will consider a sovereign state as a distinct type of community one of whose functions is to resort to force *under some circumstances*. There is then an undeniable connection, in our minds, between a country's sovereign statehood and war – a kind of linkage which, significantly, we do not normally see between, say, a 'province' (contained in, and subordinate to, a constitutionally independent country) and war.

Under what circumstances we consider it to be the sovereign state's function to resort to force will depend on what **theories** of international politics we subscribe to. By 'theories of international politics', I mean, for example, Martin Ceadel's (1987) five types of thinking about peace and war: militarism, crusading, defencism, pacific-ism and pacifism. Martin Wight's (1991) traditions of international theory – **realism**, **rationalism**, **revolutionism** and inverted revolutionism – are similar.

Ceadel's 'pacifism' and Wight's 'inverted revolutionism' correspond to 'absolute pacifism', which sees *no* circumstances that justify war. By contrast, 'militarism' in Ceadel's classification, or an extreme form of 'realism' in Wight's, glorifies war. Between these two extremes, Ceadel's 'crusading' and Wight's 'revolutionism' consider war justifiable as a means to bring about a revolutionary change to the world, whereas Ceadel's 'pacific-ism' and 'defencism' broadly correspond to Wight's 'rationalism' and gentler form of 'realism', for which war is an appropriate means with which to maintain international order or protect **national interests**.

Which type of thinking about war and peace prevails within a society of sovereign states is a crucial factor which shapes the conditions of life in that society and, in particular, that society's war-proneness. What kinds of issue are deemed to be worth resorting to war for is an aspect of this (Luard 1986; Wendt 1999; Lebow 2008). These observations are vital in understanding the causes of war and the conditions of peace – for if a community of states emerges where resort to war is effectively ruled out as a means of solving their differences, war will become obsolete there. In IR, such a community is called a 'pluralistic security community' – 'pluralistic' because it comprises a number of sovereign states and '**security community**' because there is no threat of war inside it (Deutsch et al. 1957). The US, Canada and Britain form such a community, as do Norway, Sweden and Finland.

Even outside such communities, the dominant idea about state sovereignty and its relation to war has changed considerably over the past 100 years and gradually reduced the freedom of sovereign states to resort to war. However, the post-September 11 US practice of preventive war is one illustration of the precariousness of this evolving process, just as the al-Qaeda attacks were an acute reminder that the legal control of the use of force by sovereign states is not an adequate response to violent challenges facing the world (see Box 13.1 and Chapter 15).

BOX 13.1: DISCUSSION POINTS

Self-defence, preemptive strikes and preventive wars

UN members have the right of individual or collective *self-defence* 'if an armed attack occurs' (Art. 51). This is interpreted by some to mean that a target state is permitted to resort to *a preemptive strike* where an attack is imminent. However, A's war against B is said to be *preventive* typically if A attacks B, thinking that war with B is inevitable in the near future and that it is better to start a war earlier than later because B's military power is increasing. Removing the sources of future threat to a country's security, as in the US/UK war against Saddam Hussein's Iraq (2003), may be 'preventive' but not 'preemptive'.

If war is no longer sovereign states' prerogative in their foreign affairs, neither is it a phenomenon only observable in their external relationships. There are wars inside what was once a functioning sovereign state – between the existing regime and rebel groups, for example, in Afghanistan, or between the government forces and secessionist groups – the latter sometimes gaining independence as did, for example, Bangladesh from Pakistan in 1971. There are also wars between all kinds of warring factions encompassing those inside and outside a country in a complex pattern, as in the Bosnian war (Kaldor 2006) (see Chapter 14).

Wars, however, are always fought between organised social groups. Fights between individuals do not constitute what we normally mean by 'war'. It is not impermissible, of course, to define 'war' to include conflict between individuals. There is a significant difference, however, between 'fights' between individuals and 'wars' between societies.

Conflict between societies requires an ability and inclination to form social groups, each with a requisite degree of solidarity to make it possible for its members to fight for their respective groups. Those who wish to reserve the term 'war' specifically to denote violent inter-group conflicts are attaching special importance to this, which is a significant move. It makes us aware that for 'war' to occur, it is not enough for human beings to have a capacity to inflict lethal violence upon one another; it is also necessary that they distinguish between 'us' and 'them' in some way and that they have a capacity for a considerable degree of cooperation, even altruism, inside their respective social groups. We often consider war as a manifestation of our animalistic aggressiveness or selfish human nature. However, animals fight but do not make war (Huntington 1989) and much selflessness is exhibited within social groups at war. War occurs not because human beings are selfish and aggressive. It does so because they are sociable, capable of living in organised societies – though not, or not yet, so overwhelmingly sociable as to form a universal community of humankind without any deep divisions. This is the rationale behind reserving the term 'war' to denote an armed conflict between social groups and, in particular, sovereign states and similar entities. I should add here that the existence of pluralistic security communities, mentioned earlier, is especially noteworthy because it demonstrates the possibility of a new form of sociability in the world of sovereign states.

Necessary causes of war?

As noted earlier, IR scholars investigating 'the causes of war' have searched for 'necessary causes of war', 'regular causal paths to war', and 'contributory causes of war'. A search for war's necessary causes has not produced very good answers, however.

Perhaps this is not surprising. For some item to be war's *necessary* cause, it is not enough that, in its absence, war does not happen. We must have a good reason to believe that war could not happen in its absence. This feature of a necessary cause is clear when we consider a familiar case. The presence of oxygen is a necessary cause of a fire; in its absence, a fire does not, and could not, occur because a fire is a form of 'oxidisation'.

IR specialists now broadly agree that there has not been any clear case of war between uncontentiously **liberal** democratic states (see Chapter 3). But 'democratic **peace**' is much discussed precisely because it is an exception that proves the rule – that there are no rules to speak of in this area (Levy and Thomson 2010: 104–8, 124, n. 38). What the researchers have established, in any case, is the fact that there has not been any clear case of war between well-established **democracies** so far. We may find some reasons to suppose that between such entities war would be rare. But there is no plausible reason why war between such entities is impossible – like a fire without oxygen. The absence of democracy from at least one of the two parties cannot therefore be treated as a necessary cause of war.

Nevertheless, erratic belligerency is not a very likely feature of foreign relations among democracies for a number of reasons: institutional and normative constraints, mutual trust reinforced by the record of unbroken peace, **alliance** against common undemocratic enemies, commercial **interdependence**, among others (Levy and Thomson 2010: 108–17). One or more of these factors, perhaps in combination with some others, may explain some instances of peace between some democratic countries.

Erratic belligerency, or a trigger-happy attitude, is certainly not a necessary cause of war. But it is fairly common to suppose that war begins because both parties consider they have a good chance of winning (Blainey 1988). Optimism for victory, however, is not a necessary cause of war. A country may go to war realising that the chances of victory are slim, as did Japan against the US in 1941 (Sagan 1989). As this case illustrates, it is enough for a war-initiator to calculate that, even though the chances of victory are small, it is better to fight now because what fighting now can probably bring is better than almost certain and unacceptable consequences of not fighting.

Sheer unwillingness to accept what we see as the iniquitous conditions which our opponents have imposed on us goes a long way towards making us fight. In such circumstances we might attack them, calculating, or hoping, that we may be able to harm them sufficiently to gain some concessions from them. Egypt did this to Israel in the 1973 October War, which, through a remarkable turn of events, led to the Egyptian-Israeli Peace Treaty of 1977.

Regular causal paths to war?

War comes about in many ways. But there are some familiar ways in which couples come to break up or children become delinquent, and similarly there may be some common ways in which countries come to fight. Paul Senese and John Vasquez (2008) have tried to articulate one such path. This comprises a number of steps. The presence of a dispute between two states roughly equal in power increases the probability of war between them, especially if it is a territorial dispute. A territorial dispute tends to breed other territorial disputes and a crisis more crises. Responding to the deteriorating conditions by alliance formation further increases the probability of war. Arms races also increase the probability of war, as does a history of rivalry.

However, it is important to see Vasquez and Senese's 'steps to war' for what they are. Even though the impact of each step along the path may cumulatively increase the probability of war at the end, the path itself is one of many possible routes. If those things which they present as the signs of war do occur, war will be a likely outcome. But this does not necessarily mean that most actual wars have come about, or will do so in the future, along the path they have constructed.

The causal path they have constructed is precisely that – constructed by them. In essence, it is in the nature of a *cautionary tale*; it is a model causal path whose steps recur here and there, individually or in combination, in this order or that in various actual paths to war. But actual causal paths to war contain a wider variety of steps, or contributory causes, than are included in Senese and Vasquez's model. There are some more cautionary tales to tell.

Contributory causes of war

Many factors contribute to war; they are either 'things that happen' or 'things that are done'. 'Things that happen' may occur by chance or follow automatically as the conditions are ripe and nothing is stopping them. When we add 'things that are done' to these two, we have a set of three types of contributory cause regarding war: chance occurrences directing the sequence of events towards war; war-conducive mechanisms; and actions and inactions of certain key actors contributing to the coming of a war (Box 13.2).

BOX 13.2: DISCUSSION POINTS

Three kinds of contributory causes concerning war

1. Chance coincidences, directing the sequence of events towards war
2. War-conducive mechanisms
3. War-conducive actions and inactions of the key participants.

Chance occurrences

Things that happen by chance always involve at least two things occurring at the same time and perhaps in the same place. One of the best-known cases of chance occurrence contributing to war is seen in the June 1914 assassination of Archduke Ferdinand, heir to the Austrian throne, in Sarajevo by a Serbian nationalist, Princip, opposed to Austria's takeover of Bosnia. Princip's presence in Sarajevo at that time was of course no coincidence; he went there with intent to harm the Archduke. But the circumstances were such that Princip would most likely have failed if Ferdinand's car, driving fast, had not had to stop. The chauffeur, having taken a wrong turn, was told to halt, back up, and get back on course. And this occurred yards away from where Princip happened to be, enabling him to shoot Ferdinand and his wife at point-blank range.

The incident is commonly characterised as a spark that ignited the fire, it being generally understood that without the highly inflammable circumstances of Europe and of its major powers around that time, World War I would not have broken out. But without that particular spark no fire would have been ignited then, and it is not easy to imagine how, through another causal path, a war like World War I would have come about. It is conceivable for the system to have survived without a major war for some time (Lebow 2010: ch. 3).

How much weight the whole incident, and the chance factor, had as a cause of the war is a matter of interpretation. If you are in search of a *common* contributory cause of large-scale wars involving several **great powers**, the assassination of a foreign dignitary will not score high on the list. You may, accordingly, not put much causal weight on Ferdinand's assassination, or on the chance which enabled it, in your explanation of this particular war; you may wish to highlight those other features of the causal process which are more likely to be replicated elsewhere.

It is undeniable, however, that the assassination, and the chance that enabled it, played an indispensable causal role in the particular sequence of events that led to the Austrian declaration of war on Serbia – which, in the circumstances, escalated to what we now call World War I and without which such a war might not have come about after all. A chance factor therefore can be said to have played a significant contributory causal role in relation to World War I.

War-conducive mechanisms

A 'mechanism' is said to be in operation in a literal sense when a mechanical device functions as designed and, by extension, when something, not itself a machine, works in a machine-like manner without anyone bringing about the outcome by design. The latter occurs when, for example, the workings of our body or mind shape our behaviour, or the structural characteristics of our society encourage a particular pattern of thought and behaviour to become dominant, or our actions lead to unintended consequences as we interact with others within a particular social structure.

Such mechanisms work in all directions, some reinforcing and some counteracting one another, and in situations where chance happenings and human actions intervene, so that the operation of mechanisms does not necessarily lead to any specific outcomes. It is difficult to ascertain, therefore, that a particular mechanism exists, and was at work, in a given case.

Suppose that two democratic states A and B have not engaged in war for decades. However, inasmuch as they live under '**anarchy**' – without any overarching sovereign authority above them – we may expect them to have been subjected to war-conducive mechanisms associated with an 'anarchical' **international system**: the structural fact that there is no other entity that can be trusted to help them when they are under attack encourages them to adopt a worst-case scenario, strengthen their military capabilities, engage in an arms race, adopt a preventive stance against potential sources of future threat, and respond preemptively against an imminent threat (Waltz 1959). Yet there may also be a variety of peace-conducive mechanisms at work due, among other things, to their shared democracy.

How do we know, then, which of the two sets of mechanisms is going to be stronger in the A–B relations? The answer may be that we do not know until we know the outcome. In this case, the outcome is decades of peace, so we may work backwards from that to suggest that peace-conducive mechanisms associated with shared democracy must have prevailed. But how do we know that such mechanisms operated at all in this instance? The only way is to trace how A and B have behaved towards each other and see if there is any evidence to support a hypothesis that certain peace-conducive mechanisms associated with shared democracy were at work in their interactions.

Similarly, a detailed reconstruction seems to be a way towards supporting a hypothesis that there were certain causal mechanisms in operation in the collision course which led to a particular outbreak of war. For example, there is a much-discussed psychological mechanism called the 'groupthink syndrome': 'a concurrence-seeking tendency which can increase resistance to policy change through illusion of unanimity and invulnerability, moral certainty, self-censorship, and collective rationalization' (Levy 1986: 214). Such a mechanism may reduce decision-makers' flexibility in a crisis where much innovative thinking is required to avert a war. But whether such a psychological mechanism really worked in a given case is a question concerning which we can only gain some limited insight through a close study of the decision-making process itself.

However, it is one thing to try to reconstruct the details of a particular causal path that led to a war; it is another to be made aware of a wide variety of causal mechanisms which have potential to work as steps to war. IR's search for the causes of war, as surveyed expertly in Levy and Thomson (2010), has suggested a wide range of such mechanistic steps. These include mechanisms rooted in the structural characteristics of a given type of international system or **bilateral** relations, those stemming from the governmental and social structures of certain kinds of states, and individual and group psychological mechanisms.

However, none of these war-conducive mechanisms single-handedly explains the phenomenon of war. These mechanisms are among war's many contributory causes, neither necessary, nor sufficient by themselves, to bring about a war.

Key actions and inactions

War typically requires one party (A) to decide to force upon the other (B) a choice between immediate surrender and war, and the other party (B) to choose not to surrender immediately without a fight. A may take that decision in a number of different ways. For example, it might resort to war in a premeditated and aggressive manner against a totally innocent victim B. Or A's decision to go to war against B may be an act of exasperation against B's aggressive acts.

The first kind of case is illustrated by Germany's invasion of Belgium at the beginning of World War I and the second by the 1991 punitive war by the US-led coalition against Iraq's invasion of Kuwait. Between these two poles are cases of preventive war: for example, Pakistan's war against India in 1965, and more recently the US/UK-led war against Saddam Hussein's Iraq.

Long-premeditated aggressive wars, however, are relatively rare and the decision to resort to war usually comes at the end of a meandering process of interactions between the countries involved. Such interactions include a number of typically war-conducive acts and these, too, form important *steps to war*. Among them are 'insensitive acts', 'reckless acts', and 'acts of contributory negligence'.

A's act is 'insensitive' in relation to B when it does not realise the extent to which what it is doing is seen by B to be offensive. Argentina's 1982 invasion of the Malvinas/Falkland Islands is an archetypal example: its leaders appear to have supposed that this would force the British government to undertake a negotiated settlement over the disputed territories rather than fight back to repossess them.

A 'reckless act' is committed when A realises that B may respond by force to the course of action it is about to undertake but goes ahead with it even though it is clearly aware that B's military intervention would bring a serious disaster to A. Hitler's 1939 invasion of Poland, which forced Britain to declare war on Germany, is an archetypal example.

'Contributory negligence' occurs when (as in the appeasement of Nazi Germany in 1937–39) B fails to take appropriate measures against A's aggressive foreign policy early on, thereby unintentionally encouraging A to become more daring, and ends up having to fight A at a later date. Importantly, however, it was the fear of repeating this mistake that influenced some key decisions by the US (e.g. in its invasion of Cuba in 1961) and Britain (e.g. in its war against Egypt in 1956) in the post-world War II era.

Conclusion

War comes about in many different ways. This chapter has examined a standard type of war brought about, in the hope of achieving some gains or avoiding some worse outcomes, by sovereign states whose functions are generally assumed to include fighting a war under certain circumstances. Wars of this kind tend to have a relatively clear beginning and ending.

But war may also grow out of an exchange of increasingly more hostile moves and countermoves between two parties which, through their very interactions, come to form their identity as war-fighting entities. This was seen, for example, in the war of Croatian independence against Serbia, a key component of the dissolution of the former Yugoslavia in the early 1990s.

In such cases, we may find the seeds of war in the less than solid foundations upon which the two parties had coexisted earlier. But the knowledge of the background conditions would not be sufficient to make full sense of the process of deterioration in their relations. For this we need to trace the sequence of events that propelled the process. And this is where we need to see how chance coincidences, if any, and war-conducive mechanisms and actions and inactions of the key actors worked together. The framework of analysis presented in this chapter will be applicable to a causal investigation of any transition to war.

Many cautionary tales can be told of how war comes about, and one of the traditional concerns of IR has been to identify their key ingredients. For this purpose, a detailed study of particular cases has been just as indispensable as an attempt to see whether there may be some crisscrossing over a number of cases. There may not in the end be any regular causal paths to war, but some family resemblances are noticeable in a wide range of particular causal paths because some contributory causes of war will appear here and there, from time to time, in combination or in isolation.

QUESTIONS

1. Is war an effect of aggressive and selfish human nature?

2. Explain the relationship between state sovereignty and war.

3. How significant a causal factor is 'chance' in bringing about a war?

4. Give two examples of war-conducive mechanisms.

5. Are all wars intended?

FURTHER READING

Levy, J. S. and Thompson, W. R. 2010, *Causes of war*, Chichester: Wiley-Blackwell. Impressive overview and analysis of the theoretical and historical arguments about war's causes.

Suganami, H. 1996, *On the causes of war*, Oxford: Oxford University Press. Theoretical examination which engages with philosophy of history to make sense of war's causes.

Waltz, K. N. 1959, *Man, the state and war: a theoretical analysis*, New York: Columbia University Press. Classic account of three levels at which war's causes may be located.

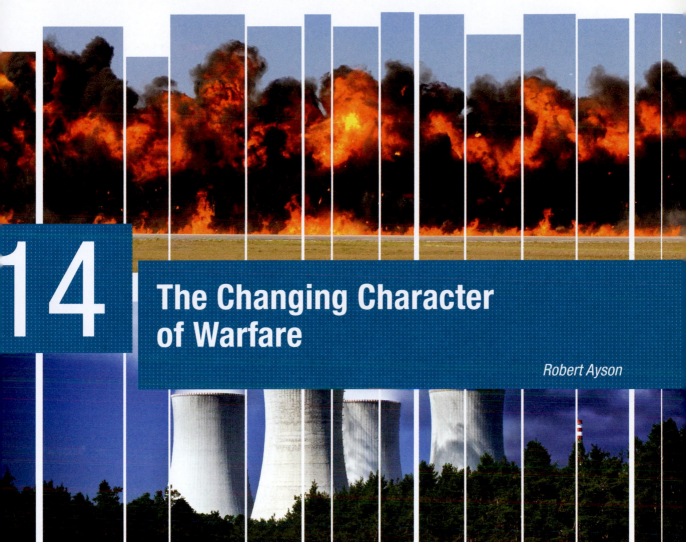

14 The Changing Character of Warfare

Robert Ayson

Introduction	200
The diversity of warfare	200
Sebastian Kaempf: Digital battlespaces and virtual media wars	202
War as *violence*	204
War as *organised* violence	206
War and *politics*	208
War as a case of *between*	210
War as *large-scale*	211
David Kilcullen: Contemporary war	212
Conclusion	215
Questions	215
Further reading	216

Introduction

The **discipline** of International Relations owes its origins to the study of **war** and **peace**. But do the wars of the early twenty-first century differ so fundamentally from their predecessors that they need to be considered in quite different ways? This chapter provides a barometer on the character of warfare and its implications for contemporary international relations. It begins with some comments on the diverse ends and means of warfare before considering five leading issues: the role of violence in warfare; the extent to which that violence is organised; the political nature of war; the interactive nature of warfare; and the scope and scale of war. The overall argument presented here is that while war today may look rather different to wars of earlier periods, much of its essential nature has remained intact. This should make us a bit sceptical about claims that the role of war in international relations has somehow been revolutionised.

The diversity of warfare

Students of International Relations need little reminding that they are traversing a discipline whose leading concepts are hotly contested. But we might be excused for supposing that the meaning and character of something as concrete as *war* would be an open and shut case. As this author has indicated elsewhere (Ayson 2006: 10–24) the field which looks at the place of war in international politics – strategic studies – often avoids endless debates about meaning and terminology, let alone **theory**.

But war can mean quite different things to different people in different parts of the world. Aside from such unhelpful notions as the 'war on terror' and the 'war on drugs' (which are about as meaningful as the idea of a 'war on war' itself), our subject admits to a quite remarkable variety. It includes large-scale and nearly total war between **states** (and groups of **nation**-states) as seen in the twentieth century's two world wars. It includes inter-state war fought in more limited fashion for more limited goals (as in the war between Britain and Argentina over the Malvinas/Falkland Islands in the early 1980s). Also included are the messy internal wars from the American **Civil War** in the 1860s to the Chinese civil war which ended with the victory of Mao's **communist** forces in the late 1940s, to the internal fighting which besieged Iraq after the US-led invasion in 2003 toppled Saddam Hussein's regime, and the more recent battles between insurgents and counterinsurgents in Afghanistan. War can also occupy a midway point between internal and inter-state, as witnessed in Vietnam from the 1940s to the 1970s: to some observers this war was part of the global **Cold War** contest between the **superpowers** and their proxies; to others it was a war for national liberation and unity. And wars certainly do not require formal (and internationally recognised) state boundaries to operate between or within. They existed well before the **Westphalian order**, as any student of the Bible (or of Chinese history) will attest.

There has also been significant variety in the means used to wage these wars. The development of military technology following the second industrial revolution of the late nineteenth century meant that the succeeding generation had access to weapons systems its predecessors could only have dreamed of. But as Biddle argues (2004), the pace of military technological innovation is not as rapid as it may seem, and even today wars are fought with weapons of incredible simplicity as well as those of great technological complexity. On the one hand there are the simple firearms (including crude homemade weapons) employed by the irregular armies fighting on Bougainville

Figure 14.1 The diversity of war – child soldier in the Congo, by Rivkah Larkin (with permission)

Figure 14.2 An F-20 fighter aircraft firing an air-to-ground missile

Source: US Air Force/Wikimedia commons.

in Papua New Guinea in the 1990s and by groups in Ghana and some other West African countries. On the other hand we can consider the vast information-processing power behind the US weapon systems used against Slobodan Milosevic's Serbia in the Kosovo crisis in 1999 in the initial attack against Iraq in 2003, and the recent use of aerial drones against individual targets in Pakistan and Yemen. We can stretch our imaginations as well to the prospect of a war involving the only genuine **weapons of mass destruction** – nuclear weapons – although of course for the citizens of Nagasaki and Hiroshima in 1945 no such imagining was required.

Digital battlespaces and virtual media wars
Sebastian Kaempf

While Western governments until very recently were able to control the ways in which their citizens were exposed to an instantaneous, real-time (albeit one-sided and sanitised) image of war, they are now finding themselves caught up in waging an unprecedented virtual war of images alongside the physical/'real' in Afghanistan and Iraq. Today, war is no longer conducted purely by the dispatch of Tomahawks in the air or Kalashnikovs and suicide attacks on the ground but also by means of bytes, blogs, bandwidths, digital images and computer simulations.

Digital new media technology has challenged a key aspect of Western warfighting strategy: the ability to control the visualisation and representation of its own wars. In the case of the US, for instance, this perceived need to control the (visual) representation of war stems from the political fall-out caused by the Vietnam War. The prevailing view among key decision makers in the Pentagon and the White House was that the war in Indochina would have been won if it had not been for the alleged misrepresentation of the conflict by the American print media, radio and television networks. As a consequence, the Pentagon has subsequently set up the so-called 'pool system' and invented 'embedded journalism' as a means to manage the media and – most importantly – to control the (visual) representation of US wars (Carruthers 2000). By putting in place a system of media management, the Pentagon regained the ability to control the (visual) representation of US wars among the American public (and a wider Western audience). Set up with the invasion of Grenada in 1983, this system has continued through the 1991 Gulf War until today. Over the past four decades, identical developments have been under way in other Western militaries, including Australian and British (Rid and Hecker 2009).

The controversial phenomenon of 'embedded journalism' therefore needs to be understood as a response by Western militaries to the increasing mediatisation of war; war has become a spectacle where warring factions use and manipulate media entertainment networks as part of their military strategy. This does not necessarily mean that the conventional 'old' media (radio, printing press and television) has lost all of its political independence, but that the sources it accesses, the information it publishes and the images it uses are more susceptible to control by the militaries' media management (Münkler 2008).

Media management has been central to not only creating but also sustaining popular notions of 'costless war', an imaginary scenario underwritten by repeated replays of 'bomb's eye views' transmitted from precision-guided missiles as they hurtle to their targets. Carefully selected images conveyed by Western military operations present US, British and Australian operations as precise, discriminate and clean, suggesting a 'grammar of killing' that avoids the unnecessary spilling of blood (Der Derian 2001). This ability to frame the perception of their operations as humane and surgical has been regarded by Western militaries as essential to creating and sustaining the legitimacy of warfare in the public's eyes.

The situation has changed fundamentally, however, with the emergence of digital new media technology. New media technology has enabled adversaries to break Western militaries' hitherto exclusive ability to frame the perception and visual representation of warfare by creating virtual counter-realities that aim at scrutinising and delegitimising US, Australian and British operations in their global 'war on terror' (Kaempf 2008). Public beheading videos and images showing the devastation and civilian costs of war (to name just two examples) have been produced as deliberate juxtapositions to the sanitised visualisations of warfare offered by Washington, London and Canberra. With the West's attempt to humanise warfare (by making war appear bloodless), non-Western adversaries have actively tried to dehumanise war (by exposing and celebrating the shedding of blood). New media technologies have thus afforded non-state actors unprecedented capacities to erode Western electoral support for the 'war on terror', while simultaneously enabling them to use these very same technologies to radicalise and mobilise globally dispersed constituencies in support of **jihadist** terrorism.

Through these new media outlets Western adversaries have been able to reconceptualise public media as a battlespace and to employ public relations as a weapon. New media technology in that sense provides a cheap and user-friendly means to produce and disseminate competing virtual realities and create rival narratives in order to influence the perception of a certain conflict. As a result, some of the most critical battles in the 'war on terror' – the first conflict waged in the new media age – have not been fought only in the mountains of Afghanistan or the streets of Baghdad, but also in American, British and Australian newsrooms and – just as importantly – in various internet forums, through YouTube, Twitter, on Facebook, in chatrooms and in the blogosphere. Most of these new media outlets are removed from the tight control of defence ministries' PR specialists and thereby offer platforms through which the uninterrogated virtual reality offered by Western operations can be put into question. This development has started to transform the experience of war, for it allows for the production of competing virtual realities. This is why, for the first time, we are witnessing a new media war, or what Paul Virilio calls a 'cybernetic war of persuasion and dissuasion' (Virilio 2002: ix) where the prime strategic objectives are no longer exclusively the elimination of the enemy's military forces but also the (re)shaping of public opinion. With terrorists and insurgents vying for 'hearts and minds', and Western support for the war effort hinging on the idea of 'costless wars', the new media has become an important, even decisive, conduit and arena for the 'war on terror'.

Sebastian Kaempf is a Lecturer in Peace and Conflict Studies at the University of Queensland, and a Research Associate of the US Studies Centre at the University of Sydney. He has published on contemporary security, the relationship between ethics and the laws of war, and digital new media wars. With Peter Mantello he is the producer of a new documentary film on war in the digital age (www.thevisionmachine.com).

This diversity should give us pause before we accept any notion that war's nature (what is at its essence) or even war's character (how it is represented on the battlefield) has changed substantially between one period and another. Nonetheless it is tempting to go along with such assertions, especially when they are linked to periods of major change in international politics. A common example here is the argument that the end of the Cold War has seen intrastate (or internal) wars rise to take the place of inter-state armed conflict. We should be wary of such sweeping propositions. For example, some research has suggested that while 'civil wars are breaking out at an all-time record rate', the respective frequencies of inter-state and intrastate wars have remained stubbornly consistent over many decades (Sarkees et al. 2003: 62). The Cold War, famous for the tensions between states (and for inter-state wars in places like the Korean peninsula), was also an era of the collapse of colonial empires and struggles for independence – an era characterised by a good deal of intrastate warfare. (The term '**guerrilla**' goes back even further to the resistance mounted by sub-state groups in Spain against Napoleon's armed forces in the early nineteenth century.)

Nonetheless we need to take seriously arguments that there have been significant changes in the way wars are fought, in who does the fighting, and in why they do so. But to do this we need a handle on war. Useful here is a definition of war proposed by Jack Levy (1998: 141) as 'large scale organised violence between political actors'. Focusing on the main terms which comprise this definition will provide some important insights into this thing called war and into whether and how its character might be said to be changing.

War as *violence*

Because it involves violence and because of the damage, death and sheer trauma that violence can involve, war represents an extreme form of political action. In international politics, there is no more important decision for a country's leaders to make than to go to war. And there is no more serious threat that one country can make towards another than to indicate that it is prepared to resort to war over the issue at hand. For **realists** at least (and for some other international relations scholars too) the capacity to wage war is the *sine qua non* of **power** in the **international system**.

The violence inherent in war reminds us that war is a clash rather than a picnic. The use of force can have its own destructive logic. The capacity for war as violence to get out of control is well recognised. For example, the mobilisation crisis of August 1914, as each country responded to the preparations of the other, led to a world war that nobody seemed to want. And what would have happened if US president Kennedy had decided to bomb Cuba during the 1962 missile crisis with the Soviet Union? It is anyone's guess as to how hard it would have been to rein in the violence once it had begun (especially once the first nuclear weapons were used). The greatest philosopher of war, Carl von **Clausewitz** (see Box 14.1) – a Prussian officer who saw first hand the capacity for violence which the French **Revolution** allowed Napoleon to wield on the battlefield – saw it thus:

… war is an act of force, and there is no logical limit to the application of that force. Each side, therefore, compels its opponent to follow suit; a reciprocal action is started which must lead, in theory, to extremes. ([1832] 1989: 77)

Clausewitz also spoke wisely about the curious and unintended consequences of war as violence. One of these is friction where pretty much anything that can go wrong does in the heat, noise and confusion of battle: misunderstood or misleading communications; failing machinery and weapons systems; accidents and mistakes made under stress. A related concept is the fog of war – those things which may seem clear before the first shot is fired become extremely opaque as violence corrodes everything in its wake. War breeds confusion and a sense of chaos.

BOX 14.1: KEY FIGURES

Carl von Clausewitz

Clausewitz's *On war*, first published in 1832 (a year after his death), has something for almost anyone. For a number of German military thinkers in the build-up to World War I, Clausewitz was the prophet of the offensive. For American strategists grappling with the destructive nature of nuclear weapons, his ideas of limited war for limited aims had obvious appeal. But therein lies both the beauty and the hazard of his writings. *On war* is philosophically ambitious and full of paradox. We can find ammunition today for arguments that war is destined to get messy and out of control, and counter-arguments that violence can be adjusted to fulfil the ends of policy. Clausewitz's greatest contribution was to highlight the political context in which war occurs, but because the relationship between force and power can be so difficult, we should be wary of attempts to understand his work in just one dimension.

This sets up a challenge for modern armed forces: with the benefits of advanced technology and training: can they master friction and pierce the fog of war? Some observers argue that the information age has ushered in a new **'revolution in military affairs'** which has completely transformed the way that wars can be fought and the ways that armed forces are organised to fight them. Pictures have been painted of a situation where pilots and their commanders can have complete awareness of the battlespace around them and are able to deliver their precision-guided munitions to destroy targets with unerring accuracy and minimal wider casualties and damage.

Others are more sceptical about claims of revolution and seek to place any such changes in a wider political context (Freedman 1998). But there is no doubt that the experience of the US's technologically sophisticated forces since the 1991 Gulf War encouraged the view that the old obstacles no longer applied. They offered a surgically precise warfare which suited a democratic society's preference for wars without excessive violence. Some of the after-action reports suggested, however, that these campaigns had not been quite as precise or limited as had been hoped. More importantly, the deaths of over 4000 US service personnel in the violence which filled the political vacuum in Iraq in 2003 indicated that the friction and fog of war was all too real. Similar factors have also been apparent in the war in Afghanistan since 2001 where the Taliban have staged a strong and costly comeback in a number of provinces, challenging their more heavily armed international opponents. And interspersed with the apparent successes of the 1990s were images of confusion and fear in Mogadishu as the US's Somalian adventure came undone, and stories of millions of dead from the brutal war in the Democratic Republic of Congo. The record is therefore mixed, at the very least. The characteristics of violence in some wars or in some portions of these wars may have changed. But there is also enough to suggest that it is very hard to seal off the discharge of violence from the old problems of friction and the confounding and destructive logic of war.

War as *organised* violence

All this might suggest that war is inherently uncontrollable and chaotic. Certainly this is an easy conclusion to reach for those caught up in its intensity. But war is not only violent behaviour. War is purposeful and organised violence. In other words there is a reason for war (even if we do not agree with it). Clausewitz states that 'war is ... an act of force to compel our enemy to do our will' ([1832] 1989: 75). Even though war may have a logic of its own and seem self-perpetuating, it is not an end in itself. It has a wider aim which, says Clausewitz, is policy.

The idea of war as organised violence differentiates it from non-organised or semi-organised violence. While a street riot may involve violence, this sort of generally spontaneous activity is not a war. There are some grey areas here. For example, the riot in the Solomon Islands capital of Honiara which followed the 2006 election result was a curious mixture of spontaneity and political purpose (and it helped achieve a clear political result with the unseating of the prime minister-elect only days afterwards). We might also ask: at what stage does civil unrest involving violence become a civil war? Another grey area is whether we consider **terrorism** to be war. One approach here is to regard terrorism as a means of war rather than as a separate form of it. Groups who are seeking to bring down the ruling authority in a **revolutionary** war may use acts of terror as part of their struggle, which may also include hit-and-run tactics and more conventional forms of organised violence. But what of groups who seem defined by and in some ways limited to terrorism? Al-Qaeda is an interesting case in point. Are they at war? And, if so, with whom?

One group well known for acts of terrorism thought that it was in a war: this was the Provisional IRA in Northern Ireland, and IRA stood for Irish Republican *Army*. This leads to another point about war as organised violence: our tendency to see it represented in organisations designed to fight wars. These armed forces generally consist of three services: armies, navies and air forces. This takes us back to our understanding of the international system because it is the main actors in this system – states – who are the largest and main organisers of armed forces. Indeed, at least in theory, **sovereign states** are expected to maintain a monopoly on the preparation for and use of armed force (see Chapter 9). Wars occur in two main ways here: the first is as organised violence between the armed forces of two or more of these sovereign states. The second is when that domestic monopoly breaks down and there are challengers within states – **insurgent** groups, **secessionists** and others – who often maintain their own unofficial and irregular armed forces. Examples of this second category include the long civil war between the Sudanese government based in the mainly Muslim north and the Sudan People's Liberation Army/Movement (SPLA/M) of the mainly Christian south, and the contest for Mindanao between the Philippines armed forces and the Moro Islamic Liberation Front (MILF) and other groups.

Some analysts suggest, however, that it is obsolete for states to concentrate on organising their own armed forces in preparation for possible wars with other states or to prevent war by credible **deterrent** strategies. Martin van Creveld (1991) (see Box 14.2), for example, suggests that these large, cumbersome military machines are heading for extinction. Instead, the wars of the future will be mounted and fought by irregular, non-state armed forces including paramilitary groups, organised criminal gangs and other sub-state actors. This goes hand-in-hand with his thesis that the Westphalian order of sovereign states is also passing away.

BOX 14.2: KEY FIGURES

Martin van Creveld

Few scholars have had a larger impact on the way we think about war today than the Israeli military historian Martin van Creveld. In terms of the serious study of warfare, van Creveld's work on technology's impact on warfare and the often undervalued significance of logistics stand as important contributions. But his *On future war* (also published as *The transformation of war*) has attracted greatest attention. Van Creveld attacks **Clausewitzean** war as obsolete because of the demise of the state's monopoly on armed violence. Israel's own challenges in coping with an undeclared war with sub-state actors in the occupied territories clearly had a bearing on this thesis. Some readers may find van Creveld's treatment of Clausewitz akin to the demolition of a straw man. But in a world preoccupied with transnational terrorist groups, weak states and insurgency, there is no doubting the appeal of his logic.

This critique needs to be taken seriously. We seem to live in an age of weak and even **failing states**, many of which are unable to maintain effective armed forces, thereby posing a greater threat to their own civilians than to the adversaries they are purportedly designed to fight. And if states are fragile and collapsing, then so too is their monopoly on organised violence. But even strong states are challenged by what is often called 'asymmetric warfare' – where the nominally weaker actors (including sub-state groups who use terrorism, such as the insurgents in Iraq) seem to have pinpointed chinks in Goliath's armour. Indeed, in one of its more notable observations about the contemporary international system, the administration of George W. Bush declared that the US 'is now threatened less by conquering states than ... by failing ones' (US National Security Strategy 2002: 1).

The organisation of armed force by strong states is not quite a thing of the past. War between the European states, and between almost any Western democracies, may now seem unthinkable. But the same does not apply in Asia where, thanks to the rise of China and India and the long-standing economic weight of Japan, global power will increasingly be concentrated. Asia features a raft of states for whom the building of armed forces with the potential to wage organised violence is far from an outdated practice. And, at least for now, a somewhat precarious sense of balance in that part of the world is maintained by the substantial regional military presence of the US, whose spending on its own armed forces exceeds the combined military expenditure of all other countries on the globe (IISS 2011). States in this part of the world will continue to maintain and develop organised armed forces to deter armed conflict and to fight if that deterrence fails.

War and *politics*

The next part of Levy's definition we turn to is the notion that war is organised violence involving *political actors*. This immediately brings to mind the most quoted statement about our subject – again from Clausewitz – that 'war is not merely an act of policy but a true political instrument, a continuation of political intercourse, carried on with other means' ([1832] 1989: 87). Rather than having the notion that war starts when diplomacy ceases, we are encouraged to regard war as an extension of the political relationship which states (and other political actors) enjoy and endure with one another. The American strategic thinker Thomas Schelling characterised this situation very colourfully by referring to the 'diplomacy of violence' (1966: 1–34).

For students of IR this puts war at the heart of their discipline which, at least traditionally, is the study of political relationships between the key actors of the international system, namely states. And by political relationships here we mean relationships involving power: who has it and how it is distributed and used in the international system. War is one means (although a highly unpleasant one) through which states – as political actors – attempt to affect the behaviour of others in the pursuit of their interests.

Clausewitz's famous statement will be recognised as an example of classical realism since it supposes a **state-centric** world full of self-interested actors. War is not an end in itself – it is a servant of the political interests of these states. We should be wary of this sort of logic, for at least two related reasons. The first reason is that it appears to legitimise war. This formulation encourages us to think of war not so much as the product of a faulty international system and poor institutions and practices (as **liberals** like Woodrow Wilson might encourage us to believe). Instead we might be encouraged to regard war as just another mechanism by which states seek to achieve their political aims in a world where there is a premium on self-help. Of course this may not be an objectionable proposition in some instances. For the allied powers in September 1939 war was not difficult to justify as a necessary means to a legitimate political end: the defeat of Nazi aggression and tyranny. But after the largely unintended catastrophe of World War I, one could argue that war could be far from a rational decision taken to further **national interests**.

Second, since war can have a destructive logic of its own it can be somewhat hazardous to see war as just another instrument of the state. War has a habit of changing and corrupting the reasons for which it is originally fought. As Azar Gat has observed, for Clausewitz the political nature of war was organic as well as functional: the nature of war reflects the political nature of the society which wages it and which brings it into being (Gat 1989: 215). Even in its purely inter-state variety, war reflects the domestic politics of those states which are fighting it. One cannot understand the frequency and the character of war between India and Pakistan since the partition of 1947 without an appreciation of these two states, and the passions which these energetic societies evoke (Ganguly 2001). Domestic politics can also serve to constrain a state's participation in war, as the US government of Lyndon Johnson learned in the Vietnam War era (Karnow 1994) and as the Soviet government learned in Afghanistan (Evans 2005). Hence, in referring to *political* actors we mean domestic as well as international political dimensions.

Of course if we agree with van Creveld we might be inclined to argue that the political actors responsible for war are leaving the stage. Rather than seeing strong states prosecuting war we might need to focus on sub-state actors. But before we dismiss the Clausewitzean/Westphalian universe and the war–politics nexus, we need to look more deeply at some of these supposedly non-traditional actors who are said to dominate today's warfare. First we might consider some of the groups who wage war against established states, either to bring them down or to carve out a piece of the territory for themselves. The MILF is not a state, but that does not mean that its approach to war is apolitical. It seeks separate statehood, something that the SLA/M has achieved with the arrival of South Sudan. War is a profoundly political activity between them and the respective incumbent governments involved.

We can apply a similar logic to the role of **identity** as a cause of modern warfare. Using such examples as the Balkan wars which precipitated and accompanied the break-up of the former Yugoslavia in the early 1990s, Mary Kaldor (1999) reminds us that elites can manipulate the politics of identity to justify war. These wars are very much acts of political ambition: for Milosevic in Serbia and Tudjman in Croatia warfare was a servant of, and also a product of, politics. There is in fact not that much of a gap here from some of the independence movements which followed World War II: identity and independence are both bedfellows of **nationalism** (see Chapter 10). Mao Zedong's revolutionary strategy, developed as his Red Army fought for the control of China, is a superb example of the idea of using force for explicitly political purposes and a recognition that those who wage war operate in an intensely political environment.

Of course not all sub-state wagers of war are involved in movements of national liberation, independence or secession. Some at least seem to act out of rather different motivations. In the wake of the September 2001 attacks on the US a number of analysts suggested that there was a difference between old and new terrorism. In the earlier type, prominent in the late 1960s and early 1970s, groups like the Palestinian Liberation Organisation (PLO) and Euskadi Ta Askatasuna (ETA) used acts of terror in the quest for limited political goals: for example, independence within a particular territory. They were avowedly political actors waging a form of internal war with their target states – in this case with the governments of Israel and Spain respectively. But in the new terrorism, it was unclear what if any political aims motivated groups like al-Qaeda, which seemed interested only in causing the maximum death and destruction possible. Such groups almost seemed caught up in the theatre (rather than the functionality) of violence. A related argument suggested that radical Islamist groups using terrorism were motivated by religion (often with apocalyptic worldviews) rather than by politics.

These claims deserve serious consideration but are also open to question (Tucker 2001: 1–14). First, it is clear that al-Qaeda has had an interest in perpetuating mass casualty terrorist attacks. But this does not necessarily mean that Osama bin Laden and his colleagues lacked a political agenda. Their motives appeared to include the removal of Western and especially US forces from parts of the Middle East, and the downfall of incumbent regimes including in Saudi Arabia. Second, the distinction between religion and politics is questionable. There is no reason why political aims cannot have religious connotations: consider the idea of a caliphate in the Middle East and the support which the theocratic government of Iran gives to Hezbollah and other groups arraigned against Israel. Of course, one might ask whether all groups who use terror are engaged in a war, and whether there are always clear political goals involved wherever terrorism occurs. Small groups operating on the basis of individual grievance (as seems possible in the 2005 London bombings) might be disqualified on both counts as perpetrators of war. But it would be a brave person who argued that Hamas and Israel had been engaged in something other than a war.

Other instances of organised violence may strain the nexus between war and politics in a more resolute fashion. Some actors seem motivated by economic gain and lack any sort of obvious political agenda. Such claims have been made about the Lord's Resistance Army (LRA) in Uganda. For this 'Army' organised violence seemed either an end in itself or was used for reasons of financial greed. But it is still rare for politics to be completely absent. First, such a group often needs a particular political situation in which to operate – in this case a virtual vacuum of state power. Second, its leaders have interests in their own positions of power and in the survival of their organisation. Third, as Vinci has argued (2005: 360–81), the LRA has used violence to breed fear for political purposes. A group does not need to publish formal policy statements or be interested in setting up a government to be regarded as a political actor. Even so, for states familiar with engaging with other states, it is not easy to know how to win wars against actors whose interests, resources and tactics can seem so different.

War as a case of *between*

This leads us to a fourth observation – that war is more like a game of poker than a game of patience. War is an activity between two or more political actors who are using force (and threats of force) to affect each other's behaviour. The notion of war as a clash of wills, each trying to impose themselves on the other, comes into play here. And it is this violent interaction which helps give war some of its truly horrible elements – friction, uncertainty and confusion are elevated when you are facing an intelligent opponent who is trying to do you harm.

At times war can be more or less symmetrical. This was the case on the Western Front in World War I, which led to a multi-year stalemate. It was also the case on the Eastern Front in World War II as the armed might of Germany was absorbed at great cost and then repelled by the Soviet Union (USSR). It would have been the case in an especially catastrophic sense had the US and USSR gone to war in the nuclear age. That a third world war was avoided suggests that the capacity for mutual destruction may act to prevent the use of force and that peer competitors can agree to tacit rules of the game by which they constrain the violence which might erupt between them. In this sense, as Schelling (1960) argues, war and threats of war can be treated as bargaining relationships where the sides find some sort of ugly compromise which prevents massive mutual damage (see Box 14.3).

BOX 14.3: KEY FIGURES

Thomas Schelling

It probably needed an unconventional economist like Thomas Schelling to show us how much war (and attempts to avoid and limit it) could resemble a bargain between self-interested strategic actors. Drawing on theories of the firm, game theory, and organisational theory,

Schelling developed a theoretically appealing approach to strategy in a nuclear age where not finding a tacit agreement with the other side could mean mutual devastation. This was spelled out with particular rigour in *The strategy of conflict*. Schelling was also a pioneer of **arms control** theory and later turned his hand to the study of international environmental problems. He was awarded a Nobel Prize in economics in 2005.

But war can also occur between unequals, both in size and in type. In terms of the former, we live in an age of US political and military supremacy, where the world's leading power (and the only real superpower) is likely to dwarf any state it fights – with the possible exception some time down the track of an undesired war with a re-emerging China. Indeed the 1990s in particular were an age of unfair strategic contests between the US (and its allies) on the one hand and an assortment of small **rogue states** on the other. These included Saddam Hussein's Iraq (twice) and Serbia. Such was the US advantage in these contests that it is a bit difficult to call them real wars in the interactive sense of the term. Indeed the US was able to fight these wars in the way and time of its choosing. This bred a certain amount of overconfidence in its own power. It also went along with what might be called **unilateral** notions of strategy – in the sense that war was simply the application of violence to achieve one's own ends almost in the absence of anything coming back the other way. War was not a case of 'between' here.

But looking back on 2003, it might be argued that the adversaries of the US in Iraq knew that they could not win such an asymmetrically pitched battle and waited for the moment when the US would be most exposed – as a rather modestly sized occupying force responsible for a huge and fractious country in the post-invasion period. Something came back the other way then, and the interaction, friction and confusion of war returned. Strategy became more like Schelling's (1960: 3) notion, adapted from game theory, where 'the best course of action for each player depends on what the other players do'. Such an approach, he argued, encourages us to 'focus on the interdependence of the adversaries' decisions and on their expectations about each other's behaviour'.

Insurgent groups, which we also see in Afghanistan, represent a different type of political actor as well as a different size of actor, extending the asymmetry of the interaction even further. In general terms, states do not fare well in wars against non-state groups. Warlike acts designed to help stabilise a country so that new institutions of government may be built are fraught with difficulty. The fact that wars are between opposing and intelligent parties is one reason why the use of force remains an extremely blunt stick in international politics. Hence, while the capacity and intent to use military force may stand as the *sine qua non* of power in the international system, it is a form of power one should be especially reluctant to unleash. The 'between' factor is an essential reason for this reluctance.

War as large-scale

Keeping wars small and under control is a risky art-form, not least because it takes two sides to agree on any such limits. The escalating US commitment to Vietnam in the 1960s, which left Hanoi largely unmoved in its resolve, is a good case of how such limits can be hard to negotiate. That failure encouraged the US view (known as the Powell Doctrine after General Colin Powell, who later became secretary of state) that

Contemporary war   David Kilcullen

Warfare is the most enduring human social activity, present in virtually all societies. War's character changes, however, through technological development, alteration in political, economic and social order, and the evolution of norms (including international law). *Technology*, *sociopolitical change* and *international norms* can thus help frame a discussion of contemporary war.

Technology

The US emerged from the Cold War in the early 1990s with unprecedented dominance in 'conventional' – state-on-state, force-on-force – warfare. The one-sided coalition victory in the 1991 Gulf War underlined this supremacy. The US and its allies have since invested heavily in technology – information and communications systems, surveillance and reconnaissance platforms, precision guided munitions and autonomous robotics – to maintain that ascendancy. By the turn of the twenty-first century this technological **'revolution in military affairs'** had convinced some that a transformation of warfare was underway.

But as events since 2001 have shown, US preeminence in one narrow, hyper-conventional style of warfare forces adversaries into new approaches. Opponents are sidestepping Western dominance – using terrorism and guerrilla warfare, disruptive technologies, or weapons of mass destruction (WMDs). Globalisation also has a levelling effect, spreading lethal weapons technology to smaller groups and individuals. Non-state armed groups (militias, guerrillas, pirates) now pose threats that only states once mustered.

Social and political change

Globalisation and its discontents are the strongest sociopolitical forces shaping contemporary war. Globalisation brings divergent communities into intimate contact, often conflict, and creates a world culture and economy that threatens and corrodes traditional ways of life. This prompts a violent backlash, exploited by military actors (such as transnational extremist groups) that are themselves highly networked and globalised, using the new tools of globalisation – the internet, and international financial, communications and transportation systems – to exacerbate local animosities, motivate diasporas and aggregate disparate traditionalist militant groups into global threats.

This dynamic lay behind the terrorist attacks of 11 September 2001 that prompted the US to mount a 'global war on terrorism'. The invasion and occupation of Afghanistan and Iraq has been accompanied by Western military interventions in dozens of countries worldwide, and the patterns of conflict prompted by this series of campaigns have defined warfare into the first decade of the new century. The effects of the Global Financial Crisis, political upheaval in the Middle East and North Africa, and an ongoing arms race in the Asia-Pacific underline this pattern: globalisation enabling aspiration for change, but also creating opposition and empowering non-state groups – a dynamic that extremists can exploit, prompting Western intervention which in turn provokes further violent opposition.

New international norms

Just as technological and sociopolitical developments dating back to the 1990s are affecting patterns of warfare today, so new international norms are also having an effect.

During the 1990s a new set of international norms began to emerge in relation to the acceptability of intervention where states were engaged in humanitarian abuses against their populations. This developed in part from the wars in Bosnia, Croatia and Kosovo during the break-up of Yugoslavia, and from interventions in Somalia, Rwanda, East Timor, Liberia, Haiti and Sierra Leone. An interventionist mood surfaced, in which state sovereignty was deemed to be conditional on proper treatment of civilian populations. Some major powers, notably China, opposed this departure from the original spirit of the United Nations. Nonetheless, the creation of an international war crimes tribunal for the former Yugoslavia, an International Criminal Court, and the new UN doctrine of the '**responsibility to protect**' civilians (see Chapter 31) gave institutional and conceptual substance to this interventionist stance.

After 2001, US interventionism drew in part on these norms, but the administration's **unilateralism** in invading Iraq in 2003, and its disregard of international institutions including the UN was only partly remedied during President George W. Bush's second term, undermining international consensus in favour of armed humanitarian intervention. US interventionism was often cloaked in the rhetoric of human rights, democracy and the 'freedom agenda', exacerbating this loss of credibility. As a result, conflicts like Somalia, Darfur, Southern Sudan and Cote d'Ivoire, and egregious abuses in Zimbabwe, were not subject to the muscular interventions that might have been possible before Iraq. Only in 2011, with a US and **NATO**-led intervention to protect civilians in Libya, did the international community again begin formally invoking the 'responsibility to protect' language of **humanitarian interventionism** that had been so prevalent before September 11.

The future

State-on-state conflict remains both possible and important in contemporary warfare. The potential for large-scale conventional war in the Middle East, on the Korean Peninsula, or between India and Pakistan remains very real, and could have extremely dire consequences, including the use of nuclear weapons. Ongoing great-power military competition could also lead, deliberately or through miscalculation, to major war.

The fact that major powers must hedge against the slim but dangerous possibility of future conventional conflicts means that countries like the US will continue to focus on, and probably to dominate, this form of conflict. In turn, potential or actual adversaries will therefore continue to sidestep Western conventional superiority, through terrorism, guerrilla warfare, WMDs or disruptive technologies such as cyber-warfare or economic warfare. For this reason, inter-state wars will almost certainly remain the minority of conflicts, as they have been over the past 200 years, when such wars have accounted for only about 17 per cent of total conflict on the planet. Although the consequences of inter-state conflict are so huge that states must continue to prepare for and hedge against them, the practical day-to-day reality of conflict in the twenty-first century will likely continue to be one of guerrilla wars, armed criminal and insurgent movements, terrorism and civil wars.

One thing seems certain, however: without a fundamental (and highly unlikely) change in human nature, war will remain an endemic and intimate part of human society, and will continue its role as an important shaping force on the evolution of states, and of the international system of which they form a part.

David Kilcullen is an author and consultant on counter-insurgency and counter-terrorism who is the founder and CEO of Caerus Associates, a Washington DC-based consultancy firm. He was a Lieutenant Colonel in the Australian Army, and has served as an advisor to US Secretary of State Condoleezza Rice, Commander of Multi-National Forces-Iraq, General David Petraeus, and the International Security Assistance Force, Afghanistan. He is the author of *The accidental guerilla* and *Counterinsurgency*, along with a section of the US Army and Marine Corps' Manual, FM 3–24 *Counterinsurgency*.

---

force should only be employed in an overwhelming fashion to achieve the objective quickly rather than through 'a little surgical bombing or a limited attack', which he argued is often followed by 'talk of just a little escalation – more bombs, more men and women, more force' (Powell 1992–93: 40). But it is important to note that Powell's argument is against the notion of gradually intensifying war rather than limited war per se. Examples abound of the resort to limited force for limited purposes, an approach which is entirely consistent with the ends–means relationship in Clausewitz's writing. China, for example, sought to teach Vietnam a 'lesson' through a limited war in 1979 (after Vietnam had invaded Cambodia to dislodge the murderous Khmer Rouge), and India and Pakistan have conducted limited wars including one which occurred under the nuclear umbrella in Kargil in 1999.

This raises the question of how large such an exchange of armed violence needs to be before we consider it to be warfare. Partly because they need agreed data sets to test their hypotheses about the occurrence of war, a good many IR scholars in the US have agreed on thresholds which allow them to count some events as wars and others as less than wars. The Correlates of War Project established at the University Michigan in 1963 is one such example. As Levy notes (1998: 141), that project's threshold of 1000 battle deaths per year as a defining requirement for a war to be counted has been adopted widely.

There are some advantages to such an approach. Generally speaking, the more extensive and costly the violence, the fewer questions there will be about whether war has in fact occurred. At one extreme, there is little doubt that World War II qualifies, with millions of battle deaths in some years. And there is no doubt that a global nuclear exchange would constitute war, although there might not be many political scientists left to record it. But at the other extreme, what of the occasional exchange of gunfire along the Line of Control in Kashmir? Is war occurring every time this happens?

But size does not always matter, at least not *absolute* size. The 1000 deaths per year threshold, for example, would exclude at least two conflicts in the South Pacific which have had serious consequences for small states: the civil war in the Solomon Islands and at least some portions of the armed conflict on Bougainville. Especially in light of the small populations involved in these places, just a few hundred deaths might be truly catastrophic. Indeed, using these somewhat arbitrary quantitative thresholds may allow a good number of intrastate wars to pass under our radar. What is important in establishing that war is taking place is a question of quality rather than quantity. And those qualitative factors are the ones we have discussed above – the use of armed violence between organised political actors. Whether these are superpowers with potentially millions of combatants and casualties or small rival tribes, the essence of war remains markedly similar.

Conclusion

If Napoleon and Clausewitz had been cryogenically frozen before their deaths and were revived today, they would likely be amazed by many of the features of contemporary warfare. They would probably marvel at what the microchip had done for modern weapon systems. Their jaws might drop as they considered the implications of including air and space as environments for battle. The intercontinental ballistic missile and the nuclear warhead, the air–land battle doctrine used by the US in the Middle East, the possibility of instantaneous and direct communication between commander and soldier, and the depth of the modern battlefield would all be new.

But having absorbed the implications of all of these new characteristics of war, Europe's greatest strategist and strategic thinker respectively might argue that not all that much has really changed. War is still as confusing and as destructive (if not more so) as it was in their day. It still reflects the political interests of the actors who wage it and the moods and energies of the societies in which they are based. As a clash of wills, war retains a logic of its own, even if it now wears rather different clothing. If correct, this conclusion implies that the title of this chapter, 'The Changing Character of Warfare', deserves to be followed by a rather large question-mark.

QUESTIONS

1. What is war? Is there agreement about what it is?
2. Is Clausewitz's theory of war still relevant to today's world? How have thinkers argued it should change?
3. To what extent does technology change war?
4. Is terrorism a form of war? What is at stake in describing it as such?
5. How do we stop today's wars?

FURTHER READING

Clausewitz, Carl von [1832] 1989, *On war*, trans. Michael Howard and Peter Paret, Princeton: Princeton University Press. Classic and indispensable treatise that shaped modern understandings of war and strategy.

Freedman, Lawrence 1998, *The revolution in strategic affairs*, Adelphi Paper 318, Oxford: Oxford University Press for the Institute for Strategic Studies. Excellent analysis that emphasises the political rather than technological factors in contemporary warfare.

Kaldor, Mary 1999, *New and old wars: organised violence in a global era*, Stanford: Stanford University Press. Controversial account of how globalisation has changed the character of warfare.

Figure 14.3 Wars since 1990

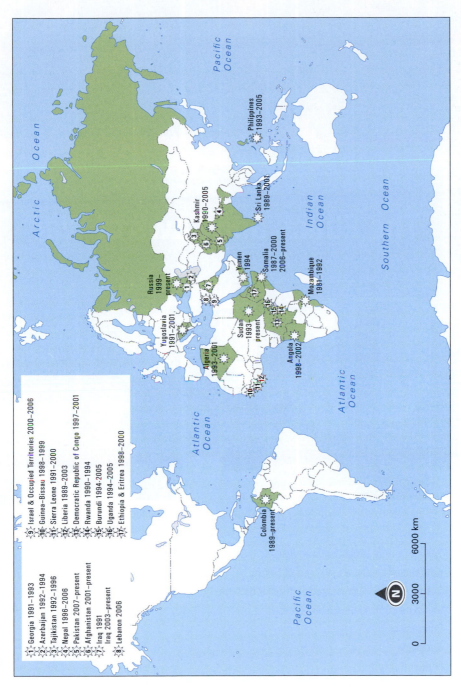

Legend:
1. Georgia 1991–1993
2. Azerbaijan 1992–1994
3. Tajikistan 1992–1996
4. Nepal 1996–2006
5. Pakistan 2007–present
6. Afghanistan 2001–present
7. Iraq 1991
   Iraq 2003–present
8. Lebanon 2006
9. Israel & Occupied Territories 2000–2006
10. Guinea-Bissau 1998–1999
11. Sierra Leone 1991–2000
12. Liberia 1989–2003
13. Democratic Republic of Congo 1997–2001
14. Rwanda 1990–1994
15. Burundi 1994–2005
16. Uganda 1994–2005
17. Ethiopia & Eritrea 1998–2000

Map labels:
- Colombia 1989–present
- Yugoslavia 1991–2001
- Algeria 1993–2001
- Sudan 1993–present
- Angola 1998–2002
- Mozambique 1981–1992
- Russia 1999–present
- Kashmir 1990–2005
- Yemen 1994
- Somalia 1987–2000 2006–present
- Sri Lanka 1989–2001
- Philippines 1993–2005

Oceans: Arctic Ocean, Pacific Ocean, Atlantic Ocean, Indian Ocean, Southern Ocean

Scale: 0   3000   6000 km

N

Source: Based on slightly revised data from 'Armed conflicts dataset', compiled jointly by the International Peace Research Institute, Oslo and the Department of Peace and Conflict Research, Uppsala University. Available at www.prio.no/CSCW/Datasets/Armed-Conflict/UCDP-PRIO.

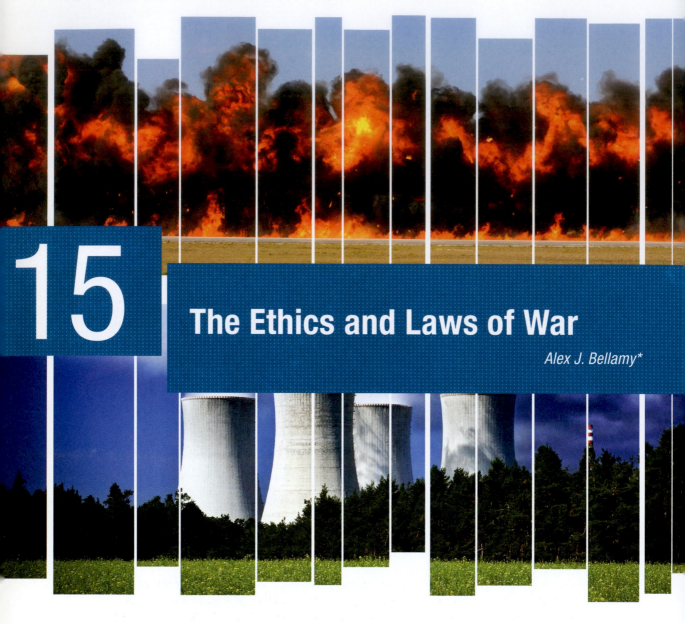

15

The Ethics and Laws of War

Alex J. Bellamy*

Introduction	219
When is it right to fight? (*jus ad bellum*)	219
How should war be waged? (*jus in bello*)	222
Jus ad bellum dilemma: preemptive self-defence	225
Jus in bello dilemma: cluster bombs	227
Conclusion	229
Questions	229
Further reading	230

* This chapter derives its argument and some of its text from Bellamy 2006b.

Introduction

This chapter provides a brief introduction to the ethics and laws of **war** in three parts. The first part outlines what **international law** and the '**just war**' tradition have to say about recourse to force, the second section explores the conduct of war and the final section explores two recent issues as examples of moral and legal debate: the legitimacy of preemptive self-defence and the use of cluster bombs.

In early 2003, millions of people took to the streets of capital cities throughout the West to protest their government's decision to join the US in the invasion of Iraq. Protesters argued that the invasion was immoral (because innocent civilians would die), illegal (because it was neither an act of self-defence nor explicitly authorised by the **UN** Security Council) and unnecessary (because they did not believe – rightly as it turned out – that conclusive evidence of Saddam's **weapons of mass destruction** (WMD) program had been presented). In response, the US and its allies mixed legal justifications with moral and strategic claims. They argued that the war was legal because it had been tacitly authorised by UN Security Council resolutions dealing with Iraq's invasion of Kuwait in 1990; morally just, because it aimed to overthrow a tyrannical regime that had butchered hundreds of thousands of its own citizens; and strategically important because Saddam's WMD program threatened regional **security** and raised the possibility of a nightmare scenario long predicted by **terrorism** experts – a rogue regime passing WMD capabilities to terrorist groups.

Once the war was underway there were also important debates about how it should be conducted and especially about how the coalition should respond to the **insurgency** that erupted in 2004. For example, the mistreatment of Iraqi prisoners at Abu-Ghraib prison and the large number of civilian casualties inflicted by US forces during the two battles for Fallujah in late 2004 raised serious doubts about the legality and legitimacy of the coalition's war conduct and seriously undermined the coalition's standing in the eyes of ordinary Iraqis.

Questions about when it is legitimate to go to war and how war must be conducted are central to public and political debates and play a significant role in policy-making and military decision-making, especially in the West. Although some realists argue that there is no place for morality in decision-making about war, in fact the politics of war is deeply imbued with moral and legal arguments. Decisions to invade countries like Iraq or Afghanistan, participate in wars such as Vietnam and World War I, or to send **peacekeepers** to East Timor or Darfur are only partly strategic choices. Indeed, the strategic question of whether we *can* achieve our aims through force is secondary to the question of whether we *ought* to do so. Likewise, decisions about how to fight are shaped by our politics and our ethics.

When is it right to fight? (*jus ad bellum*)

Contemporary international law on the use of force is based upon the **UN Charter**. Prior to the Charter (which was agreed in 1945), it was widely considered that **states** had an inherent right to wage war whenever they believed that they had a case for doing so, be it to defend themselves, protect their interests, or claim a territory. After the horrors of World War II, it was agreed that this regime was too permissive. Thus, Article 2(4) of the UN Charter explicitly forbids the use or threat of force in international relations. This is considered a fundamental rule of international relations, from which there are only two exceptions. First, all states have an inherent right to self-defence when they are attacked, set out by Article 51 of the Charter. Second, the UN's peak body for **peace** and security issues, the Security Council, has a right under Article 39 of the Charter to authorise collective enforcement action. To pass a so-called 'Chapter VIII' resolution, the Council needs to identify a threat to international peace and security, nine of the fifteen Council members must vote in favour, and none of the permanent five (P5) members (the US, UK, Russia, China and France) must vote against it. This gives the P5 effective veto on collective action.

Contemporary 'just war' writers have tended to criticise the UN Charter system for forbidding aggressive war and downplaying the role of justice in determining a war's legitimacy. As J. T. Johnson (1999: 57) has argued, labelling a war as 'aggressive' does not resolve the question of whether or not it is just, yet the UN Charter makes precisely that presumption. The Charter's drafters chose this highly restrictive model to help prevent future world wars. The key to conflict prevention, they believed, was to remove any ambiguity in the legal framework by building a 'presumption against aggressive war' into the Charter. This presumption may have contributed towards the steady decline of inter-state war since 1945. It has also produced some perverse effects, however. In 1979, Vietnam invaded Cambodia to remove Pol Pot, a genocidal dictator whose regime murdered at least two million Cambodians. The presumption against aggressive war forced Vietnam to justify its invasion by claiming that it was acting in self-defence, which was rejected by many states who imposed sanctions on Vietnam, demanded its immediate withdrawal from Cambodia and even offered indirect support to the *genocidaires* (Wheeler 2000: 78–110). This tension between law's presumption against aggressive war and an ethical 'presumption against injustice' (Johnson's term) is arguably the central dilemma of *jus ad bellum* today. The moral rules governing recourse to force found in the 'just war' tradition are more permissive than positive law in that they permit war in a wider number of instances. But they also impose more conditions. There are three types of rule: substantive, prudential and procedural. *Jus ad bellum* contains four substantive criteria (see Box 15.1).

The first criterion is *right intention*. Individuals must wage war for the common good, not for self-aggrandisement or because they hate the enemy. Right intention is seldom discussed nowadays and it has recently been suggested that it should be dropped because it is not clear why actors must have right intentions when they wage war (Chris Brown 2002: 108–9). This argument overlooks the role that right intentions play in the justification of killing itself. The just war tradition insists that a soldier's intention is absolutely critical because killing for personal gain or through hatred or envy is wrong. When soldiers kill, therefore, they must do so because it is the only way of defending the common good or righting a wrong.

The second substantive rule is that war may only be waged for a *just cause*. This is usually limited to self-defence, defence of others, restoration of peace, defence of rights and the punishment of wrongdoers. Just cause is often viewed in absolute terms: a combatant either has a just cause or does not. Today, this tendency is supported by legal **positivism**, which holds that actors either comply with the law or violate it (Walzer 1977: 59). However, since Vitoria (1991) in the sixteenth century, most 'just war' writers separated objective or true justice (knowable to God) from subjective justice (knowable to humans). Thus, wars can appear just on both sides. There are two ways of coping with this. First, as Vitoria argued, princes should show due care before they wage war. They should seek advice from learned people and listen to the opponent's arguments. Second, the just cause rule should be understood in relative terms. It is not a matter of either having or not having a just cause, but of having more or less of one. Sometimes this is labelled 'sufficient cause': do we have a sufficiently just cause to legitimise the actions we plan to take? This, of course, requires an assessment of two factors: the reason for war and the intended strategy.

Proportionality of ends asks whether the overall harm likely to be caused by the war is less than that caused by the wrong that is being righted. Vitoria suggested (1991) that proportionality played a significant role in judgments about the legitimacy of war. While war was legitimate to right wrongs, not all wrongs legitimised war. Some wrongs were neither grievous nor widespread enough to legitimise the inevitable evils that war entailed. On this view, proportionality is more than a prudential calculation. After all, prudence is always viewed from the eye of the beholder. A prudential account of proportionality would ask only whether the likely costs to us are greater than the likely benefits. Proportionality in the Vitorian sense requires a calculation of all the likely costs.

The final rule is that of *last resort*. Is the use of force the only, or most proportionate, way that the wrong is likely to be righted? Last resort does not require the exhaustion of every means short of force. If it did, force would never be licit because one can always continue to negotiate. Instead, last resort demands that actors carefully evaluate all the different strategies that might bring about the desired end, selecting force if it appears to be the only feasible strategy for securing those ends.

BOX 15.1: TERMINOLOGY

Jus ad bellum criteria

1. Substantive criteria
   – right intention
   – just cause
   – proportionality of ends
   – last resort
2. Prudential checks
3. Procedural requirements.

Prudential criteria impose important checks on decisions to wage what would otherwise be justifiable wars. The principal prudential check is *reasonable chance of success*. This criterion holds that as war always entails some degree of evil, it is wrong to wage war for a justifiable purpose unless those instigating it can reasonably expect to prevail. From a **realist** perspective, prudence includes both the overall likelihood of success and calculations about the costs of success. In other words, a state may be able to prevail but the cost of prevailing may be higher than it wishes to pay to satisfy a particular just cause. Because, from a realist perspective, political leaders have a primary moral responsibility to the welfare of their own citizens, they may not sacrifice that welfare unless their vital interests or fundamental values are at stake.

The third type of constraint covers the procedural requirements of *right authority* and *proper declaration*. In the Middle Ages, canon lawyers and scholastic intellectuals resolved the first question in favour of sovereign princes. Only those leaders with no clear superior could legitimately authorise war. In the modern era this translated into **sovereign states**, and from the eighteenth until the mid-twentieth centuries states were effectively given a free hand to authorise war whenever they saw fit. This right was heavily restricted, however, by the 1945 UN Charter, as we saw earlier. The question of who has the right to authorise war remains a moot point today. Positive law suggests that only states under attack and the UN Security Council have this right. Others hold that individual states and coalitions may legitimately wage war in other instances. Furthermore, it is widely accepted today that other actors, such as national liberation movements, may also legitimately wage war in some circumstances.

The requirement for proper declaration had its origins in the Roman system. During the Middle Ages, the declaration requirement supported the right authority test because only those princes with the **power** to declare war and not be removed from power had the right to wage war. The requirement also forced those about to embark on war to clearly state their case, providing an opportunity for peaceful restitution. Nowadays, the declaration can serve a third purpose: it clearly marks the transition from peace to war and hence the type of legal rules that ought to be applied.

How should war be waged? *(jus in bello)*

The legal and moral rules governing the conduct of war are much more clearly defined than the *jus ad bellum* rules (see Box 15.1), and today there is even an International Criminal Court (ICC) to prosecute those charged with war crimes, crimes against humanity and **genocide** in cases where the host state is either unwilling or unable to prosecute offenders.

International society's first attempt to grapple with *jus in bello* issues after World War II came in the form of the four **Geneva conventions** of 1949. The International Committee of the Red Cross/Red Crescent (ICRC) convened a meeting of experts in 1947, which produced a draft convention that was then put to states at a conference in Geneva in 1949. Although there was considerable agreement on the fundamentals, such as the need to afford further protection to non-combatants and prisoners of war, and the need for some sort of oversight, a number of issues proved contentious. The ICRC's draft had envisaged a convention that applied to all forms of armed conflict, but many states – particularly newly **decolonised** states and colonial powers – did not want protection afforded to rioters, **guerrillas** and terrorists. On the other hand, countries that had been recently occupied by the **fascists** worried that a rule giving

Figure 15.1 *White house*, Omarska, by David Kozar (with permission)

states a free hand to suppress local insurgents could be used by unjust aggressors to justify brutality towards the host population and insisted that the convention recognise that partisans had liberated parts of Europe. The result was a compromise. Common Article 3 committed parties in 'non-international' wars to respect **human rights** without specifying any particular privileges for insurgents, and the Convention on the Protection of Civilians (Convention IV) offered comprehensive legal protection to non-combatants in occupied territories. The upshot, however, was that the victims of international wars received more protection from the laws of war than the victims of **civil wars**.

The Geneva conventions comprised a comprehensive code of *jus in bello*, granting wide protection to non-combatants, the wounded and sick and prisoners of war. By the 1980s, it was widely held that the conventions had the status of customary law binding on all. Consequently, grave breaches of the conventions were universally punishable, though there remained no instrument for punishing perpetrators. Moreover, within a decade or so of their enactment, it became clear that there were significant gaps in the conventions. Not least, there was no prohibition on indiscriminate bombardment and no proportionality clause in the four conventions (Best 1994: 106–7). Furthermore, decolonisation and the overwhelming preponderance of internal wars created an impetus for extending the protections afforded in international wars to internal conflicts. Between 1974 and 1977, states returned to Geneva to negotiate additions to the conventions.

BOX 15.2: KEY TEXTS

International humanitarian law: some important documents

Hague Conference (1899)

- Convention (II) with Respect to the Laws and Customs of War on Land
- Declaration on the Launching of Projectiles and Explosives from Balloons
- Declaration on the Use of Projectiles the Object of Which is the Diffusion of Asphyxiating or Deleterious Gases

Hague Conference (1907)

- Convention (IV) Respecting the Laws and Customs of War on Land

Geneva Conventions (1949)

- Convention (I) for the Amelioration of the Condition of the Wounded and Sick in Armed Forces in the Field
- Convention (II) for the Amelioration of the Condition of the Wounded, Sick and Shipwrecked Members of the Armed Forces at Sea
- Convention (III) Relative to the Treatment of Prisoners of War
- Convention (IV) Relative to the Protection of Civilian Persons in Time of War

Additional Protocols to the Geneva Convention

- Additional Protocol (I) Relating to the Protection of Victims of International Armed Conflict (1977)
- Additional Protocol (II) Relating to the Protection of Victims of Non-International Armed Conflicts (1977)
- Additional Protocol (III) Relating to the Adoption of an Additional Distinctive Emblem (2005)

The first Geneva Protocol significantly extended the protection afforded to non-combatants. It insisted that attacks be strictly limited to military objectives, defining these as 'those objects which by their nature, location, purpose or use make an effective contribution to military action and whose total or partial destruction, capture or neutralization, in the circumstances ruling at the time, offers a definite military advantage' (Article 52, Protocol I). In other words, soldiers were forbidden from attacking non-combatants or their property, though so-called 'dual use' facilities remained lawful targets. Soldiers were also obliged to evaluate the proportionality of their attacks, with Article 51(5) outlawing attacks on military objects which 'may be expected to cause' excessive civilian casualties. The Protocol also forbade the indirect targeting of non-combatants through attacks calculated to destroy vital civilian infrastructure and cause starvation. The Protocol's principle of discrimination provided the catalyst for conventions banning weapons considered inherently indiscriminate. For example, the 1980 Convention on Conventional Weapons and subsequent amendments banned booby traps, lasers, and weapons that injure by creating fire and heat, on the grounds of inherent indiscriminacy. The 2000 Convention prohibiting the manufacture, sale and use of landmines was also justified on this basis. Of course, the question of discrimination made it problematic for the nuclear powers to adopt the Protocol because it is very difficult to see how nuclear weapons could be used discriminately. Despite the non-signature of states such as the US, UK and Russia owing to concerns about the legality of their nuclear arsenals, all three have indicated that they believe the Protocol to be binding and that the legality of the use of nuclear weapons is indeterminate, a position confirmed by the International Court of Justice (ICJ) in the *Legality of Nuclear Weapons* case.

Protocol II regulated how states might respond to internal insurgents. Above all, it reinforced the basic idea behind human rights law, that states were not free to treat their own citizens however they liked, though Protocol II afforded states considerable latitude in deciding whether or not a particular insurgency could be labelled an 'armed conflict', thereby bringing the Protocol into play. Nevertheless, some states – particularly the US – complained that Protocol II gave too many rights to 'terrorists' and tied the hands of states combating them.

Through the Geneva conventions and protocols and other instruments such as the Genocide Convention (1948) and Convention against Torture (1987), a comprehensive system of positive law designed to moderate the use of force and protect non-combatants has been created. The system did little, however, to deter despots such as Pol Pot and Idi Amin from systematically massacring non-combatants. Furthermore, in the so-called 'new wars' of the 1990s, the direct targeting of non-combatants once again became a war strategy. As a result of this seemingly growing impunity before the law, the question of enforcement was raised once again, culminating in the creation of the ICC in 2002.

The moral restrictions on the use of force are very similar to the legal prohibitions. There are three basic rules. First, the principle of discrimination: non-combatants must never be deliberately attacked. Second, the principle of proportionality: military targets may only be attacked when their military value outweighs the foreseeable destruction that will result. Third, combatants must not use prohibited weapons or conduct themselves in ways that violate the laws of war.

Underpinning the *jus in bello* is the doctrine of double-effect, first articulated in the thirteenth century by St Thomas Aquinas. According to Aquinas, the doctrine holds that any act may have two consequences: one that is intended and one that is not. Even if we intend good, our actions may cause unintended negative consequences. According to the doctrine of double-effect, unintended negative consequences are excusable if four conditions are satisfied:

1. The desired end must be good in itself.
2. Only the good effect is intended.
3. The good effect must not be produced by means of the evil effect.
4. The good of the good effect must outweigh the evil of the evil effect (proportionality) (Ramsey 1961: 43; 48–9).

There is a major flaw with this rendition and double-effect injunctions ought to be treated sceptically. It is worth quoting Walzer (1977: 156) at length here:

> Simply not to intend the death of civilians is too easy … What we look for in such cases is some sign of a positive commitment to save civilian lives. Not merely to apply the proportionality rule and kill no more civilians than is militarily necessary … Civilians have a right to something more. And if saving civilian lives means risking soldiers' lives, the risk must be accepted.

The idea that it is possible to separate intent and act, particularly when referring to individuals in combat, has often been criticised. Critics argue that there is no practical difference between *intending* the deaths of non-combatants near military targets and merely *foreseeing* it (McKeogh 2002). According to Walzer and the contemporary laws of war, although we can never fully know an actor's intentions, we can ascertain something approximating intentions by focusing on actions. To display an intention not to harm non-combatants, combatants must demonstrate *both* that they did not deliberately seek to kill non-combatants and that they have taken every reasonable precaution to minimise the likelihood of harming non-combatants (due care). However, there remain significant differences over *how much* additional risk should be accepted. These debates cannot be resolved in the abstract, but only through empirical assessments of individual cases.

The remainder of the chapter outlines two important contemporary debates, one in relation to recourse to force and the second in relation to the conduct of war.

Jus ad bellum dilemma: preemptive self-defence

After 11 September 2001, the US and many of its allies put forward a case for preemptive self-defence. Thus, the National Security Strategy presented by the US in 2002 insisted that:

> [G]iven the goals of **rogue states** and terrorists, the United States can no longer solely rely on a reactive posture as we have in the past. The inability to deter a potential attacker, the immediacy of today's threat, and the magnitude of potential harm that could be caused by our adversaries' choice of weapons, do not permit that option. We cannot let our enemies strike first (US 2002).

This doctrine was condemned by many states, especially in Asia and the Middle East, and by opponents of the government in the US and elsewhere, but is it illegal and/or unjust?

Since 1945, interpretations of Article 51 of the UN Charter have tended to fall into one of two camps, restrictionist and counter-restrictionist. Restrictionists insist that Article 51 expressly rules out pre-emption, arguing that states have a right to use force in self-defence only after an armed attack has occurred, a view supported by the ICJ in the *Nicaragua v. US* case. They argue that if these limits were loosened, states would be encouraged to abuse the right to self-defence, eroding the distinction between aggression and defence (Cassese 1986: 515–16). Although there is evidence that the Charter's drafters intended Article 51 to provide only a limited right of self-defence, the idea that a state should wait to be attacked before taking measures to defend its citizens has been widely criticised. Sir Humphrey Waldock (in G. Roberts 1999: 483) described it as 'a travesty of the purposes of the Charter'.

Counter-restrictionists argue that Article 51 does not diminish a state's inherent right to preemptive self-defence. There are at least three justifications for this view. First, it is implied in the Charter's language. Article 51 explicitly endorses a state's inherent right to self-defence. That inherent right is said to include a right of pre-emption. Second, states have tended to judge pre-emption on the merits of each case. When the threat is demonstrably imminent, international society has shown itself willing to tolerate pre-emption. The paradigmatic case of this was the world's reaction to Israel's 1967 preemptive attack on Egypt. Although some states condemned Israel, many others accepted that it was necessary for Israel to use force to defend itself (C. Gray 2000: 112–13). Finally, there is a strong tradition of moral thinking in favour of preemption. Historically, prominent writers like Grotius and Pufendorf in the seventeenth century, and Vattel in the eighteenth century, have tended to identify a limited right of pre-emption.

The balance of argument suggests a right of self-defence that permits pre-emption in some cases but forbids 'preventive' attacks before a threat has become imminent. In what situations is pre-emption justifiable? Where do we draw the line between pre-emption and prevention? We can begin to answer these questions by considering the exchange of diplomatic notes between the UK and US concerning the sinking of the *Caroline* in 1837 (Box 15.3).

BOX 15.3: CASE STUDY

The *Caroline* affair

In 1837, there was an armed insurrection against British rule in Canada. The rebels used a US-owned ship, the *Caroline*, to transport supplies from the US side of the Niagara River. On 29 December 1837, Canadian troops loyal to Britain boarded the ship, killed several US citizens, set the ship alight and allowed it to drift over the Niagara Falls. At the time of the attack the *Caroline* was docked on the US side of the border, not in its usual port on the Canadian side. The US protested against the attack, claiming that its **sovereignty** had been violated, but the British insisted that they were exercising their right to self-defence.

The British defended their action by blaming the US for failing to prevent the use of its territory by the Canadian rebels, and justified the attack as 'a necessity of self-defence and self-preservation'. Not surprisingly, the US rejected this argument, insisting that the level of threat that could justify 'hot pursuit' must be 'imminent, and extreme, and involving impending destruction'. In 1840, the US government invited the British government to apologise for the incident and pay compensation in return for the dismissal of charges against a soldier imprisoned in connection with the incident. The British Minister agreed immediately and despatched an apologetic note to the US government. In an 1842 reply to the British, the US Secretary of State, Daniel Webster, explained that for the claim of self-defence to be justifiable Britain was required to 'show a necessity of self-defence, instant, overwhelming, leaving no choice of means, and no moment for deliberation'. The action taken must also involve 'nothing unreasonable or excessive; since the act, justified by the necessity of self-defence, must be limited by that necessity and kept clearly within it' (see Bellamy 2006b: 161–2).

According to the *Caroline* case, in order to invoke a right of pre-emption, a state has to demonstrate (1) the imminence of an attack, (2) the necessity of pre-emption and (3) the proportionality of its intended response.

States therefore have a limited right of pre-emption in cases that satisfy these three criteria. Jurists worry, with good reason, that expanding the right beyond the *Caroline* formula would blur the boundary between legitimate defence and unjust aggression. In the post-September 11 world, we are confronted with a tricky dilemma – defining what 'imminence' means in relation to terrorism. As George W. Bush (2002b) put it, when it comes to terrorism, 'we cannot wait for the final proof – the smoking gun – that could come in the form of a mushroom cloud'. One way of rethinking 'imminence' without undermining the legal and moral balance would be to suggest that an attack is imminent if the enemy has demonstrated an intention to attack and has acquired the means to do so. In relation to terrorism, this might suggest that states are entitled to use force to pre-empt an attack even if they do not know the precise timing and location of an expected attack. It is imperative, however, that those using force in this way provide compelling evidence of the target's intent to attack and ability to do so.

Jus in bello dilemma: cluster bombs

Cluster bombs are designed to deliver a large amount of smaller submunitions over a significant area, increasing the overall radius of destruction that a bomb can achieve. They are generally meant for use against troop concentrations, airfields – especially runways – and air defence units. Even when targeted at military objects, cluster bombs present two sets of problems: first, because the submunitions are not individually targeted there is a high chance that the bomb attack itself could cause casualties among non-combatants. Second, unexploded submunitions effectively become anti-personnel landmines. As a result, in 2007 a group of states and **non-government organisations** led by Norway began a campaign to ban the use of cluster bombs. The following year, a Convention on Cluster Munitions was agreed in Dublin. The Convention prohibits the manufacture, use and stockpiling of cluster munitions. At the time of writing, forty-seven countries had signed and **ratified** the agreement, including the UK, whose forces had used cluster munitions in Kosovo and Iraq and whose government undertook to destroy its stockpile of weapons. A further seventy states had signed but not yet ratified. However, major powers such as Brazil, China, India, Pakistan, Russia and the US rejected the treaty on the grounds that cluster munitions are necessary weapons and not inherently indiscriminate.

The key question in this debate is whether the inability to direct each submunition and the threat that unexploded submunitions pose to non-combatants make the weapon inherently indiscriminate. The 1977 Protocol I provides guidance. The Protocol prohibits attacks 'which employ a method or means of combat which cannot be directed at a specific military target' (Article 51(4)(b)) and forbids bombings that treat 'separate and distinct' military targets as one (Article 51(5)(a)). At the very least, this suggests that cluster bombs can only be discriminately used against military targets that are well away from civilian areas. Even if this condition is satisfied, however, cluster bombs may still have an indiscriminate *effect*. Protocol I defines indiscriminate attacks as including those 'which employ a method or means of combat the effects of which cannot be limited as required by this Protocol' (Article 51(4)(c)). Coupled with the requirement to take 'all feasible precautions' to protect non-combatants, it is difficult to see how an attack in an area likely to be frequented by non-combatants before those that launched the attack have had the opportunity to remove unexploded submunitions can be considered discriminate (Cryer 2002: 61 n.137).

The US made widespread use of cluster bombs against frontline targets in Afghanistan and this example highlights the merits in both sides of the debate. In several cases, cluster bombs killed non-combatants on impact. According to Human Rights Watch, the choice of cluster bombs to strike targets relatively close to residential areas constitutes a failure to take 'all feasible precautions'. Indeed, it argues that the use of cluster bombs near residential areas should be presumed indiscriminate (2002: 24). The element of indiscrimination comes into play when a cluster bomb hits its intended target but some of its submunitions nevertheless harm non-combatants. However, in many cases the non-combatant casualties may have been the result of bombs *missing* their target, meaning that the killings were a mistake rather than a direct consequence of the type of munitions used. Given this, it is worth posing the proportionality question of whether the danger posed by large numbers of small munitions is greater or less than that posed by the alternative – a single unitary bomb. The US Defense Department is on the record as arguing that unitary bombs cause more **collateral damage** than cluster bombs because they have a larger blast range (Human Rights Watch 2001: 10 n.33). While the submunitions damaged civilian buildings, unitary bombs would have flattened them.

The much more problematic issue in relation to cluster bombs is their indiscriminate *effects*. Each submunition that fails to explode on impact effectively becomes a landmine – commonly believed to be inherently indiscriminate because it detonates irrespective of whether it is touched by a combatant or non-combatant. Do these ostensibly indiscriminate effects mean that the use of cluster bombs themselves should be deemed indiscriminate? One could argue that cluster bombs are much like any other weapon in that all weapons pose an indiscriminate threat when they malfunction. However, has the US taken every feasible precaution to minimise the damage that unexploded ordnance causes to non-combatants and civilian property?

At war's end there were between 12 221 and 53 772 unexploded submunitions in Afghanistan. Even at the lower end, this posed a significant threat to non-combatants. The first way to reduce this threat would be to lower the failure rate. The failure rate of newer weapons is considerably lower than older weapons but there are reports that the US made extensive use of old munitions weapons in Afghanistan. Because unexploded submunitions pose a continuing threat to non-combatants after the cessation of hostilities, those that delivered them have a responsibility to do everything feasible to remove them. Anything short of this breaches the principle of due care. Although de-mining and the removal of unexploded munitions have progressed apace in Afghanistan, the overwhelming bulk of the effort was conducted by the UN Mine Action Programme and non-governmental organisations such as HALO. By the end of 2002, 111 cluster bomb sites had been cleared out of an estimated total of 227, with much of the remainder being cleared in 2003–4 (Human Rights Watch 2002: 33). The most troubling issue was the very limited role played by the US government, the actor with the primary moral responsibility for removing the weapons. Most de-mining agencies in Afghanistan told Human Rights Watch that the US government provided little or no help, and that it had not even provided accurate information to de-miners. In the first eight months after the war, the US donated only $7 million in cash and equipment to the de-mining effort (Human Rights Watch 2002: 37–8).

On two counts, therefore, the US failed the due care test. First, it used old weapons with relatively high failure rates in close proximity to residential areas. Second, having dropped cluster bombs, the US and its allies failed in their responsibility to remove the threat to non-combatants posed by unexploded submunitions. But it is more difficult to say whether cluster munitions proved to be inherently indiscriminate and whether their use was more harmful than using conventional unitary bombs. This is something that should be debated more extensively, both in general and in relation to specific cases.

Conclusion

Without ethical and legal constraints on both the decision to wage it (*jus ad bellum*) and its conduct (*jus in bello*), war is nothing more than the application of brute force, logically indistinguishable from mass murder. But it need not always be this way. Today there is a well-developed set of moral and legal rules governing the use of force, and international institutions designed to enforce them.

Nonetheless, it is the ever-present danger of the descent into barbarism that makes the ethics and laws of war so important today; in democracies especially, every individual has a responsibility to use their own judgment to interrogate the morality of violence employed in their name. To return to where we started, debate about whether or not to invade Iraq and when to withdraw demonstrates only too well the practical veracity of the rules and ideas set out in this chapter. Neither advocates nor opponents rejected the existence of rules. Instead, they disagreed about the guidance the rules gave in this specific instance. This is entirely as it should be. The principles described in this chapter do not provide answers; they simply set out ways of having meaningful conversations about the myriad dilemmas presented by war. These are not idle or unimportant debates because they determine not only the future trajectory of politicians' careers but also the future life-chances of countless thousands, if not millions, of people.

QUESTIONS

1. What is the relationship between the 'just war' tradition and the laws of war?
2. In what ways should the 'just war' tradition be reformed to bring it up to date?
3. Are some weapons, like cluster bombs and nuclear missiles, inherently immoral or does it all depend on how they are used?
4. Why was there so much opposition to the 2003 invasion of Iraq? Do you think this opposition was justified?

5. Is it fair that both the just side and the unjust side in war have to abide by the same rules?

6. Does the 'just war' tradition serve to limit war or enable it by providing moral justifications for killing?

FURTHER READING

Best, G. 1994, *War and law since 1945*, Oxford: Clarendon Press. The most comprehensive account of international humanitarian law since 1945.

Johnson, J. T. 1999, *Morality and contemporary warfare*, New Haven: Yale University Press. Excellent account of 'just war' thinking grounded in the tradition's history.

Walzer, M. 1977, *Just and unjust wars: a philosophical argument with historical illustrations*, New York: Basic Books. Modern classic account of the 'just war' tradition.

16

International Law

Donald R. Rothwell

Introduction	232
Contemporary development of international law	233
Institutions	233
Sources of international law	234
Major areas of international law	238
Contemporary controversies	240
Conclusion	241
Questions	241
Further reading	242

Introduction

This chapter considers the development, sources and significance of contemporary **international law**. Particular attention is given to the sources of international law, including treaties and customary international law, and some of the distinctive fields of international law such as that governing the use of force. Comment is also made on current international law controversies.

International law is the system of law developed by **states** which governs the relationships between states at either a **multilateral**, regional or **bilateral** level. To that end, international law has traditionally been considered '**state-centric**' in that it is dominated by states which both make international law and are the predominant objects of that law (Shaw 2008: 1). The modern system of international law is often identified as having begun to develop at the time of the **Treaty of Westphalia** in 1648, though there is evidence of its gradual emergence prior to that time. Many prominent international law scholars also existed during the sixteenth and seventeenth centuries, such as the Dutch publicist Hugo **Grotius** whose famous seventeenth century work *De jure belli ac pacis* ('The rights of war and peace') ([1625] 2005) was pivotal in identifying the legal framework between states during times of war and peace. Grotius, who is often described as the 'father' of international law, was also embroiled in the so-called 'battle of books' following the publication in 1609 of his work *Mare liberum* ('The open seas') which was responded to in 1635 by the English author John Selden with *Mare clausum* ('The closed seas') (Brownlie 2008: 224). These two works were fundamental to resolving debates over the developing international law governing the sea (see Grewe 2000: 257–75).

From the seventeenth century onwards international law continued to develop with a principal focus upon the core relationships that at the time existed between states such as trade and commerce, boundaries and territoriality, **war** and **peace**. It was only in the late nineteenth century that international law began to develop an interest in the individual with the 1864 **Geneva Convention** providing protections for soldiers no longer able to take any further part in a battle as a result of being wounded or taken prisoner. In the early part of the twentieth century significant and rapid developments took place in international law, partly due to the efforts of the League of Nations and various conferences that promoted international law. In 1922 the first international court was established – the Permanent Court of International Justice (PCIJ) – located at The Hague in the Netherlands.

The most significant modern development in international law came with the adoption of the **United Nations Charter** in 1945. The Charter, which is a treaty for the purposes of international law, places considerable emphasis on the importance of international law to the **United Nations (UN)**. This is reflected, for example, in Article 1, which identifies one of the purposes of the UN as being to 'bring about by peaceful means, and in conformity with the principles of justice and international law' the settlement of international disputes. To that end, one of the principal organs of the UN established under Article 7 of the Charter is the International Court of Justice (ICJ). Often referred to as the 'World Court', the ICJ is a permanent court located in The Hague and is a successor to the PCIJ. The court is open to all UN members, and to non-UN members who accept its jurisdiction.

Contemporary development of international law

International law has witnessed significant growth and expansion since the adoption of the UN Charter as states have increasingly sought to regulate their affairs through an ever widening web of multilateral, regional and bilateral treaties which have addressed an expanding array of topics. This growth has been partly driven by the significance attached to international law by the UN Charter, and the prominence given to it through the establishment of the ICJ. The UN has also been directly responsible for the making of new international law, whether through international treaties arising from UN sponsored conferences, or through the adoption by the UN Security Council of resolutions which are binding on UN member states. Other UN affiliated organs and institutions which have promoted the development of new international laws include the Food and Agricultural Organization (FAO), International Labor Organization (ILO) and International Maritime Organization (IMO).

As new international issues have arisen, the response of the international community at both the multilateral and bilateral level has often been to seek to develop new international laws. Therefore, since 1945 there has been a significant growth in new international law addressing maritime boundaries, telecommunications, the regulation of outer space, international health, transnational crime and **terrorism**. This has resulted in a significant expansion in the number of international treaties that states are parties to, thereby increasing the extent of their international legal obligations. However, while international law has steadily developed post 1945, the level of implementation, compliance and enforcement has remained variable. This has raised two significant issues. The first is that international law is lacking in strong enforcement mechanisms, a point emphasised by **realists** (see Chapter 2). Unlike national legal systems, there is no 'international police force'. The UN Security Council certainly plays an important role in monitoring the actions of so-called '**rogue states**', but unless there has been an egregious breach of international law such as the territorial invasion by one state of another, the Council's ability to apply and enforce international law is circumscribed. The second issue is that international law often relies upon strong national legal systems for local enforcement. This is especially the case with international **human rights** law (see Chapter 32). As there are many different national legal systems there is considerable scope for variable interpretation and implementation of international law.

Institutions

Unlike national legal systems, where there are often a number of law-making institutions such as a parliament, or assembly, there are no predominant international law-making institutions. The UN (see Chapter 21) has certainly played an important role in the post-war development of international law, however UN General Assembly resolutions are not legally binding upon states. UN Security Council resolutions are legally binding under Article 25 of the Charter, although this will still depend upon the precise nature of the resolution and the wording that is used within it. Similar issues exist for other international organisations such as the Organization of American States and the European Parliament, which may or may not adopt laws and resolutions that are binding upon member states.

Organisations which have oversight of particular international issue areas have a capacity to influence the development of international law. The **World Trade Organization (WTO)** and International Atomic Energy Agency (IAEA) are prominent examples. In addition, under Article 13 of the UN Charter the UN General Assembly established the International Law Commission (ILC) as a permanent body promoting the progressive development of international law and its codification.

The ICJ as the only true world court, is the most significant global judicial institution. The court is composed of 15 judges, from varying legal systems and different countries, who serve nine-year terms. The court is able to adjudicate on contentious cases between two or more states, and can also deliver non-binding advisory opinions. In recent years the number of permanent international courts and tribunals has significantly expanded: as a result of the creation of a range of mechanisms under the WTO for the resolution of trade disputes; the establishment of the International Tribunal for the Law of the Sea (ITLOS), located in Hamburg, to consider law of the sea cases; and, perhaps most significantly, the International Criminal Court (ICC), which is also located in The Hague. The ICC joins two non-permanent international criminal tribunals for Yugoslavia and Rwanda as true international criminal courts with jurisdiction over war crimes, crimes against humanity and **genocide**. Building on the precedent of the post-World War II international military tribunals at Nuremberg and Tokyo, the ICC seeks to ensure that war crimes do not go unpunished, no matter the military rank or political status of the perpetrators. However, the effectiveness of the ICC will be constrained as long as major states such as China, Israel and the US remain resistant to their citizens being held accountable before the court.

Sources of international law

National legal systems have recognisable sources for their laws. Predominantly, these include the statutes, acts, decrees and proclamations made by a parliament, legislature or the executive (e.g. president or presidential council). In addition, the decisions of the courts and tribunals within national legal systems have a great deal of significance, not only for those parties whose disputes are adjudged by those courts, but for the legal system itself due to the precedent created by those decisions. In developed legal systems, where there is a **hierarchy** of courts at a local, regional, or provincial level, there is often an appellate structure which allows for appeals from lower to higher level courts. The decisions of appellate courts (e.g. Supreme Court, High Court, House of Lords) are binding upon lower courts in national legal systems.

International law does not mirror national legal systems in this regard; it has a distinctive set of recognised sources which are outlined in Article 38(1) of the ICJ Statute (see Box 16.1). Although Article 38(1) strictly only identifies the sources of international law to which the ICJ can refer in its decisions, it is also widely accepted as identifying the sources of international law more generally to which all states in the international community would look. The sources can be divided into two groupings as follows:

- treaties
- customary international law
- general principles of law,

and as subsidiary sources:

- judicial decisions
- teachings of the most highly qualified publicists.

BOX 16.1: KEY TEXTS

Statute of the International Court of Justice

Article 38(1)

   The Court … shall apply:

a. international conventions …;
b. international custom …;
c. the general principles of law recognized by civilized nations;
d. … judicial decisions and the teachings of the most highly qualified publicists of the various nations, as subsidiary means for the determination of the rules of law.

Treaties

Treaties are one of the most significant sources of international law and are an integral part of the conduct of international relations. During the UN era treaties have grown considerably in their importance and number. A treaty is defined by the Vienna Convention on the Law of Treaties (1969) as:

an international agreement concluded between States in written form and governed by international law, whether embodied in a single instrument or in two or more related instruments and whatever its particular designation.

An instrument which does not meet these criteria is therefore not a treaty and does not create any legally binding obligations between states. Examples would include 'Declarations' issued following a meeting of world leaders at the **G8**, **G20** or regional organisations such as the EU, **APEC** or **ASEAN**. While these documents are written, and often outline agreed positions and commitments, they are not intended to be legally binding and therefore fall short of treaty status. As treaties must be in a written form, an oral treaty is not recognised by international law. While a treaty must be in writing, there is no requirement as to the language in which the treaty is written, and this will often depend upon the official language of each state party to the treaty. Multilateral treaties negotiated under the auspicious of the UN are also written in the six official UN languages (Arabic, Chinese, English, French, Russian and Spanish).

Treaties are entered into between states which are recognised as such for the purposes of international law and international relations. The only exception to this rule applies in the case of recognised international organisations. The constituent units of federal states cannot, therefore, enter into a treaty. Agreements entered into between New York state and the province of Ontario would not be legally binding under international law. The requirement that the treaty be governed by international law goes to the actual intention of the parties, and is an important point of distinction between a legally binding international instrument and a pure political declaration.

'Treaty' is a generic term and not a required title for a legally binding international instrument between states. Other titles may be used of which the terms 'convention' or 'agreement' are also common (see Box 16.2). A treaty may comprise more than one international instrument, and amending or supplementary instruments – often referred to as 'protocols' – will also need to be read alongside the treaty.

Treaties are a preferred source for the development of new international law because of the flexibility associated with their negotiation. They can be adopted by states at a multilateral level, by a regional international organisation or by a collective of states interested in a regional issue, or by two states bilaterally. Once negotiated at a **diplomatic** gathering, a treaty will often be available for signature by states. However, it is now rare for a treaty to enter into force as a result of signature alone, and the formal act of **ratification** is most commonly required before a treaty will eventually enter into force. Each treaty will have its own particular formula before it enters into force. For multilateral treaties there will be a designated number of states which need to become a party before the treaty enters into force. For bilateral treaties, both of the relevant states need to have ratified prior to entry into force. Some multilateral treaties allow states to lodge written 'reservations', which effectively modify the extent of the legal obligation under the terms of the treaty. In turn, other states which reject the legitimacy of a reservation may seek to lodge an objection to a reservation the consequence of which is that the treaty relationship between the reserving and objecting state will be adjusted. Some treaties also permit the making of 'declarations', which permit a state to indicate its particular interpretation of certain provisions in the treaty. The effect of a declaration is that it places other states on notice as to how one state will interpret particular provisions of the treaty.

The importance of treaties is that once they enter into force the principle of '*pacta sunt servanda*' (treaties must be observed) applies, which means they are legally binding as a solemn undertaking between the states and are to be applied in good faith. As Scott (2004b: 213) has observed 'a treaty is meant to mean just what it says and States are supposed to comply with the obligations they have assumed'. In this respect a treaty is equivalent to a contract between two private parties. It is a legal instrument from which consequences will flow, and if a dispute arises between the parties then certain mechanisms may be available between the parties to resolve their differences. In order to discourage the existence of secret treaties, Article 102 of the UN Charter requires states to register their treaties with the UN Secretariat as soon as the treaty enters into force. A treaty which has not been registered in this manner may not be relied upon before a UN organ, which includes the ICJ.

Customary international law

The longest standing and continuously dominant source of international law has been customary international law. Though it is now losing some of its previous influence because of the growth of treaties during the UN era, custom remains of considerable

BOX 16.2 : TERMINOLOGY

Titles given to treaties

Convention: a multilateral treaty commonly adopted at UN conferences; e.g. United Nations Framework Convention on Climate Change.

Protocol: an additional treaty that amends or expands the operation of a Convention; e.g. Kyoto Protocol to the United Nations Framework Convention on Climate Change.

Statute: a multilateral treaty outlining the mechanisms and procedures of an international court; e.g. Rome Statute of the International Criminal Court.

Charter: a multilateral treaty outlining the constitutional framework of an international organisation; e.g. Charter of the Organization of American States.

Agreement: a bilateral or regional treaty; e.g. Australia-US Free Trade Agreement.

importance; it and treaties comprise the two predominant sources of contemporary international law.

Customary international law is based upon the practice of states and relies upon a consistency in that practice by individual states, combined with equivalent practice by states around the world. As outlined by the ICJ in the 1969 *North Sea Continental Shelf* case, customary international law requires state practice combined with *opinio juris* – which is a belief by a state that it is under a legal obligation to act in a certain manner. Unlike treaties, which rely upon a written document, custom relies the actions of states, which can be identified through statements and declarations of presidents, prime ministers or ministers, or the acts of state organs such as the military, or border and customs officials. Single, one-off actions are insufficient to establish state practice. There is also a need for consistency in state practice among states from around the world which are representative of differing regions and political, legal and cultural systems. The actions of Western states are not on their own, therefore, capable of creating new customary international law with respect to terrorism, for example. Nevertheless, the ICJ has accepted that in certain instances 'regional custom' may be created.

The significance of customary international law is that it is binding upon all members of the international community once it has been established. Therefore, unlike treaties which are only binding upon the treaty parties, custom is capable of having universal application to all states, even newly emerging states such as East Timor or Kosovo. The only exception to this rule applies in the case of a 'persistent objector' – that is, a state which continually objects to the development of a new rule of customary international law. To do so, however, the state must be vigilant in its protest against the development of the new rule. Custom is also capable of rapid evolution as a result of developments in state practice. Depending on its text, a unanimous UN General Assembly resolution may be an example of 'instant custom'.

General principles of law

The third principal source of international law referred to in Article 38(1) of the ICJ Statute is general principles of law recognised by the legal systems of states. This source utilises the common legal principles which are found across all legal systems throughout the world, irrespective of whether the national legal system is based upon a common law, civil law, or an Islamic law system. The principle of equity is an example of such a general principle drawn from national law which applies in international law and is of significance in maritime boundary delimitations.

Subsidiary sources: judicial decisions and teachings of publicists

Article 38(1) effectively creates a two-tiered system of sources when it identifies two 'subsidiary means' for determining the rules of international law. The first is judicial decisions, which principally encompasses the judgments of international courts and tribunals such as the ICJ, ICC, ITLOS and European Court of Human Rights. It would also extend to relevant decisions of national courts, when those courts are adjudging matters of international law such as the interpretation of a treaty which has significance at the national law level. The second of these sources is the writings of 'the most highly qualified publicists' which includes academic writings of eminent international law professors, retired international judges, and current or former diplomats with acknowledged international law expertise. However, as these are only subsidiary sources, they can only be legitimately referred to when the other sources prove to be inadequate. Nevertheless, as the jurisprudence of the ICJ continues to grow there has, perhaps inevitably, been a reliance upon its decisions as evidence of what the international law is in certain particular areas.

Soft law

A modern phenomenon in international relations is the plethora of multilateral and regional meetings convened by international organisations, conferences of parties to international treaty **regimes**, and ad hoc gatherings of states assessing new issues of international importance. A common outcome of these meetings is the adoption of political declarations representing the views of the states as to how certain issue areas should be addressed (see Box 16.3). Alternatively, groups of experts issue reports including draft treaties designed to influence the development of international law. While these declarations, statements and reports are not legally binding, they are commonly recognised as being a part of 'soft law' and capable of influencing the development of new treaties or, as a result of state practice and *opinio juris*, over time forming customary international law.

BOX 16.3: DISCUSSION POINTS

Non-legally binding international instruments

Ad hoc Political Declarations: adopted following an ad hoc meeting of states to discuss matters of common importance; e.g. Johannesburg Declaration on Sustainable Development.

Institutional Declarations: adopted by consensus by an international institution; e.g. APEC Leaders' Declaration, 'The Yokohama Vision – Bogor and Beyond', November 2010.

International Organisation Declarations: adopted by an international organisation following a determinative vote; e.g. The Universal Declaration of Human Rights, UN General Assembly Resolution 217A(III) (1948).

Major areas of international law

A feature of international law is that it has developed distinctive major fields, which have effectively extended the operation of international law into an ever increasing array of issue areas that are the subject of inter-state and international concern. Some of these are now identified.

Use of force

The international law governing the use of armed force is one of the fundamental areas of contemporary international law, and was a critical area for resolution in the UN Charter, coming as it did at the conclusion of World War II. The Charter did two things in this respect. First, in Article 51 it restated the fundamental right of all states to exercise the right of self-defence by way of a right of either individual or collective self-defence. The US response to the 2001 terrorist attacks upon New York and Washington, in which the US along with coalition partners such as the UK and Australia launched an armed response upon Afghanistan, is an example of the exercise of the right of self-defence. Second, Article 39 of the UN Charter also recognised the right of the UN Security Council to authorise military action in response to a 'threat to the peace, breach of the peace, or act of aggression' by way of a range of possible measures taken under Chapter VII of the Charter. Security Council resolutions adopted in 1990 following the Iraqi invasion of Kuwait authorising military action in Iraq are an example of this approach.

Law of the sea

Based upon some of the seminal writings of Hugo Grotius, the law of the sea is principally outlined in the 1982 United Nations Convention on the Law of the Sea (UNCLOS), which is often referred to as the 'constitution of the oceans'. The Convention details the extent of coastal states' rights to multiple maritime zones ranging from the territorial sea to the continental shelf, and the parallel rights of the international community to exercise the rights of freedom of navigation and freedom to fish.

Human rights

Contemporary international **human rights** law is founded upon the 1948 Universal Declaration on Human Rights (UDHR) adopted by the UN General Assembly. The UDHR is widely considered to reflect customary international law. The two 1966 international covenants, on Civil and Political Rights (ICCPR) and Economic, Social and Cultural Rights (ICESCR), further expand and develop the operation of the UDHR. In turn this legal base is supported by additional treaties dealing with a range of specific human rights issues such as racial discrimination, torture and the rights of persons with disabilities.

International humanitarian law

The law governing the use of force in armed conflict and its impact upon the participants in that conflict is referred to as **international humanitarian law** (IHL). It is principally based upon the four 1949 Geneva Conventions, and two 1977 Additional Protocols. Together these six treaties provide for a range of protections for combatants who become '*hors de combat*' (unable to further participate in the conflict), prisoners of war, and civilians who are caught up in an armed conflict.

International trade law

The international trading system was significantly reformed following the end of World War II, initially via the **General Agreement on Tariffs and Trade (GATT)** and then in 1994 by the Marrakesh Agreement establishing the World Trade Organization (WTO) (see Chapters 24 and 25). The WTO established a multilateral trading framework which includes compulsory mechanisms for the resolution of trade disputes. This regime is supplement by regional trade treaties, such as those which exist in Europe and North America, and numerous bilateral **free trade** agreements (treaties) between trading partners which are designed to reduce trade barriers and permit the flow of goods between states.

International environmental law

Since the 1970s there has been a global upsurge in environmental consciousness and this has resulted in the gradual development of a distinctive body of international law dealing with the environment. While there is no overarching global treaty framework in this area, the 1992 Rio Declaration on the Environment (a soft law instrument) does set important parameters for this field, especially with respect to principles such as the precautionary approach and sustainable development. Conventions such as those dealing with climate change, biodiversity, marine pollution and world heritage address a range of global environmental issues (see Chapters 34 and 35).

Contemporary controversies

One of the most contentious areas of international law and international relations is the use of force (see Lowe, Roberts, Welsh and Zaum 2008). The UN Charter was designed to provide an international security framework that would place significant constraints upon the use of armed force in the conduct of international relations, and Article 2(4) of the Charter sought to maintain the territorial integrity and political independence of states against the threat or use of force. Balanced against this, the Charter also recognised the Article 51 right of a state to exercise self-defence. Since the adoption of the Charter, and especially since the end of the **Cold War**, there have been increasing examples of states adopting an expansive interpretation of self-defence. This has resulted in some tension between states, the UN Security Council, and the ICJ. While the international community did not challenge the right of the US to exercise self-defence following the 2001 terrorist attacks on New York and Washington, the US-led invasion of Iraq in 2003 was much more contentious, as it predominantly relied upon UN Security Council resolutions adopted under Chapter VII of the UN Charter dealing with the **disarmament** of Iraq (see A. Roberts 2003). As the Security Council had not expressly endorsed military action against Iraq in 2003, the US and its allies sought to rely upon previous resolutions adopted in 2002 and as far back as 1990. The ambiguity of these resolutions – and the refusal of the US to allow the UN to conclusively determine the matter because of its fear that Iraq possessed **weapons of mass destruction** which would be used to launch an armed attack – ultimately resulted in the US and its allies adopting a **unilateral** interpretation of international law which had little global support from other states, or from international lawyers. These actions contributed to significant doubts being cast over the effectiveness of international law.

Since 2001 international law has also been dealing with the rise of the **non-state actor** (Scott 2004a: 296): that is, participants in international affairs who are not states yet possess some of the capabilities of states, such as **non-governmental organisations** and terrorist organisations. This phenomenon has been pervasive in the response to international terrorism and created significant difficulties in constructing a legal response to terrorist acts. Debates have arisen in a number of fields, such as international human rights law and international humanitarian law, concerning the rights of terrorists to take part in an armed conflict and the way in which military forces should respond to those non-state actors. Some parallels in this debate have also arisen following the upsurge in pirate attacks off the coastlines of states in Africa and Asia. While piracy has been regulated under international law from as far back as the time of Grotius, its modern version has raised difficult issues with respect to criminal jurisdiction over pirates once they have been detained, and whether states have an obligation to prosecute pirates for their crimes.

Conclusion

Contemporary international law has undergone enormous growth since the creation of the UN and has expanded into areas of international activity that previously would have been unthinkable. The large number of multilateral and bilateral treaties adopted by states is impressive; however, much remains to be done to ensure that the international legal obligations contained within those instruments are being properly adhered to. Some institutions, such as the WTO, have strong implementation and compliance mechanisms with compulsory dispute settlement. Human rights mechanisms, on the other hand, are not as well developed, notwithstanding UN compliance frameworks. Here there is an interesting contrast between the lack of an international human rights court at the global level, and the existence of regional human rights courts in the Americas and Europe. Nevertheless, despite its high-profile weaknesses and apparent failings, many areas of international law operate at a satisfactory level on a daily basis, underpinning multiple forms of international discourse and engagement at both a state level and an individual level. International telecommunications, air travel, navigation by sea, trade, and the movement of peoples are all dependent upon international law frameworks, and these by and large operate without dispute.

A test for international law is its responsiveness to matters of global concern, and here the track record appears variable. There is still no internationally agreed definition of international terrorism, notwithstanding the events of the early twenty-first century. Likewise, the international community has yet to come to agreement on a replacement regime for the **Kyoto Protocol** to the UN Convention on Climate Change. These examples reinforce the state-centric nature of international law and the need for state cooperation to work collaboratively to solve matters of common concern.

QUESTIONS

1. By what authority do the United Nations and other multilateral international institutions seek to adopt new international law, such as conventions and treaties, for all countries?
2. International law is often said to only operate on the basis of consent – that is, countries agree to be bound by international law. What would happen to the international legal system if countries elected to opt out of international law?
3. Is the legitimacy of the international legal system diminished by the action of a political body such as the United Nations Security Council adopting legally binding resolutions?
4. Compared to other systems of law (contract law, criminal law), is international law really law?
5. Can international law only be as effective as the mechanisms for its implementation and enforcement? Would it be assisted if there was an international police force?
6. What impact does international law really have upon the conduct of international relations?

FURTHER READING

Brownlie, Ian 2002, *Basic documents in international law*, 5th edn, Oxford: Oxford University Press. Collection of key public international law documents, including treaties and conventions.

Brownlie, Ian 2008, *Principles of public international law*, 7th edn, Oxford: Oxford University Press. Leading student and practitioner text on international law authored by one of the leading international lawyers of the late twentieth century.

Grewe, Wilhelm 2000, *The epochs of international law*, trans. Michael Byers, Berlin: Walter de Gruyter. Classic history of international law from the Middle Ages to the end of the twentieth century.

Reus-Smit, Christian 2004, *The politics of international law*, Cambridge: Cambridge University Press. Wide-ranging collection of essays at the intersection of international law and international relations.

Triggs, Gillian 2010, *International law: contemporary principles and practices*, 2nd edn, Chatswood: LexisNexis Butterworths. Comprehensive text which includes core materials from ICJ judgments and key conventions and treaties.

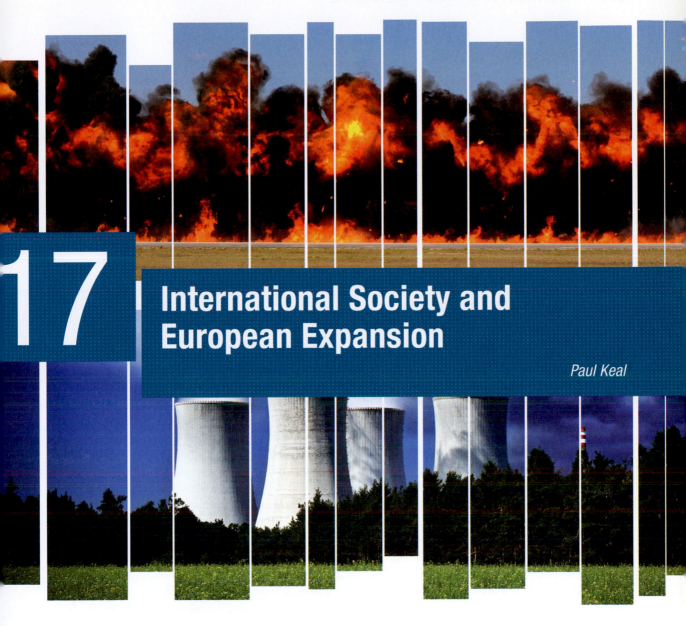

17

International Society and European Expansion

Paul Keal

Introduction	244
International society	244
The nature of international society	246
The limits of international society	249
European expansion	250
Conclusion	254
Questions	255
Further reading	255

Introduction

This chapter examines the evolution of **international society** through European expansion. It considers, first, the nature of international society: does such a society exist? What are its features? What purpose does it serve? And does it have the requisite unity to act as an agent in international relations? The discussion here draws upon the work of the **English School**, which pioneered the notion of international *society*. Second, the differing approaches to international society taken by solidarism and pluralism will be navigated. Third, the history of international society through **colonialism** and **decolonisation** will be charted, revealing the neglected story of an ongoing capacity for 'international society' to colonise the space of non-liberal **states**. Such a capacity throws up a challenge to international society to act as a standard bearer for countries and indigenous peoples who continue to be subjugated to the interests of greater powers.

International society

'International society' is a central term and focus of the English School (see Box 17.1). It is used to refer to both an influential concept and an actual society of states that is fundamental to world politics. This distinction matters because it is very easy to slip between these two meanings when thinking about international society; the concept doesn't easily correspond to how the world is actually constituted. Bearing this in mind, international society as an actual entity in world politics involves two stories; one of which is familiar and the other neglected. The familiar story presents international society as having its origins in newly formed sovereign European states, and recognising the need to regulate their mutual relations. Essential to this is an acceptance of plural conceptions of what is good and the entitlement of each **sovereign state** to conduct its internal affairs as it chooses. Cultural, religious and political differences are not seen to be a source of conflict, so long as there are rules of coexistence to guide states in their mutual relations. Largely as a consequence of the overseas expansion of Europe, and of colonisation and then decolonisation, the sovereign territorial state became the primary mode of political organisation, with practically all states becoming members of international society. From its inception international society constituted a moral community, meaning that members, at least in theory, treated each other as they would themselves be treated. Throughout the history of international society **great powers** have been central actors with both privileges and duties. Of these the most important duty has been to contribute to international **order**. At the core of this version of international society is a success story of the state as a form of political organisation and the historical maintenance of the society of states.

BOX 17.1 DISCUSSION POINTS

The English School

The English School has grown in popularity over the past twenty years as a school of international relations. Though some scholars see the English School as an offshoot of **realism**, its proponents believe it offers a middle way between and beyond realism and liberal **idealism**.

Ironically, the English School came into existence in the process of a polemical attack on international relations scholars closely associated with the London School of Economics. Roy Jones (1981) launched a withering assault on Hedley Bull, Michael Donelan, Alan James, C. A. W. Manning, Fred Northedge and Martin Wight, who he thought formed a more or less coherent School. He called for the School's closure, arguing that their defence of the 'classical approach' to international relations was **idealist**, unempirical and ignorant of scientific procedure.

Tim Dunne's (1998) pioneering 'history of the English School', to borrow from his book's subtitle, made the case for viewing the English School as an outgrowth of the British Committee on the Theory of International Politics, a group of international relations scholars that began meeting at the University of Cambridge from the late 1950s onwards. Its members included its leading figure, the historian Herbert Butterfield, as well as Wight, Bull, Michael Howard and Adam Watson among others. Dunne (1998: 6–11) argues that these scholars shared a particular tradition of inquiry, an interpretive approach to the subject, and an acknowledgment of the subject's inherently **normative** content. Interestingly, and controversially, Dunne also includes E. H. Carr as a member of the English School.

Andrew Linklater and Hidemi Suganami (2006) have recently presented an impressive reassessment and reconstruction of the English School. They question the inclusion of Carr in the School and argue instead for the inclusion of Manning, who heavily influenced the thought of Hedley Bull, the Australian who has arguably been the most significant theorist to emerge from the School. Whatever their differences regarding who's in and who's out of the English School, for Dunne – as for Linklater and Suganami – the School's key contribution to the study of international relations lies in the notion of international society. The English School argues that states exist in an international society, based on common rules, institutions and **norms**. This establishes and maintains order among states and supports the proposition that while states exist in a formal **anarchy**, they nonetheless make up a society of states. In this respect, the English School continues a line of thought that extends from Hugo Grotius in the seventeenth century (Bull, Kingsbury and Roberts 1990), which is why it is sometimes known as a **Grotian** approach.

The second, but neglected, story of international society concerns the adverse and lasting impact of European expansion on non-Europeans and **non-state actors**. As well as extending international society from Europe to cover the globe, European expansion involved the subjugation, colonisation and 'civilisation' of non-European others. It often involved the brutal treatment of non-Europeans, including acts of **genocide**. This is consequently a story of dispossession and injustice, a story in which political **theory** and **international law** progressively served, until quite recently, to justify the appropriation of lands occupied by non-Europeans. European expansion was, however, not a simple story of domination and subjection. There are many important examples of Europeans adopting the cultures that surrounded them, with some making 'really dramatic journeys across cultures' (Dalrymple 2002: 10). Even so, colonised and dispossessed peoples were generally excluded from the moral community of people entitled to the same rights and treatment that Europeans conceded to each other. In spite of decolonisation in the second half of the twentieth century and earlier, many peoples did not gain **self-determination** and remained in what they perceived as a state of internal colonialism. In spite of decolonisation there was no **self-determination** for many peoples within post-colonial states. They consequently made and continue to make rights claims against states and keep alive unresolved issues related to the harm caused by how they have been represented, by historic injustices and the moral legitimacy of the states in which they are located. This then is a story of the failure of states to resolve divisions in them and of international society to act as standard bearer for the marginalised and dispossessed.

What follows elaborates aspects of both these interwoven stories of international society, and has as its starting point what Martin Wight regarded as one of the primary questions of international theory: what is the nature of international society? Again, the discussion draws heavily from the work of English School scholars such as Wight, Bull and R. J. Vincent.

The nature of international society

International society is first and foremost a society of states. In the same way that individuals sharing a common bond or interest form a society, of which the simplest example is a club, territorial sovereign states with common interests are the members and principal actors in international society. Sovereign states are, in theory, independent actors in world politics, and in international law have equal rights with all other states. At the same time that they have authority over the people and territory within their borders, sovereign states are supposedly independent from other states and have no higher authority standing above them (see Chapter 9). From this follow two fundamental points.

First, international society is a society of mutual recognition. The states that constitute international society mutually recognise their right to **sovereignty**, independence and equality in international law. They recognise, in effect, each other's right to exist and have freedom of action as long as they do not threaten the sovereignty of another state. Without this recognition there can be no international society and from this follows the rule of non-intervention, which has been called the cardinal rule of international society (Vincent 1974) (see Box 17.2). Without the approval of the **United Nations (UN)** Security Council, or unless falling under limited and justified conditions, states are not to interfere in the internal affairs of other states. This raises the question of whether and under what circumstances it is permissible to intervene in sovereign states (Wheeler 2000).

BOX 17.2: DISCUSSION POINTS

R. J. Vincent on egg boxes

R. J. Vincent (1986: 123) proposes thinking about international society as an 'egg box'. In this metaphor, 'States are the eggs, the goodness within contained by a (fragile) shell. The box is international society, providing a compartment for each egg, and a (less fragile) wall between one and the next. The general function of international society is to separate and cushion, not to act'.

Second, within states, order and the rule of law are maintained by institutions of the state, such as courts, police forces and various administrative bodies. International society has no government of this kind. Except for the UN (see Chapter 32) – which, it should be emphasised, is an association of states and is often ineffective – there is no supranational authority able to impose or maintain order in international society. For this very reason Hedley Bull (1977) called it an 'anarchical society'; which is to say a society without government. The question arising from this, then, is: how is order between states maintained? One way to approach this is through asking a further question: how do we know that there is an international society?

Bull defined international society 'as a group of states' which is 'conscious of certain common interests and common values', and which accordingly sees itself as bound by a common set of rules 'and as sharing in the working of common institutions' (Bull 1977: 13). According to him, we know there is an international society because states behave as if there is one (see Box 17.3). Most states, most of the time, respect the rules of coexistence and participate in common institutions (Bull 1977: 42). In particular, they articulate common interests and values and also norms and rules, which their behaviour is in turn shaped by. The rules and norms might (but need not) have the status of international law. Equally, they need not be written or openly stated, but can be unspoken or tacit (Keal 1984). Rules and norms, whether written into law or not, are fundamental to international society because they guide the behaviour of states if they are to avoid conflict with each other. Unspoken or tacit rules are a response to situations where states either cannot or will not communicate openly.

BOX 17.3: DISCUSSION POINTS

Hedley Bull on system and society

A *system of states* (or **international system**) is formed when two or more states have sufficient contact between them, and have sufficient impact on one another's decisions, to cause them to behave – at least in some measure – as parts of a whole. (Bull 1977: 9).

A *society of states* (or international society) exists when a group of states, conscious of certain common interests and common values, form a society in the sense that they conceive themselves to be bound by a common set of rules in their relations with one another, and share in the working of common institutions. (Bull 1977: 13).

In important cases the coordination of common interests in international society involves the creation of mutual expectations coupled with reciprocity. For example, a state might decide not to develop or deploy a potentially destabilising weapon system if it has reason to expect another state or group of states will respond by also choosing not to deploy a similar weapon system. For such expectations to work and achieve a common interest of this kind, it must be mutually understood that their reciprocity depends on expectations being reinforced. The more expectations are met the more likely there is to be reciprocity, and this is a process that requires decision-makers in one or more states to put themselves in the shoes of decision-makers in other states. It is a process known as **intersubjectivity**. We cannot know what is in the minds of decision-makers in other states, but we can imagine what they might do. And if they then do that, our expectation is confirmed, and in this way norms and rules emerge and can become settled.

For Bull, the common interests that define international society are ones that require powerful members, from time to time, to set aside their own perceived interests and act in the interests of the society of states as a whole, especially if the survival of the society of states itself is at risk. In relation to this, it is important to ask whether international society serves the interests of all states, or only some, thus promoting the interests of a particular group of states. Among others, Chris Brown (1995) has suggested that international society might not amount to more that an inner circle of rich **liberal** states concerned mainly with promoting their own interests. Around this inner core is an outer circle whose membership in international society is less secure, and whose interests and values may be in opposition to those of the inner core. The importance of this is that far from setting aside their own interests for the sake of the international society as a whole, particular states might, by pursuing their own interests, undermine it.

Martin Wight's (1977) approach to probing the nature of international society was to identify the distinguishing marks of historic state-systems. These corresponded closely to what Bull represented as the institutions of international society, which together contribute to the maintenance of order. These institutions include:

- great powers, which have special duties and responsibilities for maintaining order
- **diplomacy**
- international law
- **war**, which has been a major mechanism of change, and
- the **balance of power**, which in Vattel's words has had the role of 'preventing any one power from becoming too powerful and laying down the law to others' (cited in Bull 1977: 7).

In other words, its historic role has been to prevent **hegemony**, which would spell the end of the states-system. Towards the end of the **Cold War** Bull warned of the danger that would ensue were the two great powers of the day to neglect their responsibilities to international society as a whole and become 'great irresponsibles' (Bull 1980). Since the **terrorist** attacks of 11 September 2001, critics of the US have asked whether this term applies to it, particularly at a time when there appears to be no meaningful balance of power and the US is widely perceived to be a hegemonic **power**, or possibly even a new imperium (Dunne 2003; Hurrell 2005). It is easy to understand how other powerful states, and groupings of them, have agency. But it is less easy to think of examples in which all states have acted together, and this comes back to the concern that international society might not amount to more than a particular group of states.

Even if this is true, international society has a wider significance. The rules and norms generated by states and other actors, including **non-governmental organisations (NGOs)**, extend beyond merely guidelines for coexistence. They also include prescriptions for how states should treat both the people within their borders and distant strangers beyond them. Like a club that stipulates conditions for membership and imposes a code of conduct, international society has always been concerned with the question of which states have the legitimacy to be included. As Ian Clark puts it, 'legitimacy lies at the heart of what is meant by an international society' (Clark 2005: 5). It is the collective judgment of international society that determines the legitimacy of states in world politics. International society is a moral community and it does have the capacity to decide which states belong to it. States that do not meet certain standards are excluded from being treated in the same way as members. International society acts in this way as a standard bearer for all states; this raises the problem of whether the values upheld by international society are those of a select group of liberal states imposed upon other cultures, or of more universal application.

The foregoing account of the nature of international society has emphasised the idea of it being an association that accommodates plural conceptions of the good. There is, however, tension between this idea and actions taken either to uphold particular norms of international society – for instance, the defence of a population against genocide – or in the interests of international society as a whole. An example of this would be going to war to expel the armed forces of a state that had violated the sovereignty of another, which was ostensibly the reason for the 1991 Gulf War. Actions such as these are examples of solidarism among states and in the literature on international society it is contrasted with pluralism (Wheeler 1992). The essence of this contrast is that pluralists take a more restrictive approach to what is required to justify, for instance, intervention. Pluralists also have a narrower view of the capacity of international society to represent the interests of human beings as a whole. Solidarism, in contrast, extends beyond calculations of what is simply in the interests of the system of states, to consider the well-being of individual human beings. It is consequently essential to humanitarian actions across borders and vital to the moral purpose of international society (see Chapter 28). In other words, international society has a moral purpose to the extent that it furthers the well-being of individuals around the world (Dunne 1998: 35). As with many other dichotomies, the decision that one is either a pluralist or a solidarist should be firmly resisted (see Linklater and Suganami 2006: 59–68). There will always be circumstances in which the principles that animate one of these views are more appropriate than those informing the other. To maintain a rigid adherence to one rather than the other might result in sacrificing the good of others in favour of dogmatism.

The limits of international society

The focus of this chapter so far has been on depicting international society as an association of sovereign states recognisable as a society because its members articulate norms and rules that then guide their actions and inactions in their mutual relations. They do this to achieve order in their mutual relations. The central concern of Bull's *Anarchical society* is the pattern of order in international society. It is, at the same time, the 'pattern of order that developed in the European states-system, through relations between European rulers and nations'. This is, in a number of ways, an incomplete and inadequate account which involves at least three important omissions.

The first is that at the same time as states are the most important units of political organisation they are not the only, or even the most important, actors in world politics. Non-governmental organisations (which are regarded as part of an emerging global civil society), **transnational corporations** (some of which have incomes far in excess of many states) (for both see Chapter 22) and sub-state groups all have important roles in international society. Through **human rights** laws and norms, individuals also have increasingly gained legal standing in international society (see Chapter 29). Appeals to the standards set by international society are often the only recourse individuals – and particular classes of individuals, including women, children, indigenous peoples and other minorities – have against the states in which they are citizens or alternatively in which they are being accommodated as **refugees**.

Second, sovereignty has generally been perceived as being located in a single source of authority and as being indivisible (see Chapter 9). At this juncture of history, sovereignty appears to be more fluid. It is being contested at sub-state and supra-state levels and is recognised as something that has in practice always been divisible.

Third, international society was, in its inception, European. The generally accepted account of this is that as the modern state emerged from the medieval world of Christendom, in which there had been a number of authorities, sovereign states began to look for ways of governing their mutual relations. In this process the 1648 **Peace of Westphalia** is generally presented as having marked the inauguration of the states-system which has been in place at least up until the **UN Charter**. The states-system established in Europe was then exported to other parts of the globe colonised by Europeans. By this means international society gradually spread to encompass the whole globe. In short, the story of international society has been told as a success story of states in which the sovereign form of state was universalised, with all states ascending, or at least aspiring, to full membership. Obscured by this is the second story of dispossession, dominance and oppression that has led to lasting resentments against 'the West', and to claims against former colonial powers and a number of the states they first established as colonies. As well as this, there was the question of how non-European states came to be accepted as members of international society. Consequently the next section turns to European expansion and deliberately construes this as more than simply expansion of the international society of states.

European expansion

Edward Keene argues that 'alongside the pattern of order that developed in the European States system' a second pattern 'developed roughly simultaneously in the colonial and imperial systems that were established beyond Europe' (Keene 2002: xi). Within Europe ('the family of civilized nations'), 'the main point of international political and legal order was to encourage respect for the equality and sovereignty of individual states or nations'. However, in the non-European world it was 'to promote the civilization of decadent, backward, savage or barbaric peoples' (Keene 2002: 7). With few exceptions, Europeans did not regard non-Europeans as part of the 'civilised' world. They did not see non-Europeans as belonging to the same moral community and consequently these peoples did not have the same rights as Europeans accorded to each other in their mutual relations. From the first significant European encounters with non-European others, European states set the conditions for membership in international society and engaged in practices that have resulted in divisions, exclusions and injustices that have lasted to the present.

The first significant encounter between Europeans and non-Europeans was marked by Columbus's arrival in Central America (Pagden 1993), which was soon followed by the conquest of Mexico led by Hernando Cortés. When the conquest began in 1508 the population of Mexico was estimated to be 20 million. By 1600 it had been reduced to 1.5 million (Sterba 1996). The encounter with Amerindians provoked a debate about whether they were human and whether they had sovereign rights against Europeans. If so, what were these rights? Debates about the encounter contributed to the development of international legal thought and political theory. Europeans progressively moved from supporting rights for non-Europeans to denying them. Through the way non-Europeans were represented, both international law and political theory had a role in justifying the dispossession of non-Europeans of the lands they had traditionally occupied, in some cases since 'time immemorial'. In the earlier phases of European expansion, the treatment of non-European others was determined by whether they had the capacity to be Christian. In the wake of the **Enlightenment** it became a matter of whether the others could be counted as rational beings; and by the end of the nineteenth century, under the influence of social Darwinism, many peoples were regarded as simply not civilised, and not entitled to the rights Europeans gave to one another (McGrane 1989). With some notable exceptions (Muthu 2003), non-Europeans were typically represented in European political thought in ways that dehumanised them, thus making it easier to justify a denial of their rights (see Box 17.4).

BOX 17.4: DISCUSSION POINTS

Racial hierarchy and dispossession of Australian Aboriginal peoples

'During the eighteenth century it became common to distinguish different types – or races – of men and to arrange them in hierarchical sequence. The Europeans were invariably placed on the top, with non-Europeans strung out down the chain till savages merged with the more advanced monkeys ... Such ideas of racial **hierarchy** were carried to the Australian colonies and were widely disseminated' (Reynolds 1987: 110).

'[R]acism furthered the material interests of most settlers. It made it so much easier to take Aboriginal land without negotiation or purchase, to crush resistance to the dispossession and then keep survivors "in their place"' (Reynolds 1987: 129).

These observations apply only to the peoples Europeans regarded as more primitive on the ladder of human development. Europeans distinguished between peoples they did and did not recognise as living in societies with social and political organisation. Those regarded as more advanced clearly were located in a civilisation. By the end of the nineteenth century, international law varied according to whether it governed relations between: European states; European and civilised non-European states; or Europeans and less civilised states, lower in the perceived order of social and political organisation. Indeed, the criterion for accepting a state into international society was whether or not it met the so-called 'standard of civilisation' (see Box 17.5). This required that non-Europeans had a form of political and social organisation that was recognised as such, and that could give Europeans the level of protection they would enjoy in their own countries.

BOX 17.5: TERMINOLOGY

The 'standard of civilisation'

According to Gerrit Gong (1984: 3) a 'standard of civilisation' embodies tacit and explicit assumptions used to distinguish civilised from the uncivilised societies. It formed a benchmark against which Europe's self-proclaimed 'civilised' powers measured and excluded non-European societies from membership in international society. The 'standard' not only differentiated Europe from the rest of the world, it also elevated it to a position of superiority. Most importantly, for several centuries (even into the twentieth century) it governed the way Europe dealt with non-European peoples, treating them as 'backward', 'primitive', 'savage' and 'barbarous'.

The development of law is a crucial aspect of European expansion, and of considerable importance for Keene's argument concerning two patterns of order. Part of his argument is that in contrast to the states of European international society, in which sovereignty was located in a single authority, in the non-European world sovereignty was divided between the colonial or imperial power and local authorities. Complicating this was that boundaries of authority between culturally different social and legal systems had to be drawn. The result was a process in which the 'structure of legal authority and the creation of cultural hierarchies [were] inextricably intertwined' (Benton 2002: 2). There was, Benton (2002: 3) observes, no uniform location of political authority

across the international system. Yet international order depended on the ability of different political authorities to recognise each other, even if that recognition fell short of formal diplomacy or treaty making. The law worked both to tie disparate parts of empires and to lay the basis for exchanges of all sorts between politically and culturally separate imperial or colonial powers.

As well as this connection with law, culture had a still wider significance in the European expansion. Non-European others were indispensable in gauging what it meant to be European. A significant example of this is the relationship between the Ottoman Empire and Europe, the relevance of which continues into the ongoing debate over whether Turkey should be admitted to the European Union. The Ottoman Empire became progressively drawn into the international relations of Europe, and Turkey was the first non-European state to be accepted as a full subject of the law of nations regulating relations between the members of international society. Turkey was, in this way, accepted as being *in, but not of,* Europe. The Muslim peoples of Turkey had the vital role of revealing to Europeans what they were not, and so helping to define European identity (Neumann and Welsh 1991). Turkey is today a member of **NATO** but has yet to be admitted to the European Union. One of the arguments deployed against its inclusion continues to be that its Islamic identity makes it fundamentally alien to Europe.

Probably the most influential statement of the idea that 'the orient has helped define Europe' is Edward Said's *Orientalism* (1979: 1). By 'orientalism' he did not mean simply the study of the Orient but instead 'a Western style for dominating, restructuring, and having authority over the Orient' (1979: 3). For him it was about the control, manipulation, even incorporation of 'what is a manifestly different … world; [and is] … above all, a discourse' that exercises power (1979: 12). As a discursive practice, orientalism uses knowledge as a means to power. It involves the 'construction' of others, primarily by Europeans for their own purposes. When others are constructed in negative ways and represented as inferior, physical and structural harm can more easily be done to them. How we perceive others impacts the way in which they are treated and the rights that are extended to them (Fry 1997). Stereotypes 'confirm the necessity and desirability of colonial government by endlessly confirming the positional superiority of the West over the East'. The result is an 'unchanging image of "a subject race, dominated by a race that knows them and what is good for them better than they could possibly know themselves"' (Ghandi 1998: 77, citing Said). Colonialism thus 'marks the process whereby the "West" attempts systematically to cancel or negate the cultural difference and value of the "non-West"' (Ghandi 1998: 16). This cancellation or negation of cultural difference is fundamental to the neglected story of international society in relation to European expansion.

It must, however, not be overlooked that colonialism was not a simple story of the subjugation and denial of non-European cultures. 'At all times colonialism has involved complex interactions between cultures and there has not been simply colonialism but colonialisms' (Keal 2003: 47). In other words, colonial encounters and the practices of colonialism differed from one time and place to another and involved complex interactions. In late eighteenth- and early nineteenth-century India, for example, there was 'widespread cultural assimilation and hybridity … Virtually all Englishmen in India at this period Indianised themselves to some extent' (Dalrymple 2002: 10). Colonialism invariably involved intersubjective relationships in which the colonisers and the colonised constructed each other. There have been, and continue to be, numerous cases in which cultures have not been and are not irreconcilable. In spite of this the outcome of colonialism was generally that the identity of colonised peoples was submerged, or at least altered, to suit the purposes of the colonisers (N. Thomas 1994: 191).

With decolonisation the majority of former colonies became not just states, but members of international society. The hitherto subjugated peoples belonging to the new states gained self-determination and the chance to be the authors of their own identities. Importantly, decolonisation did not result in self-determination for either the indigenous peoples contained in settler states that had long since ceased to be colonies, or particular groups that did not necessarily wish to be subject to the sovereignty of the new states. In the name of order, self-determination was tied to the principle that colonial boundaries were not open to revision. The political world that resulted from decolonisation threw into sharp relief the problem of difference within states; which takes us back to the tension between the two stories of international society canvassed at the beginning of this chapter. The dominant story is one in which the Peace of Westphalia not only established sovereign independent states, but also dealt with the problem of 'difference' in international relations (Inayatullah and Blaney 2004). The Westphalian system of sovereign states assumed that difference would be contained within the inviolable borders of each state. It did not address the problem of difference within states, which has often impacted on international order and has become more rather than less important with the passage of time. It is all too obvious that in important cases cultural, religious and ethnic difference between peoples within states has been and continues to be a source of deadly violence.

In the particular case of indigenous peoples, the subjugation and dispossession of indigenous peoples resulting from European expansion has left a legacy of problems yet to be fully resolved. These include arguments over how best to deal with historical injustices, the harms caused by dehumanising representations of indigenous peoples and questions about the moral legitimacy of the state. It has, for instance, been argued that Australia is morally illegitimate to the extent that it was 'founded on European denial of the continent's prior ownership by indigenous people' (Rowse 1993). It follows that until such issues are resolved through mutual negotiation between states and their indigenous inhabitants, the moral legitimacy of particular states will remain in doubt. Further to this, given that one of the crucial purposes of international society is to preserve the system of sovereign states, it might also be complicit in perpetuating structures of oppression and domination. If some of the states that constitute international society are morally illegitimate and the business of international society is to preserve those states, then international society itself could also be seen to be morally illegitimate. An important difference between states and the society to which they belong is nevertheless that the latter has the capacity to act as a standard bearer for the just resolution of relations within states.

Conclusion

The first story of international society in this chapter depicted it as being constituted by the rules and norms which guide the behaviour of individual states in their mutual relations. This image of the world holds that by taking notice of these rules and norms the behaviour of the majority of states in the world is evidence for the existence of international society. Sovereign territorial states are regarded as the primary mode of political organisation and, with few exceptions, as members of the society of states. Too often this neglects what Martin Wight (1991: 49) proposed as the most fundamental question that needs to be asked about international society: how far does it extend? Who or what is excluded? Both Halliday (1994) and C. Brown (1995) have suggested that international society might, in important ways, not extend far beyond the influence and interests of the economically and politically powerful states of the world; represented now by the **G20**. If this is correct then focusing on international society as an approach to the study of world politics inevitably restricts the scope of thought about world politics.

The immediate and lasting consequences of the expansion of Europe, which is the core of the second story, speaks to this concern. The Westphalian system, upon which international society has been built, addresses the problem of difference *between* but not *within* states (Inayatullah and Blaney 2004). In important cases the cultural, religious and ethnic differences between people within states have been and continue to be a source of deadly violence and international disorder. This has particular importance with regard to states containing active secessionist movements, and for minority peoples denied rights and oppressed by the governments of the states in which they are encased. In his penetrating study of multiculturalism in international politics, political philosopher Will Kymlicka forcefully argues that the need to defend multiculturalism has resulted in twin processes which are global in scope. One is the diffusion of a set of ideals to which all states should aspire, and this is coupled with the codification of a set of minimum standards for the treatment of minorities. His contention about these twin processes of diffusing multiculturalism and minority rights is that they 'are fundamentally reshaping the traditional conceptions of state sovereignty, nationhood, and citizenship that have underpinned the international system of states'. For him the treatment of minorities is a matter of legitimate international concern and should be 'subject to international norms and standards' (Kymlicka 2007: 4). To this end, international society can both act as a standard bearer and have agency in transforming the traditional notions of state sovereignty, nationhood and citizenship and, by extension, the nature of political community. Related to this is Andrew Linklater's (1998: 60–61) suggestion that the competing claims of universal ethical principles and cultural difference can be reconciled in a post-Westphalian state 'by breaking the nexus between sovereignty, territoriality, nationality and citizenship'.

While Kymlicka and Linklater are not necessarily writing about non-European peoples their suggestions about the revision of traditional notions of state sovereignty have especial value for peoples still dealing with the consequence of European expansion. If nothing else, they provoke questions about the meanings that can be and are now given to sovereignty. With respect to indigenous peoples one of these is *cultural sovereignty*, understood as indigenous peoples conceptualising nationhood and sovereignty in terms of their own culture. This links cultural rights to sovereignty and, in turn – as a consequence of cultural rights being an integral part of human rights – it has considerable relevance for reconceptualising not merely sovereignty but also states and the political communities they contain.

The experience of a number of the states which resulted from European expansion suggests that the form of state introduced by Europeans has not worked and is not an ideal form of political organisation. There are many cases of dysfunctional states, often referred to as '**failed states**' (see Chapter 30). It may be more useful to think of these in terms of polities which, while not possessing a model of sovereign authority based on the European-exported modern state (see Chapter 9), nevertheless function as political societies. Accepting differentiated forms of state could be part of a transition from an international to a global society in which the Westphalian sovereign territorial state is not considered the only model of political community. In contemporary IR this holds great importance not just for the continuing legacies of European expansion, but also for the way that international society continues to evolve.

QUESTIONS

1. What are the differences between an international system and an international society?
2. Are the rules of international society Eurocentric?
3. Was the 'standard of civilisation' a legitimate means of establishing an international society of uniform states and shared norms?
4. Does international society exist today? And, if it does, does it still bear the legacy of its colonial expansion?
5. Can international society endure the degree of ethnic, cultural and religious diversity that presently exists?
6. How does US hegemony impact on the rules and norms of international society?

FURTHER READING

Bellamy, Alex (ed.) 2006, *International society and its critics*, Oxford: Oxford University Press. Excellent collection of essays, both sympathetic and critical, on the English School's notion of international society.

Bull, Hedley and Watson, Adam (eds) 1984, *The expansion of international society*, Oxford: Clarendon Press. Large and indispensable collection of essays on the expansion of international society from its European origins to its global limits.

Keal, Paul 2003, *European conquest and the rights of indigenous peoples: the moral backwardness of international society*, Cambridge: Cambridge University Press. Expanded version of the argument presented here.

Keene, Edward 2002, *Beyond the anarchical society: Grotius, colonialism and order in world politics*, Cambridge: Cambridge University Press. Valuable historical account of tensions between two types of international order promoted by international society: toleration and civilisation.

Linklater, Andrew and Suganami, Hidemi 2006, *The English School of international relations: a contemporary reassessment*, Cambridge: Cambridge University Press. Impressive assessment of the English School's contribution to the study of international relations by two leading theorists.

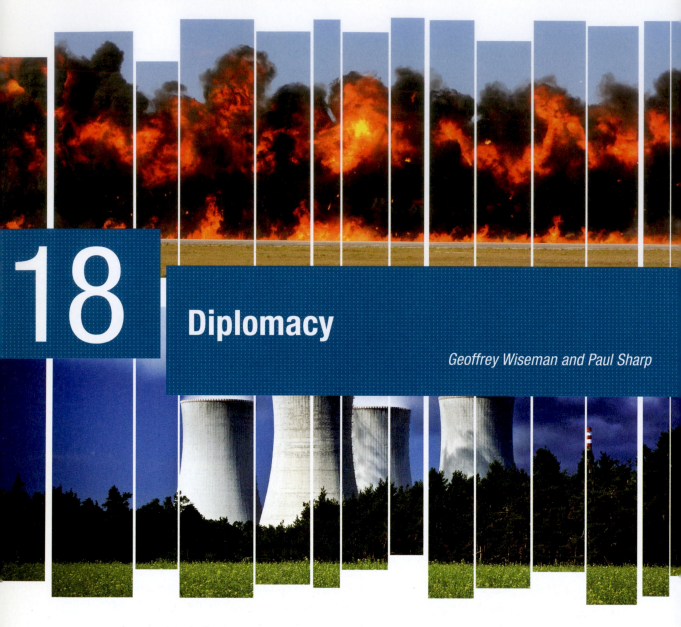

18

Diplomacy

Geoffrey Wiseman and Paul Sharp

Introduction	257
Defining diplomacy: what is diplomacy and who are the diplomats?	257
The evolution of diplomacy	258
Trends	264
Diplomacy and the study of IR	265
Conclusion	266
Questions	267
Further reading	267

Introduction

This chapter makes three main arguments: first, that ideas and practices of **diplomacy** have a multi-millennial history, much longer than is generally thought. Second, that this long history has been characterised by both continuity and change. As a result, diplomacy has been as much adaptive as resistant to change. And, third, that diplomacy is not diminishing in importance and that it – and the diplomats who carry it out – should be regarded as evolving and as important to the **theory** and practice of international relations. To assess these claims, the chapter first addresses the issue of defining diplomacy, then it examines the evolution of diplomacy in terms that may be characterised broadly as pre-modern, modern, and **postmodern**, and finally the chapter evaluates the relationship between diplomacy and the study of International Relations (IR).

Defining diplomacy: what is diplomacy and who are the diplomats?

Diplomacy is conventionally understood as the processes and institutions by which the interests and identities of **sovereign states** are represented to one another. Diplomats are understood to be people accredited by those they represent to undertake this work. We should be careful with definitions, however (see Box 18.1 for examples). They clarify the ways in which people use a term; they do not capture its true meaning, if there is such a thing, or its best use. Thus, some definitions of diplomacy emphasise a particular diplomatic *activity*: for example, negotiation (Nicolson [1939] 1969). Others stress the *manner* in which the activity should be undertaken: for example, with honesty, tact and understanding (Callières [1717] 2000; Satow [1917] 1979) or peacefully (Berridge 2010). Still others pay attention to *who* is entitled to undertake it and on behalf of whom – claiming, for example, that only the official representatives of sovereign states and international organisations may be properly viewed as engaging in diplomacy (Vienna Convention 1961). Rather than trying to pin down the best definitions of diplomacy and diplomats, therefore, it is more interesting to chart how and why the popularity and use of different ones changed over time and from place to place.

BOX 18.1: TERMINOLOGY

Some definitions of diplomacy

'Diplomacy is the application of intelligence and tact to the conduct of official relations between the governments of independent states, extending sometimes also to their relations with vassal states; or, more briefly still, the conduct of business between states by peaceful means' (Ernest Satow [1917] 1979: 1).

'Diplomacy is the management of international relations by negotiation; the method by which these relations are adjusted and managed by ambassadors and envoys; the business or art of the diplomatist' (Harold Nicolson [1939] 1969: 4–5).

'[Diplomacy is] the conduct of relations between states and other entities with standing in world politics by official agents and by peaceful means' (Hedley Bull 1977: 162).

'Diplomacy is concerned with the management of relations between states and other actors. From a state perspective diplomacy is concerned with advising, shaping and implementing foreign policy' (R. P. Barston 1988: 1).

'Diplomacy is the conduct of international relations by negotiation rather than by force, propaganda, or recourse to law, and by other peaceful means (such as gathering information or engendering goodwill) which are either directly or indirectly designed to promote negotiation' (G. R. Berridge 1995: 1).

Diplomacy is 'the peaceful conduct of relations amongst political entities, their principals and accredited agents' (Hamilton and Langhorne 2011: 1).

Why, for example, did Edmund Burke feel the need in 1797 to anglicise the French term *diplomatie* (E. Burke [1797] 1899: 450)? Why, in America, is the distinction between diplomacy and foreign policy less acknowledged than in Europe (Kissinger 1994, David Clinton 2011)? And why, nearly everywhere, do people now seek to broaden the use of the term and call a wide range of humanitarian, cultural and commercial activities diplomacy, and whoever undertakes them diplomats (Leonard and Alakeson 2000)?

The evolution of diplomacy
Pre-modern diplomacy

Something like diplomacy must have occurred between peoples in pre-history once messengers were granted immunity from unfriendly **protocols** governing relations with strangers (Nicolson [1939] 1969). Archaeological and anthropological research, however, casts doubt on the idea of communities evolving separately until encountering others. Rather, the record suggests a single group from which peoples separated early on, and processes of peoples both coming together and pulling apart ever since (Diamond 1997; Buzan and Little 2000). There are historical records of negotiations in the Old Testament, and older fragments exist including an archive of relations between pharaohs, their clients and other great kings in the fourteenth century BC (Amarna). From the latter, we obtain glimpses of missions travelling with trade caravans to arrange dynastic marriages, secure gifts, reassure allies and negotiate with rivals. For some this is the first diplomatic system and illustrates how diplomacy is 'hardwired' into the human species (Cohen and Westbrook 2000). For others, the Amarna period fails the test of being a proper diplomatic system because the parties exhibit no self-restraint in the interests of preserving their system (Butterfield 1970) and achieve no institutional expression of that system; for example, resident embassies (Berridge 2010).

The answer to when diplomacy started, as argued above, seems bound up with how diplomacy is defined and by whom. For example, until very recently it has been conventional in the Western world to interpret the earlier diplomatic experience of humanity as a precursor to the emergence of modern diplomacy in seventeenth-century Europe. In this story, while most peoples only managed to send missions when there was something to negotiate, the Greeks are distinguished by their permitting *proxenoi* (local citizens) to represent them, although without plenipotentiary (negotiating) powers (Hamilton and Langhorne 2011). The Romans, as **hegemons**, are presented as uninterested in the give-and-take of diplomacy (Nicolson 1954). The Renaissance Italians, in contrast, are credited with preparing the ground for modern diplomacy (Mattingly 1955). They established permanent resident missions (embassies) whose ministers (ambassadors) had plenipotentiary powers and developed a collective sense of themselves as a diplomatic corps sharing common professional interests and values (Sharp and Wiseman 2007). As for the rest of the world – China, India, the Americas and Africa – its diplomatic achievements are judged unimportant since it was eventually absorbed by the expansion of Europe's international society (Bull and Watson 1984).

As we shall see below, this story of how modern diplomacy emerged and was perfected in its essentials remains important and useful. However, as **power** now appears to be shifting away from Europe and America, and power itself may be transforming in such ways as to make sovereign states less powerful and important, there is a growing sense that the conventional story does not exhaust all the possibilities for diplomacy. Recently, therefore, interest has revived in how diplomacy used to be conducted in Europe before its states-system was consolidated, in other parts of the world before the Europeans arrived, and between the Europeans and indigenous peoples they encountered (Jennings et al. 1985). Interest has also revived in how so-called primitive peoples conducted (and in some cases still conduct) their diplomatic relations with others (Numelin 1950).

Modern diplomacy in the Westphalian era

Modern diplomacy is generally associated with the traditional agenda of sovereign states (especially the larger, more powerful ones), the **balance of power**, **war**, and **international law** (Bull 2002). Modern diplomacy can essentially be divided into two forms, **bilateral** and **multilateral**. Seen as the older more traditional form, bilateral diplomacy is the conduct of relations between two political actors with 'standing', usually sovereign territorial states. Multilateral diplomacy, the conduct of relations between three or more such states, is seen as a 'newer' form of diplomacy.

As noted above, diplomatic historians tend to see modern diplomacy in its bilateral form emerging on the Italian Peninsula during the Renaissance. The key diplomatic players of the time included Florence, Venice, Naples, Milan and the papacy in Rome. Machiavelli, the Florentine diplomat who authored *The prince* ([1513] 1998) and other works on how best to negotiate with other sovereigns, did so in terms that are now synonymous with a **power politics** worldview (Berridge et al. 2001: 13). Thus, as we noted above, Renaissance Italy's main contribution to the development of the ideas and practices of diplomacy was the creation of resident ambassadors. On this model, and unlike in the past when ambassadors tended to go on short-term diplomatic missions, ambassadors would reside in the host country for years, sending reports to their governments back home by whatever means were available. A product of the exchange of resident diplomats, as noted earlier, was the development of a diplomatic corps, the corporate collection of diplomats in any one capital, from Constantinople to London (Sharp and Wiseman 2007).

Many scholars regard the **Treaty of Westphalia** (1648) that ended Europe's Thirty Years' War between Protestants and Catholics, as formalising (but by no means inventing) the principle of state **sovereignty** and thus 'ushering in the era of modern diplomacy' (Stanger 2009: 56). Thus, Westphalia's association with the sovereign state became synonymous with modern diplomacy. Even though the resident bilateral diplomatic mission emerged earlier, in the fifteenth century as we have seen, Westphalia's importance in the seventeenth century was that it both represented and constituted the notion of modern diplomacy. However, while Westphalia's significance is usually associated with the rise of modern sovereign-state diplomacy, it is equally significant as a major step in the development of multilateral diplomacy (Hamilton and Langhorne 2011; Davis Cross 2007). In short, Westphalia reinforced bilateral diplomacy, which was already recognisable on the Italian Peninsula, while also pointing to a more multilateral future for diplomacy.

With bilateral diplomacy (the resident mission) and multilateral diplomacy (such as the congresses surrounding Westphalia) in place by the seventeenth century, other innovations followed. Notable here was the invention by Cardinal Richelieu – first minister of France under Louis XIII from 1624–1642 – of the foreign ministry: the now taken-for-granted institution under one roof in a country's capital that works with government ministers to formulate foreign policy and supervises a country's international network of diplomats and embassies (Berridge et al. 2001). Thus was born the idea of the professional diplomat as a key feature of modern diplomacy and international relations.

For most writers on diplomacy, the diplomacy of the **great powers** mattered most. They were supposed to be responsible for maintaining the balance of power but, as the Napoleonic Wars had demonstrated, were also capable of posing deadly threats to the peace of Europe. Great-power dominance of modern diplomacy's evolution is well demonstrated by the Concert of Europe, an informal yet powerful periodic meeting of European states that negotiated treaties, but typically did not meet in a single assembly (plenary) which would have allowed the smaller powers a larger voice in proceedings. Thus, the Concert was dominated by small, exclusive meetings of the leading statesmen from Austria, Prussia, Russia, Britain and France, such as Prince Metternich (Austria), Lord Castlereagh (Britain) and Prince Talleyrand (France). The Concert is widely associated with a period of relative **peace** in Europe for much of the nineteenth century and up to the outbreak of war in 1914.

In diplomacy's long history, World War I (1914–1918) stands out for two reasons. One, the war was blamed on diplomats conducting the 'old diplomacy' of secret treaties, shifting **alliances** and great-power backroom deals. Two, in the war's aftermath, the multilateral method was taken to a new institutionalised level with the creation of the League of Nations (the 'new diplomacy'). Under the League, diplomats conducting multilateral diplomacy would no longer meet for a few days at a time in a European capital and then return home (on the Concert model). Now, some diplomats at least would be permanently accredited to an international organisation, rather than to a country. This represented an important conceptual shift – albeit one that failed in this instance, with the disbandment of the League during World War II, which it manifestly failed to prevent.

However, the establishment of the **United Nations (UN)** in San Francisco in 1945 (Schlesinger 2003) represented a further, and this time more successful, attempt at institutionalising the multilateral diplomatic method. An important lesson seemed to be that sovereign states were willing to try again, rather than give up on a promising idea. World War II had also initiated renewed interest in the role of public opinion in the formation of foreign policy, and to some extent in its conduct by professional diplomats. After the war, the ideological conflict known as the **Cold War** (roughly 1945–1989) saw the re-emergence and general acceptance of institutionalised multilateralism (Thakur 2002), with the establishment of the extensive UN system, even if there was a sense that the UN was not central to the diplomacy of the great-power contest that was surfacing at the time (Mazower 2009). Traditional bilateral diplomacy, so vilified after World War I, continued in a new conceptual guise known as **bipolarity** – under this wider concept, large numbers of countries lined up, some of them reluctantly, behind the US and Soviet **superpowers**. The main features of this Cold War diplomacy included nuclear diplomacy, crisis diplomacy and summit diplomacy (White 2001: 392–3). The advent of nuclear weapons and their use by the US in 1945 against Japan introduced a novel and sharply dangerous element into the management of crises and the convening of high-level meetings by political leaders. If the over-riding strategic concept of the nuclear age was mutual nuclear **deterrence**, the underlying foreign policy concept was **containment** – an idea advanced by George Kennan, a serving professional US diplomat, that Soviet **communism** could be managed (contained) without the use of military force (see Box 18.2).

BOX 18.2: DISCUSSION POINTS

George Kennan's view of the emerging bipolar Cold War

Soviet communism is 'a political force committed fanatically to the belief that with US there can be no permanent *modus vivendi* … [The] problem of how to cope with this force [is] undoubtedly greatest task our diplomacy has ever faced and probably greatest it will ever have to face … But I would like to record my conviction that problem is within our power to solve – and that without recourse to any general military conflict.'

Source: The February 1946 Kennan 'Long Telegram' (Jensen 1993: 28, 29).

Decolonisation provided an important context in which Cold War diplomacy played out. This process whereby the colonies of the European powers achieved their independence had a dramatic impact on international relations in general, and diplomacy in particular. First, as just noted, while many of the newly independent countries identified and allied with one or the other superpower, many others sought to keep some political distance from them, forming groupings such as the Non-Aligned Movement (NAM) and the Group of 77 (**G77**) in order to strengthen their independence from the Cold War giants. A small minority of the new states, such as China, Cuba and Libya, branded themselves, or were seen by others, as revolutionary states, at first rejecting but later accepting diplomatic **norms** and procedures (Bull and Watson 1984; Armstrong 1993).

BOX 18.3: DISCUSSION POINTS

Proliferation of sovereign states

1919: 25 states participated in the Paris Peace Conference, formally ending World War I and setting up the League of Nations.

1945: 51 states participated in the 1945 San Francisco Conference, establishing the United Nations.

1990: the United Nations has 159 member states.

2010: the United Nations has 192 member states.

A second effect of decolonisation was a dramatic proliferation of sovereign states in the international system. Some 51 countries signed the **UN Charter** in 1945. By 1989, the UN's membership had grown to 159. In 2010, the world body had 192 members (see Box 18.3). At the UN, the impact of the proliferation of new states had two almost contradictory effects: radicalisation and socialisation. *Radicalisation* was manifested in claims for economic and social development and declarations like the infamous 1975 Zionism is Racism General Assembly resolution. *Socialisation* was manifested, for example, in acceptance of the idea that the UN now acted as the membership committee for the international community (where previously this had been left to countries acting bilaterally). In addition, new members generally accepted the norms and routine practices of UN-style multilateral diplomacy (Wiseman 2011). In short, the trappings of sovereignty – embassies, ambassadors and UN membership – were attractive at a time when the political goal was sovereign independence. Given the divisions created by the Cold War and the decolonisation process, it is striking that the international community could come together to agree – in the 1961 Vienna Convention on Diplomatic Relations – on the formal rules governing their diplomatic conduct (Langhorne 1992). The Convention set out the five key tasks of diplomacy (See Box 18.4). It also codified the immunities and privileges accorded to diplomats while serving abroad (see Box 18.5).

BOX 18.4: KEY TEXTS

The 1961 Vienna Convention: functions of a diplomatic mission

According to Article 3 of the 1961 Vienna Convention, the functions of a diplomatic mission consist, among other things, in (emphasis added):

(a) *Representing* the sending State in the receiving State;

(b) *Protecting* in the receiving State the interests of the sending State and of its nationals, within the limits permitted by international law;

(c) *Negotiating* with the Government of the receiving State;

(d) Ascertaining by all lawful means conditions and developments in the receiving State, and *reporting* thereon to the Government of the sending State;

(e) *Promoting friendly relations* between the sending State and the receiving State, and developing their economic, cultural and scientific relations.

How does diplomacy operate under hegemonic conditions? Until recently, it has been common to talk of a **unipolar** world, as distinct from a bipolar or even **multipolar** one, revolving around the sole remaining superpower, the US. The Cold War's end in 1989 led to yet another expansion of international society, with the addition of over twenty new countries from the disintegrating Soviet Union and former Yugoslavia, a series of events that reinforced the persistence of sovereignty and a state-based diplomatic culture (Wiseman 2005). And, even as the rise of emerging powers such as Brazil, India, China and South Africa challenges any unipolar US claims, the new powers in no way suggest that these power shifts will be undertaken without diplomacy and diplomats.

This early post-Cold War conventional wisdom was that the US conducted a form of hegemonic diplomacy, not unlike imperial Rome. As former UN Secretary-General Boutros Boutros-Ghali (1999: 198) remarked pointedly in his memoirs: 'The Roman Empire had no need for diplomacy. Nor does the United States'. In fact, the US conducts its relations unilaterally, bilaterally, and multilaterally. The George W. Bush administration tended to emphasise the unilateral (while in practice operating in all three spheres); the Obama administration tends to emphasise the multilateral (while also in practice operating in all three spheres) in ways that no other country can presently match (Schlesinger 2008).

BOX 18.5: KEY TEXTS

The 1961 Vienna Convention: diplomatic immunity

Under the 1961 Vienna Convention on Diplomatic Relations, diplomats cannot be arrested, no matter what their crime; they cannot be forced to testify in court proceedings, unless their home state 'waives' (lifts) their immunity. The host state may expel them, declaring them *persona non grata* (Leguey-Feuilleux: 155–6).

On 4 January, 1997, 16-year-old Jovine Waltrick was killed in a five-car pileup at Dupont Circle in Washington DC caused by the second-ranking diplomat at the Georgian embassy, Gueorgui Makharadze, who was allegedly intoxicated. The US State Department formally requested that the Georgian government not withdraw the diplomat from the US, and that it 'waive' his diplomatic immunity so that he could stand trial. Secretary of State Warren Christopher reaffirmed these requests in a letter to the President of Georgia, Eduard Shevardnadze. On 10 January 1997, President Shevardnadze announced in the Georgian capital, Tblisi, that he would waive Makharadze's diplomatic immunity. The State Department described the gesture as 'unusual' and 'courageous'. Several months later, on 17–18 July, Shevardnadze visited the US, meeting with President Clinton, Vice President Al Gore and senior State Department officials. Makharadze's trial opened on 21 July 1997. He was convicted of manslaughter and sentenced to 7–21 years in a federal prison. In 2000, Makharadze was transferred from the US to Georgia to serve the rest of his term.

Case written by Minta N. Spencer. See also 'Jailed Georgian Sent Home,' *The New York Times*, July 1, 2000.

Yet, as we discuss further below, there are countervailing trends, pointing to a world less dominated by a state-based diplomatic culture grounded unmistakably in sovereignty. The UN today is not simply a meeting place for over 190 sovereign state diplomats, but is becoming an amalgam of players from the sovereign, business, and non-governmental worlds, where sovereignty-questioning norms such as the **responsibility to protect (R2P)** – the idea that the international community could intervene with force after the state had failed to protect its own citizens – are evolving (Evans and Sahnoun 2002) (see Chapter 31).

To sum up this section, the norms, assumptions and practices of the modern Westphalian institution of diplomacy have some of their origins in ancient forms of practice dating back to the Amarna era. But they are also impressively different and, as we now argue, still useful.

The future of diplomacy in a post-Westphalian world

Prediction is always difficult, especially in the social sciences. The relationship between the social world and people's ideas about it is complex, and scholars argue over what is changing and what is meant by change. Consider the question of whether or not sovereign states and their diplomacy are disappearing. Common sense suggests they are not. In fact there are probably more states and more diplomatic missions now than at any time before the unifications of Italy and Germany in the nineteenth century (1861 and 1871 respectively). Reflection suggests they might be disappearing. It is possible that states and their diplomacy are no longer what they used to be presented as being: namely, the most important actors and processes in international politics. The world no longer turns on cable traffic between the embassies and chancelleries of a few great powers as it did at the start of World War I in August 1914. To complicate matters further, however, empirical analysis reveals that states were never as sovereign or as important as was assumed in their heyday. August 1914 was an exceptional and decisive moment, perhaps, but outside the parameters set by that great-power crisis there was a great deal of international relations going on to which sovereign states, their foreign offices and their diplomats were not central. In considering the future of diplomacy, therefore, we begin by acknowledging that at any given moment one can identify a number of possible trends, and that the present is always capable of yielding multiple possible futures, although some seem more likely than others (Henrikson 2006).

Trends

Modern diplomacy still rules

The most obvious trend is the persistence of the Westphalian or modern system of diplomacy noted above and outlined in the previous section. In general, sovereign states are still regarded as the most important actors in international relations and they continue to deploy an extensive system of embassies and consulates by which they and their interests are represented to each other. In particular cases this claim can be modified. Budgetary constraints, for example, can result in the closure of missions or, together with political developments like regional associations such as the European Union (EU), can result in various forms of shared or collective representation. The claim that **globalisation** – developments in the technologies of travel, communication and information-transfer, together with the ensuing 'collapse of distance' (see Chapter 28) – has rendered on-the-spot diplomatic representation unimportant has so far not been substantiated. Indeed, the need for such representation, especially in the great diplomatic cities of big powers and international organisations, continues unabated, leading some to speak of a 'diplomatic counter-revolution' in terms of the persistence and extension of traditional diplomatic practices (Berridge 2010: 253–55).

Less negotiating, more representation and lobbying

There has been a shift away from traditional diplomatic functions like negotiating and reporting towards both traditional and new forms of representation. Sovereign states may still be the most important actors, but their sovereignty seems to buy them less independence, security and prosperity than in the past, on an international stage that they now have to share with other sorts of international actors. Increasingly they must engage in 'polylateral' or 'triangular' diplomacy (Wiseman 2004; Strange 1992). As a result, diplomats spend more time lobbying important political and economic actors in their host states than would have been previously thought appropriate given the core diplomatic principle of non-interference in internal affairs and domestic matters. They spend more time engaged in representation contributing to the construction of favourable images of their own country's identity, interests and values through public diplomacy than would have previously been thought important, given that these activities do not typically target governments (Cull 2009; Fitzpatrick 2007). And diplomats spend more time building local and temporary coalitions of private and public actors to influence policy networks in their host states, internationally and in their home states (Hocking 1999).

Getting out of the embassy

Some diplomats, particularly those of developed and Western states, are increasingly engaged in 'transformational' or 'civilian power' diplomacy, working in state and civil society 'capacity-building' teams with other experts, especially in countries from which terrorist movements operate (Rice 2007; Clinton 2010). However, this is one of those trends of which the strength and significance remain unclear. It seems very novel to have diplomats leaving their missions to work out in the field alongside aid workers, civil engineers, doctors and soldiers, helping communities to build schools, clinics and systems of governance capable of resisting the pressures of terrorists, smugglers and gangsters. It is not clear, however, the extent to which the fate of these activities is bound up with the fate of the wars in Afghanistan and Iraq, and whether diplomats will be seen to have much of a role to play in them after all. Nor is it clear how these activities differ from those of the political officer in the old European empires, although this is a parallel which none of the parties involved have an interest in drawing. One possible indicator of growing significance will be if rising powers like China and India adopt the same technique of attaching diplomats to their own development teams around the world.

The rise of the hyphenated diplomat

The terms diplomat and ambassador are increasingly applied to people who are not officially engaged in the representation of sovereign states and the adjustment of their interests. As noted above, international and regional organisations like the UN and the EU have long enjoyed diplomatic standing and the right to diplomatic representation among states. Individuals working independently or in a semi-official capacity have long been employed by states to seek agreements and secure interests when conventional diplomacy has been judged to be ineffective or inappropriate. To these can be added field-diplomats and track two-diplomats, who work in zones of conflict to secure ceasefires between warring militias and protect non-combatants when fighting is going on (Reychler 1996). Goodwill-ambassadors and celebrity-diplomats work to raise consciousness of humanitarian and environmental issues, lobbying those in a position to help and pressuring those causing problems (Cooper 2008). Citizen-diplomats may seek to advance the profile and interests of their home towns in trade delegations and through cultural exchanges, act as international civil society lobbyists, or seek to get round or subvert a particular aspect of their own country's foreign policy with which they disagree – for example, US citizen diplomacy toward Cuba (Sharp 2001).

The rise of the hyphenated diplomats nicely illustrates the problems with considering the future of diplomacy. To the question 'what will the future look like?' has to be added another question 'what will people in the future regard as significant in it?' A European cardinal from the fifteenth century, for example, might be reassured to see the network of Vatican diplomacy still in place today, but slow to recognise that people's attitudes to it are now very different from those of his own time. There will likely be a British ambassador in Paris fifty years from now, but will she be a 'go-to' person for French people seeking to influence their British counterparts, or will both sets of citizens, along with the other 6 billion inhabitants of the world, basically engage in their own direct diplomacy with one another? If so, then what, if anything, will be diplomatic about those relations? How would setting up opportunities for commercial, social or cultural partnerships between people from different countries be distinguishable from similar efforts between people from the same country? Is diplomacy changing, therefore, or is it in the process of fading away as international relations become more like other ordinary human relations?

Diplomacy and the study of IR

The contemporary study of diplomacy is beginning to explore questions such as these. Like anyone else, IR scholars bring to the task their own assumptions about what is going on and what is important. Thus **neorealists** insist that there is an unavoidable dynamic to international politics which persists whether we like it or not (Waltz 1979). States and their diplomacy, or something so very like both that they may be treated as the same, will always exist because people live in a law-governed natural universe that constrains possibilities. Witness, they argue, the way the EU, set up as an attempt to break from the violent international politics of sovereign states, is rapidly acquiring the characteristics of a great power, including its own diplomats in the form of its External Action Service. **Constructivists**, in contrast, suggest that the social world is much more produced by the way we think about it than people realise (Wendt 1999). Sovereign states and the sort of diplomacy associated with them exist only insofar as people accept the claim that they do. In principle at least, people could consciously think and act themselves into an entirely different set of social relations in which the claims of states to sovereignty would be no longer accepted and diplomacy, as their privileged form of intercourse, would fade into irrelevance. Indeed, some people suggest that this may already be happening and that today's hyphenated diplomats are harbingers of a post-sovereign and post-state world (Wellman 2004). Others, in contrast, note what they regard as people's capacity for wishful thinking in the face of underlying, unchanging and brutish facts (Mearsheimer 2001; Carr [1939] 1946).

As noted above, however, an alternative to fitting diplomacy into broader theories of IR is to examine the circumstances in which people use terms like diplomacy and ambassador. There are shallow reasons, to be sure. Both terms are associated with power and status. Thus public *diplomacy* was so named by US officials because they thought public *relations* would put them at a disadvantage in the competition for resources and influence (Fitzpatrick 2007: 189), and all sorts of people are proclaimed 'ambassadors' when they seek support for causes generally regarded as good. Both terms surface, however, when people talk about relations with people whom they regard as 'other' and 'outsiders' from whom they feel different. This sense of difference may be malign and take the form of an alienation and estrangement that allows us to treat people badly (Der Derian 1987). It can also be benign, however, acknowledging the value of diversity and the different ways in which human communities can live (Constantinou 1996b). Either way, the sense of separateness and difference leads to a special sort of human relations, different from those within groups, requiring special handling and, arguably, a special class of people (diplomats) adept at handling them in such a way as to avoid unwanted conflict (Sharp 2009). To the extent that this is so, then we should neither want nor expect diplomacy to disappear, even if sovereign states and their foreign policies do.

Conclusion

Our review of the premodern, modern, and postmodern ideas of diplomacy confirms a very long history indeed. Even if there is disagreement about the premodern origins of diplomatic practices in forms that we would recognise today, there is little doubt that diplomacy preceded the sovereign states-system. Throughout these three broad historical periods, our review provided many examples of a diplomatic system that is capable of reproducing itself, but also of reconstituting itself in significantly different forms. The evidence of diplomacy from the pre-Westphalian period is important, because it seriously challenges the state-diplomacy link assumed in the literature and indeed by many, but by no means all, contemporary practitioners. We can therefore imagine a future without the state. But as we have conceived of the subject here, we cannot imagine any future without diplomacy. Even within the context of a state-based international order, diplomacy is becoming more important because it and the people who are said to practise it are increasingly needed (Sharp 2009). Moreover, if indeed international relations are moving in a post-hegemonic direction, then diplomacy is more likely to prosper. In one form or another, the US, China and other major players see advantage in returning to it. Moreover, there is clear evidence of an emerging non-state diplomatic conception in which well-organised groups are now acting, or claiming to act, diplomatically, at least in a minimal sense even if not yet in the full Vienna Convention sense. Students of IR therefore need a good understanding of diplomacy and diplomats (and the many conceptual issues involved).

QUESTIONS

1. Can we continue to place trust in diplomacy in universal organisations such as the UN, or do we need to build regional and even localised diplomatic structures?

2. Do you think that the concept of diplomatic immunity serves a useful purpose in today's mixed-actor world of states and non-state actors? Make the best possible case in favour of the concept and then make the case for its abolition. Can and should diplomatic immunity exist in a future non-sovereign-state world?

3. Identify the ways that we as human beings all think diplomatically on a day-to-day basis – for example, in the ways we present ourselves to a professor as a student and our communications reflect the presumed etiquette, protocols and power relations involved.

FURTHER READING

Berridge, G. R. 2010, *Diplomacy: theory and practice*, 4th edn, Basingstoke UK: Palgrave. Standard text on the diplomacy of states focusing on the activity of negotiation, bilateral and multilateral modes of diplomacy plus summitry and mediation.

Hamilton, Keith and Langhorne, Richard 2011, *The practice of diplomacy: its evolution, theory and administration*, 2nd edn, London: Routledge. Wide-ranging historical treatment of how the institution of diplomacy developed.

Jönsson, Christer and Hall, Martin, 2005, *Essence of diplomacy*, Basingstoke UK: Palgrave Macmillan. Sociological study of diplomatic practice, which interprets diplomacy as a subset of standard human behaviours that seek to mediate between universals and particulars through communication, representation and reproduction.

Nicolson, Harold 1954, *The evolution of the diplomatic method*, London: Macmillan. These essays take great liberties in terms of the national stereotyping of diplomatic methods but are valuable for their insights and for what they reveal about the outlook of the classical diplomatist.

Seib, Philip (ed.) 2009, *Toward a new public diplomacy: redirecting U.S. foreign policy*, Basingstoke, UK: Palgrave Macmillan. Set of essays reflecting the recent wave of public diplomacy scholarship, including essays on views of the US from other countries.

Sharp, Paul 2009, *Diplomatic theory of international relations*, Cambridge University Press. Argues that diplomats have a characteristic way of viewing international relations and what is important in them which is neglected by academics and other experts, but from which much is to be learned.

Sharp, Paul and Wiseman, Geoffrey (eds) 2007, *The diplomatic corps as an institution of international society*, Basingstoke UK: Palgrave Macmillan. Presents a series of case studies testing the thesis that diplomats stationed in the world's capitals constitute an epistemic entity with significance for international society.

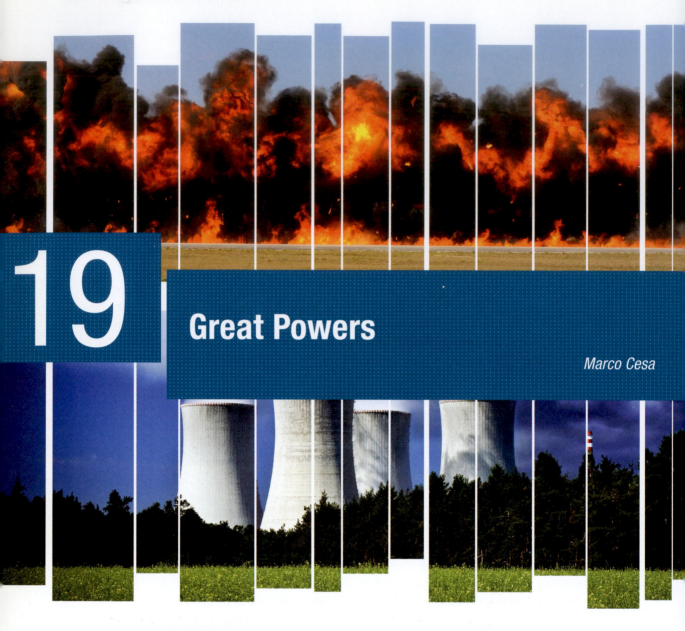

19

Great Powers

Marco Cesa

Introduction	269
What is a great power?	269
The great powers in historical perspective	271
The great powers in the theory of international relations	273
The great powers after the Cold War	276
Conclusion	278
Questions	279
Further reading	279

Introduction

One of the fundamental characteristics of any international system is the distribution of **power** among **states**. The sheer fact that states are unequal in terms of power entails a number of important implications for international politics. For example, while the desires and concerns of weak states are often neglected, the demands of strong states usually shape the international agenda; relations among strong states, in turn, significantly affect patterns of international stability, **order** and change. In short, if you want to shed light on some basic dynamics of international affairs, for analytical or practical purposes, always ask yourself a set of very simple questions: how is power distributed among states? Who are the strong states? How do they stand vis-à-vis each other? Although the relationship of forces is by no means the only explanatory variable at play, it frequently goes a long way in accounting for the 'who gets what, when and how' on the international stage.

What we have generically called 'strong states' are often referred to as '**great powers**'. At first sight, the definition of 'great power' seems unproblematic. After all, do we not know who are the great powers today? And do we not know who were the great powers in, say, the nineteenth century? Do we not recognise a great power when we see one? Yet if we look closer and try to come up with a working definition, things immediately become more complicated. The next section of this chapter will therefore focus on the attributes of a great power, on the elements – or the combination of elements – that allow us to tell a great power from other states. Such a conceptual effort will be followed by a brief historical regression whose purpose is to show the role played by the great powers in the modern and contemporary **international systems**. Next, we will examine the main theories of international relations that claim to explain broad patterns of cooperation and conflict between great powers. Some emphasise the special *functions* that great powers perform; some rely on the *number* of the existing great powers; some identify in the *rise and decline* of the great powers the basic force behind international change. The last section will assess the relevance of the established knowledge for the post-**Cold War** international system.

What is a great power?

In the social sciences, the notion of 'power' refers to a *relationship*: A exerts power over B when A induces B to do something that it would not otherwise do. Once this relational dimension has been established, analysis often shifts to the *means* through which A is able to affect B's actions. What are then the ingredients of power in international politics? Scholars usually offer detailed lists, mostly of a descriptive nature: size of population and territory, resource endowment, economic capability, military strength, political stability and competence, technological development, national character and morale. The most convincing conceptualisation is presented by the French sociologist and political theorist Raymond Aron, who groups the various components of power into three main categories. In his words (Aron 1966: 54),

the power of a collectivity depends on the theater of its action and on its capacity to use available material and human resources. *Milieu, resources, collective action*, such are, from every evidence, whatever the century and whatever the forms of competition among political units, the determinants of power.

In other words, in assessing the power of any given state at any given time we must look at the space that it occupies and within which it is active, the quantity and the quality of implements and combatants, and finally the organisation of the armed forces, the quality of military and civilian leadership in **war** and **peace**, the way in which citizens react to the test of war. While the three terms have some universal value, they also suggest how to investigate change: resources and collective action are always a function of historical contingencies. Only the environment – or, more precisely, the terrain (e.g. mountains, deserts, sheer size) – seems to display some persistent implications: from the nineteenth century to the present day, the British, the Russians and the Americans have all found it hard to pacify Afghanistan. Yet, depending on the existing technology, insular powers such as Britain and the US have been invulnerable or vulnerable, what used to be a strategic chokepoint may become a simple geographical detail, and the air and the sea offer always new communication lanes. Not to mention the broad geographical context in which action takes place. For most of human history, power projection capabilities were limited to a region or to a continent. But ever since the sixteenth century, although one can still conceive of 'regional great powers' – Prussia in the eighteenth century, or Habsburg Austria throughout its history – the major actors on the international scene have had world-wide interests, as well as the means to protect those interests.

The multidimensional nature of power should never be forgotten. Great powers do not achieve and keep their rank by scoring high on a single item. Australia and Canada are endowed with large territories, yet they hardly qualify as great powers. Japan can now rely on the world's second (or third) largest GDP, and yet its formidable economic resources do not translate into a commensurate political weight. One might be tempted to argue that the military potential is perhaps the single most important indicator of great power status. After all, many definitions of great power refer to its war capabilities. To Martin Wight (1978: 18), a great power 'can afford to incur a war'; in Georg Schwarzenberger's view (1964: 115), 'the total warpower of a country is the ultimate test of its status in the international **hierarchy**'; and even Aron's implicit benchmark is war: the 'resources' he has in mind are above all those susceptible of being transformed into weapons and troops. And yet the relevance of sheer military strength should not be exaggerated. At the very least, there must be some connection between economic resources and military resources. It has often been noted, for example, that during the Cold War the USSR – in many ways like Russia before it – was a 'lopsided great power' that compensated for economic weakness with military might, discipline and a vast territory; eventually, the shaky economic foundations of the country played a large role in its sudden collapse. Austria in the early twentieth century and Japan in the 1930s could similarly rely on remarkable military forces, but their economic essentials could not sustain a large military effort; in fact, the very size of their military complex made their relative economic backwardness even more acute. By contrast, Britain in the nineteenth century and the US in the twentieth century were able to work out a better combination of military and economic power; this, in turn, allowed them both to remain at the top of the international hierarchy for decades. In short, and as a general rule, 'the better the symbiosis between the military and the economic arms of power … the more likely would be the prolongation of a Great Power's tenure' (Kennedy 1994: 374).

While in time of war power is mostly a function of military might and its economic basis, in time of peace power rests upon other elements as well, such as the ability to convince other nations by means short of the use of force. In **diplomatic** practice it is often assumed that peacetime power and wartime power are somewhat related to each other. Many international agreements, for example, tend to reflect the relation of forces among the parties involved, as the weak are induced to accept the terms suggested by the strong. Yet calculating power, both in wartime and in peacetime, is a most difficult enterprise, and the net result is at best a vague approximation. Carl von Clausewitz ([1832] 1989: 101) wrote memorable words in this vein: 'War is the realm of chance … Chance makes everything more uncertain and interferes with the whole course of events'. Nor are things less complicated in time of peace. Aron (1966: 62–70) has persuasively shown how problematic it can be to select the economic indicators that will accurately measure the military potential of any given **nation**. In addition, the number of people that can be mobilised in the war effort is above all a function of something that cannot be precisely gauged: that is, organisational and administrative skills. Finally, although we may easily anticipate that in a prolonged and costly conflict the war effort will be sustained only by reducing the standards of living of the civilian population, not even this is of great help in making predictions: rich countries would seem better equipped than poor countries to deal with a redefinition of such standards, but the former can find it more difficult to do without things that may well look superfluous to the latter.

The great powers in historical perspective

Great powers can be found, almost by definition, in any historical age. Think, for example, of the famous rivalries of classical antiquity, such as Athens–Sparta and Rome–Carthage; or of the long period of Roman **hegemony** over most of Europe and the Mediterranean world. Although the Middle Ages witnessed in turn the fragmentation of Europe into a number of decentralised political entities that could hardly mobilise significant resources, nevertheless some hierarchy among them existed, and kingdoms, dynasties and city-states frequently struggled to emerge above the rest. Despite all this, however, both historians and political scientists usually reserve the term 'great power' to the political units that have been active in the modern and contemporary state-system: solid, centralised states entertaining constant relations of all sorts. It is only when you have an established 'system' of states – that is, a set of political units that interact on a regular basis – that the role of the great powers can be fully appreciated. Such conditions were historically met in the European continent at the beginning of the modern age (Kennedy 1987). Although centres of power existed in Asia as well (Ming China, the Mogul Empire, Tokugawa Japan), it was in Europe that economic growth, military effectiveness and political organisation reached levels unmatched in the rest of the globe.

The evolution of the European state-system from its origins to its end – arguably in 1945 – can indeed be interpreted as a succession of struggles among great powers for expansion, influence and security. Periodically, a great power would rise to a position of predominance that seemed to jeopardise the independence, if not the survival, of the other great powers; the latter, in turn, would join forces in order to contain hegemony. Spain, France and Germany, each twice, tried to reach some form of control over most of the continent; each was defeated, every time, by coalitions made up of those that refused to submit, in what remain the best historical illustrations of the **balance of power** (Dehio [1948] 1962).

From the beginning of the sixteenth century up to the **Peace of Westphalia** (1648) the policies of a dynastic and religious bloc, centred on Spain (and Austria) and led by Habsburg rulers, were seen as aiming at a 'universal monarchy'; accordingly, they prompted the opposition of other great powers – such as France and the Ottoman Empire – and of nations that became great powers precisely during that long struggle, such as the Netherlands and Sweden. But it was only in the following century that the European state-system acquired a more stable and more familiar physiognomy. By the middle of the eighteenth century the decline of the Netherlands, Sweden and Spain was plain for all to see; next to the traditional great powers, France and Austria, now stood Russia, Britain and Prussia. It should be noted that rank had been lost or gained, kept or upgraded, thanks to a long series of wars. In a famous article published in 1833, the German historian Leopold von Ranke hailed the rise of the eighteenth-century great powers as the safest barrier against France's hegemonic designs, as implemented first by Louis XIV, and later by Napoleon (Ranke [1833] 1950) (see Box 19.1). To Ranke, the very existence of several great powers and their balance-of-power policies had performed the historical function of guaranteeing the freedom and particular development of all.

BOX 19.1: DISCUSSION POINTS

Ranke on the rise of the great powers in Europe

'As we have seen, it was a necessity of the seventeenth century that France be checked. This had now occurred in a manner that exceeded all expectation. It cannot really be said that an artificial, complex political system had been formed to this end. It merely appeared so, but the fact was that great powers had raised themselves by their own strength and that new independent national states in all their original power had taken over the world stage … In their rise and development … lies the principal event of the hundred years which preceded the outbreak of the French Revolution' (Ranke [1833] 1950: 205–6).

Be that as it may, the five great powers that emerged in the eighteenth century would fight not only in the Napoleonic wars but – if you substitute Germany for Prussia – in World War I and in World War II (with the deletion of Austria) as well (Hinsley 1963: 4–5).

It was at Vienna, in 1814, that the rank of great power was first recognised in diplomatic practice: in the words of the British foreign minister of the time, Castlereagh, the control of negotiations was to remain in the hands 'of the six Powers most considerable in population and weight' (quoted in Wight 1946: 19). The 'Concert of Europe' that followed, and that managed the international system until the outbreak of World War I, reflected a strategic equilibrium supported by the joint efforts of the great powers; neither the Crimean War nor the wars related to the national unification of Italy and Germany escalated to a continental conflict (see Box 19.2). Thanks to this relative stability and its industrial superiority, Britain reached its peak as a world power, in naval and commercial terms, in the second half of the century. Shortly afterwards, however, the traditional Eurocentric international system was challenged by the spreading of industrialisation and modernisation to other areas of the world. While several economic indices pointed at a relative decline of France, Austria and Italy, the US and Japan were now moving to the forefront; even Russia, despite its backwardness, was making considerable progress. Yet, neither Soviet Russia nor the US, for different reasons, played a significant role in the international system that resulted from World War I. Britain and France, although challenged by Italy, Germany and Japan, remained at the centre of the diplomatic stage. It took World War II for the two giants to finally emerge in what was to be a completely new configuration: a world system structured around two major powers, only one of which was (partially) European.

BOX 19.2: DISCUSSION POINTS

Different views on the great powers in the Concert of Europe

Scholars disagree on the interpretation of the great powers' policies during the Concert of Europe.

'The impressive thing about the behavior of the Powers in 1815 is that they were prepared, as they had never previously been prepared, to waive their individual interests in the pursuit of an international system' (Hinsley 1963: 197).

'The success of the Concert … was the result rather than the cause of this pacification, which was primarily due to the fact that Britain, Russia and France had at that time apparently limitless opportunities of independent expansion outside Europe, while Prussia was busy conquering Germany' (Wight 1946: 22).

Size, population, military might, economic strength, political organisation – for most of the Cold War period, the two **superpowers** were unmatchable by any combination of those indicators. Their military superiority, in particular, was further reinforced by their massive build-up of nuclear weapons. Although the diplomatic and strategic landscape of the second half of the twentieth century was thus totally different from that of the previous decades (let alone centuries), some familiar traits of international politics persisted: each superpower had its own **sphere of influence**; each kept the other in check, in some revisited form of balance of power; **bilateral** agreements on certain issues would exert a strong, persuasive pressure on all the other nations, just as bilateral crises would threaten to involve allies in a general war. In one word, the international agenda was shaped by the policies of, and the relations between, the two great powers, possibly to an extent unmatched before: they both were global powers, with global interests and the appropriate means – ideological, diplomatic, economic and military – to pursue such interests.

The progressive reduction in the number of the great powers reached a new stage with the end of the Cold War. Since the early 1990s, the US has been the only superpower left. Before we examine the post-Cold War international system, however, let us take a look at some of the most relevant theories of international relations that are centred on the great powers.

The great powers in the theory of international relations

Although there is no such thing as a comprehensive 'great powers theory', in their analysis of several important issues scholars have always devoted a good deal of attention to the great powers. For our purposes, at least two main themes must be mentioned.

The great powers and international order

Arguably, the most relevant function performed by the great powers is related to the creation and preservation of some international order. According to Hedley Bull (1977: 200–29), great powers claim, and are usually granted, special rights and responsibilities in managing issues of **security** and stability. They can carry out such a function in two basic ways: by handling their relations with one another and by exploiting their superiority vis-à-vis the other nations. The great powers are the main actors behind the implementation of the balance of power: when relations with each other become tense, they can engage in measures of crisis prevention and management; finally, if a war does break out, they can try and limit its escalation. As for the exercise of preponderance over weaker nations, this can take various forms, ranging from the establishment of some outright dominance, to hegemony, or to milder techniques of control, such as spheres of influence. In short, the great powers restrain the policies of the other nations and prevent the latter from taking unsettling initiatives. While those measures of coercion and persuasion are likely to impose a cost on the weak, they also strengthen the stability of the international system as a whole. The Concert of Europe offers a nice illustration of all this: the great powers, after finding a collective *modus vivendi*, moved on to promote joint policies that affected the entire international system (Clark 1989: 170).

Similarly, during the Cold War the two superpowers kept each other in check; in addition, they managed their respective spheres of influence and, albeit sporadically, enforced common policies (e.g. nuclear non-proliferation) (Gaddis 1986).

If management is a key function, what are the conditions that make it more, or less, likely? One influential answer suggests to look at the *number* of great powers. Ever since the beginning of the Cold War, scholars have compared and contrasted two basic types of international system: the **multipolar** system – whose historical reference was of course the classical European state-system – and the bipolar system that had come out of World War II. At first, the former was considered more reliable. When several great powers exist, so the argument went, they can always adjust to changes in the relation of forces. If one of them grows too powerful, its partners can leave the **alliance** and create a new coalition, according to classical balance-of-power principles. Multipolar systems are based on *flexible alliances* because when there are more than two significant players realignment is, by definition, always an option. This is why multipolarity may seem better equipped than bipolarity to absorb shocks related to shifts in the distribution of capabilities among the main actors (Morgenthau [1948] 1973: 349–50). The opposite view, whose most outspoken supporter has been Kenneth Waltz (1979: 163–70), argues that in multipolar systems friendships and rivalries are often ambiguous; in addition, it is frequently uncertain who will take the leadership, in case of need. Such a systemic complexity predisposes the great powers to make two serious mistakes: they may tie themselves too tightly to some adventurous ally whose support is considered vital (*chain-ganging*), or they may be encouraged to behave as free riders, hoping that somebody else will pull the chestnuts out of fire (*buck-passing*). The crisis leading to the outbreak of World War I illustrates the first mechanism, while the general failure to prevent Germany from becoming more and more aggressive in the late 1930s is a nice example of the second. By contrast, a bipolar system is not afflicted with such problems. Here, who is a friend to whom – just as who is a foe to whom – is well known. It is clear who will take responsibility for managing the system: the Big Two will. Waltz acknowledges that in multipolarity alliances are flexible. But he adds that such a flexibility can induce the great powers to adopt rigid strategies in times of crisis. On the contrary, while bipolarity is characterised by rigid alliances, this allows the Big Two to adopt flexible strategies. What does that mean? Take a multipolar crisis, such as the one that struck Europe in the summer of 1914. Precisely because it could not afford the luxury of losing its only reliable ally, Germany – far from restraining Austria – actually encouraged Vienna's bellicose posture and ended up tying its own hands, which contributed to the collective loss of control over events. Take now the 1956 Suez crisis, in a bipolar context. In this case, the US knew that its own allies had no credible realignment option; in addition, even if they had defected, this would not have altered the overall strategic balance, because the power gap between the Big Two and all the others was simply too wide. These systemic conditions allowed the US to restrain France, Britain and Israel, and the crisis was over in a matter of days.

The great powers and international change

Although great powers are always there, their identity varies across history. Some keep their rank for quite some time, while others go through a much quicker cycle. Yet all great powers rise and fall. In this simple fact lies the key to understanding two fundamental phenomena of international politics: systemic change and the origin of major wars.

Drawing upon Thucydides's diagnosis of the causes of the Peloponnesian war (Thucydides [c.431 BC] 1972: 48–9, 87, 103) and some general insights on the evolution of universal history (Toynbee 1934 and 1939), a number of contemporary scholars have explained international change as the reflection of a fundamental shift in the relation of forces among the great powers. 'Power transition theory' (Organski and Kugler 1980), 'power cycle theory' (Doran 1971 and 1991), 'hegemonic war theory' (Gilpin 1981 and 1988), 'long cycle theory' (Modelski 1987): although those frameworks differ in many respects, they all share the basic idea that patterns of *relative growth* and *relative decline* between the great powers decisively affect the dynamics of international politics. According to Paul Kennedy (1994), the differential in terms of economic and technological development among nations predisposes the strong and rich to expand their political influence with the help of military means, either by establishing veritable empires (as Spain, Britain and France did at their zenith) or by getting rid of dangerous rivals (as the US did in the twentieth century). Such predominance, however, is sooner or later challenged by those powers that are now rising and filling the initial gap. While the dominant power may still be growing in absolute terms, other powers are growing even faster – which means that the former has now entered a phase of relative decline. Such was the position, for example, in which the Netherlands and France found themselves in the mid-eighteenth century and at the beginning of the twentieth century respectively. At this point, the declining great power is likely to have all sorts of obligations (dependence on foreign markets and raw materials, overseas military bases, alliances) and less means to deal with them. Its instinctive response to the rise of challengers is usually to spend more on defence, thereby diverting resources from productive investment and further accelerating its own decline. The cases of imperial Spain in the seventeenth century, of Britain on the eve of World War I, and of the USSR in the last phase of the Cold War illustrate the point.

Although Kennedy emphasises the mismatch between economic potential and military spending, neither he nor other scholars who write in a similar vein argue that economic variables alone are always decisive. As we have seen, 'power' is a multidimensional concept – space and domestic organisation play just as important a role. Robert Gilpin (1981: 186–97) argues that the declining great power has two broad strategies at its disposal: it can try to increase its resources, or to reduce its costs. Accordingly, not only can it extract some tribute from its clients or manipulate the terms of trade with other countries, it can also try to increase its own efficiency via social and institutional reform. On the cost-reduction side, the declining great power can design a new defensive perimeter with the help of new alliances, can make concessions to the challenger, or can withdraw **unilaterally** from the most exposed areas.

Although great powers such as Venice or China were able to slow down their decline for centuries thanks to a skilful use of their resources, in other cases the shifting distribution of power between the main players has ended up in a 'hegemonic war' characterised by: a) a direct clash between the former dominant power and the rising challenger; b) the use of unlimited means; c) the general scope of warfare. In other words, this type of war is different from other armed conflicts because of what is at stake: the governance of the international system. In the modern age, the Thirty Years' War (1618–1648), the Napoleonic wars and the two world wars illustrate the point: in each case, what followed was a new international system, with a new distribution of territory, new political and economic arrangements, a new hierarchy between the great powers (Gilpin 1988).

The great powers after the Cold War

Do 'hegemonic wars' as a repetitive phenomenon rule out peaceful change? Of course not. What we witnessed between the end of the 1980s and the beginning of the 1990s was precisely the peaceful resolution of a long great-power competition and a smooth transition to a new international system. Does all this affect the relevance of what we have discussed so far? Not really, for at least two reasons. First, the sudden collapse of the USSR vividly reminds us of the multidimensional nature of power. The USSR was a formidable military power – too formidable, in fact, to be sustained by the economic means at its disposal. In addition, the Soviet political system was no longer able to mobilise any significant support among its citizens at home and its allies abroad. Except for its military might, in other words, the USSR could no longer be considered a credible challenger to the US. The peaceful end of the Cold War is thus less surprising than it might seem, for the typical preconditions for a 'hegemonic war' simply failed to materialise.

Second, a great-power analysis along traditional lines can still shed some light on several basic features of the current international system. To that purpose, Table 19.1 compares the contemporary major powers on the basis of a few indicators. While the overall picture is far from being exhaustive, it nevertheless suggests some significant considerations.

In military terms, the US is in a class of its own. No other country comes even close to match the amount of money that it allocates to defence. The US is a distant first in terms of GDP too. If these two gross indicators are combined, one can indeed find some compelling evidence for this rare power configuration called unipolarity.

Table 19.1 The great powers in 2010

	United States	Russia	EU-27	France	Germany	United Kingdom	Japan	China	India
Population (millions)	315	140	500	62	81	62	130	1350	1200
Size (million km²)	9.3	17	4.3	0.5	0.3	0.2	0.4	9.5	3.2
GDP (trillion $)	14.2	1.6	16.3	2.6	3.3	2.2	5	4.9	1.3
Growth rate (%)	1.6	5	1	0.6	2.2	1.2	0.1	10	8.6
Defence outlays (billion $)	660	53	300	64	45	58	51	100	36

Sources: www.tradingeconomics.com, Eurostat, IMF, World Bank, SIPRI.

the international system is now structured around one major power only. Table 19.1, however, also points at the potential of the European Union as a great power. As independent players, even the three most important European nations are no more than pygmies; however, the twenty-seven members of the EU combined constitute the richest area of the planet, the third largest concentration of population and the second biggest military spender. In other words, a politically cohesive EU – something like the 'United States of Europe' – would be a natural candidate for great power status and role. More importantly, Table 19.1 shows some trends that, if confirmed in the future, might have large repercussions. If we look at growth rates, we cannot help noting the impetuous rise of China and India, which makes for a strident contrast with the very modest pace at which the US and the EU are growing. While it is too soon to say if this is the beginning of a new 'power transition', it is important to keep in mind that large economic shifts have in the past very often preceded the rise of new great powers.

Table 19.1 also reminds us that great power status still rests upon a number of attributes. Since the end of the Cold War, many have been concerned about nuclear proliferation. Whether the spread of nuclear weapons would have stabilising or destabilising consequences is open to debate. For our purposes, it is enough to say that nuclear weapons alone do not transform nations into great powers. During the Cold War, Britain and France were not great powers, despite their strategic arsenals (Morgenthau 1972). After the Cold War, Pakistan did not become a great power following its first nuclear test. In purely defensive postures, however, nuclear weapons may have altered the connection between economic means and military might: if a minor power adopts a strategy based on nuclear **deterrence**, it can easily complicate whatever plans of intimidation a bigger power might have, its modest economic capability notwithstanding (Waltz 1993). Another recurrent theme is that in the contemporary international system power has become more diffused; as a result, the importance of non-material resources, including culture, ideology and institutionalised **norms**, has been enhanced. Such

Figure 19.1   US President Obama in discussion aboard *Air Force One*, June 2009

Source: Wikimedia commons.

ingredients make for what is called '**soft power**' (Nye 1990), and the US is usually believed to have more of it than other countries. One may wonder, however, if this is a feature only of contemporary world politics. In the past as well, a great power's culture and ideology have attracted other nations and conferred legitimacy on the former's policies. In addition, 'soft power' is influential insofar as it is connected with 'hard power'. The spread of cultural models throughout the ancient world was certainly an integral part of Roman hegemony; however, such a hegemony was in the first place based upon material resources and organisation. Likewise, France, at its peak in the seventeenth and eighteenth centuries, exerted a remarkable 'soft power' over the other European nations as it set the standards for literature, language and arts. But France was above all a rich, centralised, very populous, well-armed, big country. Finally, just as for 'hard power', it is difficult to measure the impact of 'soft power': while American cultural models (e.g. Hollywood movies) may reinforce the influence of the US, they may also unleash bitter anti-American reactions (Kennedy 1994: 375).

Conclusion

One of the historical functions of the great powers has been the management of the international system: it is only when the most relevant players concur that collective action can be taken. To a large extent this is still true. The blooming of international institutions over the past decades has led many to conclude that states are no longer the only relevant actors in world politics. Yet the functioning of the main international organisations essentially depends on the preferences of the great powers. Both during and after the Cold War, security issues have been successfully addressed by the **United Nations (UN)** only when the five permanent members of the Security Council have agreed. **NATO**'s profile has always been shaped by US policies, just as the European integration process has always reflected – and keeps reflecting – French and German priorities and leadership. Not to mention those international fora whose membership is officially restricted to the strong, such as the **G20**, the self-appointed, exclusive association of the largest economies in the world. At the same time, there are also significant discontinuities. In the past great powers have often balanced each other, thus preventing one of them from growing too strong; yet since the end of the Cold War no balance of power has emerged to contain the US. This may be due to a number of factors: unlike many previous hegemonic great powers, the US is not interested in territorial expansion; it is a democracy; and it accepts some self-restraint, as reflected in its participation in a number of international institutions (Ikenberry 2002). Thus, although a formidable great power, the US does not pose a threat to other nations. There are, however, more familiar explanations that cannot be neglected. First, in structural terms, the power gap between the US and the other nations may simply be too wide to be filled by any coalition. Second, after the Cold War US diplomacy has been very good at preserving (in Western Europe, the Far East, the Middle East) and expanding (in Eastern Europe and in Central Asia) its network of alliances on a global scale while keeping strong regional actors (e.g. Russia, China, Iraq and Iran) at bay (Joffe 1995; Huntington 1999). Such a policy places the US in continuity with what great powers have traditionally done to defend and enlarge their spheres of influence.

QUESTIONS

1. Geography, or what Raymond Aron calls *milieu*, has often played a large role in defining great-power status. What is its role in the contemporary international system?
2. Under what conditions might India and China emerge as great powers in the next two decades or so? Will this affect the tone and content of their relations with the US?
3. Why does **realism** assign a special place to the great powers?
4. What are the functions performed by the great powers in the United Nations (UN)? Are those functions significantly different from those carried out by the great powers prior to the UN's existence?
5. Discuss how Hedley Bull's ideas about great-power politics can be illustrated in a past international system of your choosing.

FURTHER READING

Grygiel, Jakub J. 2006, *Great powers and geopolitical change*, Baltimore: The Johns Hopkins University Press. Sheds light on the importance of geopolitical variables (stability of state boundaries, location of resources, trade networks) in establishing and keeping power in the international arena. Case studies include Venice, the Ottoman Empire and China in the fifteenth century.

Holbraad, Carsten 1970, *The Concert of Europe: a study in German and British international theory, 1815–1914*, London: Longman. Discusses how British, Austrian and German statesmen and intellectuals alike looked at the Concert of Europe in different periods of the nineteenth century and shows the ambivalent connections between the Concert and the old balance of power.

Joffe, Josef 1998, *The great powers*, London: Phoenix. Examines the post-Cold War international system and the role of the great powers therein. Analysis is combined with the major theoretical paradigms of the field for explanatory and predictive purposes.

Mearsheimer, John J. 2001, *The tragedy of great power politics*, New York: Norton. Offers a general realist theory about the behaviour of the great powers, with special emphasis on war. Illustrations range from the eighteenth century to the present.

Pastor, Robert A. and Hoffmann, Stanley H. (eds) 1999, *A century's journey: how the great powers shape the world*, New York: Basic Books. Looks at the continuities and discontinuities in the grand strategy and foreign policy of the US, Japan, China, Russia and the major European powers in the course of the twentieth century.

Rasler, Karen A. and Thompson, William R. 1994, *The great powers and global struggle, 1490–1990*, Lexington: The University Press of Kentucky. Focuses on the rise and fall of the great powers, and the way in which these shifts have set the stage for the outbreak of major wars over the past five centuries.

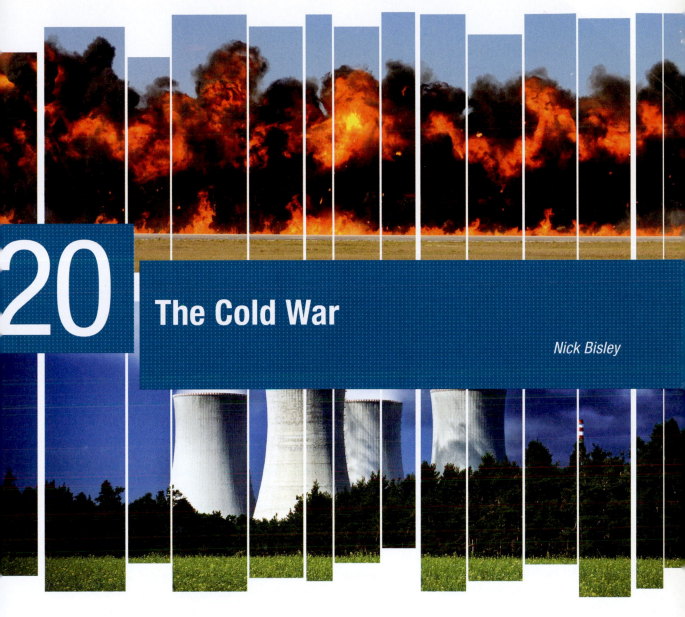

20

The Cold War

Nick Bisley

Introduction	282
The beginnings of the Cold War: 1945–53	282
The Cold War spreads: 1953–69	286
Détente and the 'second' Cold War: 1969–85	287
The end of the Cold War: 1985–91	288
The Cold War and International Relations	290
Conclusion: echoes of the Cold War	291
Questions	293
Further reading	293

Introduction

The **Cold War** was the most important feature of the **international system** in the second half of the twentieth century. The rivalry between the Soviet Union (USSR) and the United States (US) shaped the contours of conflict and cooperation among **states** and peoples between 1945 and 1991. Although the conflict did not drive all aspects of international relations, its force permeated every corner of the globe. Whether in Santiago, Sydney or Shanghai, the influence of **geopolitical** and ideological conflict was unmistakable. More importantly, the Cold War created rivalries and political fault lines which continue to shape international relations long after the conflict has passed.

The Cold War was a conflict between the USSR and the US (see Box 20.1). The two powers who emerged from World War II as preeminent in world politics became engaged in a protracted global contest which, although actual combat between them never eventuated, involved the largest and most destructive military arsenals in history. The two camps could destroy the entire planet thousands of times over with their nuclear weapons, and each side's military was on a hair trigger for the conflict's duration. It was a dispute that was driven both by traditional concerns about **security** – each felt the other threatening to their survival and their interests – as well as by ideological antagonism. Both embodied universal ideologies which assumed the superiority of their social system over all others. In this respect the Cold War was as much a contest about how to organise society as it was a competition for strategic influence and nuclear superiority.

BOX 20.1: TERMINOLOGY

Cold War: meanings and temperature

The term Cold War is generally used in two ways. First, it refers to the conflictual relations between the US and the USSR and their respective allies. Second, it is used as a label for the broader period in which the conflict was the preeminent feature. In spite of the many wars that were caused directly or indirectly by Soviet-American rivalry, such as in Korea, Vietnam and Afghanistan, the conflict is referred to as 'cold' because although there were near misses, such as Cuba in 1962, direct military action between the two protagonists never eventuated.

In contrast to traditional **wars**, which can be dated with some precision, a declaration of war or an invasion or attack, there is no clear starting date for the Cold War; instead there existed a gradual escalation of tensions. Some historians have argued that the Cold War had its origins in the Russian **Revolution** of 1917 (Powaski 1998) – understandable given that the tension of the Cold War was in part a function of the revolutionary ideology at the heart of Soviet **power**. However, as an overt geopolitical and socio-economic contest, the Cold War began in the wake of World War II, with the collapse of the Grand **Alliance** between the US, Britain and the Soviet Union that had been struck to defeat the Axis powers (Germany, Japan and Italy). Likewise, its termination has no clear surrender date or 'armistice day', although two dates commonly cited are those of the fall of the Berlin Wall on the night of 8–9 November 1989 and the dissolution of the USSR on New Year's Eve, 1991.

The beginnings of the Cold War: 1945–53

During the planning for the post-war world that had commenced towards the end of World War II, tensions between the Soviet and American allies began to emerge. They were already clear when US President Franklin D. Roosevelt, British Prime Minister

Figure 20.1   Allied leaders Winston Churchill (UK), Franklin D. Roosevelt (US) and Joseph Stalin (USSR) at the Yalta Conference, February 1945

Source: Wikimedia commons.

Winston Churchill and Soviet Premier Joseph Stalin met at the Yalta Conference in February 1945 (see Figure 20.1). The death of President Franklin Roosevelt in April 1945 contributed further to the breakdown of the alliance as his successor, Harry Truman, was distinctly more anti-Soviet than his predecessor. After the defeat of Japan in August 1945, the alliance that had been formed in 1941 began to unravel swiftly. When the Soviet Union reneged on commitments to **self-determination** in Eastern Europe, failed to withdraw troops from Iran and demanded territorial concessions as well as bases from Turkey, US policy took a more confrontational line. This approach was informed by George Kennan's 'Long Telegram' of February 1946, where the Moscow-based diplomat argued that an accommodation between the Soviets and the Americans was impossible due to the essential character of Soviet power (see Box 20.2).

BOX 20.2: DISCUSSION POINTS

Containment and George Kennan

George Kennan was one of the most influential figures in the early years of the Cold War and is thought by many to be the father of America's grand strategy of **containment**. The 'Long Telegram' was first sent as a diplomatic cable in February 1946. It was subsequently published in 1947 in the influential US journal *Foreign Affairs*, with the author described as 'X' (Kennan 1946). In the text Kennan argued that the best US response to the Soviet

Union was to establish lines of containment to limit the spread of Soviet power. This would constrain Soviet influence and allow the natural superiority of the US system to win out over what he saw to be a deeply flawed USSR. The policy of containment, limiting Soviet expansion but not interfering around the world, took on a more interventionist dimension as the Cold War developed, most notably in Vietnam. Kennan felt that this interventionism was counterproductive to US interests.

The mistrust and suspicion soon turned into geopolitical and ideological competition (Yergin 1978). In 1947 the US pursued what came to be known as the **Truman Doctrine** whereby the US provided military assistance to Turkey and Greece as part of a broader response to Soviet aggression and expansion. The view that the USSR sought to take advantage of post-war Europe's vulnerability, where **communism** had considerable appeal in the ashes of war, was the motivating force behind the **Marshall Plan**'s economic reconstruction of Western Europe. The US believed that an economically robust Western Europe would be politically stable and much less susceptible to the challenges of communism. The Plan involved large-scale loans which underwrote the economic reconstruction of Europe and added momentum to the creation of the European Communities, the precursor to the European Union. The Plan was offered, somewhat disingenuously, to the Soviets, who turned it down as they recognised that it would compromise their strategic and economic interests in Eastern Europe.

The status of Berlin was the source of the first significant crisis of the conflict. Post-war Germany had been divided into four sectors, each run by an Allied power. Berlin was similarly divided but was located in the centre of East Germany, which was under Soviet control. The Soviets sought to claim Berlin and in mid-1948 severed road and rail communications to the entire city. A massive airlift, which lasted nearly a year, ensured West Berlin remained out of Soviet control, but political tensions had escalated considerably as a result.

A year later the USSR successfully tested an atomic bomb. Now the animosity and rivalry were backed with the terrible power of atomic weaponry. This led to the creation of the **North Atlantic Treaty Organization (NATO)**. NATO was intended to provide a formal structure for an American military presence in Europe that was to deter Soviet aggression. In response, the Soviets created the **Warsaw Pact** as a counter-weight in 1955. Thus, ten years after they had fought so successfully to defeat Nazi Germany, the allies were now lined up against one another. Europe was divided between a Soviet-dominated East, where liberated states were run by communist **regimes** loyal to and propped up by the Soviet Union, and a democratic West whose security relied on American military power. Concerns about Soviet expansionism in the West appeared to be confirmed by Berlin and the bomb; fear in the East about American threats was realised by the ongoing presence of US conventional and atomic weapons in Western Europe.

The Cold War had its origins in, and was in its primary motivation, a conflict over Europe. From the outset, however, its challenge was global (see Figure 20.2). Two events in Asia brought this home. The defeat of Japan had reignited the Chinese **Civil War** which had been running since the fall of the Manchu Dynasty in 1911. The surprising victory of Mao Zedong's Soviet-supported communist forces meant that the world's largest state, as well as its most populous one, were now communist.

Figure 20.2 The Cold War: NATO and Warsaw Pact countries (1949–89)

Legend: NATO members – light shade

Warsaw Pact members – dark shade

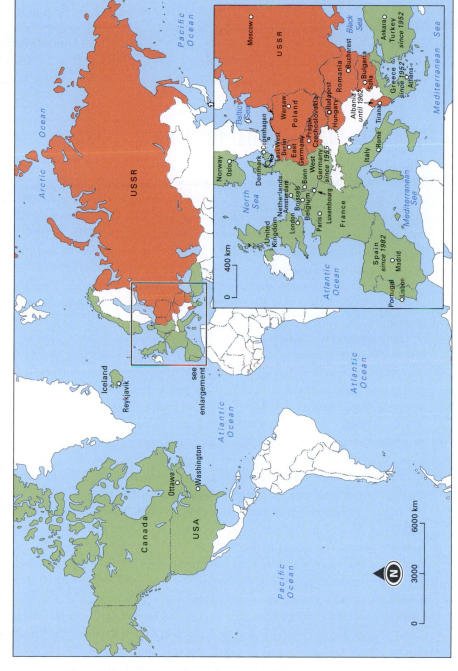

Viewed from Washington, Soviet forces and allies spread from the Baltic Sea across the Eurasian landmass to the South China Sea. The second element of the Cold War's spread was in Korea. The Korean peninsula had been a Japanese colony since 1895 and was hastily divided in the wake of Japan's defeat. In June 1950 the Soviet-backed North launched an attack on the US-supported South which confirmed, in the minds of the Western allies, that communist forces were not only aggressive but emboldened by success in China and elsewhere. Aided by the newly formed **United Nations (UN)**, the US and its allies fought a long and bloody war where more than 3 million lost their lives. In 1953 an armistice was signed but to this day the border remains a geostrategic flashpoint.

The Cold War spreads: 1953–69

The Korean War convinced the Americans and their allies that communism was aggressive; it also reinforced the sense that it was a monolithic bloc. Soviets, Chinese and Koreans appeared to be part of a unified system with global ambitions. As such, a concerted global response was thought to be necessary. This prompted the US to sign a series of alliance treaties in the Asia-Pacific, including **ANZUS** in 1951 and **SEATO** in 1954. It was also a key factor driving US policy in Indochina. In Europe, NATO was organisationally and militarily strengthened, with the US committing to a long-term and large-scale military presence to deter Soviet conventional forces. Through the 1950s and 1960s both Soviets and Americans enhanced both their conventional and nuclear arsenals.

After Korea, the dynamics of East–West confrontation began to spread and interact with regional developments across the world. It had particular purchase in the struggles that were prompted by the dismantling of European empires. In Iran, Guatemala and the Middle East in the early 1950s, local political elites attempted to gain domestic advantage by playing on US and Soviet perceptions of their relative strategic importance. Although Stalin's death in March 1953 brought the more conciliatory Nikita Khrushchev to power, Soviet support for national liberation movements such as in the Congo and Cuba, along with its intervention in Hungary in 1956, confirmed the perception in Washington that the USSR continued to pose a threat to the US and its allies, and to their economic and strategic interests around the world.

Tensions reached a high point in the Berlin crisis of 1961 and the **Cuban missile crisis** in 1962. The first involved a dangerous military stand-off that led to the construction of the infamous Berlin Wall which prevented East Berliners moving to the West. The heavily fortified physical division of the city was a potent symbol of the split and its tragic human consequences – hundreds were killed trying to cross from East to West during the wall's twenty-eight year existence. The second, where the USSR secretly deployed missiles 90 miles off the American coast only to withdraw them after tense negotiations, led to a humiliating climb-down for Khrushchev. The Soviet leader had attempted to place strategic pressure on the US but, in spite of achieving a trade-off removal of US missiles from Turkey, was perceived to have been outfoxed by President Kennedy. His position at home was fatally weakened and US decision-makers began to believe that they were gaining an upper hand in the global contest. Both crises had brought the world extraordinarily close to nuclear annihilation and this resulted in improved communications between Washington and

Moscow and a somewhat more stable platform for Soviet-American relations for the next ten years or so.

This did not slow down the rate of the arms race, which continued apace during this phase (see Box 20.3), and did not deter their indirect rivalry across the world. In 1965 the US made the fateful decision to escalate its support for South Vietnam in its struggle with the North, and to participate in a large-scale ground war which ultimately led to an embarrassing withdrawal in 1973 after political support for the conflict collapsed. US policy was driven by the ultimately unfounded fears that defeat of South Vietnam at the hands of Ho Chi Minh's communist forces would destabilise the region and strengthen the appeal and success of communism in Southeast Asia.

BOX 20.3: DISCUSSION POINTS

The arms race

One of the central features of Cold War rivalry was the competition over strategic arms. In the years following World War II technological sophistication in weaponry was growing at a considerable pace and each advance appeared to give the holder a decisive advantage. The arms race was the acute end of the conflict and involved both conventional and nuclear weapons. It began with Soviet efforts to break the US atomic monopoly, in which they succeeded in 1949. It was a race that involved an expansion in the quantity of weapons as well as the development of more sophisticated delivery systems such as intercontinental bombers, ballistic missiles and multiple independently targeted re-entry vehicles (MIRV). In 1950 the US had a stockpile of around 450 atomic weapons and the USSR had several. By 1985 the US had over 11 000 nuclear weapons and the USSR around 9500, including both bombs and missile warheads.

These fears did not come to fruition, in part due to the breakdown of Chinese-Soviet relations. While the West had perceived a monolithic communist entity in the Soviet-China alliance, relations had always been uneasy. After Stalin's death, personal clashes between Mao and Khrushchev, along with ideological differences and competition for leadership of the communist movement, as well as Soviet refusal to pass on atomic technology, led to the deterioration of relations. Few in the West realised that relations had become so bad and it was not until the short 1969 Sino-Soviet border war that it became clear that the communist bloc had fragmented.

Détente and the 'second' Cold War: 1969–85

The policy of **détente** was a deliberate attempt to improve Soviet-American relations, and the hostility that had emerged between China and the USSR provided the strategic opening that made it possible. The US, led by President Nixon and Secretary of State Henry Kissinger, sought to improve relations with China and Russia – which their mutual antagonism now allowed – so that the US could extricate itself from Vietnam and contain Soviet nuclear weapon acquisition. US recognition of the People's Republic of China in 1972, the signing of the Strategic Arms Limitation Treaty in the same year and the Helsinki Final Act of 1975 were the key achievements of détente. The latter was notable for establishing principles of **human rights** as the basis for future Soviet-American discussions. Symbolically, détente was embodied by the meeting of a US Apollo and Soviet Soyuz spacecraft in orbit in July 1975.

Yet the achievements in **arms control**, improvements in communication and the civility of diplomatic language did not remove the underlying hostility between the two sides, and their mutual distrust was never far from the surface. Both sides were entangled in the Arab-Israeli war of 1973 and by the mid-1970s the mood began to shift. The USSR was thought to have been taking advantage of the improved relations to escalate its support for revolutionary movements around the world. The success of revolutions in Ethiopia, Iran, Cambodia, Angola, Afghanistan and Nicaragua in the second half of the 1970s and, most particularly, the Soviet intervention in Afghanistan in 1979, were seen by many as the results of détente.

This prompted in the US a sense of weakness in its foreign policy that was matched by a poorly performing economy, which had been badly affected by the oil shocks of the 1970s and the decline of its manufacturing base. These palpable concerns propelled Ronald Reagan to the US presidency. Reagan had campaigned on taking a harder line on the USSR, and upon accession to the White House began to put pressure on the Soviets. This involved large increases in military spending, active intervention in Soviet allied states such as El Salvador and Nicaragua, and an increasingly bellicose rhetoric. The shooting down of a Korean Air Lines passenger jet which had strayed over Soviet airspace in 1983 was symptomatic of the increase in tensions and sense of risk at the time. Arms control negotiations collapsed, the US increased its interventions in Central America and elsewhere, and Reagan launched a space-based missile defence initiative, dubbed 'Star Wars'. By the end of his first term as president, Europe was experiencing levels of tension unseen since the early days of the Cold War, and a sense that nuclear war was a very real possibility had returned (Halliday 1986).

The end of the Cold War: 1985–91

The transformation of the Cold War was as radical as it was rapid and was a function of both individual roles and the broader structural circumstances of international relations. The key development was the selection in 1985 of Mikhail Gorbachev as General Secretary (see Box 20.4) by the Politburo, the Communist Party's key policy-making and governing body. The USSR's economy had been stagnant since 1978 and its strategic position was being compromised as its capacity to fund its geopolitical commitments was severely tested – to say nothing of the cost of trying to maintain technological parity with the US. Gorbachev determined to undertake a reform program which was intended to revitalise the Soviet economy and society. A central element of the program was the belief that a peaceful international environment was necessary for domestic revitalisation, and to that end Gorbachev launched a program of foreign policy reform.

Following his first-term hostility, Reagan undertook a significant change in attitude towards the USSR during the re-election year of 1984. After a summit meeting in Geneva in late 1985 he became receptive to the arms reduction proposals set out by Gorbachev, and together they enhanced the two states' sense of trust (Garthoff 1994). The USSR's foreign policy reform program involved a massive reduction in conventional and nuclear weapons, a shift to a purely defensive military doctrine, the adoption of a liberal posture towards the international system – that is, one focused on institutions, human rights and the international rule of law – and the cessation of support for revolutionary movements and 'fraternal' communist regimes.

BOX 20.4: KEY FIGURES

Mikhail Sergeevich Gorbachev

The final leader of the Soviet Union was, other than Lenin, the only one to have graduated from university. He was made General Secretary of the Communist Party in March 1985 following the death of Konstantin Chernenko. He was a surprise choice, having only been elevated to the Politburo in 1978 and being one of its youngest members. Following decades of dour and elderly political leaders in Moscow, Gorbachev, and his foreign minister, the charismatic Eduard Shevardnadze, represented an important shift in generation, experience and worldview. Gorbachev was educated, had travelled and, most crucially, did not follow the traditional Kremlin path in his dealings with outsiders. British Prime Minister Margaret Thatcher famously declared that he was a man 'with whom we can do business', and it was this capacity to 'do business' that was central to his success. Many individual leaders played important parts in the development of the conflict, but none can match the significance Gorbachev played in bringing the curtain down on the Cold War.

The reforms developed in a piecemeal fashion between 1985 and 1989 and famously culminated in the 'velvet revolutions' in Eastern Europe. As Gorbachev was reforming the USSR with policies of *perestroika* (restructuring), *glasnost* (openness) and **democratisation**, popular dissatisfaction with the regimes in Eastern Europe emerged. This sentiment was led by movements for change, most famously embodied in Poland by Lech Walesa's Solidarność (Solidarity) – the Eastern Bloc's first independent trade union – and created huge pressure on Soviet control mechanisms. The Soviet leadership determined that the time had come for an end to the situation whereby the USSR essentially determined the direction of politics and strategy in Eastern Europe (known as the Brezhnev doctrine). Gorbachev felt that the regimes, if they stood for anything, would have to stand for themselves, which they proved utterly incapable of doing. After 1989 the reform program within the USSR also began to spin out of the Communist Party's control, as democratisation and new freedoms mixed with an explosive **nationalism** that eventually destroyed the Soviet Union. As an entity, the USSR was replaced by a series of new **sovereign states** which were based on the organisational structure of its constituent republics, and the geopolitical map of Central and Eastern Europe was rewritten as their Soviet-supported governments were rejected en masse (see Box 20.5).

It was the shift within the USSR, and the acceptance of this by the US-led West, which brought about the end of the Cold War. It had been a conflict between competing ideologies as well as a geopolitical struggle between states. It came to an end with the rejection by elites within the Communist Party of the USSR's revolutionary ideas, and the policies that sprang from them. While the Cold War had been very much about strategic threats and nuclear weapons, they were a means through which the contest was played out but not the contest itself. Many tend to think that Reagan won the Cold War through out-spending the USSR in the military competition. There is little evidence to support this view. The Soviets were most certainly at a decisive strategic disadvantage by the late 1970s but the motive force behind the foreign policy reform program was not strategic but political and economic.

BOX 20.5: DISCUSSION POINTS

A new European map

The end of the Cold War transformed the geopolitical map of world politics, bringing a raft of new states into the international system. From the collapse of the USSR came the following new sovereign states: Armenia, Azerbaijan, Belarus, Estonia, Georgia, Latvia, Lithuania, Moldova, Kazakhstan, Kyrgyzstan, the Russian Federation (Russia), Tajikistan, Turkmenistan, Ukraine and Uzbekistan. Russia became the legal heir of the USSR's international commitments, such as its seat at the UN, and founded the Commonwealth of Independent States (CIS), incorporating twelve of the USSR's republics, to try to assert some vestiges of its **hegemony**. In Eastern and Central Europe, more states were created. Czechoslovakia peacefully divided into the Czech and Slovak republics. The collapse of Yugoslavia involved a series of bloody wars that created new states from the constituent republics of Bosnia and Herzegovina, Croatia, Slovenia, Macedonia, Serbia and Montenegro.

The Cold War and International Relations

International Relations **theory** has a close relationship with the Cold War, as many of the **discipline**'s theoretical developments were in response to changes in the dynamics of conflict. The rise of **realism** was produced by the dominance of geopolitics during the early phases of the Cold War. Détente's optimism helped revive liberal internationalism and brought the cooperative possibilities of **interdependence** to the table; and the role that ideas played in the Cold War's demise helped facilitate the rise of **constructivism**. Beyond this, the Cold War provokes many questions which theory can help answer. Why did the US-Soviet alliance, which had worked so well during World War II, break down? Why did the US and the USSR never come to blows? What role did the leaders play in shaping the conflict? Why did it end so suddenly? Why did no one predict its demise?

Of the many issues, the question of causation is perhaps most important. What were the causes of the Cold War? The answer to this complex question depends on which theory one turns to and thus which assumptions one makes. For realists, the answer lies in the power vacuum in the international system after 1945 (see, for example, Gaddis 1990; Wohlforth 1993). Prior to World War II, both the US and the USSR were significant powers but neither was dominant and neither was interested in projecting its power much beyond its borders. Germany, Britain, France and Italy were all major powers with expansive international interests and considerable military force. The calamity of World War II destroyed the basis of these states' power and into this vacuum stepped a largely unscathed US and a battle-damaged but militarily dominant USSR. Here, the Cold War was a product of the inexorable workings of the international system, whereby major powers are compelled to expand their interests or fall prey to others who have expanded. In Western Europe there was no dominant power and thus the system induced American and Soviet rivalry; this went global as **decolonisation** provided further opportunities for advantage. For realists, the Cold War was a contest of **power politics** in which ideology was little more than window dressing. From this perspective, the roots of rivalry lay in the structure of the international system and the distribution of power across the states.

A different theoretical approach, that of **liberalism**, does not look at the system so much as the attributes of its constituent states. While liberals do not deny the importance of the military rivalry, for an explanation of the conflict they look to ineffective policies, misperceptions and miscommunication between political elites (see, for example, Jervis 1976; Larson 1985). While realists see conflict as inevitable, liberals see it as contingent on specific actions. The Cold War was not caused by a power vacuum but instead was the product of **diplomatic** blundering and misunderstanding. Rivalry was not inevitable, but was the product of a mutual sense of insecurity that could have been resolved. Improved communication and better understanding of the other side's intentions and concerns could have produced a workable and cooperative international system and a much more peaceful post-war setting.

There are a host of other explanations as well, with some arguing that the Cold War was a product of **capitalist** international relations, which fosters militaristic competition among states. For others, the Cold War was not really a clash of values and interests but a military exercise that was used by both sides to establish and further their respective domination of domestic society (Chomsky 1982; Kaldor 1990). These theories produce different answers because they place explanatory emphasis on different aspects of the conflict. They can help clarify thinking but careful attention must be paid to the basic assumptions about social behaviour which they make and upon which they place explanatory weight.

The most enduring conundrum of the Cold War relates to something that did not happen. Why did the US and the USSR avoid military conflict? The greatest source of concern for all who lived through the Cold War was the apocalyptic prospect of nuclear war. There are many reasons put forward to explain the absence of war. Some point to good communication and effective diplomacy in times of crisis, others argue that it was their lack of physical proximity that kept the peace. The most influential answer to this question is also one of the most controversial: that **peace** between the US and the USSR was brought about by nuclear weapons. So massive was the price that would have to be paid if conflict eventuated that both sides were forced to adopt less bellicose policies. From this point of view the long post-war peace (at least between the chief protagonists) was kept by the very weapons they had acquired to destroy one another. The idea that peace was enforced by a balance of terror is hard to refute, for the simple reason that it is logically impossible to say why something did *not* happen. It is no doubt true that the weapons inspired caution, as indeed did the scale of conventional weapons, but we cannot say with any certainty that peace was the product of nuclear weapons. More importantly, the level of risk that is involved in structuring the international system around nuclear deterrence is massive and, as many have argued, it must surely be the least rational means of managing international peace yet devised.

Conclusion: echoes of the Cold War

For its duration, the Cold War rivalry played a dominant role in world politics. Nowhere was its influence more evident than in anti-colonial struggles and in the politics of post-colonial states. From Tehran to Tokyo, Jakarta to Johannesburg, East–West rivalry put local conflicts into a global context. The political struggles to fill the holes created by departing European powers had a broader consequence as both the USSR and the US saw the other's gain as its loss in the battle for hearts, minds and strategic influence in the decolonising world. A communist North Vietnam or South Yemen was thought to be not only a loss from the ledger of capitalist states but also a decisive strategic advantage for Soviet communism. Just as Soviet–US rivalry had consequences far from home, the Cold War has left a legacy with which we are still coming to terms (Westad 2005).

Three of the most pressing issues in world politics – the nuclear crisis on the Korean peninsula, the status of Taiwan and the war on **terrorism** – have their roots in the Cold War. In Korea, the Cold War divisions are most glaring. The peninsula is still divided. North Korea is one of the few states that retains a command economy and a Stalinist political system, and added to this has been its recent acquisition of nuclear technology. Cold War tension continues to shape the strategic balance in Northeast Asia. Taiwan's uncertain political status is also the unfinished business of the Cold War. Created by the nationalists who had lost the Chinese Civil War, Taiwan was initially recognised by the US as the legitimate China, only to have this recognition removed as the US improved its relations with the People's Republic of China during détente. Tension across the Taiwan Straits has grown precipitously in recent years and US commitment to its recently democratised ally Taiwan makes it one of the most likely locations of major power conflict in the international system.

As the horror of the terrorist attacks of 11 September 2001 unfolded before a television audience of billions, few realised that they were witnessing an after-shock of the Cold War. Yet it was the Soviet intervention in Afghanistan and the US funding of **guerrilla** insurgents that gave birth to al-Qaeda and its fellow travellers. Soviet forces were defeated by a combination of Afghan militias and guerrillas of a militant Islamist variety whose funding and organisation were heavily assisted by the US. Most of the militant Islamists active today, from members of the Islamic Salvation Front (FIS) in Algeria to Hambali and Imam Samudra in Indonesia, learnt their trade in Afghanistan in the 1980s. The 'war on terror' which has taken centre stage in the foreign policy of the US and many of its allies is a conflict which is a direct, though utterly unintended, consequence of the Cold War's strategic competition and the indirect manner of its prosecution.

The decade following the Cold War's demise was one of distinct optimism in international relations. Long-unrepresented peoples were able to enjoy self-determination; the prospect of imminent nuclear annihilation had receded; and the strife associated with East–West rivalry had largely faded into the distance. Yet developments in international relations do not spring forth from the ether. They have a history, both political and economic, and in the history of contemporary crises and challenges the Cold War has a heavy weight. In Korea, Taiwan and Islamist terrorism we see only the most acute examples of this legacy. From ethnic conflicts in the states of the former Soviet Union to environmental problems in Eastern Europe, from civil war in Angola to the still unresolved political problems in Cambodia, the Cold War's imprint can still be seen around the world. Some argue that it is not only in the events that we feel its effect: in the very way in which the US and its allies think about international politics we can detect the continuing influence of a Cold War approach to the world. In the search for an enemy to defeat, and for military threats to snuff out, one sees an approach to international politics that is born of the East–West **bipolar** conflict. The Cold War may be twenty years gone, but it will be a long time before its influence has passed from being among the central concerns for scholars, policy-makers and analysts of international relations.

QUESTIONS

1. Could the Cold War have been avoided?
2. Does the Cold War confirm or refute the view that conflict is inevitable in the international system?
3. The Cold War began as a dispute in Europe. Why did it spread around the world?
4. How important was the Cuban missile crisis to the dynamics of Cold War conflict?
5. Was the American historian John Lewis Gaddis right to describe the Cold War as a 'long peace'?
6. Did détente fail?
7. What role did nuclear weapons play in the Cold War?
8. Who should take credit for the end of the Cold War?
9. In what ways is the Cold War still visible in the contemporary international system?

FURTHER READING

Crockatt, Richard 1995, *The fifty years war: the United States and the Soviet Union in world politics, 1941–1991*, London: Routledge. Systematic and thorough assessment of Soviet-American relations in the broader context of international relations.

Gaddis, John Lewis 2005, *The Cold War: a new history*, New York: Penguin. Concise but comprehensive account of the diplomatic and military manoeuvring by the doyen of American Cold War history.

Oberdorfer, Don 1998, revised edition, *From the Cold War to a new era*, Baltimore: Johns Hopkins University Press. Best single overview of the events of the end of the Cold War, written by a senior *Washington Post* journalist.

Walker, Martin 1993, *The Cold War and the making of the modern world*, London: Fourth Estate. Erudite overview of the history, benefiting from Walker's experiences as *The Guardian*'s Moscow correspondent during the final years of the USSR.

Westad, Odd Arne 2007, *The global Cold War: Third World interventions and the making of our times* Cambridge: Cambridge University Press. Best assessment of the global impact of the Cold War and its continuing legacy, written by a leading international historian based at the London School of Economics.

The New Agenda
GLOBALISATION AND GLOBAL GOVERNANCE

PART 3

21 **The United Nations**   296
    Ian Hurd

22 **Non-State Actors: Multinational Corporations and International
    Non-Governmental Organisations**   310
    James Goodman

23 **Religion and Secularism**   322
    Elizabeth Shakman Hurd

24 **Global Economic Institutions**   336
    Marc Williams

25 **Global Trade**   348
    Maryanne Kelton

26 **Global Finance**   360
    Leonard Seabrooke

27 **Global Poverty, Inequality and Development**   372
    Heloise Weber and Mark T. Berger

28 **Globalisation and Its Critics**   386
    Steven Slaughter

29 **Global Terrorism**   398
    David Wright-Neville

30 **Post-Conflict State-Building**   414
    Beth K. Greener

31 **Humanitarian Intervention**   426
    Thomas G. Weiss

32 **Human Rights**   440
    Anthony J. Langlois

33 **Migration and Refugees**   450
    Sara E. Davies

34 **Global Environmental Politics**   462
    Robyn Eckersley

35 **Climate Change**   475
    Peter Newell

21

The United Nations

Ian Hurd

Introduction	297
The UN in the Charter	297
The UN's principal organs	299
The UN as actor, forum and resource	304
Conclusion	308
Questions	309
Further reading	309

Introduction

The purpose of this chapter is to explain the legal and political features of the **United Nations (UN)**. The chapter begins with a short introduction to the **UN Charter** in **international law**, which shows the framework, limits and authorities within which all UN activity takes place. It then puts these into a more practical setting, emphasising how the organisation can be seen as at once an actor, as a forum and as a resource (or some combination of all three).

The UN Charter has near-constitutional status in the inter-state system as it performs two crucial functions that make contemporary inter-state relations fundamentally different from any previous era. First, the Charter defines the essential obligations that governments owe to one another, which include a strict regulation on the use of force to settle disputes, the aspirations to universal **human rights** and gender equality, and the subordination of **states** to the collective decisions of the UN Security Council. Second, it creates a set of institutions with formal and specific competencies to oversee those obligations. These institutions, including the Security Council, the General Assembly and the Trusteeship Council, have their own **powers**, limits and practices, and therefore their own legal and political lives. Since its **ratification** in 1945, the Charter has been the centrepiece of international law among states, setting the post-1945 era apart from anything that had come before. The organisation has come to include all **sovereign states** in the world, or at least all states that are widely recognised as being states (where who counts as a 'state' is largely endogenous, that is: it is defined by who the UN will accept as a member), and so its rules and powers have come to make up the constitutional structure for inter-state relations.

The complexity, authority and breadth of the UN mean that its decisions and its peculiarities matter a great deal for world politics. At the same time, an important and intriguing gap exists between the UN's formal powers and its life in practice, which means that it is worth examining both the legal terms set out in the Charter and the interaction between the Charter and the real-world practices that arise around it.

The UN in the Charter

The UN Charter is the international treaty that states sign to become members of the United Nations organisation. It is an inter-*state* treaty and it makes the organisation a strictly **state-centric** entity: in law, it has power over states only and not individuals, firms, or other groups. The Charter was negotiated in 1945 among the fifty or so countries that participated in the San Francisco conference as World War II was ending, and it was conceived as a formal foundation for the new international organisation and also a place to express what were thought of as universal values and goals in need of reinforcement after the traumas of the first half of the twentieth century. It therefore contains two kinds of clauses: those that affirm values and goals in aspirational terms, and those that express formal legal content. The former are exemplified by the Preamble, which says among other things that 'We the Peoples of the United Nations [are] determined … to practice tolerance and live together in peace with one another as good neighbors' and pledge to 'employ international machinery for the promotion of the economic and social advancement of all peoples'. The latter are much less poetic (for example, Article 29 says 'The Security Council may establish such subsidiary organs as it deems necessary for the performance of its functions') but they set the legal framework within which much of international politics takes place. They spell out the commitments that states make to each other and to the organisation as a consequence of joining the UN, and they define the organs of the UN and their various powers and limits. This section explores the three main areas in which membership in the UN creates specific legal constraints or obligations on states.

The main obligations that arise from membership in the UN are these: to pay one's financial contribution to the organisation (Art. 17(2)); to support the decisions of the UN Security Council (Art. 25); and to refrain from using force to settle disputes with other states (Art. 2(4)). These are commitments that are binding on every individual state that is a member of the UN. They constitute only a small proportion of the entire Charter but they have an enormous influence over the content and direction of international relations. Some UN organs (notably the Security Council) can create further obligations, but these remain encapsulated within the core powers from which they derive. For instance, the Security Council decided in 2001 (Resolution 1343) that no country should import rough diamonds from Liberia, on the belief that the revenue of the diamond trade was funding the Liberian leader's support of **war** and atrocity in west Africa, and this automatically became a mandatory obligation for UN members as a result of the language of Article 25 (and further of Chapter VII) of the Charter.

The UN itself is delimited by two very important clauses in Article 2 of the Charter. The first says that 'The Organization is based on the sovereign equality of all its Members' (Art. 2(1)), and the second that 'Nothing contained in the present Charter shall authorize the United Nations to intervene in matters which are essentially within the domestic jurisdiction of any state' (Art. 2.(7)). These create both an internal and an external limit on all of the UN's activities. Internally, Article 2(1) requires that everything that happens in the organisation must treat all members equally. The UN cannot behave in any way that favours one group of members over any others. All members have the same rights and duties under law, no matter how powerful or weak they may be. Externally, Article 2(7) establishes that the UN has no authority over states' domestic affairs, and everything it does in the wider world must either deal with the *international* rather than domestic affairs of states, or be done with the permission of the state with which it is dealing. These are strict and serious limits on the power of the UN – although both are subject to ambiguities in their interpretation which make for some interesting and unexpected developments. For instance, the key to understanding Article 2(7) is understanding the term 'essentially within the domestic jurisdiction' of a state – and this language is not further explained anywhere in the Charter. It is open to interpretation, and is frequently argued over. It is often understood as the obverse of a 'threat to international **peace** and **security**' from Article 39, such that any issue that threatens international peace and security is by definition not within the domestic jurisdiction of the state. Putting these two clauses together means that when the Security Council decides that a matter is a threat to international peace the restrictions on intervention contained in Art. 2(7) are not relevant to the case. So, when the Council decided in 2006 that North Korea's nuclear weapons program constituted a threat to international peace and security (Res. 1718), North Korea could no longer claim that it had the right under international law to develop these weapons for its own defence. Similarly, Sudan cannot maintain that the atrocities in Darfur constitute a matter within its domestic jurisdiction, following the decision of the Council in 2004 (Res. 1564) that identified them as a problem of international peace and security.

The UN's principal organs

The Charter defines the central institutions (the 'principal organs') of the UN as the General Assembly (GA), the Security Council (SC), the UN Secretariat, the International Court of Justice (ICJ), the Trusteeship Council, and the Economic and Social Council (ECOSOC). The last three of these are much less significant than the first three and I treat them briefly here before turning to the GA, the SC and the Secretariat.

BOX 21.1: KEY TEXTS

UN Charter: ECOSOC

Article 61

1. The Economic and Social Council shall consist of fifty-four Members of the United Nations elected by the General Assembly.

Article 62

1. The Economic and Social Council may make or initiate studies and reports with respect to international economic, social, cultural, educational, health, and related matters and may make recommendations … to the General Assembly, to the Members of the United Nations, and to the specialized agencies concerned.
2. It may make recommendations for the purposes of promoting respect for, and observance of, human rights and fundamental freedoms for all.

Article 67

1. Each member of the Economic and Social Council shall have one vote.
2. Decisions of the Economic and Social Council shall be made by a majority of the members present and voting.

The ECOSOC (see Box 21.1) is best seen as a subsidiary organ to the General Assembly and so fits into the discussion of the GA below. The ICJ (see Box 21.2) hears cases that arise from legal disputes between states and it issues binding decisions in response. The court is set out in the UN Charter but it is largely governed by the separate Statute of the ICJ and its docket of contentious cases is entirely separate from the UN.

BOX 21.2: KEY TEXTS

UN Charter: the International Court of Justice

Article 92

The International Court of Justice shall be the principal judicial organ of the United Nations.

Article 93

1. All Members of the United Nations are *ipso facto* parties to the Statute of the International Court of Justice.

Article 94

1. Each member of the United Nations undertakes to comply with the decision of the International Court of Justice to which it is a party.

The Trusteeship Council (see Box 21.3) was once the legal overseer of territories governed by other states as mandates or in trusteeship, and it was responsible for ensuring that this near-colonial relationship did not degenerate into outright **colonialism**. The system came to an end when Palau, the last of the trust territories, declared independence and was recognised as a sovereign state in 1994. The Trusteeship Council is therefore dead in practice, though it remains alive in law given that its permanence is written into the Charter; it still has members, still chooses its president and vice-president, and until 2005 it still held annual meetings that were without content.

BOX 21.3: KEY TEXTS

UN Charter: the Trusteeship Council

Article 75

The United Nations shall establish … an international trusteeship system for the administration and supervision of such territories as may be placed thereunder by subsequent agreements.

Article 77

1. The trusteeship system shall apply to …
   a. territories now held under mandate;
   b. territories which may be detached from enemy states as a result of the Second World War; and
   c. territories voluntarily placed under the system by states responsible for their administration.

Article 87

The General Assembly and, under its authority, the Trusteeship Council, … may:

   a. consider reports submitted by the administering authority; …
   b. provide for periodic visits to the respective trust territories …; and
   c. take these and other actions in conformity with the terms of the trusteeship agreements.

The core of the UN's mission is performed by the the Security Council, General Assembly and the Secretariat. The division of authority among them establishes that the Council has the authority to take decisions regarding international peace and security on behalf of all UN members (Box 21.4), the General Assembly may make recommendations to members on any topic within the scope of the Charter (Box 21.6), and the Secretariat supplies the administrative support to make these two function (Box 21.7).

This distribution of powers reflects the interests of the **great powers** in 1945: the US, the USSR, and the UK wanted a centralised enforcement vehicle that would represent the entire UN membership and a forum for global debate that could encompass the broad range of that membership. These two functions had to be institutionally separate because they reflected contradictory impulses of domination and legitimation. The great powers (see Chapter 19) wanted to ensure that the enforcement function could not operate outside of their control, and thus the Security Council's broad power to intervene in world politics is set inside an institution of very limited membership (fifteen states, after the reforms of 1965) in which each of the five permanent (P5) members has a veto (Art. 27(3)) (see Box 21.5).

The General Assembly was intended as a deliberative body with universal membership, space for open-ended discussion and a majoritarian-decision rule. It operates by majority rule (two-thirds majority for 'important' matters: Art. 18(2)) and without a veto, and the consequence of this relatively **democratic** structure was that the great powers in 1945 restricted its powers to making recommendations to states or international organisations (Arts 10, 13). There is an intentionally inverse relationship between democratic structure and decision-making authority. the Council stands in an authoritative position over states with respect to matters of international peace and security, and the framers of the Charter in 1945 were not willing to allow this power to leave the hands of the great powers. The General Assembly functions as the meeting place for the international community of states, and its diversity and pluralism were thought safe only in a body that was limited to making recommendations.

BOX 21.4: KEY TEXTS

UN Charter: the Security Council

Article 23

1. The Security Council shall consist of fifteen Members of the United Nations. The Republic of China, France, the Union of Soviet Socialist Republics, the United Kingdom … and the United States of America shall be permanent members of the Security Council. The General Assembly shall elect ten other Members.

Article 24

1. In order to ensure prompt and effective action by the United Nations, its Members confer on the Security Council primary responsibility for the maintenance of international peace and security.

Article 27

1. Each member of the Security Council shall have one vote …
2. Decisions of the Security Council … shall be made by an affirmative vote of nine members including the concurring votes of the permanent members.

Article 39

The Security Council shall determine the existence of any threat to the peace, breach of the peace, or act of aggression and shall … decide what measures shall be taken … to restore international peace and security.

The Security Council is granted 'primary responsibility for the maintenance of international peace and security' (Art. 24(1)), and to that end states are required to: cede their own right to use force to settle disputes (Art. 2(4)); respect the decisions about peace and security the Council makes on their behalf (Arts 24, 25, 39, 42); and commit some of their military forces to the collective (Art. 43). The logic behind the Council is something like what Hobbes had in mind in *Leviathan* ([1651] 1968) to solve the problem of the state of nature: individuals must disarm and the central authority must monopolise the use of force. The Security Council has been given a legal monopoly over war-making, which it can activate by following the two-part procedure set out in Chapter VII of the Charter: first, the Council must determine that there exists a breach of or threat to international peace and security (Art. 39); second, it must decide to call on the collective military forces of its members and deploy them to remedy the breach or threat (Art. 42). These resources are loaned to the UN by states for the specific operation in question; the Council controls no military forces of its own, despite the intention of Article 43 that states should set aside for the Council some of their militaries.

The two-stage process is illustrated by the reaction to Iraq's invasion of Kuwait in 1990. By Resolution 660 (2 August 1990) the Security Council identified 'a breach of international peace and security as regards the Iraqi invasion of Kuwait' and in Resolution 678 (29 November 1990) it authorised 'Member States co-operating with the Government of Kuwait … to use all necessary means to uphold and implement resolution 660'.

The Iraq war stands as a singular example of the UN's centralised system of international enforcement in practice. It may also be *the* singular example, since no other UN operation under Chapter VII has been as legally coherent and uncontroversial, and many military adventures by states have been launched in the face of the Charter's prohibitions. International history since 1945 is littered with wars, threats and violations of international peace, and yet the Council has used its authority to intervene only very conservatively. The practical political questions of when to intervene, against whom, for what goals, with what precedential effect and at whose expense have almost always prevented the Council from activating its full military potential. A very small number of peace-enforcement operations have been launched by the Council, notably in Kuwait in 1990–91 and in Korea in 1950. Most of the Council's activity has involved pressuring states to change their policies while holding the threat of UN intervention in the background.

BOX 21.5: KEY ACTORS

The P5: permanent members of the UN Security Council

- China
- France
- Russia
- UK
- USA

The General Assembly's authority is wider in scope but less binding than that of the Council. Its powers are set out in Articles 10 through 13. As a general matter, the Assembly 'may discuss any questions or any matters within the scope of the present Charter' (Art. 10). The Assembly is the plenary body of the UN, meaning that it includes as members all of the **nation**-states in the UN. Each state gets one vote in the Assembly, and decisions require supporting votes of two-thirds of the members present and voting. While Article 10 authorises the Assembly to discuss 'any questions or any matters' of concern to the UN, the Assembly's power over those topics is limited to making 'recommendations' to states or to the Secretary-General, issuing reports and launching studies (see Box 21.6). General Assembly resolutions are therefore not legally binding. States' obligations to these recommendations are very limited: the Charter implies that members have a duty to take these recommendations seriously, but it does not create any formal legal obligation to implement or even consider them, let alone to force states to do anything. The General Assembly's power is therefore broad but very shallow.

It can consider and make recommendations on many topics but its outputs have no coercive authority.

The one exception to this pattern is the Assembly's decisive power over the UN expenditure budget and the allocation of costs among member states. This authority is established by Article 17, and it is noteworthy because it means that the sensitive matters of revenue and spending are decided by the Assembly by two-thirds majority vote, without any special influence reserved for the highest-contributing states. The UN's critics, particularly conservatives in the US, have taken this as evidence that UN spending is disconnected from or unaccountable to the rich states who contribute the largest shares of the UN's income (see, for instance, B.D. Schaefer 2006). This is not correct. That the UN is organised this way reflects the fact that in 1945 there was a dominant view that the spending decisions of the organisation were of interest to the general membership and not just to the great powers. In this case, the democratic impulse trumped the usual tendency for the strong states to keep close control over important decisions. However, the power of the big contributors is accommodated in more subtle ways: the draft budget only reaches the Assembly after having passed through a committee that contains the major contributors and that operates by consensus. This committee (the Advisory Committee on Administrative and Budgetary Questions (ACABQ)) has sixteen members, elected from the General Assembly, and it receives the draft budget from the Secretary-General before sending it on to the Assembly. By customary agreement, the US always has a member on the committee. In practice, therefore, the US can veto the budget in its drafting stage – no budget can reach the Assembly without US approval. In a second accommodation to the influence of political power, the budget for **peacekeeping** missions is organised separately from the 'regular' budget described in Article 17, in an effort to insulate the regular budget from the disagreements that arose when the GA, rather than the SC, launched peace operations in the 1950s and 1960s.

BOX 21.6: KEY TEXTS

UN Charter: the General Assembly

Article 9

1. The General Assembly shall consist of all the Members of the United Nations.

Article 10

The General Assembly may discuss any questions or matters within the scope of the present Charter … [and] make recommendations to the Members … on any such questions or matters.

Article 18

1. Each member of the General Assembly shall have one vote.
2. Decisions of the General Assembly on important questions shall be made by a two-thirds majority of the members present and voting.

The constitutional arrangement of the Assembly means that it is the closest thing that currently exists to a comprehensive deliberative body of states. It may sometimes look like a global legislature but it lacks the crucial ingredient of the capacity to pass legislation. Decisions of the Assembly come in the form of resolutions, and these are defined in the Charter as recommendations rather than decisions. Nevertheless, the Assembly's deliberations and resolutions can, when the political forces align in their favour, take on political weight that is greater than their legal authority. They can sometimes be successfully presented as reflecting the view of the 'international community' of states. Several of the most famous GA resolutions illustrate the fact that their political impact sometimes far outweighs their very limited legal status. For instance, the Universal Declaration of Human Rights began its life as a declaration (not a resolution) by the General Assembly in 1948. This declaration is an excellent example of how the Assembly can be used to reinforce **norms** or rules of customary international law. Similarly, the GA Resolution known colloquially as 'Uniting for Peace' (GA 377) is influential, though far more legally uncertain. It includes the claim that the Assembly can use its recommendatory power to create new peace operations in cases when the Security Council fails to execute its 'primary' responsibility for peace and security under Article 24. In 1975, the Assembly passed a resolution (A/3379) declaring that 'Zionism is a form of racism because it privileges one religious or ethnic group over all others'. This was revoked in 1991 by Resolution 46/86, but the controversy it attracted shows the political power of GA instruments beyond their purely legal authority.

The UN as actor, forum and resource

The UN on paper can be very different from the UN in practice. While the rules and institutions described in the Charter set formal boundaries around its behaviour, much of what makes the organisation interesting and important arises as states and others strive to operate in and around those boundaries. The assorted complexities of the UN's structure and practice mean that it displays itself in different ways to different observers and in different contexts. At times, the UN behaves like an independent actor in world politics, making its influence felt on states and others and taking action in the world. At other times, it operates like a forum where states and others come to discuss among themselves, with the UN providing an institutional setting where negotiations can take place. At still other times, the UN is a resource in the hands of other players, acting as an instrument or tool by which these others hope to advance their goals. The three functions of actor, forum and resource must be combined by scholars in order to get a more complete picture of the power and nature of the UN (I. Hurd 2011).

The UN as an actor

International organisations such as the UN are actors in world politics. They are constituted by international law as independent entities, separate from the states that are their founders and their members. The practical expression of this independence varies greatly across organisations, but in a formal sense they are corporate 'persons', much like firms are 'persons' in domestic commercial law. At a minimum, this means that they have legal standing, with certain rights and obligations. These qualities were explicitly recognised for the UN in the ICJ opinion on *Reparations for Injuries suffered in the Service of the United Nations* in 1949, but that case merely affirmed what had existed in prior custom and practice: inter-state organisations are legally independent from their founders. Beyond this legal minimum, being recognised as an actor requires some kind of social recognition, plus some kind of capacity for action. For the UN, these are evident in the ways that states treat the UN as a player of consequence in world politics – states appear to believe that it matters what the UN does and says. They feel the need to respond to unfavourable reports by the organisation, to influence the direction of UN action and to gain membership on important committees. These behaviours indicate that the UN has a conceptual status separate from its member states, with the potential to hinder or advance their interests.

The UN as a forum

International organisations are also places in space and time. They are buildings, conferences, schedules of meetings and lists of members. Part of their utility is that they facilitate discussions among states, reducing their transaction costs and changing their political symbolism. The UN may have no role in these discussions other than providing a physical and political focal point; but this can be an important contribution, and very different to the 'UN-as-actor' function.

In its role as forum, the UN represents an extension of the nineteenth-century European practice of holding *ad hoc* themed conferences among governments, such as those that produced the first **Geneva Convention**. This practice became largely institutionalised in the UN after 1945, with major UN-sponsored conferences on environment and development (Rio 1993), human rights (Vienna 1994), and the status of women (Mexico City 1975, Beijing 1995) among others. The value of the UN in these cases is that it can provide experienced logistical support for such large meetings, even though it itself may not be present as a formal participant. They represent the 'forum' function of international organisations in its clearest form. Most international organisations include a plenary body in which all members are represented, and whose purpose is general deliberation about the work or themes of the organisation. The General Assembly is perhaps the best example of an international organisation in the shape of a forum. But beyond the UN, most organisations include a similar component: the International Criminal Court (ICC) has an Assembly of States Parties; the **World Trade Organization (WTO)** has its General Council; the International Labor Organization (ILO) has the International Labor Conference. The procedures for discussion in these bodies are relatively inclusive and open so that all members have the opportunity to participate. As a consequence, they tend to have either few executive powers or high standards of consensus for decisions. The UN General Assembly fits the former category: it can make recommendations but has few powers to take legally binding decisions. The WTO fits the latter: its Dispute Settlement Board can take important decisions such as overturning dispute settlement panel decisions, but only when all members agree (or at least when none is willing formally to oppose the decision).

The deliberative functions of these assemblies can have a powerful legitimating effect on the organisation and its decisions. They are also useful for facilitating side-negotiations among members. For instance, the original motivation behind the UN General Assembly was to have a place where states that were not great powers could express their views regarding the work of the organisation (Bosco 2009), but its annual meetings in New York have come to include both the formal speeches by governments and the large and unknowable number of informal meetings on the sides that are made possible by virtue of so many diplomats and leaders being in one city at the same time. The transaction costs for **diplomacy** are thereby reduced, and a benefit is achieved even if the formal speeches do not solve any particular problem.

The UN as a resource

Finally, the United Nations can be seen as a political resource (or a source of political resources) that states use as they pursue their goals, domestic and international. States use the statements, decisions and other outputs that come from the UN as material to support their own positions, and many international disputes include competing interpretations of these materials. States fight over what international organisations should say and what they should do, and then fight over what these acts and statements mean for world politics. For instance, does Security Council Resolution 242 really require that Israel withdraw immediately from the Palestinian territory it seized in the 1967 war, as the plain text would indicate, or only that it should negotiate a withdrawal in due time? Competing interpretations allow the parties to maintain that the Council supports their policies, and that the other side is violating its obligations. They use the resolution as a political tool to further their goals. This could not happen in the absence of the UN. Much of what comes out of international organisations is useful to states in this way, and one might even say that anything that is not useful in this way is not likely to have any impact at all. This can be a source of power and autonomy for the organisation to the extent that it can control who uses its symbols and outputs. The Security Council, for instance, controls 'UN peacekeeping' as if it were a trademarked brand, and when it has allowed countries' military operations to be called 'peacekeeping' missions it has demanded that they adhere to standards set by the Council. The General Assembly has much less capacity to act as a gatekeeper.

Seeing international organisations as resources rather than as solutions in themselves to problems also helps to emphasise some limits on their power and usefulness. The UN can be influential when circumstances are favourable, but it can also be marginalised when powerful states see no advantage in activating it. For instance, in the early 1980s the Secretary-General (see Box 21.7) had prepared a diplomatic solution to the contested governance of Cambodia, but he and the entire UN were largely kept out of the process by a few states of the Association of Southeast Asian Nations (**ASEAN**) group who refused to negotiate with the Vietnamese government that controlled Cambodia (Pérez de Cuéllar 1997; Annabi 1995). Only after the **geopolitics** of ASEAN changed in the late 1980s did his plan come to be implemented as the Paris Peace Agreement of 1991. The apparent 'failure' of the UN to deal effectively with the Cambodia problem in the 1980s was actually a result of the fact that some powerful states insisted that the UN *not* be used as a tool for solving the problem. The 'resource' view is an antidote to the common but misleading assumption that there is always in principle an international-organisation answer to every diplomatic problem or humanitarian crisis. From Darfur to the Haiti earthquake to the Rwandan **genocide**, the contribution of international organisations to international problems is in part defined by the utility that states see in putting them to work.

The three aspects of actor, forum and resource coexist in tension in the UN, and each perspective provides a distinct, though incomplete, view of the organisation. To see the UN exclusively as a forum leads to the mistake made by John Bolton (cited in Perlez 2001), who maintained that the UN 'does not exist'. What does exist, he implied, is a collection of independent states who sometimes choose to meet in the rooms of the UN building, and perhaps to add a UN label to their collective endeavours (i.e. a 'forum' and nothing else). This is a radically reductionist view of international politics

BOX 21.7: KEY TEXTS

UN Charter: the Secretariat

Article 97

The Secretariat shall comprise a Secretary-General and such staff as the Organization may require. The Secretary-General shall be appointed by the General Assembly upon the recommendation of the Security Council. He [or she] shall be the chief administrative officer of the Organization.

Article 99

The Secretary-General may bring to the attention of the Security Council any matter which in his [or her] opinion may threaten the maintenance of international peace and security.

Article 100

1. In the performance of their duties the Secretary-General and the staff shall not receive instructions from any government or from any other authority external to the Organization. They shall refrain from any action which might reflect on their position as international officials responsible only to the Organization.

---

and law: it claims that everything that is done through or by the UN can be reduced analytically to the behaviour of individual states without losing any meaning. It denies the possibility of corporate personhood for international organisations, and thus also the possibility that they might have positions or take actions independent of their members. This is an impossible position to sustain, since it requires that we deny that there is any difference between states acting alone and states acting through the UN. The real-world of international relations is full of examples that states react quite differently to what other states do as opposed to what international organisations do. Consider the US effort to gain Security Council approval for its invasion of Iraq in 2003, while John Bolton was in the US Department of State: the premise of that effort was that the Council could provide collective legitimation for the invasion and this would change how other states reacted to it. The US strategy of seeking Security Council support presumed that the audience of states would see a UN-supported invasion as more legitimate than one without Council approval, or than if the US gained the state-by-state support of governments individually through **bilateral** efforts. If there is a difference in how the action is perceived depending on whether it is supported by a collection of individual states and supported by those states through the Council, then the reductionist view must be wrong. That difference represents the independent contribution of the Security Council to world politics, beyond its role as a forum or meeting place.

It is equally hard to sustain an entirely actor-centric view of the UN, or of most international organisations. The independence of even the strongest international organisation is always conditional on an alignment of social forces that is outside of its control. The Security Council, for instance, has the authority to intervene in world politics in any way it sees fit in response to anything it identifies as a threat to international peace and security. And yet its ability to take action on international security depends on the voluntary contributions of military resources by individual member states. As a result, the actor-like qualities in the international system that are legally enshrined by the Charter are drastically undercut in practice by member states. Both the independence of international organisations and their limits are central to some versions of the 'delegation' approach, which suggests that international organisations can be understood based on the act of delegation by which states endow them with authority (Hawkins et al. 2006). Once empowered by this delegated authority, the organisation may have considerable autonomy to deploy its powers as it wishes, and it may be a challenge for member states to control it. To overstate the independence of international organisations is as much a mistake as to understate it, and anywhere along this spectrum all claims about the autonomy of international organisations must be grounded in an empirical study of the organisation in question. There are no general answers to questions about the distribution of power and authority between states and international organisations. The challenge for the scholar is to figure out how to combine them and where to put the emphasis to best suit the research problem at hand. Michael Barnett (2003) provides a good model in his book on how the UN came to abandon Rwanda at the time of the genocide in 1994: he examines the positions that the strongest states on the Security Council brought to the question (a 'forum' view of the UN); he also looks at the position of the Secretary-General and his staff (thus recognising that the UN was also an actor in the process); and how the collective decisions of the Council would be perceived and manipulated by other states and by the *genocidaires* themselves (i.e. how the UN would be used as a tool by other players).

Conclusion

As actor, forum and resource, the UN is the world's most comprehensive international organisation in terms of both its membership and its scope of authority. It encompasses all countries and potentially all policy areas that carry international implications. Its salience in international politics is remarkable given that most of its organs do not have the legal authority to take decisions that are binding on its members. The General Assembly and ECOSOC are explicitly limited to making recommendations rather than taking decisions, and the Secretariat has no authority at all over member-states. The few exceptions to this pattern are interesting precisely because they stand out so clearly from the norm, and because they subvert the conventional wisdom that international organisations are legally subordinate to their members. The binding powers in the UN include the General Assembly's power over the budget and the Security Council's authority to enact military interventions. The most controversial moments in the life of the UN arise when its powers come up against the interests of strong players, and in the resulting contests of legal and political strength we see the power (and limits) of the UN most clearly. However, much of the UN's contribution to the world takes place in a quieter register, in moments where its resources and its subtle political influence are put to use in the pursuit of the goals of the Preamble. These are less visible than the episodes of high tension, but they likely contribute more towards realising the collective values of the UN than is accomplished during the news-making crises.

QUESTIONS

1. Assess John Bolton's claim that the UN does not exist. In what ways is it true, and in what ways not? Explain your own position.

2. What should be done with the Trusteeship Council, now that it has no more territories to manage? Consider its utility and its liabilities in the contemporary world, one that includes failed states and a commitment to anti-colonialism.

3. The Security Council has considerable freedom to interpret the meaning of 'international peace and security' and thus can redefine the only limit placed on it by the Charter. How has the content of that phrase been understood by the Council over the course of its history? Is the Council expanding its authority by reinterpreting those crucial words?

4. How different might the United Nations look if we were writing the Charter today? Would this be an improvement over the organisation as we have inherited it from 1945?

FURTHER READING

Alvarez. José E. 2006, *International organizations as law-makers*, Oxford: Oxford University Press.

Bailey, Sydney D. and Daws, Sam 1998, *The procedure of the UN Security Council*, Oxford: Oxford University Press.

Bosco, David 2009, *Five to rule them all: the UN Security Council and the making of the modern world*, Oxford: Oxford University Press.

Chesterman, Simon, Franck, Thomas M. and Malone, David M. 2008, *Law and practice of the United Nations: documents and commentary*, Oxford: Oxford University Press.

Hurd, Ian 2011, *International organizations: politics, law, practice*, Cambridge: Cambridge University Press.

Russell, Ruth B. 1958, *A history of the United Nations Charter: the role of the United States 1940–1945*, Washington DC: The Brookings Institution.

22

Non-State Actors: Multinational Corporations and International Non-Governmental Organisations

James Goodman

Introduction	311
MNCs: transnationalised material power	311
INGOs: transnationalised normative power	316
Conclusion	320
Questions	321
Further reading	321

Introduction

World politics has always had a plurality of players. The key is not so much to determine which have primacy, but how they interact to produce the prevailing **order**. This chapter is structured around a discussion of **multinational corporations (MNCs)** and international non-governmental organisations (INGOs) respectively. Each is discussed in terms of: first, the degree to which it has **transnationalised**; second, the extent to which it constitutes a social formation able to exert international agency; and third, the degree to which it is able to marshal political influence and status. It is argued that there is no necessary antagonism between **state** and non-state realms. Instead, relations between state and non-state forces are intermeshed and shaped by broader systemic conflicts. The chapter charts material class antagonisms that shape the role of MNCs and INGOs, and argues that these generate patterns of transnational contestation within international relations.

In the post-**Cold War** context, **globalisation** theory made considerable headway. For hyperglobalisationists at least (see Chapter 28), newly powerful transnational forces were overwhelming state and inter-state incumbents. With US **power** embedded in a range of inter-state frameworks, a model of multilateral **unipolarity** appeared to be emerging – a model wherein US dominance was embedded in and restrained by a network of **multilateral** institutions. More recently we have seen the advent of a significantly more **unilateralist** unipolarity, as the US has increasingly disengaged itself from multilateral institutions by adopting exceptionalist and preemptive doctrines. The consequences for globalisation **theory** have been wide-ranging. By the mid-2000s not only had the hype been exposed as ideology, but the ideology itself was claimed to have been superseded (see McGrew 2007).

A key reason for the collapse was the assumed impact of globalisation on state power. As Rosenberg argued (2000: 15), the return of state-centred politics has been 'as devastating for globalisation theory as it has always been for alternative approaches which have left untheorised the terrain of **geopolitics**'. This chapter attempts to clarify the role of **non-state actors** in relation to states and the states-system, and posit a more 'genuinely social theory of the international system' (Rosenberg 2000: 15), one that does not abstract states from broader social and economic processes and structures.

MNCs: transnationalised material power

The definition and role of multinational corporations is hotly debated. **Transnational corporations (TNCs)** are usually defined as corporate entities that have no clear national base; MNCs are then presented as nationally centred entities with international interests. The UNCTAD World Investment Report finds most corporations operating across national borders fall into the MNC category: its 'index of nationality' measures the foreign proportion of assets, sales and employment for large corporates and finds the bulk are nationally centred (UNCTAD 2005). But while it may be more accurate to use the MNC category, this does not mean the impact of MNCs is primarily national. If we examine the ways that MNCs behave, we find their qualitative impact is much broader than their operational scope would suggest. The power that MNCs exert is embedded within existing inter-state **hierarchies** and power structures, but MNCs are not simply tools of nationally centred elites. They operate against as much as within national contexts and, as social formations, allow an interlocking of national elites to the extent of forming a class bloc, what Leslie Sklair calls the 'transnational capitalist class' (Sklair 2001).

Transnationalisation: MNCs

The central driver and rationale for MNCs is the exercise of material power across national jurisdictions. Across finance, production and distribution, MNCs exploit power-gaps between spatially fixed governments and fluid cross-national flows of money and commodities. Transnational finance relations express hierarchies of risk – in effect, assessments of the future potential for capital accumulation – with each national context measured against the other. Transnationalised productive relations reflect the strategies of dominant multinational firms in exploiting and reproducing divergent relations of production and consumption. Trading, distribution and retail relations express hierarchies of international dependence through unequal exchange, embedded in a diffused culture-ideology of consumerism.

Finance MNCs set the pace. In 2004 the assets of the top ten financial MNCs amounted to US\$13 trillion while the assets of the top ten non-financial MNCs stood at \$3.1 trillion (UNCTAD 2006: A.1.11; A.1.14). Finance MNCs have ascended the corporate league tables: in 1989 none of the world's fifty largest companies was based in the finance sector; in 2003 there were fourteen such companies on the list (UNCTAD 2005: 19). The success of finance houses is reflected in a wholesale financialisation of assets. Finance and business accounted for 25 per cent of total foreign direct investment in 1990; by 2004 it accounted for 47 per cent (UNCTAD 2006: A.1.3). Total international private lending stood at about a tenth of global income in 1980; in 2006 it stood at nearly half of global income (McGuire and Tarashev 2006). In 1978 finance flows were ten times the value of world trade; in 2000 they stood at about fifty times the value of world trade, with total flows amounting to \$1.5 trillion per day. In large part this reflects the explosion in financial derivatives: there were 478 million derivatives created in 1990, by 2004 there were 6144 million (International Monetary Fund 2006a: Statistical Annex, Table 6). In terms of value, in 2003 options and futures stood at \$36786 billion; in just three years that had risen to \$84020 billion (Bank for International Settlements 2006: Statistical Annex, Table 23A). With global GDP (gross domestic product) standing at about \$40 trillion, this suggests a remarkable process of global concentration and financialisation.

In terms of manufacturing MNCs, in 1971 there were 7000 companies with overseas subsidiaries in operation; by 2005 that number had risen to 77000, with close to 800000 affiliates (UNCTAD 2006: 9; Annex Table A.1.6). In 1996 MNCs accounted for one-fifth of global manufacturing output and one-third of private assets. In 1982 MNC assets stood at about one-fifth of global income; in 2005 MNC assets were marginally higher than world income (calculated from UNCTAD 2005: 9). Perhaps most importantly, MNCs control 50 per cent of global research and development funding (UNCTAD 2005). At the same time there has been an upsurge in cross-national mergers and acquisitions. Centred on the developed countries of the north, in 2004 alone total merger activity accounted for at least \$3800 trillion, or approximately 9 per cent of global GDP (UNCTAD 2005: 14). The result has been an increased concentration of economic power across the various sectors of economic activity. Aside from finance, a key emerging sector is in the provision of services, reflecting the global wave of infrastructure, telecom, power and water privatisation (accounting for one-fifth of the largest 100 MNCs in 2003) (UNCTAD 2005: 15).

MNCs also play a central role in trade and retail activity, and in associated media and advertising industries. A small coterie of media empires span the globe, providing much of what suffices for global entertainment, advertising and news (McChesney 2001). Four conglomerates account for half of global advertising and public relations; one conglomerate, WPP, claims 300 of the Fortune Global 500 companies (a list of the world's 500 richest corporations) as clients (Miller and Dinan 2003). Meanwhile, the retail sector has created the world's largest private employer, Wal-Mart, with 1.7 million workers. In 1982 total MNC sales were equivalent to about a quarter of global income; by 1995 this had risen to 50 per cent (calculated from UNCTAD 2005: 9). In 1998 UNCTAD estimated that about half of MNC trade was intra-firm trade, allowing MNCs to routinely declare profit in the lowest-taxing economies (see Box 22.1).

BOX 22.1: DISCUSSION POINTS

MNCs and tax avoidance

MNCs routinely avoid tax. In 2002 US MNCs 'sheltered' more than half of their total offshore profits in low-tax jurisdictions. In 2006 the Australian Tax Commissioner stated that MNCs accounted for the bulk of tax avoidance in Australia.

In an effort to address this, in 2003 the Pacific Association of Tax Administrators, a group that draws together tax authorities in Australia, the US, Canada and Japan, produced a scheme to enable corporate compliance with **Organisation for Economic Cooperation and Development (OECD)** guidelines. Tellingly, the scheme was voluntary.

In practice, tax minimisation and sheltering have become legitimate, accepted by the OECD as unavoidable. Governments, meanwhile, compete with each other to cut corporate taxes in order to attract investment funds.

The USA – the world's most powerful state – has been ahead of the pack in this 'race to the bottom'. In 2004 the American Jobs Creation Act provided a one-off tax cut on repatriated profit from 35 per cent to 5.25 per cent, explicitly to encourage MNCs to bring funds back to the US.

In March 2006 the American Shareholders Association, a strong supporter of the Act, reported that 350 US MNCs would be repatriating a total of $307 billion in 2005 (up from $36 billion in 2004), and that this could rise still further in 2006 (see Webb 2004).

International agency: social formation

In the wake of MNC growth, global material power has become increasingly concentrated. A report on global wealth found the wealthiest 2 per cent own 51 per cent of the world's wealth (Davies et al. 2006: 26). In terms of income, the gap between the richest fifth and the poorest fifth has widened from 31:1 in 1960 to 74:1 in 1997 (Pieterse 2004: 63). The high-income, high-wealth class has become increasingly self-aware and able to act for itself, forging strategies that deliver discernible political leverage for MNC elites.

In the first instance, MNCs create a bidding war between governments. They impose a systemic restraint on government measures that delimit rates of return, such as labour protections, corporate taxation, environmental regulation or other limits to 'market access'. Deregulated corporate enclaves – 'offshore' financial havens, 'export processing zones' (or 'free trade zones'), 'flags of convenience' (registering merchant ships to countries other than the ships' owners), *maquiladoras* (factories on the Mexican side of the US–Mexico border manufacturing goods for export back to the US) and 'special economic zones' – emerge as aberrations or exceptions that over time become institutionalised into **norms** of 'good governance'. In 1975, for instance, there were seventy-nine export processing zones worldwide; in 2002 there were 3000 (Hayter 2004). Such norms are then expressed as conditionalities imposed by financial institutions such as the **International Monetary Fund (IMF)**, or as corporate guidelines generated by **hegemonic** blocs such as the OECD, or as international standards-setting **regimes** for 'market access' such as the **World Trade Organization (WTO)**, or indeed as direct corporate rights regimes with trade and finance agreements such as the North American Free Trade Agreement (NAFTA). MNCs, and the structural incentives they create, are chief instigators in the emergence of these regimes.

MNCs 'cascade' across the globe: while 80 per cent of MNC parents are based in high-income countries, about 60 per cent of their branch plants are located in low-income countries. MNCs create global supply chains, webs of outsourced risk that exert influence at arm's length. Their power extends into the 'domestic' sphere through franchises, licensing arrangements, contract growing, supply contracts, equity investment, cross-ownership and joint ventures. One good example is the McDonald's franchise restaurant, where all the risk rests with the owner-franchisee. MNCs set the pace for the 'domestic' economy: as observers of 'Macdonaldisation' and 'Walmartisation' attest, MNCs establish transnational industry standards. Not surprisingly, the management consultancy industry, concentrated on just four companies, underwent phenomenal growth in the 1990s. Three global credit ratings agencies – Standard and Poor's, Moody's and Fitch – now set the framework for national policy-making worldwide. Governments pay the agencies six-figure sums to provide a 'sovereign' rating that determines access to international finance. In 1975 Standard and Poor's conducted three country ratings; in 2004 it produced more than a hundred.

Political status and influence

Corporations pursue joint political interests through international business associations. The International Chamber of Commerce, for instance, has been in place since 1919. Over the last thirty years these international business NGOs have proliferated and become increasingly integrated (Carroll and Carson 2003). A key approach is to disseminate the notion of popular **capitalism** – an approach that has generated whole media conglomerates such as *Fortune* and *Forbes* dedicated to ranking global corporations, engendering pride in global business, and recruiting aspirants. At the same time, transnational **alliances** of free-marketeering think tanks have emerged, funded by MNCs, with remarkable access to the international policy-making process (Struyk 2002).

The MNC lobby is most clearly manifested in the World Economic Forum (WEF) (Robinson and Harris 2000). Created in 1987, the WEF draws major MNCs to its annual conference in Davos, Switzerland. The Forum self-consciously develops strategy: the theme at Davos 2007 was 'Shaping the Global Agenda'. The Forum commissions a yearly survey gauging corporate reputation: conducted in thirty countries with 20 000 interviewees, it shows a decline in the trust accorded to corporates since 2001. In response to this 'trust deficit' the WEF aspires to 'entrepreneurship in the global public interest', and positions itself as the leading global policy forum, actively recruiting non-corporate 'Global Leadership Fellows'. Lobbying is not always successful: from the late 1990s several states in Asia and Latin America have intervened to constrain finance flows, demonstrating abiding state capacity (Higgott and Phillips 2000). Nevertheless, as UNCTAD reports, of the 271 government measures affecting foreign investment in 2004, 87 per cent favoured MNCs, reducing the average tax for MNCs from 29.7 per cent to 26.5 per cent (UNCTAD 2005: 26). One of these 2004 measures was the American Jobs Creation Act, discussed in Box 22.1.

MNCs have also influenced international public policy agendas. MNC interventions into the sustainability debate, such as through the Business Council on Sustainable Development and the Global Climate Coalition (GCC), are especially significant (Sklair 2001). The GCC was set up by a group of oil and energy MNCs in 1989 to target the 1992 UN Conference on Environment and Development (UNCED), and helped to limit the Climate Change Convention to declarations of intent. After the 1997 **Kyoto Protocol** put some limited commitments into place, the GCC successfully campaigned for the US to renege on its commitments. In 2002 the group was officially wound up, declaring it had 'served its purpose'. Corporate PR now sits at the heart of the **UN**, with a 'Global Compact' that explicitly offers MNCs the possibility of 'leveraging the UN's global reach and convening power' (Coleman 2003).

Finally, there is recourse to legal offence, to sue critics and claim compensation. The corporate use of SLAPPs – 'strategic lawsuits against public participation' – became so prevalent in the US in the 1990s that by 2006 more than thirty-five US states had introduced legislation to protect freedom of speech. But governments themselves are not beyond the reach of corporate litigation. From 1994, under Chapter 11 of NAFTA, corporations gained the right to sue signatory governments for discriminatory regulation. NAFTA's investor protection provisions, which treat corporations 'as an equal subject of **international law**, on a par with governments', have since been extended into other free trade agreements and investment agreements (Gal-Or 2005: 122). Cases taken against states under these clauses have 'risen dramatically' (UNCTAD 2005: 3) (see Box 22.2).

BOX 22.2: DISCUSSION POINTS

Investment protection and corporate–state litigation

Investor protection commitments and rights to arbitration for corporates have been written into a growing proliferation of international investment agreements. There were fewer than eighty such agreements in 1990. By 2004 there were more than 400.

Increasingly, corporations have used these rules to sue governments. When a corporation believes it has suffered from government actions, and believes those actions violate investment agreements, it can make a claim for lost earnings. The claim then goes to an international arbitration court for decision.

In 2006 there were 255 such cases, taken against seventy countries (including thirty-nine cases against the Argentine Government following the country's financial crisis). Several cases have led to large pay-outs. In 2002 Ecuador was required to pay $71 million. In 2004 Slovakia paid $834 million. In 2006 Argentina was instructed to pay $165 million.

Developing countries, UNCTAD notes, are especially 'vulnerable'. Increasingly, though, arbitrators are ruling against corporate claims. After awarding claims against the Argentine Government, arbitrators have accepted the financial crisis created a 'state of necessity' that absolved it of obligations under investment treaties (see UNCTAD 2005).

Overall, MNCs are transnational actors, 'oligopolistic at a global level', capable of exerting significant influence on the world stage, influence expressed in various forms of legal recognition of their role and status (Nolan et al. 2002: 101). Such legal personality is hardly new – it can, for instance, be thought of as 'transnational **mercantilism**' (Graz 2004). Nevertheless, it is clearly growing, complemented by an expanding international law of state–MNC arbitration (Teubner 1997).

INGOs: transnationalised normative power

INGOs are most simply defined as international organisations that represent sectors of society independently of governments. The UN's Economic and Social Council (ECOSOC) defines an INGO as any international organisation that is not established by inter-state treaty. In order to be accorded consultative status with ECOSOC, INGOs must be of recognised standing, representative, accountable, transparent, democratic and funded by voluntary non-government sources. The Union of International Associations uses a similar seven-point definition, including requirements for autonomy from governments and operations in more than two countries. These definitions encompass a wide variety of organisations, including business NGOs. The focus here is on public interest INGOs that engage in international advocacy in the name of a cause or issue.

Transnationalisation: INGOs

In recent years an INGO 'explosion' has paralleled the MNC 'explosion' (Josselin and Wallace 2001: 1–2). In 2002 the UNDP described the INGO boom as a 'revolution', noting that one-fifth of the 37 000 INGOs in place in 2000 had emerged since 1990, and that these had generated more than 20 000 INGO networks, a 'revolution [that] parallels the rapid growth of global business over the same period' (UNDP 2002: 102).

Since 2000 the Centre for Global Governance (CGG) has used data from the Union of International Associations to map the INGO phenomenon. Its data show a worldwide 43 per cent rise in the number of INGO secretariats (to 17 428) between 1992 and 2002, with the rise in low-income countries standing at 27 per cent (Kaldor, Anheier and Glasius 2003: Record 15, 327–33). Membership growth, however, has been faster in lower and middle-income contexts (Anheier and Katz 2004: 338). Secretariats remained concentrated in high-income contexts: of the fourteen cities housing more than a hundred INGO secretariats, two were in the US, one in Japan and nine in Western Europe, and one each in Africa and Latin America. The CGG project thus identifies the geopolitical heartland of Northwest Europe as the centre of global INGOism, with much of the South as peripheral.

The CGG findings confirm the expansion of INGOs while suggesting INGO distribution mirrors inter-state hierarchies. The pattern is replicated at the UN, where only 251 of the 1550 registered NGOs are based in developing countries (UNDP 2002: 111). Indeed, another assessment finds the North–South divide in INGO participation to be proportionately deeper than North–South income divides (Beckfield 2003).

International relations of advocacy are clearly conjoined with inter-state relations: we may further argue that INGOs are simply an international version of the 'extended state', an expression of inter-state hegemony over 'global civil society' (Hirsch 2003). If INGOs are to be seen as an emergent force, capable of mobilising alternate sources of power, a different distribution would be expected. Researchers in political geography have tested these possibilities, in one case looking at connectivity between INGOs as an alternate measure of INGO geography (Taylor 2004). The resulting maps of INGO connectivity reveal a different pattern, where 'Nairobi, Bangkok, New Delhi and Manila [are] at least as important as Brussels, London and Washington', suggesting INGOs are indeed creating their own autonomous trans-urban geography (P. Taylor 2004: 272).

Whether or not hierarchies among INGO coalitions directly mirror inter-state hierarchies, INGO advocacy has different drivers from inter-state politics and forces into view an alternative geopolitics centring on **normative** claims (Bebbington 2004). Policy advocacy to address global problems such as environmental change, global development, labour rights and gender division rests on the capacity to mobilise legitimacy across the North–South axis. Clearly INGOs are inadequate as channels for formal political representation (Chandhoke 2005). Yet INGO power relations, unlike MNC relations, rest on normative claims to legitimacy grounded in transnational consciousness (Hudson 2001).

International agency: social formation

There is no doubt INGOs have an important influence on international political agendas. As Halliday (2001: 2) argues, 'the climate of international opinion, be it that of states or informed public opinion, *has* been significantly affected by what these NGOs, linked to social change, have brought about' (emphasis in original). INGOs have drawn on a vast font of legitimacy as representatives of public opinion in their confrontations with corporations and governments, establishing something of a 'pro-NGO norm' (Reimann 2006). Reflecting this, the WEF-funded survey mentioned above found that NGOs attracted remarkable levels of trust, with between 80 and 90 per cent agreeing that NGOs would 'operate in the best interests of our society'.

The influence of INGOs is often seen as extending the domestic public sphere into international contexts (Price 2003). Advocacy INGOs can be seen as vehicles for 'globalisation from below', offering an antidote to 'predatory globalisation' (Falk 2000b). Such vehicles can be seen as prefiguring new forms of 'cosmopolitan **democracy**', filling political vacuums between transnationalised power sources and national democratic structures (Held 1995). In the process, INGOs may be interpreted as extending forms of global citizenship, enabling the application of universal principles of citizen rights beyond state borders (Linklater 1998).

INGOs do indeed act as semi-autonomous institutional nodes, promoting a deepened globalisation. They mediate and translate normative principles and discourses from one context to another, creating a politics of flows that constitutes a less hierarchical transnational politics (R. B. J. Walker 1994). While INGOs find their inspiration in transnational fields of contention, they find political traction in relation to states and inter-state regimes (Joachim 2003). INGOs make claims on states and inter-state bodies, and reproduce state centrality. Their leverage rests on the capacity to deploy normative and informational power, provoking public argument about the most desirable or necessary course of action for governments and for inter-state bodies (Holzscheiter

2005). Confined to the non-state realms of 'global civil society', they constitute a self-limited 'loyal' opposition, that respects **Lockean** liberal categories of state and non-state, public and private, and reproduces these as naturalised universals (Chandhoke 2005). INGOs are therefore not necessarily pitted against states: like MNCs, INGOs constitute transnational realms of action that realign rather than transcend inter-state power relations. We may see INGOs, then, not so much as harbingers of a new order but as key players in reforming the existing one.

Political status and influence

A central factor in the growth of INGOs as players in international relations is the capacity to politicise cross-national issues under-addressed by state and inter-state sources of authority. Benefiting from the increased connectivity that results from transnational communication, INGOs are able to expose the inadequacies of existing frameworks, and mobilise public opinion to challenge both the policies and legitimacy of inter-state agencies. Through the 1990s INGOs actively constructed their own capacity, primarily through coalition-building targeted on MNCs and inter-state bodies, with considerable success (Yanacopulosi 2005). Reflecting this, INGOs are more prominent in countries that are engaged with inter-state institutions (J. Smith and Wiest 2005). These 'transnational advocacy networks', and the sources of political leverage they provide, have become a crucial aspect of INGO activity (Keck and Sikkink 1998). Indeed, given their orientation to transnational concerns, INGOs have at times had an advantage over MNCs in inter-state policy-making (Kellow 2002).

INGO coalitions play a formative role in a range of international policy issues, from the development of international **human rights** regimes to the management of global environmental change, to the creation of international norms on the status of women. On these and other issues INGOs have become key agents in instigating and encouraging the emergence of inter-state normative and policy regimes (Reimann 2006) (see Box 22.3). In the process INGOs 'find themselves involved in setting the agenda for political negotiations and decision-making' (Hirsch 2003: 250).

BOX 22.3: DISCUSSION POINTS

UN – INGOs 'catalyse change'

Since 1990 the United Nations Development Programme (UNDP) has published the yearly *Human Development Report*. The Report has been instrumental in promoting a holistic measure of international development.

In 2002 the Report was subtitled 'Deepening democracy in a fragmented world', and focused on democratic involvement as a key aspect of development. The Report discussed deepened democracy at the global level, pointing to INGOs as key agents for cross-border democratisation.

The UNDP Report cited six examples of INGO campaigns that had forced the creation of new inter-state agreements and regimes. The six campaigns are:

- Jubilee 2000 campaign for debt relief
- campaigns for essential HIV/AIDS drugs
- the campaign for an International Criminal Court
- anti-dams campaigns

- anti-poverty campaigns, and
- campaigns for corporate responsibility.

All had been led by INGO coalitions, demonstrating INGO capacity and 'potential to catalyse change'. According to the Report, INGO campaigns herald a 'new global politics' (UNDP 2002).

The role that INGOs play is formally recognised, but only in a limited sense. In 1986, for instance, the Council of Europe recognised INGOs, with the proviso they first be recognised in a national jurisdiction. The 1996 resolution regulating the role of NGOs in the UN conferences clearly states that 'active participation of non-governmental organisations therein, while welcome, does not entail a negotiating role'. In 2002, the UNDP outlined a series of responsibilities for INGOs, effectively imposing ground rules for INGO engagement (UNDP 2002). While inter-state bodies may seek to circumscribe their formal role, INGOs have become deeply engaged with inter-state regimes, to a significant degree influencing intergovernmentalism, such as at the UN Millennium Forum (Alger 2002).

As central players in 'complex multilateralism' INGOs have tailored their proposals for inter-state bodies and have become increasingly professionalised (Martens 2006). In response, inter-state bodies have adapted procedures to enable structured dialogue with INGOs, such as through inclusion in government delegations, consultation, involvement in convention drafting, acceptance of alternative reports and accreditation arrangements (Cooper and Hocking 2000). In some contexts INGOs have entered into tripartite relations with corporations and intergovernmental institutions – whether in service delivery, in compliance monitoring, or indeed in projecting influence (Ottaway 2001). Such engagement comes at a price as INGOs are required to accept the institutional legitimacy of inter-state bodies and of their dominant policy frames (Kamat 2004). A good example drawn from the field of global environmental policy is the role of the Climate Action Network in negotiations over the Climate Change Convention, and the subsequent Kyoto Protocol. The Network aggregates opinion within the transnational environment movement, correlating and calibrating its proposals to the negotiating agenda (Paterson et al. 2003). In the process, the inter-state regime is bent to the needs of environment NGOs, but also vice versa (Haas 2002).

While INGOs play a key role in generating and collaborating with some inter-state initiatives, they have also been successful in exposing and halting others. These interventions are embedded in transnational perspectives, but gain political leverage by exploiting inter-state divisions. An important and relatively early example was the campaign against the Multilateral Agreement on Investment – a corporate rights agreement proposed by the OECD in the mid-1990s. Here INGO campaigners deliberately played national jurisdictions off against each other (J. Goodman and Ranald 1999). This same 'monkey-wrenching' approach was used successfully to block the WTO's 'Millennium Round' in 1999, and also the subsequent WTO 'Development Round', which finally unravelled in 2006.

INGOs have also sought to generate their own positive programs. The World Social Forum (WSF), first staged in Porto Alegre, Brazil, in 2001 as a deliberate counter to the WEF, was deliberately geared to developing such agendas (Soeane and Taddei 2002). The WEF Davos forum had been the focus for protesters in 1998. In 1999 a counter-conference was organised in Davos, and in 2000 an anti-Davos 'global forum' was held in Paris (Houtart and Polet 2001). In 2001 the World *Social* Forum was convened to debate alternatives to the WEF, and symbolically located in Brazil, part of the developing world (Byrd 2005). Since 2001 the social forum process, expressed as a dialogue for alternatives in the WSF Charter of Principles, has been highly influential. It has attracted many tens of thousands of participants, and has been replicated across the globe. Subsequently the WSF moved to countries of Asia and Africa, deepening its legitimacy beyond the Latin American context. INGO involvement in the WSF lent an infrastructure to the global justice movement that emerged in the early 2000s. Latterly, in the face of the so-called 'war on terror', INGOs and wider social movements were able to proactively engage the states-system, deploying their autonomy to influence the agenda, and in 2003 mount the largest mobilisation the world has seen in anti-**war** demonstrations in capital cities across the world (Rupert 2003).

Positioned at the nexus between transnational flows and national jurisdictions, INGOs have charted channels for influence, in the process broadening the logic of inter-state politics. They have been key players in a 'new public diplomacy' where governments exercise power with an eye to normative INGO agendas (Vickers 2004). They have also charted alternatives to official channels, constructing their own shadow structures (J. Goodman 2007). These are highly uneven, especially in their North–South dimensions, reflecting the contingent and limited logic of transnational awareness and consciousness (Kiely 2005). But the leverage remains, both as a contingent present-day reality and as a transformative potential.

Conclusion

MNCs and INGOs have a central and abiding **constitutive** role in international relations. As non-state actors, though, they are embedded in the inter-state system. From Cold War **bipolarisation** to post-Cold War US predominance and the revival of American exceptionalism after the **terrorist** attacks of September 11, non-state forces have been harnessed as constituent elements of **sovereign states**. They have also persistently constituted themselves and exercised their own autonomy: international antagonism between corporate power exemplified by MNCs and 'people power' expressed by advocacy INGOs is thus much more than an inter-state conflict. States and inter-state bodies clearly play a role as the vehicle for the corporate rights agenda and as the main focus for INGO appeals. But it is the non-state players, MNC business associations and advocacy INGOs, which define the terms of the conflict. This non-state dynamic of agency and contestation generates its own autonomy, shaping definitions of the global common good. In this respect their role is not so much political as meta-political.

Such transnational contestation is most clearly expressed in the conflict between the WEF and WSF. The similarities between the two are instructive: both seek to frame the public sphere through agenda-setting strategic interventions; both are predicated on the principle of dialogue and engagement on how best to address mutual problems. In both there is a deliberate attempt to articulate and assert legitimacy on the world stage and thereby influence governmental and inter-state bodies. Both the WEF and WSF are not so much policy-making institutions as discursive interventions, geared to concertising and coalescing political blocs, and to manifesting principles and values that can guide inter-state and state authorities. Taken together they constitute a clash of guiding principles framing the states-system. More generally, their role demonstrates the need for an approach that apprehends the co-constitutive international relations of states and non-state actors. Following Halliday (2001), to understand the role of non-state actors today we need a political sociology of state power rather than an international relations of state-ness. Such an approach offers us the critical scope we need to identify the overarching or meta-antagonisms of international relations, and to highlight strategic fractures and sources of instability and transformation.

A decade on, Halliday's call for political sociology rings true. In 2011, in the midst of a 'hydra-headed crisis' of global governance, the importance of MNCs and INGOs is, if anything, growing (Held, Kaldor and Quah 2010). If nothing else, the 2008–9 financial crisis and ensuing economic crisis demonstrated the power of the global financial sector to secure its interests at taxpayer expense (UNCTAD 2009). The stasis in inter-state governance in other fields, notably in climate change, security and food, opens the door to growing INGO influence, as a normative crisis envelops governing structures. The contest for influence is increasingly waged on this terrain, where states, together with MNCs and INGOs, are conduits for wider social forces and meta-conflicts.

QUESTIONS

1. What are the similarities and differences between MNCs and INGOs?
2. Have non-state actors shifted power away from states and the states-system?
3. How do you explain the rise in number and influence of MNCs and INGOs?
4. To what extent have MNCs influenced state economic management?
5. To what extent have INGOs influenced the exercise of state power?
6. How do MNCs and INGOs impact on the North–South divide?

FURTHER READING

Websites

Centre for the Study of Global Governance 2001–, *Global civil society yearbook*, London: Sage. Compiles commentary and data on the role of INGOs in global politics. Available online at www2.lse.ac.uk/globalGovernance/research/globalCivilSociety/publications.aspx.

International Labour Organization 2004, *Report of the World Commission on the social dimensions of globalization*, Geneva: ILO. Collection of papers on social aspects of globalisation, including the role of MNCs, housed under the heading 'Knowledge Networks' at www.ilo.org/public/english/fairglobalization.

United Nations Conference on Trade and Development (UNCTAD) 1991–, *World investment report*, New York: United Nations, www.unctad.org, housed under the heading 'Main publications'. A mine of information on all aspects of MNCs, including their role in international politics.

United Nations Development Programme (UNDP) 1990–, *Human development report*, New York: United Nations, http://hdr.undp.org/reports. Invaluable resource for debates on global issues affected by INGOs and MNCs.

World Social Forum: www.forumsocialmundial.org.br. The WSF English version contains a 'Library of Alternatives', effectively an archive of WSF perspectives since 2001.

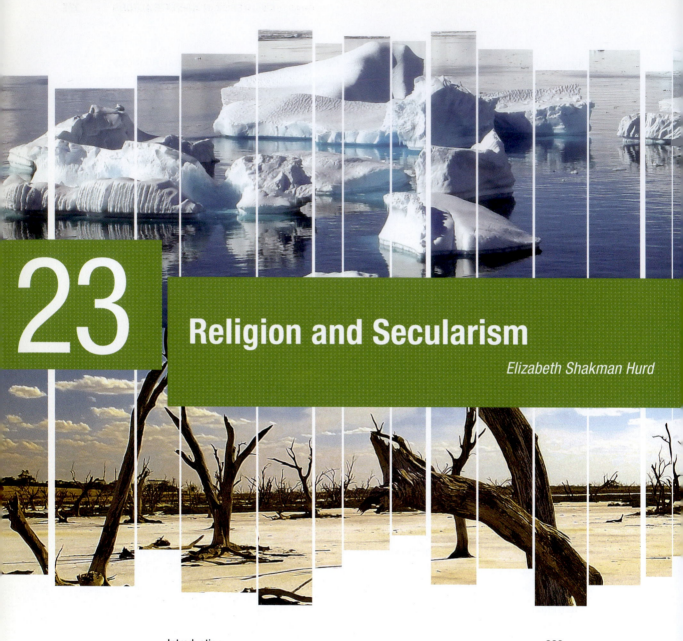

23

Religion and Secularism

Elizabeth Shakman Hurd

Introduction	323
Religion and international relations	323
History of a concept: secularism	325
Secularism and world politics	326
The politics of secularism in the Middle East and North Africa	329
Conclusion	333
Questions	334
Further reading	334

Introduction

This chapter introduces a new research program for understanding the politics of religion and **secularism**. It argues that a focus on the politics of secularism offers a productive port of entry into the study of religion and international politics. Following a brief introduction to religion and international relations, it offers a basic historical introduction to the concept of secularism (see Box 23.1), explains why the politics of secularism is significant to the study of global politics, and concludes with two short case studies of the politics of secularism in the Middle East and North Africa.

Religion and international relations

The study of the global dimensions and implications of religion and secularism is relatively new to the discipline of International Relations (IR) (E. S. Hurd 2008; Katzenstein and Byrnes 2006; S. M. Thomas 2005; Petito and Hatzopoulos 2003; Falk 2001). The power and authority of different forms of secularism and the force they command in many parts of the world, and in global politics, has received little attention. There are a number of reasons for this lack of attention.

First and most significantly, religion has been marginalised due to the sheer power and authority of secularism to define the terms of the debate in such a way that religion is understood as (at best) irrelevant to politics and (at worst) an existential threat to rational public **order**. This consensus has been so powerful in IR and in the world that for many years to question it was considered nonsensical. The conviction that religion should be privatised – and that particular religions may threaten this process more than others – cuts to the core of modern political thought and practice. The privatisation of religion is 'mandated ideologically by **liberal** categories of thought which permeate not only political ideologies and constitutional **theories** but the entire structure of modern Western thought' (Casanova 1994: 215). As a foundational principle of modern politics, secularisation is seen as having contributed to democratisation and liberalisation. In Europe and its settler colonies (the US, Australia, Canada, etc.), **secularist settlements** of the relation between religion and politics are associated with notions of the public interest, public good, freedom, toleration, justice and legitimacy. Secularist laws, traditions, institutions and sensibilities provide 'a set of parameters, focal points, or even points of contention around which political discourse revolves' (Bukovansky 2002: 25). They facilitate closure and agreement around received cultural, political and legal settlements of the relation between religion and politics.

Secularism, it turns out, is a powerful 'pattern of political rule' (Asad 2006: 219). Secularist settlements are sustained by a variety of assumptions, including: secularisation as the most recent step in the worldly realisation of Christian or Judaeo-Christian morality; secularisation as the natural evolution toward a universal morality that has transcended the need for metaphysical moorings; secularisation as a commendable side-effect of democratisation and economic and political modernisation; and secularisation as the triumphant **globalisation** of a modern states-system in which religion has been privatised once and for all. Though often jostling with each other for supremacy, and sometimes colliding head-on, these powerful narratives and projects serve to manage religious diversity, imbue **state** interest and **identity** with meaning, secure an image of contemporary international order as modern, secular and **democratic**, and normalise particular religions and religious actors as either fit or unfit for participation in politics within and outside the state.

Like everyone else, IR scholars have been subject to this powerful secularist consensus. As a result a number of assumptions about religion have been taken for granted. One is that there are two kinds of religion: 'good' and 'bad.' 'Good' religion is associated with a modern ideal subject who has interiorised religion as a set of privately held beliefs that are largely irrelevant to politics. 'Bad' religion is associated with the violent history of Europe's past, particularly the sectarian violence of the Wars of Religion during the European Reformation and afterwards, and, increasingly today, with **terrorism**. Most **realist**, liberal, **constructivist** and **English School** approaches to international relations have picked up on these working definitions of 'good' and 'bad' religion and adapted them to their theoretical paradigms. Consequently most operate on the assumption that 'good' religion is that which has been confined to the private sphere or has disappeared altogether, while 'bad' religion is that which obstinately refuses the terms of this confinement. Many more recent contributions to the study of religion in and world politics have put a slightly different spin on the story by seeking to marginalise 'bad' religion, associating it with division, violence and intolerance, while attempting to resuscitate 'good' religion and ensure its proper place in international politics and public life as a contributor to global justice, engineer of **peacebuilding** and post-conflict reconciliation, and countervailing force to terrorism (Toft, Philpott and Shah 2011; Sisk 2011; E. K. Wilson 2010).

A second reason for the lack of attention to religion in the field of international relations is that both structuralist and materialist approaches to international relations view religion (whether 'good' or 'bad') as largely epiphenomenal, meaning that religion is seen as an effect of or cover for more fundamental material considerations including economic interest and **power politics**. As Talal Asad (1993: 46) has observed, materialist approaches such as **Marxism** (Chapter 4) dismiss religion as 'a mode of consciousness which is other than consciousness of reality, external to the relations of production, producing no knowledge, but expressing at once the anguish of the oppressed and a spurious consolation'. Structuralist approaches such as **neorealism** (Chapter 2) on the other hand tend to proceed on the assumption that states have fixed interests and that state behaviour is constrained by international structure defined by factors such as the distribution of **power**, technology and geography. In both cases secularism and religion are viewed as ideologies that are essentially 'contingent upon, and thus reducible to, material configurations of power or resources' (Bukovansky (2002: 19).

A third and final reason for the marginalisation of religion in international relations is that questions of religion and secularism tend to fall just beyond the peripheral vision of the **empiricist** and **positivist** methods that have dominated mainstream political science for several decades. Consequently these questions have only recently been subject to sustained analysis (see E. S. Hurd 2008).

In today's globalising world, however, to take at face value these assumptions about the nature of 'good' and 'bad' religion, the terms and status of its alleged privatisation, and/or its role as a cover for material interests, is no longer an option. In a world of diverse foundational commitments, to dismiss 'religion or the 'religious' in this way is to miss some of the most interesting and important political developments of our time. And the same must be said for secularism: to take 'secularism' as a given or as merely the absence of religion, is to miss an important part of the story of contemporary

BOX 23.1: TERMINOLOGY

Key concepts

Secularism: A pattern of rule intended to deprive religion of practical, political effects in the public sphere. While the meaning of secularism has changed over time, the dominant contemporary meaning – which emerged in the nineteenth century – refers to a movement aimed at cultivating spheres of social and political life without references to a deity or the afterlife.

Secularist settlement: A mode of containing, managing, remaking, and reforming religion in a manner consistent with secularist agendas. Challenges the idea that secularism is a fixed, final achievement of modernity; instead viewing it as a historically and politically contingent attempt to determine the relationship between politics and religion.

world politics. Secularism and religion are co-**constitutive** concepts – you can't have one without the other. The study of religion, secularism and world politics requires grappling with not one but many varieties of secularism, and not one but many varieties of religion.

As this paradigm shift takes hold, the presumed or desired separation of 'religion' and 'politics' can no longer be taken for granted. Rather, social scientists now speak of secularist 'settlements': powerful and evolving religio-political, legal and institutional constructs with diverse and contested histories, both global and local. No longer seen as fixed and final achievements of European-inspired modernity, these settlements are understood as modes of managing, remaking and reforming religion (Cady and Hurd 2010). In this new research program, concepts and practices associated with the secular and the religious are relationally defined and understood to assume disparate meanings and associations across time and space. It assumes a world of compressed time and space, in which Christianity can no longer be assumed by default to play the role it once did in Christian-majority countries, and in which secularisms are increasingly understood as historically contingent constructs with complex assumptions built into them. Social scientists are responding to these developments by historicising and politicising the categories of the secular and the religious (Calhoun, Juergensmeyer and VanAntwerpen 2011). Secularisms are patterns of political rule with their own complex and contested political histories and implications. Failure to acknowledge this has led to a selective blindness in the study of world politics, as the blanket usage of the categories 'secular' and 'religious' has masked the complex politics surrounding claims to secularism, secularisation, secular democracy, secular human rights and related concepts. This chapter provides a framework for addressing these issues.

History of a concept: secularism

Though often perceived as static, the notion of the secular in Europe and its settler colonies has assumed a surprising range of meanings over time. William E. Connolly (1995: 189) describes the secular as having 'emerged historically within North American and European Christian culture as a subordinate space in which the mundane and the material could be given due attention'. Within this broad definition, however, at least three distinct transformations have occurred in the meaning of the secular in Latin Christendom (now Western Europe). First, as early as the thirteenth century, 'secular' was used in English, usually with negative connotations, to distinguish clergy living in the wider world from those residing in monastic seclusion. Priests who withdrew from the world formed the religious clergy, while those who lived in the world formed the secular clergy (Casanova 1994: 13). Second, by the sixteenth century, the term had shed its affiliation with godlessness and the profane: 'the word "secular" was flung into motion and used to describe a world thought to be in motion: to "secularise" meant to make someone or something secular – converting from ecclesiastical to civil use or possession' (Keane 2000: 6). At this time, to secularise meant to take possession of that which had been associated with the ecclesiastical. In the 1648 **Treaty of Westphalia**, for instance, secularisation referred to the laicisation of church lands. Casanova describes this meaning of secularisation as the 'passage, transfer, or relocation of persons, things, functions, meanings, and so forth, from their traditional location in the religious sphere to the secular spheres' (Casanova 1994: 13). In a third transformation, and from the nineteenth century onward, secularism took on the meaning that it has today in the vernacular, referring to a movement that was 'expressly intended to provide a certain theory of life and conduct without reference to a deity or a future life' (Tamimi 2000: 14). Modern secularists came to be associated with the marginalisation of religion – with the idea that the 'Church and the world are caught up in an historical struggle in which slowly, irreversibly worldliness is getting the upper hand' (Keane 2000: 7).

Secularist divisions between religion and politics are not only constantly evolving within societies but also take different shapes across societies. Adapting sociologist Craig Calhoun's insight about **nationalism**, secularism may be understood as 'not the solution to the puzzle [of politics and religion] but the *discourse* within which struggles to settle the question are most commonly waged' (Calhoun 1997: 76). Secularism is an authoritative discourse, or a 'tradition of argumentation' (Shotter 1993: 200). Secularising claims, projects and institutions produce authoritative settlements of religion and politics, while simultaneously claiming to be exempt from this process of production. Secularism serves as a resource for collective mobilisation and legitimisation, and a language in which moral and political questions are contested. Like nationalism, it contributes to the consolidation of inclusionary and exclusionary group identities, whether at the global, national or **transnational** level. Secularist traditions both rely upon, and help to produce, particular understandings of religion, of political Islam, of religious resurgence, of what is understood as 'normal' politics and so forth. Consider as an example the fact that one hears relatively few references to political Christianity, or political Judaism – this is subsumed for the most part under 'normal politics'. Yet we hear a great deal about political Islam. This is due to the influence of particular secularist settlements, which often carry within them assumptions about particular religious traditions and their relation to different forms of governance. This brings us to the question of world politics.

Secularism and world politics

Most discussions in political science and IR presuppose a fixed definition of the secular and the religious and proceed from there. Realist, liberal, English School, **feminist** and Marxist approaches to international relations treat religion as either private by prior assumption, or as a cultural relic to be handled by anthropologists or religious studies scholars. Even constructivists have paid scant attention to the politics of secularism, focusing instead on the interaction of pre-existing state units to explain how international norms influence state interests and identity, or looking at the social construction of states and the states-system with religion left out of the picture.

This **disciplinary** convention fixes in advance key definitions and terms of inquiry, with some of the most vital aspects of contemporary world politics systematically excluded from consideration. The presumption that religion has been privatised and is no longer operative in modern politics, or that its influence can be neatly encapsulated in anthropological studies of a particular religious tradition and its influence (always from the outside) upon politics, has led IR scholars to miss or misconstrue some of the most significant political developments of our time. This narrow vision is in part attributable to a rigid and de-historicised approach to the 'secular' that pre-structures the academic fields of political science and IR. These fixed concepts patrol the borders of what counts as 'politics,' what counts as 'religion', and how they relate to each other.

I do not want to suggest that the categories of the secular and the religious lack any analytical or political salience. What I do want to suggest is that these categories cannot be taken for granted, and that it is important to look closely at what is actually meant when they are used (see Box 23.2). This is necessary in order to account for the limitations of these categories, for the power relations they reflect and reproduce, and for the histories that they carry with them into the present. Accepting these categories at face value makes it difficult to perceive the shifting and contested relation of secularism not only to religion but also to other political phenomena cast in opposition to it. Failing to attend to the politics of secularism imposes a simplistic and distorted template on world politics by stabilising particular, historically contingent definitions of both secularism and religion. This makes life easier for social scientists looking for answers in the short run, but it is costly in a world in which it is vital to explore how these categories came to be defined and what they signify in different contexts.

BOX 23.2: DISCUSSION POINTS

Religious – secular

Secularism is not the absence of religion. The secular and the religious are concepts that can only be defined in relation to each other, and so to talk about the 'secular' presumes an understanding of the 'religious'. But there is no consensus on the meaning of these key terms. The study of religion, secularism and IR therefore requires recognising not one but many varieties of secularism, and not one but many varieties of religion.

Framing the question of religion and global politics through the lens of the politics of secularism has at least six implications for the study of international relations. First, there are many varieties of secularism (Turkish Kemalism, French *laïcité*, American 'Judeo-Christian' secularism), each representing a contingent yet powerful political settlement of the relation between religion and politics (E. S. Hurd 2008).

Second, secularist settlements are not fixed in stone. They are produced and renegotiated through laws, practices, customs, traditions and social relations, including international relations. Despite their contingency, particular forms of secularism often become so entrenched that they are perceived as exempt from this process of production. In other words, secularist settlements, like nationalist settlements, become 'naturalised'. They operate below the threshold of public debate and contestation and are taken as given, and not made. Secularisation may be understood as the social and historical processes through which these settlements become authoritative, legitimated and embedded in individuals, the law, the state and other societal relations.

Third, a focus on the politics of secularism offers a new understanding of the return of religion to world politics by shifting the focus away from religious actors and institutions. Instead, the focus is on the politics involved in defining the 'religious' and contesting the 'secular'. Forms of secularism that emerged from Christianity differ from those that emerged from other religious traditions, including Islamic traditions which have a long history of separation between civil and religious authorities. Different forms of secularism exist within Europe and outside it. Multiple forms of secularism exist in both Christian and Muslim-majority societies. Challenges to these formations of secularism are often designated as 'religious resurgence': Kemalists in Turkey and laicists in France, for example, are no longer able to monopolise the public debate over what it means to be a secular state. Challengers to authoritative forms of secularism are defined by those in power as 'religious'; hence 'religious' resurgence. Challenges to Kemalism in Turkey and to republican *laïcité* in France are parallel movements, part of the politics of secularism. Similarly, debates over what it means to live in a Christian or post-Christian state are a perennial feature of US politics, and whether India is a Hindu, multi-religious or post-Hindu state is hotly contested. Religious resurgence, from the standpoint of the politics of secularism, is not simply a rise or return of 'religion' taken in a pre-defined way, but an acceleration of challenges to dominant secularist settlements and to the laws and institutions that underpin them. These movements, whether understood as religious or not, contest particular secularist settlements of the relationship between religion, politics and the state (E. S. Hurd 2007).

Fourth, insofar as they operate on the assumption that religion was privatised and rendered irrelevant to power politics after the Westphalian settlement, realist, liberal and constructivist theories of international relations need to be reconsidered. As Peter Katzenstein has observed, 'conventional renderings of the historical origins of the modern European state system and religious politics are intellectually suspect … Religion continues to lurk underneath the veneer of European secularization' (Katzenstein 2006: 32–3). Modern forms of secularism emerged out of a Christian-influenced Westphalian moral order and its influence upon them makes it difficult to subsume the current international order into realist and liberal frameworks which assume that religion has been privatised. Put differently, modern forms of secularism contribute to the constitution of a particular idea and practice of state **sovereignty** that claims to be universal by defining the limits of **state-centred** politics with 'religion' on the outside. To delimit the terms and boundaries of the political by defining religion as a private counterpart to politics, however, is a historically variable claim. Modern European and American forms of secularism perpetuate this claim about the limits of modern politics, operating beneath the threshold of public debate and yet deeply implicated in the politics of sovereign authority.

Fifth, studying the global politics of secularism involves taking a second look at the moral foundations of **international law** and international **human rights**. Many European and American varieties of secularism aspire to provide a theory of life and conduct without reference to a deity. Although this sounds laudable to most **Enlightenment**-trained ears, it is more complex than it may seem at first glance. The assumption that an individual, institution or political collectivity is equipped to distinguish unambiguously between transcendent and temporal is in many quarters a controversial one. In defining the secular, secularists assign a place for something else, which is designated as religious. Casanova (1994: 20) notes that 'the secular, as a concept, only makes sense in relation to its counterpart, the religious'. Given this situation, we might ask: what would a politics look like that claimed *neither* to transcend religious and cultural particularity once and for all (as in most liberal varieties of secularism) *nor* to identify the only possible source of order in a single religious or cultural heritage (as in many forms of politicised religion)? What would happen if one were to begin with the premise that there is no basic, secular authority, command or contract that must be placed above questioning for ethical life to proceed? (Connolly 2002a: xix). To escape the cycle of violence on both sides of the secular–religious divide it may be necessary to break 'both with a secularism that seeks to confine faith to the private realm and with a theo-centered vision that seeks to unite people behind one true faith' (Connolly 2002a: 16).

Finally, secularisms in Europe, the Middle East or elsewhere cannot be understood without reference to European and global history, including **colonial** history. This is a point at which I part ways with Charles Taylor's argument in *A secular age* (2007) – for me it cannot be fully understood without this global context. Secularisms have been created through actions and beliefs and cannot be abstracted from the specific global historical contexts and circumstances in which they emerged, and in which Europe has played a crucial global role in recent centuries. While on the one hand French *laïcité* emerged out of and remains indebted to the Enlightenment critique of religion and Christian reform, for example, on the other it has been constituted through global relationships, including colonial relations in North Africa and the Middle East and negative representations of Islam. The examples in the next section illustrate some of the complex legacies of imperial power and its entanglement with the politics of secularism.

The politics of secularism in the Middle East and North Africa

The politics of secularism in the Middle East and North Africa is a complex and varied story involving: interactions between global and local forms of separation and accommodation; the cooptation of authoritarian secularist discourse by leaders in search of power; colonial and postcolonial politics and history; and religious politics of staggering variety. In conceptual terms, the turn to this region offers a window onto the extraordinary complexities that come with using a term that emerged out of predominantly Christian Europe's religious and political history but that has circulated globally – and been dramatically reinterpreted – in non-Christian majority contexts. Daunting though this may seem, there is no choice but to grapple with the globalisation of secularity because particular Christian, now post-Christian, categories (namely, 'secular' and 'religious'), have become globalised, hybridised and transformed through interactions with other societies. According to Casanova, 'the very fact that the same category of religion is being used globally across cultures and civilizations testifies to the global expansion of the modern secular–religious system of classification of reality which first emerged in the modern Christian West' (Casanova, forthcoming 2011). Given this state of affairs, Europe is 'both indispensable and inadequate' (Chakrabarty 2000: 6). In other words, European conceptions of secularism and secularisation are both indispensable and inadequate to the task of understanding non-European forms of modernity and trajectories of secularisation (Davison 2006: 388–9).

A brief introduction to the politics of secularism in Tunisia and Iran illustrates the capacity of discourses of secularism and secularisation to assume different meanings in different contexts, and offers a glimpse of the global power dynamics of the politics of secularism. I do not claim to offer a comprehensive schedule of religious separation and accommodation in the Middle East. What it means to be *laiklik* in Turkey differs from what it means to be *laic* in France or secular in the US. There is no agreement as to the proper translation of the term 'secularism' into Arabic: it is sometimes translated as *ilmaniyah* (from *ilm*, science) or as *alamaniyah* (from *alam*, world). Others argue that it is more accurately rendered by *dunyawiyah*, or worldly, mundane and temporal (Tamimi 2000: 13).

With these complexities in mind, both President Habib Bourguiba in Tunisia and the Shah of Iran adopted forms of state-sponsored secularisation to entrench their domestic power while maintaining the allegiance of powerful Western allies. Both leaders developed and imposed national-cultural projects that involved explicit reference to the need to imitate what were perceived as 'Western' secularist settlements, including a public, state-sponsored marginalisation of Islam. These narratives were later picked up by oppositional Islamists and used as an indictment of enforced privatisation of Islam, autocratic state power and tacit support for European and American **hegemony** in the Middle East. Given these associations, it is hardly surprising that secularisation was widely unpopular in these two countries. What is interesting from the perspective of the global politics of secularism is that in the Tunisian case it was the secular autocrats who ultimately prevailed, at least in the short term, while in Iran it was their opponents.

Tunisia

European forms of secularism emerged for the most part indigenously within Europe – largely, though not exclusively, out of internal disputes within Christianity. In Tunisia, secularisation was from the beginning a state-sponsored political project. In the Middle East and North Africa the politics of secularism intensified in the mid-nineteenth century as a result of increasing interactions with Europe in which both the 'crown' and the 'cross' weighed heavily. The study of the politics of secularism in this region therefore requires particular attention to colonial and postcolonial influences, without assuming that this context is the only relevant one. Like global modernity in general, processes of secularisation in the region are both related to Europe and developed in distinctive ways in the Middle East (Abu-Lughod 1998: 22).

In Tunisia, secularisation became associated with the attempt by a powerful state to denigrate local conceptions of community and authority in the name of centralised state power, in support of Western interests. Under the leadership of Habib Bourguiba (r. 1956–1987) and backed by Western governments, Tunisia's post-independence government pursued an aggressive program of state-imposed secularization. The government abolished the *sharia* courts, closed the Zaytouna (a renowned centre of Muslim learning), banned the headscarf for women, and debilitated the *ulama* (Islamic scholars) (Esposito 1999: 161). It was clear that 'for Bourguiba, Islam represented the past; the West was Tunisia's only hope for a modern future' (Esposito 1999: 161).

These developments led to the formation of the oppositional Islamic Tendency Movement (Renaissance Party), led by Rashid Ghannoushi. Though initially an apolitical cultural society, the group's status changed in January 1978 when President Bourguiba used the military to crush protesters associated with the group. Combined with the success of the Islamic Revolution in Iran, this 'convinced Ghannoushi and the movement of the need to move beyond broad ideological statements and relate Islam directly and specifically to the real, everyday political, economic, and social problems of the people' (Esposito 1999: 164–5). Ghannoushi hence became the leader of the more overtly politicised Islamic Association (*Jamaah al-Islamiyya*), which developed the concept of a 'living Islam' concerned with wages, poverty, worker's rights and national and cultural identity. Two years later, in 1981, Ghannoushi's Islamic Association became a political party, the MTI (Islamic Tendency Movement). Bourguiba refused to issue a licence legalising the MTI, a decision described by one analyst as a fatal political error: 'The brutality of Bourguiba's response to any and all opposition and the restrictive policies of his government alienated many Tunisians … MTI proved effective in attracting many of the disaffected, not only students, workers, and union members but also middle-class professionals, professors, teachers, engineers, lawyers, scientists, and doctors' (Esposito 1999: 166). In 1981 Bourguiba cracked down on the MTI, imprisoning and torturing Ghannoushi and other leaders. Although Ghannoushi was released in 1984 in response to popular pressure, severe repression of Islamic groups, customs, symbols and traditions continued, followed by another violent crackdown in 1987. The MTI became increasingly radicalised as a result, with the government using the excuse of a **fundamentalist** threat to cement their hold on state power and shun political liberalisation. Bourguiba's replacement, Zine El Abidine Ben Ali, also refused to allow the MTI to participate in public life. Ben Ali, who was forced to flee to Saudi Arabia on 14 January 2011 after being overthrown in a popular uprising, cited a 'firm belief in the need not to mix religion and politics, as experience has shown that anarchy emerges and the rule of law and institutions is undermined when such a mixing takes place' (cited in Esposito 1999: 170).

Yet the MTI did not seek to establish a militant Islamic state. Instead it called for 'a reassertion of Tunisia's Islamic-Arabic way of life and values, restriction of Tunisia's Westernised (Francophile) profile, and promotion of democracy, political pluralism, and economic and social justice' (Esposito 1999: 166). However, leaders acting in the name of the secular state classified MTI alongside pro-Iranian groups such as Islamic Jihad and Hezbollah and banned it, despite its legitimacy among the Tunisian people and progressive nationalist agenda. In this case, the modernising autocratic state prevailed, at least until Ben Ali was forced out by the Tunisian people in 2011 as a result of the corruption, economic mismanagement and political repression associated with his regime.

Iran

Iranian political history offers an interesting counterpoint to the Tunisian experience because in this case opponents of the modernising autocratic state prevailed, at least in the first instance. In Iran under the Shah and his father Riza Shah (r. 1925–41), secularism became a legitimising principle for the suppression of Islamic thought and practice. A state-centric model of imposed modernisation sought to excise Iran's Islamic heritage in favor of what was portrayed by the Iranian government as Western and pre-Islamic political traditions (Mirsepassi 2000). The discourse of secularisation was associated with the US attempt, through the proxy rule of the Shah, to take possession of Iran economically, politically and culturally in the name of US economic (namely, oil) and political interests (namely, support during the **Cold War** and support for Israel).

Opposition to the Shah culminated in the Iranian revolution of 1978–79. Revolutionaries of strikingly disparate political persuasions, who might be labelled secular, religious or perhaps neither, all sought to refashion the Shah's state-imposed secularist settlement. The Iranian **revolution** was not simply a religious backlash against secular modernity, as often portrayed. It was a challenge to the *specific* form of secularisation and modernisation undertaken by the ruling regime, rather than to secularism in general, and a response to the economic and cultural dislocation set in motion by that regime's policies. The Shah had become associated with Western interference in Iran's internal affairs. As one analyst concluded, 'the goal of the Islamic Revolution in Iran, then, was not only to free Iranians politically from the Shah but also to liberate them conceptually from Western ways of thinking' (Juergensmeyer 1993: 19).

Rather than an attempt to return to a fixed and ahistoric form of Islamic governance, the revolution sought to overturn and renegotiate the prevailing state-sponsored secularist settlement, perceived as connected to illegitimate and culturally distant outside economic and political interests. After the revolution, many Iranians favored a non-dogmatic and non-hegemonic tradition of secularism legitimised through reference to Islamic tradition. They called for a politics that was neither 'secular' in the Shah's impositional sense, nor 'religious' in the theocratic sense espoused by Ayatollah Khomeini and his followers, who ultimately triumphed. Khomeini's governance was a dramatic departure from Islamic tradition; at the time of the revolution Iran had no direct historical precedent for governance by the clergy: 'The basis for Khomeini's theory of Islamic governance – the guardianship of the religious jurist (*veliyet-e faqih*) – rests on a novel and almost unprecedented reinterpretation of religious canon that continues to be contested by senior theologians' (Maloney 2002: 98). The Iranian revolution replaced an imperial form of secular modernity with an imperial form of religious modernity – the 'rule of the jurisconsult'. It was a shift 'from temporal to theocratic absolutism' (Arjomand 1988: 89–174). This rejection of Western interference in Iran's internal politics and the West's bid for cultural and political hegemony 'signified the emergence of a new political sociability and the dominance of a new political discourse' in which 'imperialist domination of Islamicate societies was seen to have been achieved not through military or economic supremacy, as earlier generations of nationalists and socialists had argued, but through the undermining of religion and culture mediated through women' (Najmabadi 2008: 41).

Beyond the politics of 'secular versus religious'

Not all claims to the secular or secularisation in the Middle East have been a front for authoritarian state power, cooperation with the West, or the marginalisation of Islam. There are many different secularisms in this region, as diverse in their foundations as they are in their political and religious expressions (see Box 23.3). Understanding the politics of secularism requires attention to how the secular and the religious are mobilised in particular contexts. Not all of these contexts involve state power. In the case of religious movements, for example, a variety of pietist movements throughout the region have attempted to ethically socialise pious subjects, playing a large role in public Islam but working almost exclusively outside the state (Mahmood 2005). In addition, European imperial power has involved more than simply the imposition or sponsorship through proxy of European-style secularism. The focus here on the politics of secularism in relation to imperial power is not intended to exclude other dimensions of these histories but to call attention to the significance of the politics of secularism in understanding these global dynamics. It is also worth mentioning the many religio-political discourses circulating in the region that resemble neither Bourguiba's Tunisia nor Iran under the Shah. Such alternative approaches to questions of religion and politics have sought to move beyond and operate outside of politicised divisions between 'secularist' and 'Islamist'. An example is the writings of Iranian scholar and philosopher Abdolkarim Soroush, who draws explicitly upon resources within Islamic tradition to legitimise forms of separation between religious and political authorities (Soroush 2002). Another example is feminist activism in contemporary Iran, which has refigured the restrictive terms of the 'secular versus Islamic' oppositional binary (Najmabadi 2008). Criticising those who insist upon a rigid Islamic-versus-secular divide, Najmabadi concludes that:

Those who resist and oppose this totalizing outlook have every stake in resisting not only the specific lines being drawn as to what constitutes Islam and what un-Islam, what is secular and what is religious, but the very notion of drawing any lines that would demarcate a religious domain from a secular domain (Najmabadi 2008: 43).

The recent histories of Tunisia and Iran point to the complexity and contestation surrounding the politics of secularism. They illustrate that different significations have become tied to secularist politics in different times and places. Secularisation in the Middle East and North Africa is not merely a Western power play or an imperial imposition, but a plural set of competing discourses and governing practices that evoke very different meanings of 'secular' and 'religious' than those conventionally used in the West. Scholars and analysts need to be attentive to these distinctions.

BOX 23.3: DISCUSSION POINTS

Popular revolutions 2011

The revolutions in the Middle East in 2011 produced new secularist settlements in which relations between religion and politics were open for renegotiation. They were not Islamic revolutions but popular democratic revolts against authoritarian regimes supported by Western governments. Part of creating a more democratic society includes opening space for a broader range of political parties, many of whom (like the Muslim Brotherhood) had been outlawed by leaders such as former Egyptian President Mubarak.

Conclusion

This chapter has sought to bring into focus a paradigm shift in the study of religion and world politics. Opening the black box of secularism which had remained closed due to the conviction that modernisation theorists had long ago resolved the question of religion and politics, removing the theoretical and conceptual blinders which insist that there is only one secularism and not many, and recognising the simultaneous indispensability and inadequacy of Europe to understanding the politics of secularism on a global scale clears a path for new responses to the vexing questions raised by a pluralising world in which religions have always been and are likely to remain significant in public life. Yet much work remains to be done.

The study of religion, secularism and international affairs requires a suspension of (dis)belief (E. S. Hurd 2011). It requires a suspension of belief in the 'secular' as a given, and attention to how it came to be what it is, and do what it does, in different contexts. This requires framing new research questions that do not presume a particular understanding of the 'secular', and that are attentive to the power relations, histories, struggles and even violence that take place under the heading of the secular. This can be uncomfortable for those socialised in European and American forms of secularism, which are kept afloat by a high degree of certainty, stability and even comfort. Approaching the secular and religious relationally, as unstable, historically contingent constructs, allows the ground to shift in interesting directions.

And this ground is shifting. Developments in late modern politics, including an increasing cultural pluralism within societies, rising global **interdependence**, the retreat of Christendom, the questioning of Enlightenment universality, and a rise in religiously-inspired forms of collective political identification demand a rethinking of the basic terms and binaries (secular rational versus religious irrational, philosophical versus theological, reason versus faith, secular law versus religious law) that have structured inquiry on this subject. Scholars need to pose research questions that do not presuppose fixed definitions of these terms or relations between them. Doing so opens the door to new perspectives on power, authority, and history – and not just religion – in international and comparative politics.

QUESTIONS

1. What are some of the contentious issues involving the politics of secularism where you live?
2. If you wanted to learn more about the global and comparative politics of secularism, which states or non-state actors or organisations do you think would be most interesting to study, and why?
3. What is the role of international courts such as the European Court of Human Rights in adjudicating issues involving the politics of secularism and religion? What other international institutions are involved in these issues, and in what ways?
4. In what ways does the politics of gender and sexuality intersect with the politics of secularism?
5. How does globalisation, including its economic, political, cultural, demographic and technological dimensions, affect the ways in which secularism is lived and understood in different locations?
6. How do different international human rights actors and organisations, such as Human Rights Watch and Amnesty International, approach questions involving secularism, religion and religious difference?
7. What sources would you use to study the politics of secularism and religion? Policy statements? International treaties? Speeches? Opinion polls? Court decisions? Academic conference proceedings? All of the above?

FURTHER READING

Bender, Courtney and Klassen, Pamela E. 2010, *After pluralism: reimagining religious engagement*, New York: Columbia University Press. Interrogates the concept of religious pluralism as a solution to issues posed by religious difference.

Cady, Linell E. and Hurd, Elizabeth Shakman (eds) 2010, *Comparative secularisms in a global age*, New York: Palgrave Macmillan. Explores the history and politics of secularism and religion in France, India, Turkey and the US and interrogates presumption of European origins of modern forms of secularism.

Grillo, Ralph, Ballard, Roger, Ferrari, Alessandro, Hoekema, André J., Maussen, Marcel and Shah, Prakash (eds) 2009, *Legal practice and cultural diversity*. London: Ashgate. Considers how cultural and religious diversity challenges legal practice and how that practice is changing in the encounter with the cultural diversity occasioned by immigration.

Jakobsen, Janet and Pellegrini, Ann (eds) 2008, *Secularisms*, Durham: Duke University Press. Scholars of religious studies, gender and sexuality studies, history, science studies, anthropology, and political science challenge the binary conception of 'conservative' religion versus 'progressive' secularism.

Snyder, Jack (ed.) 2011, *Religion and international relations theory*, New York: Columbia University Press. Reconsiders realist, liberal and constructivist approaches to international relations theory and practice in light of new attention to the history and politics of secularism and religion.

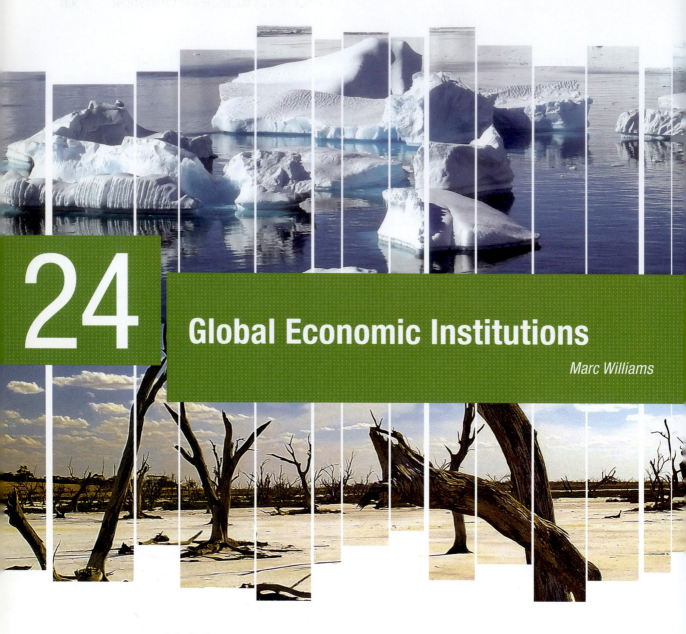

24

Global Economic Institutions

Marc Williams

Introduction	337
Global governance and the global economy	337
Global economic institutions and the management of the global economy	340
Legitimacy, democracy and global economic institutions	345
Conclusion	347
Questions	347
Further reading	347

Introduction

This chapter explores the role of three global economic institutions (GEIs) in contemporary economic governance: the **International Monetary Fund (IMF)**, the **World Bank** and the **World Trade Organization (WTO)**. As we will see there is no single vantage point from which to view these institutions or from which to assess their importance. In the first part of the chapter we discuss global governance and **globalisation** and examine competing perspectives on international organisations. Controversies over the role of the GEIs in the global economy have focused on the economic impact of their activities and their representative nature as institutions of governance. The second part therefore explores the historical evolution of the IMF, World Bank and WTO as they adapted to the challenges of an evolving global economy. In this section we will examine competing claims concerning their competence as economic managers. Recently, the legitimacy, accountability and representative nature of GEIs have been called into question. The final part of the chapter focuses on the debate over the **democratic** credentials of the GEIs.

In 2008 a financial crisis with its origins in the US spread to the rest of the world ushering in a global financial crisis with deep and profound consequences for most countries in the world. The Global Financial Crisis (GFC) of 2008–09 was the most severe experienced by credit markets since the Great Depression of the 1930s (Collyns 2008). The financial crisis in turn sparked an economic recession as economic output fell. It was apparent from the outset that individual nations could not return to economic prosperity through reliance on their own economic measures. In other words, both national and international action was necessary to repair the damage wrought by the GFC. Under these circumstances forms of global regulation and management came under intense scrutiny and the focus turned to the key institutions of global economic management with many commentators debating the relevance of the **Bretton Woods** institutions (the IMF and World Bank) to the twenty-first century economic landscape (Boughton 2009; Pisani-Ferry and Santos 2009). One major innovation in the area of global governance was the rise of the Group of 20 (**G20**), and while the implications of the shift from the **G8** to the G20 certainly marks an important evolution in the institutionalisation of global economic governance (Beeson and Bell 2009; Helleiner and Pagliari 2009), the global economic crisis served to highlight the continuing relevance of the Bretton Woods institutions and the WTO to contemporary global governance. This chapter focuses on the World Bank, IMF and WTO – arguably, the most important GEIs in contemporary world politics. In order to understand the activities of these institutions and the controversies surrounding them it is necessary to look at both their historical evolution and the various ways in which writers analyse international organisations.

Global governance and the global economy

There are, of course, many definitions of the term 'global governance'. For the purposes of this chapter governance will be taken to mean the sum of the many ways that individuals and institutions, public and private, manage their common affairs. (Commission on Global Governance 1995). Following from this definition of governance, global governance will be understood as the system of governance mechanisms (institutions, rules, **norms** and **regimes**) designed to regulate human affairs in the world (O'Brien and Williams 2010:

425). GEIs are key actors in global economic governance. Although the World Bank, IMF and WTO are now inescapable features of the international economic landscape, permanent global economic institutions are a relatively recent historical creation.

As World War II drew to a close the **United Nations (UN)** Monetary and Financial Conference was held in July 1944 at Bretton Woods, New Hampshire, US. This conference laid the foundations for the post-war international economic **order**. At the Bretton Woods conference two organisations were formed – the International Bank for Reconstruction and Development (IBRD), which was later called the World Bank, and the IMF. These two organisations were meant to be two parts of a tripartite structure of international economic organisations that would provide the foundations for post-war recovery and prosperity. The third part of the economic architecture was meant to be created at the Havana Conference on Trade and Employment in November 1947, but although the delegates agreed to form an International Trade Organization (ITO) this institution never came into existence since its charter was never **ratified**. With the failure of the ITO, the **General Agreement on Tariffs and Trade (GATT)** became a forum for the reduction of tariffs and for international trade policy until it was replaced in 1995 by the WTO.

The rationale for the creation of a **multilateral** economic order underpinned by formal institutions lay in three considerations. First, many policy-makers believed that one of the major causes of the war was the economic instability of the 1930s (Calleo and Rowland 1973: 35–7). The international economic system experienced a number of shocks in the inter-war period including the Wall Street Crash of 1929, the Great Depression of the 1930s and a breakdown in international economic cooperation. These policy-makers believed that the rise of **fascism**, Nazism and militarism in the 1930s was a direct result of economic instability and economic rivalry. They therefore set out to establish an economic framework that would provide a firm foundation on which to build a peaceful post-war world. Second, policy-makers believed that an open trading system and a stable monetary and financial system were essential prerequisites for the recovery of European economies devastated by the war. Third, policy-makers believed it necessary to preserve **national interests** while encouraging international cooperation. Thus, they established an economic system based on what has been termed 'embedded **liberalism**' – that is, compromise between **state** intervention to secure domestic markets and liberal economic principles (Ruggie 1982).

While there is no single answer to the question 'do we need global economic institutions?', since the end of World War II leading governments have answered this question in the affirmative. In the immediate aftermath of World War II the positive answer to this question was conditioned by their experience of the Great Depression, war and the challenge of reconstruction. In the contemporary world an answer framed in relation to globalisation also appears to be a positive one, given the reaction of governments to the recent GFC. While recognising that globalisation remains a contested term, with disputes taking place not only over its meaning but also over its very existence (Scholte 2005), no better concept exists that captures the profound changes that have taken place in economic, political, social and cultural dimensions of society.

Arguably, globalisation is not a recent phenomenon, but contemporary globalisation is distinct from other historical forms of the phenomenon. There are three key features of contemporary globalisation. First, central to contemporary globalisation is a 'widening, deepening and speeding up of worldwide interconnectedness' (Held et al. 1999: 2). Second, globalisation is a multidimensional affair covering economic, political, social, technological, ecological and cultural dimensions of social life. Third, globalisation is inclusive of both material and ideational/**normative** dimensions. Globalisation refers not simply to changes in material structures and processes but also to ideological and ethical issues. This three-fold approach suggests that globalisation is a set of processes rather than an end state, and highlights the contested nature of the debate concerning global governance as a response to the pressures created by globalisation.

Globalisation is an uneven process and therefore it poses both challenges and opportunities for the global economy and GEIs tasked with forms of economic management (Woods 1999: 25–34). On the one hand, global economic **interdependence** is a process which brings national economies closer together, thus requiring better coordination and harmonisation of policies (UNDP 2005). On the other hand, globalisation unleashes forces which appear to speed up the processes whereby the gap between winners and losers in the world economy widens more quickly (Amoroso 2007; Kacowicz 2007) and with more serious consequences than at previous times. GEIs are thus faced with the task of ameliorating these adverse consequences of globalisation. These challenges have been central to the higher profile that GEIs have experienced in the past decade.

Frequently globalisation is confused or conflated with a particular type of economic policy, namely **neoliberalism**. However, neoliberal economic policy is just one response to globalisation and not the only available mix of economic policies. Neoliberal economic policies, in this context, refer to policies supportive of market solutions to economic problems, increased emphasis on the private sector, a lessening of government intervention in the economy, and a reduction in welfare provisions. Many of the critics of the GEIs focus on their role as instruments in the spread of economic liberal ideas and strategies. In the 1980s and 1990s the World Bank and IMF adopted a neoliberal approach known as the Washington Consensus (see Box 24.1). While some analysts have discussed the emergence of a post-Washington Consensus (Öniş and Şenses 2005) in the wake of the Global Financial Crisis no consensus exists on the current economic philosophy of these organisations. But before we examine the contested record of the GEIs it is necessary to take a brief look at contrasting perspectives on international organisation, since assessment of the possibilities and limitations of GEIs is conditioned by the perspective held by the analyst.

BOX 24.1: TERMINOLOGY

The Washington Consensus

The Washington Consensus is a term coined by the economist John Williamson. It refers to a set of policies designed to foster economic development that had broad support among officials and economists in the US Government (especially the US Treasury), IMF and World Bank. Although Williamson's original thesis applied solely to Latin America the term has been given wider applicability. These policies included fiscal discipline (balancing budgets), liberalising trade, freeing exchange rates and interest rates, privatising state industries, deregulation, tax reform to broaden the tax base, redirecting public expenditure to increase economic returns and redistribute income, and securing property rights.

Perspectives on global economic institutions

While there are numerous questions that scholars and practitioners pose concerning the role played by GEIs in global governance, these can be seen to be variations on two central questions: Are GEIs important? And whose interests are served by GEIs? These two questions contain both positive and normative components. That is, they embrace issues relating to what has been accomplished by these organisations and also issues surrounding the goals or purposes of these bodies. Views about GEIs are related to beliefs about international cooperation and international organisation more generally (Pease 2006). Liberal **theories** have been dominant in approaches to thinking about international organisation because liberal theories take international organisation seriously (see Chapter 3). For liberals there are a number of core assumptions which lead them to think that GEIs are important. First, liberals believe that international cooperation is a rational response to an interdependent world economy (Rittberger and Zangl 2006: 16–20). Liberals believe that states are rational actors and they thus see GEIs as a rational response to the complexities of international economic transactions. No single state can secure its economic goals in an interdependent world economy, and therefore mutual vulnerabilities will lead states to create GEIs. Second, liberals believe international cooperation on the basis of reciprocity increases mutual gains for all parties (Karns and Mingst 2010: 37). Thus, GEIs can benefit all members since they promote efficiency and stability in the world economy.

While liberals provide positive answers to both questions, **realists** tend to take the opposite view. All forms of realism take the state as the basic and most important unit in international relations (see Chapter 2). Thus, from a realist perspective GEIs are only important to the extent that they serve the interests of the states which created them. Because international organisations are viewed from this focus on power realists will tend to argue that international organisations will reflect the interests of the dominant states (Waltz 2000: 26). Therefore, a GEI will serve the interests of the most powerful state in the organisation.

From a **constructivist** perspective (see Chapter 7) international organisations can be important and independent actors in international relations (Barnett and Finnemore 2004). Constructivists focus on norms and **identity** formation and from this perspective GEIs both reflect the normative consensus underlying their creation and influence their members through changing their beliefs and understandings and shaping their behaviour (Karns and Mingst 2010: 50–2). While there is no settled view on the interest served by GEIs the dominant liberal constructivist view focuses on the dissemination of liberal norms (Barkin 2003).

Critical Theory approaches to the global economy emphasise the nature of oppression and the struggle for justice (O'Brien and Williams 2010: 25). While there is no single critical perspective (see Chapters 4–7) it can be argued that critical approaches are united in an attempt to understand the roles that international organisations play in maintaining or challenging the **status quo**. Critical perspectives thus focus on the dominant interests served by international organisations.

Global economic institutions and the management of the global economy

This section presents a brief sketch of the performance of the three major global economic institutions. As mentioned above, different theorists will arrive at different conclusions about the impact of a specific GEI since there are no agreed criteria by which to measure the performance of the GEIs. Moreover, different approaches to international relations will emphasise different values. Is the key goal of global economic governance the promotion of **security** and stability (realism); efficiency (liberalism); equity (critical approaches) or **democracy** (liberal and critical perspectives)? Analysts who place emphasis on stability will differ in their assessments of the performance of GEIs from those who place greater emphasis on efficiency or equity. Of course, these goals need not necessarily be in conflict and a well-functioning governance system is likely to seek to achieve all of them. Nevertheless, in practice, it often proves difficult to reconcile the demands of stability, efficiency and justice in ways satisfactory to specific constituencies.

The International Monetary Fund

GEIs exist within a changing global environment and one measure of their success is their ability to adapt to change. In some respects the IMF has responded creatively to the challenges posed by a changing international financial order, but in other respects it has failed either to provide appropriate regulatory oversight or develop polices suitable for its membership.

Supporters of the IMF point to its changed lending portfolio as an example of its adaptability and continued relevance. Initially the IMF was essentially a short-term lending (12–24 month loans) institution providing loans through its Stand-by Arrangements. It has progressively expanded its lending role and developed lending facilities to cope with specific problems: for example, the Extended Fund Facility, established in 1974 for countries suffering serious balance of payments; the Supplemental Reserve Facility, devised in 1997 to provide short-term financing on a large scale; and the Compensatory Financing Facility, initiated in 1963 in response to pleas for special financial resources by countries experiencing **balance of payments** difficulties as a result of fluctuating commodity prices. The IMF was also at the forefront of adjustment efforts in the management of the 1980s debt crisis, in the transition to **capitalism** of the command economies of Eastern and Central Europe, and the search for solutions to financial crises (the Mexican crisis in 1994, the Asian financial crisis in 1997, the Russian crisis in 1998, the Argentine crisis in 2000–01 and the 2008–09 Global Financial Crisis). In the context of the GFC the G20 has underlined the continuing relevance of the IMF's role as a lender to emerging markets, a provider of loans to low-income countries, a framework for advocating fiscal stimulus and a key institution in the reform of the international financial system. This commitment has resulted in an increase in the IMF's lending resources by up to US$500 billion (International Monetary Fund 2010) through an injection of funds (under the New Arrangements to Borrow). Overall this has resulted in the tripling of the IMF's lending capacity to US$750 billion.

Although the IMF has clearly responded to a changing global financial system, many critics question the appropriateness of IMF polices and the continuing relevance of the organisation to a global economy in which global financial integration creates instability and the diffusion of financial autonomy to banks, **transnational corporations** and markets significantly weakens national monetary autonomy. There has been a long-running debate over the impact of IMF policies on recipient countries (Vreeland 2003; Williams 1994). As the Fund became more heavily involved in structural adjustment lending (see Box 24.2) following the onset of the debt crisis in 1982, the criticisms became more widespread. Essentially the critics argue that IMF policies have a negative impact on economic growth, result in adverse distributional impacts and lead to political instability. The IMF has argued that the overall record of its programs is positive and that the initial conditions in borrower countries have a significant impact on the success of adjustment programs. Moreover, it has progressively moved from the hard conditionality of the 1980s and 1990s to more varied and flexible forms of conditionality. In response to the GFC the IMF has promised greater flexibility in its loan programs. Despite these reforms the debate on the impact of its programs will continue. The second issue concerns the role of the IMF in stabilising the international financial system. While debate over the IMF's surveillance policies and its prescriptions to countries experiencing financial crises (Mosley 2004) has highlighted both the moral hazard of IMF intervention and the impact of its policy prescriptions, its very existence has also recently been called into question. The onset of the GFC exposed the limitations of the fund as a governance mechanism. The G20 (2009a), in admitting that 'major failures in the financial sector and in financial regulation and supervision were fundamental causes of the crisis', recognised the limitations of the IMF as a global regulatory agency and has proposed the creation of a Financial Stability Board (G20 2009b). Further issues relating to the governance of the IMF will be discussed below.

> **BOX 24.2: TERMINOLOGY**
>
> **Structural adjustment policies**
> A typical structural adjustment package contains prescriptions leading to:
>
> - devaluation of the national currency
> - cuts in government expenditure
> - reduction of the role of the state in production and distribution
> - liberalisation of foreign trade
> - price liberalisation and deregulation, and
> - restructuring government expenditure through privatisation.

The World Bank

Like its twinned institution, the World Bank has shown a degree of flexibility and adaptability to a changing international economic order. The International Finance Corporation (IFC) was established in 1956 to promote private sector growth in developing countries through investing in private projects, supporting the growth of private capital markets and encouraging flows of domestic and foreign capital. The International Development Association (IDA), created in 1960, is the Bank's soft loan affiliate and provides loans to the poorest developing countries on very favourable terms. The Multilateral Investment Guarantee Agency (MIGA), established in 1988, aims to encourage the flow of direct investment to developing countries through the lessening of non-commercial investment barriers.

The World Bank has also adapted its approach to development over time. Since its early years the Bank has had four identifiable shifts in its approach to the financing of economic development. Its early lending programs focused on industrialisation and large infrastructure projects. A central belief at this time was that economic growth would trickle-down from rich to poor and thus no specific anti-poverty measures were required. Beginning in 1973 the Bank embarked on what became known as the Basic Needs strategy. The focus in this era was on poverty-oriented polices designed to meet the basic needs of target populations. While industrial projects remained heavily favoured there was increased funding of agriculture and the rural sector. The Basic Needs policy was supplanted by adjustment lending in 1980. The move to structural adjustment loans, which were the key feature of adjustment lending, saw a shift from poverty alleviation to one of improving the balance of payments and overall economic performance of client states (see Box 24.2). A renewed emphasis on poverty alleviation characterises the current Bank approach. The sustainable development paradigm has shifted Bank priorities towards governance reforms, an increased role for the private sector in development and a greater focus on poverty reduction (Pincus and Winters 2002). The current focus of the Bank is on achieving the Millennium Development Goals (MDGs) (see Box 24.3 and Chapter 27).

BOX 24.3: DISCUSSION POINTS

The Millennium Development Goals

Goal 1: Eradicate extreme poverty and hunger.

Goal 2: Achieve universal primary education.

Goal 3: Promote gender equality and empower women.

Goal 4: Reduce child mortality.

Goal 5: Improve maternal health.

Goal 6: Combat HIV/AIDS, malaria and other diseases.

Goal 7: Ensure environmental sustainability.

Goal 8: Develop a Global Partnership for Development.

While the impact of the GFC on developing countries is not uniform it is widely agreed that it has led to an increase in global poverty and makes attainment of the MDGs more difficult. A World Bank study estimated that there would be 64 million more people living in extreme poverty (less than $1.25 per day) by the end of 2010 (World Bank 2010). In response to the increased economic vulnerability faced by most of its membership the World Bank has significantly increased lending. In fiscal year 2009 the IBRD and IDA made commitments of US$46.9 billion, which was almost double the $24.7 billion in commitments made in fiscal year 2008. Overall World Bank loans, grants, equity investment and guarantees increased by 54 per cent between fiscal year 2008 and fiscal year 2009 to total $58.8 billion (World Bank 2009: 2). Apart from increased lending the Bank has devised new programs in response to the GFC. The Vulnerability Finance Facility (VFF) focuses on agriculture and employment and social safety nets; the Infrastructure Recovery and Assets Platform provides counter-cyclical lending to protect existing assets and future projects.

Nevertheless, the World Bank remains a deeply controversial institution. Supporters of the Bank contend that it provides developing countries with much-needed capital, and maintain that the projects it supports are vital in the fight against world poverty. In their view these resources provide important supplementary assistance for the governments of developing countries and enhance the perceived stability of the economy to international investors. Supporters of World Bank policies think that the conditions it attaches to its loans provide a framework of sound financial management for the governments of its borrower nations (Picciotto 2003). On the other hand, critics accuse the Bank of putting profits before people, and of distorting development (Cammack 2004; Caulfield 1996). To the critics these resources are often insufficient, inadequate and ineffective. They contend that the specific conditionality imposed by the Bank privileges external interests over those of the recipients and is focused on repayment of the loan rather than on improving welfare.

The World Trade Organization

Assessment of the World Trade Organization's (WTO) contribution to global governance has varied depending on the view taken of the organisation's ability to affect countries' trade policies and analysis of the beneficial effects of trade liberalisation. The WTO provides a complex framework for the organisation of international trade.

First, as an international organisation the WTO is primarily a legal agreement which provides a framework of rules, norms and principles to govern the multilateral trading system. The Global Financial Crisis resulted in the most severe contraction in world trade since the Great Depression (WTO 2010) and it was feared that rising **protectionism** would further constrain economic recovery. It can be argued that the existence of the WTO was instrumental in ensuring that a widespread return to protectionism was kept at bay. In support of the liberal trade order the G20 was quick to 'reaffirm our commitment to fight all forms of protectionism and to reach an ambitious and balanced conclusion to the Doha Development Round [of trade negotiations]' (G20 2009c).

Second, it is a forum for multilateral trade negotiations. The organisation, itself the outcome of a round of multilateral trade negotiations, presides over the process through which further trade liberalisation is achieved. Negotiations under the auspices of the WTO specify the principal contractual obligations determining trade negotiations and trade legislation, and the Trade Policy Mechanism facilitates the evolution of trade relations and trade policy through its surveillance of the policies of WTO member states.

Since its inception the WTO has presided over piecemeal liberalisation but has yet to oversee a round of substantial reduction in barriers to trade. The currently stalled Doha Round provides ammunition for supporters and critics alike. The critics argue that the failure to conclude the round shows the importance of the rich countries' interests in managing outcomes in the WTO. Supporters of the WTO argue that the stalemate is proof that a multilateral institution is necessary.

Third, the WTO through its Dispute Settlement Understanding (DSU) facilitates dispute resolution. The DSU provides the machinery for settling members' differences on their rights and obligations. For some this function is crucial because it contributes to the stability and further evolution of the world trading system, since liberalisation will not take place in the absence of effective dispute settlement procedures (Jackson 2008). For others, the dispute settlement procedures give authority to unelected judges to make decisions affecting the livelihoods of groups unrepresented in the process (Wallach and Woodall 2004: 239–61).

The WTO is committed to the promotion of a liberal trading order. Its policies are predicated on an assumption that trade is better than no trade, and that barriers to trade are harmful to national and international welfare. As a successor to the GATT the WTO widens and deepens global regulation of international trade and payments. It extends GATT disciplines into areas previously governed by protectionist devices in the post-war global trade regime – agriculture and textiles – and brings 'new' issues such as intellectual property rights and investment measures under regulatory control. For supporters the WTO provides a level playing field and thus can be effective in constraining damaging economic **nationalist** policies (Blackhurst 1997). Moreover, they emphasise the beneficial impact of trade liberalisation for all countries (Bhagwati and Srinivasan 2002). Critics of the WTO argue that major states dictate the rules of the organisation (Kwa 2003). Furthermore, they contend that further unfettered trade liberalisation can be damaging to poor countries (Chang 2005) and the environment (Conca 2000).

Legitimacy, democracy and global economic institutions

Like many organisations, GEIs have been the subject of intense debate concerning their democratic credentials, accountability and legitimacy (J. Glenn 2008; Woods and Lombardi 2006; Zweifel 2006). In this debate supporters of the status quo have attempted to defend the current arrangements against a wide variety of critics. In order to understand this controversy I will first outline the defence of current arrangements, followed by the arguments of the critics. The defence of the status quo can be called a statist approach. It begins from the assumption that the accountability of GEIs is situated with the state actors that constitute their membership (Keohane and Nye 2001). That is, multilateral economic institutions are accountable to their membership – to states and not to other actors in the international system. It follows that a GEI is legitimate to the extent that its members accept its authority.

On the basis of these assumptions the extent to which the World Bank, IMF and WTO are democratic institutions has been made the subject of three tests. The first concerns the extent to which the organisation is representative of the members of **international society**. At its simplest level representation therefore refers to inclusiveness of the membership. In this sense an international organisation is democratic if its membership actually covers all states that potentially have an interest in the selected issue-area(s), and an organisation is undemocratic if it deliberately excludes from membership states that meet the criteria for membership and have a legitimate interest in its activities.

Using these criteria the World Bank, IMF and WTO are democratic institutions, since all three organisations boast a wide membership (see Box 24.4). Not only are most of the world's states members, but in terms of the activities covered by these organisations no significant states are denied membership.

BOX 24.4: KEY FIGURES

Membership of the GEIs*

International Monetary Fund: 187 members.
World Bank: 187 members.
World Trade Organization: 153 members.

*As at July 2011.

Second, representation can be conceived as a process of fair decision-making. In this sense democracy refers to the decisional rules of an international organisation. The statist perspective rejects criticism of the weighted voting mechanism of the World Bank and the IMF. Statists argue that in a financial institution a weighted voting system is necessary to protect the interests of the major shareholders without whose contributions a pool of finance for borrowing states would not exist. With respect to the WTO the statist perspective contends that the consensus decision-making rules are ultra-democratic since every member country has a voice. The third criterion is that of transparency, and supporters of the status quo emphasise recent developments, especially at the Bank and the WTO, to increase access to information. They defend the necessity of secret negotiations and argue that further openness is the responsibility of national governments.

A number of critical voices have been raised in opposition to these arguments. They argue that in the contemporary world a focus on inter-governmental relations is too limiting since the forces of interdependence and globalisation have reduced the degree of autonomy and independence implied in the traditional statist concept of **sovereignty**. Globalisation, it is argued, poses fundamental questions for the exercise of global democratic governance. Critics reject the claim that these institutions are democratic because they are accountable to their member states. First, there are limitations on state sovereignty in the sense that the authority and power of national authorities is undermined by the activities of the GEIs. The conditionalities imposed by the World Bank and IMF and the expanded mandate of the WTO mean that national governments and their citizens are increasingly subject to new forms of regulation over which there is little direct control (Woods 2001: 88–90; Williams 1999).

Second, critics contend, it cannot be assumed that the decision-making structures are fully representative. The weighted decision-making of the World Bank and IMF results in a system in which poorer countries are inadequately represented (Woods 2003: 84–7). Moreover, the critics reject the argument that decision-making in financial organisations should reflect the interests of the most powerful. They argue that a fair decision-making system should take into account those most affected by the decisions taken. Furthermore, a restriction of decision-making to governments does not satisfactorily capture the range of stakeholders likely to be affected by the activities of the GEIs. Critics argue that the conventional answer that states represent their citizens and therefore the politics of GEIs reflect the interests of diverse groups in national society is no longer tenable (if it ever was), given the direct organising sub-nationally and transnationally of groups who believe that current state structures marginalise their interests (Williams 1999; 2005).

Furthermore, critics have argued that the GEIs are not sufficiently transparent either in terms of their decision-making – which is often conducted in secret – or in terms of the provision of access to information. This absence of transparency reduces accountability, since it limits public scrutiny of decision-making and curtails the potential effectiveness of specific GEIs by reducing public debate and input into policy-making.

The debate on the democratic deficit of the GEIs, which can be traced to the mid-1990s, was given increased political salience by the Global Financial Crisis. In one sense the GFC was perceived as a crisis of governance, and in that respect the issue of who controls the GEIs became a politically sensitive one. The ensuing debate exposed the hollowness of the statist defence of the status quo. It has been recognised that institutional effectiveness is linked to representation and accountability. In the IMF the Executive Board's Agreement of April 2008 on the reform of quotas and voice only entered into force on 3 March 2011, despite the political salience of the issue. The increased political salience of governance reform in the GEIs has not to date resulted in significant transformation. Moreover, the international discussions have been limited in nature. And finally, while the G20 has called for increased voice and participation of developing countries in the IMF and World Bank through increased voting power for these countries, it is also important to note that the G20 itself has limited legitimacy.

Conclusion

The activities of the International Monetary Fund, World Bank and World Trade Organization have far-reaching consequences for the livelihood of people around the globe. The IMF's macroeconomic policy coordination, crisis management skills and role in economic development have all sparked debate and controversy. The World Bank, as the world's leading multilateral development agency, has a crucial role to play in poverty alleviation. While the Bank has not been a static institution and has changed its priorities over time its credibility as a development agency remains in question. The creation of the WTO signalled a stronger institutional base for the multilateral trading system, but the tension between further trade liberalisation and sectional interests has stymied its ability to fulfil this role.

In respect of all three institutions persistent criticisms remain of their ability to contribute to stability, efficiency and justice in the global economy. In a very stark manner the Global Financial Crisis raised pertinent issues about the governance role of these institutions and brought to the forefront the dilemmas of reforming their internal governance structures to address the perceived crisis of legitimacy they face.

QUESTIONS

1. To what extent are global economic institutions indispensable pieces of global governance?
2. Why does governance reform in the IMF and World Bank matter?
3. Does the IMF still have an important role to play in the governance of the international financial system?
4. What are the key constraints faced by the World Bank in achieving its stated goal of poverty alleviation?
5. What conclusions can be drawn from the stalled Doha Round concerning the future of the World Trade Organization?

FURTHER READING

Lanoszka, A. 2009, *The World Trade Organization: changing dynamics in the global political economy*, Boulder and London: Lynne Rienner. Excellent introduction to the WTO and the global trade regime.

O'Brien, R. et al. 2000, *Contesting global governance*, Cambridge: Cambridge University Press. Detailed examination of the relationship between the IMF, World Bank, WTO and environmental, labour and women's movements.

Woods, N. 2006, *The globalizers: The IMF, the World Bank and their borrowers*, Ithaca: Cornell University Press. Examines the effects of IMF and World Bank lending in Africa, Mexico, and Russia.

25

Global Trade

*Maryanne Kelton**

Introduction	349
Free trade and the international trading system	350
An imperfect system	352
Preferential trade arrangements	354
Reform of the trading system?	355
The Global Financial Crisis and trade	356
Prospects for recovery	357
Conclusion: systemic recovery and reform	358
Questions	359
Further reading	359

* My thanks to Alex Stephens and Owen Covick for their assistance with this chapter.

Introduction

This chapter examines both the concepts and the structures of the global trading **regime** before considering the ensuing debates. First, it explains the international **free trade** regime and the opportunities it affords. Second, it identifies some of the problems that have beset this system. Third, it notes the growth in preferential trade agreements. Fourth, it considers the prospects for reform of the global trading system; and fifth, it examines the impact of the Global Financial Crisis on global trade, before examining the prospects for recovery. Key terms relating to global trade are explained in Box 25.1.

The global trade regime has been variously praised as providing the engine for global growth and critiqued for exploiting weaker players in the international system. The intense protests at the **World Trade Organization (WTO)** Millennium Round's Third Ministerial Meeting in Seattle in November and December 1999 were a dramatic illustration of the disputes being fought over the operation of the world trading regime. These public battles reflected both intellectual and policy concerns surrounding the nature of global trade. In particular, this major dispute reveals a broad coalescence of dissatisfaction with the **liberal** international economic **order** that was established immediately after World War II. Born after a period of devastation wrought through

---

BOX 25.1: TERMINOLOGY

Key global trade terms

Economic liberalism: Perspective that favours free and open trade, separate from politics, believing that this approach maximises economic efficiency and thereby prosperity.

Economic nationalism: Government policies designed to protect local industries from foreign competition.

Embedded liberalism: Compromise struck between the free market and government control in managing the international economy.

Mercantilism: Trade policies designed to maximise state power/wealth, often at the expense of others.

*Most favoured **nation***: GATT Article I principle of non-discrimination between trading partners.

National treatment: The principle, enshrined in GATT Article III, that requires imports receive the same treatment as domestically produced goods.

Non-tariff barriers: Protection measures other than direct taxes designed to limit foreign competition. These may include quotas (or limits), sanitary regulation or import licensing.

Orderly market arrangements: Bilateral arrangements where the exporting country cooperates to limit exports. Voluntary Export Restraints (VER) and Voluntary Restraint Arrangements (VRA) are similar mechanisms.

Protection: Barriers designed to defend local producers from foreign competition.

Public goods: Goods that can continue to be enjoyed despite others' use. Benefits can extend across borders and generations; for example, a lighthouse.

Radicalism: Perspective that critiques a competitive and conflictual capitalist trading regime and argues for system change.

Rules of origin: These rules set the criteria for the assessment of the country of origin of a product.

Tariff: Customs duty on imported merchandise. Protects local goods from competition. Revenue raising for governments.

Terms of trade: Ratio of the price of export commodities against import commodities.

two world **wars** and the Great Depression, the new economic order attempted to remove barriers to trade, promote prosperity and thereby prevent a repeat of past tragedies. The emergent system sponsored by the US aimed to implement a liberal trading regime that both espoused and practised free and open trade. Part of the post-war reconstruction process involved countries profiting from access to markets and removal of barriers to capital movement. Towards the latter half of the twentieth century this process was given greater impetus through rapid developments in transportation and communication. Market internationalisation increased significantly and countries became increasingly **interdependent**. In short, international trade and prosperity expanded enormously during this period.

By 1999, however, opposition to the global trading regime had become widespread. Not only were there intellectual criticisms directed at the theoretical limitations of the free trade paradigm, but also practical concerns over the injustices of the trading regime. Criticisms mostly coalesced around the inability of the current arrangements to redress global inequities. Critics pointed to the inherent lack of distributive justice in the system (see Chapter 8). Some remonstrated that the trading regime was manipulated to advantage by a few industrialised, powerful **states**. Others protested the largesse of the profits taken from the system by **multinational corporations**. Labour groups in some industrialised countries protested the erosion of their wages as they competed with cheaper wage arrangements in developing countries, while environmentalists railed against the ever-increasing **capitalist** demands on resources.

Free trade and the international trading system

Prior to the Gobal Financial Crisis (GFC) in 2008, global trade peaked in 2004 with approximately US$8.9 trillion of merchandise goods and US$2.1 trillion in commercial services traded across national boundaries globally. In real terms export growth for 2004 was 9 per cent, which surpassed world gross domestic product (GDP) growth. The WTO documented that the dynamic traders of 2004 – and, indeed, the traders who would lead the return to global trade growth in 2010 with a 16 per cent rise in export trade through the first half of 2010 – were located in Asia, Central and South America, and the Commonwealth of Independent States (CIS, i.e. Russia and other republics of the former USSR). Some of this was fuelled by solid commodity prices and, as always, exchange rates exerted a significant influence on trade flows (World Trade Organization 2005; WTO 2010).

Trade has always been part of people's lives throughout the globe. With the extension of the Roman Empire in the West and that of the Chinese in the East, through the age of discovery to the peak of **colonial** rule in the nineteenth century, trade has been partner to the **security** agenda. It is, however, the nature of the current trading system and its origins that concern us most here. In the interwar period of the 1920s the major international economies increasingly employed protection to shield their domestic industries from imports from their international competitors. As a consequence world trade declined dramatically, with the end result being the Great Depression. With the Depression came the rise of militarism and **fascism**, culminating in World War II. Trade was perceived to be inextricably connected not only to prosperity but also to **peace**. As the US emerged from the war in a position to oversee any new international economic order and had drawn a line from economic *nationalism* to the devastation of war, it was intent on overseeing a post-war economic order based on principles of economic liberalism. Undoubtedly it was in the interests of the US to establish a system of free trade, as it would be a significant beneficiary of its ability to produce goods and services in demand by other countries. Nonetheless, the argument crafted affirmed the benefits that would be distributed to all traders in the international system. It was a positive-sum game.

These free trade arguments were derived from the work of both Adam Smith (1723–90) and David Ricardo (1772–1823), who argued that free trade, through the encouragement of competition, advanced economic efficiency and created better products and cheaper prices of goods for consumers. Smith attempted to demonstrate that 'the invisible hand' of the market, in allowing individuals to pursue private gains, would ultimately benefit the collective public interest (Adam Smith [1776] 1998: 292; see Box 3.1). Ricardo built upon this advocacy of free trade by developing the **theory** of comparative advantage. In the international economy, states received a net gain in welfare where they specialised in what they produced. This specialisation could result from their natural endowments or policy prescriptions and were those items they could produce more efficiently, relative to other countries. These products could then be traded for items produced by other states as a consequence of their comparative advantage (Ricardo [1817] 1973). For example, when we compare Australia's climate, space and topography with that of China's, we find that Australia has a comparative advantage vis-à-vis China in the production of wool versus clothing. (That is, Australia has one comparative advantage in the production of wool, whereas through the abundance of labour one of China's comparative advantages lies in the mass production of apparel.) Liberal economists argue that through this division of labour efficiencies are maximised and the international trading system can deliver benefits to all.

This theory of liberal economics was given material form in 1944 through the meeting of forty-four states at **Bretton Woods**, New Hampshire, where the new liberal economic order was constructed and the multilateral institutions of the **World Bank**, **International Monetary Fund (IMF)** and **General Agreement on Tariffs and Trade (GATT)** were established (see Chapters 24 and 26). Originally the Bretton Woods states had envisioned the International Trade Organization to establish and implement the new trading regime. However, US Senate opposition prevented its formation. Although at its formal instigation in 1947 the GATT was intended as a temporary institution, it oversaw the reduction of tariffs, particularly on manufactured goods, through multilateral trade negotiations rounds or talks until its transformation into the WTO in 1995. The driving tenet of the GATT was its category of most favoured nation (also now normal trading relations) status and national treatment rules based on principles of non-discrimination. These principles aimed to encourage trade on an open multilateral basis.

Yet, despite the intention that the GATT should be a vehicle for comprehensive trade liberalisation, there were some notable exceptions. These exemptions were granted as a consequence of the political nature of its inception and were testimony to the compromise wrought between *laissez-faire* economists and domestic interventionists, and later became known as 'embedded liberalism'. Keen to protect their farmers, the US and Western European countries exempted agricultural barriers from discussion. Discriminatory trading blocs such as the European Economic Community and the British Commonwealth, which conducted preferential trading within their membership group, were granted exemptions. Services trade, too, was initially outside the boundaries of the negotiations, principally because of its lesser import in the 1940s. Nonetheless, in much of the American literature at least, stability and maintenance of the system would be brokered by the US as a **hegemonic** power. Hegemonic stability theory posits that the dominant economy would ensure that in the liberal economic system free trade rules would be enforced (Gilpin 2001). In addition, the hegemon's responsibilities were to manage global macroeconomic policy. This included overseeing the international monetary system and acting as lender of last resort for those states in financial crisis. In the trading system the US provided the 'club good', the non-discriminatory access to US markets that underpinned the GATT (Kerr 2005). Control over production, markets and capital would not only provide collective or public goods for all but undoubtedly would benefit the hegemon.

Today, however, the US is fighting to maintain its preeminent position as production centres have moved to the East. Not only have trade 'miracles' been wrought in the East Asian environment over the past half century, but now China is increasingly asserting itself as a dominant trade partner to many states internationally. China's ascension to the WTO in 2001 and its twelve-year transition period from that point also signals the multilateral trade regime's increasingly comprehensive global nature. Moreover, that the US and China have instituted a Strategic and Economic Dialogue attests to the importance of smooth trading relations in the **bilateral** affairs between the hegemonic power and the rising power in the international system.

An imperfect system

Given that a system of autarky, a closed national trading system, is now neither efficient nor desirable, many states in the post-World War II environment sought a system where trade between countries could be conducted more freely, the barriers to trade could be reduced and as a result the prospects for prosperity and peace would be made more likely. Nevertheless, while the post-war liberal economic system was designed to remove obstacles to free trade, many still exist – and for an array of reasons. As tariffs were gradually reduced or removed an assortment of non-tariff barriers were deployed to serve the same function. In addition to both import and export quotas, financial subsidies exist to assist specific industries and producers. For example, the EU's Common Agricultural Policy (CAP) subsidies in 2008 were estimated to be worth €43 billion (although as a proportion of the EU budget this figure has been slowly declining), while in 2002 the US Farm Bill provided US$190 billion over ten years in assistance for its farmers. Some countries stringent quarantine regulations occasionally have been perceived as a vehicle for **protectionism** by stealth, by preventing the import of a range of foreign agricultural products. Furthermore, both countervailing duties (taxes on imported goods that are believed to have benefited from government subsidies) and antidumping duties (taxes designed to counteract markets being swamped by the sale of goods at below-cost prices) have been utilised to counter foreign governments' suspected use of subsidies.

These vehicles designed to promote and preserve a state's trading advantages are components of a government's strategic trade policy. In theoretical terms this is known as economic **mercantilism** and is derivative of **realist** politics. From the 1960s onwards the effects of foreign states' use of mercantilist policies were felt acutely in the US. This coincided with the threats felt by the US to its hegemonic position, arising as a consequence of the resurgence of the Japanese economy and the newly industrialising economies of Asia but also with the ongoing reconstruction of the European economies. Countries hitherto given concessions by the US as part of the **Cold War** were increasingly thought to be free riders on the US economy. That is, they were enjoying the benefits of the international system as sponsored by the US but their outlays were comparatively small. There was no question that many of the Asian states pursued a mercantilist model of economic development and that the Europeans had consistently managed a system of preferential trading.

US preparedness to underwrite the system snapped in 1971 when President Richard Nixon announced that the US would no longer guarantee fixed exchange rates, thus signalling that it was no longer prepared to underwrite the international financial system (see Chapter 26). Following this action, the **protectionist** ante was upped across the next two decades in the trade domain. The US implemented a plethora of orderly market arrangements, including voluntary export restraints to preserve domestic industries, and attempted to redress the proclivity for overextension. Consequently, by the end of the 1980s the politics of neo-mercantilism became more predominant and the international system was seen by some in increasingly **zero-sum** terms. Where possible the costs of structural adjustment would be transferred offshore through a trade policy of aggressive **unilateralism**. Competitor wheat growers were particularly affected in their third country markets by the US Export Enhancement Programme (EEP), implemented in May 1985, in which the US provided subsidies to farmers for the export of specific commodities to certain countries.

Nonetheless, the problems with the system were more widespread than those of competition between developed countries. While there were arguments, expressed particularly by the European Union and Japan, that in certain circumstances the state had a legitimate role in preserving food security in addition to sponsoring local and community interests, these multifunctionality arguments were exacerbated by the difficulties experienced by developing and least developed countries within the system. As Friedrich List (1798–1846) had theorised, government intervention was necessary to ensure the individual's interest in acquiring personal assets did not conflict with the interests of the nation. Yet, liberal economic theory remained dominant. And as Dani Rodrik has claimed, 'in many "emerging" economies traditional developmental concerns relating to industrialisation and poverty have been crowded out by the pursuit of "international competitiveness"' (Rodrik 1999: 1). Furthermore, it was argued that free trade of itself was not responsible for growth, but that macroeconomic stability and investment were more significant determinants (Rodrik 1999). Outside the mainstream discourses, radicalism developed in response to the dominance of the liberal economists. While **Marxism** informed the structure of the **communist** economies and trade between the central and Eastern European **Warsaw Pact** countries, through the 1960s and 1970s radical theorists posited that liberal economic policies and the international trading regime only exacerbated the problems of inequality. Dependency theorists argued that capitalism entrenched the wealth of the powerful states and left the developing countries in a fixed state of exploitation. **Feminists**, too, critiqued the trading regime for neglecting the effect of the system on women. The discourse of fair trade in this respect contested the ability of the existing system to provide for all in a just manner. Moreover, critics argued that instead of everyone benefiting from the rising tide of free trade, frequent storms often swamped the opportunities of some.

Currently the trading regime is beset by problems arising from these tensions. By November 1999 these critiques from both right and left coalesced around the impending WTO meeting in Seattle. The Seattle meeting was convened to establish a new round of multilateral trade negotiations. Although the critics succeeded eventually in altering the focus to one of development, by 2010 the 150 member participants in the Doha Development Round (as it came to be known) struggled to find agreement, particularly on the reduction of agricultural subsidies. If the Round collapses completely, questions will remain as to the possible marginalisation of the WTO itself and a return to a global trading system riven by competing preferential trade blocs.

Preferential trade arrangements

The inability of the current system to maintain the pace of multilateral liberalisation has provided some of the impetus for the recent spate of preferential trade arrangements. While states often refer to these arrangements as free trade agreements (FTA) or regional trade agreements (RTA), most are discriminatory in structure. Nevertheless, the WTO rules allow for these agreements as long as they incorporate substantially all sectors of trade and do not exclude others from trading. It is generally understood that the phase-in period for these arrangements should not exceed ten years. Midway through 2010 the WTO had been notified of 371 free trade agreements, of which 193 were currently in force. Not all of these agreements comply with WTO rules. For the US, the failure of the Fifth WTO Ministerial Conference in Cancun, in September 2003, to reach consensus – particularly over investment, competition, government procurement and trade facilitation measures – compounded the problems of the Seattle gridlock and drove it away from **multilateralism** and down the bilateral and regional track that led to its interest in a string of FTAs, including the Chile, Australia, Morocco, Bahrain, Peru, Oman, Singapore and Jordan FTAs. More widely it has signalled its interest in a Free Trade Agreement of the Americas.

Adding to the quest for greater access to partner country markets, there exist a number of other rationales for FTA negotiations. For those countries wishing to broaden inter-state relations FTAs can act positively to foster relations between states. As the consultations accompanying the Australia–US FTA negotiations evidenced, there is no doubt that the Congressional liaison and business links established by the Australian Embassy in Washington considerably raised Australia's profile in the US. Other factors stimulating negotiations include the weakness of existing regional institutions and attempts to hasten domestic reforms by coupling restructuring to international agreements. Some negotiations attempt to implement 'WTO plus' or 'third wave' considerations that reach beyond border constraints into areas traditionally regarded as public policy concerns. Related to this is the demonstration effect for other countries' consultations, as agreements incorporate attempts to write rules for new areas to be integrated into trade agreements. The strengthening of intellectual property rights in the US–Singapore FTA can be regarded as demonstrative of this modelling. And if the US–Israel FTA signed in 1985 was principally concerned with security objectives, arguably more of the recent FTAs are also motivated by geostrategic themes. If it can be contended that some of these contemporary FTAs demonstrate little economic benefit, then these alternate explanations such as the securitisation of trade must be considered. It should also be noted that some of these motives for bilateral or regional agreements have proved no less contentious in the public domain, as the opposition to the NAFTA (North American Free Trade Agreement) has testified.

It is also evident that the current US interest in a trans-Pacific partnership agreement (TPP) with Chile, Australia, New Zealand, Vietnam, Brunei, Singapore and Peru flags its interest in moving the trade liberalisation agenda forward after this process was stalled, not only in the Doha Round but also in the current trans-Pacific forum of **APEC**. What is more, this agreement also declares the US pursuit to maintain its trade presence in Asia and its concurrent interest in surmounting oppositional forces which may have designs in orchestrating more exclusivist Asian forums.

Reform of the trading system?

Clearly, world trade is affected by the expansion in the integration of economies internationally. As communications and transport technologies improve, so too does the opportunity for product supply chains to be internationalised, for more rapid and integrated financial coordination to occur, for multinational corporations to conduct business and for the movement of people to occur more freely. These changes, as part of the processes of **globalisation** (see Chapter 28), can increase the prospects for trade exchanges to occur. However, the trade consequences of globalisation remain hotly debated. Proponents argue that the global production and marketplace has resulted in increased opportunity and unprecedented prosperity, together with a consequent reduction in conflict. It is axiomatic, however, that those beneficiaries have most likely been the mature economies with strong governance structures.

Yet others have argued that prior to World War I, where significant tracts around the globe were integrated into the British Empire, the forces of globalisation were much more persuasive. Critics both then and now argue that these liberalising changes have only brought heightened prosperity to those best placed to maximise opportunities, and have magnified the North–South divide. Hence, they say, globalisation is not operating on a level playing field and has only exacerbated the disparity between rich and poor at both intra- and inter-state levels (see Box 25.2). Others argue that trade liberalisation as a consequence of globalisation also functions to dissipate the power of the state and corrode state sovereignty. The 'third wave' trade agreements that affect social policy would be cited as illustrative of this point.

BOX 25.2: DISCUSSION POINTS

Agricultural trading reform and the Cairns Group

In August 1986 a group of disparate agricultural 'fair traders', separate to the major players but producers of approximately 25 per cent of agricultural trade, met in Cairns, Australia, to plan a strategy for the GATT Punta del Este meeting to launch the Uruguay Round of trade negotiations. Their intent was to maximise their negotiating clout to liberalise the trade in agriculture (Snape et al. 1998). Ultimately the Cairns Group achieved some limited success in forcing agriculture onto the multilateral agenda, but nonetheless the intransigence of the major states to eliminate subsidies remained robust.

Overall it would seem that as the Bretton Woods agreement endeavoured to produce a mix of market forces and government control to manage the international economy some sixty-five years ago, the policies of embedded liberalism within the trade regime may be most appropriate to allow for both economic growth and development. Not only does the improvement of people's quality of life internationally require the conditions for peace and stability with strong governance structures at the intrastate level, but Joseph Stiglitz argues that reforms to the global trade regime are inherent in the process. He cites reforms which include: the granting of 'special and differentiated treatment' for least developed and developing countries in trade agreements; extended market access to poor countries (similar to the EU's 'Everything but Arms' policy decision to provide quota- and tariff-free access for all imports except armaments from the fifty least developed countries); the reduction of rich country agricultural subsidies, non-tariff and technical barriers to trade; and, the review of the rules of origin arrangements whereby poorer countries can be isolated from the profits of the production process (Stiglitz 2006). He also argues for greater scrutiny of preferential trade agreements and reform of the institutions governing the trade regime to counter the problems of unfair agenda setting, negotiations and enforcement (Stiglitz 2006). Ultimately, too, those interested in reform remain cognisant of the benefits that a fairer trading system will have in the promotion of international security.

The Global Financial Crisis and trade

World trade has experienced long periods of extended expansion and delivered some spectacular profits, but it has also suffered some severe recessionary setbacks. These were induced in 1974–75 by the oil price rise shocks, in 1982–83 by the combination of inflation and unemployment (i.e stagflation), and in 2001–02 by the 'techwreck' (Baldwin 2009). Trade volume contractions over these periods were 0.2 per cent, 2 per cent and 7 per cent respectively. Figure 25.1 reveals the extent to which world imports of goods and services were affected by these crises.

However, the most significant contraction in world trade began in late 2008 as a consequence of a financial crisis emanating out of the US housing market and banking system, where the shock of the Lehman Brothers merchant bankruptcy induced a consumption and lending crisis that spread globally and dramatically (see Chapter 26). Not since the Great Depression had world trade suffered such a significant setback (see Figure 25.1). And as Figure 25.2 demonstrates, the Global Financial Crisis (GFC) was more precipitious in its immediate effect than even the Great Depression.

Figure 25.1   The great trade collapses in historical perspective, 1965–2009

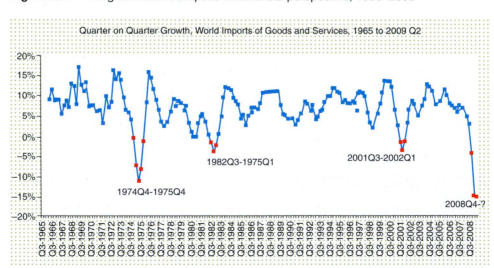

Source: OECD Quarterly real trade data.

Figure 25.2   The volume of world trade, now vs then

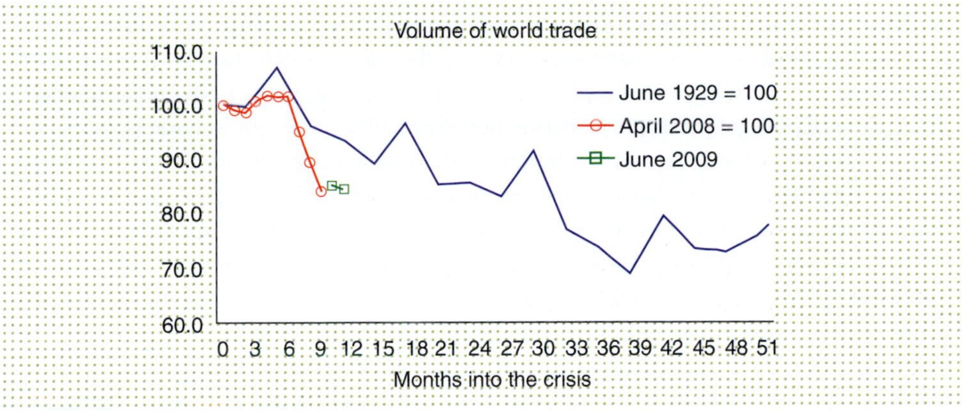

Source: Barry Eichengreen and Kevin O'Rourke, 'What do the new data tell us' *Vox*, 8 March 2010, and 'A tale of two depressions: now and then', *Vox*, 6 April 2009, www.voxeu.org/index.php?q=node/3421#jun09.

By 2009 world trade had contracted by 12.2 per cent (WTO 2010a: 18). So why the fall in trade of such magnitude and also immediacy? Economists have agreed on a few key explanations. Principally, the real estate crisis and attendant banking crisis precipitated a collapse in demand initially in the US and then elsewhere in the globe. It also limited the availability of credit in the international system. The extent to which the banking sector but also global supply chains are interconnected is explanatory of the synchronised effects of the crisis. In short, people delayed purchases of consumer goods, such as cars, as they carefully weighed up their financial future. For businesses, the lack of credit in some cases delayed investment decisions, and in others foreclosed factories. The flow-on effect of an employment crisis further reduced demand. In industry too, the iron and steel producers were intimately affected by factory shutdowns and the shrinking purchase of machinery together with the collapse of construction in the real estate sector. Moreover, both the global and 'just in time' production features of the supply chain not only sensitise the system to downturns in other geographic regions but also ensure that it is immediately responsive (Baldwin 2009). An additional statistical effect of the global supply chain is to skew the impact on trade results. On each occasion where a good in the production process transits a national boundary it is recorded in the trade data. Although ultimately only one product may be manufactured, its component parts may all have been recorded in the trade statistics. Hence, the double counting factor may exacerbate the picture of the dramatic decline in trade as partner to the contemporary recession.

Prospects for recovery

The drive to recovery from the GFC included the restoration of global trade, in part fuelled by government stimulus packages. As a result, employment opportunities were undergoing a revival in most countries. In the first half of 2010 world trade expanded almost as dramatically as it had contracted in the previous year. So quick was this year-on-year expansion that it was the fastest recorded since 1950. Albeit off this low base, the WTO economists predicted that in 2010 trade growth would reach 13.5 per cent (WTO 2010b), with the developing countries recording a higher level of growth than the advanced economies. However, as the government assistance measures conclude the pace of growth is unlikely to be maintained. Two of the dangers here are that the structural adjustment that has occurred as a consequence of the recession will have enduring effects in the form of political pressures to pursue neomercantilist protectionist trade policies, and that the prospects for reform of the trading system which will require the rich countries to offer concessions to the least developed countries will be less likely. Given the unmet expectations in the mature economies that the crisis has wrought, the polity may be less able but also less inclined to assist those outside their immediate national concern. The test for the newly constituted **G20**, which attempts to reflect the new exigencies of power in the international system, will be to address these problems in an equitable fashion and by doing so confirm its legitimacy as a preeminent global institution.

One particular trade aspect of any recovery is the need to manage the likely revitalisation of the trade in, and the volatility of prices of, natural resources: namely, the trade in mining and energy resources, fish stocks and forestry products. Water may also eventually be considered in this group. History is replete with examples of conflict emanating from the limitations of resource availability. One only need look to the restrictions on Japanese access to resources in the 1930s to realise how the road to conflict is exacerbated by the uneven distribution of resources. Thus, specific problems to be managed that are associated with this resource group include its uneven availability to countries intent on industrialisation and the converse problem of 'the Dutch disease' for those countries whose abundant natural resource stocks delay the development of a manufacturing, technological or service base. These concerns, together with the problem of global resource exhaustion and the environmental impact of resource misuse, will mandate greater international cooperation and regulation (WTO 2010a).

Conclusion: systemic recovery and reform

There is no question that trade has contributed significantly to many people's quality of life globally. The current test for governments and the international trading regime, however, is to ensure that a durable recovery occurs after the worst financial crisis in eighty years and that the gains derived from international trade can be sustained and are more equitably distributed. By doing so they will act to reduce the likelihood of conflict both at the local and international level. The challenge also falls to the G20 and the WTO to assist in coordinating efforts to do so and to sponsor the openness of the trading regime. By fostering a prosperous trading regime the G20 will also ensure its prospects for legitimacy. No doubt, however, trading tensions between countries will persist and the battles over the nature of the trading regime will continue. Current questions also remain as to whether the attention that states have devoted to bilateral and regional trade agreements have detracted from their capacity to focus resources on the WTO regime, or whether they will spur the resolution of the multilateral negotiations. Although the Doha Round of talks have stalled for some years, the WTO is well aware that if a complete collapse or an eventual hollow finale is agreed upon it is likely that damage will be inflicted on the legitimacy of the WTO itself. If it survives – and it is improbable that a wholesale dismantling of the current regime will occur – it is reasonable to insist that the system be modified to incorporate greater attention to issues of distributive justice and resource management.

QUESTIONS

1. Is economic efficiency the only consideration in determining the nature of the trading regime?

2. Is trade fair? If not, how can this be resolved? Should this be resolved?

3. How does domestic politics affect trade?

4. To what extent should domestic policy be influenced by trade policy and 'third wave' trade agreements?

5. Does trade reduce poverty?

6. How has the Global Financial Crisis affected trade? How can the system recover?

FURTHER READING

Baldwin, Richard (ed.) 2009, *The great trade collapse: causes, consequences and prospects*, London: Centre for Economic Policy Research.

Capling, Ann 2001, *Australia and the global trade system: from Havana to Seattle*, Cambridge: Cambridge University Press. An excellent account of Australia's place in the global trading system.

Gilpin, Robert 2001, *Global political economy: understanding the international economic order*, Princeton: Princeton University Press. A comprehensive account of the history and competing ideologies of international political economy.

Keohane, Robert O. and Nye, Joseph [1977] 1989, *Power and interdependence*, 3rd edn, Boston: Little Brown.

Stiglitz, Joseph 2006, *Making globalization work*, London: Norton. The former World Bank senior vice president and chief economist's endeavours to improve and shape the global trading system.

World Trade Organization, 2010a, *World trade report 2010*, Geneva, www.wto.org/english/res_e/booksp_e/anrep_e/world_trade_report10_e.pdf.

26

Global Finance

Leonard Seabrooke

Introduction	361
Death of the last great financial globalisation, 1900–45	362
The rise and fall of the Bretton Woods system, 1946–71	363
Domestic stagflation and international over-lending, 1972–81	364
Debt crises at home and abroad, 1982–92	365
Talking about architecture, 1993–2000	366
Promises, promises: credit booms and liquidity busts, 2001 to the present	368
Conclusion: how should we study global finance?	369
Questions	370
Further reading	370

Introduction

This chapter presents a fleeting history of key changes in global finance during the past century based around the themes of crisis, architecture and socialisation, with an emphasis on the role of US **power** in shaping global finance. Through these three themes we can see why global finance has become increasingly internationally institutionalised, as well as how it is having an ever-greater impact on our everyday lives. The first section of the chapter discusses global finance in the first half of the twentieth century. The second section considers the emergence of the post-World War II **Bretton Woods regime**. The third section outlines the rise of private capital in the 1970s. The fourth section traces the impact of the debt crisis of the 1980s. The fifth section considers discussions of global financial architecture in the 1990s. Finally, the sixth section discusses the role of surveillance and re-regulation in our contemporary global financial system. Key international regimes are listed in Box 26.1.

Who is afraid of the global financial system?

Within international relations, calls for the study of global finance were initially based on fears that market actors had gained the upper hand over **states** after the collapse of the Bretton Woods system of international finance (explained below). It was thought that the international political economy would be prone to frequent and severe economic crises, with advanced industrial economies forced to dismantle their welfare regimes at the behest of international financial competition. Increased power to financial markets, the logic followed, would also increase developing states' structural economic dependence on the West as the drive for increasing profits led to a more aggressive extraction of resources and exploitation of cheap labour.

Since this foundational work, the study of global finance in international relations typically considers three key themes: (1) crisis – why the contemporary world economy is prone to international financial crises; (2) architecture – how to combat crises through international institutions and organisations; and, most recently, (3) financial socialisation – how financial innovations in domestic systems are changing global finance. The most common aspect of all three is the role of the US as the '**hegemon**' within the global financial system, as it respectively exercises: market power through financial competition and innovation; state power through its treatment of international regimes on global finance; and a combination of state and market power as it propagates new financial practices among its population to broaden and deepen its domestic financial system, with global implications (see Seabrooke 2006a). The US economy is also critical to the character of global finance since the size of its capital and current account deficits directly influence world interest rates.

BOX 26.1: KEY ORGANISATIONS

Key international regimes for global finance

African Development Bank – www.afdb.org
Asian Development Bank – www.adb.org
Bank for International Settlements – www.bis.org
European Bank for Reconstruction and Development – www.ebrd.com
European Central Bank – www.ecb.int

Financial Stability Board – www.financialstabilityboard.org
Group of Twenty (**G20**) – www.g20.org
Inter-American Development Bank – www.iadb.org
International Accounting Standards Board – www.iasb.org
International Association of Insurance Supervisors – www.iaisweb.org
International Monetary Fund – www.imf.org
International Organization of Securities Commissions – www.iosco.org
Islamic Development Bank – www.isdb.org
Joint Vienna Institute – www.jvi.org
Organisation for Economic Cooperation and Development – www.oecd.org
Paris Club – www.clubdeparis.org
United Nations Conference on Trade and Development – www.unctad.org
World Bank Group – www.worldbank.org
World Federation of Exchanges – www.world-exchanges.org

Death of the last great financial globalisation, 1900–45

It is difficult to imagine the death of financial **globalisation**, but it has happened before. In fact, the world experienced intense financial globalisation a century ago and has only returned to a period of high international capital mobility in recent decades, after decades of **war** and national **capitalism**. The earlier form of financial globalisation differed greatly from our own in the nature of its financial crises, the extent to which the international financial **order**'s architecture was centred on international organisations, and the depth of financial socialisation within domestic economies. First, the centre for this earlier international financial order was not New York but the City of London. Some 40 per cent of all debt securities in the world were issued from London, and it has been suggested that one-third of British wealth was invested abroad (the US financial market today is overwhelmingly domestic). Most of this investment was going into what we would now call 'emerging market economies', which, in this earlier period of globalisation, included states like Australia, Argentina, Denmark, the US and others. Nearly one-fifth of investment went to Latin American states, and the common form of investment was in government debt and heavy industries such as railways, mining and metallurgy (see Seabrooke 2006b: 151). In fact, compared to our own period of financial globalisation, there was much greater investment from advanced economies into emerging market economies. Financial crises during this period were quite different from now. While today's crises are short, sharp shocks, crises over a century ago were slow-burning affairs. The most recent financial crisis (2008–09), for example, provided massive amounts of financial bursts in a short period of time, fuelled by capital that was more transatlantic than it was from advanced economies to emerging market economies. One reason why nineteenth- and early twentieth-century crises were slow to be addressed was that the international financial order lacked centralised organisations that could resolve information problems concerning a state's creditworthiness. Instead, private associations, like the Corporation for Foreign Bondholders (Lipson 1985), coordinated information to assess creditworthiness and sent it back to London investors to judge. Given this rickety system, foreign investors called for state support to protect their investments, as occurred with the sending of British warships to Latin America in the early 1900s.

The pairing of intense financial globalisation and the threat of the use of state-sanctioned force led many actors to call for international regulation that could separate private investment from public violence. During ongoing conferences in The Hague, various national elites called for the formation of a new international financial architecture. Particularly prominent here was Luis Drago, an Argentinean lawyer, who in 1907 successfully called for an agreement among states that public violence should not be used to enforce private investments. This 'Drago Doctrine' was strongly supported by the US and can be seen as an extension of Monroe Doctrine principles: that European powers should keep their noses out of Latin America. Within Europe itself, there was a long-standing perception that global finance was becoming too speculative. In 1912 an international convention to create an international register of securities trading was supported by European states but rejected by the US and the UK as too invasive on individual rights and economic freedoms.

The US and UK choice to reject the close international monitoring of speculative capital in global finance was not a reflection of mass public will. Financial socialisation in the leading financial powers did not extend to the general population. Rather, especially in the British case, it was based on 'rentiers' – those who earn money from 'unproductive' passive investments, like being a landlord or investing in government debt (Seabrooke 2006a: ch. 3). In part as a consequence of financial wealth being concentrated among a small elite, the principal centres of global finance were very prone to external shocks. World War I provided an enormous shock as high levels of international capital mobility collapsed. Many investors were caught out with financial relationships in states that were now enemies, clearly unable to see the link between their dependence on **imperialist** forms of investment and the rising militarism associated with it. During the reconstruction of global finance in the 1920s, domestic financial systems once again were concentrated among small elite groups and with thin governmental regulations. The lack of financial socialisation encouraged speculation and herd-like behaviour in domestic and international financial markets (only 1.2 per cent of Americans had brokerage accounts; see Seabrooke 2001: 61). The Great Depression of the late 1920s and early 1930s was indicative of a general contraction of economic activity throughout the world. This was only corrected by a change in thinking to **Keynesian** economics and more interventionist governments in the 1930s and 1940s during World War II.

The rise and fall of the Bretton Woods system, 1946–71

The formation of the Bretton Woods system in the late 1940s was centred on the idea that global finance should serve national purposes. The system was embodied in its new key international institutions, the **International Monetary Fund (IMF)** and the International Bank for Reconstruction and Development (the **World Bank**). For monetary affairs, in particular, the IMF's Articles of Agreement set out that all of its member states should seek to maintain high levels of growth and employment, and that they should avoid the types of predatory currency practices seen during the Great Depression. This system ideally provided the 'embedded **liberalism** compromise'

(Ruggie 1982), where states engaged in pro-growth international finance and trade while also retaining the right to steer their domestic welfare regimes. The key for the new system was the rule that states would keep in check their domestic currencies in relation to a fixed exchange rate of US$35 per ounce of gold. This 'gold-dollar' standard would ideally ensure that all states in the global system would not fall into 'fundamental disequilibrium' with global standards (J. Best 2005).

The key financial crises that occurred during the duration of the Bretton Woods system reflected its purposes and ambiguities; they were primarily the problem of states dealing with their currencies and capital accounts to stay within the official system. So, while we think of the IMF as an organisation that deals only with developing states, during the 1960s many Western states organised loans from the IMF (this has only recently returned, with countries such as Iceland, Greece and others under IMF packages following crises). One important source of financial problems during the 1960s was that much financial trading increasingly took place through an unofficial system. From the mid-1950s the development of 'Euromarkets' allowed financial actors to wrestle autonomy away from the state – an autonomy it had maintained since the Great Depression. The Euromarkets are a bit of a mind-bender. The markets were named 'Euro' because they were primarily located in London and Paris, although legally they operated in no-man's land. The markets were anonymous, untaxed and highly liquid secondary markets for securities (meaning the trading of IOUs among third parties, not the issuer) and for currency trading. Between 1960 and 1970 the size of the 'Eurocurrency' market expanded from US$2 billion to US$57 billion, while 'Eurobond' and foreign bond markets grew from US$0.8 billion to US$5.3 billion (Webb 1995: 98). This private system for global finance provided states and financial institutions with more options than the official system. The US Government also implicitly supported it, since it favoured the expansion of US banks overseas during a period in which they were trying to maintain high growth with little inflation inside the US. Within the US, the growth of 'People's Capitalism' included greater participation in the stock market from the population, and the generation of institutions for financial socialisation: VISA and Mastercard, for example, both started up business during this time (Seabrooke 2001: 60–1).

In this period the key problem for global finance was that the US dollar was the world currency. It was controlled by governments with international responsibilities but a domestic electorate. Given the growth of Euromarkets, there was a great degree of uncertainty and speculation about the real value of the US dollar in relation to an ounce of gold. The architecture for global finance groaned under the weight of such speculation. In the late 1960s and early 1970s many central banks called the US's bluff by exchanging their US dollars for gold at $35 per ounce, when in private markets the rate was thought to be US$41 per ounce. Eventually, under such pressure, President Richard Nixon closed the 'gold window' in August 1971, claiming that the US had been subsidising the world economy for too long (Seabrooke 2001: 73–80).

Domestic stagflation and international over-lending, 1972–81

Nixon's closing of the 'gold window' and the sheer weight of private capital now in the world economy signalled a change in global finance away from state-led to market-led forms of governance (Helleiner 1994). The collapse of the 'gold-dollar' exchange rate system soon gave way to a 'paper-dollar' system, despite attempts to coordinate a new fixed exchange rate regime based on the IMF's currency, Special Drawing Rights (Seabrooke 2001: 85–7). The new floating and flexible system was fuelled also by the massive amount of private capital generated by the Organization of the Petroleum Exporting Countries' (OPEC) oil crisis of 1973–4. During this crisis, Arab oil-producing states strongly signalled their opposition to Western support for Israel during the Arab-Israeli 'Yom Kippur' War by using the 'oil weapon' to quadruple oil prices for Western states. The huge sums of capital transferred to OPEC states then became recycled 'petrodollars' through the Euromarkets.

Financial crises during this period reflected the increased privatisation of global finance, as well as states learning to manage and regulate a global financial order with a capacity for self-implosion not seen since the 1920s. In particular, Keynesian economic thinking was given a shock as states experienced high unemployment and high inflation at the same time (a phenomenon called 'stagflation' that had previously been thought unlikely). Western economies slowed down despite vast increases in the amount of private capital within the world economy. International banks then began to compensate for weak domestic lending activity by using petrodollars (capital derived from the oil crisis invested in the Euromarkets) for lending to developing states. Such 'over-lending' boomed during the mid-1970s as mainly US banks, within international bank syndicates (where, say, ten banks each take a share in a loan), lent 'jumbo' loans of US$500 million and 'mammoth' loans of US$1 billion. Eighty per cent of these loans went to the governments of developing states. At the same time as such over-lending, banks dropped their 'capital adequacy ratios', the amount of money they keep aside in proportion to their loans in case there is a crisis (Seabrooke 2001: 95). Banks also engaged in increasingly speculative activity on foreign currency trading, leading to major bank collapses in Germany and the US, with the Bank for International Settlements (BIS) calling for a new international financial architecture to improve banks' capital adequacy ratios.

Within Western states the liberalisation of banks' activities in international markets saw a parallel in domestic markets, with customers calling for greater flexibility in how they managed their accounts and for more competitive interest rates. In the US, in particular, the development of cash management accounts and the removal of interest cap restrictions signalled the forthcoming wave of financial socialisation.

Debt crises at home and abroad, 1982–92

Most of the jumbo and mammoth loans of the 1970s were issued by US banks and in US dollars. The governments within emerging market economies who had to repay these loans needed foreign export earnings to pay off their loans. In the early 1980s the ongoing stagflation in Western economies and an international problem of 'surplus capacity' in production (basically a glut) made it very difficult for borrowing governments to repay their loans – which meant that borrowing states faced an export earnings trade deficit crisis. Given this, in 1982 the Mexican Government declared that it needed four months of non-payment or it would face a major crisis. Similar experiences occurred throughout the Americas and also in Eastern Europe. This debt crisis shook the US financial system to its core, since the top US banks had grossly overcommitted capital within syndicated bank loans. The consequence was that the big international banks went to the London Club where borrower repayment negotiations for private interests were coordinated, while the G5 states (the US, UK, France, Japan and Germany) discussed coordinating debt repayments at the 'Paris Club'. International organisations, namely the IMF and the World Bank, were also brought in to reform the affected borrower states. The use of structural adjustment programs in Latin America gave international organisations, and especially the IMF, bad reputations for decades to follow because of stringent conditions imposed on the way governments managed their finances.

Changes to the global financial architecture were, of course, directly informed by the debt crisis. The most prominent change was the development of the first of the Basel Accords in 1988 from the Basel Committee on Banking Supervision (BCBS), which is under the auspices of the Bank for International Settlements. This new regime for international financial regulation introduced different risk weightings for the different kinds of assets banks held. The regime gave a clear advantage to US banks and was a clear disadvantage to Japanese banks, which had to buy an enormous amount of safe assets, namely US Treasury bonds. The US was able to exercise its structural power in the global financial system by changing the rules of the game in its favour (Strange 1988).

The US was able to extend its advantage, not only through shaping the rules of the game internationally but also through innovations that spurred on financial socialisation in its domestic system. In particular, one key effect of the debt crisis was that banks moved away from traditional loans and towards disintermediation and securitisation (see Box 26.2). During the 1980s and early 1990s the US Government supported these changes by enabling regulations for en masse mortgage securitisation (where financial institutions can package a dedicated income stream from a mortgage into new debt to be sold to an investor in return for capital to keep lending) (Seabrooke 2006a: 123–7), as well as permitting commercial banks to trade securities (which was banned during the Great Depression). Financial socialisation spurred further innovations within the US domestic market that gave US financial institutions a competitive advantage in global finance, as well as attracting international investment into US markets.

Talking about architecture, 1993–2000

By the mid-1990s the intensity of financial globalisation present at the beginning of the century had returned. The number of financial crises reflected the increased intensity of capital mobility in the system. These financial crises, like those in earlier decades, were primarily concerned with the repayment of debts. However, unlike in the 1980s debt crisis, in the 1990s the problem was

---

BOX 26.2: TERMINOLOGY

Disintermediation and securitisation

To understand many of the changes during our most recent period of financial globalisation, two processes are crucial to keep in mind.

The first is *disintermediation*. Disintermediation is the process of moving away from traditional forms of lending, like bank loans, into the use of debt securities (essentially 'IOUs') by states and markets. Basically, banks have been increasingly behaving more like brokers than lenders.

The second process is *securitisation*. Securitisation is the process of backing or supporting debt securities with steady streams of income, like a home mortgage or even a car loan payment.

Both processes, originated in the US, have revolutionised global finance since the 1980s and led to a much stronger international emphasis on creditworthiness and surveillance.

not typically a lack of export earnings but a liquidity problem (having the ready cash) at moments when investors chose to withdraw their capital. Such problems were related to the spread of disintermediation as a preferred way of doing finance, with financial institutions choosing to use short-term bonds that could easily be withdrawn from the borrower, rather than using more traditional loans.

Many emerging market economies embraced this new way of financing, with their issuance of bonds for government debt increasing from US$13.9 billion in total in 1991 to US$127.9 billion in 1997 (L. Mosley 2003: 108). By the late 1990s most emerging market economies were using bond financing rather than loans as their principal means of financing. And with opportunity comes risk. To engage in global bond markets states were required to liberalise their capital accounts, with many emerging market economies permitting rapid inward investments with weak regulations or oversight of whether the investments were sound.

As a consequence of these processes, the 1990s was peppered with crises related to nervousness over the value of a home currency where borrowers had to repay on short-term debt securities in US dollars. This scenario occurred in Mexico in 1993–94 when government debt denominated in dollars faced massive capital flight when US investors thought the peso was overvalued. It happened in Southeast Asia in 1997 when mainly Japanese and European investors became nervous about the value of their investments in real estate and the stock market, given a potential currency collapse. And it happened in Russia in 1998, as investors and international organisations clamoured to save investments when the stock market, and the government's capacity to repay debts, collapsed (Seabrooke 2001: 165–85). In all of these crises, changes in the value of the US dollar, altered through US interest rates, played a crucial role, especially as many states had adopted 'currency pegs' where they moved the value of their own currency in accordance with the dollar. In short, an interest rate spike in the US sent quick shockwaves to emerging market economies, which had to push up their own currencies, in turn feeding speculation over their capacity to do so. In all of these crises the role of the US in international organisations was questioned during a period in which the changing shape of global finance gave it more power over decision-making. For example, within the IMF the approval of a 'special decision' for an extraordinarily big loan requires 85 per cent of members' votes. Votes within the IMF are allocated according to subscriptions and the US held between 17 and 18 per cent of the vote throughout the 1990s. As such, loans to Mexico, Thailand, etc. came under the scrutiny of the US Congress, which did exercise its right to veto loans. The consequence was that large international loans for crisis financing were increasingly cobbled together by the IMF in association with the BIS and wealthy member states (Seabrooke 2006a: 187–8). The IMF was then criticised as a puppet for US foreign economic policy, leading it to try to publicly demonstrate its own transparency and accountability through the establishment of an Independent Evaluation Office in 2001.

More generally, there was a shift in the global financial architecture in the 1990s as international organisations placed less stress on enforcement and more emphasis on common global standards. There was an efflorescence of forums to increase cooperation among international organisations, including agreements between the IMF, BIS, World Bank, and Organisation for Economic Cooperation and Development (OECD), on data-sharing. Finance ministers within the most powerful states held numerous meetings on the 'global financial architecture' to try to harmonise financial regulations. In 1999 they created a Financial Stability Forum, which now includes twenty-six states (including Australia), the BIS, IMF, OECD and the World Bank, as well as expert committees.

Finance ministers and international organisations were right to be concerned with introducing greater means for data-sharing and surveillance in the global financial system, since the creation and diffusion of financial innovations continued apace. Within the US in particular, financial socialisation led to greater securitisation of mortgages and even consumer debt, as well as greater investment in stock and bond markets as institutional investors, especially those controlling workers' pension funds, became ever more prominent.

Promises, promises: credit booms and liquidity busts, 2001 to the present

Once dust settled from the big financial crises of the 1990s, work in the 2000s was initially focused on surveillance and containment. During the first half of the decade financial crises were short, sharp shocks based around currency speculation or asset overvaluation. They were highly localised within corporate scandals, such as the accounting scandals at Enron and World Com. After the mid-2000s the growth of credit and the intensification of short-term capital flows escalated, while regulation gave more and more control to banks who could demonstrate that they had adequate risk-management technologies. There was also a consensus around creditworthiness and surveillance by private and public international organisations. With faith in this expanding system of self-regulation and the failure to pop asset bubbles, the conditions for the most recent financial crisis – the Global Financial Crisis – were established.

Particularly important in the 2000s was the growth of what we can call 'quasi-regulators' with private authority for governance of the global financial architecture. Especially important here is the role of bond rating agencies. These agencies, such as Standard and Poor's and Moody's, provide evaluations of the creditworthiness of governments' and corporations' debt securities. While it is difficult to deny that they raise classic conflict of interest concerns, their opinions are considered crucially important by financial market traders in the global financial system (Sinclair 2005: 147). International organisations embraced the role of these agencies, including the integration of Basel Accord II (2004) risk-weightings and stress on self-regulation into broader international standards and codes, leading to the questionable logic of applying rules designed for financial institutions in advanced industrial economies to those in frontier economies. In principle, the increased role of surveillance and creditworthiness assessments provides emerging market and frontier economies with some capacity to provide clear signs of their creditworthiness and attract more investment. It also makes them conform to what could be called a 'global standard of market civilisation' (Seabrooke 2006b). States and economies that fail to do so are increasingly punished in the global financial system, not only through a lack of access to capital, but also through international 'naming and shaming' techniques from international organisations. The OECD's campaign to 'blacklist' small island tax havens provides one particularly interesting case (Sharman 2006).

Much of the increased surveillance and checks for creditworthiness in global markets can be attributed to their prominence within the US domestic financial system and its now intense financial socialisation. The GFC demonstrated the ill effects of excessive financialisation. While the US leads the world in minority shareholder protection legislation to protect those with pensions (Gourevitch and Shinn 2005), the expansion of credit post-2003 in the US occurred during a period of no real wage growth and left many vulnerable to economic doldrums should the bubble burst. And it did. The most recent financial crisis has frequently been pinned on 'subprime' markets in the US: loans provided to borrowers with impeded creditworthiness. In reality, this was only the headline for financial recklessness and the real culprit was the risk-management models and persistent short-termism that led such volumes of capital to search for yield from seemingly mundane investments such as mortgages. In considering the origins of the crisis and the likely prospect of a new crisis following the next bubble, a number of influential scholars and commissions have suggested that the most important element to be considered is how we evaluate risk at the systemic level, and how credit, market and liquidity risks are tied to both the function of institutions and the market as a whole (see University of Warwick 2009). Others have considered how the financial system is intimately linked to the 'real' economy, including national welfare needs. These are all important questions in thinking through who was to blame for the crisis and who is to pay for its consequences.

The GFC was the biggest crisis in advanced industrial economies since the Great Depression and required huge 'bailouts' from governments to help the financial sector in various economies. These taxpayer-funded rescues were initially offered on the basis that national and international financial architecture would be reformed. Other than the creation of the Financial Stability Board in 2009 and hopes for broader international fora to provide better financial governance, not much of substance has occurred. We can see a lot of movement from the Group of Twenty Finance Ministers and Central Bank Governors (G20), which replaced the former Group of Eight (**G8**) as the most relevant international forum for discussing economic and financial international cooperation. The expansion of the G20's powers has arguably led to greater inclusiveness among what were quite exclusive clubs composed of wealthy northwestern European economies and North America and Japan. The BCBS, for example, expanded its membership to the current twenty-seven, including countries such as India, Indonesia and Saudi Arabia. An expanded and more representative membership does not, by itself, create change (this is a common theme for scholars of International Organisation). The Basel III regime, to be phased in by 2019, places emphasis on fighting procyclical lending and has reconsidered its risk frameworks, but there is no fundamental change in how the framework favours large banks in advanced industrial economies. One explanation is that socialisation among regulators and bankers alike has been particularly intense and changing rules requires fundamental changes in behaviour and incentives.

Conclusion: how should we study global finance?

This chapter has provided a lightning history of global finance in the twentieth century until the present, with an emphasis on US influence in global finance. Let us finish by considering how the processes discussed here relate to theories of international relations. The two main approaches to studying global finance within international relations are those associated with **realism** (Chapter 2) and **neoliberalism** (Chapter 3), on the one hand, and neo-**Gramscian** Critical Theory (Chapter 4) and constructivism (Chapter 7), on the other. Neoliberals and realists commonly focus on states as actors competing with each other for financial power and the determination of currency values; seeing private financial relations as an extension of a state's foreign economic policy; and 'principal–agent' problems between international organisations and their member-states (basically, asking 'who is in charge?') (see L. Mosley 2003). This perspective tries to map assumed self-interests (wanting more wealth and power) and sees national structures as more or less having fixed characteristics over time. Most of the time these approaches get it right in being able to *explain* a lot. However, constructivists and neo-Gramscian Critical Theorists place more emphasis on seeking to *understand* how actors form their preferences on the grounds that self-interest is not automatically given to actors but framed within a social context. As such, the neo-Gramscian literature has typically focused on explaining the evolution of long-term material structures for global finance by identifying actors who are able to use a mixture of coercion and consent to legitimate policy changes (Germain 1997). Separate to this, the constructivist literature has focused on how ideas can be used as weapons to change the appropriateness of certain financial policies (see Kirschner 2003), as well as studies of how financial power rests on social legitimacy (Seabrooke 2006a). After all, if the stability of the global financial system is dependent on increasingly complex webs of regulation and surveillance, it is crucial that all the players have the right idea about how the game should be played.

QUESTIONS

1. Why is the global financial system naturally prone to crisis?
2. What were the key features of the Bretton Woods system?
3. What are the main features of contemporary global financial regulation?
4. To what degree are global financial markets shaped by private authorities?
5. How have developments in global finance changed the character of states?
6. What caused the Asian financial crisis? What caused the subprime crisis? How are the causes different?

FURTHER READING

Germain, Randall 2010, *Global politics and financial governance*, New York: Palgrave. Fine book suggesting that long-term trends in international financial governance are likely to lead to a system based on global governance and national responsibility as national interest is reasserted.

Helleiner, Eric 1994, *States and the reemergence of global finance*, Ithaca: Cornell University Press. Classic text tracing the evolution of the politics of the post-war global financial system, clashes between key states, and the transition to more market-driven forms of power.

Helleiner, Eric, Pagliari, Stefano and Zimmermann, Hubert (eds) 2010, *Global finance in crisis*, London: Routledge. Excellent volume exploring the regulatory responses to the crisis at the national, regional and international levels, including a range of public and private actors.

Schwartz, Herman M. 2009, *Subprime nation*, Ithaca: Cornell University Press. Investigates the foundations of the 2007–9 international financial crisis, especially the international links to American housing and financial markets.

Schwartz, Herman M. and Seabrooke, Leonard (eds), 2009, *The politics of property booms*, New York: Palgrave. Edited volume that brings together a range of scholars working on how the transnationalisation of housing finance intersects with the national systems for housing and welfare. The authors explore a range of cases in the OECD, including the origins of the 2007–9 crisis.

Seabrooke, Leonard 2006a, *The social sources of financial power*, Ithaca: Cornell University Press. Discusses how state intervention in everyday finance contributes to the state's international financial capacity when the majority of the population view the normative (not material) structures underpinning taxation, credit and housing to be legitimate. It explores two historical periods and four cases (US, UK, Germany and Japan).

Sinclair, Timothy J. 2005, *The new masters of capital*, Ithaca: Cornell University Press. Traces the emergence and importance of bond-rating agencies in global finance that have the power to punish and reward governments and corporations.

Singer, David Andrew 2007, *Regulating capital*, Ithaca: Cornell University Press. Focusing on the US case, this book applies a principal–agent framework to how regulators create rules in both national and international financial systems.

Underhill, Geoffrey R. D, Blom, Jasper and Mügge, Daniel (eds) 2010, *Global financial integraton thirty years on*, Cambridge: Cambridge University Press. Edited volume exploring issues of legitimacy and who holds authority – the public or the private sector? – in tracing the evolution of modern finance.

University of Warwick 2009, *The Warwick Commission on international financial reform*, Coventry: University of Warwick. Report of independent commission discussing regulatory responses to the crisis; puts forward the argument that we have to consider how risk is determined and what the financial system is for in different economies.

Journals

Key international relations journals that commonly discuss global finance include: *International Organisation, International Politics, International Studies Quarterly, New Political Economy, Review of International Political Economy*, and *World Politics*.

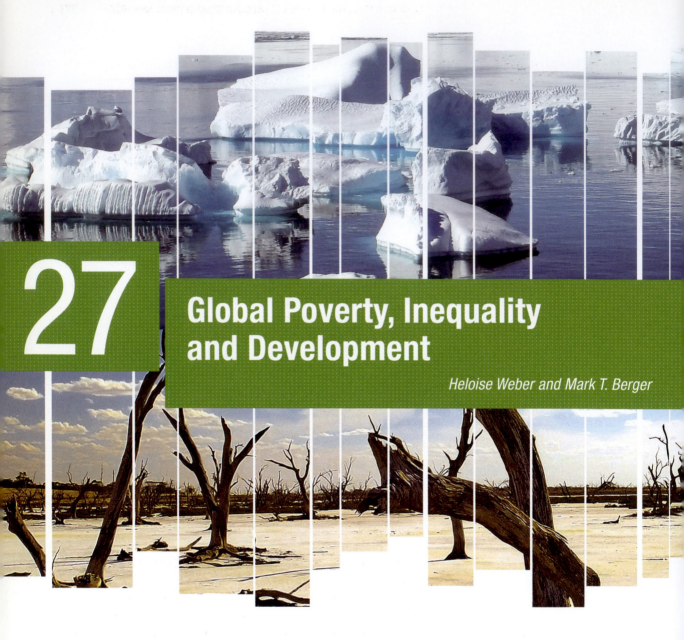

27

Global Poverty, Inequality and Development

Heloise Weber and Mark T. Berger

Introduction	373
Background to understanding poverty and inequality	373
A relational approach to global poverty, inequality and development	376
From the Washington Consensus to the Millennium Development Goals	379
Perspectives on the Millennium Development Goals and global poverty	381
Conclusion	384
Questions	384
Further reading	385

Introduction

This chapter examines poverty and inequality in global politics. The first section provides the background for our analysis of global poverty and inequality. We demonstrate the importance of beginning with an appreciation that poverty and inequality are complex, and that how they are understood and theorised in development is contested (McMichael 2010). We illustrate that any meaningful discussion of poverty and inequality necessarily has to be in relation to development. This is partly because understandings of poverty and inequality are already deeply informed by a preconceived idea of what development is and how it should be achieved. The second section discusses key contemporary initiatives for global development. The final section focuses on the **United Nations' (UN)** Millennium Development Goals (MDGs) initiative. Through an analysis of the MDGs we reconnect to the key points put forward in the first section of this chapter.

Background to understanding poverty and inequality

Global poverty and inequality have been high on the agenda in world politics since the start of the new millennium. This is not surprising, as not only is the worldwide gap between the rich and the poor growing, but there has also been an unprecedented rise in insecurities and vulnerability in the everyday lived experiences of many people, specifically the poor. There is no shortage of figures and statistical evidence to draw upon in order to substantiate these claims (see, for example, the **World Bank**'s *World development* reports since 1990 and the United Nations' *Human development* reports). Two highly visible issues can be drawn upon to illustrate the growth of inequality and poverty in global development. These are the growth of slum-dweller and/or squatter communities globally, and the rise of food insecurities for many, also globally. For example, Mike Davis's recent work, presented in his book *Planet of slums*, on the rise and expansion of slums across the globe, has drawn attention to the rapid increases in precarious living conditions in urban and peri-urban areas (Davis 2006). The expansion of slum dwellings occurs in direct relation with development processes, including industralisation and urbanisation. In the case of food insecurities, the rise in the incidence of food riots globally since the 1980s has also been taking place in the midst of high technology-oriented, high mass-scale production of food for the global market (Patel 2008). Activists, **non-governmental organisations (NGOs)**, policy-makers, politicians and scholars are all engaged in rigorous debates about the scale and character of global poverty and inequality, and have embarked on various campaigns to 'make poverty history'. However, first and foremost, it is important to carefully reflect on the history of poverty and inequality; any meaningful discussion of these two issues is incomplete without addressing their corollary: namely development, or the lack thereof (see Box 27.1).

We need to keep two more points in perspective, which are important for understanding what is at stake in debates about poverty and inequality. First, that debates about global poverty and inequality have not always been situated within, or in relation to, the wider debate about development. Instead, these debates have oftentimes been conducted from *within* a particular modernisation-centred development framework.

Figure 27.1   Slums built on swamp land near a garbage dump in East Cipinang, Jakarta, Indonesia

Source: Jonathan McIntosh, 2004/Wikimedia commons.

This is not to say that 'development' was not always contested, whether in terms of workers' struggles, resistance to slavery or resistance to gender and race inequalities, but only that modernisation-based liberal approaches have been dominant in international political institutions. Approaches to poverty and inequality have also been guided by this conception of development. Broader questions about development and its relation to poverty and inequality thus were not always at the forefront of social and political analyses. Second, debates about development in turn have historically centred upon the erstwhile Third World. Today, however, concepts such as the First, Second and Third World have little analytical utility. This is partly because the idea of the three worlds of development was historically specific. During the **Cold War**, the First World was identified with the core capitalist **nation**-states, the Second World with the nation-states of the socialist bloc and the Third World generally with a loose coalition of post-colonial nation-states. The latter sought, in theory, to pursue a developmental path between the liberal **capitalism** of the First World and the state socialism of the Second World.

Despite the passing of the Cold War and the dramatic and uneven transformation of the one-time Third World, the high ground in the development debate continues to implicitly take the idea of 'developing' versus developed states as its point of reference. Some observers and institutions engaged in the **theory** and practice of development, however, have turned to a more historically informed global perspective on the dynamics of development and inequality, one that seeks to transcend understandings

BOX 27.1: TERMINOLOGY

Poverty

When people (or, as often happens, *a people*) are described as 'poor', we tend to make a whole range of associations relating to material lack, vulnerabilities and visions of precarious existences more generally. However, as Ashis Nandy has shown, there are very good reasons to be mindful of how easily the discourse of poverty leads to misidentifications and potentially quite severe adverse consequences for those who have poverty falsely attributed to them. Consider the following two scenarios:

1) A band of hunter-gatherers set out on a food-gathering trip, which takes them a long way from their homestead. On the way, they tell each other stories in light, makeshift camps, and subsist on a rich diet of foodstuffs gathered along the way (the Australian film *Ten Canoes*, for instance, tells such a story). They get to their destination, where they go hunting for a migratory species which comes through annually, and they eventually return to their homestead with what they can transport of their prey.

2) A young mother of three children aged between three and nine leaves the two younger ones in the care of the nine-year-old to trek 5 km from her make-shift shack in a slum on the outreaches of Kampala to a suburb where, on occasion, she has been lucky in getting paid by wealthier locals for helping out with the laundry. For the fourth day in a row she is unsuccessful, going from door to door, and returns home having purchased some cassava flour with some of the little money she has left from a microloan she took for her 'laundry business'. Her partner has spent the whole day moving from building site to building site looking for casual employment as a day-labourer, and has been unsuccessful too. The loan-repayments are due every fortnight, and there are only three days left.

Nandy's point is that both these scenarios, as different as they are, tend to fall under the description of poverty. This is problematic for the following reasons:

a) In the first case, those identified as 'poor' may themselves not conceive of themselves as such, but actually experience themselves as living in conditions of some abundance, within lives they value.

b) The family in the second case experiences hardship, but their hardship is not an original condition, even if it is represented as such. Rather, their situation, or their hardship is an *outcome* of processes of development itself.

By representing the vulnerable or destitute as living in an original condition of poverty, the processes by which they ended up in this condition are obliterated. For instance, the family may have been forced off their subsistence farm in the countryside by developers (see Nandy 2002; McMichael 2006).

of global poverty and inequality in terms of binaries and spatially defined categories such as 'developed–developing', 'developed–underdeveloped', or 'First World – Third World' (McMichael 2008; Saurin 1995).

We find this latter approach more useful for analysing and understanding global poverty and inequality. This is mainly because the former approach is premised on a **state-centred** perspective in the sense that it takes the nation-state as its key analytical referent. This means that development and poverty are primarily conceptualised in terms of the territorial and spatial categories of conventional international relations theory, rather than in terms of social networks and relations constituted within a global context. Additionally, approaching development in these terms disconnects development as a process from its global dimensions, and presents it as just one issue that should be associated with 'developing states'. The understanding of development we operate with, then, is one which takes it as a relational process, treats inequalities and poverty as comprising sets of globally constituted social relations, and avoids analyses in terms of state-centred categories.

A relational approach to global poverty, inequality and development

Often when we think about global poverty and inequality we tend to associate these with a lack of development or the unfulfilled promises of development. This is misleading. Global poverty and inequality are outcomes of a long historical process of uneven global development. This means that there is an intrinsic *relationship* between development and inequality. Let us illustrate this briefly. Have you ever wondered why very poor people live in slum dwellings on the edge of cities, or sometimes within cities? Have you ever wondered how their condition came about? Unless their circumstances have been 'voluntary' (which is generally unlikely), they have usually found themselves living in urban poverty as a result of having been displaced from their rural homes and lands as part of a wider process of modernisation-based national or international development (see Box 27.2). Often such displacements occur because decisions have been taken at a national level (in coordination with international networks) to build, for instance, large dams, so that local, national or regional industrial plants can be facilitated by new energy sources. However, not everyone benefits from such a model of development and, more importantly, not everyone even subscribes to such a conception of development.

The case of the Narmada Valley dam in India (see Box 27.3) is just one example that captures the complexity of the ongoing power struggles over development: what it is and how to achieve it. The dam project in question was an ambitious proposal to develop the Narmada River, a proposal which would, it was estimated, benefit some 50 million people. The costs, on the other hand, include ecological damage and

BOX 27.2: TERMINOLOGY

Modernisation theory

Modernisation theory (MT) is premised on a stages-of-growth approach to development. From this perspective all countries and their societies will transcend their specific social, cultural and material forms and converge on the Western liberal model through the mechanism of the market (albeit under the tutelage of the **state**, and not necessarily a democratic state, and foreign intervention). MT emerged from the US in the context of the Cold War, although it has its roots in European philosophical thought about progress more generally. Modernisation as development was generally accepted by many of the erstwhile 'Third World' states. However, they disputed the conditions under which they were to modernise, identifying the legacy of the **colonial** and international division of labour as an obstacle. Modernisation theorists on the other hand identified 'domestic' factors (culture, society and economy) as key obstacles to development. (Hoselitz 1952; Rostow 1960).

displacement of millions of peasants who live in villages along the course of the river. What it illustrates is that conditions of inequality and poverty are neither natural nor given. Rather, they are outcomes of the complex historical and political dynamics of the pursuit of development as a planned project (McMichael 2008: 45). Furthermore, development is conceptualised differently by different people, and as such it is continually contested and infused with relations of **power** and identity (see Box 27.4). We can build on this relational understanding of development and say that global poverty and inequality are outcomes of ongoing historical and political struggles over development. While specific examples may be situated locally or nationally, to varying degrees they will have historical roots and political similarities with distant locales and peoples. For example, the historical development and modernisation of contemporary European states was facilitated through colonial and **imperial** relations that extended well beyond the territorial boundaries of the modernising imperial states concerned. Similarly, the European encounter with distant peoples not only influenced how Europe developed culturally and materially but also influenced the development path of their former colonies and protectorates (Hobson 2004; F. Cooper 2005). Neither of these encounters was experienced in a homogeneous way. Thus, for instance, the drive for modernisation in India after independence from Britain in 1947 was grounded in the legacy of the colonial experience. Today, in an increasingly **globalising** world, social relations and experiences are not only more interconnected, but have taken on an even more global dimension (McMichael 2008; 2010).

BOX 27.3: CASE STUDY

Narmada Valley dam, India

The villagers of Jalsindi (a group of villages identified for submersion in order for a dam to be contructed in the Narmada Valley, India) did not wish to give up their lifestyle and their cultural links with their ancestral lands. While not totally cut off from the 'modern' world, the villages of Jalsindi were fairly self-sufficient and were living only partly in exchange with the cash economy. In a cash economy, how well one survives materially is contingent upon what one earns in cash. If jobs are scarce, as in many poorer societies, and there is no formal welfare system in place to support the under- or unemployed, such persons effectively become destitute. Importantly, displacement and destitution affect not just the material well-being of people, but also their dignity, their senses of identity and belonging, and recognition by others. The identity of the villagers, including their own conception of development, is not valued or understood by the developers, for whom development is the pursuit of modernisation. Resistance to the Narmada Valley dam project is ongoing, with the villages of Jalsindi continuing to struggle against their displacement (see www.narmada.org/gcg/gcg.html).

By now you should have some appreciation that there are foundational questions central to debates about development, global poverty and inequality which need to be engaged with: for example, what *is* development? What is the *relationship* between development and poverty and inequality? Let us now reconnect some of these issues to the **discipline** of International Relations (IR). Today, any introductory course in IR will include at least a basic introduction to concerns about development, global poverty and inequality. It is also likely that these concerns will be set in the context of national and international **security** and questions about global governance. You will more than likely be asked to write an essay on such topics, including perhaps one on the MDGs initiative, adopted as part of the UN's Millennium Declaration. The MDGs initiative is one of the more recent approaches adopted globally as a response to international poverty and inequality. This observation already indicates that there is some recognition that there is a *global* dimension to the everyday and localised lived experiences of poverty and inequality.

It is important to remember that poverty, inequality, and development are not new to world politics. Before we further develop the above themes, we should summarise the key points we have made:

- Global poverty and inequality are not natural or inevitable. On the contrary, contemporary problems of inequality and poverty are the outcomes of a long historical process of uneven global development.
- Development in turn is also not a natural phenomenon, but a process that is socially and politically organised and contested.
- There is no such thing as an apolitical development perspective or process. How we explain global poverty and inequality is highly political because ultimately it has implications for our understanding of the *causes* of poverty, and hence how we organise political responses to it. This in turn will be contingent upon our respective conceptions of development.
- Development is much more than a linear process of material advancement and modernisation. Development and modernisation involve issues of identity and power, and conceptions of justice.

BOX 27.4: DISCUSSION POINTS

Dimensions of poverty and inequality

In this chapter we narrate the relationship between development on the one hand and poverty and inequality on the other, predominantly through the lens of economic well-being. Indeed, most people will probably associate development, in the first instance, with economic well-being, even for perspectives that maintain economic growth to be instrumental for living a good life. However, this is not quite accurate; while we do not have the room to discuss this exhaustively, we want to flag some aspects of relations of development, poverty and inequality which are too often side-lined.

In the case of the Narmada Valley dam (Box 27.3), for instance, many of the people displaced are *indigenous*, and from different ethnic and cultural identities within the state. Their expropriation is therefore also an act of **power** of particular majorities and interests *vis-à-vis* a distinct people and their way of life. Likewise, the history of development and inequality can only be understood properly if, for instance, questions of slavery and forced labour are taken into account, not least because these cast long-lasting shadows with significant contemporary implications. They also bring out the extent to which race and the way in which framing others as non-human or inferior has played a significant role in the history of development (see James [1938] 2001).

We examine global poverty and inequality in a way that foregrounds these broader issues. First, we demonstrate that there is an intricate relationship between conceptions of development and experiences of poverty and inequality. How one *conceptualises*

BOX 27.5: TERMINOLOGY

Dependency theory

Dependency theory has argued that the asymmetrical structure of world politics, in particular the way in which the global economy has been organised, is biased in favour of the Western capitalist states. The Third World was situated in a subordinate position as a consequence of **colonialism** and the colonial division of labour, which did not change after political independence. There are variants of this argument. The general thrust of dependency theory, however, was structural, in the sense that the development of capitalism was theorised as a structural process resulting in uneven and combined development. Inequality and poverty were conceived as inherent to the overall structure of economic development (Amin 1990; Frank 1967).

development will inform how one responds to poverty and inequality. Second, and related to the above point, we argue that the **method** one chooses to evaluate and analyse development also has implications for poverty and inequality. Choice of method is both contingent upon a prior theory or understanding of poverty and inequality and related to conceptions of development. Third, we suggest that development has always been, and will continue to be, the focus of political and social debate and struggle. The reason for this is that whichever way development is conceptualised and pursued in practice 'it is not just a goal, but a method of rule' (McMichael 2008: 49). The relevance of these observations for the study of development, global poverty and inequality will become clearer as you proceed through the chapter.

We proceed with an outline of the contemporary context of development and explore this through the example of the MDG initiative. The purpose of this exercise is to set the scene for the discussion by starting with 'where we are now'. There are, of course, any number of ways to introduce the study of global poverty and inequality, particularly when the emphasis is on the history and politics of development. We could, for instance, start with the famous 1949 speech by former US President Harry S. Truman, which for many symbolically, if not substantively, divided the world into the 'developed' and the 'underdeveloped' and led to what became known as the Point IV Program. On 20 January 1949, in his inaugural address at the start of his second term as president, Truman concluded by sketching out an expanded **foreign aid** policy to assist the 'freedom loving nations' to develop (Berger 2004: 43). This was a decisive moment in the history of development. However, we intend to 'fast-forward' our historically informed approach to global poverty and inequality and focus on the MDGs of the early twenty-first century, which may in retrospect also eventually be seen as an important turning point for development and world politics. As the brief discussion of the Point IV Program makes clear, global poverty and inequality did not start and will not end with the MDGs. We do not intend to provide a comprehensive account of the MDGs per se, but it is important to recognise the extent to which contemporary debates about development have come to the fore both in relation to previous debates such as dependency theory and also in relation to contemporary political trends (see Box 27.5).

From the Washington Consensus to the Millennium Development Goals

As the world entered the twenty-first century a new consensus was emerging among key policy-makers and politicians about global poverty and inequality. This new consensus is seen as a departure from the dominant development policies of the 1980s and 1990s. In particular the new consensus has been presented as a shift away from the '**Washington Consensus**' (see Box 24.1) advocated by key global institutions such as the World Bank and the **International Monetary Fund (IMF)** (see Chapter 24). The Washington Consensus maintained a focus on macro-political restructuring, such as managing national budgets in a more austere style in the hope this would facilitate 'economic growth' in the long run, enable sovereign debt repayments and also reduce poverty. Structural adjustment programs (SAPs) gained increasing influence in the 1980s and included policy initiatives such as privatisation, liberalisation and cutbacks on state subsidies for basic staple foods and other products, and more general welfare programs (see Box 24.2). In a substantive sense, the Washington Consensus was seen as the best approach to development, which in turn, it was hoped, would redress the *social* crises of global poverty and inequality.

However, as a consequence of the negative social and political implications of SAPs, the Washington Consensus came under critical scrutiny from various quarters. In the context of this crisis of legitimacy of development the shift to integrate micro-political experiences with an ostensibly more poverty-focused macro-political governance agenda emerged in a comprehensive way. This entailed a radical shift in the representation of poverty and the articulation of development policy. These important changes were reflected in development policy processes at various levels, particularly at the level of key **multilateral** economic institutions, which included the World Bank, the IMF and the **World Trade Organization (WTO)**.

For example, in contrast to their position in the 1980s and 1990s, all three institutions have now come to represent their *raison d'être* in terms of development. The shift in focus, from concerns with macro-economic and political processes of development to concerns about the everyday lived experiences of poor people, came to be labelled the post-Washington Consensus. This is generally understood to entail two substantive departures from the Washington Consensus. In addition to the foregrounding of concerns about poverty and how to alleviate it, the post-Washington Consensus is generally understood to imply a change in the process of development policy formulation itself. It is assumed that poverty reduction and development policy will not be premised on a preset general framework, but rather be the outcome of context-specific concerns premised on a more inclusive policy-making process. In particular, there was an expectation that there would be more participation and input from the global poor. Thus, the thrust of the post-Washington Consensus approach to development ostensibly gives priority to the 'voices of the poor'.

Let us briefly consider three key development initiatives that were formalised under the post-Washington Consensus. First, in 1999 the World Bank and the IMF adopted the Poverty Reduction Strategy Paper (PRSP) initiative over the previous SAP process. A PRSP is compulsory for countries wishing to access credit from the World Bank and the IMF to finance development. The PRSP sets out a comprehensive national development plan that ought to encompass in an integrated way macro-political aspects of governance with micro-political concerns. This means that a typical PRSP will have policies, including projected expenditure, for various sectors (such as health, education, poverty and so on) set out on the basis of three- to five-year plans. These plans are in turn correlated to the projected national budget (based on anticipated income and expenditure) of the state concerned. The PRSP initiative has generally been represented as a country-specific document that sets poverty reduction as the core objective. To the extent that it focuses on poverty reduction, there is little to disagree with. It is also correct to say that the PRSP initiative goes beyond the SAPs approach, in that it legalises a comprehensive national development plan linking local level policies to a globally constituted framework for development.

Second, in keeping with the consensus that poverty reduction and development are key rationales of multilateral economic institutions (MEIs), the WTO has also agreed to facilitate this objective. The WTO 2000 Doha Round of Talks was represented in terms of a comprehensive 'development' agenda.

Third, the MDGs were also adopted as a way of monitoring concrete outcomes of the reorientation in global development. While there is no doubt that under the post-Washington Consensus global poverty and inequality have been put centre stage, debates continue over the global politics of development and poverty (Higgott and Weber 2005; H. Weber 2004, 2006; Weber and Berger 2009). For this reason, we will not refer to the vision or, most significantly, the practice of development as espoused by MEIs in terms of the post-Washington Consensus but rather as a reconfigured, while still orthodox, modernising approach to development, as this more accurately captures the substantive issues at stake.

Not everyone shares this reconfigured orthodox modernising vision of development and the processes through which it is to be achieved (Munck and O'Hearn 1999; Rahnema with Bawtree 1997). For example, the diverse groups that coalesce under the umbrella of the World Social Forum (WSF) exemplify a fairly large and globally constituted alternative **globalisation** movement (see Chapter 25). Within this movement there are, for instance, peasant organisations who are interested in pursuing ecologically sustainable food production systems which reflect a comprehensively different development vision to the orthodox one (McMichael 2006). To make clear what is at stake in the ongoing debates about development we now turn to the specific example of the Millennium Development Goals.

Perspectives on the Millennium Development Goals and global poverty

Through a brief examination of divergent perspectives on the MDGs (see Box 24.3) we demonstrate the degree to which these debates are reflective of differences over how development is conceptualised, and over how the root causes of poverty are viewed. These divergent perspectives can be captured through a few select quotations on the MDG initiative.

For advocates of the MDG initiative – including Kofi Annan, the former Secretary-General of the UN, under whose leadership the UN adopted the MDG declaration – it 'was a seminal event in the history of the United Nations' (Annan 2005a). Other advocates are cautiously optimistic about the potential value of the MDG initiative, and suggest that the initiative has at least made global poverty a key focus in world politics (Fukada-Parr 2004).

For some critics, the MDG initiative is better conceived as a strategy to further justify and entrench a **neoliberal** conception of development, and hence they call for a rejection of the MDG approach (Amin 2006; Bond 2006). Thomas Pogge (2004), on the other hand, argues that it is morally objectionable to focus on reducing a *proportion* of the poor when there are sufficient resources to meet the basic needs of all of humanity. Jeffrey James (2006), in contrast, cautions over the emphasis the MDG initiative places on quantitative goals and targets. While for advocates quantifiable targets can demonstrate in a concrete way whether poverty reduction goals are being achieved, for critics it displaces what development *ought to be* about. James illustrates his point through a simple example. Primary school enrolment is an MDG target: is this in itself an adequate measure of development? Or should there be a meaningful consideration of the *quality* of the education and what one can do with it after that? Following Amartya Sen, such critical perspectives place an emphasis on the quality of life rather than targeting outcomes per se. These arguments do not deny that poverty and inequality exist and that we ought to redress the lived experiences of those subject to vulnerabilities. Instead, they resonate with foundational questions about what development actually is, or is about.

These are what we might call the first-order questions that underpin debates about development. Whether we are talking about the PRSPs, or the WTO Doha agenda, or indeed the MDGs themselves, it is possible to discern some fundamental differences between the critical and orthodox approaches. On closer examination these different perspectives can be seen to diverge precisely with reference to first-order questions about development, global poverty and inequality:

• What *is* development?
• What is the *relationship* between development and poverty and inequality?
• Development for *whom*, and for *what purpose*?

Let us extrapolate these differences by carefully considering what is substantively at stake in the divergent perspectives on the MDG initiative. Why is it that for its advocates the MDG initiative reflects a seminal event in world history, while others remain so critical of this initiative specifically, and the orthodox development and modernisation project more generally?

Advocates of the MDG initiative

From this perspective development is broadly conceptualised in terms of modernisation; for example, it places faith in the value of modern, scientific knowledge and technology, and accepts that development is to be achieved through the implementation and regulation of forms of private rights. This entails an intensification of a market-based approach to public goods and services. Thus, the orthodox approach is ultimately premised on expanding a growth-based framework for development, within which individuals can compete to enhance their private gains. This perspective is underpinned by a set of foundational assumptions about development and poverty. First, it takes for granted that everyone in the world thinks about their everyday lives in individualistic terms *and* values modern scientific knowledge and technology as progress. It assumes that society is comprised of atomistic individuals who prioritise individual gain through competition. This view of the world is premised on a perspective that begins with a fixed conception of human beings. They are, in this view, rational agents acting in accordance with individual decisions made on the basis of explicitly economic calculations: profit maximisation, consumption needs and desires in the context of available information about the more general workings of the economy. Given that such a conception begins with the individual rather than society as a whole, poverty and inequality in turn are not conceptualised as an outcome of development (a socially and politically organised system), but rather as an outcome of *individual* failure to successfully pursue development.

From such a perspective, global poverty and inequality are understood not as an outcome of development but rather as a condition extraneous to the process of development. The orthodox approach does have a conception of *a* relationship between poverty and inequality and development, but it is conceptualised in a non-relational way. That is to say, the orthodox conception and theory of development ultimately rest on an *abstraction* from social relations, presupposing an individualistic perspective congruent with private property rights that renders invisible the social, historical and political contexts.

From this perspective, a social **order** that is beset with the injustices of class relations, gender inequalities and racial hierarchies is treated as if it were 'given', rather than socially and politically constructed. Instead of proceeding from the basis of historically specific experiences and struggles, the orthodox proponents of development and modernisation see the promises of development as a linear vision of progress tied to the future. In this sense, the orthodoxy is premised on a temporal vision (future time) and also spatial stratification. The MDG initiative exemplifies both these observations. It focuses on a future date to realise the promise of development and retains a spatial conception of the political organisation of development to the extent that 'national development', conceived in terms of a stages of growth logic, remains the dominant frame of reference.

Critics of the MDG initiative

From the perspective of critics, the MDG initiative is not only inappropriate, but is also set to reproduce and entrench global poverty and inequality because it is conceptualised from within an orthodox approach to development. The core of the critique is not so much an outright dismissal of the goals of the MDGs (even if they might be limited) but rather on its conceptual framework. Amin (2006) argues that: (a) it does not adequately address the relationship between development and poverty; and (b) it does not act on a conception of development that moves beyond an economic and technocratic frame of reference. Let us consider these two points in more detail. For critics, what is particularly problematic is the way in which the MDG conceptual framework remains premised on a neoliberal conception of development and associated policy processes. The MDGs are to be *realised* through the wider context of the development process, including the PRSP process, the WTO framework and so on, which are all firmly grounded within a set of 'free market' policies and strategies. This relies on growth rather than redistribution, which was precisely the cause of much social distress in the 1980s under SAPs (C. Thomas 2000).

From a critical perspective such an approach is tantamount to a form of governance based on what Stephen Gill has called 'disciplinary neoliberalism', advanced through an associated regulatory framework of 'new **constitutionalism**' (Gill 2002). This approach is *ahistorical* because it continues to conceive of development in a way that abstracts it from the social relations of power and the concrete forms of dispossession it engenders; it does not take into account the way in which development is – and came to be – organised. For instance, the legacy of **colonialism**, which, among other things, instituted an asymmetrical international division of labour between the North and the South with precarious terms of trade, is not factored into the MDG conceptual framework. The current organisation of the production of goods and services continues to be precarious and impacts adversely on the lived experiences of many. From the perspective of the critics, presuming social contexts to be primarily constituted in terms of rational self-interested agents acting in the image of consumption-oriented and profit-maximising individuals is flawed. To understand the politics of inequality and poverty, it is just as important to appreciate the complex nature of development as it is to historicise development and inequality. This would entail asking questions about the relationship between knowledge about development and social power relations (Saurin 1996).

Conclusion

Global poverty and inequality are not new phenomena to international relations, though they may appear so depending on one's theoretical perspective. If we see the world as a system of discrete territorial units (states) then we may find reasons to celebrate the MDGs. On the other hand, we may still find comfort in the narrative of a global system of discrete territorial states, but hope to struggle for alternative approaches to development as modernisation. Under both scenarios, we would be *abstracting* from the social reality of everyday lived experiences of historical and contemporary social relations, which have configured the global project of development and inequality. From such a state-centred perspective we are unable to account for '**transnational**' relations which constitute the making of, and resistance to, global development through inequality. Development implies progress; conceived as a linear approach it involves the subordination of the present to the past and the future. Human beings, however, are complex: we *live* the present in relation to memories (real or imagined) of the past and aspirations (real or imagined) of the future. While it can be said that the orthodox and critical perspectives of development both operate within conceptions of time and space, they nevertheless differ fundamentally. The orthodox approach to the temporal dimension of development is linear, projecting a particular conception of the history of development into the future. The history of development is conceptualised in non-relational terms, spatially and socially. On the other hand, critical perspectives are premised on substantive aspects of the social and political contexts of development. If we are to respond to global poverty and inequality, it is our contention that we must return to first-order questions about development itself. To do so, we would have to engage ultimately with a much wider range of issues than we have been able to deal with in this chapter. In the many dimensions of relations of poverty and inequality, questions of culture, identity, race and ethnicity are often central, as are questions of material and symbolic power, and problems related to conceptions of time and space. Focusing on socio-economic issues and relations helps to uncover some of the most important components of the conflictual and problematic ways in which relations of poverty and inequality are constituted and lived out.

QUESTIONS

1. What differentiates orthodox and alternative approaches to development?
2. What is the relationship between conceptions of development and the method we use to 'measure' development?

3. How are poverty and development related?

4. To what extent are assumptions about development relevant for how we respond to poverty?

FURTHER READING

Berger, Mark T. 2004, *The battle for Asia: from decolonization to globalization*, London: Routledge Curzon. Detailed overview of the history of theory and practice of international development from the end of World War II to the Asian financial crisis of 1997 and beyond.

McMichael, Philip 2008, *Development and social change: a global perspective*, 3rd edn, Thousand Oaks: Pine Forge Press. Engaging and accessible account of the history of development that challenges the reader to rethink problematic assumptions about development.

McMichael, Philip (ed.) 2010, *Contesting development: critical struggles for social change*, London and New York: Routledge. Brings together a rich and diverse collection of essays that foregrounds development as a relational, social and political process; presents the contradictions of development and the struggles for social change.

Rahnema, Majid with Bawtree, Victoria (eds) 1997, *The post-development reader*, London: Zed Books. Unconventional collection of essays on development and poverty; challenging and inspiring.

Weber, Heloise and Berger, Mark T. (eds) 2009, *Recognition and redistribution: beyond international development*, London: Routledge. Collection of essays reflecting alternative perspectives on development from an interdisciplinary perspective.

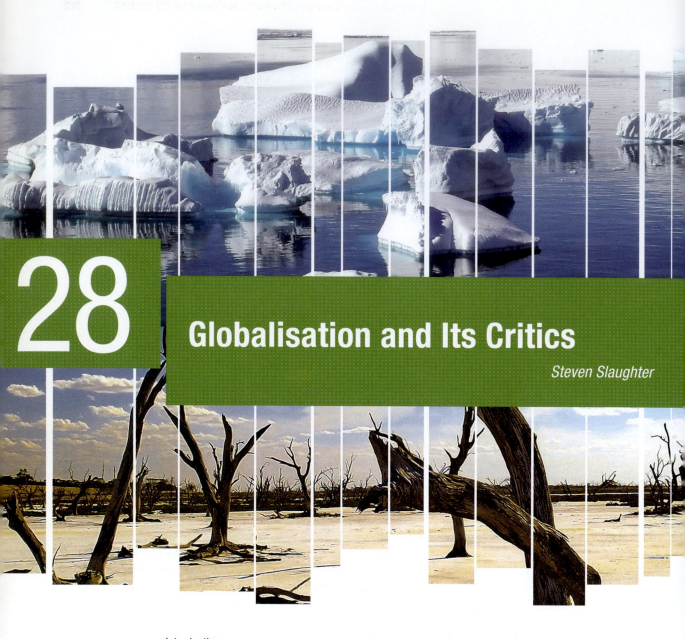

28

Globalisation and Its Critics

Steven Slaughter

Introduction	387
Understanding globalisation	387
The anti-capitalist movement	392
Scholarly critiques of globalisation	396
Conclusion	397
Questions	397
Further reading	397

Introduction

The purpose of this chapter is to introduce the contemporary theoretical debates surrounding **globalisation**. It illustrates the main features of protests against the social consequences of a globalised economy, and it identifies some of the key political issues that scholars and students of International Relations (IR) must face when addressing the promotion of justice and effective governance within a more densely connected world.

Since the mid-1990s the term globalisation has entered common usage and become a central issue in public debates in most countries around the world because of the apparently changed structure of world politics and economics. Globalisation has become associated with the controversial social outcomes that have stemmed from an increasingly integrated global economy, and the resulting public disquiet and controversy around the world, as particularly symbolised by the 1999 protests in Seattle against the **World Trade Organization (WTO)** and more recent protests in the aftermath of the Global Financial Crisis of 2008–9. Globalisation has also become an important – although essentially contested – concept within the field of IR and other social science **disciplines**. It is therefore essential to understand what globalisation means.

Understanding globalisation

Globalisation is a messy term that encompasses a wide variety of human activity. As you may be aware there are trade statistics and other economic facts that suggest the world is becoming increasingly globally integrated (Held et al. 1999: 169–75). Nevertheless, facts do not tell the whole story. Consequently, in an effort to systematise the examination of globalisation, a variety of scholars have advanced arguments about what globalisation means. The seminal globalisation work, *Global transformations*, offers a systematic study of the history and nature of globalisation and suggests three explanations for contemporary global integration (Held et al. 1999) (see Box 28.1). The first is '*hyperglobalisation*', a position held by liberals like Kenichi Ohmae (1995) who claim that globalisation represents a recent and near-complete triumph of liberal values and global markets that is tightly integrating **states** and people around the world. They argue that globalisation is a significant force for human progress.

BOX 28.1: TERMINOLOGY

Three explanations of globalisation

Hyperglobalist

Globalisation is:	Real and new.
Why?	Globalisation is the consequence of information and communications technology as well as **capitalism**.
Main elements:	Global economy.
Role of the state:	End of effective state capacity.
Moral stance:	Positive process.
Proponents:	Thomas Friedman, *The Lexus and the olive tree* (1999); Kenichi Ohmae, *The end of the nation state* (1995).

Sceptical

Globalisation is:	Nothing new – either is not real or is a long-standing process.
Why?	Globalisation is a myth – there is a continuing international economy.
Main elements:	Capitalism as usual.
Role of the state:	Persistence of 'normal' state capacity for policy-making.
Moral stance:	Globalisation is imaginary.
Proponents:	Paul Hirst and Grahame Thompson, *Globalization in question* (1996); Linda Weiss, *The myth of the powerless state* (1998).

Transformationalist

Globalisation is:	A real but long-standing spatial process.
Why?	Long-term processes of technology, ideas and institutions have stretched human activity across time and space.
Main elements:	Globalisation is a multifaceted social process – different aspects of life are becoming global in varying degrees.
Role of the state:	State capacity is undergoing transformation. The line between the foreign and domestic policy has become blurred.
Moral stance:	An ambiguous process that is producing both 'winners' and 'losers', as well as reconstituting traditional political communities.
Proponents:	David Held et al., *Global transformations* (1999); Anthony Giddens, *Runaway world* (1999).

The second position is a *sceptical* set of observations which suggest that globalisation is overstated and largely a myth because the level of global integration during the 1990s is less than in the period between 1870 and 1914 (Hirst and Thompson 1996: 2). Far from being a world where markets have trumped states, the world economy is still shaped by state-to-state interaction; there remain significant differences between the strategic choices made by states in response to the world economy; and strong states are still 'able to work the system to their advantage' (Waltz 1999: 7). **Marxists** are also sceptical, on the grounds that global interconnections are an essential part of the capitalist mode of production; globalisation is seen as a 'long standing process always implicit in capital accumulation rather than a political-economic condition that has recently come into being' (Harvey 1997: 421).

The third account of globalisation is the *'transformationalist'* perspective that seeks to locate globalisation in a more historical framework and that has become the predominant explanation of globalisation. The transformationalist position conceives globalisation as a spatial process whereby various forms of human activity are increasingly traversing the world and connecting people in differing parts of it more densely and more quickly than in previous times. This spatial interconnectedness is largely due to developments in transportation and communications technology that enable long-distance social relations. Anthony Giddens (1990: 64) exemplifies this account when he defines globalisation as 'the intensification of world wide social relations which link distant localities in such a way that local happenings are shaped by events occurring many miles away and vice versa'. In this process national borders are transcended on a regular basis by various flows of resources, people and ideas. It is important to emphasise that this account contends that globalisation is multifaceted in that it is not restricted to the economic realm alone, as people are increasingly affected by various forms of economic, cultural and political activity. Equally important, the transformationalist position argues that globalisation is not novel to the late twentieth century as individuals and polities have been interconnecting across the world for at least 500 years, with some dynamics of globalisation evident even earlier.

There are four main political implications of this spatial process for world politics. First, while **nation**-states remain important actors in world politics, global connections and the development of communications technology have empowered a new range of actors to operate in politically significant ways (Held et al. 1999: chapter 1). Clearly, globalisation has made it easier to develop **non-government organisations (NGOs)** that promote and disseminate a certain set of political values, but it has also made it easier for **terrorist** groups and organised crime to transfer people, resources and harm across national borders. **Transnational corporations** have also been greatly empowered – if not enabled – by these accelerated forms of global linkage. Second, globalisation leads to global connections and ramifications that are more authentically transnational and universal. Indeed,

political communities and civilisations can no longer be characterised simply as 'discrete worlds': they are enmeshed and entrenched in complex structures of overlapping forces, relations and movements … But even the most powerful among them – including the most powerful nation-states – do not remain unaffected by the changing conditions and processes of regional and global entrenchment (Held et al. 1999: 77–80).

However, these overlapping forces are often uneven and have greater local or regional implications for some people or states. For instance, the GFC of 2008–9 demonstrated the interconnected nature of economic systems but had different economic and social impacts around the world. Third, in many senses, the lines between foreign and domestic policy have blurred due to the intense and widespread forms of global integration and connection. This leads to issues such as terrorism, organised crime and environmental impact that intersect national borders and thereby can only be addressed by elaborate international cooperation.

Fourth, as a result of the previous points, there are increasingly complex forms of international and transnational cooperation that have become referred to as 'global governance'. The previous points create the situation where the nation-state cannot be assumed to be the only major political actor in issues like **security**, economic prosperity, or environmental sustainability. It is now the case that international or intergovernmental forms of organisation such as the **United Nations (UN)**, the Group of Twenty (**G20**), regional bodies like the EU or non-public bodies like transnational corporations, business councils or NGOs are increasingly important to understanding the enactment of policy-making. Jan Aart Scholte (2005: 138–9) indicates that these public and private bodies are 'supraterritorial constituencies' that are external influences over the operation of state policy-making. As we will see in the last section of this chapter, this is problematic because it can be seen to undermine **democracy** within nation-states.

It is important to be aware that some scholars are sceptical of the incidence or significance of the spatial implications of globalisation. As I mentioned previously, sceptics claim the **power** of the state is still largely intact – and there is plenty of evidence, especially in the post-September 11 context, to demonstrate the power of the state. Even transformationalist scholars argue that globalisation is not a monolithic force: different states and groups of people are affected by global integration in differing ways. However, there are also scholars who believe that while the spatial implications of contemporary global integration may be largely correct, they ignore any examination of the ideas and interests that are dominating and championing the contemporary shape of global economic integration. Some critically minded scholars (see Chapter 4) emphasise the importance of *neoliberal* and free market capitalist ideologies and policies in shaping the way the global economy has developed since the 1970s (Cox 1997; Gill 1998).

Neoliberalism (also known as economic **rationalism**) is a strand of liberal thought that advances a range of policies ushered in by many Western – especially Anglo-Saxon – countries and the **multilateral** economic institutions (MEIs), such as the **International Monetary Fund (IMF)** and the **World Bank** (see Chapter 24). Neoliberalism is an ideology and philosophy based on the principle that human welfare is best promoted by economic growth, which in turn is best enabled by reducing the interference of governments in the private sector. Neoliberals also support measures that enable trade and finance to have unrestricted movement across national borders. These policies attempt to 'roll back' the state and the role of government, and leave decisions about allocation, production and distribution in the economy to the global market, thereby excluding or limiting measures that restrict or redistribute the wealth of individuals (Gill 1998). These 'market friendly' policies are evident in: the policies of *deregulation* that remove 'political' interferences and rules from the operation of markets; *privatisation*, which entails the sale of state assets to the private sector or the 'contracting out' of public services to the private sector; and the *liberalisation* of restrictions on the movements of capital or trade across state borders. Neoliberals claim that an unregulated market is the best way to promote individual freedom and increase global economic growth, which will ultimately benefit – and 'trickle down' – to everyone. These policies have been influential around the world and replaced the more moderate **Keynesian** liberalism that sought economic growth and social stability by allowing an active domestic role for the state.

Consequently, we can see a close relationship between neoliberalism and contemporary processes of global integration. Indeed, the hyperglobalist position best captures the perspective of many Western governments, which conceive globalisation as an inexorable economic force. From the early 1980s onwards, globalisation was seen as an external technological and economic force compelling countries around the world to adjust their economic policies, largely through liberalisation and deregulation. This idea of globalisation being a monolithic external force was challenged by scholars who claimed that governments have used the idea of 'globalisation' to mask the neoliberal agenda driving economic policy (Cox 1997; Gill 1998). While it is now generally accepted that globalisation is a broader phenomenon encompassing more than just economics, there is no doubt that neo-liberal ideas and policy-making are an important component of political life at a national and global level.

At the global level there have been mounting efforts by states to manage globalisation. The **G8** and the G20 forums have played central roles in managing global forms of economic and social integration. The 'G' system has its origins in the 1970s when the leading industrialised democracies created an annual forum for executive level deliberations to coordinate policy in respect to transnational economic and social issues. As a forum for finance ministers, the G20 has its particular origins in the late 1990s response to instability in the global financial system, as demonstrated by the Asian Financial Crisis. The role of the G20 continued to grow, and replaced the G8 as the preeminent site for economic diplomacy in 2009 in response to the Global Financial Crisis of 2008–9. Consequently, the formation of the G20 represents the current resting-point of executive level deliberations to manage globalisation.

The G20 plays a crucial role in stabilising globalisation and in coordinating the actions of states and international organisations to address global crises when they arise. There is a sense that the G20 fills a glaring gap in global governance. An important aspect of the G20's role in global governance is that its membership has expanded beyond Western states to include emerging economic powers such as China, India, and Brazil (see Box 28.2). Furthermore, while the G8 and G20 have a clear focus on economic issues, these forums have addressed a range of non-economic issues – from terrorism to global warming and global health – with mixed results. The potential of the G20 to address an array of issues broader than promoting global capitalism, or coordinating responses to economic crises, points to the potential significance of creating and sustaining a body that plays a coordination role in global governance that extends to address social issues and promote public goods in world politics. However, despite this broadening agenda, many observers claim that the 'G' system has played – and continues to play – an important role in articulating and legitimating neoliberal principles (Beeson and Bell 2009: 69).

BOX 28.2: DISCUSSION POINTS

Timeline of the 'G' system of forums

G6 – 1975: Executive leaders (i.e. the presidents or prime ministers of member states) from France, West Germany, Italy, Japan, the UK and the US.
G7 – 1976: Canada added.
G8 – 1997: Russia added.
G20 Finance Ministers – 1999: The G20 is made up of the finance ministers and central bank governors of Argentina, Australia, Brazil, Canada, China, France, Germany, India, Indonesia, Italy, Japan, Mexico, Russia, Saudi Arabia, South Africa, Republic of Korea, Turkey, UK, US and the EU.
G20 Leaders Forum – 2009: At the 2009 meeting it was announced that the G20 had replaced the G8 as the central forum for executive leaders.

The focus of neoliberal ideas and policies is on unleashing innovation, profitability and economic growth through encouraging unimpeded transnational economic linkages. Neoliberal ideas underpinned the formation of the '**Washington Consensus**' orthodoxy of the MEIs in the 1980s (see Chapter 24), expressing a view articulated by the US Government and development economists that neoliberal policies were the only path to prosperity and development. This orthodoxy has been evident in the policies of the IMF and World Bank, especially the policies of structural adjustment, in directing developing countries to introduce neoliberal measures. Substantiation of the impact of neoliberalism is also evident in the rising tide of public concern over its implications. While trade liberalisation can promote public disquiet – because jobs are often affected and the losers in this scenario tend to be more vocal than the winners – during the 1990s the focus throughout the Western world shifted towards a broader concern for global justice. This concern broadened further in the 2000s when the instability of deregulated globalisation was evident in the GFC. This public concern is an indication that globalisation as a spatial process had impacted on public awareness and that neoliberal policies have some unpalatable social implications. We now turn to the substance of these public concerns and protests.

The anti-capitalist movement

Although NGOs like Oxfam and Greenpeace have been interested in the global economy for many years, and people in developing parts of the world have likewise contested the policies of the IMF for some decades, since the mid-1990s individuals and NGOs concerned with global social justice grew exponentially in number and voice. It has become common to refer to these protests as a social movement – the 'anti-globalisation' or, more accurately, the 'anti-capitalist movement' (ACM). However, the unity of this movement is open to debate. The ACM is a global social movement (or collection of movements) that challenges the domination of transnational corporate interests and neoliberal/free market policies because of the perceived impact of this type of global capitalism on social justice. Sometimes this movement is referred to as the 'global justice movement'. Ultimately, the groups involved in this movement seek to challenge the orthodoxy of trade liberalisation and neoliberalism that exclude efforts to regulate or redistribute economic activity (N. Klein 2001). They do not accept the economic assumptions and arguments associated with neoliberalism, and they see that economic gain and the interests of market actors need to be considered along with other public goals such as good labour standards, environmental protection and **human rights**. They claim that the defenders of neoliberalism and **free trade** frequently fail to acknowledge the needs of vulnerable people around the world in favour of the economic interests of the affluent (N. Klein 2001).

While most people became aware of the ACM with the protests against the WTO meeting in Seattle in 1999, the real beginnings of the movement against global capitalism began in 1994 with the Zapatista struggle against neoliberalism (see Box 28.3). On 1 January 1994, a grassroots rebellion in the impoverished southern Mexican state of Chiapas began against the introduction of the North American Free Trade Agreement (NAFTA), a regional treaty animated by explicit neoliberal principles. While the Zapatistas employed some forms of active resistance, the true impact of the movement was its explicit recognition of the importance of challenging neoliberal ideas and an effective use of the internet to communicate their cause. This played a crucial role in mobilising a wide variety of campaigns from around the world on the question of neoliberalism. These events were followed by a global internet campaign against the Multilateral

Agreement on Investment (MAI). The MAI was an agreement being devised by the Organisation for Economic Co-operation and Development (OECD) in secrecy from 1995, with the aim of applying trade liberalisation principles to the realm of investment. It was feared by those in and beyond the ACM that this would have eliminated the right of states to control many aspects of policy-making such as regulated working conditions or environmental standards (Goodman and Ranald 1999: 34). Once a copy of the MAI draft treaty was leaked onto the internet it catalysed a worldwide campaign that exacerbated the differences within the OECD and in 1998 negotiations collapsed, leading to the treaty being scrapped. The successful anti-MAI campaign was quickly followed up by large-scale physical protests at Seattle in 1999 and a protest against the World Economic Forum (WEF) in Melbourne on 11 September 2000, which, despite some violence, involved the heavy use of entertainment and carnival-like themes to capture public attention.

BOX 28.3: DISCUSSION POINTS

A brief timeline of the global anti-capitalist movement

January 1994:	EZLN (Zapatista) revolt against North American Free Trade Agreement (NAFTA) begins in Chiapas, Mexico.
1998:	Internet-coordinated protests publicising details of secret negotiations on the Multilateral Agreement on Investment (MAI) bring about their collapse.
18 June 1999:	The first Day of Global Action holds protests against financial centres in forty-one countries.
December 1999:	60 000–80 000 people from around the world demonstrate as part of the Day of Global Action at the WTO meeting in Seattle.
September 2000:	20 000 protest against World Bank and IMF in Prague; and more than 20 000 protest against the WEF meeting in Melbourne.
April 2001:	80 000 protest against the Free Trade Area of the Americas (FTAA) in Quebec.
July 2001:	During protests by 200 000 people against the Group of 8 (G8) meeting in Genoa, the police kill one protester.
September 2004:	Protests against the WTO in Cancun; WTO dialogue between the member states stalls and collapses (again).
July 2005:	Protests are held against the G8 meeting in Gleneagles, Scotland; the Live 8 concerts.

An important development for the ACM occurred in January 2001 when the World Social Forum (WSF) was created in Porto Alegre in Brazil. The WSF was created as a political space to discuss and formulate alternatives to neoliberal globalisation and thus challenge the ideas of the WEF, which meets annually in Davos, Switzerland and intermittently in other places. The WSF annual meetings have been growing in size and in 2006 there were simultaneous meetings in Mali, Venezuela and Pakistan (see Box 28.4).

BOX 28.4: DISCUSSION POINTS

World Social Forum attendance at a glance

The World Social Forum is not a formal organisation, but:

… an open meeting place for reflective thinking, democratic debate of ideas, formulation of proposals, free exchange of experiences and inter-linking for effective action, by groups and movements of civil society that are opposed to neoliberalism and to domination of the world by capital and any form of imperialism, and are committed to building a society directed towards fruitful relationships among Humankind and between it and the earth (World Social Forum 2002).

2001: Porto Alegre – 10 000.

2002: Porto Alegre – 40 000.

2003: Porto Alegre – 70 000–80 000.

2004: Mumbai – 100 000+.

2005: Porto Alegre – 155 000.

2006: Bamako (Mali), Caracas (Venezuela) and Karachi (Pakistan) – 120 000+.

Sources: www.glovesoff.org/columns/cooney_2005wsf.html;
www.forumsocialmundial.org.br/main.php?id_menu=14_6&cd_language=2

The terrorist attacks of 11 September 2001 had a significant impact on the ACM, with the political climate moving away from social justice concerns. However, in the lead-up to the US-led war in Iraq, the increased public concern about the defensibility of that war led to a high level of cross-pollination of anti-war and global social justice concerns. This was followed in 2005 with the 'Make Poverty History' campaign and the 'Live 8' concerts aimed at galvanising public awareness about the impact of global poverty. It should be noted, however, that there is some controversy about the coherence of the Make Poverty History campaign with the previously stated goals of the ACM. In particular, while the ACM has sought to significantly reform or dismantle global capitalism, the Make Poverty History campaign seemed to accept the core aspects of global capitalism coupled with measures that promote 'trade justice', 'drop the debt' and offer 'more and better aid' (Make Poverty History campaign 2005). Whether this is a maturing or a weakening of the ACM's agenda depends ultimately on your perspective.

There have been, and continue to be, significant differences within the ACM over the goals of protest and the tactics that should be utilised. There are groups that advocate violence and vandalism against capitalist icons, those who support non-violent protests and those who wish to engage in constructive dialogue with transnational corporations and the MEIs. There are socialist groups that aspire to move beyond capitalism and some groups that seek to reform the capitalist system. However, while the diversity and global extent of the protest movement speaks volumes about the social problems facing the world and the diversity of moral viewpoints of those resisting neoliberalism, developing political coherence amidst such diversity is the most significant challenge facing the protest movement. It is important, also, to note that the ACM itself has been actively countered by the MEIs and the many pro-capitalist business councils and lobby groups that continue to play an important role in supporting the development of economic globalisation. There are, as Leslie Sklair (1997) has pointed out, 'social movements for global capitalism' in developing and defending economic globalisation.

Economists and business councils play a crucial role in supporting and legitimating neoliberal ideas and the type of global capitalism we take for granted.

Also, while there has not yet been a momentous transformation in the economic orthodoxy away from neoliberalism, the impact of these forms of contestation is not insignificant. It is clear that the protest movements have brought the structure and neoliberal policies of the MEIs to world attention when previously they were not significant topics of public consideration. The protest movement has politicised the global economy and opened up some avenues for dissenting ideas and voices by making clear that contemporary globalisation is a political and cultural structure as much as an economic one. The ACM has essentially politicised the ideas and private bodies that stand behind the institutional infrastructure of contemporary globalisation, such that corporate think tanks and transnational business councils have been taken out of the realm of conspiracy theory and placed into the discourse of any reasonable explanation of the contours of contemporary globalisation. The increasing attention paid to the social and institutional underpinnings of prosperity by the MEIs can also be seen to reflect a reaction to outside voices as much as internal learning processes inside the MEIs (O'Brien et al. 2000: 228). In some cases the ACM has frustrated and slowed the development of the **institutionalisation** of neoliberalism. The Seattle protest and the anti-MAI campaigns are examples of protests that amplified the divisions *within* the intergovernmental negotiations and that were consequently successful at slowing down the institutional growth of neoliberal globalisation.

Most significantly, it appears that in terms of organising global economic affairs we are witnessing a shift away from conventional inter-state cooperation towards a more complicated model of cooperation where NGOs and social movements have some impact. This is a significant departure from the **Westphalian** idea of international relations being about state-to-state interaction. Indeed, some scholars suggest that this is the emergence of 'complex **multilateralism**' where states are overlaid by **non-state actors** (O'Brien et al. 2000: 207). The consequence of this is simple: the institutions that states have set up are not alone in making public decisions – they have to interact with NGOs in order to work effectively. The days of international bodies making decisions in splendid isolation are over – increasingly people are questioning the legitimacy and competency of these bodies (Esty 2002). The operation of the NGOs complicates the 'smooth' operation of the MEIs and can be seen to play a blocking role even if they cannot or do not play a constructive role. This is a trend that is unlikely to go away: people are concerned that trade liberalisation and economic globalisation may be increasing inequality, poverty and environmental degradation. These public perceptions are important because NGOs play a growing role in the nature of world politics through informing the public and through promoting alternative perspectives on the desirability of neoliberal ideas and assumptions.

The significance and future prospects of these protests against global capitalism depend heavily upon how the ideas and energy created by the ACM are interpreted by citizens around the world, and especially upon how powerful political and economic actors respond to future social problems that are directly or indirectly connected to global capitalism. The future of these protests, and indeed of globalisation itself, also depend heavily upon what we consider as being the appropriate political structures that should be maintained or developed in future. Should we develop extensive forms of global democracy or protect state **sovereignty**? Consequently, questions of international relations **theory** and political theory are tremendously significant to the future shape of globalisation.

Scholarly critiques of globalisation

One of the core questions facing IR scholars, and indeed everyone on our planet, is: how are we to organise political authority and effective governance within the context of globalisation? Despite significant public disquiet about the type of globalisation that currently exists, the fact remains that over the past two or three decades various forms of international cooperation and governance have developed so that global capitalism and other forms of global integration are able to secure their existence. The role of non-state actors has also increased. These forms of international and transnational governance, coupled with processes of economic and cultural globalisation, have called into question the nation-state's future role in a world system that promotes stability or justice. We are witnessing a double displacement of state authority – towards private market influences and towards global and regional bodies that are external to any state (Slaughter 2005: 71). There are real questions about whether states around the world, even the most powerful, can control their domestic affairs in the face of globalised structures and forces.

Consequently, in IR literature the idea of 'cosmopolitan democracy' has become a significant conjectural alternative to contemporary globalisation. Contemporary scholars such as Richard Falk, Anthony McGrew and David Held have argued we need to institutionalise the idea that people are 'citizens of the world'. While the idea of **cosmopolitanism** has been around for some time (see Chapter 9), in recent times cosmopolitans are more forthright in their support for global institutions and a single global democratic space. They contend that the various processes of globalisation have fundamentally limited the capacity of the nation-state to have any real sense of control over its destiny because its populace is now routinely affected by 'outside' decisions and forces (Falk 1995; Held 1995). Held claims that 'the idea of a political community of fate – of a self-determining collectivity which forms its own agenda and life conditions – can no longer meaningfully be located within the boundaries of a single nation-state alone' (1998: 21). In the context of globalisation, cosmopolitans argue that the only way to overcome these disjunctures is to include in decision-making processes everyone who stands to be affected by them, thereby making the appropriate site for democracy, at least on some issues, a global one. In pursuing this alternative and globally extending democracy *across* states borders, the state and other actors such as transnational corporations will be increasingly bound by global laws and standards (Held 1995: 234–5), and individuals – not states – will be the primary moral agents in world politics.

Obviously, there are many critics of cosmopolitan proposals. After all, the idea of global democracy seems a far-fetched and **utopian** attempt at world government. While the proponents of cosmopolitan democracy suggest that we need to think creatively about a more just form of global **order**, the **communitarian** critics of cosmopolitanism claim that cosmopolitans understate the power and utility of national forms of identity and loyalty (D. Miller 1999). More particularly, communitarian and republican critics claim that a global democracy is not necessary for global cooperation and that citizens of democratic states ought instead to direct their states to be more just and cooperative with respect to their foreign policies (Slaughter 2005). While it is easy to be critical of the feasibility of cosmopolitan democracy, it is harder to be critical of calls to promote an increased concern for human rights at home and abroad. It is also difficult to dismiss the claim that global forms of deliberation between people from different civilisations, nation-states and belief systems are needed to justly and effectively manage globalisation (Dryzek 2006). In terms of the future, it is hard to avoid the conclusion that we need new forms of governance and political community, and while cosmopolitan claims may not square with the political realities of a world where nation-states are still predominant, cosmopolitans are posing important questions.

Conclusion

This chapter has indicated the variety of ways in which world politics is increasingly important to our everyday lives. Contemporary globalisation entails a blurring of local, national and world politics. Neoliberal policy-making's emphasis on promoting economic growth and excluding efforts to regulate or redistribute economic activity is having profound effects around the world and is provoking public concern as to whether this is the path to a sustainable and socially just future. This chapter has also illuminated the way that ordinary people around the world have become engaged with the question of how global political life should be organised in the hope of promoting a more just and stable world. Consequently, the level of our knowledge of world politics and our stance in relation to how we could achieve effective governance and justice are fundamental questions to us as citizens and as students, as we live a shared future in an increasingly globalised world.

QUESTIONS

1. Do you think the hyperglobalists, the sceptics or the transformationalists provide the better account of globalisation?
2. Why has globalisation stimulated so much resistance? Is this resistance justified?
3. Why has democracy become such a central issue in globalisation debates?
4. Do protests against globalisation make a difference? If so, how?
5. Who or what should the anti-capitalist movement target? Has the position of the anti-capitalist movement been strengthened by the Global Financial Crisis?
6. Do protests against globalisation reflect cosmopolitan or communitarian sentiment?

FURTHER READING

Dryzek, John 2006, *Deliberative global politics: discourse and democracy in a divided world*, Cambridge: Polity Press.

Held, David 2006, 'Reframing global governance: apocalypse soon or reform!' *New Political Economy* 11(2):157–76.

Stiglitz, Joesph 2006, *Making globalization work*, London: Penguin Books.

29

Global Terrorism

David Wright-Neville

Introduction	399
What is terrorism?	399
Some secondary warnings for the unaware	401
Contemporary terrorism in context	403
The globalisation of terrorism	406
Some final misperceptions	409
Conclusion	410
Questions	412
Further reading	412

Introduction

This chapter provides an overview and analysis of global **terrorism**. Its main argument is that any understanding of modern terrorism requires an appreciation of how individuals and groups with localised grievances seek to change perceived injustices through acts of violence targeted at a wider national and even global level. The chapter begins with a brief overview of the vexed issue of defining terrorism – a topic that has divided policy-makers and scholars for over a century – and presents a broad working definition of what terrorism is. It then addresses some of the reasons why terrorism is such a controversial subject. The third section shifts focus to the need to understand acts of terrorism within their social and historical contexts – each act of terrorism has its own unique set of historical circumstances even when part of the same general campaign. The fourth elaborates how terrorism is being transformed under conditions of **globalisation**, focusing in particular on two uniquely modern aspects: the inclination of a growing number of people to redress local grievances through violent actions far from the source of their anger; and the increasing tendency of individuals with no cultural, historical or social ties to a particular conflict to identify with its protagonists and either enlist in faraway terrorist groups or to take matters into their own hands and pursue a violent agenda of their own accord. The chapter concludes with a brief dicussion designed to clear up some misconceptions surrounding terrorism's root causes.

What is terrorism?

Very few concepts in politics can provoke as negative a reaction as terrorism. Even the debates that swirl around the classification of a person or a government as 'despotic' or 'dictatorial' pale in comparison with the near-universal opprobrium carried by the concept of a 'terrorist'. After all, one can claim to be a 'benign despot' or a 'benevolent dictator', and there are also circumstances in which authoritarian or dictatorial governance is deemed (rightly or wrongly) as acceptable and legitimate. For instance, many people argue that during periods of warfare or social turmoil there is a need to suspend **democracy** until **order** is restored. Others argue that authoritarian and non-democratic governance can be culturally sanctioned, which is an argument that is used to legitimate the regimes of countries as diverse as Saudi Arabia and Singapore. However, while some people might be willing under some circumstances to accept being called despotic, dictatorial or authoritarian, almost nobody accepts the label of 'terrorist'. Even Osama bin Laden rejected strongly the charge that he or his followers were terrorists.

Despite the widespread acceptance that terrorism is a bad thing, debates about what terrorism actually is remain politically contentious and clouded by confusion. Indeed, perhaps the most commented-upon issue in terrorism research is that there is still no definition that attracts anything close to universal approval. What is more, this definitional ambiguity is not confined to academe but stretches into the domestic and international policy realms. For example, the definition of terrorism used by the US Central Intelligence Agency is slightly different from that used by the Federal Bureau of Investigation, which is different again from the definition used by the Pentagon and US Department of Defense. At the international level, almost five decades after beginning the debate the **United Nations (UN)** has still not settled upon a definition that satisfies all members. Much of the disagreement centres on when violence by **non-state actors** should or should not be considered legitimate. For many smaller countries, especially those that have experienced **colonialism**, there are occasions when organised violence by non-state groups can be considered justifiable. It is often pointed out, for example, that Nelson Mandela was charged, convicted and imprisoned as a terrorist in the early 1960s by the apartheid government of South Africa. There are few today who are prepared to criticise Mandela for the small acts of targeted violence against apartheid era infrastructure he coordinated while leader of the banned African National Congress's military wing, *Umkhonto we Sizwe* ('Spear of the Nation'). Rightly or wrongly, many members of the UN view the actions of Palestinian groups and other organisations – in the Indian province of Kashmir, Sri Lanka, the Caucasus region in Russia, the Basque region of Spain and many other places – in a similarly sympathetic light.

Any blanket definition that encapsulates all acts of politically motivated violence by non-state groups is therefore seen by many smaller states as an implicit rejection of their own struggles for independence and as diminishing the legitimacy of causes that they continue to see as just. For similar reasons, many states with large Muslim populations reject any possible UN definition of terrorism that has the potential to delegitimise the cause of genuine Palestinian independence.

The intricacies of this definitional merry-go-round need not concern us here. For the purposes of understanding the contemporary significance of global terrorism a useful working definition is as follows: 'terrorism is the actual or threatened use of violence against a civilian population undertaken in the pursuit of a political cause'. To be sure, such a definition raises more questions than it answers, but it is useful because it captures four of terrorism's most important and less controversial features.

1. Violence (or the threat of violence) has a purposive value for terrorists in that it is used to generate fear and uncertainty within a community, and to elevate this fear to such a level that it becomes so psychologically unbearable that it elicits a change in the political or social behaviour of that community, or it forces them to pressure their political leaders to change their behaviour or policies.
2. The fact that the violence is directed at achieving political goals is similarly important. Threats of violence for personal financial gain constitute criminal extortion or blackmail. Terrorism is in a class of its own; it is of course a criminal act, but at its core it is motivated by political rather than private financial objectives.
3. I have suggested confining our definition of terrorism to actual or threatened violence against civilian targets, for the simple reason that to include threats against military or police targets introduces the complicating issue of **insurgencies** and **guerrilla warfare**. There are insurgency groups in many parts of the world that not only engage in conventional military combat against soldiers and police but that also occasionally resort to acts of terrorism against civilian targets; however, once again the nexus between insurgency and terrorism is complex and introducing it here would unnecessarily confuse an already complicated issue.
4. The definition above also recognises the uncomfortable truth that terrorism is a tactic that is used not only by non-state actors but also by some governments against their own populations or against the populations of other states. However, as with the relationship between insurgencies and terrorism, the phenomenon of

state terrorism is complicated and, although it is an important and often overlooked part of the more complex terrorism equation, there is insuffient space to explore it in any detail here.

Some secondary warnings for the unaware

At first reading, the brief introductory points set out above are unlikely to appear controversial. Sadly, however, in the field of terrorism studies there is precious little that can sustain a consensus for anything but a brief moment. Therefore, for those about to embark on 'terrorism studies', it is worth keeping in mind that very little of what you encounter and study will ever be without its critics. As pointed out in the preceding section, even the concept of 'terrorism' itself is contested. Perhaps the most famous aphorism in the field, that 'one man's terrorist is another man's freedom fighter', remains as true today as when it was first coined in the 1970s (see Box 29.1).

Terrorism is, therefore, a highly emotive issue. Just as political debates about terrorism are inevitably highly charged and sometimes highly divisive affairs, so too is terrorism scholarship often highly volatile. Indeed, even the premise of this very chapter – that to understand global terrorism we need to understand its root causes – would not be accepted by some scholars. For such critics the search for root causes of terrorism weakens the moral clarity that our society needs if it is to defeat terrorism (see Newman 2006). They worry that any discussion about *why* terrorists kill risks legitimising such actions at a time when what is needed is universal condemnation. For others, including this author, not only is this argument logically flawed – we can understand why a person might murder a business rival without accepting the act as morally legitimate, so why can we not apply the same principle to understanding global terrorism? – but it is also a potentially dangerous argument. Allowing our justifiable outrage at the murder of innocent human beings to divert us from the search for an understanding of what motivates terrorists to kill ignores the obvious point that to manage a threat effectively we first need to understand the forces that drive it (see Silke 2004). Having an understanding *of terrorism* is not the same as having an understanding *with terrorism*.

Second, conceiving of terrorism as a phenomenon with its roots deeply embedded in the society in which it takes place obliges us to develop an understanding of what we mean by 'society'. This is not the place to interrogate the various ways in which the concept of society has been and is currently debated in domestic and international politics (for example, is there such a thing as a 'society of states'?), but it is important to note that the concept is critical to understanding terrorism. In fact, one way of viewing terrorism is as a tactic used by individuals who see themselves as at **war** with other groups in society, or indeed at war with other societies altogether – the latter a theme common in terrorism carried out in the name of religion (Jones 2008). Typically, the terrorists have as their goal an alternative vision of society, or even the establishment of their own separate society.

Historically speaking, individuals who might have felt alienated, disempowered and inclined to lash out almost always targeted local symbols of power within the society in which they resided – politicians, police, national governments or neighbouring ethnic groups. However, because of globalisation (see Chapter 28) the idea of 'society' has expanded, with individuals taking on a much broader understanding of who are their neighbours and which groups or governments might have an influence over their own lives. Social grievances have therefore taken on an increasingly global character: with anger born of events both at home and abroad, blame is attributed to both local and global forces; violence is aimed at both local and global targets. This is what is meant when we speak of the 'globalisation of terrorism'; it is the emergence of global issues as a source of local anger and the development of global networks as a way of lashing out violently against the perceived causes of this anger.

BOX 29.1: CASE STUDY

The first terrorists?

Around the first century of our common era, violent groups emerged in the area of Judea, a region now located in present-day Israel. Among them were the 'Sicarii' and the 'Zealots', made up of members from Jewish sects opposed to Roman rule in Judea (see M. Goodman 2007; Horsley 1979). Forced to pay taxes to their Roman conquerors, to display reverence for Roman gods, with limited or almost no influence over Roman policy, and confronting what was a far superior and highly professional Roman army, some of these individuals resorted to terrorism as the only conceivable way of liberating themselves from occupation. The tactics employed to drive the Romans from Judea included the stalking and execution of Roman soldiers, officials, Greek merchants and even fellow Jews considered to be collaborating with the Roman authorities. For the Sicarii and the Zealots, the utility of their violence lay in its potential to strike fear into the Roman community and those who supported them, and by so doing to either drive them from Judea or cause an implosion of the Roman administrative apparatus so that Judea was rendered ungovernable. However, it is important to note that Zealot and Sicarii terrorism was not a function of their Judaism, or of any innate hatred of Romans or Roman collaborators. Rather, their terrorism sprang from feelings of alienation and humiliation experienced as a subjugated people, which – when combined with the psychological effects generated by an overwhelming sense of political impotence in the face of exclusionary political structures and a substantially more powerful occupying army – triggered in some people an urge to strike out violently against their perceived oppressors. Understanding how the economic, political and social structures of Roman **imperialism** in Judea generated feelings of alienation is thus the first step to understanding Zealot and Sicarii terrorism.

It is therefore always worth keeping in mind that no one is born a terrorist and that those who eventually become terrorists do so only after passing through an evolutionary progression involving a complex mix of social, political and psychological forces. Putting the argument slightly differently, terrorism is a form of learned behaviour and rests upon a highly personal and symbiotic relationship between potential and actual terrorists and the society in which they exist. And because the societies in which we live are becoming increasingly global in character, it is not surprising that the grievances that inspire terrorists, and the methods that they use to try to rectify these grievances, are also becoming increasingly global.

Terrorism by individuals and groups associated with al-Qaeda is a useful example of this phenomenon. Forged by Osama bin Laden (a Saudi), Ayman al-Zawahiri (an Egyptian) and others in Afghanistan in the 1980s and 1990s, al-Qaeda is often misrepresented as a vanguard movement intent on a global Islamic revolution. However, if we look behind the surface-level rhetoric of its leaders and adopt a more forensic approach to the group's origins and evolution in the decade after the attacks in the US on 11 September 2001, we see an amorphous network of loosely connected individuals motivated by a disparate array of local grievances but united by a shared view that the sources of their local concerns are corrupt local governments sponsored by the US and its allies. In other words, the disaggregation of al-Qaeda into a network of loosely affiliated franchises – such as al-Qaeda in Iraq, al-Qaeda in the Arabian Peninsula, al-Qaeda in the Islamic Maghreb and so on – gives violent voice to the modern terrorist phenomenon of local grievances being perceived through an increasingly global lens (Riedel 2010). Individuals and groups angry with local circumstances and frustrated at their inability to change things through peaceful means are increasingly inclined to follow the global connections of their perceived oppressors and strike out against them anytime, anywhere. Under conditions of globalisation, anger and violence do not require passports.

The idea that terrorism is a political act motivated by anger brings us to the third and final issue which needs to be clarified. It is not possible to begin to understand the complexity of terrorism until we combine the idea of terrorism as an increasingly global phenomenon with the act of violence itself as something more than an act by 'evil' or 'mad' people. Nobody is born a terrorist; terrorists are made from a combination of social circumstances and individual psychologies. Terrorism does not spring forth spontaneously but, as shown in the biographies of individual terrorists and the histories of terrorist movements, it typically emerges only after a long gestation period whereby the anger and frustration eventually erupt into hatred and violence (see Atran 2010; McCauley and Moskalenko 2008; Moghaddam 2005; J. Davis 2004; Sageman 2004; Silke 2003). However, this does not mean there is a single magic formula that, once identified, will allow us to understand the precise mix and measures of ingredients that when combined will produce a terrorist. Terrorism is essentially an 'acting out' of accumulated feelings usually associated with alienation, anger, frustration and humiliation, but this does not mean that *every* person who experiences such feelings will become a terrorist or even sympathise with terrorist causes. For example (as has been pointed out by many authors), prolonged exposure to the deprivations of an authoritarian state might breed a deep sense of non-violent anomie in some people, while a shorter exposure can inculcate an energised embrace of violence in others. There is no single avenue along which all terrorists have travelled in their journey towards violence. Rather, to paraphrase Taylor and Horgan, there are only 'individual routes to terrorism, and furthermore those routes and activities as experienced by the individual *change* over time' (Horgan and Taylor 2006: 597; see also McCauley 2007).

Contemporary terrorism in context

A decade after the tragedy of September 11 and former US President Bush's declaration of the 'war on terror', the threat of terrorism seems more pervasive than ever. Not only have terrorist attacks been a sad feature in conflict zones such as Afghanistan and Iraq, and in states where conventional political authority is undermined and being challenged by new grass roots movements in places such as Pakistan, Somalia and Yemen. Local and international agents of these and other movements and ideologies have also used or attempted to use terrorism against civilian, commercial, military and political targets across a diverse terrain – including Australia, Britain, Canada,

Denmark, France, Germany, Jordan, India, Indonesia, Italy, Norway, the Philippines, Russia, Saudi Arabia, Spain, Turkey and the US. At the same time, although they have not attracted as much attention, less spectacular terrorist strikes have imposed similarly serious economic, social and psychological costs on communities in sub-Saharan Africa and in Central and South America. The net effect of this pattern of violence has been a steady supply of media-friendly outrages that have kept terrorism at the forefront of the Western imagination and turned counter-terrorism into a new organising principle within domestic and international politics (see Box 29.2).

BOX 29.2: DISCUSSION POINTS

Some recent terrorist plots

21 December 1988:	UK – bombing of Lockerbie/Pan Am flight 103
26 February 1993:	US – attack on and partial destruction of World Trade Center
20 March 1995:	Japan – Sarin gas attacks, Tokyo underground
19 April 1995:	US – Oklahoma City bombing
7 August 1998:	East Africa – bombings of US embassies in Nairobi and Dar es Salaam
11 September 2001:	US – attacks on World Trade Center and Pentagon
12 October 2002:	Indonesia – Bali bombing
11 March 2005:	Spain – Madrid bombings
7 July 2005:	UK – London bombings
1 October 2005:	Indonesia – Bali bombing
11 July 2006:	India – Mumbai train bombings
14 August 2007:	Iraq – four coordinated suicide bombings kill over 500
18 October 2007:	Pakistan – suicide bombings near Karachi
25 April 2008:	Sri Lanka – bombing of commuter bus in Colombo
13 May 2008:	India – coordinated bombings in Jaipur
26–29 November 2008:	India – terrorist attacks in Mumbai
7 March 2009:	Northern Ireland – two unarmed British soldiers shot dead
17 July 2009:	Indonesia – coordinated bombings at two Western hotels
27 November 2009:	Russia – bomb on railway track derails train
25 December 2009:	US – Nigerian citizen attempts to blow up a flight from Europe with explosives hidden in underpants
29 March 2010:	Russia – two female suicide bombers attack Moscow subway
1 May 2010:	US – New York's Time Square evacuated after discovery of car bomb
11 July 2010:	Uganda – Somalian terrorist group bombs venues showing World Cup
30 September 2010:	Britain, France, Germany – discovery of coordinated bombing plot

| 29 December 2010: | Denmark – discovery of plot to launch attacks in Copenhagen |
| 24 January 2011: | Russia – suicide bombing at Moscow airport |

This has not always been the case. Although there have been periods in history when individual **sovereign states** have wrestled with the threat of terrorism – such as Tsarist Russia's battle with anarchist groups in the 1870s and 1880s and Britain's struggle in the 1970s and 1980s with violence by Irish terrorists – the emergence of a globally networked terrorist menace marks a new development in international affairs. Indeed, for some writers the emergence of transnational terrorists with an ability to strike almost anywhere at any time signals the end of an **international system** in which **states** enjoyed a virtual monopoly over the ability to wage war (Beck 2009; Bauman 2002; Kaldor 1999).

What are the forces that are leading a growing number of individuals to detach from the protective membrane of the state and try to rectify perceived injustices by taking matters into their own hands? Why are a steady stream of mainly young people abrogating national allegiances and defining themselves in transnational religious or cultural terms and in ways that sit in high tension with the dominant identities of the societies into which they were born? The answers to these conundrums provide vital clues to the deeper forces that are driving the spread of global terrorist networks and the ideologies that sustain them. Unfortunately, the complex multidimensional character of these issues means that easy answers are elusive. Explaining *how* this evolution in global politics has occurred requires the student of IR to sift through a complex amalgam of economic, political and technological forces. The task becomes even more difficult if we want to understand *why* a growing number of individuals appear willing to engage in or even support the use of terrorist violence. To address this part of the terrorism puzzle we also need to add insights from psychology and sociology so that we can understand how attitudes and behaviour are shaped by the increasingly global character of economic, political and social issues. In short, global terrorism is a highly complex phenomenon and there is no single academic **discipline** that holds the key to understanding its root causes.

However, there are some general attributes that have recurred with terrorist movements in different historical epochs and that allow us to make some general claims about the political and social character of terrorism. The most important of these characteristics is that terrorism rarely bursts forth spontaneously. It is almost always the result of a period of increasing alienation and anger among those who perpetrate the violence. Another important but often ignored historical fact is that even though terrorism has always been a feature of organised human societies, the causes of the anger that inspire it – and the types of violence used – differ over time. In this sense, as we shall see, in recent years terrorism has become both more deadly, as terrorists adopt new destructive technologies, and more global, operating across a wider international terrain as a result of globalisation (see Chapter 28). Putting this point in a slightly more controversial way, the root causes of terrorism lie not in religion or culture but in the economic, political and social structures of the society in which it emerges. This is as true for early terrorist groups such as the first century Sicarii and Zealots (see Box 29.1) as it is for contemporary terrorist movements as diverse as violent Christian **fundamentalist** groups in the US and al-Qaeda and its various international components.

The globalisation of terrorism

As mentioned above, one of the defining features of terrorism today is the enhanced role played by global contact in shaping the different routes that individuals take towards violence. This aspect of the contemporary terrorism phenomenon should alert us to the extent to which the emergence of terrorist groups that are international in their aims and contacts – such as the different components of the al-Qaeda franchise – is part of the same general trend that is also leading to other problematic developments in terms of **peace** and **security**. Under conditions of globalisation there has emerged a wide array of issues that elude resolution by states acting alone. Among the most obvious is the rapid deterioration in the sustainability of the Earth's ecosystems (see Chapters 34 and 35), but into the mix we also need to include the re-emergence of militarily significant private armies, crime syndicates with sufficient financial and fire-power to intimidate, and perhaps even control, the governments of small nations.

Looking at this development from a different angle, globalisation is eroding the protective **power** of national borders and diminishing the utility of conventional military doctrines and equipment as the fulcrum upon which national security rests. There is very little that the best-equipped and most technologically advanced army in the world can do to protect the welfare of a **nation** suffering the effects of drought or floods, exacerbated by climate change that in turn is caused by the actions of the entire global community (although clearly some members cause more damage than others). Similarly, there is little that conventional military forces can do to combat the threat to national security posed by individuals whose anger is invisible but intense, who might live anonymously among us, travel with legitimate visas and passports, carry legally mandated identity cards, and who have learnt from the internet how to make a bomb from products found in almost every modern kitchen or laundry. In this way, globalisation is feeding a curious development which might be called the 'privatisation of violence'; a situation whereby states are losing their erstwhile monopoly over the means to wage war. Although it is true that states are likely to remain the sole proprietors of cutting-edge military technology costing billions of dollars, globalisation is feeding the development of new forms of warfare which are allowing enemies of the state, such as terrorists, to 'level the playing field' through the use of simple, cheap but highly deadly technologies and tactics. Reflecting on the implications of the attacks of September 11 for international politics, the distinguished scholar Robert Keohane (2002: 89–90) observed that:

[t]he terrorist attacks on New York and Washington force us to rethink our theories of world politics. Globalism should not be equated with economic integration. The agents of globalization are not simply the high-tech creators of the Internet, or multinational corporations, but also small bands of fanatics travelling on jet aircraft and inspired by fundamentalist religion. The globalization of informal violence has rendered problematic our conventional assumptions about security threats. It should also lead us to question the classical **realist** distinction between important parts of the world, in which **great powers** have interests, and insignificant places, which were thought to present no security threats although they may raise moral dilemmas. Indeed, we need to reconceptualise the significance for homeland security of geographical space, which can be as much a carrier of malign informal violence as a barrier to it.

Implicit in Keohane's observation is another aspect of the nexus between globalisation and terrorism, albeit one that is often absent from conventional studies: the role played by the cultural, economic and political consequences of globalisation in generating and feeding a new generation of terrorist motivations. As mentioned above, terrorism has always been a feature of human societies, but it is only recently that it has broken free of local issues and environments and assumed a genuinely global presence – most particularly in the form of al-Qaeda, the organisations with which it is most frequently affiliated, and the individuals who, although not formal members of any sub-group, are nevertheless motivated by its ideology. Within this context, although the late Osama bin Laden and other senior al-Qaeda figures have been most energised by the plight of Muslims in the Middle East, from where they themselves came, they see Western economic and political interference in these countries, along with the simultaneous spread of Western cultural values, as the main reason for the plight of the people they claim to represent. Just as the Zealots and Sicarii attributed the secondary status of Jews in ancient Judea not so much to the corruption of Jewish leaders but to the cooperation of those leaders with the oppressive occupying Roman forces, so too does al-Qaeda see the oppression of Muslims as resulting from a coalition of corrupt local leaders with more powerful foreign forces.

Under conditions of globalisation, however, the dominance of external powers does not have to take the form of direct military occupation or overt political interference. The occupation and humiliation of the weak by the strong can now be secured through the more subtle manipulation of cultural, economic and political institutions by the powerful. It is partly for this reason that the al-Qaeda leadership believes that by provoking the West, particularly the US and its allies, into wars in Afghanistan and Iraq they have revealed to the rest of the world how Western economic and cultural power is ultimately underpinned by a willingness to use force to defend their de facto control over the cultural, economic and political destinies of non-Western peoples. Consistent with terrorists throughout history, al-Qaeda sees its own violence as a legitimate way of fighting back against an oppressor of overwhelming economic, cultural and military superiority. The failure to fight back in this way, for the terrorists, constitutes a form of submission that will only prolong the powerlessness and humiliation of the weak. As the Harvard scholar of terrorism, Louise Richardson, noted of bin Laden:

Bin Laden's statements and interviews constantly reassert his desire to redress Muslim humiliation. Declaring to his followers 'Death is better than life in humiliation,' bin Laden calls on his Muslim brothers 'to expel the enemy, humiliated and defeated, out of the sanctuaries of Islam' (L. Richardson 2006: 126).

However, under conditions of globalisation the boundaries of the 'sanctuaries of Islam' are much less clear than were the 'sanctuaries' of Judaism that motivated the Zealots and Sicarii two millennia earlier. People's senses of **identity** and belonging increasingly transcend the state, cutting across the local and encompassing the regional and the global.

This latter point has been given especially dramatic voice by the actions of individuals who despite having no obvious cultural, religious, historical or familial connections with a given conflict have nevertheless developed a psychological affiliation with its protogonists and sought to engage in terrorist actions on their behalf. In the decade

Figure 29.1   Members of the National Guard at the World Trade Center, New York, 19 September 2001

Source: Andrea Booher/FEMA News Photo.

since the events of September 11 this phenomenon of 'self-radicalisation' has become increasingly prominent, with the conflict in Iraq, the ongoing war in Afghanistan and simmering violence in places such as Somalia, Pakistan, Yemen, the Russian Caucasus region and elsewhere, providing young people in places far from the sites of actual battles with an entrée to radicalism and terrorist violence and an outlet for pre-existing existential frustration and anger.

The complex mix of individual and psychological processes that drive this phenomenon of self-radicalisation need not concern us here: suffice it to say that under conditions of globalisation alienated individuals can use a variety of new communication technologies to tap into issues that in earlier times would have been remote and invisible. So, an alienated young man born and raised in Daphne, Alabama can undergo a metamorphosis that leads him to enlist in the al-Qaeda–linked group al Shabab in far away Somalia. This is the life trajectory of Omar Hammami, who – despite the Middle Eastern tone of his name – was born in the US South, raised a Baptist and elected president of his school sophomore class before drifting towards terrorist violence (see Elliott 2010). Similarly, Adam Pearlman was born in Oregon and raised a Protestant in California, where he played Little League Baseball before immersing himself in the heavy metal scene and, just a few years later, making his way to Afghanistan and Pakistan where he adopted the name Azzam al-Amriki and became al-Qaeda's main English-language spokesman. He now lives life on the run with a multi-million dollar bounty placed on him by the US Government (see Khatchadourian 2007). These are just two cases, out of thousands, involving young people with no obvious cultural or historical links to a terrorist cause becoming radicalised through information and contacts channelled through new information and communication technologies. Under conditions of globalisation individuals experience a greater array of cultural raw materials with which to craft their own identities, and terrorist organisations are proving increasingly adept at influencing identity politics to generate fresh waves of new recruits from distant lands.

Some final misperceptions

This final section casts a critical eye over three propositions that are often held to explain core aspects of contemporary terrorist behaviour, but which on closer examination are highly suspect.

The first is the often-heard view that religion causes terrorism. Regardless of the religion involved, there are a sufficient number of life histories of terrorists claiming to be acting in the names of various Christian, Hindu or Muslim causes to question the view that religion in general, or some religions in particular, are prone to fomenting violence. Very few of those terrorists who claim to be acting in the name of religion have been pious for the majority of their lives. Contrary to popular belief, the vast majority of terrorists are radicalised by their anger or frustration and embrace violence *prior* to becoming religious. Indeed, biographical surveys of members of violent Islamist, Christian and Hindu groups suggest that fundamentalist interpretations of religion appeal mostly to individuals who are already radicalised, because they provide a pseudo-ethical justification for a *preexisting* urge to act out violently against those who are perceived to have acted unjustly against the individual concerned and his or her 'in-group' (Jones 2008; McCauley 2007; Moghaddam 2006). In other words, they do not become angry or violent *because* they are fundamentalists, they become fundamentalists because they are already angry and open to extremist ideologies and violent impulses (Wiktorowicz 2005).

Second, it is often argued that terrorists suffer from some form of psychopathological condition that impairs their capacity to make informed rational judgments. Indeed, of all the myths that cloud our understanding of terrorism it is this view that has proven one of the most difficult to debunk. Sustained by media sensationalism and the melodramatic instincts of political leaders, the mistaken assumption that terrorists are 'mad' has led to a series of poorly calibrated counter-terrorism policies that habitually underestimate the operational and strategic intelligence of the vast majority of terrorists. While it is impossible to speak of a single terrorist personality type, there exists a growing body of evidence that terrorists possess high levels of political and social literacy and are directed by a clear capacity for rational decision-making. In short, most terrorists are 'dangerously normal' (Horgan 2005).

The final misconception is that terrorists are motivated to violence because they 'hate us for our way of life', which in the modern Western context translates into the argument that they are moved to violence because they despise the secular **liberalism** and democracy that characterises Western societies. Those who make this claim tend to base their argument on the rhetoric of terrorist leaders such as the late Osama bin Laden and in the erroneous assumption that his utterances were taken as gospel by all terrorists who might act in his name. But close examination of the individual motives of terrorists evinces very little proof that this is the case. More influential in shaping the attitudes of individual terrorists than an innate rejection of dominant cultural and political structures of the society in which they live is a sense that these structures have failed them and impede their efforts to empower themselves and improve their own lives. In this sense, the ideologies that sustain terrorists grow out of perceived failures in the existing social order and are not independent of it. Terrorist ideologies do not grow in a vacuum; they are built out of the life experiences of those who live in a system but who have also experienced its failures. In other words, rather than saying the terrorists hate our democracy because they hate the idea of freedom, it is more accurate to say they hate our democracy for a perception that it fails to accommodate them and their own aspirations for freedom (see Wieviorka 2004).

Conclusion

Terrorism is a dynamic phenomenon, which means that it is inherently fluid and changes along with wider shifts in the character of human society. And just as human societies are becoming increasingly interconnected and **interdependent** in terms of their ecological, economic, political and social needs, so too is the ancient practice of terrorism changing and evolving a global logic. Just as the terrorism of the Zealots and the Sicarii cannot be understood without interrogating the economic, political and social structures of local customs, social habits and political character of the Roman Empire in Judea, contemporary terrorism cannot be understood without being contextualised within the increasingly global nature of modern social structures. In terms of the issues that can motivate people to anger and violence, in terms of the new technologies that allow for the emergence of formal and informal networks of individuals who share this anger, and in terms of the new destructive technologies that allow these communities to act out their anger, the forces of globalisation have unleashed a powerful force that is likely to challenge states for the foreseeable future.

It is argued by some (e.g. Bauman 2002; Beck 2009) that we are on the cusp of a new era in which the forces of globalisation have unleashed new dynamics that are reshaping how people define themselves and their interests, and how they respond to political and social disappointments and frustrations. Global terrorism signifies one of the most extreme manifestations of this wider social process – which also encompasses a wide variety of other social movements, very few of which resort to violent means but all of which constitute a challenge to traditional forms of political behaviour. The 'war on terror' launched by the administration of former US President George W. Bush in the wake of the September 11 attacks and supported by many of its allies including Britain, other members of NATO and Australia represents an attempt to deal with this problem mainly through conventional military means (see Box 29.3). However, more than a decade after the declaration of this 'war' there is little evidence that the risk of global terrorism has been reduced, and by the turn of the decade almost all governments around the world had abandoned the term. Even intelligence services in the West now agree that since 2001 the threat of terrorism has shifted and morphed rather than decreased.

BOX 29.3: DISCUSSION POINTS

US President Barack Obama on the terrorist threat

'Now, this generation faces a great test in the specter of terrorism. Unlike the Civil War or World War II, we cannot count on a surrender ceremony to bring this journey to an end. Right now, in distant training camps and in crowded cities, there are people plotting to take American lives. That will be the case a year from now, five years from now, and – in all probability – ten years from now.

'Neither I nor anyone else standing here today can say that there will not be another terrorist attack that takes American lives. But I can say with certainty that my Administration – along with our extraordinary troops and the patriotic men and women who defend our national security – will do everything in our power to keep the American people safe.

'And I do know with certainty that we can defeat al Qaeda. Because the terrorists can only succeed if they swell their ranks and alienate America from our allies, and they will never be able to do that if we stay true to who we are; if we forge tough and durable approaches to fighting terrorism that are anchored in our timeless ideals.'

(President Barak Obama, 'Protecting our Security and our Values', speech delivered at National Archives Museum, Washington DC, 19 May 2009).

What is needed is a new global approach to combating the threats posed by global terrorism which involves bold decisions that have thus far eluded governments. This will not happen if emerging generations of scholars and policy-makers retreat into analytical comfort zones which refuse to acknowledge how globalisation has changed

Table 29.1 Recent trends in terrorist violence

	Terrorist incidents	Injuries	Fatalities
2001	1732	6403	4571
2002	2649	7349	2763
2003	1899	6200	2349
2004	2647	1704	1129
2005	4995	15 062	8194
2006	6660	20 991	12 071
2007	4526	20 963	10 232
2008	2846	14 434	5909
2009	560	1957	1197

Source: RAND Database of Worldwide Terrorist Incidents (http://smapp.rand.org/
nsrd/projects/terrorism-incidents.html)

the nature of terrorism and which reproduce simplistic explanations that reduce terrorism to unicausal factors such as religion, culture or the alleged 'madness' of the perpetrator.

QUESTIONS

1. How do you define terrorism?
2. Has globalisation facilitated the growth of terrorism?
3. What are the root causes of terrorism?
4. What are the motives behind al-Qaeda's attacks on Western targets?
5. Do you agree with the saying that 'one person's terrorist is another person's freedom fighter'?
6. Has the character of terrorism changed in recent years? If so, how? And what has caused this change?

FURTHER READING

Burke, Jason 2003, *Al-Qaeda: casting a shadow of terror*, London: I. B. Tauris. Measured and insightful analysis of the origins and motives of al-Qaeda.

Guelke, Adrian 2006, *Terrorism and global disorder*, London: I. B. Tauris. Useful overview of how global forces unleashed since the end of the Cold War have changed the nature of terrorism and turned it into a new organising principle in international politics.

Horgan, John 2005, *The psychology of terrorism*, London: Routledge. Accessible yet thorough examination of the complex mix of individual, group and social forces that shape the evolution of terrorist personalities.

Jackson, Richard et al. 2011, *Terrorism: a critical introduction* Basingstoke: Palgrave Macmillan. A useful introduction to the field of critical terrorism study whereby a new generation of terrorism scholars interrogate and find wanting many of our accepted assumptions about twenty-first century terrorism.

Richardson, Louise 2006, *What terrorists want: understanding the terrorist threat*, London: John Murray Publishers. One of the most wide-ranging introductory analyses of terrorism in its historical and modern forms.

Riedel, Bruce 2010, *The search for al Qaeda: its leadership, ideology, and future* (rev. edn), Washington DC: Brookings Institution. Excellent overview of the manner in which the twenty-first century's first transnational terrorist network has evolved and adapted to meet the counter-terrorism strategies arrayed against it.

30

Post-Conflict State-Building

Beth K. Greener

Introduction	415
The rise of post-conflict state-building	415
The post-conflict state-building agenda	418
The politics of contemporary post-conflict state-building	419
Critics of the current agenda	420
Impacts of post-conflict state-building	422
The future of post-conflict state-building?	422
Conclusion	424
Questions	424
Further reading	425

Introduction

This chapter introduces students to the current post-conflict state-building agenda. Identifying the end of the **Cold War** (see Chapter 20), the rise of the discourse of **humanitarian intervention** (see Chapter 31) and the events of September 11 (see Chapter 29) as key to the development of this agenda, the chapter canvasses the main areas of contention and debate in this field. It seeks to highlight the debates over the political content of post conflict state-building, with critics tackling the notion from a number of different perspectives. The chapter closes with a brief consideration of the impacts of the current post conflict state-building agenda and asks where that agenda might head from here.

The rise of post-conflict state-building

Roland Paris (2003: 451) recently argued that 'there is no logical requirement for international agencies to resurrect **failed states** *as states*, rather than allowing war-torn regions to develop into some other kind of polity'. Paris's argument provocatively suggests that current demands to rebuild the state as the apparently automatic response in post-conflict situations may not be the ideal answer to the difficulties at hand. Yet state-building remains the predominant response of the international community when attempting to address the various problems that arise in post-conflict situations.

State-building has become the international community's default answer when presented with the need to respond to calls for help by severely weakened or beleaguered governments (as in the Solomon Islands), the dissolution of certain regimes (as in Afghanistan and Iraq), or the complete creation of new political authorities (as in Kosovo and East Timor).

Although there are some historical precedents in the form of the post-World War II rebuilding of Japan and Germany, as noted in Box 30.1, the drive by external actors to be involved in the building of states in post-conflict sites has predominantly been a post-Cold War and post-September 11 affair.

BOX 30.1: CASE STUDY

Post-war state-building in Japan

Japan was occupied by the Allied powers from its defeat in World War II until 1952. President Truman's 'US Initial Post Surrender Policy for Japan' set out two main objectives: 1) to prevent Japan from being able to wage war again in the near future; and 2) to turn Japan into a pro-American Western style democratic state.

Statebuilding efforts therefore focused on supporting the **institutionalisation** of **democracy** and **human rights**. These were to be enshrined in the new Constitution of 1947, which also limited Japan's military capabilities and formally renounced the right to **war**. In addition to this, the education and police services were decentralised, land reforms undertaken and universal suffrage introduced.

Economically, the powerful *zaibatsu* companies were dismantled, and government ministries such as the Ministry of International Trade and Industry (MITI) were empowered to help drive economic recovery after the devastations of war. US investment and aid also helped stimulate growth. The perceived success of Japan's post-war recovery has at times been cited as a positive rationale for the continuing US involvement in post-conflict state-building.

Strategic competition prior to the 1990s meant that the notion of 'post-conflict state-building' – understood here as a broad-ranging set of activities as opposed to more specific tasks such as propping up friendly regimes in various countries, **peacekeeping**, or measures such as election organisation in Namibia in 1989 – was not part of our common terminology. The 1990s, however, saw the rise of 'humanitarian intervention' discourses. Driven by the demand to 'do something', and released from the competitive frame of the Cold War, the **United Nations (UN)** in particular sought to respond to international **peace** and **security** issues of the day by becoming increasingly involved in more comprehensive and often more interventionist peace operations. Efforts undertaken in places such as Cambodia in 1994 began with limited mandates for specific peacekeeping missions, but slipped into more comprehensive responses as local needs grew. Even more ambitious projects were being undertaken by the end of the millennium, such that the UN, for example, was in effect responsible for the day-to-day administration of populations in Kosovo and East Timor (see Box 30.2).

BOX 30.2: CASE STUDY

Post-conflict state-building in Kosovo

NATO's Kosovo Force (KFOR), originally comprising some 50 000 personnel, began operations on 12 June 1999. UNMIK, the UN Mission in Kosovo, was created to work alongside KFOR. KFOR had been mandated to keep the peace in Kosovo by UN Security Council Resolution 1244 in June 1999, while UNMIK's task was to rebuild a lasting peace in Kosovo.

This meant that 'international officials took over key administrative functions, from taxation to garbage collection, in what amounted to the creation of a UN protectorate' (Paris 2004: 213). The transitional administration therefore assumed the authority and functions of the state, with these tasks being divided into four broad areas: police and justice; civil administration; democratisation and institution-building; and reconstruction and economic development (Dwan 2006: 268).

Critics argued that 'no master plan existed against which implementation [of state-building policies] could be measured' (Heinemann-Gruder and Grebenschikov 2006: 44) and that the focus on administration and order as emphasised both in Kosovo and in East Timor encouraged a very technical view of the state that resulted in the people and institutions that deliver these being seen as unresponsive to local views and inputs (Dwan 2006: 269).

On 17 February 2008 Kosovo declared independence but, despite a recent International Court of Justice ruling (July 2010) supporting the claim to independence, it is still not recognised by Serbia which considers the territory a UN-governed entity, and a significant international presence remains in situ.

Moreover, humanitarian imperatives to help with building or re-building institutions in post-conflict situations have been further compounded by post-September 11 fears of the destructive potential of 'failed states'.

Figure 30.1   US Defense Secretary Robert M. Gates boards a UH-60 Blackhawk on Camp Montieth, Kosovo, 7 October 2008

Source: US Air Force Tech. Sgt Jerry Morrison/US Dept of Defense.

'Failed states' are said to be 'tense, deeply conflicted, dangerous, and contested bitterly by warring factions' where there is an enduring violence aimed at the government, and where **state** authorities are unable to control borders or spiralling crime rates (Rotberg 2003: 5–6). After September 11, security concerns have seen a great deal of interest in this notion that states may fail, as policy-makers have feared that failed states could potentially harbour **terrorist** bases or training camps (Mallaby 2002). This fear that a non-functioning state may allow, among other things, for terrorists and criminals to operate with impunity, combined with the interrelated advent of major state-building projects in Iraq and Afghanistan, has therefore meant that the term 'post-conflict state-building' has become part of our lexicon.

The importance of post-conflict state-building is due to a number of interrelated political and **normative** assumptions at play in contemporary international affairs. Central here are three assertions. First, that the **sovereign state** is currently the best form of political organisation available for helping to secure peace, justice and development. Second, that state-building can and ought to be pursued with vigour by the international community (Whaites 2008; Ghani and Lockhart 2008; Fukuyama 2004; OECD 2008). Third, that so-called 'failed states' constitute an active threat to the security of others that must be addressed (Rotberg 2003; Mallaby 2002).

Some of these points of view suggest that sovereign states currently constitute the dominant and ideal form of territorially based political and economic units for our world (and some argue that this situation *should* endure into the future, contrary to some **cosmopolitan** aspirations). Perhaps more importantly when thinking about the actual shape of current efforts to build or rebuild states in post-conflict situations, it is clear that particular models of statehood are favoured over others in the current rush to build or rebuild states.

The post-conflict state-building agenda

The concept of 'post-conflict state-building' has two major components, both of which lack definitional clarity. The idea of something being *post*-conflict is both optimistic (hopeful that conflict has passed) and pejorative (for while violent conflict has ceased all is not yet well). Additionally, it can be difficult to ascertain when something is in fact post-conflict, if a situation remains somewhat unsettled if not in a state of outright violence (see Brown, Langer and Stewart 2008). These definitional issues continue into a consideration of the idea of state-building too.

As noted in Chapter 9, modern states may be described in a variety of ways. They may be viewed as institutions that provide certain functions and services or, alternatively, as expressions of **power**. There are also many possible manifestations of 'statehood', and scholars have created different ways of categorising or classifying the types of states that exist today, depending on what aspect of the state they wish to focus on. Comparativist Joel Migdal (2001) assesses states in terms of the state–society nexus – identifying, for example, how states may be strong in terms of institutional capacity but weak in terms of conceptualisations of a complementary society.

Scholars therefore seek to understand how these entities called states may differ wildly yet still retain some essential characteristics. Attempts to define the basic premises of the state tend to emphasise that these are predominantly legal entities based on fixed territorial boundaries that emerge out of some sort of political settlement, claim some sort of legitimacy domestically and internationally, and include a political executive and separate, permanent and professional administrative structures to implement policy.

In thinking about how to 'build' such entities, Lakhdar Brahimi (2007: 5) claims that state-building is 'a description of exactly what it is that we should be trying to do in post conflict countries – *building effective systems and institutions of government*' (italics added). State-building writ large is often viewed as an ongoing dynamic process that involves the enhancement of the state's ability to function. Alan Whaites (2008: 6) therefore suggests that state-building involves three necessary areas of progress: political settlement; survival functions; and expected functions such as the provision of security. David Chandler (2006: 1) further argues that state-building refers to 'constructing or reconstructing institutions of governance capable of providing citizens with physical and economic security'.

Post-conflict state-building is therefore a term that seems simply to denote particular kinds of technically oriented activities such as:

- the (re)writing of a constitution
- the (re)creation of the different offices of state
- the (re)creation of a criminal justice system
- the (re)creation of national police and/or military forces
- the (re)creation of a national taxation office, and so on.

These sorts of activities can be seen at work in a number of post-conflict situations in the world today (see Box 30.3), and are at times described by alternative but similar terms such as capacity building, reconstruction, stabilisation or institution building.

BOX 30.3: CASE STUDY

Regional assistance to the Solomon Islands

At the request of that country's beleaguered Prime Minister, Allan Kemakeza, the Regional Assistance Mission to Solomon Islands (RAMSI) was deployed in mid- 2003 to help restore law and order following years of civil strife. This law and order restoration phase has on the whole been hailed as a success so far (R. Glenn 2007).

However, RAMSI was intended to do more than just provide for a security pause. As noted on the RAMSI website (www.ramsi.org/about/what-is-RAMSI.html), its mandate as agreed under the Solomon Islands Government-RAMSI Partnership Framework allows for wide-ranging programs that aim to:

- ensure the safety and security of the Solomon Islands
- repair and reform the machinery of government, improve government accountability, and improve the delivery of services in urban and provincial areas
- improve economic governance and strengthen the government's financial systems
- help rebuild the economy and encourage sustainable broad-based growth
- build strong and peaceful communities.

RAMSI is therefore aiming to provide support and mentoring across a broad range of government initiatives, and this has meant activities such as promoting women in politics, restructuring financial and economic institutions, and providing electoral support.

Critics such as Hamieri (2009) have, however, voiced their concerns about issues such as neo-**colonialism** and a lack of 'fit' of the types of institutions being promoted by RAMSI.

However, descriptions such as these that focus on 'function' or 'capacity' obscure the fact that the state-building process favoured in present-day circumstances is a political rather than merely technical process. Contemporary state-building is therefore not a neutral phenomenon: it promotes certain types of political, social and economic institutions and relationships to the exclusion of others.

The politics of contemporary post-conflict state-building

Advocates of contemporary post-conflict state-building efforts often operate under the assumption that outsiders can, and indeed should, help with or even drive this process – a notion that parallels the theme of the democratisation literature of the 1990s, which argued in essence that **democracy** can and should be 'manufactured' (Di Palma 1990). Thus, although the Organisation for Economic Co-operation and Development (OECD 2008) suggested that state-building is an 'endogenous' process with which international actors can 'align', in practice there may be little in the way of shared local interest or capacity in post-conflict situations to drive the process from within. Even 'partnerships' between international and local actors have often been unbalanced in favour of the former. In practice, the term post-conflict state-building therefore tends to refer to the role of external actors – predominantly members of the international community (including regional bodies, the **UN**, or various coalitions of states) – who have the resources and motivations to shape other states.

Usually there is an accompanying assumption, either implicit or explicit, within much of these state-building activities as prescribed by those external actors – namely, that certain types of states are more desirable to build than others. **Critical** scholars have therefore argued that projects to rebuild the state mask 'an implicit preference for a particular set of social and political relationships and the institutional arrangements supportive of this. Contemporary state-building interventions … are particularly shaped by a **neoliberal** institutionalist notion of state capacity' (Hamieri 2009: 57).

The particular model of statehood being promoted in post-conflict state-building efforts is one that seeks to embed certain Western or liberal democratic characteristics such as market economies, individual rights, political representation and the rule of law. These characteristics are touted by institutions, such as the UN in Kosovo and Timor or NATO in Afghanistan, as the ideal type of political institution to help solve the various problems faced by post-conflict populations, with influential academic figures such as Francis Fukuyama also promoting these values.

Fukuyama (2004) sees the role of state-building as creating political and economic institutions that will be capable of democratic governance and economic development – in other words, modelled on neoliberal forms of politics and economics. Asraf Ghani and Clare Lockhart (2008: 59) further argue that:

our world today is one of literal and symbolic connections between the public, the private, and the citizen and that value is derived from chains of relationships among these stakeholders … a framework has been devised that balances the activities of the state, the market and the citizen. This recognises a public sphere of accountability and the rule of law; the market as a competitive space in which law allows freedom to contract, as well as the means of regulation; and a space for civil society where voluntary association is permissible. The citizen in this world is knowledgeable and may participate in all three spheres.

The concept of modern political, economic and social life outlined by Ghani and Lockhart and necessarily involving state-building is, they argue, key to settled peace and prosperity. This particular state-building agenda is, however, under siege from a number of critics for a number of different reasons.

Critics of the current agenda

Post-conflict state-building efforts have, first of all, been criticised for focusing too narrowly on 'just' establishing certain institutions and mechanisms such as constitutions, offices of state, police services or legal systems. In the case of the Solomon Islands, for example, critics have argued that closer attention needs to be paid to broader efforts vis-à-vis relationship-building between different sectors of government and society and to the encouragement of civil society participation in general (Lambourne and Herro 2008: 286). Similar sentiments are expressed by Peter Schaefer (2008: 101) who questions the focus on state-building rather than **nation**-building in Iraq and Afghanistan, while Stein Sundstol Eriksen (2009) argues that overly rigid state-building strategies used in the Democratic Republic of Congo have contributed to state weakness.

Sinclair Dinnen (2007) helps to clarify state-building projects as distinct from nation-building ones. Dinnen asserts that 'state-building comprises the practical task of establishing or strengthening state institutions, while nation-building is more concerned with the character of relations between citizens and their state', noting that:

The workings of many institutions of the modern state rely on the willingness of individuals to identify with – and be able to participate as members of – a common political community. This is essential if states are to be held accountable effectively by the citizens they exist to serve. The construction and reproduction of national identity remains a live, continuous and, often, contested issue in most nation-states (2007: 2).

Other critics have focused on the impacts of state-building in post-conflict situations by asking how the focus on states may impede the **peacebuilding** process (Call with Wyeth 2008). After all, these are sometimes only recently or tenuously post-conflict situations where the building of an effective state will be, in part at least, dependent on a sustainable peace. Certain aspects of post-conflict efforts that contribute to this broader peacebuilding effort are not in state form, as mechanisms to help polities resolve rival claims may or may not be state-based, and an exclusive focus on state-building may therefore have negative effects (Cousens 2001: 12).

Other critics have focused on the political nature of these state-building efforts. The drive towards democratic polities as part of these efforts, for one, has met with a variety of critiques. The difficulties faced by historical and recent democracy promotion programs in countries in Melanesia, the Middle East, Central Asia and Africa have, for example, demonstrated a number of problems with the dogged pursuit of democratisation along Western models (Zakaria 2003). Here, as Benjamin Reilly (2006: 812) notes, any cultural or social features existing in tension with the adoption of such practices are particularly complicated by a post-conflict situation where 'pressures for politicization of identity issues' can result in those oppositional politics occurring along (potentially violence-inducing) ethnic or other lines.

Another assumption in much of the theory that drives contemporary state-building practice is that **capitalist** market economies with liberalised trading practices are desirable counterparts to the state. The liberalisation of trade, the promotion of foreign direct investment and export-driven economies, the downsizing of the public sector in favour of private competition, and so on, have become the dominant model for promoting successful economic development. Yet the work of Roland Paris (2004) outlines how political stability and economic prosperity have proved difficult to achieve in post-conflict sites despite countries undergoing a process of democratisation, adopting a market economy and following advice from international organisations.

Lastly, as Necla Tschirgi (2004: ii) points out in relation to the likely result of such state-building efforts in post-conflict sites, the post-September 11 necessity of preventing state failure in order to enhance one's own security is a formulation 'driven by external demands' and therefore 'likely to undermine the basic premise of peacebuilding that peace, security and stability cannot be imposed from the outside'. The agendas of international actors in places such as Afghanistan (Suhrke 2007) and the Solomon Islands (Hamieri 2009) have therefore been called into question, with critics questioning who post-conflict state-building processes serve in these places, and why. This brings us back to one of the central assumptions at play, that outsiders can and should promote or even control state-building efforts in post-conflict situations.

Criticisms about post-conflict state-building therefore often focus on the motivations behind particular state-building agendas, most notably the concern that these agendas might not serve the local populations but rather reflect post-September 11 security measures implemented to make interveners feel more secure. These concerns are also related to others about the relationship between state-building, peacebuilding and nation-building, and hence to the suitability of the models of state-building that are promoted in post-conflict situations, with concerns expressed over the extent of the social engineering that is taking place (Zaum 2007).

Impacts of post-conflict state-building

A number of consequences have emerged from the recent post-conflict state-building agenda. Some positive impacts could arguably be seen in the restoration of law and order, for example, in the Solomon Islands (Glenn 2003), or in the tentatively successful trial of liberalised economic models in the Rwandan coffee trade (Boudreaux and Ahluwalia 2009). Advocates of post-conflict state-building would also suggest that many of the recent activities undertaken in Iraq and Afghanistan are yet to yield the benefits of what are essentially long-term commitments and processes. Some of the potential negative impacts of recent state-building efforts include the abovementioned mismatch between the interests of the local populations and those of the intervening 'state-builders', or the potential for state-building efforts to exacerbate underlying conflicts.

Other impacts are, however, more generic than these localised and practical concerns. The state-building agenda also feeds into an obsession with the state, despite debate over what constitutes a legitimate state. The concept of 'state failure' (or 'state fragility') means there is a spectrum of more or less legitimate institutional forms in international relations. This is a spectrum in which Western developed states constitute the ideal but their characteristics have not held much relevance to the rest of the world (Boas and Jennings 2005). Indeed, there now exist 'Failed States Indexes' to try to quantify the quality of the state in question (see: www.foreignpolicy.com/failedstates). This may be a useful or destructive development, depending upon one's point of view.

Similarly, in more specific terms, funding for certain post-conflict projects has been prioritised along the neoliberal lines highlighted above, with state-based agencies – particularly security agencies such as police, border guards and the military – being major focal points of international efforts. After all, states are heavily defined by their claimed monopoly over the legitimate use of force and their ability to provide for the security of their citizens. Again, these developments may be seen in more positive or negative light depending upon interpretation. Also open for interpretation is the likely future of the current post-conflict state-building agenda.

The future of post-conflict state-building?

Pinned together somewhat tenuously by broad characteristics of territorially based centralised political units – internal and external forms of sovereignty, at least nominal monopoly over the legitimate use of force, some form of citizenship and, importantly, independence under international law – states can differ significantly. This useful flexibility of form, combined with various pressures to retain a state-based **international system** (or **society**) as noted throughout this textbook, make it difficult to think beyond the concept of the state as described in this manner when we consider the question of 'what to do' with post-conflict societies. Yet post-conflict state-building also has its critics, and it has been argued that 'learning to do state-building better is central to the future of world order' (Fukuyama 2004: 120).

One of the key questions to be asked of the current state-building agenda is therefore: 'if not states, then what?' Paris (2004) may have suggested that there is no requirement to rebuild post-conflict polities as states, but it remains difficult to fully understand what alternatives may exist. This question as to 'if not states, then what?' has in part been considered in Chapter 8, where cosmopolitan authors argue for new modes of global governance. Others consider the new regionalism to be an alternative mode for political community, though regionalism tends to begin with building on shared economic functionalism between member states, and it is unclear what starting premise could replace this. This question of what else might be possible can also be considered through a highly localised lens – whereby there could be a return to a new technologically advanced form of *neo-medievalism* (a term that is mentioned in conjunction with the Kosovo situation) comprising some localised governance in addition to other shifting loyalties in the commercial or regional sphere, for example.

In the post-conflict state-building literature there is one term that has begun to resonate somewhat in asking 'what is to be done?': this is the notion of hybrid approaches that may draw on all of the above. Some scholars have questioned the apparent necessity to build or rebuild states by asking: 'what might constitute a viable political community?' (Boege et al. 2009: 602). Volker Boege, Anne Brown, Kevin Clements and Anna Nolan identify a number of areas where the logic of the formal state exists alongside and in relationship with both a traditional 'informal' societal order and the effects of globalisation and associated social fragmentation. Here 'in short, these hybrid political orders differ considerably from the Western model state', and these authors 'seek a broader understanding of, and advocate, a greater appreciation of hybridity, beyond the limits of its negative connotations' (Boege et al. 2009: 606).

These authors draw on the work of Wiuff Moe (2009) and Hagmann and Hoehne (2007) in arguing that Somaliland is an example of an emerging state grounded in a hybrid political order: a 'state' that enjoys a great deal of local legitimacy yet is not yet recognised internationally; that does not claim full monopoly over the use of force, with security being dealt with in a decentralised manner; and that exists in a situation where customary, Islamic and statutory norms and practices offer up alternative forms of justice. However, these re-conceptualisations of what might constitute legitimate political entities may be a step too far for international institutions and some scholars who seek to retain a firm control over the accepted shape and nature of what we consider to be legitimate political actors (states) in international relations today.

An alternative approach is to temper, though not substantially challenge, the current agenda, by allowing for more local contextualisation in state-building efforts, while maintaining key tenets of democratic governance and liberal economic models as much as possible. The OECD has worked up a number of principles to this effect (see Box 30.4).

BOX 30.4: DISCUSSION POINTS

OECD Principles for Good International Engagement in Fragile States
- Take context as the starting point.
- Ensure all activities do no harm.
- Focus on state-building as the central objective.

- Prioritise prevention.
- Recognise the links between, political, security and development objectives.
- Promote non-discrimination as a basis for inclusive and stable societies.
- Align with local priorities in different ways in different contexts.
- Agree on practical coordination mechanisms between international actors.
- Act fast ... but stay engaged long enough to give success a chance.
- Avoid pockets of exclusion ('aid orphans'). (Source: OECD 2007)

The Principles were field-tested in nine countries over 2006–07:

- the Solomon Islands (facilitated by Australia and New Zealand)
- the Democratic Republic of Congo (facilitated by Belgium)
- Haiti (facilitated by Canada)
- Sudan (facilitated by Norway)
- Guinea Bissau (facilitated by Portugal)
- Nepal (facilitated by the UK)
- Somalia (facilitated by the **World Bank** and the UK)
- Yemen (facilitated by UNDP and the UK).

Conclusion

State-building has been pursued with great vigour in recent times as it is seen as the only viable option for helping to solve post-conflict development and security needs. Such efforts are, however, highly political acts as they have promoted particular models of states, and state-building efforts have therefore met with a number of critiques along the way. The relevance and sustainability of the politically and economically liberalised and centralised state institutions required by recent state-building attempts have been questioned by a number of critics, and alternative suggestions have spoken of the possibilities of 'shared sovereignty' or 'hybrid political orders'. The future of state-building in post-conflict situations may therefore look somewhat different from the experiments of the 1990s and the first decade of the new millennium as we continue to reconceptualise the role of the state and statehood in the international arena.

QUESTIONS

1. Consider Tilly's suggestion that '[w]ar made the state, and the state made war' (1975: 42): what might this assertion mean for contemporary post conflict state-building efforts?

2. What is the relationship between state-building and peace-building? Which of these should be prioritised in addressing the problems of post-conflict situations, and why?

3. Find a 'Failed States Index' on the internet. How useful is this type of classifying exercise? What are the consequences that emerge from the creation of such an index?

4. What are the various obstacles in international relations that would make it difficult to move away from the post-conflict state-building agenda as currently construed? What is the likely future of post-conflict state-building?

5. What does the case of Kosovo say about the problems and prospects for post-conflict state-building, particularly given that states still need to have their authority recognised by others?

FURTHER READING

Boege, Volker, Brown, Anne, Clements, Kevin and Nolan, Anna 2009, 'Building peace and political community in hybrid political orders', *International Peacekeeping*, 16(5), 599–615.

Call, Charles with V. Wyeth 2008, *Building states to build peace*. Boulder CO: International Peace Institute/Lynne Rienner.

Chandler, David 2006, *Empire in denial: the politics of state-building*, London: Pluto Press.

Fukuyama, Francis 2004, *State-building: governance and world order in the 21st century*, Ithaca NY: Cornell University Press.

Ghani, Ashraf and Lockhart, Clare 2008, *Fixing failed states; a framework for rebuilding a fractured world*, Oxford: Oxford University Press.

Paris, Roland 2004, *At war's end: building peace after civil conflict*, Cambridge: Cambridge University Press.

31

Humanitarian Intervention

Thomas G. Weiss

Introduction	427
The origins of humanitarianism	427
A short history of humanitarian intervention	431
The responsibility to protect	433
Noel Morada: Responsibility to protect (R2P) and prevention of mass atrocities	435
Conclusion	438
Questions	438
Further reading	439

Introduction

This chapter introduces students to an idea which has enjoyed a remarkable, if hotly contested, development in the post-**Cold War** era: **humanitarian intervention**. Based on a commitment to principles of humanity, humanitarian intervention seeks to alleviate the unnecessary human suffering caused by violent conflict by intervening in another state with force under certain limited conditions. The chapter first outlines the origins of **humanitarianism**; second, it sketches a short history of humanitarian intervention; and third, it discusses the shift from humanitarian intervention to **responsibility to protect (R2P)**. As the context of world politics becomes ever more complex, debate about global responsibilities to protect suffering strangers through humanitarian action will continue to shape the theory and practice of international relations.

For the last two decades, humanitarian organisations have careened from one major disaster to another. The end of the Cold War unleashed a pent-up demand for acute humanitarian action – that is, protecting and assisting individuals caught in war zones. Analyses of this period typically highlight three defining trends that explain this expansion, as well as second thoughts about the overall direction (Barnett and Weiss 2011). The first is the growing willingness and ability of outsiders to help those at risk. Radical improvements in information technology and logistical capacities, growing international support for coming to the rescue of victims, multiplying numbers of relief organisations, and substantial increases in available resources promised an enhanced collective capacity to provide relief, rescue and reconstruction. The second trend reflects the mounting dangers that aid workers confront in war zones where access is difficult, where they are often perceived as a threat or as a resource to be captured, where their own physical safety is in doubt, and where civilian populations are the intended victims (Kaldor 1999; Duffield 2001). In addition, the deployment of military force in such arenas for human protection purposes has raised new kinds of questions about the ability of aid workers to remain faithful to their principles (Hoffman and Weiss 2006).

This chapter focuses on the peculiar dynamics of what until recently was called 'humanitarian intervention' (forcefully coming to the rescue of civilians without the consent of political authorities in the territories where victims are located) but is now more commonly called 'R2P', the emerging norm of the responsibility to protect. First, however, it provides a basic introduction to humanitarianism, as well as to the early history of humanitarian intervention, before reviewing the contemporary phenomenon.

The origins of humanitarianism

Charity and expressions of care and concern are certainly not a modern phenomenon; kith and kin have long sought to extend helping hands, which is symbolised by the Biblical tale of the Good Samaritan. In the late eighteenth and early nineteenth centuries in Europe, however, the Industrial Revolution produced ugly social conditions and new instabilities that led to the modern humanitarianism. Changes in the economy, society and culture led to the founding of religious and social movements, of which the anti-slavery movement was the most famous. Importantly, many of the same reform societies, social movements and leaders who spearheaded campaigns to humanise domestic society also became deeply troubled by unnecessary suffering outside their borders (Calhoun 2008). If the suffering of neighbors was unacceptable when something could be done to alleviate it, why should artificially drawn frontiers define the limits of concern?

The official beginning of war-related international humanitarianism is usually dated to the aftermath of a bloody battle in northern Italy in 1859. The Swiss businessman Henry Dunant was appalled by what he saw at the Battle of Solferino and the needless suffering during the last engagement of the second war of Italian independence between Austro-Hungarian and Franco-Piedmontese troops (see Box 31.1). Dunant pulled together friends and acquaintances from Geneva, and also persuaded the Swiss Government to convene a diplomatic conference, which resulted in the official establishment in 1864 of the International Committee of the Red Cross (ICRC). This gathering also led to the signature of the first **Geneva Convention**, the foundation for what would eventually be codified as **international humanitarian law**, which is also called 'the laws of **war**' (Bugnion 2003).

BOX 31.1: KEY TEXTS

Extracts from Henry Dunant's *Memory of Solferino* ([1862] 1986)

'I was a mere tourist with no part whatever in this great conflict; but it was my rare privilege, through an unusual train of circumstances, to witness the moving scenes that I have resolved to describe' (4).

'Here is hand-to-hand struggle in all its horror and frightfulness; Austrians and Allies trampling each other under foot, killing one another on piles of bleeding corpses, felling their enemies with their rifle butts, crushing skulls, ripping bellies open with sabre and bayonet. No quarter is given; it is sheer butchery; a struggle between savage beasts, maddened with blood and fury … A little further on, it is the same picture, only made the more ghastly by the approach of a squadron of cavalry, which gallops by, crushing dead and dying beneath its horses' hoofs' (5).

'But why have I told all these scenes of pain and distress, and perhaps aroused painful emotions in my readers? Why have I lingered with seeming complacency over lamentable pictures, tracing their details with what might appear desperate fidelity?

It is a natural question. Perhaps I might answer it by another.

Would it not be possible, in time of peace and quiet, to form relief societies for the purpose of having care given to the wounded in wartime by zealous, devoted and thoroughly qualified volunteers?' (27).

'Humanity and civilization call imperiously for such an organization as is here suggested' (29).

From those conventions and their updates in 1949 and 1977, along with efforts in what are called the Hague conferences of 1899 and 1907, humanitarian action has customarily followed the ICRC's core principles of humanity, impartiality, neutrality and independence (see Box 31.2). The industry grew, particularly during and after the first and second world wars; both **non-governmental organisations (NGOs)** and intergovernmental ones – now of the **United Nations (UN)** system – dominate the provision of assistance to war victims. Although aid organisations have come to disagree on when the operating principles of independence and neutrality lead to desired outcomes (as we see below), the principles of impartiality and humanity are defining features of their identities.

BOX 31.2: KEY TEXTS

The ICRC's Mission Statement

The International Committee of the Red Cross (ICRC) is an impartial, neutral and independent organization whose exclusively humanitarian mission is to protect the lives and dignity of victims of war and internal violence and to provide them with assistance.

It directs and coordinates the international relief activities conducted by the Movement in situations of conflict. It also endeavours to prevent suffering by promoting and strengthening humanitarian law and universal humanitarian principles.

Established in 1863, the ICRC is at the origin of the International Red Cross and Red Crescent Movement.

Source: www.icrc.org/eng/who-we-are/mandate/overview-icrc-mandate-mission.htm

---

Humanitarian action is intimately related to **cosmopolitanism** – the claim that each person is of equal moral worth and a subject of moral concern, and that everyone at risk, regardless of his or her background or affiliation, and regardless of religion or ethnic background, deserves equal attention. Humanitarian organisations are expressing a cosmopolitan ethic as they relieve suffering and save lives; and thus fundamentally they distinguish themselves from other entities with resources to devote to 'saving strangers' in an international society of states (Wheeler 2000).

It would be useful to have a sense of the magnitude of the contemporary 'humanitarian enterprise' (Minear 2002). Many accounts proceed as if humanitarianism began with the end of the Cold War, a clear demonstration of overlooking history. While the absence of longitudinal data on basic categories such as expenditure, income, number of organisations and activities makes certain comparisons difficult, nonetheless the humanitarian sector has undergone significant growth since the end of the Cold War – most noticeably in its density, resources and activities.

To start, the sheer increase in organisational numbers is striking. Notwithstanding debate about whether a particular organisation is or is not humanitarian, presently there are at least 2500 NGOs in the humanitarian business, but only about one-tenth of them are serious players – based on a 2003 roster (no longer updated) by the UN Office for the Coordination of Humanitarian Affairs (OCHA). In fact, in 2001 the half-dozen or so largest NGOs controlled between US$2.5 billion and US$3 billion, or about half of all global humanitarian assistance (Development Initiatives 2003: 56).

A detailed survey of US-based private voluntary agencies engaged in relief and development suggests a picture of growth more generally over the last three-quarters of a century. In 1940, shortly after the start of World War II, the number rose quickly to 387 organisations (from 240), but the numbers dropped to 103 in 1946 and 60 in 1948. They rose steadily thereafter and reached 543 in 2005. The growth was especially dramatic from 1986 to 1994, when the number increased from 178 to 506 (McCleary 2009: 3–35).

UN organisations are also prominent in the sector. The Office of the UN High Commissioner for Refugees (UNHCR), the UN Children's Fund (UNICEF) and the

Figure 31.1   UN chopper

Source: Jude Ewing, used with permission.

World Food Programme (WFP) were born as humanitarian organisations and now are the mainstays of the intergovernmental humanitarian system. Other international organisations were created to foster development but are increasingly involved in relief and reconstruction because of humanitarian demand and the availability of resources, including the UN Development Programme (UNDP) and the **World Bank**.

There has also been a growth in the number of international and regional organisations whose primary responsibility is to coordinate humanitarian assistance, including the European Community Humanitarian Aid Office (ECHO), the UN's Inter-Agency Standing Committee (IASC) and OCHA (preceded by the Department of Humanitarian Affairs, DHA). The same phenomenon exists for NGOs in the US and Europe, including InterAction in Washington, DC, the International Council for Voluntary Action (ICVA) and Emergency Committee for Humanitarian Response (ECHR) in Geneva, and Voluntary Organisations in Cooperation in Emergencies (VOICE) in Brussels. In addition, states, not-for-profit disaster firms, other businesses and various foundations are increasingly prominent contributors to humanitarian action.

Private contributions have increased, but most impressive has been the growth in official (i.e. governmental) assistance. Between 1990 and 2000 aid levels rose nearly threefold, from US$2.1 billion to US$5.9 billion – and in 2005–6 were over US$18 billion, up around $3 billion from the previous year (Global Humanitarian Assistance 2009: 2).

A short history of humanitarian intervention

The European scramble for colonies in the nineteenth century gave birth to the term 'humanitarian intervention' (Bass 2008). Many colonial powers rationalised the use of overwhelming force with the use of humanitarian rhetoric. But they selectively applied such might to geographical areas with immediate strategic and economic interests, and often stayed long after the territory was more politically stable. No wonder, then, that the former subjugated peoples who are living in now independent countries that constitute the global South harbour tremendous doubts and frequently express outright hostility toward the claim from the West (which is where all the former **colonial** masters are located) that military interventions for human protection purposes are self-sacrificing and disinterested.

The first international legal references to humanitarian intervention appeared after 1840 (Stapleton 1866; Stowell 1921). Two interventions, in particular, were directly responsible for stimulating such analytical interest: the intervention in Greece by England, France and Russia in 1827 to stop Turkish massacres and suppression of populations associated with it; and the intervention by France in Syria in 1860 to protect Maronite Christians. In fact, there were at least five prominent interventions undertaken by European powers against the Ottoman Empire from 1827 to 1908 (Danish Institute of International Affairs 1999: 79). By the 1920s, the rationale for intervention had broadened to include the protection of nationals abroad as well when they were under attack from colonial peoples or local authorities (Brownlie 1963: 338–9).

Intervention thus was invoked against a state's abuse of its sovereignty for brutal and cruel treatment of those within its power, both nationals and non-nationals. Such a state was regarded as having made itself liable to intervention by any state or coalition of states that were prepared to act. Such intervention has frequently been surrounded by controversy, mainly because humanitarian justifications were oftentimes a none-too-subtle alibi for meddling motivated by strategic, economic or political interests. Even when objectives were more laudable, the cultural arrogance and paternalism of intervening powers undermined the credibility of their claim to be acting on behalf of affected populations rather than protecting their own self-interests.

The noted international lawyer Ian Brownlie concluded that 'no genuine case of humanitarian intervention has occurred with the possible exception of the occupation of Syria in 1860 and 1861' (1963: 340). The scale of the atrocities in that case may well have warranted intervention – more than 11 000 Maronite Christians were killed and 100 000 made homeless in a single four-week period. But by the time some 12 000 European soldiers arrived the violence was largely over; and after undertaking some relief activities the troops withdrew.

At the end of the nineteenth century, some legal commentators argued that a doctrine of humanitarian intervention existed in customary **international law**, but a considerable number of their colleagues adamantly disagreed. At present, contemporary legal scholars continue to debate the significance of these conclusions. Some argue that the doctrine was clearly established in state practice prior to 1945 and that only the parameters, not the existence, of that doctrine are subject to question. Other public international lawyers reject this claim and point to the inconsistency of state practice, particularly in the twentieth century, and the substantial number of legal scholars who have categorically rejected the proposition.

The UN Security Council was paralysed for many of the Cold War years because a veto by any one of the permanent five members (the US, the UK, France, China and the Soviet Union) meant no binding decision could be made (see Chapters 20 and 21). The end of the Cold War permitted robust decisions that abruptly catapulted the UN to the centre of the international conflict-management business. In a departure from previous practice, in the 1990s the world body either authorised or sub-contracted to regional organisations the use of military force to protect human beings (Durch 2006; L. Howard 2008). Beginning with the 1991 authorisation to use all necessary means to protect the Kurds from Saddam Hussein in the aftermath of the Gulf War, a host of Security Council decisions authorised the use of force for human protection purposes in Bosnia, Somalia, Rwanda, Liberia, Sierra Leone, Kosovo and East Timor. As a result, many NGO and UN humanitarian agencies were able to engage in activities to protect and succour populations in insecure arenas, whereas earlier the ICRC had had a virtual monopoly in such circumstances.

Whether the results of these 'military–civilian interactions' have been, on balance, beneficial (Weiss 2005a) or counter-productive (Chandler 2002; Rieff 2002) remains controversial. However, the earlier notion that the Security Council could not apply the provisions of Chapter VII of the **UN Charter** to make binding decisions about humanitarian crises became moot (see Box 31.3). The Council effectively set precedents in taking action on numerous cases by labelling humanitarian disasters 'threats to international peace and security', the agreed basis in the Charter to justify such decisions. This power of self-definition explains why there are continual demands to reform the composition and procedures of the Security Council; but to date no agreement has been reached because all of the proposals create as many problems as they solve (Weiss 2005b).

BOX 31.3: KEY TEXTS

Chapter VII of the UN Charter

Chapter VII: Action with respect to threats to the peace, breaches of the peace, and acts of aggression

Article 39

The Security Council shall determine the existence of any threat to the peace, breach of the peace, or act of aggression and shall make recommendations, or decide what measures shall be taken in accordance with Articles 41 and 42, to maintain or restore international peace and security.

Article 41

The Security Council may decide what measures not involving the use of armed force are to be employed to give force to its decisions …

Article 42

Should the Security Council consider that measures provided for in Article 41 would be inadequate or have proved to be inadequate, it may take such action by air, sea, or land forces as may be necessary to maintain or restore international peace and security …

While this is not the place to discuss them, the Security Council also made decisions under the UN Charter's Chapter VII to authorise coercive measures short of military force. Economic sanctions and international criminal pursuit, beginning in the 1990s, are not usually considered part of humanitarian intervention per se. However, they too oblige the entire UN membership to take specific actions against the expressed will of a targeted state, and a partial or total justification for many was humanitarian. In what was called 'the sanctions decade' (Cortright and Lopez 2000), Council decisions reflected the specific desire to elicit dramatic changes by the targeted regimes whose policies were creating humanitarian disasters. Ironically, the sometimes catastrophic humanitarian consequences of sanctions on innocent civilian populations within targeted states (Weiss et al. 1997) led the Security Council away from the comprehensive measures toward 'smart sanctions' (Cortright et al. 2002). It also created a number of international criminal tribunals, beginning in the early 1990s with those for the former Yugoslavia and Rwanda; and in 2002 states created the International Criminal Court (Goldstone and Smith 2008). While many of the persons brought to the dock had been responsible for war crimes and other crimes against humanity – including the former presidents of Serbia and Liberia, and warrants issued for the sitting presidents of Sudan and Libya – international criminal pursuit is also not typically classified as part of humanitarian intervention.

Clearly the notion of coming to the rescue of affected populations evolved substantially before the appearance of a well-developed international system with institutions responsible for maintaining international order and protecting human rights. That the 'H' word was all too often a transparent pretext for interest-based rather than unselfish intervention continues to colour the contemporary debate. As Ramesh Thakur points out, developing countries 'are neither amused nor mindful at being lectured on universal human values by those who failed to practice the same during European colonialism and now urge them to cooperate in promoting "global" human rights norms' (Thakur 2001: 31; see also Ayoob 2004).

The responsibility to protect

Since it appeared as the title of the 2001 report by the International Commission on Intervention and State Sovereignty (ICISS), the responsibility to protect (R2P) has shaped international responses to egregious violations of human rights (see Box 31.4). Given R2P's declared goal to change the terms of humanitarian discourse and the controversy that continues to swirl around it, questions arise as to how far it presently is from the status of an agreed international **norm** as part of 'revolutions in sovereignty' (Philpott 2001). Most importantly, R2P attempted to move beyond the toxic topic of humanitarian intervention.

BOX 31.4: KEY TEXTS

The responsibility to protect: Report of the International Commission on Intervention and State Sovereignty (2001)

Basic principles:

A. State sovereignty implies responsibility, and the primary responsibility for the protection of its people lies with the state itself.

B. Where a population is suffering serious harm, as a result of internal war, insurgency, repression or state failure, and the state in question is unwilling or unable to halt or avert it, the principle of non-intervention yields to the international responsibility to protect.

Available at www.iciss.ca/pdf/Commission-Report.pdf

In referring to 'two sovereignties' (that is, of individuals and of states) in several speeches, UN Secretary-General from 1997–2006 Kofi Annan (1999) created unease and even open hostility among numerous countries of the global South. They disputed his contention that individual sovereignty and human rights could on occasion trump sacrosanct state sovereignty. Beginning with the international response in northern Iraq in 1991 to protect Kurds from Saddam Hussein's regime in the aftermath of the Gulf War, largely circular and poisonous tirades took place around Security Council decisions about the agency, timing, legitimacy, means, circumstances and advisability of using military force to protect human beings. The R2P agenda, however, comprises more complex and subtle responses to mass atrocities than the use of force, ranging from prevention to post-conflict rebuilding to protecting civilians at risk (Thakur 2006; Weiss 2007; Evans 2008; Bellamy 2009; and Badescu 2010).

The central **normative** tenet of the responsibility to protect, as envisaged first in the 2001 ICISS report and its accompanying research volume (Weiss and Hubert 2001) and embraced later by the consensus decision at the September 2005 UN World Summit (Bellamy 2006b), is that state sovereignty is contingent and not absolute (United Nations 2005: paras 138–140). Each state has a responsibility to protect its citizens from large-scale **ethnic cleansing**, mass killings and other conscience-shocking suffering. If a state, however, is unable or unwilling to exercise that responsibility, or actually is a perpetrator of mass atrocities, its sovereignty is abrogated while the responsibility to protect devolves to the international community of states, ideally acting through the Security Council. The two-fold responsibility in this framework – internal and external – draws upon earlier work by Francis Deng and Roberta Cohen on 'sovereignty as responsibility' to alleviate the plight of internally displaced persons (IDPs) (Deng et al. 1996; Cohen and Deng 1998; see also Weiss and Korn 2006).

The ICISS as well as the World Summit consciously sought to distance themselves from the perceived anachronistic language of humanitarian intervention. Both emphasised the need to do everything possible to prevent mass atrocities so that deploying military force would be an option only after other alternatives had been considered and had failed. In the Summit's language, such actions would only apply to cases of '**genocide**, war crimes, ethnic cleansing and crimes against humanity'.

The removal of the 'H' adjective from intervention underlined a point that was of especial significance to former colonial peoples: the merits of particular situations should be evaluated rather than blindly given the imprimatur of 'humanitarian'. Because of the number of sins justified by the use of that adjective during the painful period of colonialism, this change was more than semantic. The language marked a dramatic shift away from the rights of outsiders to intervene toward the rights of populations at risk to receive succour and protection and the responsibility of outsiders to come to their rescue.

Gareth Evans calculates that the evolution has taken place in 'a blink of the eye in the history of ideas' (2008: 28). Whether one agrees or not with that perspective, the developments since the release of the ICISS report in December 2001 suggest that R2P has moved from the prose and passion of an international expert commission to a mainstay of international public policy. The responsibility to protect also has potential to evolve in customary international law and to contribute to ongoing conversations about the responsibilities of states if they are to be legitimate sovereigns.

Responsibility to protect (R2P) and prevention of mass atrocities   Noel Morada

Translating an emerging political norm from words to deeds

The idea of the responsibility to protect (R2P) was put forward in 2001 by the International Commission on Intervention and State Sovereignty (ICISS), which conducted a series of intensive collaborative research and consultations on how the international community should respond to humanitarian crisis situations across the globe. This stemmed from various humanitarian crises in the 1990s (e.g. Rwanda, Bosnia-Herzegovina, Sudan, etc.) that forced the United Nations and its member states to seriously consider the appropriate principles and mechanisms to respond effectively to these problems. R2P redefines state sovereignty as one that also includes the responsibility of the state to protect its people or populations against mass atrocities. Specifically, it includes the responsibility to prevent (i.e. to address the direct or root causes of internal conflicts or humanitarian crises), the responsibility to react (i.e. respond to humanitarian crisis situations with appropriate measures, including military intervention as a last resort), and responsibility to rebuild (i.e. provide assistance for post-conflict rehabilitation and **peace building**). R2P as a political **norm** also advances that, if states fail to protect their own people, the responsibility shifts to the international community to respond to humanitarian crisis situations in accordance with international law and the Charter of the United Nations. Initially, a number of developing states were quite uncomfortable with the idea of R2P because it goes against the traditional principle of promoting respect for state sovereignty and non-intervention. Some of them feared that it could be used and abused by powerful Western countries as a pretext for intervention in other states as the ICISS report gave heavy emphasis to the coercive aspect of R2P. There were also concerns about how the United Nations would decide on when to invoke R2P to justify military intervention in humanitarian crisis situations.

In 2005, following the World Summit of Leaders in the United Nations, a consensus on R2P emerged, which was reflected in paragraphs 138–140 of the World Summit Outcome Document. In particular, member states agreed that the responsibility to protect rests primarily on states and that the international community should assist states in building the capacity to prevent genocide and mass atrocities. They also agreed that R2P should cover only four crimes – genocide, ethnic cleansing, war crimes, and crimes against humanity – and that international assistance to states should focus on prevention measures such as developing early warning capabilities. It is important to note that the pertinent paragraphs in the Outcome Document did not mention military intervention per se and focused on the use of 'appropriate diplomatic, humanitarian, and other peaceful means' to protect populations from the four crimes. Nonetheless, it also included reference to member states of the United Nations being prepared to take collective action 'in a timely and decisive manner' in accordance with Chapter VII of the UN Charter, which allows for military intervention, 'on a case-by-case basis and in cooperation with relevant regional organizations as appropriate'. This third pillar of R2P remains controversial as many developing states, including China, regard it as an opening for misuse or abuse to justify intervention. For example,

Russia in August 2008 inappropriately invoked R2P to justify its military intervention in Ossetia, Georgia, while France for the wrong reasons used it to call for collective international humanitarian intervention against the Myanmar military junta in May 2008 following Cyclone Nargis when the latter refused to accept humanitarian assistance from Western countries. Through the mediation of the Association of Southeast Asian Nations (**ASEAN**), however, the military junta relented and allowed international humanitarian assistance to come in through the regional organisation. Even so, some member states in ASEAN remain reluctant supporters of R2P as they still cling to the organisation's traditional norms of respecting state sovereignty and non-interference in domestic affairs. Post-colonial states in the region are also facing a number of armed challenges to the legitimacy of the state even as they are also in the process of building nations from multi-ethnic societies. Indeed, these pose serious challenges to the exercise of state sovereignty with corresponding responsibility to protect populations from the four crimes. At the same time, the region has experienced a range of human rights violations and mass atrocity crimes, notably in the case of Cambodia under the Khmer Rouge, East Timor prior to its independence, and the Maguindanao massacre in the Philippines in 2009.

In an effort to implement the international consensus on R2P, global and regional centres were set up with the support of some member states of the United Nations. Specifically, these organisations were tasked to do research aimed at developing tools in preventing genocide and examine the root causes and preconditions for mass atrocities, as well as developing or enhancing capabilities of states for protection of civilians, especially in armed conflict areas. Advocacy work is also needed in promoting R2P in various regions, particularly in building awareness about what the norm is about as well as in creating constituencies that would contribute to enhancing the capability of states to prevent mass atrocities.

As an emerging political norm, R2P must be internalised at various levels – international, regional, national, and local or community – in order for the idea to resonate deeply and effectively promote the protection of populations from genocide, ethnic cleansing, war crimes and crimes against humanity. States may sign international agreements or conventions on human rights and international humanitarian law, or become parties to the International Criminal Court. But these are inadequate in preventing the commission of the four crimes if there are no corresponding domestic laws that punish perpetrators and if states overall remain incapable of addressing the root causes and preconditions for mass atrocities. In the context of conflict-prone, multi-ethnic societies in Southeast Asia, for example, so much may be expected of states whose legitimacy is continually being challenged while they continue to invoke the traditional definition of sovereignty and non-interference. At the end of the day, R2P is about changing the mindset of political leaders: that sovereignty, more than a right, is also a responsibility. And the international community of nations must remain vigilant and ensure that perpetrators of mass atrocities are held accountable for their crimes.

Noel Morada is Executive Director of the Asia-Pacific Centre for the Responsibility to Protect. He was formerly Professor of Political Science at the University of the Philippines Diliman and was a Distinguished Visiting Professor, Southeast Asian Program at the School of Advanced International Studies (SAIS) at the Johns Hopkins University, Washington DC in Spring 2008.

The advance of rhetoric is impressive. In 2004 in the preparations for the UN's sixtieth anniversary, the High-level Panel on Threats, Challenges and Change issued their report *A more secure world: our shared responsibility*, which endorsed 'the emerging norm that there is a collective international responsibility to protect' (para. 203). Former UN Secretary-General Kofi Annan lauded it in his 2005 report, *In larger freedom*. The most significant normative advance came in September 2005, when more than 150 heads of state and government gathered in New York unanimously supported the R2P. In addition to the official blessing of the World Summit's separate section that was approved by the UN General Assembly in October 2005, the Security Council also made subsequent and specific references to R2P: the April 2006 Resolution 1674 on the protection of civilians in armed conflict expressly 'reaffirms the provisions of paragraphs 138 and 139'; the August 2006 Resolution 1706 on Darfur was the first to link R2P to a particular conflict; and the 2011 Resolution 1973 approved the no-fly zone in Libya.

In addition, UN Secretary-General Ban Ki-moon appointed a special adviser for the prevention of genocide and a special adviser tasked with promoting R2P. The Secretary-General has referred to R2P as one of his priorities, and in January 2009 released a comprehensive report on *Implementing the responsibility to protect*. This report puts forward the details of 'three pillars' for implementing R2P, which comprise: (1) the protection responsibilities of individual states; (2) international assistance and capacity-building for feeble states; and (3) timely and decisive international responses when states fail to meet their responsibilities toward civilian populations (United Nations 2009).

The UN General Assembly debates in the summers of 2009, 2010 and 2011 represented the latest fledgling step in R2P's normative journey. In preparation, the states members of the 'Group of Friends' of the responsibility to protect in New York, the UN special adviser and civil society picked up the mantle from previous norm entrepreneurs and mobilised around the Secretary-General's report. Initially, many feared that the 2009 debate would produce a resolution diluting the September 2005 commitments, or normative backpedalling: *The Economist* (2009) described opponents who 'have been busily sharpening their knives' on the eve of the debate. A troubled start had critics trying to paint R2P in **imperialistic** colours, including the opening harangue by the Nicaraguan president of the General Assembly, Father Miguel d'Escoto Brockmann (*Economist* 2009), who went so far as to dub R2P 'redecorated colonialism', and suggested that 'a more accurate name for R2P would be the right to intervene'.

However, a close reading of remarks by the representatives of ninety-two countries and two observers who took the floor showed faint support for undermining the responsibility to protect. Virtually all supported its implementation, with only four countries directly questioning the 2005 World Summit agreement – namely, the usual suspects of Cuba, Nicaragua, Sudan and Venezuela. Of especial relevance were remarks from major regional powers that had previously been reticent or even hostile, including Brazil, Nigeria, India, South Africa and Japan. The R2P agenda item ended without any resolution, but a resumed 2009 General Assembly debate in September reaffirmed the consensus. Similar decisions followed in 2010 and 2011.

Despite disagreement and contestation, the most sensible interpretation is that the responsibility to protect is at the beginning of an arduous normative process. All humanitarian initiatives – including the venerable Geneva Conventions after more than a century and a half – require considerable time before new norms stimulate routine change and compliance. As David Rieff summarises, 'there is considerable evidence of changing norms, though not, of course, changing facts on the ground' (2008: 41).

Conclusion

While we do not normally think of anything other than positive precedents as laying the groundwork for normative advances, in fact both applications and misapplications – in rhetoric and in reality – can foster normative consolidation. While this chapter has analysed the accumulation of positive precedents, it is worth noting that the humanitarian and R2P labels were misapplied to the invasion of Iraq (after the links to Al-Qaeda and **weapons of mass destruction (WMDs)** disappeared) as well as to the 2008 Russian invasion of Georgia and to foot-dragging that same year by the Burmese authorities after Cyclone Nargis.

With the possible exception of the international reactions to the violence following the December 2007 elections in Kenya (Weiss 2010), R2P lacked adequate specific applications in practice and concrete examples of compliant behaviour until the dramatic 2011 action to protect civilians in Libya. As such, it is also worthwhile to track actors' reactions and changes in discourse produced by recent misapplications of the norm. In fact, debate and contestation after misapplications and abuses can constitute steps in the direction of norm advancement just as the positive precedents of the 1990s put the issue on the international policy map (Badescu and Weiss 2010). Misuses and violations prompt discussion and contribute to clarifying the scope and boundaries of a new norm. In turn, such clarifications can foster compliance and what ultimately is the desired impact of this norm – namely, increased protection of affected populations.

Despite ongoing grousing about the norm's relevance and purpose, the General Assembly debates and the Security Council's 2011 action in Libya suggest that the responsibility to protect is unlikely to be dislodged from **multilateral** diplomatic discourse. At the same time, it would be foolhardy to assume that governments and humanitarians will react similarly in all emergencies. Politics and national-interest calculations explain why we sometimes do and sometimes do not respond to conscience-shocking humanitarian disasters.

Hence, the term humanitarian 'impulse' is the more accurate description of likely efforts to come to the rescue of strangers, although humanitarian 'imperative' has become the preferred description within virtually all discourse in the field (Weiss 2004). The latter entails an obligation to treat victims similarly and react to all crises consistently – in effect, to deny the relevance of politics, which consists of drawing lines and weighing options and available resources. Yet humanitarian action remains desirable, not obligatory. The humanitarian impulse is permissive; the humanitarian imperative peremptory.

QUESTIONS

1. What does 'humanitarianism' mean in the context of international relations?
2. Do states have a responsibility to protect their own citizens?
3. Does international society have a responsibility to prevent a state from systematically violating the human rights of its own citizens?

4. Can and should force be used against sovereign states for humanitarian reasons?
5. Is there a norm of humanitarian intervention in international relations?
6. Is R2P an instrument of Western imperialism?

FURTHER READING

Barnett, Michael and Weiss, Thomas G. (eds) 2008, *Humanitarianism in question: politics, power, ethics*, Ithaca: Cornell University Press. Comprehensive collection of essays by leading scholars on the manifold dimensions of humanitarianism and armed intervention.

Barnett, Michael and Weiss, Thomas G. 2011, *Humanitarianism contested: where angels fear to tread*, London: Routledge. Succinct but sophisticated analysis of ongoing dilemmas and tensions that have accompanied humanitarianism since its origins in the nineteenth century.

Bellamy, Alex J. 2009, *The responsibility to protect: the global effort to end mass atrocities*, Cambridge: Polity Press. Lucid and thoughtful account and evaluation of the rise of R2P.

Holzgrefe, J. L. and Keohane, Robert O. (eds) 2003, *Humanitarian intervention: ethical, legal and political dilemmas*, Cambridge: Cambridge University Press. Useful collection of essays on the ethical, legal and political debates surrounding humanitarian intervention.

Weiss, Thomas G. 2007, *Humanitarian intervention: ideas in action*, Cambridge: Polity Press. Succinct and accessible study of humanitarian intervention and the debates that it has sparked.

Wheeler, Nicholas J. 2000, *Saving strangers: humanitarian intervention in international society*, Oxford: Oxford University Press. One of the most important books on the subject; engages English School theory to compare Cold War and post-Cold War instances of humanitarian intervention.

Zolo, Danilo 2002, *Invoking humanity: war, law and global order*, trans. Federico and Gordon Poole, London: Continuum. Formidable critique of humanitarian intervention by leading Italian realist.

32

Human Rights

Anthony J. Langlois

Introduction   441

The historical development of an idea   442

The human rights idea today   444

The politics of liberal universalism   445

The future of human rights   447

Conclusion   449

Questions   449

Further reading   449

Introduction

This chapter examines the rise and growth of **human rights**. First, it discusses the historical development of human rights. Second, it outlines how human rights are understood today. Third, it explains how the liberal universalism that lies behind human rights has come up against cultural resistance. Finally, the chapter touches on some challenges that lie ahead in the struggle for human rights.

The doctrine of human rights has become one of the central political doctrines of international politics. This is a remarkable state of affairs, given that only sixty years ago the idea, while championed by some, had little or no traction on the behaviour of states with one another. The end of World War II was the key marker in the birth of the human rights movement as we know it today. Prior to that **war**, human rights – or 'the rights of man' as they were known – had few political supporters in international relations. The doctrines of **realism**, or *realpolitik*, seemed an accurate description of international politics and stood opposed to the kinds of **idealism** and moralism which the idea of human rights was thought to embody. Importantly, too, the idea of universal rights had fallen on hard times in intellectual terms, being subject to various critiques which undermined its authority and persuasive power.

World War II was one of a series of tragedies that gripped the world in the twentieth century. The particularly horrific atrocities manifested by Germany through the Holocaust precipitated a radical change in the structures of international politics, and in the place that moral concerns were given within those structures. The **international system** underwent a crisis of legitimacy, and one component of the restoration of that legitimacy was the emergence of the modern human rights movement. Above all else, this movement sought to establish minimum standards for the behaviour of states, in order for them to have legitimate standing in the international community.

These standards were expressed through, and were to be monitored and implemented by, a new organisation founded after World War II, the **United Nations (UN)**. Human rights were articulated in the **UN Charter**. In 1948, the key document of the human rights movement was promulgated by the UN: The Universal Declaration of Human Rights. This document was created pursuant to an international drafting effort, which sought to capture in declaratory form the essence of those values which, when adopted, would prevent the atrocities of World War II from being repeated.

From the beginning, however, there were political difficulties. The Declaration was itself not binding in **international law**: it was a document of aspiration, in the first instance. Second, the document did not receive universal acceptance among the states of the postwar era. The USSR and five of its allies refused to endorse it, and they were accompanied by South Africa and Saudi Arabia. These refusals were not surprising, not least because – despite the universalist rhetoric of the human rights movement – the values embodied in the Universal Declaration of Human Rights are a distilled version of the political **liberalism** which animated the allied West.

The greatest obstacle of them all was that of giving human rights teeth – a genuine capacity to do something other than make pious statements about how the peoples of the world might live together more harmoniously. In the first instance, this capacity was found in the drafting of two international treaties, known as covenants. These were the International Covenant on Civil and Political Rights, and the International Covenant on Economic, Social and Cultural Rights. These were promulgated in 1966 – almost two decades after the original Declaration. They had to wait a further decade before a sufficient number of states had signed up for the treaty to take any kind of effect.

It is still the case that not all states have signed these two basic human rights treaties: of the 190-odd states that comprise the international system, only 140 have signed both. There have been many other human rights instrumentalities which have been developed under the auspices of the UN since the promulgation of the Covenants – some of the more well known would be those on the Rights of the Child, and the Convention on the Elimination of all Forms of Discrimination Against Women (see Box 32.1). It represents a major shift in international politics that we can say that all states have signed on to at least one such human rights law instrument. Despite the inevitable problems of compliance and politicisation, this fact nonetheless represents a significant change in the politics and structures of international relations since the end of World War II.

BOX 32.1: DISCUSSION POINTS

Key human rights instruments of the UN

United Nations Charter (1945)

Universal Declaration of Human Rights (1948)

International Covenant on Civil and Political Rights (1966)

International Covenant on Economic, Social and Cultural Rights (1966)

International Convention on the Elimination of All Forms of Racial Discrimination (1965)

Convention on the Elimination of All Forms of Discrimination against Women (1979)

Convention against Torture and Other Cruel, Inhuman or Degrading Treatment or Punishment (1984)

Convention on the Rights of the Child (1989)

International Convention on the Protection of the Rights of All Migrant Workers and Members of Their Families (1990)

The historical development of an idea

As noted above, the idea of human rights was invoked after World War II as a way of expressing both moral outrage and a determination to prevent the recurrence of the events that provoked that outrage. But this raises the question: why was it that human rights were not already there, in action, to prevent the atrocities of that and other wars? If they are indeed *universal* rights – the rights of all peoples in all places at all times – why were they not available in the lexicon of international politics until after World War II?

The term 'universal human rights' is a modernised, updated version of a number of other terms which have, in fact, been around for a very long time. These are the ideas of natural law, natural right and the rights of man. These ideas together provide the foundation for many of the political structures that we in the West take for granted today. And it was these ideas that the West looked to in its crisis of legitimacy after World War II. The difficulty is that these ideas themselves are not unproblematic; indeed, we can see that a number of the key political problems associated with human rights today have their roots in the way in which these older political and moral ideas were appropriated by the modern human rights movement.

The Nuremburg and Tokyo trials held after World War II convicted people of committing crimes against humanity. The natural law was the basis for this justice. This same natural law is often appealed to as the basis for human rights. But it is by looking at this appeal that we can see what some of the difficulties with the idea of human rights are, and why it is that the idea – or the earlier forms of the idea – had come to be viewed as problematic. The idea of natural law is the idea that there is a moral or ethical law which is built into our nature as human beings – that, in fact, is built into the nature of the cosmos. This idea has strong pre-Christian antecedents but it finds its fullest expression in the Western tradition in Christian theology, to the extent that once Christianity started to be doubted and repudiated by Western thinkers, the idiom of the natural law was also fundamentally challenged.

The great irony of the history of the human rights idea is that the same historical period furnished both the most damaging criticisms and the most important political victories for the idea. During the period that is known as the **Enlightenment**, or the Age of Reason, in Western intellectual history, universal rights became both politically efficacious and intellectually passé.

This period was marked by famous rights declarations: 1776 saw the 'unanimous declaration of the thirteen united States of America'; and in 1789 we have the French 'Declaration on the Rights of Man and Citizens'. Rights language was in vogue, and it was making very significant political gains for the new political classes. However, the foundations of these claims were being questioned by many of the philosophers of the day. These thinkers were appealing to new ways of thinking which challenged many of the intellectual pieties of the past. Human reason was the standard these thinkers appealed to, not class privilege, religious revelation or social authority. And for many, the language of rights, with its foundation in natural law, was too tainted with false premises from older ways of thinking to remain legitimate.

The most famous critique of all from this period, perhaps because of its rhetorical excess, is that put forward by the **Utilitarian** thinker Jeremy Bentham. He said: 'Natural rights is simple nonsense: natural and imprescriptable rights, rhetorical nonsense – nonsense upon stilts'. These rights were 'unreal metaphysical phenomena'. Why so? Again, the common point here is the association with the Christian intellectual tradition. Natural rights came via the natural law which was given by God. But if you take away God, you appear to have no foundations for natural rights or natural law. The only rights you have are in fact those provided by people through political institutions; all other rights are merely idle talk. As we will see, however, this position has its own difficulties.

From this we can start to answer our earlier question: why it was that human rights were not there to prevent the atrocities of World War II, if they are universal in the way claimed by the Universal Declaration of Human Rights? Our brief excursus into intellectual history – the history of ideas – helps us to see that the idea of rights itself does not stand alone, but is linked to the broader intellectual and political climate of the day. This climate had been unfavourable to the idea of universal rights for some time before the mid-twentieth century. In the eighteenth century natural rights were in their heyday; by the twnetieth the idea had lost both its intellectual justification and its political limelight. That was until the atrocities of mid-century which caused the West to reach into its past for a set of terms that would adequately articulate its sense of moral outrage about what members of its own civilisation had done to one another.

The human rights idea today

It is tempting to respond to these historical considerations by claiming that the development of the Universal Declaration on Human Rights (UDHR) represents a break from the past – both the immediate past of Holocaust atrocity and the longer past of intellectual prevarication about the nature of human rights. The UDHR, it might be said, sets new standards and is justified by the participation of the members of the international community in its creation and extensions via subsequent human rights law instrumentalities. From this point of view, troubling ourselves with past philosophical debates about the nature and justification of rights is to miss the main game: that we now have an international human rights **regime**, mandated and overseen by the UN; that this regime sets the standards for human rights matters; and that this regime has a secure place within the architecture of international politics today.

This argument is one that is called the argument from legal **positivism** – and it is not unlike that argued by Jeremy Bentham, as mentioned above. His claim was that the only rights you in fact have are those which are provided by political institutions. This appeal to the realities of contemporary human rights law as an antidote to the philosophical problems with human rights, however, has serious shortcomings at both the conceptual and the political level. So much so that if we allow it to stand, we find that the language of human rights itself will fail to play the role that was envisaged for it by those who sought to introduce it as a medium for justice in international politics. To see this, we need to recognise the fatal flaw of the argument from legal positivism.

The legal positivists' way of answering the question, 'what are human rights?' is to point us to international human rights law: to the Universal Declaration of Human Rights, to the Covenants, and to the various other legal instrumentalities which operate at state, regional and international levels. The problem with legal positivism is that, in this manner, it is reductionist: it reduces human rights to these laws. Rather than seeing these laws as instruments which *protect* human rights, human rights are reduced to *being* these instruments. Human rights, then, do not exist whenever these structures are not in place. Human rights are created when these structures are created. Human rights change when these laws change.

Because international human rights law, then, is law that is created by **states** working together, and because human rights laws within states are created by states, this legal positivist argument has as one of its key consequences – albeit one that is not always immediately apparent – that human rights can be reduced to the will of the state. If human rights are reduced to laws which are created by states, and states then decide to change those laws, the implication is that human rights change as well. And the logic here dictates that should states repudiate human rights, these rights go out of existence. But this leaves us powerless against the state when it seeks to act unjustly against people; it leaves us with no defence against the kind of behaviour that led to World War II.

The argument from legal positivism is appealing because it seems to short-circuit the endless debate of moral philosophers about the nature of justice. However, it appears that if we want to ensure justice, we need to appeal to more than the human rights-respecting legal structures that were developed at some point in history; we need to appeal to the moral and philosophical reasons which tell us why such legal structures are good things, and why it is claimed that they are universally good: good for all human beings.

The politics of liberal universalism

It is the universalism of human rights that has made it so powerful as a tool of political and moral critique. The claim is that there are universal moral standards that the laws of all states should conform to. It is this claim to universality that gives human rights their moral bite – it is a claim to something that goes beyond the interests or laws of any given state (or, for that matter, **non-state agent**). And for precisely this reason, it is the claim that this 'something', being greater than all of us, applies to all of us. The challenge is to articulate what that 'something' is. For the modern human rights movement, the **norms** and values that are translated into human rights are derived from the liberal tradition of political thought. It is this tradition that is the inheritor of the notions of natural law and right, and that has transformed them into documents such as the Universal Declaration of Human Right.

Liberal universalism is a particular kind of universalism. It makes the claim that a certain set of values *should* be applied to all peoples in all states at all times. Thus, it is not a claim about **empirical** universality – it is not a claim that these values do now exist or can now be seen in all societies. Rather it is a **normative** claim: these values can be justified as being good for all human persons, and so we should strive to implement them universally.

The values in question are liberal values. That is, they are centred around the idea that each individual is important as an individual, that each individual has equal value, and should be free to follow his or her own interests. The conception of the person that is implied here emerges out of Western political and cultural history. It owes it provenance to such broad movements as the Renaissance, the Protestant Reformation, and – preeminently – the European Enlightenment. The liberal values articulated via the new doctrines of rights were individualistic, rational, universal, secular, democratic and radical. The focus here is squarely on the individual as the building block of society. The individual is conceptualised as a willing self – hence the importance of freedom: I must have the space in which to act the way that I will myself to act (see Box 32.2). This conception of the individual – often called the transcendental self – is a key aspect of the way in which theorists have justified the universality of human rights. If all human persons have these characteristics, and if these characteristics lead us to posit human rights, then human rights can be universal. In this view, it is the self that is considered to be the core of our humanity, despite all the differences between individuals or groups of individuals: differences such as religion, culture, socialisation and politics.

BOX 32.2: DISCUSSION POINTS

Three generations of rights

First generation rights: these are the civil and political rights, that form the basis of the human rights tradition, and which are represented in the International Covenant on Civil and Political Rights. These rights emerged to protect the interests and negative liberties of the individual against the power and encroachment of states. They include rights such as freedom of speech, religion and association.

Second generation rights: this generation of rights represents the recognition that people need a certain set of political and economic circumstances to be provided before they can flourish as human beings – indeed, before they can even properly take advantage of their civil and political rights. The second generation thus includes rights to basic levels of economic subsistence, education and work, among others. These rights are enumerated in the International Covenant on Economic, Social and Cultural Rights.

Third generation rights: also known as group rights, these rights attend more to the communal aspects of human being; thus, these rights extend the reach of human rights to matters such as the recognition of minority groups, social identity and cultural issues. These rights are often provided for by dedicated UN human rights instrumentalities.

This is a key issue, because it is factors such as religion, culture, socialisation and politics that lead people to engage in behaviour that is not acceptable on the basis of human rights standards. It is at this point that the political nature of human rights comes to the fore. One of the consequences of the universalist rhetoric of human rights has been that the political nature of human rights has often remained hidden. The politics of human rights is most often revealed, however, in the transition from the grand claims of universalism to the very specific changes that need to be made to legal and political systems to make them conform to international human rights standards. The legal instrumentalities of the international human rights regime do not merely urge states to cease behaving in undesirable ways; they prescribe specific standards which must be met.

The universalism of the human rights regime foundered from the very beginning because of these political tensions. The world was prepared to unite in its condemnation of the events of the Holocaust. But agreement on a rights regime that required something more that claiming the moral high ground was harder to come by. The principal disagreement on human rights issues was one which sundered the world, and was aligned with the political and economic differences between the post-war **superpowers**. The **Cold War**, among other things, was a dispute about which kinds of rights should take precedence in a given society: political and civil rights, or economic and social rights. Both types of rights were included in the UDHR. Human rights became a pawn in a larger conflict; rights became politicised and for a period the ability of rights discourse to advance the well-being of all persons was severely constrained by the refusal of Soviet and aligned states to accept either the spirit or the letter of human rights law.

More recently a similar set of claims have been played out in the Asian region (see Box 32.3). In this debate, authoritarian political elites have claimed that because the human rights doctrine is centred around the Western idea of the individual as the preeminent building block of society, it is a doctrine which has less application in their societies. In Asian societies, so it was claimed, the community, not the individual, is preeminent. This means that the rights and freedoms of individuals are always subservient to the state, and not vice versa. A similar debate has been had in other regions of the world – notably Africa.

What is at stake in these debates is the idea that a cultural, religious or philosophical tradition that is less disposed to viewing individual rights favourably may be put forward as a legitimate alternative way of organising society. The outcome of these alternatives is that many of the standards claimed by international human rights law may come into question. Particular issues that arise have to do with female **emancipation**, religious freedom, the rights of children, family and criminal law, the standing of social minorities (indigenous peoples, gays and lesbians, and others) and various political and economic freedoms.

BOX 32.3: DISCUSSION POINTS

Asian values

The 'Asian values' debate followed the end of the Cold War and a period of unprecedented economic growth in Asian economies. The debate was spearheaded by political elites from Malaysia, Singapore, China, Burma, Indonesia and Japan. The principal claim was that because Asian societies have different cultural backgrounds from those of the West, they need not be subject to the same standards of human rights and democracy as those asserted by the West. The argument from culture fails, however, because the claims of political elites to be the only legitimate spokespersons for a culture are spurious. Many Asians, including some political leaders, spoke out against Asian values, demonstrating that cultures are dynamic and contested, and cannot be easily enlisted by the powerful **status quo** political elite. Along with the argument from culture was an argument from economic development: that human rights needed to be rolled out sequentially, and that economic and social rights come before political and civil liberties. Asia is not as economically developed as the West and therefore should not be expected to live by the West's standards. But the real question here is not whether rights must develop sequentially, but whether the provision of economic rights *requires* the deprivation of political rights. Another issue here is the threshold issue: Singapore, for example, is clearly well developed, and yet is reluctant to give its citizens full first generation rights. Asian states also argued using the principles of state **sovereignty**, claiming that the norm of non-intervention protects them from external critique. The Asian Financial Crisis of the late 1990s saw the end of the Asian values debate as an expression of political hubris; this, however, does not mean the end of the issue. Asia is a broad region with many diverse values systems which do not all sit easily with the international human rights regime, even when they are not being exploited by self-interested political elites. How to manage such global pluralism is one of the key challenges facing the doctrine of human rights.

In most cases, the legitimacy of this debate is brought into question because the proponents of these views tend to be the same strongmen who run the countries in an authoritarian fashion. A conflict of interest is immediately apparent, in that the arguments presented serve to preserve the status quo of the political elites and their interests. Moreover, dissenting voices are not difficult to find. Indeed, it is these voices that are the more significant and interesting, and who represent the real challenge to the universal claims of liberal values; for while these dissenters criticise their own governments, they may also have reservations about the liberal predisposition of international human rights standards. Thus, we see, for example, religious organisations from all the world religions crafting alternative bills of rights which diverge on crucial key issues from those of the UN. With the renewed salience of religion to international affairs since the end of the Cold War, these groups and movements represent a significant political challenge to the prevailing international human rights regime.

The future of human rights

Human rights has proven to be a revolutionary political tool for those concerned with ethical standards in international politics. While human rights has often been derided as 'soft', because of its fundamental subservience to sovereignty in international affairs, it has nonetheless changed the landscape of international politics since the end of World War II. The UN and other human rights organisations have been at the forefront of this transformation of international politics which, along with developments in the international political economy, have introduced new and powerful non-state actors into the international arena. Moreover, human rights have become central to the standard-setting rhetoric of all states, and while in many cases critics will be frustrated at the 'it's just words' nature of this development, in many other cases human rights standards-setting has led to the creation of institutions which have led to transformations in the processes of both domestic and international politics. Institutionally, then, human rights have become an entrenched fixture in both domestic and international politics (see Box 32.4).

BOX 32.4: DISCUSSION POINTS

Human rights promotion: difficult cases

Since the establishment of the UN human rights regime, Australia has been an important human rights supporter on the global stage. However, different Australian governments have had different policy approaches to the issue of human rights, ranging from more liberal internationalist perspectives to the more conservative, realist approaches. Controversy about method often focuses on difficult cases. The current Australian government has chosen to use the mechanism of 'dialogue' in order to engage with some difficult cases: China, Vietnam and Iran are countries who have been involved with dialogue processes. In a similar vein, Australia has also engaged Burma by offering human rights workshops there. These policy responses by government represent a particular way of engaging with states that have poor human rights records. They are controversial policy responses because, while they seek to support the UN human rights regime in general terms, they are not conducted under the UN auspices. Here, the fundamental question is whether more is gained for human rights by using a **bilateral** policy approach rather than that of engagement via international human rights regimes. A second fundamental question also arises from these examples: to what extent do you promote human rights by direct confrontation over rights-abusive state behaviour, and to what extent do you try to change that behaviour by indirect engagement in other areas? In addition to the states mentioned above, Australia's relationship with Indonesia is a key illustration of this issue, in particular with what is now the world's newest independent state, East Timor, and with respect to Australia's policy towards other regions of Indonesia which have strong separatist movements, members of which routinely suffer human rights abuses at the behest of state institutions.

There remain political challenges. The key one of these is directly linked to the main conceptual challenges regarding the nature of human rights. Our answer to the question 'what are human rights?' will lead us directly to substantive issues about what values should be enshrined by our human rights laws and institutions. Some countries, for example, press for different legal systems for members of different religions. This has implication for the way in which we think about the universality of freedom of religion, of women's rights, of children's rights and of criminal law. This in turn leads to troubling questions about how different human rights regimes should then interact with one another; and about how people who cross jurisdictions will be treated in different places: is it possible to speak of human rights being universal, when your rights appear to change as your geography changes?

The liberal universalism of human rights, which stands at the foundation of the international human rights regime, is under challenge then, in these various ways and others. The key developments in the future of human rights will lie with the way in which the philosophical, institutional and political issues entwined at the heart of this challenge are engaged over coming decades.

Conclusion

This chapter has examined the way in which the concept of human rights has become one of the central doctrines of global politics. It has examined the institutional development of human rights through the United Nations and the Universal Declaration of Human Rights. It has also considered the importance of the philosophical justification of human rights and the challenges that this task presents, particularly in the face of global cultural diversity. The universalist political liberalism which underlies the human rights movement has been contested by various constituencies, and the way in which the movement responds will shape the future of the global politics of human rights.

QUESTIONS

1. Are human rights a Western prejudice?
2. Are there 'Asian values'? And how, if at all, do they impact on human rights?
3. Why have human rights grown in stature and popularity in recent decades?
4. Is the prevailing international human rights regime effective?
5. Should all sovereign states be compelled to apply human rights standards to their own citizens?
6. Should human rights be balanced against the demands of security?

FURTHER READING

Dunne, T. and Wheeler, N. (eds) 1999, *Human rights in global politics*, Cambridge University Press. Excellent collection comprising various theoretical perspectives.

Forsythe, D. 2000, *Human rights in international relations*, Cambridge University Press. Very good overview of human rights.

Langlois, A. 2001, *The politics of justice and human rights: Southeast Asia and universalist theory*, Cambridge University Press. Theoretically informed account of human rights and cultural difference.

Shue, H. 1980, *Basic rights*, Princeton University Press. Excellent philosophical defence of human rights.

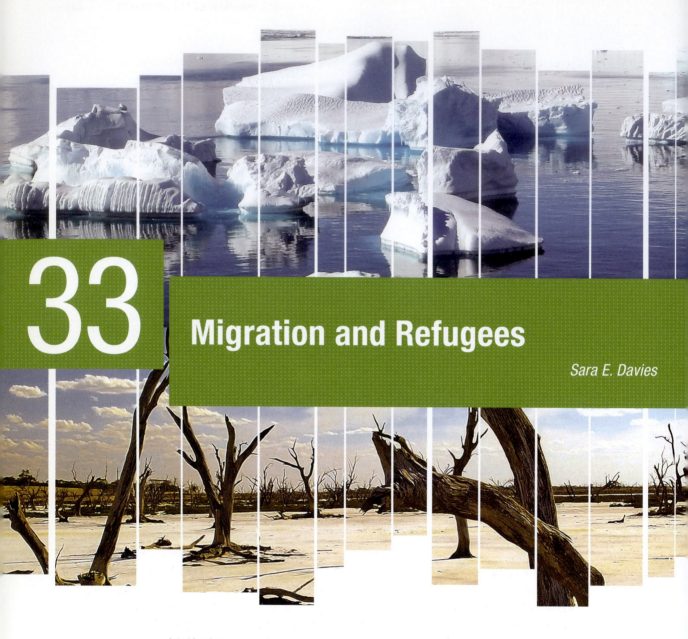

33

Migration and Refugees

Sara E. Davies

Introduction	451
States, refugees and immigrants	451
Controlling migration: a brief history	451
The origins and purposes of refugee law	453
The distribution of refugees around the world	455
The present situation	458
Conclusion	460
Questions	460
Further reading	461

Introduction

This chapter proceeds in four sections. The first looks at how the two terms, 'migrant' and '**refugee**', came to be defined as distinct from each other in the context of the modern **state**. As the reification of borders intensified in the nineteenth and twentieth centuries, citizenship became an essential part of 'belonging' to a state as well as indicating the strength of the state itself. Hence, the categorisation of those 'outside' the state developed as a way of ascertaining who belonged and who did not. The second examines how states define and categorise refugees through laws that seek to contain and limit their flow. The third is concerned with the consequences of limiting the definition of a refugee, which has led to an unequal burden between developed and developing states. The final section will canvass the various options presented to reduce the present imbalance where the vast majority of the world's 'people of concern'[1] eke out an existence in refugee camps in developing countries. Ultimately, this chapter seeks to demonstrate that the choices made by states in border protection become the key determinants of how refugees will be accepted. Adherence to international refugee law will not necessarily address all the problems associated with refugees, but nor will seeing refugees as unwanted intruders in contrast to 'desirable' migrants.

States, refugees and immigrants

The former Prime Minister of Australia, John Howard, campaigned in the 2001 federal election under the banner 'we will decide who comes to this country and under what circumstances' (Marr and Wilkinson 2003: 277). As this slogan demonstrates, there is arguably no greater control than determining who is a 'legitimate' citizen of the state – that is, determining who can and cannot live within your borders. Being able to secure borders and identify when they are being breached is essential to state **sovereignty**. Entry into a state without permission is seen as an 'illegal' breach of sovereignty, or even a threat to sovereignty. Consider Canadian Prime Minister Stephen Harper's comments in relation to the arrival of Sri Lankan asylum seekers who stowed away on a cargo ship: 'It's a fundamental exercise of sovereignty and we're responsible for the security of our borders and the ability to welcome people or not welcome people when they come' (*Sydney Morning Herald* 2010). The determination of whether an individual's crossing of a border is deemed as illegal, threatening or permissible is part of how a state constructs its **identity** and territoriality. Therefore, this chapter will first look at how states define an individual's entry, through tracing the development of the term 'refugee', contrasting it to the term 'migrant' and exploring how this delineation affects the lives of people seeking entry into states.

Controlling migration: a brief history

Even before the creation of the 'modern state' (see Chapter 9), there were attempts to 'territorialise' borders in order to control who could and could not enter and exit political communities. Evidence of early migration policy exists in China's political

---

[1] This term is mainly used by the Office of the United Nations High Commission for Refugees (UNHCR) to collectively describe asylum seekers, persons with refugee status, displaced persons and stateless people.

history from at least the second millennium BC. From then until AD 800, planned migration was a constant feature of Chinese population movement. What has changed with the advent of modern states is how they have responded to foreigners entering sovereign territory.

In the new world of **nation**-states, individuals needed to be 'territorialised'. Since the seventeenth century many terms have been used by states in an attempt to distinguish new entrants from residents – foreigner, exile, alien, refugee, migrant. In more recent times, the tendency to classify people has become a central feature of the bureaucratic state and reflects the concern of bureaucrats to attach people to domiciles where 'they can be registered, enumerated, taxed, drafted and watched' (Tilly 1978: 49).

Today, a migrant is defined as a person who chooses to move from their country of origin to another which will accept them (see Box 33.1). The causes of migration are important because the term 'migrant' is associated with choice – a choice that the person makes to seek a life elsewhere and a choice by the state to accept that person. When new states such as Canada, Australia and the US were being industrialised and urbanised, migrants were a welcome addition – though some were considered more preferable than others, as is still the case today. For instance, the US, UK and Canada all had Alien Laws in the 1800s and early 1900s, which prohibited 'undesirables' such as Asians and Jews from entering their state. The first Act the new Australian federal government passed was the Immigration Restriction Act of 1901, better known as the White Australia Policy. These policies were reflective of most new industrialising states' dual tension – while they needed migrants for labour, they were fearful of taking on groups deemed to be 'inassimilable'. This would lead to practices, such as in the US and Australia, where there were annual quotas on the number of Asians, for example, who could enter per year, as well as language and health tests (which allowed migrant officials to randomly apply them to those who were, by appearance, deemed undesirable). Nonetheless, the idea of choice when thinking about migration is very important – the premise here is that you have a will to leave your country of origin with the knowledge that the receiving state will accept you.

By contrast, the term 'refugee' has no association with choice. It is a relatively new term, first arriving in English usage at the end of the seventeenth century. Originally referring in French to someone searching for refuge and assistance, the term 'refugee' came to be associated with people fleeing some form of persecution. When it first came into English usage, it was used to describe the Protestant Huguenots who fled Catholic France in the seventeenth century, fearing persecution because of their refusal to convert to Catholicism. The Netherlands and England, the primary receiving states of the Huguenot population, were not resistant to accepting the Huguenot population because a large proportion of them were wealthy, aligned with aristocracy (which particularly suited England's form of state rule), of similar religion and, in some cases, skilled.

BOX 33.1: TERMINOLOGY

Migrants and refugees

A *migrant* is a person who leaves their state by choice, and whom the receiving state accepts by choice.

A *forced migrant* is a person who did not leave their country by choice, but nor are they eligible for refugee status under the 1951 Convention (see Box 33.2).

An *illegal migrant* is a migrant who enters another state without first seeking permission to do so, and who will often remain in the host state without a visa which allows them to stay or work there.

A *refugee* is often forced to flee, to enter a state without its permission and is not always welcomed in the state in which they seek refuge.

Conversely though, if the population had been poor, uneducated and without social or religious links to their host country, there arguably would not have been such acceptance, and it is this *lack* of guaranteed state reception, alongside the forced nature of flight, that distinguishes the refugee from the migrant in the modern state. Though the term 'refugee' is associated with fleeing and a lack of choice, it is also associated with an imposition upon the receiving state. The state has little choice to accept or refuse because the refugee has nowhere else to go. This was never more marked than after the Russian **Revolution** of 1917 and at the end of World War I, when approximately 20 million refugees existed in Europe and could not, due to changes in state identities, borders and citizenship, return to where they originally lived. This left Western European countries with large numbers of displaced people that newly emerging states did not want because of this group's potential burden on attempts to rebuild infrastructure, distribute housing and provide employment and social welfare for their own population.

The origins and purposes of refugee law
Origins

Contemporary international refugee law has its origins in the inter-war period between World wars I and II. In 1921, the League of Nations was enlisted to assist with the resettlement of post-war refugees, principally Russians and Armenians. At the end of World War II, the Office of the United Nations High Commissioner for Refugees (UNHCR) was created under the **UN** umbrella to deal with the 40 million refugees across Europe. A crucial part of guaranteeing resettlement places (see Box 33.2) for these refugees was the creation of criteria that could be used to define who was eligible for such assistance and who was not, so that not just 'anyone' could be given refugee status, along with all the legal and economic benefits that came with such status.

The UN General Assembly agreed that it would be a fear of political persecution that would determine whether or not a person was a refugee. This definition had its origins in the work of the League of Nations Office for Refugees from 1926 to 1939. By the time UN member states had to vote on what the definition of a refugee would be in 1951, the association of persecution with politics became the only legitimate understanding of what makes one a refugee. The 1951 Convention relating to the Status of Refugees (hereafter referred to as the 1951 Convention, see Box 33.3) was created by the fifty-five states that were members of the Third Committee of the United Nations. The 1951

BOX 33.2: TERMINOLOGY

Definitions of a refugee according to international law

Resettlement is the relocation of a refugee from a refugee camp to another state that will accept them and provide them with the same rights and benefits as a citizen.

The 1951 Convention (Article 1A) defines a refugee as a person who:

owing to a well-founded fear of being persecuted for reasons of race, religion, nationality, membership of a particular social group or political opinion, is outside the country of his nationality and is unable or, owing to such fear, is unwilling to avail himself of the protection of that country.

The 1967 Protocol relating to the Status of Refugees was an addendum to the 1951 Convention which removed the time (prior to 1 January 1951) and geographic constraints (in Europe) from Article 1 of the 1951 Convention. This meant that a state could sign the 1967 Protocol and still follow all the remaining articles in the 1951 Convention, but without any limitations to its applicability.

Convention was created as a legal guideline for states to use. Each Article within the Convention contributes to the process of refugee determination – including the definition of a refugee, how a refugee should be treated when first seeking asylum on a foreign border, the right not to be returned to their country of origin once determined as a refugee (*non-refoulement*), and what rights and benefits a refugee should receive from their host state – that is, recognition of marriage, intellectual property, employment and so on. What was most important about this Convention, though, was that it determined who a refugee was, and thus excluded many who would claim such status.

When the 1951 Convention was created the only people who could receive the status of a refugee were those affected by events in Europe prior to 1 January 1951. States had the option to apply the definition of a refugee to those outside Europe, but it could be only due to events prior to 1 January 1951. It is also important to bear in mind that the 1951 Convention was created at the beginning of the **Cold War**. The US and France argued that the spread of **communism** across Eastern Europe was a growing cause for the flow of refugees into Western Europe, and that refuge for this group should be the primary focus for resettlement for they were fleeing the worst kind of political persecution: communism. Thus, the political overtones associated with refugee status were apparent and the 1951 Convention was used as an instrument by Western states *against* communism, and to support those fleeing it. This did not change until the end of the Cold War in 1991, although the time and geographic constraints were removed by the 1967 Protocol Relating to the Status of Refugees (1967 Protocol) (see Box 33.2).

Purposes

International refugee law has three primary purposes. The first is to provide states with a process for recognising people who have entered sovereign territory without permission. These 'recognition of refugee status' procedures permit states to identify whether the entrant is worthy of admission without punishment for arriving illicitly. Second, it gives the refugee a form of recognition that should provide them with rights – such as the right to not be returned to their country of origin, as stated under Article 33 of the 1951 Convention. Another right is encompassed in Article 31, which stipulates that a person once deemed to be a refugee is neither to be penalised nor detained for entering the host country without permission, and must be provided with legal protection by the host state. This means that a person cannot be an illegal immigrant if found to be a refugee, and that the state, if a signatory to the Convention, is required to determine the person's status first so that refugees are not wrongly punished.

BOX 33.3: KEY TEXTS

Important articles in the 1951 Convention relating to the Status of Refugees

Article 31

The host state is not to impose penalties on refugees for their illegal entry or presence when they come directly from a country where their life or freedom was threatened; provided they present themselves to authorities without delay. Nor should their movement be restricted for an undue length of time.

Article 33

Refugees bear the right not to be forcibly returned or expelled to a situation which would threaten one's life or freedom. This is the principle of *non-refoulement*.

Article 34

The host state should, upon conferment of refugee status, begin procedures to naturalise the refugee and provide citizenship rights.

The third purpose of refugee law is to provide the state with an exclusion process. Unlike a migrant, a refugee is meant to be able to enter any country without fear of return or penalisation. States wanted to be able to make sure that the person was 'worthy' of these rights; they did not want their state to be encumbered by people who just wanted to make a better life for themselves without the fuss of going through the migration application processes, or by people who could be criminals or **security** threats masquerading as refugees. However, due to its emphasis on political persecution, the definition of a refugee reflects a very narrow conception of what causes someone to flee and seek protection from another state. In practice, it is very difficult for an individual to prove a genuine fear of political persecution. The times that refugee status has been granted to a 'mass' group of refugees, such as an ethnic population or a group with defined political affiliation, have been very rare, largely because it requires the UN General Assembly to pass a resolution allowing the UNHCR to grant mass refugee status to this particular group. Examples where this has occurred are, for example, the Hungarian population fleeing a communist crackdown on the state in 1954, and Indochinese refugees fleeing communist repression from 1979 to 1989.

The distribution of refugees around the world

The global distribution of refugees exemplifies the dilemma that the world currently faces with the movement of people. The UNHCR 2009 Global Trends revealed that more than half of the world's refugees (5.5 million) have been living in what is called a 'protracted situation' – they have lived for five years or more in refugee camps in host countries that cannot or will not provide permanent residency – where they are unable to return home for fear of being persecuted (UNHCR 2010: 1). The majority of these protracted situations are in developing countries (over 80 per cent), and there are now cases where second-generation refugees are living in the camps. For example, there remains a large Afghan refugee population who fled the country's **civil war** in the 1990s and continue to live in camps and urban settlements within Pakistan and Iran; there are populations from Somalia who have been living in refugee camp settlements in Kenya since the 1990s as the civil war continues; and in Thailand, there are a vast number of asylum seekers from Myanmar who have lived as 'illegal migrants' since the early 1990s, unable to gain residency from the Thai Government but fearful of returning to the junta-ruled regime. It should be noted that the 5.5 million figure does not include the 4 million Palestinians who claimed to be displaced due to the creation of the state of Israel in 1948 (UNHCR 2010).

Added to the high number of protracted refugee situations is the rising figure of people being forcibly displaced from their homes – some 25 million people (10.5 million refugees and 15 million internally displaced) (UNHCR 2010: 1). This number has not been as high since the mid-1990s, which experienced a high number of territorial conflicts following the end of the Cold War. In addition to the protracted refugee situation and rising number of displaced persons, there is an increasing number of people refusing to return to their home countries. Since the end of the Cold War, voluntary repatriation – refugees agreeing to return home – has become the dominant practice for handling refugee populations. People are held in refugee camps or given temporary protection visas and then returned home once the **war** has ended or the regime commits to not persecuting the individuals in question. With this solution diminishing, there is going to be greater pressure on refugee camps and on states to take refugees as permanent residents. These current trends are particularly significant for developing countries as they host the majority of the world's displaced persons (four-fifths of the total population) (UNHCR 2010: 1).

Developing countries host vast numbers of displaced persons for four primary reasons: the definition of a refugee; the instability of developing countries; geography; and changes to resettlement schemes by industrialised countries.

As stated earlier, the refugee definition is narrow, and is usually granted only after the individual has proven they would face political persecution if returned to their country of origin. Anyone fleeing because of an unstable government causing generalised fear or violence does not receive refugee status until it is first proven. If a person is fleeing because of a lack of medical services or dire economic circumstances – that is, because a type of treatment is unavailable, or because they face malnutrition and even starvation – these conditions are not just cause for flight under the 1951 Convention. Further, forced uprooting due to natural disasters does not fall under the 1951 Convention definition. What this means is that even if a person is able to seek asylum in a state that is a member of the 1951 Convention, refugee status will not be granted because of a generalised fear of violence, authoritarian rule, poverty, famine, natural disaster or failed medical care. However, people still flee due to these conditions, which partly explains why such high numbers of refugees and displaced persons take flight. The number of refugees is staggering: one out of four refugees worldwide is from Afghanistan, and at least 1.8 million continue to seek refuge in Pakistan and Iran; 132 000 Somalis fled to Kenya, Ethiopia, Yemen and Djibouti in 2008, while an additional 300 000 were internally displaced in the same year (UNHCR 2010: 6–9). After the 1994 **genocide** in Rwanda, 250 000 people fled to Tanzania in forty-eight hours (Halverson 2001: 308); more than a million Iraqi refugees have fled into Syria since the 2003 Iraq war. It is impossible in such conditions to individually assess who does and does not meet the narrow definition of a refugee, yet in order for resettlement places to be offered by Western countries, this is precisely what must happen. So many refugees remain in often unsafe, unsanitary, miserable conditions in refugee camps because no other state will take them under a refugee program until the legal requirement of 'fear of persecution' is proven.

The second reason for the high number of refugees in developing countries is political instability. Much work has been done in development studies about how the era of **decolonisation** from the early 1950s through to the late 1960s left many Third World states with very little state capacity. The result is that many developing countries have had unstable governments with at best fluctuating economies and sometimes uncertain civil law. This furthered the dramatic rise in the number of people seeking refuge in the 1970s and 1980s, and in turn contributed to the increased number of people both fleeing generalised violence and requiring resettlement due to genuine fear of returning

Table 33.1 Persons of concern to UNHCR – by region

Region	2004	2009
Asia	6 112 500	13 624 502
Africa	4 285 100	10 636 239
Europe	4 242 800	1 087 700
North America	978 100	3934
Latin America and the Caribbean	1 316 400	3 898 344
Oceania	74 400	2519
Various*		7 207 068
TOTAL	17 009 300	19 197 400

*Refers to 'individuals who not necessarily fall
directly into any of the other groups but to whom UNHCR
may extend its protection and/or assistance services.
These activities might be based on humanitarian or other
special grounds' (UNHCR 2010: 30).
Source: UNHCR 2006; UNHCR 2010.

home. This situation was only exacerbated with the end of the Soviet Union and the break-up of many Soviet-ruled states in the 1990s, not to mention the regional war that was taking place between seven African nations from 1996–2002 (Democratic Republic of Congo, Uganda, Rwanda, Congo, Sudan, Angola and Zimbabwe).

The flow-on of refugees between border conflicts, as occurred in post-Soviet Europe and Central Africa, brings us to the third point of difference between developing and developed states – geography. The majority of Western, developed states either have 'buffer' states between themselves and the countries from which refugees flee, or are completely isolated from other states by water. Western Europe has, since the end of the Cold War, obligated Eastern European states wishing to join the European Union to sign on to the 1951 Convention and 1967 Protocol, so as to compel them to deal with any refugee populations moving from the East. This has relieved the pressure on Western Europe from being the only regional bloc in Europe to provide legal refugee status. The US and Canada are to some degree also protected by their geographic mass, although the US does have land-border incursions from South America and both countries have experienced unauthorised boat arrivals, despite the dangerous and difficult passage. Australia has an even easier time ensuring that no refugees surreptitiously pass a rocky border region, or thickly covered forest area that demarcates a border, because entering by sea or air is the only way to enter Australia. Entering by tourist visa or a working visa and then claiming asylum at the airport, or illegally overstaying visa conditions, are the more common ways that people seek entry into developed countries. But this too can be difficult: governments invest a lot of money in customs and immigration agencies to screen and catch those who enter and then stay on as 'illegal migrants' (consider the regional representation of peoples of concern in Table 33.1).

Finally, the options available to forcibly displaced people have significantly changed in funding and emphasis since the Cold War years. The ideological battle of the Cold War made those seeking asylum from communist states attractive propaganda to the

Figure 33.1 UN refugee tents

US and others to demonstrate the triumph of **capitalism** and democratic governance (though it should be noted that refugees from Africa and South Asia during this period had high numbers, but fewer offers of resettlement). A second pressure on the offers of resettlement from developed states was the economic downturn of major Western states during the 1980s. The large loss of jobs and the burden on domestic economies saw a rise of domestic resistance to generous refugee admission policies. The global South saw this as the global North turning its back on them when they were also hurting from the economic downturn. Nonetheless, developed countries at this point started to devote aid and political interest to refugee settlement 'solutions' that focused on local settlement (i.e. supporting 'regional solutions' where neighbouring states resettle the refugee populations) and voluntary repatriation (Slaughter and Crisp 2009). The result has been a rise in people living in protracted refugee situations in countries that are often as economically and politically fragile as the state they fled, or people integrating themselves into the local community without any permanent residency status and therefore vulnerable to forcible repatriation at any time (Jacobsen 2006).

The present situation

There has been much debate about the best way to resolve the global imbalance in the refugee intake and resettlement numbers (for example, Cohen 2007; Hathaway 2007; Haddad 2008; Price 2009; Betts 2010). The problem of how to develop an international solution that addresses this imbalance has led to debate largely centring on three concerns: definition of persecution; protracted refugee situations; and Western states adopting their share of the 'refugee burden'.

First, there is the matter of broadening what 'persecution' means under the refugee definition. Recent debate has largely centred on whether the emphasis on 'political persecution' reflects the real conditions that force the majority of people to flee their homes. As discussed above, people are forced to flee for a wide range of reasons, including: economic deprivation; natural disaster (numbers are predicted to rise with the impact of climate change); state failure to offer protection against domestic violence; attacks from organised crime gangs; or lack of access to essential medicines – for example, to treat HIV/AIDS. Why should those fleeing such life-threatening conditions not be afforded the same protections as those fearing political persecution (Cohen 2007; Betts 2010)? The debate has been divided between those who seek complementary protection and those who argue that any effort to broaden the definition would be detrimental to the refugee protection **regime**. Those in favour of broadening the justificatory reasons for people to seek asylum argue that Western states, in particular, should introduce a complementary protection regime that accepts people fleeing *any cause* of deprivation and insecurity. A form of protection that is complementary to the protection available for refugees under the 1951 Convention is essential, it is argued, because the new drivers of forced migration are no less valid reasons for people to flee than the narrow conditions outlined in the Convention more than sixty years ago (Betts 2010: 363). Opponents of this call for complementary protection have articulated two concerns. First, if the conditions under which persecution and protection can be claimed are broadened, states may not be more generous, but less so. Price (2009: 250–1) goes so far as to argue that every time a (Western) commonwealth court interprets the 1951 Convention to apply to a 'new form' of persecution, the state imposes more restrictive legislative and regulatory conditions upon those seeking asylum. The second argument against broadening the refugee definition is that asylum is a rare protection afforded those facing a threat to their bodily integrity or liberty due to expulsion from their political community as 'enemies of the state'. Their choice, if it can be called that, is to leave or die. Those facing extreme economic, medical and environment deprivation are often not enemies of the state, yet the state has not protected them from an equivalent fate. Who should protect them, for how long and under what legal status, thus remain contested questions.

Second, the protracted refugee situation has also attracted controversy. Do people stay in refugee camps because their livelihood may be better there compared to their country of origin (Jacobsen 2006)? For some, their first experience of access to education and healthcare is in a refugee camp managed by humanitarian agencies. Returning to a fragile state with no such resources would be daunting and difficult. But people also remain in camps because they do not feel – and are not – safe to return home. People stay in the hope of being granted refugee status by UNHCR, and then often wait many years for resettlement. There are thousands of applicants awaiting the same fate from the few countries with regular resettlement intake schemes. In 2009, nineteen countries provided resettlement schemes (some, such as the US, Canada, Australia, Germany, Sweden and Norway, provide annual intake quotas). In the same year the UNHCR had the highest number of people seeking resettlement since 1996 (UNHCR 2010: 12) (see Table 33.1). Inevitably, eligible refugees were turned away due to insufficient places. This situation leads to many taking matters into their own hands, primarily seeking passage in dangerous conditions (including decrepit vessels, plane cargo holds and ship containers) provided by 'people smugglers', to gain entry into developed countries. Developed countries are preferred because they are perceived to offer job opportunities, better health and education services, the chance to apply for refugee status and be granted permanent residency and, most importantly for people fleeing horrific political and social conditions, safe sanctuary.

While people will do as they always have, and continue to leave their place of origin to seek asylum elsewhere, the reception is never the same (Haddad 2008). Recently, the emphasis has been on receiving states diversifying their refugee policies (Gibney 2004). Rather than seek to divert or obstruct people's efforts to leave, there have been increased arguments for more diplomatic engagement and economic investment into preventing the conditions that drove them to leave (Haddad 2008). A controversial addition to the intake argument is to introduce temporary protection resettlements – allowing people to temporarily reside in safety but returning groups to their home country once the conditions that forced them to flee have been resolved (Haddad 2008: 207–8). Another suggestion has been for greater numbers of developed countries to establish annual resettlement quotas and for all developed states to raise annual resettlement numbers (Gibney 2004). The benefits are multiple: more protection for refugees; fewer illegal voyages and lower asylum-seeker processing costs; reduction in people-smuggling operations; upholding the rights of verified refugees; government control over refugee intake (and therefore higher chance of more intakes); and finally, burden-relief for (predominantly developing) states housing refugee camps.

Ultimately, broadening or narrowing the application of international refugee law is not the sole solution. The response also requires political solutions because refugees are the responsibility of all states (Betts 2010: 361).

Conclusion

This chapter has demonstrated that the development of refugee policy at the international level has sought specifically to differentiate between a migrant and a refugee, with the implicit idea that the term 'refugee' is a special status granted to few due to exceptional circumstances. However, as this chapter has also shown through highlighting the shared burden of the refugee population between the developing and developed world, the number seeking refuge still remains high and the need for equitable sharing of the burden among states is crucial. The imbalance between developing states and developed states does affect refugees and the choices they make in seeking asylum. The fact that four-fifths of the world's refugee population remain in mostly cramped, unsafe conditions in the developing world indicates why people seek other desperate means to have a chance of a better life.

QUESTIONS

1. What is the difference between a *migrant* and a *refugee*?
2. Should the 1951 Convention relating to the Status of Refugees have a broader definition of 'refugee' in Article 1A?
3. Do you think that the majority of Western states are protected by their borders from asylum-seeking populations? Does this mean that refugee populations are not the West's 'problem'?

4. How can people be forcibly displaced, but not considered to be a refugee?

5. Does your country have a yearly refugee intake scheme? Why/why not? If your country does, from where do the majority of refugees your country accepts come from? Why would your country receive high numbers of this refugee population?

FURTHER READING

Castles, Stephen and Miller, Mark J. 2003, *The age of migration*, Houndmills: Palgrave Macmillan. Useful account of migration in an age of globalisation.

Gibney, Matthew J. 2004, *The ethics and politics of asylum: liberal democracy and the response to refugees*, Cambridge: Cambridge University Press. Important theoretically-informed account of how liberal democratic states (Australia, Germany, UK, US) deal with refugees.

Haddad, Emma 2008, *The refugee in international society: between sovereigns*, Cambridge: Cambridge University Press. Argues that the evolution of the 'refugee problem' is directly related to the creation of the modern state, and will remain an 'inevitable' product of the modern state. Once this reality is accepted, new responses and solutions become available.

Loescher, Gil, Milner, James, Newman, Edward and Troeller, Gary (eds) 2008, *Protracted refugee situations: political, human rights and security implications*, Tokyo: United Nations University Press. An edited volume that explores the causes of protracted refugee situations, the roles of different actors in seeking to remedy these situations, and specific cases of refugees living in these situations, i.e. Afghan, Palestininan, Somali, Sudanese, Bhutanese and Burmese populations.

34

Global Environmental Politics

Robyn Eckersley

Introduction	463
The rise of the environment as a global political problem	464
The post-Cold War context	466
Theories of global environmental politics	469
The US as the reluctant environmental state	471
Conclusion	473
Questions	473
Further reading	474

Introduction

This chapter will introduce three of the most prominent global environmental discourses: sustainable development, environmental security and environmental justice. It begins by tracking the emergence of environmental problems as a 'global' political problem and tracing the discursive shift from 'limits to growth' in the early 1970s to sustainable development in the 1980s. It then highlights the environmental challenges of the post-**Cold War** period and introduces the discourses of environmental justice and ecological security. This is followed by a brief introduction to the different ways in which the basic questions of global environmental politics have been addressed by the three broad traditions of international relations: **realism**, **liberalism** and **critical theory**. Finally, the chapter turns to contemporary challenges, focusing on the failure of the US to take a leadership role in tackling the most serious global environmental problem of all – global warming.

The study of global environmental politics has emerged as a problem-oriented and multidisciplinary field of inquiry that seeks to understand: (a) how and why global ecological problems arise and persist; (b) how ecological risks are distributed through space and time; and (c) how the global community (encompassing **states** and **non-state actors**) has responded, or ought to respond. These three basic questions frame the field of inquiry of global environmental politics. They also signal the enormous political challenges facing international and transnational collective efforts to protect the Earth's ecosystems and climate in a world of 193 **sovereign states** with vast disparities in capacity, resource endowments, population, cultures and levels of economic development.

Global environmental politics is a sprawling field of study, in terms of both the sheer breadth of the object of study and the variety of disciplinary frames that are relevant to global ecopolitical problems. While the primary object of study is political responses to global and transboundary environmental problems, the distinction between global and transboundary, and national and local, environmental problems is hard to maintain. All global ecological problems produce local effects, and local environmental problems often have transboundary causes and/or consequences. For example, local ecological problems such as species extinction or deforestation are globally ubiquitous, and tied into **international systems** of investment, production and exchange. To give another example, severe local drought or deforestation can give rise to 'ecological **refugees**'. The term 'global' in global environmental politics has therefore grown to encompass all those transborder flows and relationships that are implicated in the generation and management of environmental problems, along with the global and transnational discourses that frame our understanding of these problems. This encompasses not only international relations between states but also transnational relations between state and non-state actors, ranging from scientists and **transnational corporations** to international organisations and environmental **non-governmental organisations (NGOs)**.

It is now a trite observation that ecological problems transgress political borders and that any comprehensive understanding of global environmental politics likewise requires the crossing of disciplinary borders. Reflecting these insights, the field of global environmental politics includes scholars working within a variety of research traditions in the **discipline** of International Relations as well as the broader field of global politics or **globalisation** studies (see Box 34.1). This has produced a variety of strikingly different theories of global environmental politics, ranging from explanatory to **normative** and conservative to radical. At the same time, several prominent global environmental discourses have emerged in both the practice and study of global environmental politics that cut across sub-disciplinary boundaries, anchor general debates and inform political proposals for institutional reform.

BOX 34.1: KEY TEXTS

Where can I find published research on global environmental politics?

Academic journals covering debates in global environmental politics include: *Environmental Politics*; *Global Environmental Politics*; *Global Environmental Change*; *Climate Policy*; *Environment and Planning A, B* and *C*; *International Environmental Agreements: Politics, Law and Economics*; *Environment and Organisation*; and *The Journal of Environment and Development*. Systematic reporting of global environmental trends can be found in the regular *State of the World* reports and *Vital Signs*, both published by the World Resources Institute, and the *Geo* reports produced by the United Nations Environment Programme.

The rise of the environment as a global political problem

The 'modern ecological crisis' – marked by an exponential increase in the range, scale and seriousness of environmental problems around the world – is generally understood to have emerged only in the second half of the twentieth century, although its beginnings may be traced to the processes of modernisation and globalisation that followed European global expansion and the Industrial Revolution. The long period of economic boom following the end of World War II produced a range of mass-produced goods but also a mass of ubiquitous ecological problems. In all, rapid world economic growth, the proliferation of new technologies and rising population in the post-World War II period generated increasing energy and resource consumption, new sources of waste (for example, nuclear waste) and rising levels of pollution and waste production and the rapid erosion of the Earth's biodiversity. International concern over environmental problems was heightened in the 1980s with the discovery of the 'hole' in the ozone layer and the problem of global warming.

From limits to growth to sustainable development

The systematic tracking and politicisation of global trends in population, resource and energy consumption, pollution and species extinction began in the late 1960s and early 1970s with the so-called 'limits to growth' debate, which publicised the uncanny correlation between the escalating rates of global economic growth and environmental degradation. Influential publications such as the Club of Rome's *The limits to growth* (Meadows et al. 1972) offered dire predictions of impending ecological catastrophe. This period also saw the consolidation of the modern environment movement as a persistent and ubiquitous social movement and the enactment of a raft of new environmental legislation in many OECD (Organisation for Economic Co-operation and Development) countries. The new global environmental consciousness was also reflected in the increasing popularity of the metaphor of 'Spaceship Earth' and the circulation of the first images of the planet taken from outer space by NASA. The new metaphors and images of the whole Earth, along with the oil crisis of 1973–74, contributed to the growing popular recognition of the fragility of life-support systems, the finite character of many of the Earth's resources, and the need for a collective response to global ecological problems. The first United Nations Conference on the Human Environment, held in 1972, led to the creation of the first official **UN** environmental organ – the United Nations Environment Programme (UNEP).

However, the general message of the limits to growth advocates – that environmental protection required drastic measures, including the curbing of economic growth and human population – attracted a critical backlash from technological optimists and proved to be unpalatable to political leaders. In any event, the discourse of limits to growth was soon overshadowed by the new discourse of 'sustainable development' following the publication in 1987 of *Our common future* by the World Commission on Environment and Development (WCED, otherwise known as the Brundtland Report) (WCED 1987). The WCED, chaired by Gro Harlem Brundtland, was set up in 1983 by the UN General Assembly to take stock of global ecological problems and develop a global agenda for change. After reviewing global environmental trends, the WCED called on the international community to adopt a new path of sustainable development that would meet the needs of present generations without sacrificing the needs of future generations. Whereas limits to growth advocates had called for a curbing of economic growth or a new steady-state economy, the WCED argued that sustainable development merely required the 'decoupling' of economic growth and environmental protection through constant technological innovation that reduced the amount of natural resources and energy consumed and waste produced per unit of gross domestic product (GDP). This has also served as the central claim of the more recent discourse of 'ecological modernisation', which argues that improving the environmental efficiency of production through technological innovation actually improves rather than retards national economic competitiveness.

However, the WCED not only called for improvements in the environmental efficiency of production; it also called for intra- and inter-generational equity, noting that communities that are impoverished are often forced to utilise their environment in unsustainable ways. It argued that a relatively rapid rise in per capita income in developing countries was an essential step towards sustainable development and it recommended that both the rich and poor worlds had to keep growing, with the poor world growing faster in order to 'catch up'. This argument highlights the paradoxical, and still deeply contested, relationship between economic growth and environmental quality: further growth increases societal capacity to respond to environmental degradation but also increases environmental degradation. Increasing the environmental efficiency of each unit of production merely slows the rate of increase in environmental degradation, but does not reduce aggregate levels of such degradation.

Nonetheless, the WCED's 'win-win' compromise was politically appealing and widely endorsed by governments, key environmental NGOs and business leaders. The concept of sustainable development served as the organising theme of the second United Nations Conference on Environment and Development (the 'Earth Summit') held in Rio de Janeiro in 1992. It also framed the Rio Declaration on Environment and Development (the core principles of sustainable development) and Agenda 21 (the global action plan for sustainable development). Many national, provincial and local governments around the world have developed sustainable development strategies or 'green plans', albeit with varying levels of commitment and success. In the wake of Brundtland, the 'limits to growth' idea that economic growth and environmental protection stand in a simple, **zero-sum** relationship has now been replaced with the idea that it is possible, at least to some extent, to *integrate* environment and development goals. Exactly how much remains a matter of ongoing political debate.

The post-Cold War context

From the vantage point of the twenty-first century, the 1992 Earth Summit marks the high-water mark of international environmental concern in the twentieth century. This unprecedented gathering of heads of state, NGOs and world media occurred in the wake of the Chernobyl nuclear accident in 1986, the 'discovery' of new global problems such as the thinning of the ozone layer and global warming, the publication of the influential Brundtland Report and the rise of green political parties. It also served as the meeting for the final negotiation and signing of the United Nations Framework Convention on Climate Change (UNFCCC) and the Convention on Biological Diversity. The thawing of the Cold War had prompted considerable speculation about the possibility of a new world **order** that would be not only peaceful but also ecologically sustainable. Lester Brown, for example, in the 1991 *State of the world* report, suggested that 'the battle to save the planet will replace the battle over ideology as the organising theme of the new world order' (L. Brown 1991: 3).

Instead of replacing the old ideological debates between East and West, however, the discourse of sustainable development now constitutes one of the new ideological debates of the post-Cold War period. The fall of **communism** signalled the triumph of **capitalism** as a more efficient system for allocating resources – though not for protecting nature or maintaining the viability of ecosystems upon which human well-being depends. The new, overlapping strategies of sustainable development and ecological modernisation promise improvements in the environmental efficiency of production but they provide no means of ensuring that the world economy operates within the carrying capacity of planetary ecosystems. Indeed, improving environmental productivity also fuels more investment, production and consumption. The more radical wing of the environment movement has argued that capitalism is inherently unsustainable because it is inherently expansionary, it discounts the future and it privatises profits while socialising or 'externalising' the ecological costs of economic activity. Strict environmental regulation of investment, production and consumption is defended as necessary to protect life-support systems and biological diversity. However, this critical environmental analysis runs against the dominant consensus (reflected in the Brundtland Report, and the policies of the **World Bank**, the OECD and other international organisations) that capitalist economic growth and environmental protection are, for the most part, compatible.

Ecological security

The lifting of the Iron Curtain (between the former USSR and the West) eased one form of insecurity – the imminent risk of nuclear war between the **superpowers** – only to reveal new forms of environmental insecurity, such as dwindling supplies of fresh water, fisheries and arable soil, the erosion of biodiversity and the serious threats of global warming. Instead of invading armies, citizens now contemplated the prospect of 'invading' deserts and oceans, ultraviolet radiation and malaria-carrying mosquitoes, all of which challenge traditional notions and practices of territorial defence. Predicted sea-level rises and damage to coastal infrastructure from global warming are expected to threaten human security and trigger a mass movement of 'ecological refugees' that is likely to generate political friction within and between states. Some analysts have predicted that competition over the increasing scarcity of natural resources (such as timber, arable land and especially oil and water) is likely to lead to an increasing incidence of armed conflict. Traditional strategic studies experts now frame climate change as a 'threat multiplier'. There have even been proposals for the establishment of a UN Environmental Security Council to deal with major environmental conflicts and disasters. However, critics point out that purely environmental conflicts are rare and that they are usually entangled with other conflicts. Some environmental problems have generated new forms of transboundary cooperation, particularly in relation to watersheds that straddle traditional political boundaries.

Although the concept of ecological security has not enjoyed the same notoriety as the concept of sustainable development in the international environment and development debates, it nonetheless has some influential advocates, including Gro Harlem Brundtland and former US Vice President Al Gore. Yet there are many who doubt the wisdom of employing the language of **security** in order to raise the status of ecological problems to a matter of 'high politics'. Indeed, sceptics have pointed to the potential for the concept to backfire and ultimately impede the quest for an ecologically sustainable new world order. Far from greening the state, the military and global governance, critics have suggested that the discourse of ecological security may unwittingly serve to reinforce a **Hobbesian** state system and legitimate the militarisation of state responses to environmental threats (Deudney 1990). However, proponents argue that a more comprehensive security framework enables critical reflection on the sources, moral referents, responses and conditions for long-term environmental and human security. They also claim that it has the potential to transform narrow, **state-centred** security thinking and possibly enable the redirection of military spending towards national and international environmental protection. Proponents of a more comprehensive (and critical) security framework also highlight the need to democratise societal processes of risk assessment, both nationally and internationally.

Environmental justice

The period of 'global environmental awakening' in the 1970s drew heavily on the Spaceship Earth metaphor, which underscored the common ecological fate of humankind. However, many critics on the left of the political spectrum were quick to point out that there were stark differences between those travelling first class and those working in the engine room. Indeed, the skewed distribution of environmental 'goods' (for example, urban amenity, clean air and water) and 'bads' (such as pollution) has emerged as a key moral debate and a major source of political conflict at the local, national and global levels over the last two decades. Emerging from the black ghettos of the US, the environmental justice movement has highlighted the fact that three out of five African-Americans and Latino-Americans live in communities with abandoned toxic waste sites, while no such sites can be found in leafy middle class suburbs. National and regional environmental and labour organisations have pointed out that many polluting industries have relocated from the developed to the developing world where labour is cheaper and environmental standards weaker and/or poorly enforced (such as the Mexican *maquiladora* region just south of the US border).

In international environmental negotiations, developing countries have drawn attention to the huge disparity in per capita levels of resource and energy consumption and waste production between the rich world and poor world. UNEP's Millennium Ecosystem Assessment, completed in March 2005, found that approximately 60 per cent of the ecosystem services that support life on Earth are being degraded or used unsustainably (UNEP 2005). It also found that the world's poor are suffering a disproportionate share of the harmful effects of environmental degradation. The report predicted that the continued degradation of life-support services could, in the absence of radical policy shifts, intensify over the next fifty years and undermine the achievement of the UN's Millennium Development Goals. The Intergovernmental Panel on Climate Change (IPCC) has also reported that low-income populations in developing countries, especially in tropical and sub-tropical regions, will be the most vulnerable to the risks of climate change (IPCC 2001: 9, 13). In short, many communities that consume the least energy and resources are destined to suffer the worst effects of global environmental degradation.

Environmental justice arguments have been especially prominent in the climate change negotiations. A key concern of developing countries is that the developed world may use ecological problems such as global warming as an excuse to 'kick the ladder down' and deny developing countries the opportunity to increase their consumption of energy and resources to raise the standard of living of their people relative to the developed world. These developing country concerns have been acknowledged in general terms in the Brundtland Report, the Rio Declaration, Agenda 21 and a number of major environmental treaties, including the UNFCCC and its offspring, the **Kyoto Protocol**. For example, the principle of 'common but differentiated responsibilities' (hereafter 'CBDR') enshrined in the Rio Declaration also serves as a core environmental justice principle in the UNFCCC 1992, the Kyoto Protocol 1997 and the Copenhagen Accord 2009. Applied to the climate change challenge, this principle acknowledges that the developed world should take the lead in tackling climate change because it has a greater responsibility for historical emissions, significantly higher per capita emissions and a greater capacity to absorb emission cuts and adapt to climate change than developing countries. It also acknowledges the specific development needs and special circumstances of developing countries, especially those that are particularly vulnerable to the impacts of climate change and least able to adapt. Accordingly, under the Kyoto Protocol, only industrialised countries are required to commit to mandatory greenhouse gas reduction targets in the first commitment period (2008–12). However, the rapid economic growth in major developing countries such as China and India has led the US to challenge the rigid distinction between the developed and developing world that is enshrined in the UNFCCC and the Kyoto Protocol.

Theories of global environmental politics
Realism and neoliberal institutionalism

The environment emerged as a 'new agenda issue' in international relations around the late 1970s. Most of this new environmental scholarship formed part of a larger research project on increasing global economic **interdependence** and the challenge of designing international institutions that enabled inter-state cooperation under conditions of **anarchy**. This new institutionalist turn, which has been dominated by **neoliberal institutionalism**, has produced a significant body of empirical work on both the negotiation and implementation phase of environmental treaties or **regimes** – work which has successfully refuted realist predictions that it is more rational for states to 'defect' and 'free ride' than to cooperate in international environmental treaties and strategies.

Realists had argued that the anarchic character of the international system is such that there is no solution to 'the tragedy of the commons' unless a **hegemonic** state or powerful **alliance** of states regard environmental protection as consonant with their self-interest and are prepared to absorb most of the costs of collective action. However, environmental problems have generally been regarded as matters of 'low politics' by **great powers**. More generally, realists argue that states have no incentive to take **multilateral** or **unilateral** action to protect the environment whenever this might create costs or disadvantages relative to other states. Nor is it in the interests of states to protect the environment ahead of more fundamental security and economic interests. While this approach appears to explain the US's repudiation of the Kyoto Protocol, it cannot explain why 192 parties have agreed to **ratify** the Protocol. Nor can it explain the general proliferation of environmental treaties over the last three decades. Contrary to realist predictions, concerns over relative gains have not prevented environmental cooperation.

Neoliberal institutionalists also begin with the fundamental insight that states are self-seeking, rational egoists operating in an anarchic environment, but they diverge significantly from realists in their assessment of the efficacy of the rule of **international law** and international institutions and the importance of relative versus absolute gains. They have shown that states will cooperate under well-designed environmental treaties or 'regimes' in order to avoid the 'suboptimal' consequences of international anarchy in situations of complex interdependence. In terms of the three basic questions of global environmental politics, neoliberal institutionalists regard international anarchy as the central 'problem' of global environmental politics, to which well-designed treaties are the solution. Well-designed regimes provide a better set of pay-offs than alternative self-help arrangements by lowering transaction costs, reducing uncertainty, providing mutual assurance and stabilising expectations. To the extent that neoliberal institutionalists have addressed questions of environmental justice, this has been through an examination of the incentive structure of treaties, such as whether they provide an acceptable distribution of benefits and burdens for the contracting parties in terms of relative economic costs, relative environmental vulnerability and relative capacity to adjust to environmental problems. However, the broader normative debates about environmental justice and responsibility are not part of the research agenda of neoliberal institutionalism, which is confined to explanation, prediction and problem-solving rather than fundamental critique.

From critical theory to global political ecology

In contrast to the 'problem-solving' approach of neoliberal institutionalism, the critical tradition of inquiry within international relations has explicitly set itself the task of drawing attention to structures of social and economic domination and highlighting and encouraging counter-hegemonic discourses and movements that seek to overcome such domination. Building on this broad tradition, a new school of international relations **theory**, variously referred to as 'global political ecology', 'critical political ecology' or 'Third World political ecology' emerged in the 1990s as a direct challenge to the environmental analyses and reformism of neoliberal institutionalists. Drawing on the **Gramscian**-inspired **Critical Theory** of Robert Cox, globalisation studies and radical environmental scholarship in the social sciences and humanities, this new branch of international ecopolitical inquiry has identified global capitalism, rather than the system of sovereign states, as the primary culprit for global environmental degradation, as well as for the skewed distribution of ecological risks. From this perspective, global capitalism is shown to leave highly uneven patterns of development and impacts across different human communities and ecosystems both within and between particular states, with some social classes and communities leaving much bigger 'ecological footprints' at the expense of others. Whereas traditional international political economy had always focused on investment and production, global political ecology has highlighted uneven patterns of consumption, as well as global patterns of advertising, retailing and disposal in global commodity chains. It has also highlighted the **power** of consumer and environmental organisations to redirect patterns of investment and production through consumer boycotts and green labelling.

More generally, global political ecology has highlighted the ways in which economic globalisation and the ascendancy of neoliberal economics have weakened both the steering capability and political legitimacy of states. Instead of serving as the protector and provider of public goods and services (such as environmental quality), states are increasingly acting as facilitators of privatisation, commodification, marketisation and deregulation. At the same time, global political ecology has drawn attention to a range of new public, private and hybrid forms of governance that shape environmental policy at the local, regional and transnational levels. Examples include the corporate responsibility movement, new environmental management systems, transnational environmental policy networks, the Intergovernmental Panel on Climate Change, the Commission for Sustainable Development and environmental NGO product certification schemes.

Finally, for global political ecologists, the study of global environmental politics is by no means restricted to the **norms** and structures of global *environmental* governance, such as the United Nations Environment Programme (UNEP), global environmental treaties, strategies and policy networks. It also extends to the norms and structures of *economic* governance, including organisations such as the **World Trade Organization**, the World Bank and the **International Monetary Fund** that are directly implicated in structuring global resource use and investment and development patterns. Indeed, the contradictions between international economic and environmental governance have emerged as one of the central preoccupations of global political ecology. For example, increasing attention has been directed to the ways in which the international trade and finance regimes have promoted unsustainable development patterns and undermined the effectiveness of multilateral environmental agreements.

Unlike neoliberal institutionalists, global political ecologists argue that fine-tuning environmental regimes is only part of the solution to global environmental problems. Their broader goal is to transform social structures to promote environmental justice, environmental security and more sustainable patterns of production and consumption around the world.

The US as the reluctant environmental state

The US was widely recognised as an environmental leader in the 1970s but in the post-Cold War period it has developed a reputation as an environmental laggard, especially in relation to the world's most significant global environmental challenge – climate change. For example, the US ratified 71 per cent of the environmental treaties listed in the UNEP register in the period 1970–91 but only 33 per cent in the period 1992–2007 (Eckersley 2008). The US's failure to ratify the Kyoto Protocol has attracted the most critical attention as the scientific research on the dire consequences of unchecked emissions growth continues to mount. Indeed, the lack of US support for the Kyoto Protocol has prompted the parties to the UNFCCC to commence negotiations for a second treaty, on Long Term Cooperative Action, as a means of drawing the US back into the climate talks. This treaty was scheduled to be concluded at the Copenhagen conference in 2009. However, no legal agreement was reached – only a short political agreement known as the Copenhagen Accord – and negotiations are ongoing.

One of the core sticking points for the US in the climate regime is the burden-sharing principles of common but differentiated responsibilities discussed above, which impose a leadership obligation on developed countries while recognising that developing countries' share of global emissions will need to grow to meet unmet development needs. According to these principles, the US should incur the biggest mitigation obligation. With less than 5 per cent of the world's population, the US consumes around a quarter of the world's fossil fuels. It has produced the largest share of historical or cumulative greenhouse gas emissions since industrialisation, it is ranked second (after China) in current aggregate emissions and it is one of the world's highest per capita emitters. It also has significant economic and technological capabilities. However, the US executive has never warmly embraced CBDR and the response of Congress has been even less enthusiastic, despite the growing number of climate bills that have been presented to Congress in the last five years. Although Democrat presidents Clinton and Obama have been relatively more open to CBDR than the Republican presidents Bush senior and junior, the last twenty years demonstrate more continuity than change in US climate policy output and international diplomacy. The dominant political consensus in the US is that the Kyoto architecture, which seeks to implement CBDR, is fundamentally flawed and unfair, because it requires the US to drastically restrict its emissions in order to provide room for developing countries, including rapidly growing China, to expand their emissions in the short to medium term. CBDR is at odds with the US's traditional economic and strategic interests, as well as US political elites' understanding of fair play.

While the Obama administration has rhetorically embraced CBDR, it remains chastened by the Clinton administration's failure to win Senate support for the ratification of the Kyoto Protocol. It has therefore sought to deflect attention from the US's leadership responsibilities by drawing attention to China's rapid emissions growth trajectory, as a backdrop for a recalibrated understanding of CBDR: one that requires international commitments from the major emerging emitters in the developing world in the same commitment period, rather than at some future, unspecified time *after* the US has demonstrated leadership. It has also insisted that these developing country mitigation commitments be measurable, reportable and verifiable. However, China and the **G77** remain staunch supporters of the traditional framing of CBDR and insist that developed countries should undertake a second round of commitments under the Kyoto Protocol, which is due to expire in 2012 if no further commitments are negotiated. China has argued that it has already undertaken ambitious national policies to reduce its emissions intensity and energy efficiency, for which the US has not given it due credit. However, it does not accept mandatory international reduction commitments, and at Copenhagen it refused to commit to a 2050 global emissions reduction target or a timetable for the peaking of global emissions because of its unfulfilled development needs.

Most comparative analyses of the US's failure as an international climate leader focus on the peculiarities of the US political system, which favours the **status quo** by requiring a two-thirds Senate majority for the ratification of treaties. However, while the procedures of the US Senate are certainly crucial to any understanding of US climate policy and diplomacy, they do not explain the ideational character of the US's response to climate change or the US's identity as a (liberal) superpower.

Realists would argue that the US's relationship to CBDR can be explained by US concerns over relative gains vis-à-vis a rising China and India (Grundig 2006), while neoliberal institutionalists would explain the US's position in terms of a defence of **national interests** based on a calculation of the costs of mitigation relative to vulnerability to climate disruption arising from inaction (Sprinz and Vaahtoranta 1994; Dolsak 2001). However, realists cannot explain why the relative gains enjoyed by developing countries under the climate regime are of much greater concern to the US than to most other developed states, particularly in Western Europe, which have embraced CBDR and enacted a regional emissions trading scheme. Likewise, neoliberal institutionalism cannot explain variations in climate policy over time, or climate policy variation between countries with similar levels of fossil-fuel dependence, because they assume that all states follow the same cost-benefit calculations when deciding whether to ratify an environmental treaty. Yet cost-benefit calculations can produce vastly different results depending on the nature of the costs and benefits that are included, the time horizons employed and whether a security, economic or environmental framework is applied. Such variations require an understanding of national differences in the social construction of climate change as a problem, domestic climate policy framing, strategies of capital accumulation and foreign policy identities.

For global political ecologists, a key problem for the US is that its economic and military strength was developed on the basis of cheap fossil-fuel energy and extensive land development, which Matthew Paterson has characterised as 'carboniferous capitalism' (Paterson 2009: 148). Oil has also been used as a strategic resource to maintain US hegemony both during and after the Cold War. Imposing a 'price on carbon' has therefore been rejected as a threat to US interests and the American way of life, rather than being seen as an opportunity to lead the world towards a low-carbon future. This stands in strong contrast to climate leaders such as Germany, which have pursued a strategy of 'ecological modernisation' through the imposition of increasingly aggressive restraints on carbon emissions as well as the active promotion of renewable energy and energy efficiency. Whereas the German Government has embraced CBDR and highlighted the domestic economic, technological and employment benefits that flow from stringent targets, the US Congress has rejected CBDR and focused only on the short-term economic costs of carbon constraints.

A global political ecology analysis would also draw attention to the fact that the dominant discourses of economic development, justice and security in the US are mostly at odds with the global environmental discourses of sustainable development, environmental justice and ecological security that have framed the CBDR. This dissonance is reflected in the US's grand strategy, the central pillars of which are to secure US military and economic supremacy, promote a stable world capitalist system according to US liberal ideals, and promote the spread of liberal democracy. None of these pillars has been interpreted or pursued in ways that are compatible with a low US carbon footprint, planetary sustainability or global environmental justice (although the Pentagon has recently moved to improve energy efficiency). No US administration has played an active role in promoting environmental sustainability as a whole-of-government **meta-policy** at the domestic or international levels. Although the US has sometimes taken strong domestic and international action in certain environmental policy domains, such as wildlife protection and protection of the ozone layer, environmental issues have never been considered to be, or allowed to impinge upon, matters of 'high politics'. Rather, US foreign petroleum policy, and complementary domestic policies such as energy and economic policy, have typically constrained the development of a more proactive climate policy at home and abroad.

Conclusion

As Robert Falkner has observed, 'unlike trade and monetary policy, environmental policy has never been central to the US effort to create international order' (Falkner 2005: 586). However, this will have to change if the US is to take a leadership role. This is mostly likely to happen through creative issue-linkage between energy security and climate concerns and recognition of the economic and strategic advantages derived from innovation in low-carbon technologies. During the Cold War, one of the relatively benign forms of rivalry between the US and the Soviet Union was the 'space race'. In the post-Cold War period, the productive rivalry between the US and China is likely to take the form of a 'green high-tech race'. This may be the crucial lever needed to overcome policy gridlock in the US Congress and galvanise both the legislature and the executive, including the Pentagon, to pursue a low-carbon future.

QUESTIONS

1. What is 'sustainable development'? And why did the UN World Commission on Environment and Development propose it?
2. To what extent does the states-system contribute to global ecological problems?
3. Do you think the environmental crisis (extending from dwindling supplies of fresh water, fisheries and arable soil to the erosion of biodiversity and the threat of global warming) is best conceived in terms of environmental 'security'?

4. Which international relations theory offers the best means of grasping environmental issues in international relations?

5. Why has the US been an environmental laggard in the post-Cold War period? Is this likely to change?

FURTHER READING

Bernstein, Steven 2001, *The compromise of liberal environmentalism*, New York: Columbia University Press. **Constructivist** analysis of the history of the sustainable development discourse, showing how the discourse has been constrained by the requirements of capitalist economics.

Clapp, Jennifer and Dauvergne, Peter 2005, *Paths to a green world: the political economy of the global environment*, Cambridge, MA: MIT Press. Examines the relationship between economic globalisation and the environment, including trade, investment and finance, with a particular focus on developing countries.

Paterson, Matthew 2009, 'Post-hegemonic climate change?' *British Journal of Politics and International Relations* 11(1), 140–158.

World Watch Institute 2005, *State of the world 2005: redefining global security*, Washington: World Watch Institute. Explores the underlying sources of global insecurity including poverty, infectious disease, environmental degradation and rising competition over oil and other natural resources.

35

Climate Change

Peter Newell

Introduction	476
A brief history of climate change politics	477
Explaining the global politics of climate change	482
Conclusion	484
Questions	485
Further reading	485

Introduction

This chapter gives an overview of the **theory** and practice of global climate politics. First, it provides a brief history of the politics of climate change as they play out in the international negotiations on the issue overseen by the **United Nations (UN)**. Second, it looks at the formal organisational and institutional structures that exist to manage the international community's response to climate change. Third, it reviews the ways in which different theories of International Relations (IR) have been applied to climate change, assessing both their potentials and limitations. Finally, the conclusion offers some thoughts on the evolving nature of the 'global' governance of climate change.

The issue of global climate change (see Box 35.1) has moved to the centre of the international agenda in recent years. As scientific consensus about the severity of uncontrolled warming strengthens around the idea that nations should take immediate steps to reduce their contribution to climate change, politicians are under pressure to act. Yet the fact that climate change is caused by such a wide array of everyday human activities creates a coordination and cooperation challenge of staggering proportions. Added to this, the uneven contribution of nations to the problem and the uneven exposure of different social groups to the worst effects of climate change make it an issue of social justice since, for the most part, those who will suffer the worst impacts of climate change have contributed least to the problem. This links climate change to broader North–South debates about aid, finance, technology and development. Also, despite the fact that many people in vulnerable locations are already exposed to the effects of climate change, some of the most dramatic effects will not be felt for many years to come. This introduces the complex question of inter-generational justice while providing few incentives for this generation of politicians to bear the brunt of the costs of taking actions from which unborn children will be the primary beneficiaries.

As well as being seen as a serious issue in its own right, climate change is also increasingly connected to other key issues in international relations such as development, trade and security. The connections are apparent in debates about the levels and types of financing to which developing countries should be entitled in order to pay for mitigation (emissions reductions) activities they undertake for the benefit of the international community and the adaptation measures they have to put in place to protect their citizens from the effects of climate change. They arise through concerns about the use of trade measures such as so-called 'border tax adjustments', which seek to tax imported products that have been manufactured in countries not subject to emissions controls (on the basis that without the tax they will benefit from an unfair competitive advantage when compared with products that have). **Security** concerns about 'climate refugees' fleeing from areas of the world subject to sea-level rise or extreme

BOX 35.1: TERMINOLOGY

What is climate change?

The world's climate system has always undergone dramatic change due to natural variability. What currently causes concern is the observed increase in global surface temperatures, as a consequence of radiative forcing, thought to be caused by anthropogenic greenhouse gas emissions. Concentrations of these gases – which include CO_2, methane and nitrous oxide as well as gases from the chlorine family – create a 'greenhouse effect' which traps incoming radiation from the Sun but prevents some of it from being released back into the Earth's atmosphere, hence warming the planet.

weather events, or the impact of climate change in exacerbating tensions over access to water and land viable for agriculture, have brought climate change to the attention of the military establishment.

A brief history of climate change politics

Although we often assume that the high profile that climate change now enjoys means that it is a new political issue, in fact it has a much longer legacy. The governance of climate change as a global political issue has progressed from being a cause for concern among a growing number of scientists to gaining recognition as an issue deserving of a collective global effort orchestrated by the UN (see Box 35.2). Over time there has been a deepening of cooperation and a firming up of obligations to act; a process common to many international negotiations on the environment where a general agreement identifies the need for action and a subsequent protocol contains concrete legally-binding emissions reductions commitments. What is also notable, and a theme to which we return below, is the increasing use of market or flexible mechanisms to achieve emissions reductions.

BOX 35.2: DISCUSSION POINTS

The global governance of climate change: a short chronology

1988: World Conference on the Changing Atmosphere: politicians and scientists conclude that 'humanity is conducting an un-intended, uncontrolled, globally pervasive experiment whose ultimate consequences could be second only to nuclear war'. The conference recommends reducing CO_2 emissions by 20 per cent by 2005.

1990: The Intergovernmental Panel on Climate Change (IPCC) publishes its First Assessment Report.

1991: The Intergovernmental Negotiating Committee is set up to oversee negotiations towards an international agreement.

1992: 154 countries at the United Nations Conference on Environment and Development in Rio sign the UN Framework Convention on Climate Change (UNFCCC), which aims to stabilise emissions at 1990 levels by the year 2000 as part of overall goal to stabilise greenhouse gas (GHG) 'concentrations in the atmosphere at a level that would prevent dangerous interference with the climate system'.

1994: The UNFCCC enters into force on 21 March.

1995: The first CoP (Conference of the Parties) agrees in Berlin that binding commitments by industrialised countries are required to reduce emissions.

1995: The IPCC publishes its Second Assessment Report, which argues that: 'The balance of evidence suggests a discernible human influence on global climate.'

1996: The second CoP in Geneva sees the US agree to legally binding targets to reduce emissions as long as emissions trading is included in an agreement.

1997: More than 150 countries sign the Kyoto Protocol, which binds thirty-eight industrialised (Annex 1) countries to reduce GHG emissions by an average of 5.2 per cent below 1990 levels during the period 2008–12.

2000: The negotiations at the sixth CoP in The Hague collapse amid disagreements principally between the US and Europe about the use of the Kyoto Protocol's flexibility mechanisms.

2001: US President George W. Bush announces his country is to withdraw from the Kyoto Protocol.

2001: In Marrakesh the final elements of the Kyoto Protocol are worked out, particularly the rules and procedures by which the flexible mechanisms will operate.

2004: The Buenos Aires Programme of Work on Adaptation and Response Measures is agreed at CoP 10.

2005: On 16 February, the Kyoto Protocol becomes law after Russian **ratification** pushes the emissions of ratified Annex 1 countries over the 55 per cent mark.

2005: The first Meeting of the Parties to the Kyoto Protocol takes place in Montreal at CoP 11.

2006: At the Second Meeting of the Parties (CoP 12) the Nairobi Work Programme on Adaptation and the Nairobi Framework on Capacity-Building for the CDM are agreed.

2007: The IPCC publishes its Fourth Assessment Report.

2007: At CoP 13 the Bali Action Plan is agreed, which calls for a long-term goal for emissions reductions; measurable, reportable, verifiable mitigation commitments including nationally appropriate mitigation actions by less-developed countries (LDCs), as well as enhanced adaptation, action on technology development and transfer and financial resources and investment to support the above.

2009: CoP 15 takes place in Copenhagen amid chaotic scenes and failure by negotiators to 'seal the deal'. Instead the Copenhagen Accord is produced by a limited number of countries, which is not legally binding but whose existence has been taken note of by a number of countries despite initial protests about the exclusionary way in which it was produced.

2010: CoP 16 agrees the 'Cancún agreements', which seek to keep the negotiations on track in the areas of adaptation, forests, climate finance, technology transfer and capacity-building in the wake of the fiasco at Copenhagen.

The UN Framework Convention on Climate Change (UNFCCC) was agreed at the UN Conference on Environment and Development (UNCED) summit in Rio de Janeiro in 1992. As the first major milestone in the history of climate diplomacy, the UNFCCC provided a framework for global action on the issue. It sought to emulate the apparent success of the ozone **regime**, which first produced the Vienna Convention establishing the nature of the problem and the basis for remedial action, and subsequently the Montreal Protocol which agreed a phase-out of the most damaging ozone-depleting chemicals. Given the sharp differences of opinion described above, and the relative lack of momentum behind the issue at the time, the fact the UNFCCC was agreed at all can be considered a substantial achievement. The agreement set the goal of 'avoiding dangerous interference in the climate system,' defined as aiming to stabilise concentrations of greenhouse gases (GHGs) in the atmosphere, and listed some policies and measures that countries might adopt to achieve that end. Acknowledging the vast differences in contributions to the problem, the convention established the principle of 'common but differentiated responsibility' and recognised that developing countries were not yet in a position to assume obligations to act. Efforts they could make towards tackling the issue were made dependent on the receipt of aid and technology transfer from Northern countries that were meant to be 'additional' to existing aid budgets.

Attention then turned to how to realise the general nature of the commitments contained in the UNFCCC. With scientific assessments of the severity of climate change becoming increasingly common and growing awareness of the inadequacy of existing policy responses, momentum built for a follow-up to the convention. The 1995 Berlin Mandate at the first Conference of the Parties (CoP) sought to promote quantified emissions limitations and reduction obligations (QELROs), and negotiations thus began towards a Protocol which would set legally binding targets to reduce GHG emissions. The Kyoto Protocol, concluded in 1997, was the outcome of this (see Box 35.3). Signed by more than 150 countries, it binds 38 industrialised countries (so called Annex 1 parties) to reduce GHG emissions by an average of 5.2 per cent below 1990 levels during the period 2008–12. It fixes differentiated targets for industrialised countries while setting in train a process to further elaborate 'flexible mechanisms' such as the joint implementation scheme, emissions trading schemes (ETS) and a Clean Development Mechanism (CDM). We discuss these further below. The idea was that these market mechanisms allowed for countries to pay for emissions reductions wherever it was cheapest to do so.

BOX 35.3: KEY TEXTS

The Kyoto Protocol in brief

Commitments:

- Industrialised countries will reduce their collective emissions of GHG by an average of 5.2 per cent below 1990 levels in the commitment period 2008–12.
- The US has to reduce its emissions by an average of 7 per cent; Japan by an average of 6 per cent and the EU by an average of 8 per cent. Other industrialised countries are permitted small increases while others are obliged only to freeze their emissions.
- Developed countries are obliged to provide:
  - 'new and additional financial resources to meet the agreed full costs incurred by developing country parties in advancing the implementation of existing commitments'
  - 'such financial resources, including transfer of technology, needed by the developing country parties to meet the agreed and full incremental costs of advancing the implementation of existing commitments', and
  - 'financial resources for the implementation of Article 10, through bilateral, regional and other multilateral channels' which developing country parties can avail of'.

Instruments:

- *Clean Development Mechanism*: The aim of this body is to assist developing countries in 'achieving sustainable development' and at the same time to help developed countries 'in achieving compliance with their quantified emission limitation and reduction commitments'. In effect its purpose is to oversee the implementation of projects funded by developed states wanting to accrue credits for emissions achieved overseas. Reduction credits are certified by the CDM Executive Board to ensure that projects add value to savings that would have been made in their absence (Article 12).
- *Joint Implementation*: Actions implemented jointly have to be 'additional to any that would otherwise occur' and 'supplemental to domestic actions'. Scope is provided to include 'verifiable changes in stocks of sinks' in parties' assessment of their net GHG emissions (Article 6).
- *Emissions trading* (Article 17).
- *Implementation*: Will be via national reports overseen by teams of experts nominated by the parties.

The process for finalising the rules and operational details of the Protocol was agreed at CoP 4 in 1998 as part of the Buenos Aires Plan of Action. In November 2000 parties met in The Hague at CoP 6 to try and complete these negotiations, but failed to do so amid a growing rift between the European Union (EU) and the US in particular. Having negotiated and lobbied hard for the inclusion of market-based mechanisms which would allow industrialised countries maximum flexibility, in 2001 the US walked away from the Kyoto Protocol. Part of the US's refusal to ratify Kyoto was because its economic competitors in the developing world were not required to reduce their emissions. Without the involvement of the US, many assumed the inevitable demise of the Kyoto Protocol. If the largest contributor to the problem and most powerful economy in the world was not on board, what incentive was there for others to sign up? In fact, the absence of the US served to galvanize the EU and the coalition formed by the **G77** group of less developed countries plus China (G77 + China) into further action, and with the Russian ratification of the Kyoto Protocol in 2005 it entered into force.

Subsequent negotiations have focused on detailed issues concerning the implementation and enforcement of Kyoto and, increasingly, what might come in its place as the end of the implementation period (2012) draws ever closer. At CoP 7 the Marrakesh Accords were agreed, which established the rules and procedures for the operation of the flexible mechanisms including the CDM, as well as details on reporting and methodologies. Importantly they also established three new funds: the Least Developed Countries Fund, the Special Climate Change Fund and the Adaptation Fund. This work was continued through to the Buenos Aires Programme of Work on Adaptation and Response Measures agreed at CoP 10 in 2004. This was followed at CoP 11 in Montreal with the creation of the Ad Hoc Working Group on Further Commitments for Annex 1 parties under the Kyoto Protocol. At CoP 12 in Nairobi, dubbed the 'Africa CoP,' there was significant discussion about financing issues and how to increase the number of CDM projects being hosted by the poorest regions of the world, most notably sub-Saharan Africa. The meeting produced the Nairobi Work Programme on Adaptation and the Nairobi Framework on Capacity-Building for the CDM. The Bali Action Plan, agreed a year later at CoP 13, set the path for negotiations towards Copenhagen, calling for a long-term goal for emissions reductions; measurable, reportable, verifiable mitigation commitments including nationally appropriate mitigation actions by less-developed countries (LDCs), as well as enhanced adaptation, action on technology development and transfer and financial resources, and investment to support the above. Unfortunately, the 2009 CoP 15 meeting failed to agree a new legally binding agreement despite intense pressure to 'seal the deal'. A 'Copenhagen Accord' was produced by a small number of powerful countries including China, India, Brazil and South Africa – reflecting the growing economic and political power of those countries as well as their own rising contribution to the problem of climate change. The failure of the meeting to advance progress and the breakdown in trust that occurred left the negotiations in a state of disarray. This was, at least in part, rectified by the Cancún meeting in 2010, which agreed to a series of decisions on key areas of the Bali Action Plan, on issues such as finance – most notably the creation of the Green Climate Fund – as well as technology cooperation and adaptation. These complex questions of responsibility and who pays for action on climate change continue to dominate the negotiations.

The organisation of the negotiations

The international negotiations on climate change are organised around a number of key actors, institutions and decision-making processes. In terms of international organisations, three institutions are critical to the process of negotiating climate change policy. First, there is the secretariat of the UNFCCC, based in Bonn since 1996, which organises and oversees the negotiations, prepares the necessary documentation and is responsible for overseeing reporting of emissions profiles and projects funded through the Kyoto Protocol. Guided by the Parties to the Convention, it provides organisational support and technical expertise to the negotiations and institutions and facilitates the flow of authoritative information on the implementation of the Convention. It has a key and often underestimated role to play in shaping the outcomes of the negotiations (Depledge 2005). It has an executive secretary who is responsible for trying to guide the negotiations towards a successful conclusion. Second, there is the Conference of the Parties (CoP) to the UNFCCC and Kyoto Protocol, which meets annually to review progress on commitments contained in those treaties and to update them in the light of the latest scientific advice. This is the ultimate decision-making body in the climate negotiations. Third, there are the Subsidiary Bodies on Implementation (SBI) and Science and Technology (SBSTA) and the Ad Hoc Working Groups which take forward negotiations on specific issues that the CoP ultimately has to approve. For example, there is currently an Ad Hoc Working Group on Further Commitments for Annex 1 parties under the Kyoto Protocol.

In order to shape this process, governments often organise themselves into blocs and negotiating coalitions to enhance their influence and to advance common agendas. These key coalitions and negotiating blocs emerged early on in the negotiations, but have evolved significantly since then as the issues changed and their levels of economic development dramatically altered (Paterson and Grubb 1992). At one end of the spectrum the Organization of Petroleum Exporting Countries (OPEC) grouping quickly emerged as the coalition of states most hostile to action on climate change. With revenues almost entirely dependent on the export of oil, that opposition was unsurprising. This bloc affected the pace and course of the negotiations with calls for greater scientific certainty before action could take place, the formation of **alliances** with businesses opposed to action and the use of wrecking tactics such as the call for compensation for loss of oil revenue in response to the call from many low-lying developing countries for economic compensation for impacts suffered as a result of climate change (Newell 2000).

At the other end of the spectrum, the Alliance of Small Island states (AOSIS), a coalition of island states most vulnerable to the effects of sea-level rise, has been the most strident of the negotiating coalitions in its demands for far-reaching and stringent emissions reductions targets. In 1995 it proposed its own protocol to the agreement mandating a 20 per cent cut in 1990 emissions by 2005. The AOSIS group works closely with the London-based legal group Foundation for International Environmental Law and Development (FIELD), which provides legal advice on the negotiating text. Indeed, FIELD was attributed a key role in drafting the AOSIS protocol, suggesting the fragility of rigid distinctions about who exercises power and authority in the governance of climate change (Arts 1998).

In between these two polarities lay the G77 + China coalition, which emphasised the North's primary contribution to the problem of climate change and sought to deflect calls for the South to make commitments and to ensure that funds committed to achieve the convention's goals were genuinely additional to existing money for aid. The G77, which as we will see below is now less cohesive, continues to provide a platform for shared concerns about climate change policy. The EU meanwhile has been keen to see a stronger agreement, while the US, particularly during the administrations of presidents Bush senior and junior, was resolutely opposed to legally binding cuts in greenhouse gases. Japan has adopted a position between these two, as host to the summit that produced the Kyoto Protocol but often a reluctant leader because of high levels of industry pressure to not over-commit. Both the US and Japan were part of the JUSCANZ grouping (Japan, the US, Canada, Australia and New Zealand) which argued for maximum flexibility in how countries are expected to meet their commitments.

Alongside the formal negotiations organised in plenary sessions and working groups that meet in parallel to discuss specific issues, a bewildering array of non-government, business and other organisations are registered to participate in the process. Though they do not have formal voting rights, they are allowed to make interventions and are often admitted onto government delegations, where they have access to all the meetings taking place. In many ways, these actors are non-governmental 'diplomats', performing many of the same functions as state delegates: representing the interests of their constituencies, engaging in information exchange, negotiating and providing policy advice (Betsill and Corell 2008). Demands for participation in climate change negotiations have created a massive strain on the capacity of countries to host these events. This issue came to a head at the Copenhagen CoP15 in December 2009 when the premises could not accommodate a record 900 observer organisations and the security entourages of 196 heads of states. Entry passes were rationed – often under chaotic circumstances – and many observers were shut out of the building where negotiations took place. This raises questions about the possibility of an inclusive and open process, and casts doubt on the feasibility of such a mega-process.

We can see, therefore, that the process of making climate policy involves international organisations and institutional structures established for this purpose, coalitions and blocs of state actors, and a range of **non-state actors** who have sought to influence the process of negotiation in a variety of ways.

Explaining the global politics of climate change

The issue of climate change has attracted increasing attention from IR scholars from all theoretical perspectives. Many earlier interpretations understandably fell back on familiar tools and existing theoretical canons to make sense of this 'new' challenge. **Regime** theory, which seeks to explain the emergence, evolution and effectiveness of international cooperation (Krasner 1983; Haas, Keohane and Levy 1993; Young 1998; Vogler 1995), appeared to offer a useful entry point for explaining the negotiations around the UNFCCC and subsequent Kyoto Protocol, and this is where a lot of attention has remained. Sometimes referred to as **neo-liberal institutionalism**, regime theory covers a range of perspectives that place different emphases on the role of **power** (particularly the **hegemonic** power of leading states such as the US), the extent to which institutions exercise their own degree of power which is more than the sum of their parts, and the degree to which expert or knowledge-based communities play a role in creating the enabling conditions for international cooperation (Hasenclever et al. 1997).

It is increasingly difficult, however, to account for the history and contemporary nature of responses to climate change using traditional IR theories. While growing links to security issues may mean that **realists** devote more attention to the issue than they have done in the past, their preoccupations with a narrow set of questions around **anarchy**, **order** and international security do not shed much light on the nature of global responses to climate change. Power-based regime perspectives, which place emphasis on the role of a hegemonic power in creating the conditions in which cooperation between states is possible, might point to the decisive role of the US in the climate negotiations. As historically the largest contributor to the problem of climate change, the US has played a veto role in stalling international agreements which it does not approve of, such as the Kyoto Protocol. The US's abstention from the agreement also made it easier for other countries to refuse to take action. Reaching the levels of finance now required – US$100 billion a year by 2020 according to the Copenhagen Accord – will also rely on the active support and cooperation of powerful actors such as the US, EU and Japan. Yet the climate negotiations continued in the absence of US leadership and the climate regime described above has very much developed a life of its own, with a series of institutions under its umbrella that are not readily unsettled by the shifting preferences of government administrations that come and go.

Theories of international regimes help us to understand the role of interests and knowledge in shaping the nature of responses to date. Pointing towards the ways in which institutions can reduce transaction costs, improve information flows and generate trust among parties, they draw attention to the ways in which bodies such as the UNFCCC can guide states towards cooperative outcomes (Depledge 2005). They provide useful insights into the micro-politics of negotiations and deal-brokering within institutions and between **states**. Work which emphasises the relationship between power and knowledge, particularly with reference to the forms of expertise exercised by scientists and economists in climate policy debates, usefully helps us to understand why the problem of climate is constructed and framed in one way and not another (Hajer 1997; Litfin 1994; Wynne 1994). Ideas about 'epistemic communities' (Haas 1990) have been applied to the role of the UN IPCC, which plays a consensus-building and agenda-setting role in the climate change negotiations (Paterson 1996). Many accounts within IR have also drawn attention to the importance of non-state actors in shaping outcomes in climate politics: influencing states' negotiating positions and keeping up pressure on them to go further (Arts 1998; Betsill and Corell 2008; Newell 2000). More recent work has gone beyond this to explore the governance roles played by such actors in their own right, creating forms of transnational governance which set targets, generate funding and oversee project implementation in ways which complement, as well as go beyond, the UN regime (Andonova et al. 2009; Bulkeley and Newell 2010).

Coming from a **Marxist** and **Critical Theory** perspective, some writers in IR suggest that to understand more deeply the nature of global responses to climate change, we have to look at the role of states in a capitalist global political economy and the way in which **capitalism** structures opportunities for action (Gale 1998; Levy and Newell 2002, 2005). Focusing on the relationship between the state and market (or the state and capital in Marxist terms), these accounts suggest that barriers to cooperation are less about fears of other states free-riding on the collective efforts of others to address the problem, or uncertainties about the case for action; rather, they reflect the structural relationship between states and the businesses they depend on for jobs, taxation and in some cases party funding, but whose emissions they are expected to regulate to tackle climate change (Newell and Paterson 1998). According to this perspective, therefore, change will have to come from shifts in the economic system, or at the very least the emergence of sections of the business community (fractions of capital) that see climate change as an investment opportunity rather than a threat to their business if action on the issue is to meaningfully advance (Newell and Paterson 2010).

Rather than view each of these perspectives as incompatible and in competition with one another, it is also worth remembering that they seek to explain different aspects of global climate governance. Many focus on one particular source of power (knowledge-based theories), while others seek to go beyond the regime itself to locate climate change as a feature of the organisation of political and economic power in the global economy (Marxist and Critical Theory accounts). Studies that emphasise the importance of non-state actors also bring an added dimension to those regime approaches which underscore the primary importance of states and their relationship to international institutions. There is certainly great value in keeping an open mind about which aspects of global climate politics can be explained by which theories.

As the climate change regime broadens to address new areas, enrol new actors and develop novel policy instruments, theoretical approaches face fresh challenges to their assumptions and focus about who the relevant actors are, the scales at which they operate, and the ways in which they govern. To take one example: increasingly climate politics is conducted by and for markets. Whether it is the use of emissions trading (as in the EU), the Clean Development Mechanism (between Annex 1 and non-Annex 1 parties) or the growth of voluntary carbon markets alongside the regime, the marketisation of climate governance, as with other areas of the environment, is a notable trend (Newell 2008a). These mechanisms extend the reach of global governance mechanisms to the livelihoods of millions of the world's poor in Asia, Africa and Latin America working in the forestry, energy or waste sectors, for example, raising issues of who benefits and how. They rely on elaborate networks of intermediaries and brokers, accountants, lawyers and project developers operating across a variety of scales to enable the markets to function. They operate in the shadow of hierarchy, but require systems of governance that extend way beyond what states alone can provide. Capturing and adequately explaining the nature of these governance arrangements requires an attempt to think outside conventional disciplinary boundaries.

Conclusion

It seems likely that climate change is here to stay as an issue on the global political agenda. How high a place on that agenda it occupies will depend on the extent to which, and ways in which, it is linked to other issues of 'high' politics such as trade and security and its intimate ties to key resources such as energy, water and land.

There continues to be an alarming disconnect between what we know about climate change as a scientific and social phenomenon, what this implies in terms of urgent and large-scale change, and the seeming inability of governments and private actors the world over to respond in a timely and decisive manner. Perceptions of the slow and inadequate nature of responses to the threat provide the rationale and point of departure for many of the innovations and experiments in climate governance that have mushroomed in recent years through collaborations, partnerships and private regimes involving cities, local governments, the private sector and civil society (Bulkeley and Newell 2010). Actions and initiatives such as these are perhaps more empowering than waiting and hoping that the UN machinery will deliver a new legally-binding and comprehensive agreement to cut global GHG emissions. In and of themselves, though, they may not be enough. Those who place their faith in carbon markets to trade their way out of trouble still need targets and timetables to give a steer to the market about how many permits will be available and over what time frames. Likewise, private governance and standard-setting may have an important role to play, but it cannot achieve the comprehensiveness or ability to sanction that state-backed regulation can. And while community-based mobilisations play a vital role both in mobilising people to reduce their own emissions and preparing for the effects of climate change, such initiatives would benefit from being scaled up and coordinated in a way which only states can do. The challenge, increasingly, is how to coordinate and steer multiple systems of climate governance, both public and private, that operate across numerous scales.

The discipline of IR can and should have an important role to play in explaining responses to climate change, assessing their effectiveness and suggesting ways forward for tackling this most complex and 'wicked' of problems. It remains a challenge for all of us to be thinking openly, innovatively and critically about the options before us if we are to make a contribution to ensuring that this does not come to be defined, as the title of a recent film suggests, as the 'age of stupid'.

QUESTIONS

1. What makes climate change a political issue?
2. How has the climate change regime evolved over time and how can this best be explained?
3. How far do divisions between the global North and South remain the principal barrier to progress in the climate change negotiations?
4. How significant are non-state actors to collective efforts to respond to climate change?
5. How can we best explain the global politics of climate change using different theories of International Relations?

FURTHER READING

Bulkeley, Harriet and Newell, Peter 2010, *Governing climate change*, London: Routledge. Overview of climate governance from the international regime to organised responses from cities, businesses and communities and the theoretical challenges this raises.

Newell, Peter 2000, *Climate for change: non-state actors and the global politics of the greenhouse*, Cambridge: Cambridge University Press. Assessment and explanation of the political influence of a range of non-state actors (the scientific community, mass media, business groups and environmental NGOs) upon the climate regime up to the Kyoto Protocol.

Newell, Peter and Paterson, Matthew 2010, *Climate capitalism: global warming and the transformation of the global economy*, Cambridge: Cambridge University Press. Provides a history of carbon markets and the intertwining of climate change politics and the global economy while also suggesting the conditions under which 'climate capitalism' might be possible.

Paterson, Matthew 1996, *Global warming, global politics*, London: Routledge. Assesses different strands of IR theory on their ability to explain processes of international cooperation around the UNFCCC.

Roberts, Timmons and Parks, Bradley 2007, *Climate of injustice: global inequality, North-South politics and climate policy*, Cambridge, Mass.: MIT Press. Shows how North-South conflicts in climate negotiations are a feature of broader historical inequities between developed and less-developed countries.

GLOSSARY OF TERMS

Richard Devetak

Glossary terms are highlighted in bold throughout the text. Words in italics are defined elsewhere in the glossary.

A. Q. Khan network – An illicit global network for the proliferation of nuclear weapons technology named after one of its leading figures, Pakistani nuclear scientist, Abdul Qadeer Khan.

Alliance – A formal agreement between two or more *sovereign states* to cooperate on matters of *security* and defence.

Alter-casting – A strategy wherein one actor cajoles another (or others) into a certain way of being or behaving by treating the other(s) consistently with their view of appropriate conduct.

Anarchy – The absence of rule or government. In international relations it does not mean disorder and chaos.

Anti-colonialism – The ideology and struggle opposed to *colonialism*; it helped fuel the *decolonisation* process.

ANZUS – A *security* agreement between Australia, New Zealand and the US which came into force in 1952. Each party agrees, under certain conditions, to assist others in the case of armed attack. Since 1986, when New Zealand refused entry to US ships that may have been carrying nuclear weapons, the US has not recognised its commitment to New Zealand.

APEC (Asia-Pacific Economic Cooperation) – A forum for countries of the Asia-Pacific region to discuss and negotiate matters of common economic interest, especially trade matters. Members include: Australia, Brunei Darussalam, Canada, Chile, China, Hong Kong, Indonesia, Japan, Republic of Korea, Malaysia, Mexico, New Zealand, Papua New Guinea, Philippines, Singapore, Chinese Taipei, Thailand and the US.

Arms control – The exercise of restraint in the development, acquisition, stockpiling and use of weapons. The management of this process is usually achieved through negotiated agreements or treaties.

ASEAN (Association of Southeast Asian Nations) – Formed in 1967 to promote regional stability and economic cooperation, it currently comprises 10 state members: Brunei, Burma, Cambodia, Laos, Indonesia, Malaysia, Philippines, Singapore, Thailand and Vietnam.

Balance of payments – A *state's* capital account surplus or deficit, based on the difference between the amount of money flowing in or out of the state. It is the account of a state's financial transactions with the rest of the world.

Balance of power – Refers to a mechanism that operates to prevent one *state* from achieving such a preponderance of *power* that it is in a position to lay down and enforce the law over all others. Central to *realist* theories, it can be viewed as the deliberate product of foreign policies, or as the unintended consequence of several states seeking to protect themselves. In any case, states align with others to counter-balance the growth in another's power, seeking to preserve international *order* and a degree of equilibrium.

Balance of trade – A *state's* annual net trade surplus or deficit, based on the difference in value between imports and exports. It is the account of a state's trade relations with the rest of the world.

Bilateralism – A term referring to discussions, negotiations and decisions made by two *states* on matters of mutual interest. Compare with *unilateralism* and *multilateralism*.

Bipolarity – Refers to an *international system* where two overwhelmingly powerful *states* dominate. Like magnetic poles, the two *powers* both attract and repel at the same time. They attract friends and allies, and repel rivals and enemies. The *Cold War* is the best example of a bipolar system. Compare with *unipolarity* and *multipolarity*.

Bretton Woods – Refers to the post-World War II system of international trade and finance. It saw the establishment of the *International Monetary Fund (IMF)* and the International Bank for Reconstruction and Development, popularly known as the *World Bank*. Together with the *General Agreement on Tariffs and Trade (GATT)* which was established by the *UN*, it formed the system which was intended to stabilise the international economy under liberal economic policy goals. It is named for the place in New Hampshire, US where the original agreement was struck.

Capitalism – A social system that favours free and open markets based on private property and the accumulation of private wealth. Eighteenth-century Scotsman Adam Smith is conventionally associated with the ideological defence of capitalism, while Karl Marx is capitalism's greatest critic.

Civil war – War fought largely within the territorial boundaries of a single *sovereign state*.

Clausewitzean – An adjective describing strategic thought influenced by the work of Prussian military officer, Carl von Clausewitz (1780–1831). His *On war*, published posthumously in 1832, is still widely recognised as the most important treatise ever written on military strategy. For Clausewitz, *war* is a decisive encounter between two or more armed forces of a *state*. His most famous proposition is that war is simply the continuation of politics by other, namely violent, means.

Cold War – Describes a condition of hostile encounter between two *states* or *alliances* which falls just short of 'hot war' or direct violent conflict. It is mostly used to name the conflict between the US and USSR from roughly 1946 to 1989. Though the two *superpowers* did not apparently fight one another directly, they often fought by proxy. Because it is historically unusual for two preeminent *powers* not to wage war against each other, some commentators also refer to the Cold War as a 'long *peace*'.

Collateral damage – A euphemism used to refer to the unintended damage done to civilians and civilian infrastructure by military action.

Collective defence – Draws from the Three Musketeers' motto, 'one for all and all for one', but the collective is limited to those who are members of a particular *security* or defence agreement. Examples include *ANZUS*, *NATO* and the *Warsaw Pact*.

Collective security – Also draws from the Three Musketeers' motto, 'one for all and all for one'. Rather than leave *security* in the hands of each individual *state*, security for all is shared by all. If one state is threatened or attacked, the collective will react. Collective security is embodied in the *UN Charter*.

Colonialism – The practice of occupying foreign lands by forceful or peaceful means with the intention of developing or civilising 'backward' peoples of the non-European world. In the twentieth century colonialism has earned a bad name because it often reinforces racial stereotypes or discriminatory practices. Compare *decolonisation*.

Common security – Underpinned by the idea that *security* is best achieved with others rather than against them. Common security is promoted through *arms control* and *confidence and security-building measures (CSBMs)*. It originated in the *UN* Palme Commission Report of 1982 but found energetic political support in former Soviet premier, Mikhail Gorbachev, and former Australian foreign minister, Gareth Evans. It is premised on the belief that the *security dilemma* can be overcome or at least lessened.

Communism – A social system that favours government-controlled markets based on collective ownership and the distribution of wealth according to need. Karl Marx was communism's greatest advocate. Communist ideology is also said to have governed the USSR, though Marx probably would have disagreed.

Communitarianism – A political theory that emphasises individuals' attachments to the community in which they grew up. The communities in which we grow up are thought to be the source of all moral values. Communitarianism adopts the ethical position that a person's moral obligations are always first and foremost to members of our own community and that they cannot be extended beyond that community's boundaries. Moreover, it believes that communities should not be expected to submit to abstract or universal values or obligations advocated by *cosmopolitanism*.

Confidence and security-building measures (CSBMs) – The attempt to build mutual trust and reassurance through demilitarisation, *disarmament*, *arms control*, joint military training exercises and greater consultation and dialogue. The purpose is to reduce fear, suspicion, misperception and uncertainty, the elements that make up the *security dilemma*.

Constitutionalism – The exercise of decision-making power or governance on the basis of an original constitution, charter or set of foundational rules.

Constitutive – Having the power of bringing something (an actor or set of rules) into existence. A constitutive rule specifies who counts as a legitimate actor and what kind of acts or moves are legitimate. See *regulative* rule.

Constructivism – A theory that challenges the belief that social structures are more or less natural phenomena. Constructivists argue that the social world is formed through *constitutive* linguistic and social practices, thus leaving open the possibility for societies to transform their social worlds. In this respect constructivism converges with *critical theories* such as *feminism* and *Frankfurt School Critical Theory* as well as some *Marxist* theories. However, some critical theorists believe that constructivism sometimes remains too close to *positivist methodologies*.

Containment – A *Cold War* US strategy for keeping the USSR within its extant boundaries and preventing the further spread of *communism*. The *Truman Doctrine* and *Marshall Plan* are said to be respectively the military and economic aspects of containment.

Cosmopolitanism – A political *theory* that emphasises individuals' obligations to all other human beings. It rejects the *communitarian* position that a person's moral obligations end at the political borders of our community. When asked where he came from, the ancient Greek philosopher, Diogenes the Cynic responded by saying he was a 'citizen of the world'. Cosmopolitanism does not deny local or national attachments and obligations; it just does not see why they must always be privileged. *Critical theories* often have strong inclinations to cosmopolitanism.

Counter-insurgency – The government's response to *insurgency*.

Critical theory – Any *theory* that seeks to question traditional theoretical methods and purposes. It is usually guided by a suspicion towards *empiricism* and *positivism* and a commitment to overcoming forms of social, economic and political domination. It thus includes, among others, *feminism*, *postmodernism*, *Marxism* and *Critical Theory* – all of which are sceptical of claims that the world is as it must be. In this respect it converges with *constructivism* too.

Critical Theory – A specific type of *Marxist*-inspired *critical theory* deriving from the *Frankfurt School* of social theory.

Cuban missile crisis – Occurred in 1962. The US discovered that the USSR was installing medium-range nuclear missiles in Cuba, only miles from the coast of Florida. When US President Kennedy imposed a naval blockade, a thirteen-day stand-off ensued in which the world came very close to nuclear *war*. Kennedy and Soviet leader Khrushchev eventually reached a compromise that allowed the Soviets to 'save face' and the Americans to remove the missiles. It inaugurated a period of *détente* between the *superpowers*.

Decolonisation – The process by which *colonial powers* withdrew from or were expelled from foreign territories over which they ruled. It granted *sovereign* independence to peoples formerly ruled by colonial powers. The years following World War II saw the height of this process. See *anti-colonialism*.

Deconstruction – A theoretical mode developed by Jacques Derrida aimed at destabilising taken-for-granted assumptions and binary oppositions.

Democracy – Born in ancient Athens, it is a powerful idea and popular political practice for ensuring that individuals and communities rule themselves by participating in decision-making processes that affect their lives. In his Gettysburg Address, Abraham Lincoln famously defined democracy as 'government of the people, by the people, for the people'. Democracy may be direct, as in ancient Athens where small face-to-face communities deliberated and decided on their own political futures, or indirect, where representatives are elected to govern on behalf of the people.

Democratic peace theory – The theory that democratic *states* do not fight *war* against each other. A good amount of *empirical* evidence has been collected indicating that war has never been fought between two stable *democracies*. Closely associated with Michael Doyle.

Détente – Relaxation of tensions between rivals. A period of the *Cold War* that commenced in the early 1960s after the *Cuban missile crisis* and was reinforced by the initiatives of US President Nixon and his National Security Advisor, Henry Kissinger.

Deterrence – A policy or strategy based on the threat of massive retaliation in the event of an attack. It is premised on the notion that if the destruction threatened in retaliation is great enough, it will deter any initial attack. It is mostly associated with nuclear weapons. Nuclear deterrence is also known as mutually assured destruction (MAD).

Diplomacy – The formal and informal activity by which *states* interact with each other. Somewhat romantically described as 'the art of negotiation', diplomacy involves the exchange of agents (diplomats, envoys, consular officials) who represent the *state's* interests abroad and negotiate on its behalf. Diplomacy may take place secretly or publicly, *bilaterally* or *multilaterally* (for example, at the *UN*).

Disarmament – A means and an end involving the reduction or elimination of weapons.

Discipline – A branch of learning focused on a relatively distinct subject matter, including a distinctive focus, set of institutions and traditions of thought.

Emancipation – The process and condition of being free from all forms of domination, oppression, exclusion and injustice. It is thus central to *liberalism* as well as *critical theories*, including *Marxism*, *feminism* and *Frankfurt School Critical Theory*, though how each theory defines freedom differs greatly.

Empiricism – A philosophy based on the idea that experience is the source of knowledge. Empiricist *methods* proceed through examination of phenomena that can be perceived through the senses, predominantly observable phenomena. It is sceptical of knowledge drawn from ideas, beliefs and *norms*, or any knowledge that does not appear empirically verifiable.

English School – An approach to international relations that focuses on the rules and institutions that bring *order* to *international society*. It holds the view that while *states* exist in a formal *anarchy*, they still form a society. It draws upon and is closely associated with the *Grotian* tradition.

Enlightenment – A period commencing in the late seventeenth century and culminating at the end of eighteenth-century Europe that saw tremendous intellectual change in the natural, human and social sciences, including the rise of *liberalism* and the American and French *revolutions*. It also refers to the process of employing reason to challenge received ways of thinking and acting. Though diverse, enlightenment as process includes some common features: the exercise of suspicion towards authority, especially traditional modes of religious and political thinking; the expression of moral, legal and political equality among all humans; the commitment to *emancipation* from unnecessary constraints.

Epistemology – The branch of philosophy that studies how we produce and acquire knowledge. It is concerned with establishing the conditions for producing valid knowledge, and establishing criteria for testing and justifying knowledge claims.

Ethnic cleansing – The systematic, deliberate and violent attempt to expel or eliminate targeted ethnic groups from disputed or conflict-ridden territories. Ethnic cleansing was conducted, probably by all sides, but most prominently by Serbian militia, during the break-up of Yugoslavia in the 1990s.

Explanation – A method of accounting for effects or outcomes by focusing on facts and causes that exist independently of the observer. Closely associated with *empiricism* and *positivism*. It is often contrasted with *interpretation* and *hermeneutics*.

Failed state – A state where the government is no longer able to exert authority or *power* over its people and territory.

Fascism – A twentieth-century doctrine of authoritarianism hostile to peace and characterised by militarism, aggressive *nationalism*, racism and *imperialism*.

Feminism – A *critical theory* that focuses on the place of women and on the role of gender in international relations. It highlights the way women are historically marginalised and disempowered by the prevailing structures of domestic and international politics. Additionally, it has explored the way gendered stereotypes (masculinity and femininity) shape actors' identities and expectations.

Foreign aid – The transfer of money and resources to less developed or developing countries from developed countries. Usually the aid is given as a long-term loan with conditions attached.

Foundationalism – Adherence to the belief that knowledge can and must be built on firm foundations or grounds. This quest for certainty, often associated with *positivism*, is a response to the uncertainty thought to result from *interpretive theories*.

Frankfurt School – The name given to a group of German émigrés, led by Max Horkheimer and Theodor Adorno, who fled to New York and California during World War II after working in the Frankfurt Institute of Social Research. They pioneered a form of critical social *theory* influenced by German thinkers Immanuel *Kant*, G. W. F. Hegel and Karl *Marx*, among others, that challenged prevailing social, political and economic structures in an effort to *emancipate* all individuals and communities from unjust forms of domination and exclusion. It is the inspiration behind *Critical Theory*.

Free trade – The idea that governments should not interfere in cross-border trade. Closely associated with *liberalism* and *capitalism*, it is also the governing ideology of the *WTO (World Trade Organization)*, formerly the *GATT (General Agreement on Tariffs and Trade)*.

Fundamentalism – Refers to the tendency to suppose that one's own ideological or belief system is unquestionably true and should be adhered to absolutely. Anyone who does not adhere to the purity of this system of beliefs is thought to be a heretic or infidel, and is often cast as evil. It is often associated with religions, for example, Islamic or Christian fundamentalism, but any ideology or belief may be susceptible to fundamentalism.

G20, G8 – The Group of 20, Group of 8, or 'G-system' refers to the forums established by the world's leading industrial states to manage global economic affairs. The formation of these Groups began in the 1970s and the composition and number of the Group has expanded over time to its present size of twenty members who meet to deliberate on matters predominantly of global economic concern.

G77 – The Group of seventy-seven developing countries formed in 1964 to promote the collective interests and the negotiating power of the global South, especially in relation to global economic issues.

Genealogy – A mode of doing history (or counter-history) that exposes the relations between *power* and knowledge and that questions dominant notions of origins and progress.

General Agreement on Tariffs and Trade (GATT) – Established under the *UN* to develop rules governing international trade. Founded on *liberal* principles of *free trade*, its main objectives are to reduce and eliminate tariff barriers and to provide a forum in which *states* can mediate disputes and negotiate a more open system of trade. In 1995 the GATT was replaced by the *World Trade Organization (WTO)*.

Geneva conventions – Comprised of four *international humanitarian law* treaties codified in 1949, and the additional protocols of 1977. The 1949 conventions relate to the treatment of prisoners of *war*, the treatment of military personnel when sick or wounded at sea or on land, and the protection of civilians during war. The two additional protocols of 1977 outline protections due to the victims of international and *civil wars*.

Genocide – The deliberate and systematic act of destroying in whole or in part a national, ethnic, racial or religious group. It is outlawed under the *UN* Convention on the Punishment and Prevention of the Crime of Genocide. Twentieth-century cases of genocide include the Turkish genocide of the Armenians, the Nazi genocide of the Jews and others, and the Hutu genocide of Tutsi in Rwanda.

Geopolitics – The study of the effects of geography (human and physical) on international politics. It is often closely related to the *balance of power*.

Globalisation – The stretching and intensification of social and economic relations across the globe made possible by new communication and computer technologies and advances in transport. It is thought by many to inaugurate an unprecedented degree of global interconnectedness, although some deny its novelty by pointing to similar levels of *interdependence* in the late nineteenth and early twentieth century. Still others criticise globalisation for being a vehicle of *neoliberal* ideology.

Gramscian – An adjective describing a perspective on international relations influenced by the work of Italian socialist and union organiser, Antonio Gramsci (1891–1937). Gramsci was a *Marxist* who cautioned against overemphasising the economic 'base' of society. He argued that the 'superstructure' of society, which includes schools, churches and civil society more generally, also played a vital part in the reproduction of *capitalist* societies and in their possible transformation. In international relations his work has been adapted to focus on the way ideas and *states* interact to maintain dominant world *orders*.

Great power – A state possessing, and seen to possess, multiple dimensions of *power* and its sources, including military, political, economic, ideological, territorial, natural resources, people and so on.

Grotian – An adjective describing a perspective on international relations influenced by the work of Dutch seventeenth-century jurist, Hugo Grotius (1583–1645). Closely associated with the *English School*, the Grotian tradition of international thought places great emphasis on the rules and *norms* of international relations. It aims to secure *order* and coexistence among *states* rather than the *Kantian* ideal of perpetual *peace* or the *Hobbesian* horror of '*war* of all against all'.

Guerrilla warfare – 'Hit and run' tactics employed by small, highly mobile bands of armed forces against more conventional armed, and usually invading or occupying, forces. Guerrillas operate by taking full advantage of their environment, both physical and urban. It was a tactic employed to good effect by Germanic tribes against the Roman army, and by the Vietcong against the US in Vietnam.

Hegemony – The preponderance of *power* and influence by a *state* (the hegemon). Though it involves coercive power, hegemony without ideological or political suasion is unlikely. *Gramsci* proposed thinking of hegemony as a centaur (half man, half beast).

Hermeneutics – The art or *method* of *interpretation*. Derived from Hermes, the messenger god, hermeneutics originally referred to the textual interpretation of the Bible, but in modern times it refers more generally to the interpretation of texts, *theories* and ideas, as well as the action and behaviour of social and political agents. Its main purpose is to further understanding of others' meanings or intentions. It is often contrasted with *explanation*.

Hierarchy – The structured differentiation of rank and authority. In the study of international relations hierarchy is often opposed to *anarchy*.

Hobbesian – An adjective describing a perspective on international relations influenced by the work of seventeenth-century political philosopher, Thomas Hobbes (1588–1679). He emphasised the political importance of *state sovereignty* and the necessity of *states* to be prepared to use threats and force to achieve *security*. He is thought to have likened international relations to a 'state of *war*', a lawless, insecure and conflict-ridden condition which he described as a 'war of all against all'.

Human rights – The entitlements thought to be due to all humans simply by virtue of their humanity. Human rights are enshrined in the Universal Declaration of Human Rights (1948) which is a non-binding document, and in the legally binding Covenant on Civil and Political Rights and Covenant on Economic, Social and Cultural Rights (both 1966).

Humanitarian intervention – The coercive interference in a *sovereign state* to prevent or end massive *human rights* violations. Generally thought to be prohibited by *international law* and the *UN Charter*, it has enjoyed increased international support since the brutal conflicts, *ethnic cleansing* and *genocides* witnessed in the 1990s. *NATO*'s 1999 bombing of Serbia to protect Kosovars remains the most controversial instance of humanitarian intervention. See *responsibility to protect*.

Humanitarianism – Refers to the array of moral, political, medical and logistical practices designed to alleviate human suffering, especially in the aftermath of natural or political disasters.

Idealism – A *theory* of international relations whose chief purpose is to eradicate *war*. Flourishing after World War I, it embraced the *Enlightenment* and *liberal* values of *peace* and progress, believing that peace could be achieved through *collective security* arrangements, respect for the rule of law and greater *interdependence*. See also *utopianism*.

Identity – The distinctive purpose ascribed to a state, including self-understandings. A key term in *constructivism*.

Imperialism – The projection or expansion of a *state*'s domination over foreign lands and peoples through conquest and control. Often associated with a high-handed and rather brutal treatment of those under imperial *power*.

Institutionalism – The view that institutions (both formal and informal sets of rules and norms) matter in international relations by setting standards, shaping expectations, constraining behaviour and establishing patterns of interaction. See *regime*.

Insurgency – Political violence with the subversive intent of destabilising or overthrowing a ruling government.

Interdependence – The mutual dependence developed among *states* by utilising new technologies and through the growth of international cross-border commerce, communication and travel. A term used before *globalisation* became popular.

International humanitarian law – Set of rules integrating *human rights* into *international law* with the purpose of protecting individuals (civilians and combatants) during times of *war*.

It comprises the four *Geneva conventions* and two additional protocols. The International Committee of the Red Cross (ICRC) is the custodian of these rules.

International law – Set of rules applying to *sovereign states*. Traditionally it has focused exclusively on *states*, but since World War II it has increasingly incorporated rights and duties of individuals. The sources of international law include custom, treaties, judicial decisions and esteemed legal opinion. Because they define law as orders backed by force, *realists* are sceptical that international law, which lacks an enforcement mechanism, deserves the status of law.

International Monetary Fund (IMF) – Established as part of the *Bretton Woods* system, its main task is to create a stable international exchange rate system and to provide emergency assistance to *states* facing temporary *balance of payments* problems.

International society – Exists when two or more *states* become conscious of being bound by common rules and institutions. One of the *English School*'s key concepts, international society, or the society of states, allows for cooperation in institutions such as *diplomacy* and *international law*.

International system – Exists when two or more states have sufficient contact with each other that they become conscious of existing in the same environment and conscious of the need to consider other *states*' interests and capabilities in the pursuit of their own interests.

Interpretation – A mode of giving meaning to something, whether an act, an event, a history, an art object, a novel, a poem and so on. See *hermeneutics* and, for contrast, *explanation*.

Intersubjective – Ideas and beliefs existing among conscious actors or social agents. Generally refers to the sets of ideas and beliefs shared collectively by actors (such as states in international society). Key term in *constructivim* and *Critical Theory*.

Jihad – Militant Muslims use the word to mean the violent struggle against infidels and heretics who threaten Islam. In its original theological sense it means the self-discipline or internal struggle to pursue noble goals. Western commentators often mistakenly equate *jihad* with the Christian notion of 'holy *war*'.

Just war – A *war* deemed to be conducted justly or lawfully (*jus in bello* in Latin) and for a just or lawful cause (*jus ad bellum*). The tradition of distinguishing between just and unjust wars goes back to antiquity, was continued by Christian theologians throughout the Middle Ages and persists in secular form today. Since the late nineteenth century numerous *international humanitarian law* treaties outlining prohibited conduct during war have come into force. *Humanitarian intervention* has, however, forced a reconsideration of rules relating to *jus ad bellum*.

Kantian – An adjective describing a perspective on international relations influenced by the work of eighteenth-century *Enlightenment* philosopher, Immanuel Kant (1724–1804). Most famous in international relations for his essay, 'Towards perpetual peace', Kant argued that *states* ought to subject their conduct to political, legal and moral rules consistent with *liberalism* so that *peace*, justice and freedom can flourish for the whole community of humankind.

Keynesian – Adjective describing an economic doctrine based on the thought of British economist, John Maynard Keynes (1883–1946). He argued that free market principles must be tempered by measured governmental interventions to maintain social *order*.

Kyoto Protocol – An agreement signed at the 1997 Kyoto (Japan) climate change conference to address global warming. *States*, excluding most notably Australia and the US, committed themselves to reducing greenhouse gas emissions to 5 per cent below 1990 levels by the year 2012.

Liberalism – A political *theory* that prizes individual freedom. It believes individuals should be free to do as they please, without the interference of others, so long as they do not harm or limit the freedom of others. In international relations it has tended to focus on the development of *international law*, the spread of *democracy* (*democratic peace theory*) and the expansion of *free trade*. Immanuel *Kant* is one of the leading liberal theorists of international relations.

Lockean – An adjective describing a political worldview informed by the ideas of John Locke (1632–1704). Often associated with the *English School*, and holding affinities with the *Grotian* tradition, Lockean political thought emphasises individual rights, the rule of law and the rational capacities of humankind as the key elements of political *order* within and between *states*. Locke did not conceive the state of nature as a *Hobbesian* state of war, but as a condition where reason may still prevail and foster sociability and cooperation.

Machiavellianism – A term usually employed pejoratively to criticise cunning or ruthless political behaviour. It derives from the name of Florentine diplomat, Niccolò Machiavelli (1469–1527), especially the advice he gives to rulers in his infamous tract, *The prince*, written in 1513 though not published until after his death in 1532. It would be wrong to assume, however, that Machiavelli was Machiavellian.

Marshall Plan – The US aid program designed to reconstruct and stimulate the economies of Western Europe after World War II. Introduced in 1947, it is best understood as the economic aspect of the US strategy of *containment* alongside the *Truman Doctrine*. It aimed to stabilise Western Europe's economies and immunise them against the threat of *communism*.

Marxism – An adjective describing a perspective on international relations influenced by the work of nineteenth-century thinker, Karl Marx (1818–1883). Marxism's most central feature is its powerful critique of *capitalism* for exploiting and dehumanising workers. Marxists believe that international relations is shaped by the changing patterns of capitalism and the conflict it generates between classes. It thus tends to see *states* and the *international system* as a reflection of deeper socio-economic structures and processes. Marxists believe that capitalism is only a stage on the way to a truly *emancipated* society of humankind.

Meaning – The significance or symbolic value held by an object or attributed to it.

Mercantilism – A policy-system developed by many early modern European *states* to increase national wealth for the purposes of enhancing the state's *power*. This wealth was produced by a mix of *protectionism* and favourable *balance of payments* to grow the state's stocks of gold bullion. Often contrasted to *free trade*.

Meta-theory – Theoretical reflection on *theory*.

Method – A way or means of producing or attaining knowledge. Some ways are more *hermeneutic* or *interpretive*, others are more *positivist*, *empiricist* or *explanatory*.

Methodology – The study of different ways (*methods*) of producing valid knowledge.

Multilateralism – A term referring to international structures and processes in which many *states* discuss, negotiate and decide on matters of international significance. Compare with *bilateralism* and *unilateralism*.

Multinational corporation (MNC) – A commercial actor with branches or operations in several countries and interconnected business strategies. Increasingly such corporations see the globe rather than any single national economy as their marketplace. They tend to advocate *globalisation* and *neoliberal* policy ideals. Also see *transnational corporation (TNC)*.

Multipolarity – Refers to an *international system* where more than two powerful *states* dominate. *Realism* sees multipolar systems as more unstable than *bipolar* ones.

Nation – A community of people bound together by belief in common historical, cultural, ethnic, religious or linguistic ties. Nations quite often, but not always, demand exclusive allegiance from their citizens.

National interest – A notoriously plastic term that refers to the *state*'s foreign policy aims. The national interest is said to be the same regardless of the government in *power*, but different governments will hold different ideological agendas and priorities, meaning that the national interest will change accordingly.

Nationalism – The political ideology that prizes and exults in the *nation* as the primary and exclusive source of allegiance.

NATO (North Atlantic Treaty Organisation) – A military *alliance* formed in 1949 by Western European and Northern American countries aligned against the USSR during the *Cold War*. Unlike the *Warsaw Pact*, it did not die with the end of the Cold War. Instead, it expanded by absorbing former Warsaw Pact countries into its membership.

Neoliberalism – Used in two senses. One is as a *theory* of international relations which argues, contrary to *realism* and *neorealism*, that cooperation is possible even in conditions of international *anarchy*. A revised version of *liberalism*, this neoliberalism focuses on the rules and *norms states* are socialised to accept by working through international institutions or *regimes*. It is most closely associated with the work of Robert Keohane. The other use of neoliberalism is as a late form of *liberalism* that focuses heavily on free market economic policies of trade liberalisation, deregulation of financial markets and the workplace, and privatisation of government-owned industries and utilities. In Australia this latter sense often goes by the name of 'economic *rationalism*'.

Neorealism – A *theory* of international relations which seeks to improve upon *realism* by making it more scientific (based on *positivism*) and by obtaining a more objective picture of how the structure of *anarchy* shapes and shoves *states*. Most closely associated with the work of Kenneth Waltz, neorealism argues, contrary to older versions of realism, that states seek to maximise *security* rather than *power*.

Nesting – A strategy whereby a group of actors collectively subsume themselves under a broader identity, thereby changing the identity of all the actors in the process.

Non-governmental organisation (NGO) – Specialised not-for-profit *non-state actors* that seek to raise consciousness and change the activities of governments and populations on a variety of issues. NGOs have proliferated over the last century, advocating and lobbying on issues such as *human rights*, landmines, poverty, animal rights and the environment, among many others.

Non-state actor – An actor not part of the official *state* or governmental apparatuses.

Normative – An adjective referring to the moral quality of something. For example, normative *theories* of international relations are primarily concerned with posing moral questions of actors or assessing the moral justification and evaluation of structures and processes.

Norms – Moral standards or expectations.

Ontology – The branch of philosophy that studies the nature of being. It is concerned with determining what exists in the world and the character of the different things that exist. In other words, it regards the 'furniture' of the world.

Order – A sustained pattern of social arrangements. Order should not be confused with *peace* or stability. Peace is a particular order whereby the pattern of social arrangements excludes *war*. But, unlike peace and war, order and war are not mutually exclusive conditions. Order is also distinguishable from stability because stability and instability are properties of order. That is, orders may be more or less stable or unstable.

Patriarchy – A form of social organisation where men dominate and govern at the expense of women. It is an important concept in *feminism*.

pax americana – A Latin phrase that translates as 'American peace'. Drawing upon the older phrase *pax romana* (Roman peace), it conjures ideas of American *imperialism*.

Peace – Most simply, it is the absence of *war*. This definition has been found wanting because it says nothing about the positive requirements of peace, which are usually thought to include justice and basic human needs, among other things.

Peacebuilding – Initiatives taken to rebuild political and legal institutions and civilian infrastructure, including markets, in post-conflict situations. It has the long-term objective of establishing lasting *peace* and prosperity within stable political conditions.

Peacekeeping – Military operations undertaken with the consent of all major parties to a conflict with the purpose of maintaining the terms of a truce or ceasefire. Only a temporary or provisional measure, peacekeeping is intended to open opportunities for dialogue among the parties that will lead to lasting *peace*.

Positivism – An approach to knowledge based on the conviction that the human and social sciences, including the study of international relations, must emulate the physical or natural sciences by employing *empiricist* methods. This means facts must be separated from values and beliefs to allow for objective investigation and explanation of *empirical* or observable phenomena (namely, facts). *Critical theories* dispute the feasibility and desirability of completely separating facts and values in the human and social sciences.

Postmodernism – A theoretical approach to the social and human sciences that questions not just *positivism* but aspects of *hermeneutics* too for believing that all questions can be finally resolved by attaining the Truth. For postmodernism there are likely to be as many truths as there are perspectives on any given issue since there is no single vantage point from which all social, political and moral questions can be addressed. It is closely associated with *deconstruction* and *genealogy*.

Power – Classically defined as the ability to get an actor to do what they would otherwise not do. This is power in the sense of domination or power over others. But power can also be thought of in terms of capability or power to do or act. *Realist* theories hold the belief that international relations are a constant struggle for power, usually defined in materials terms. See also *soft power*.

Power politics – A nickname given to hard-nosed *realist* policies because of the great emphasis realists place on the struggle for *power*.

Protectionism – An economic policy designed to cushion or protect national industries from international competition. Often pursued by the imposition of taxes, tariffs and quotas on imports.

Raison d'état – French for *reason of state*. It refers to the logic that drives policies employed in the service of the *state* itself. Such policies do not serve the common good or the welfare of the population, they are intended to preserve and strengthen the state apparatus alone. Commonly associated with *realist* policies.

Ratification – A legal term describing the act by which a state confirms being bound by a treaty or convention. The legislative procedures for ratification may vary from one state to another.

Rationalism – In the US the term is most commonly used to refer to theories employing *positivist methods*, in contrast to *reflectivism*. Elsewhere, rationalism is sometimes used, by Martin Wight, for example, to refer to *Grotianism*. See also *realism* and *reflectivism*.

Realism – A tradition of thought that posits the struggle for *power* and the condition of *anarchy* as two fundamental realities of international relations. These are realities with which both *states* and students of the subject must grapple.

Realpolitik – German term connoting hard-nosed *realist* politics. It is more or less a synonym of the English term *power politics*.

Reason of state – See *raison d'état*.

Reflectivism – A term used in the US to refer to *critical theories* in contrast to *rationalism*.

Refugee – A person forced to flee his or her country because of persecution. For centuries refugees have fled their homelands because their lives and livelihoods were in grave danger for no other reason than their religion, their ethnicity, their race, their gender or their political beliefs. The 1951 Convention Relating to the Status of Refugees and the formation of the *UN* High Commission for Refugees (UNHCR) have helped draw attention to the global flows and plight of refugees.

Regime – Agreed rules, norms and decision-making procedures that set standards, shape expectations, constrain behaviour and establish patterns of interaction. Also see *institutionalism*.

Regulative – Having the power of governing or controlling the behaviour of an actor. A regulative rule specifies the range of actions considered legitimate by distinguishing between proscribed and permitted actions. See *constitutive* rule.

Responsibility to protect (R2P) – The doctrine that neither individual *states* nor the international community can stand idly by while large-scale violations of *human rights* occur. According to R2P, states, individually and collectively, have a duty to undertake some form of preventative or ameliorative action. R2P was given its most important formulation in 2001 by the International Commission on Intervention and State Sovereignty chaired by Gareth Evans and Mohamed Sahnoun. See also *humanitarian intervention*.

Revisionist – An adjective used to describe *states* intent on challenging the prevailing international *order*. Also used to describe histories written to offer a different political viewpoint.

Revolution – A sudden, usually violent change of government. The great revolutions (England in 1688, America in 1776, France in 1789, Russia in 1917) promised to *emancipate* the people from the tyranny of the so-called 'old regime', although on occasion the revolutionaries have brutally *terrorised* the people after seizing *power*.

Revolution in military affairs – The transformation in the way *war* is fought. In the West, especially the US, technological advances have led to changes in the organisation and operation of armed forces, and in the military hardware and weapons systems available to them. Some commentators now speak of a 'Western way of war' which depends heavily on taking full advantage of new war technologies to fight wars from the skies or from afar so as to minimise their casualties. The accuracy of so-called 'smart' weapons is also claimed to minimise civilian casualties.

Revolutionism – A tradition of thought committed to the *cosmopolitan* ideal of realising the moral and political community of humankind. It often possesses a missionary character and is committed to the *revolutionary* transformation of international order.

Rogue state – A *state* deemed to be a serial violator of *international society*'s rules, *norms* and standards of expected behaviour. A highly subjective political term, the rogue state has been used by the US to decry its enemies, but critics of US foreign policy have also labelled the US a rogue state for its perceived violations of international rules and norms.

SEATO (Southeast Asian Treaty Organization) – Designed to serve as a collective defence organisation during the Cold War, it existed from 1955 to 1977. Its eight member states included Australia, France, New Zealand, Pakistan, Philippines, Thailand, UK and US.

Secession – Breaking away or separating from an existing *state* to become an independent *sovereign state*.

Secularism – A movement aimed at depriving religion of political effects in the public sphere. Privileging the temporal (earthly) over the transcendental, it seeks to cultivate spheres of social and political life free from references to a deity or the afterlife.

Secularist settlement – A mode of containing and managing religion along *secularist* lines. Rather than construe secularism as a fixed, final achievement, it views it as a historically and politically contingent attempt to determine the relationship between politics and religion.

Security – The condition of being free from harm or threat. Over recent decades scholars and practitioners have increasingly spoken of human security, but traditionally, the *state* is the referent of security, that is, the actor to be made secure. One of the enduring difficulties for states in achieving security, according to *realists*, is that they must deal with the *security dilemma*. But in recent decades attempts have been made to overcome the dilemma by reconceptualising security in terms of *common security*.

Security community – A group of *states* that have integrated their social, economic and political structures to a degree where *war* no longer seems likely among them. The European Union (EU) is the best example.

Security dilemma – A condition in which *states* find themselves because every measure taken to make themselves more secure may simply urge other states to respond in such a manner that all states end up feeling less secure and more anxious. The security dilemma arises because states will never know with absolute certainty what the intentions and capabilities are of other states. *Realists* believe there is nothing that can be done to overcome this dilemma. *Liberals* believe *confidence and security-building measures* may open opportunities for going beyond the security dilemma. Also see *common security*.

Self-determination – The doctrine proclaiming that each *nation* or people should possess independence and govern themselves. It is a key concept of *liberalism* and was advocated by US President Woodrow Wilson in the early twentieth century. It was also an important feature of *anti-colonial* struggles and the *decolonisation* process and has a natural affinity with *nationalism*.

Soft power – Coined by US IR scholar, Joseph S. Nye, to refer to the intangible, non-material and non-military elements of US *power*, including its ideas, ideology, culture, institutions and so on. As a form of power it works through attraction and persuasion rather than coercion ('hard' power).

Sovereign state – The modern form of political society in which authority is concentrated in a single, supreme decision-maker. See *state* and *sovereignty*.

Sovereignty – Denotes a single, supreme political decision-making authority. In early modern Europe the monarch was the sovereign. In modern *states* sovereignty tends to lie with the executive arm of government. A controversial term, sovereignty depends on authority, not *power*. That is, the sovereign claims the right or authority to decide matters of interest to the state, even if it cannot control everything that occurs within its territory.

Sphere of influence – A *geopolitical* term referring to an area (composed of multiple countries) under the informal control of a *superpower*. During the *Cold War* there was a mutual unspoken understanding between the US and USSR about the rights of the superpower to intervene within its sphere of influence.

State – A political society comprising a government that extends its authority and *power* over a territory and its inhabitants (citizens and foreign visitors). Several features have become characteristic of the modern state: *sovereignty*, *nationalism* and the monopoly over the instruments of violence.

State-centric – A view of international relations that places the *state* at the centre. State-centrism underplays the significance of *non-state actors*, believing that they have little impact on issues of international importance.

Status quo – The existing state of affairs.

Superpower – A preeminent *state* whose *power* is vastly greater than other states. The term was first used to describe the US, USSR and UK immediately after World War II. For the duration of the *Cold War* only the US and USSR retained the title.

Terrorism – The use of violence designed to spread fear for political purposes. Sometimes this violence is aimed at so-called 'legitimate' targets such as politicians or military forces; at other times it is aimed at civilians.

Theory – Reflective or abstract thought aimed at an understanding or explanation of social phenomena that goes beyond common sense. It makes us more self-conscious of our assumptions and prejudices. Some theories, such as *positivism*, may aim for universal explanatory laws. Others, such as *critical theories*, tend to be more *hermeneutic* in approach.

Transnational corporation (TNC) – A commercial actor with branches or operations in several countries and interconnected business strategies. Increasingly such corporations see the globe rather than any single national economy as their marketplace. TNCs tend to see the globe as a borderless market, which is why they advocate *globalisation* and *neoliberal* policy ideals. Also see *multinational corporation (MNC)*.

Transnationalism – The process and condition of cross-border interaction. *Globalisation* is often associated with increased levels of transnational or cross-border activity.

Truman Doctrine – US policy commitment to provide military aid to Western European countries in an effort to resist *communism*. Originally offered to Turkey and Greece, the military aid and support was eventually extended to other European countries thought to be under threat of communist subversion. Announced in 1947, it is best thought of as the political-military aspect of the US strategy of *containment* alongside the *Marshall Plan*.

UN (United Nations) – An international organisation whose membership is open to all *sovereign states*. Founded in 1945, its primary purpose is to maintain international *peace* and *security* through *diplomacy* and negotiation where possible. It comprises six principal organs: the Security Council, the General Assembly, the Secretariat, the Trusteeship Council, the Economic and Social Council, and the International Court of Justice, of which the first is the most important politically because it has the authority to pass binding resolutions.

UN Charter – The set of rules that acts as a kind of constitution for the *UN*. Among other things, the Charter prohibits *war* or the threat of war except in self-defence or when the UN Security Council authorises war. It also prohibits intervention in a *sovereign state*'s domestic affairs, unless authorised by the Security Council.

Unilateralism – A term referring to decisions and actions taken by a *state* on its own, without consulting others, not even friends and allies, on matters of international significance. Compare with *bilateralism* and *multilateralism*.

Unipolarity – Refers to an *international system* where one overwhelmingly powerful *state* dominates. Some commentators regard the post-*Cold War* era as unipolar because the US seems unchallengeable as the sole *superpower*. Compare with *bipolarity* and *multipolarity*.

Utilitarianism – A philosophical doctrine, proposed by Jeremy Bentham (1748–1832), that all of our actions should be aimed at producing the greatest happiness for the greatest number of people.

Utopianism – A belief, doctrine or ideology committed to utopia; that is, an imaginary place of ideal social, moral and political conditions. A term often used to disparage *idealism*.

War – Organised political violence or armed conflict. The opposite of *peace*. Conventionally understood, war involves two armed forces, but the term is also used to cover asymmetrical wars where an official armed force confronts an unofficial force of *insurgents*, *guerrillas* or *terrorists*.

Warsaw Pact – A military *alliance* formed in 1955 by Eastern European countries aligned with the USSR during the *Cold War*. It was largely a response to the formation of *NATO*. Its members were: USSR, Poland, East Germany, Czechoslovakia, Bulgaria, Hungary, Romania and Albania (until 1961). It dissolved when the Cold War ended.

Washington Consensus – A set of *neoliberal* policy prescriptions that find strong support among the Washington-based *multilateral* economic institutions: the *IMF*, the *World Bank* and the US Treasury.

Weapons of mass destruction (WMD) – A term referring to nuclear, biological and chemical weapons. These three classes of weapon are thought to be more destructive than conventional weapons and likely to inflict greater *collateral damage*. Each is also the subject of an international convention or treaty.

Westphalia, Peace of – Refers to the two treaties (of Osnabrück and Münster) that brought the Thirty Years' War (1618–1648) to an end. The Thirty Years' War was essentially fought over the German lands of the Holy Roman Empire to resolve disputes relating to religion and the relative political rights of the Emperor and the emerging territorial *states* under the Empire's jurisdiction. As significant as the year 1648 is, it is overstating things to say, as many scholars do, that the *sovereign state* was born in the treaties of Westphalia.

World Bank – Originally formed to help post-World War II economic reconstruction, the World Bank provides funds and long-term loans at reduced interest rates to developing countries. Part of the *Bretton Woods* system, its policy prescriptions are consistent with the *Washington Consensus*. The Bank has been subject to a good deal of intense criticism for uncritically accepting and promoting *neoliberal* principles.

World Trade Organization (WTO) – Formerly the *General Agreement on Tariffs and Trade (GATT)*, the WTO provides a more permanent institution in which *states* can work towards the reduction and elimination of tariff barriers and in which they can mediate disputes and negotiate a more open, *free trade* system.

Zero-sum game – A situation in which gains made by one actor unavoidably come at the expense of another or others.

BIBLIOGRAPHY

Abu-Lughod, Lila 1998, 'Introduction: feminist longings and postcolonial conditions' in Lila Abu-Lughod (ed.), *Remaking women: feminism and modernity in the Middle East*, Princeton: Princeton University Press.

Acharya, Amitav 2001, *Constructing a security community in Southeast Asia: ASEAN and the problem of regional order*, London and New York: Routledge.

Adler, Emanuel 2005, *Communitarian international relations*, London: Routledge.

Adler, Emanuel and Barnett, Michael (eds) 1998, *Security communities*, Cambridge: Cambridge University Press.

Adler, Emanuel and Pouliot, Vincent 2011, 'International practices', *International Theory* 3(1): 1–36.

Adorno, Theodor W. [1966] 1992, *Negative Dialektik*, Frankfurt: Suhrkamp.

Agamben, Giorgio 1998, *Homo sacer: sovereign power and bare life*, Stanford: Stanford University Press.

Alagappa, M. (ed.) 1998, *Asian security practice*, Stanford: Stanford University Press.

Alger, C. 2002, 'The emerging roles of NGOs in the UN system: from Article 71 to a People's Millennium Assembly', *Global Governance* 8(1).

Alvarez, José E. 2006, *International organizations as law-makers*, Oxford: Oxford University Press.

Amin, Samir 1990, *Delinking: towards a polycentric world*, London: Atlanta Highlands.

Amin, Samir 2006, 'The Millennium Development Goals: a critique from the South', *Monthly Review* 57(10): 1–15.

Amnesty International, *US joins arms trade treaty talks but at a high price*, 14 October 2009, www.amnesty.org/en/news-and-updates/us-joins-arms-trade-treaty-talks-high-price-20091015.

Amoroso, B. 2007, 'Globalization and poverty: winners and losers', *Development* 50(2): 12–19.

Anderson, Benedict 1991, *Imagined communities*, rev. edn, London: Verso.

Andonova, L. M. Betsill and Bulkelely H. 2009, 'Transnational climate governance' *Global Environmental Politics* Vol. 9 No. 2.

Angell, Norman 1912, *The great illusion: a study of the relation of military power in nations to their economic and social advantage*, London: Heinemann.

Angell, Norman 1932, *The unseen assassins*, London: Hamish Hamilton.

Anheier, H. and Katz, H. 2004, 'Network approaches to global civil society' in Mary Kaldor, Helmut Anheier and Marlies Glasius (eds), *Global civil society 2004/5*, London: Centre for the Study of Global Governance/Sage Publications.

Anievas, Alexander (ed.), 2010, *Marxism and world politics: contesting global capitalism*, London: Routledge.

Annabi, Hedi 1995, *UN oral history interview*, New York: United Nations Library.

Annan, Kofi A. 1999, *The question of intervention: speeches of the Secretary-General*, New York: United Nations.

Annan, Kofi 2005a, *Millennium development goals report*, www.undp.org/mdg.

Annan, Kofi 2005b, *In larger freedom: towards development, security and human rights for all*, New York: United Nations.

Archibugi, Daniele 2004, 'Cosmopolitan democracy and its critics: a review', *European journal of international relations* 10(3): 437–73.

Aristotle 2009, *The Nicomachean ethics*, ed. Lesley Brown, trans. David Ross, New York: Oxford University Press.

Arjomand, Said Amir 1988, *The turban for the crown: the Islamic Revolution in Iran*, New York: Oxford University Press.

Armitage, David 2004, 'The fifty years' rift: intellectual history and international relations', *Modern Intellectual History* 1(1): 97–109.

Armitage, David 2007, *The Declaration of Independence: a global history*, Cambridge, Mass.: Harvard University Press.

Armstrong, David 1993, *Revolution and world order: the revolutionary state in international society*, Oxford: Oxford University Press.

Aron, Raymond 1966, *Peace and war: a theory of international relations*, New York: Doubleday.

Arts, B. 1998, *The political influence of global NGOs: case studies on the climate and biodiversity conventions*, Utrecht, Netherlands: International Books.

Asad, Talal 1993, *Genealogies of religion: discipline and reasons of power in Christianity and Islam*, Baltimore, MD: Johns Hopkins University Press.

Asad, Talal 2006, 'Responses,' in David Scott and Charles Hirschkind (eds), *Powers of the secular modern: Talal Asad and his interlocutors*, Stanford: Stanford University Press.

Ashcroft, B., Griffiths, G. and Tiffin, H. 1989, *The empire writes back: theory and practice in post-colonial literatures*, New York: Routledge.

Ashley, Richard K. 1981, 'Political realism and human interests', *International Studies Quarterly* 25(2): 204–36.

Ashley, Richard K. 1984, 'The poverty of neorealism', *International Organisation* 38(2): 225–86.

Ashley, Richard K. 1986, 'The poverty of neorealism' in Robert O. Keohane (ed.), *Neorealism and its critics*, New York: Columbia University Press.

Ashley, Richard K. 1988, 'Untying the sovereign state: a double reading of the anarchy problematique' *Millennium*, 17(2): 227–62.

Ashley, Richard K. 1989, 'Living on border lines: man, poststructuralism, and war' in James Der Derian and Michael Shapiro (eds), *International/intertextual relations: postmodern readings of world politics*, Lexington: Lexington Books.

Ashley, Richard K. and Walker, R. B. J. 1990, 'Speaking the language of exile: dissident thought in international studies', *International Studies Quarterly*, special issue 34(3): 259–68.

Ashworth, Lucian 1999, *Creating international studies: Angell, Mitrany and the liberal tradition*, Aldershot: Ashgate.

Atran, Scott 2010, *Talking to the enemy: faith, brotherhood, and the (un)making of terrorists*, New York: Ecco.

AusAID 2005, *Humanitarian action plan*, Canberra, Commonwealth of Australia, available at www.ausaid.gov.au/publications/pdf/humanitarian_policy.pdf.

Ayoob, Mohammed 2004, 'Third world perspectives on humanitarian intervention and international administration', *Global Governance* 10(1): 99–118.

Ayson, Robert 2006, 'Concepts for strategy and security,' in Robert Ayson and Desmond Ball (eds), *Strategy and security in the Asia-Pacific*, Crow's Nest: Allen & Unwin.

Badescu, Cristina G. 2011, *Humanitarian intervention and the responsibility to protect: security and human rights*. London: Routledge.

Badescu, Cristina G. and Thomas G. Weiss. 2010, 'Misrepresenting R2P and advancing norms: an alternative spiral?' *International Studies Perspectives* 11(4): 354–74.

Bailey, S. H. 1932, *The framework of international society*, London: Longmans.

Bailey, Sydney D. and Daws, Sam 1998, *The procedure of the UN Security Council*, Oxford: Oxford University Press.

Baldwin, David (ed.) 1993, *Neorealism and neoliberalism: the contemporary debate*, New York: Columbia University Press.

Baldwin, Richard (ed.) 2009, *The great trade collapse: causes, consequences and prospects*, London: Centre for Economic Policy Research.

Bank for International Settlements 2006, *Quarterly Review*, September, Geneva: BIS.

Barkin, J. Samuel 2003, 'Realist constructivism', *International Studies Review* 5(3): 325–42.

Barkin, J. Samuel 2010, *Realist constructivism: rethinking international relations theory*, Cambridge: Cambridge University Press.

Barnett, Michael N. 2003, *Eyewitness to a genocide*, Ithaca: Cornell University Press.

Barnett, Michael N. and Finnemore, M. 2004, *Rules for the world: international organizations in world politics*, Ithaca and London: Cornell University Press.

Barnett, Michael N. and Sikkink, Kathryn 2008, 'From international relations to global society', in C. Reus-Smit and D. Snidal (eds), *The Oxford handbook of international relations*, Oxford: Oxford University Press.

Barnett, Michael N. and Weiss, Thomas G. (eds) 2008 *Humanitarianism in question: politics, power, ethics*, Ithaca: Cornell University Press.

Barnett, Michael and Weiss, Thomas G. 2011, *Humanitarianism contested: where angels fear to tread*, London: Routledge.

Barston, Ronald P. 1988, *Modern diplomacy*, London: Longman.

Bass, Gary J. 2008, *Freedom's battle: the origins of humanitarian intervention*, New York: Knopf.

Baudelaire, Charles 1961, 'Le peintre de la vie moderne' in *Oeuvres complètes*, Paris: Gallimard.

Baudrillard, Jean 1983, *Simulations*, trans. Paul Foss, Paul Patton and Philip Beitchman, New York: Semiotext(e).

Baudrillard, Jean 1985, 'The ecstasy of communication', trans. J. Johnston, in Hal Foster (ed.), *Postmodern culture*, London: Pluto Press.

Baudrillard, Jean 1995, *The Gulf War did not take place*, Bloomington: Indiana University Press.

Bauman, Zygmunt 1998, *Globalization: the human consequences*, Cambridge: Polity Press.

Bauman, Zygmunt 2002, 'Reconnaissance wars of the planetary frontierland', *Theory, Culture and Society* 19(4): 81–90.

Baylis, John 2001, 'International and global security in the post-Cold War era' in John Baylis and Steve Smith (eds), *The globalization of world politics*, 2nd edition, Oxford: Oxford University Press.

Bebbington, A. 2004, 'NGOs and uneven development: geographies of development intervention', *Progress in Human Geography* 28(6): 725–45.

Beck, Ulrich 2009, *World at risk*, Cambridge: Polity Press.

Beckfield, J. 2003, 'Inequality in the world polity: the structure of international organization', *American Sociological Review* 68(3).

Beeson, Mark and Bell, Stephen 2009, 'The G20 and international economic governance: hegemony, collectivism, or both?', *Global Governance* 15(1):67–86.

Beitz, Charles 1979, *Political theory and international relations*, Princeton: Princeton University Press.

Beitz, Charles 1991, 'Sovereignty and morality in international affairs' in D. Held (ed.), *Political theory today*, Cambridge: Polity Press.

Beitz, Charles 1994, 'Cosmopolitan liberalism and the states system' in C. Brown (ed.), *Political restructuring in Europe: ethical perspectives*, London: Routledge.

Belkin, Aaron and Bateman, Geoffrey (eds) 2003, *Don't ask, don't tell: debating the gay ban in the military*, Boulder: Lynne Rienner Publishers.

Bell, Daniel 1960, *The end of ideology: on the exhaustion of political ideas in the fifties*, Glencoe: Free Press.

Bell, Duncan 2001, 'International relations: the dawn of a historiographical turn?', *British Journal of Politics and International Relations* 3(1): 115–26.

Bell, Duncan 2006, 'Empire and international relations in Victorian political thought', *Historical Journal* 49(1): 281–98.

Bell, Duncan (ed.) 2009, *Political thought and international relations: variations on a realist theme*, Oxford: Oxford University Press.

Bellah, Robert N. 1970, *Beyond belief: essays on religion in a post-traditionalist world*, New York: Harper & Row.

Bellamy, Alex J. 2004, *Security communities and their neighbours: regional fortresses or global integrators?*, Houndmills and New York: Palgrave Macmillan.

Bellamy, Alex J. 2006a, *Just wars: from Cicero to Iraq*, Cambridge: Polity Press.

Bellamy, Alex J. 2006b, 'Whither the responsibility to protect? Humanitarian intervention and the 2005 World Summit', *Ethics and international affairs*, 20(2): 143–69.

Bellamy, Alex J. (ed.) 2006c, *International society and its critics*, Oxford: Oxford University Press.

Bellamy, Alex J. 2009, *Responsibility to protect: the global effort to end mass atrocities*, Cambridge: Polity Press.

Bellamy, Alex J. and McDonald, Matt 2002, 'The utility of human security: which humans? What security?', *Security Dialogue* 33(3).

Bender, Courtney and Klassen, Pamela E. 2010, *After pluralism: reimagining religious engagement*, New York: Columbia University Press.

Benton, Lauren 2002, *Law and colonial cultures: legal regimes in world history 1400–1900*, Cambridge: Cambridge University Press.

Berger, Mark T. 2004, *The battle for Asia: from decolonization to globalization*, London: Routledge Curzon.

Berger, Mark T. and Weber, Heloise 2008, *Rethinking the Third World: international development and world politics*, London: Palgrave.

Berger, Peter L. and Luckmann, Thomas 1967, *The social construction of reality*, Anchor Books.

Berlin, Isaiah 1982, 'Two concepts of liberty', in *Four essays on liberty*, Oxford: Oxford University Press.

Bernstein, Steven 2001, *The compromise of liberal environmentalism*, New York: Columbia University Press.

Berridge, G. R. 1995, *Diplomacy: theory and practice*, London: Harvester Wheatsheaf.

Berridge, G. R. 2010, *Diplomacy: theory and practice* 4th edition, Basingstoke: Palgrave.

Berridge, G. R., Keens-Soper, Maurice and Otte, Thomas G. 2001, *Diplomatic theory from Machiavelli to Kissinger*, Basingstoke: Palgrave.

Best, Geoffrey 1994, *War and law since 1945*, Oxford: Clarendon Press.

Best, Jacqueline 2005, *The limits of transparency*, Ithaca: Cornell University Press.

Betsill, M. B and Corell, E. (eds) 2008, *NGO diplomacy: The influence of nongovernmental organizations in international environmental negotiations*. Cambridge, Massachusetts: MIT Press.

Betts, Alexander 2010, 'Towards a "soft law" framework for the protection of vulnerable irregular migrants', *International Journal of Refugee Law*, 22(2): 209–36.

Bhagwati, Jagdish and Srinivasan, T. N. 2002, 'Trade and poverty in the poor countries', *The American Economic Review, Papers and Proceedings* 92(2): 180–3.

Biddle, Stephen 2004, *Military power: explaining victory and defeat in modern battle*, Princeton: Princeton University Press.

Bieler, Andreas and Morton, Adam David 2004, 'A critical theory route to hegemony, world order and historical change: neo-Gramscian perspectives in International Relations', *Review of International Political Economy*, 28(1): 85–113.

Blackaby, Frank and Milne, Tom (eds) 2000, *A nuclear-weapon-free world: steps along the way*, London: Macmillan.

Blackhurst, R. 1997, 'The WTO and the global economy', *The World Economy* 20(54): 527–44.

Blainey, Geoffrey 1988, *The causes of war*, 3rd edition, London: Macmillan.

Bleiker, Roland 2001, 'Identity and security in Korea', *The Pacific Review* 14(1): 121–48.

Bleiker, Roland 2005, *Divided Korea: towards a culture of reconciliation*, Minneapolis: Minnesota University Press.

Blight, J. G. and Lang, J. F. 2005, *The fog of war: lessons from the life of Robert S. McNamara*, Lanham: Rowman & Littlefield.

Boas, M. and Jennings, K. 2005, 'Insecurity and development: the rhetoric of the "failed state"', *European Journal of Development Research*, 17(3): 285–95.

Bodin, Jean [1576] 1992, *On sovereignty: four chapters from the six books of the Republic*, ed. and trans. Julian Franklin, Cambridge: Cambridge University Press.

Boege, V., Brown, A., Clements, K. and Nolan, A. 2009, 'Building peace and political community in hybrid political orders', *International Peacekeeping*, 16(5): 599–615.

Bohman, James 2010, 'Democratising the global order: from communicative freedom to communicative power', *Review of International Studies* 36(2): 431–47.

Bond, Patrick 2006, 'Global governance campaigning and MDGSs: from top-down to bottom-up anti-poverty work', *Third World Quarterly* 27(2): 339–50.

Booth, Ken 1991, 'Security and emancipation', *Review of International Studies* 17(4): 313–26.

Booth, Ken (ed.) 2005, *Critical security studies and world politics*, Boulder: Lynne Rienner Publishers.

Booth, Ken and Wheeler, N. J. 2008, *The security dilemma: fear, cooperation and trust in world politics*, Basingstoke: Palgrave.

Bosco, David 2009, *Five to rule them all: The UN Security Council and the making of the modern world*, Oxford: Oxford University Press.

Boudreaux, Karol C. and Ahluwalia, Puja 2009, 'Cautiously optimistic: economic liberalization and reconciliation in Rwanda's coffee sector', *Denver Journal of International Law and Policy* 37(2): 147–200.

Boughton, J. M. 2009, 'A new Bretton Woods?', *Finance and Development* 46(1): 44–46.

Boutros-Ghali, Boutros 1999, *Unvanquished: a U.S.-U.N. saga*, New York: Random House.

Brahimi, Lakhdar 2007, 'Statebuilding in crisis and post conflict countries', paper presented at 7th Global Forum on Reinventing Government: Building Trust in Government 26–29 June, Vienna, Austria.

Brodie, Bernard 1946, *The absolute weapon*, New York: Harcourt and Brace.

Brown, Chris 1995, 'International theory and international society: the viability of the middle way?', *Review of International Studies* 21(2): 183–96.

Brown, Chris 1997, *Understanding international relations*, London: Macmillan.

Brown, Chris 2002, *Sovereignty, rights and justice: international political theory today*, Cambridge: Polity Press.

Brown, G., Langer, A. and Stewart, F. 2008, 'What is "post conflict?" A typology of post-conflict environments: an overview', *CRISE Working Paper 53*, December.

Brown, Lester 1991, *State of the world report*, Washington: World Watch Institute.

Brown, Seyom 2003, *The illusion of control: force and foreign policy in the 21st century*, Washington DC: Brookings Institution Press.

Brownlie, Ian 1963, *International law and the use of force by states*, Oxford: Oxford University Press.

Brownlie, Ian 2002, *Documents in international law*, 5th edition, Oxford: Oxford University Press.

Brownlie, Ian 2008, *Principles of international law*, 7th edition, Oxford: Oxford University Press.

Brubaker, Rogers 1996, *Nationalism reframed: nationhood and the national question in the new Europe*, Cambridge: Cambridge University Press.

Bugnion, Francois 2003, *The International Committee of the Red Cross and the protection of war victims*, Geneva: ICRC.

Bukovansky, Mlada 2002, *Legitimacy and power politics: the American and French Revolutions in international political culture*. Princeton: Princeton University Press.

Bulkeley, H. and Newell, P. 2010, *Governing climate change* London: Routledge.

Bull, Hedley 1961, *The control of the arms race: disarmament and arms control in the missile age,* New York: Praeger.

Bull, Hedley 1966, 'International theory: the case for the classical approach', *World Politics*, April 18(3): 361–77.

Bull, Hedley 1972, 'The theory of international politics, 1919–1969' in Brian Porter (ed.), *The Aberystwyth papers: international politics 1919–1969*, London: Oxford University Press.

Bull, Hedley 1976, 'Martin Wight and the theory of international relations', *British Journal of International Studies* 2: 101–16.

Bull, Hedley 1977, *The anarchical society: a study of order in world politics*, New York: Columbia University Press.

Bull, Hedley 1980, 'The great irresponsibles? The United States, the Soviet Union and world order', *International Journal* 35(3).

Bull, Hedley 1983, *Justice in international relations*, the Hagey Lectures, Waterloo, Ontario: University of Waterloo.

Bull, Hedley 2002, *The anarchical society: a study of order in world politics*, 3rd edition, New York: Columbia University Press.

Bull, Hedley and Watson, Adam (eds) 1984, *The expansion of international society*, Oxford: Clarendon Press.

Bull, Hedley, Kingsbury, Benedict and Roberts, Adam (eds) 1990, *Hugo Grotius and international relations*, Oxford: Clarendon Press.

Burchill, Scott, Linklater, Andrew, Devetak, Richard, Donnelly, Jack, Paterson, Matthew, Reus-Smit, Christian and True, Jacqui 2009, *Theories of international relations*, 4th edition, London: Palgrave.

Burgess, J. P. (ed.) 2010, *The Routledge handbook of new security studies*, London and New York: Routledge.

Burke, Anthony 2001, 'Caught between national and human security: knowledge and power in post-crisis Asia', *Pacifica Review: Peace, Security & Global Change* October 13(3): 215–39.

Burke, Anthony 2006, 'Critical approaches to security and strategy' in R. Ayson and D. Ball (eds), *Strategy and security in the Asia-Pacific*, Crows Nest: Allen & Unwin.

Burke, Anthony 2007a, *Beyond security, ethics and violence: war against the other*, London: Routledge.

Burke, Anthony 2007b, 'Australia paranoid: security politics and identity policy' in Anthony Burke and Matt McDonald (eds), *Critical security in the Asia-Pacific*, Manchester: Manchester University Press.

Burke, Anthony 2008, *In fear of security: Australia's invasion anxiety*, Cambridge: Cambridge University Press.

Burke, Anthony 2009, 'Nuclear reason: at the limits of strategy', *International Relations*, 23(4): 506–29.

Burke, Anthony and McDonald, Matt 2007, 'Introduction: Asia-Pacific security legacies and futures' in Anthony Burke and Matt McDonald (eds), *Critical security in the Asia-Pacific*, Manchester: Manchester University Press.

Burke, Edmund, ([1797] 1899), 'Third letter on a regicide peace', in *The works of the Right Honourable Edmund Burke*, Vol 5, London: John C. Nimmo.

Burke, Jason 2003, *Al-Qaeda: casting a shadow of terror*, London: I. B. Tauris.

Burns, Cecil Delisle 1915, *The morality of nations: an essay on the theory of politics*, London: University of London Press.

Burns, Richard Dean 2009, *The evolution of arms control: from antiquity to the nuclear age*, Praeger.

Bush, George H. 1991, 'President George Bush Announcing the War in Iraq', January 16, 1991, transcript available at the History Place website: www.historyplace.com/speeches/bush-war.htm.

Bush, George W. 2002a, 'State of the union address', 29 January, available at http://georgewbush-whitehouse.archives.gov/news/releases/2002/01/20020129-11.html.

Bush, George W. 2002b, Speech at Cincinnati, 7 October, http://georgewbush-whitehouse.archives.gov/news/releases/2002/10/20021007–8.html.

Butfoy, Andrew 2005, *Disarming proposals: controlling nuclear, biological and chemical weapons*, Sydney: UNSW Press.

Butko, T. J. 2006, 'Gramsci and the "anti-globalization" movement: think before you act', *Socialism and democracy*, 20(2): 79–102.

Butterfield, Herbert 1955, *Man on his past: the study of the history of historical scholarship*, Cambridge: Cambridge University Press.

Butterfield, Herbert 1970, 'Diplomacy', in Hatton and Anderson (eds), *Studies in diplomatic history: essays in honour of David Bayne Horn*, London: Archon Books Longman.

Buzan, Barry and Hansen, Lene 2009, *The evolution of international security studies*, Cambridge: Cambridge University Press.

Buzan, Barry, Jones, Charles and Little, Richard 1993, *The logic of anarchy: neorealism to structural realism*, New York, Columbia University Press.

Buzan, Barry and Little, Richard 2000, *International systems in world history*, Oxford: Oxford University Press.

Buzan, Barry, Wæver, Ole, and de Wilde, Jaap 1998, *Security: a new framework for analysis*, Boulder: Lynne Rienner Publishers.

Byrd, S. 2005, 'The Porto Alegre consensus: theorising the forum movement', *Globalizations* 2(1): 151–63.

Cady, Linell E. and Hurd, Elizabeth Shakman 2010, 'Comparative secularisms and the politics of modernity: an introduction,' in Cady and Hurd (eds), *Comparative secularisms in a global age*, New York: Palgrave Macmillan.

Calhoun, Craig 1997, *Nationalism*, Minneapolis: University of Minnesota Press.

Calhoun, Craig 2008, 'The imperative to reduce suffering: charity, progress, and emergencies in the field of humanitarian action', in Barnett and Weiss (eds) 2008, *Humanitarianism in question*, Ithaca: Cornell University Press.

Calhoun, Craig, Juergensmeyer, Mark and VanAntwerpen, Jonathan (eds) 2011, *Rethinking secularism*, Oxford: Oxford University Press.

Call, C. with Wyeth, V. 2008, *Building states to build peace*. Boulder CO: International Peace Institute, Lynne Rienner.

Calleo, David P. and Rowland, B. M. 1973, *America and the world political economy*, Bloomington: Indiana University Press.

Callières, François de [1717] 2000, *On the manner of negotiating with princes*, trans. A. F. Whyte, Boston: Houghton Mifflin.

Cammack, Paul 2004, 'What the World Bank means by poverty reduction and why it matters', *New Political Economy* 9(2): 189–211

Campbell, David 1992, *Writing security: US foreign policy and the politics of identity*, Minneapolis: University of Minnesota Press.

Campbell, David 1998, *National deconstruction: violence, identity and justice in Bosnia*, Minneapolis: University of Minnesota Press.

Campbell, David 2007, 'Poststructuralism' in Tim Dunne, Milja Kurki and Steve Smith (eds), *International relations theories*, Oxford: Oxford University Press.

Canberra Commission on the Elimination of Nuclear Weapons 1996, Report, Australian Department of Foreign Affairs, www.dfat.gov.au/cc/ccreport.pdf.

Caney, Simon 2001, 'International distributive justice' (review article), *Political Studies* 49: 974–97.

Caney, Simon 2005, *Justice beyond borders: a global political theory*, Oxford: Oxford University Press.

Capling, Ann 2001, *Australia and the global trade system: from Havana to Seattle*, Cambridge: Cambridge University Press.

Carpenter, Boyd 1933, 'Review of Hans Kohn: nationalism and imperialism in the hither east, New York, Harcourt, 1932', *The American Journal of International Law*, 27(2): 374–5.

Carpenter, R. Charli 2006, 'Recognizing gender-based violence against civilian men and boys in conflict zones,' *Security Dialogue*, 27(1).

Carr, E. H. 1934, *Karl Marx: a study in fanaticism*, London: J. M. Dent.

Carr, E. H. 1945, *Nationalism and after*, London: Macmillan.

Carr, E. H. 1946, *The twenty years' crisis 1919–1939: an introduction to the study of international relations*, 2nd edition, New York: St. Martin's Press.

Carr, E. H. 1951, *The new society*, London: Macmillan.

Carroll, W. and Carson, C. 2003, 'Forging a new hegemony? The role of transnational policy groups in the network and discourses of global corporate governance', *Journal of World Systems Research* 9(1): 67–102.

Carruthers, Susan L. 2000, *The media at war: communication and conflict in the twentieth century*, Basingstoke: Macmillan/Palgrave.

Carver, Terrell (ed.) 2003, 'Forum: gender and international relations', *International Studies Review* 5: 287–302.

Carver, Terrell 2004, 'War of the worlds/invasion of the body snatchers', *International Affairs* 80(1): 92–4.

Casanova, José 1994, *Public religions in the modern world*, Chicago: University of Chicago Press.

Casanova, José 2011 forthcoming, 'Rethinking public religions,' in Alfred Stepan, Monica Toft and Timothy Shah (eds), *Handbook on religion and world affairs*, Oxford: Oxford University Press.

Cassese, Antonio 1986, 'Return to Westphalia? Considerations in the gradual erosion of the charter system' in A. Cassese (ed.), *The current legal regulation of the use of force*, Dordrecht: Martinus Nijhoff.

Castles, Stephen and Miller, Mark J. 2003, *The age of migration*, Houndmills: Palgrave Macmillan.

Caufield, C. 1996, *Masters of illusion: the World Bank and the poverty of nations*, New York: Henry Holt.

Ceadel, Martin 1987, *Thinking about peace and war*, Oxford: Oxford University Press.

Centre for the Study of Global Governance 2001–, *Global civil society yearbook*, London: Sage. Available online at www2.lse.ac.uk/globalGovernance/research/globalCivilSociety/home.aspx.

Chakrabarty, Dipesh 2000, *Provincializing Europe: postcolonial thought and historical difference*, Princeton: Princeton University Press.

Chalk, Peter 2000, *Non-military security and global order*, Houndmills: Macmillan.

Chandhoke, N. 2005, 'How global is global civil society?', *Journal of World Systems Research* XI(2): 355–71.

Chandler, David 2002, *From Kosovo to Kabul: human rights and international intervention*, London: Pluto Press.

Chandler, David 2006, *Empire in denial: the politics of state-building*, London: Pluto Press.

Chang, J.-A. 2005, *Why developing countries need tariffs: how WTO NAMA negotiations could deny developing countries' right to a future*, Geneva: South Centre.

Chatterjee, Partha 1993, *The nation and its fragments: colonial and postcolonial histories*, Princeton: Princeton University Press.

Chesterman, Simon, Franck, Thomas M. and Malone, David M. 2008, *Law and practice of the United Nations: documents and commentary*, Oxford: Oxford University Press.

Chomsky, Noam 1982, *Towards a new Cold War*, New York: Pantheon.

Chomsky, Noam 2003, *What Uncle Sam really wants (real story)*, London: Pluto Press.

Chowdrey, G. and Nair, S. (eds) 2002, *Power, postcolonialism and international relations*, London: Routledge.

Cirincione, Joseph, Wolfsthal, John B. and Rajkumar, Miriam 2005, *Deadly arsenals: nuclear, biological and chemical threats*, 2nd edition, Washington DC: Carnegie Endowment for International Peace.

Clapp, Jennifer and Dauvergne, Peter 2005, *Paths to a green world: the political economy of the global environment*, Cambridge: MIT Press.

Clark, Ian 1989, *The hierarchy of states: reform and resistance in the international order,* Cambridge: Cambridge University Press.

Clark, Ian 1999, *Globalization and international relations theory*, Oxford: Oxford University Press.

Clark, Ian 2005, *Legitimacy in international society*, Oxford: Oxford University Press.

Claude, Inis 1964, *Swords into plowshares: the problems and progress of international organization*, London: University of London Press.

Clausewitz, Carl von [1832] 1989, *On war*, trans. Michael Howard and Peter Paret, Princeton: Princeton University Press.

Clinton, David 2011 forthcoming, 'The distinction between foreign policy and diplomacy in American international thought and practice', *The Hague Journal of Diplomacy*.

Clinton, Hillary Rodham 2010, 'Leading through civilian power: redefining American diplomacy and development', *Foreign Affairs* 89(6): 13–24.

Cohen, Raymond and Westbrook, Raymond 2000, *Amarna diplomacy: the beginnings of international relations*. Baltimore: Johns Hopkins.

Cohen, Roberta 2007, 'Response to Hathaway', *Journal of Refugee Studies*, 20(3): 370–76.

Cohen, Roberta and Deng, Francis, M. 1998, *Masses in flight: the global financial crises of internal displacement*, Washington, D.C.: Brookings Institution.

Cohn, Carol 1987, 'Sex and death in the rational world of defense intellectuals', *Signs*, 12(4): 687–718.

Colas, Alex and Saull, Richard (eds) 2006, *The war on terrorism and the American empire after the Cold War*, London: Routledge.

Coleman, D. 2003, 'The United Nations and transnational corporations: from an inter-nation to a "beyond-nation" model of engagement', *Global Society* 17(4).

Collins, Alan 2007, *Contemporary security studies*, Oxford: Oxford University Press.

Collyns, C. 2008, 'The crises through the lens of history', *Finance and Development*, 45(4):18–20.

Commission on Global Governance 1995, *Our global neighbourhood*, Oxford: Oxford University Press.

Conca, Ken 2000, 'The WTO and the undermining of global environmental governance', *Review of International Political Economy* 7(3): 484–94.

Connolly, William E. 1993, *Political theory and modernity*, Ithaca: Cornell University Press.

Connolly, William E. 1995, *The ethos of pluralization*, Minneapolis: University of Minnesota Press.

Connolly, William E. 2002a, *Identity/difference: democratic negotiations of political paradox*, expanded edition, Minneapolis: University of Minnesota Press.

Connolly, William E. 2002b, *Neuropolitics: thinking, culture, speed*, Minneapolis: University of Minnesota Press.

Connor, Walker 1994, *Ethnonationalism: the quest for understanding*, Princeton: Princeton University Press.

Connor, Walker 2004, 'A few cautionary notes on ethnonational conflicts' in Andreas Joras, Ulrike Schetter, Conrad Horowitz, Donald L. Goldstone and Richard J. Wimmer (eds), *Facing ethnic conflicts: toward a new realism*, Lanham: Rowman & Littlefield.

Constant, Benjamin 1988 [1819], 'The liberty of the ancients compared with that of the moderns', in *Political Writings*, ed. and trans. Biancamaria Fontana, Cambridge: Cambridge University Press.

Constantinou, Costas 1996a, 'NATO's caps: European security and the future of the North Atlantic alliance', *Alternatives*, 20(2): 147–64.

Constantinou, Costas 1996b, *On the way to diplomacy*, Minneapolis: University of Minnesota Press.

Cooper, Andrew 2008, *Celebrity diplomacy*, Boulder, CO: Paradigm.

Cooper, Andrew and Hocking, Brian 2000, 'Governments, non-government organizations and the recalibration of diplomacy', *Global Society* 14(3): 361–76.

Cooper, Frederick 2005, *Colonialism in question – theory, knowledge, history*, Berkeley: University of California Press.

Cortright, David and Lopez, George A. 2000, *The sanctions decade: assessing UN strategies in the 1990s*. Boulder, CO.: Lynne Rienner Publishers.

Cortright, David, Lopez, George A. and Stephanides, Joseph (eds) 2002, *Smart sanctions: targeting economic statecraft*, Boulder, CO: Lynne Rienner Publishers.

Cousens, Elizabeth M. 2001, 'Introduction' in E. M. Cousens and C. Kumar et al. (eds), *Peacebuilding as politics: cultivating peace in fragile societies*, London: Lynne Rienner.

Cox, Robert W. 1981, 'Social forces, states and world orders: beyond international relations theory', *Millennium* 10(2): 126–55.

Cox, Robert W. 1983, 'Gramsci, hegemony and international relations: an essay on method', *Millennium*, 12(2): 162–75.

Cox, Robert W. 1987, *Production, power and world order: social forces in the making of history*, New York: Columbia University Press.

Cox, Robert W. 1997, 'Democracy in hard times: economic globalisation and the limits to liberal democracy' in A. McGrew (ed.), *The transformation of democracy*, Cambridge: Polity Press.

Cox, Robert W. 1999, 'Civil society at the turn of the millennium: prospects for an alternative world order', *Review of International Studies*, 25(1): 3–28.

Cox, Robert W. and Sinclair, Timothy 1995, *Approaches to world order*, Cambridge: Cambridge University Press.

Crawford, Neta 2009, '*Homo politicus* and argument (nearly) all the way down: persuasion in politics', *Perspectives on politics* 7(1): 103–124.

Creveld, Martin van 1991, *On future war*, London: Brassey's.

Creveld, Martin van 1999, *The rise and decline of the state*, Cambridge and New York: Cambridge University Press.

Crockatt, Richard 1995, *The fifty years war: the United States and the Soviet Union in world politics, 1941–1991*, London: Routledge.

Cryer, R. 2002, 'The fine art of friendship: *jus in bello* in Afghanistan', *Journal of Conflict and Security Law* 7(1).

Crystal, David 2000, *Language death*, Cambridge: Cambridge University Press.

Cull, Nicholas J. 2009, 'How we got here', in Seib, Philip (ed.), *Toward a new public diplomacy: redirecting U.S. foreign policy*, Basingstoke, UK: Palgrave Macmillan

Dalby, Simon 1997, 'Contesting an essential concept: reading the dilemmas in contemporary security discourse' in K. Krause and M. C. Williams (eds), *Critical security studies: concepts and cases*, Minneapolis: University of Minnesota Press.

Dalrymple, W. 2002, *White Mughals: love and betrayal in eighteenth-century India*, London: Flamingo.

Danish Institute of International Affairs 1999, *Humanitarian intervention: legal and political aspects*, Copenhagen: DUPI.

Darby, Phillip 1997, *At the edge of international relations: postcolonialism, gender and dependency*, London: Pinter.

Darby, Phillip (ed.) 2000, *At the edge of international relations: postcolonialism, gender and dependency*, London: Continuum.

Dauphinee, E. and Masters, C. (eds) 2007, *The logics of biopower and the war on terror*, New York: Palgrave Macmillan.

Davies, J., Sanderson, S., Shorrocks, A. and Wolff, E., 2006, *The world distribution of wealth*, 5 December, Helsinki: World Institute for Development Economics Research of the United Nations University (WIDER-UNU).

Davis, Joyce 2004, *Martyrs: innocence, vengeance, and despair in the Middle East*, New York: Palgrave Macmillan.

Davis, Mike 2006, *Planet of slums*, London: Verso.

Davis Cross, M. K. 2007, *The European diplomatic corps: diplomats and international cooperation from Westphalia to Maastricht*, Basingstoke, UK: Palgrave Macmillan.

Davison, Andrew 2006, 'Ziya Gökalp and provincializing Europe,' *Comparative studies of South Asia, Africa and the Middle East*, 26(3): 377–390.

Dehio, Ludwig [1948] 1963, *The precarious balance: four centuries of the European power struggle*, trans. Charles Fullma, New York: Vintage Books.

Deng, Francis M. et al. 1996 *Sovereignty as responsibility: conflict management in Africa*, Washington, D.C.: Brookings.

Depledge, J. 2005, *The organization of the global negotiations: constructing the climate regime* London: Earthscan.

Der Derian, James 1987, *On diplomacy: a genealogy of western estrangement*, Oxford: Blackwell.

Der Derian, James 2001, *Virtuous war: mapping the military-industrial-media-entertainment network*, Boulder, CO: Westview Press.

Der Derian, James and Shapiro, Michael J. (eds) 1989, *International/intertextual relations: postmodern readings of world politics*, New York: Lexington Books.

Deudney, Daniel 1990, 'The case against linking environmental degradation to national security', *Millennium: Journal of International Studies* 19(3): 461–76.

Deutsch, K. W. et al. 1957, *Political community and the North Atlantic Area: international organization in the light of historical experience*, Princeton University Press.

Development Initiatives 2003, *Global humanitarian assistance,* London: Overseas Development Institute.

Devetak, Richard 2008, 'Globalization's shadow: an introduction to the globalization of political violence', in R. Devetak and C. W. Hughes (eds), *The globalization of political violence: globalization's shadow*, London: Routledge.

Devetak, Richard 2009a, 'Critical theory' in Scott Burchill, Andrew Linklater, Richard Devetak, Jack Donnelly, Terry Nardin, Matthew Paterson, Christian Reus-Smit and Jacqui True (eds), *Theories of international relations*, 4th edition, London: Macmillan.

Devetak, Richard 2009b, 'Postmodernism' in Scott Burchill, Andrew Linklater, Richard Devetak, Terry Nardin, Jack Donnelly, Matthew Paterson, Christian Reus-Smit and Jacqui True (eds), *Theories of international relations*, 4th edition, London: Macmillan.

Devetak, Richard and True, Jacqui 2006, 'Diplomatic divergence in the Antipodes: globalisation, foreign policy and state identity in Australia and New Zealand', *Australian Journal of Political Science*, 41(2): 241–56.

Di Palma, Giuseppe 1990, *To craft democracies: an essay on democratic transitions*, Los Angeles: University of California Press.

Diamond, Jared 1997, *Germs, guns and steel: the fates of human societies*, New York: W.W. Norton.

Dinnen, Sinclair 2007, *The twin processes of nation building and state building*, Policy Briefing Note 1/2007, State Society and Governance in Melanesia Project, Research School of Pacific and Asian Studies, The Australian National University.

Dolšak, Nives 2001, 'Mitigating global climate change: why some countries are more committed than others?', *Policy Studies Journal*, 29(3): 414–36.

Doran, Charles F. 1971, *The politics of assimilation: hegemony and its aftermath*, Baltimore: The Johns Hopkins Press.

Doyle, Michael 1983, 'Kant, liberal legacies, and foreign affairs', *Philosophy and Public Affairs* 12(3 & 4): 205–35 and 323–53.

Doyle, Michael 1986, 'Liberalism and world politics', *American Political Science Review*, 80(4): 1151–69.

Doyle, Michael 1997, *Ways of war and peace: realism, liberalism, and socialism*, New York: W. W. Norton & Co.

Dryzek, John 2006, *Deliberative global politics: discourse and democracy in a divided world*, Cambridge: Polity Press.

Duffield, Mark 2001, *Global governance and the new wars: the merging of development and security*, London: Zed Books.

Dunant, Henry [1862] 1986, *Memory of Solferino*, Geneva: International Committee of the Red Cross.

Dunn, John 2000, *The cunning of unreason*, New York: HarperCollins.

Dunne, Tim 1998, *Inventing international society: a history of the English School*, London: Macmillan.

Dunne, Tim 2003, 'Society and hierarchy in international relations', *International Relations*, 17(3): 303–20.

Dunne, Tim 2007, 'The English School' in Tim Dunne, Milja Kurki and Steve Smith (eds), *International relations theories*, Oxford: Oxford University Press.

Dunne, Tim and Wheeler, Nicholas (eds) 1999, *Human rights in global politics*, Cambridge: Cambridge University Press.

Dupont, Alan 2001, *East Asia imperilled: transnational challenges to security*, Cambridge: Cambridge University Press.

Durch, William J. (ed.) 2006, *Twenty-first century peace operations*, Washington, DC.:U.S. Institute of Peace Press.

Dwan, Renata 2006, 'Civilian tasks and capabilities in EU operations', in Marlies Glasius and Mary Kaldor (eds), *A human security doctrine for Europe; project, principles, practicalities*, London: Routledge.

Eckersley, Robyn 2008, 'US foreign policy and the environment', in Mick Cox and Doug Stokes (eds), *US foreign policy*, Oxford: Oxford University Press.

The Economist 2009, 'Responsibility to protect: an idea whose time has come—and gone?' *The Economist*, 23 November.

Edkins, Jenny 1999, *Poststructuralism and international relations: bringing the political back in*, Boulder, CO: Lynne Rienner.

Edkins, Jenny 2004, *Whose hunger? Concepts of famine, practices of aid*, Minneapolis: University of Minnesota Press.

Eller, Jack David 1990, *From culture to ethnicity to conflict: an anthropological perspective of international ethnic conflict*, Ann Arbor: University of Michigan Press.

Elliott, Andrea 2010, 'The jihadist next door', *New York Times*, 31 January.

Elshtain, Jean Bethke 1982, 'On beautiful souls, just warriors and feminist consciousness', *Women's Studies International Forum* 5(3–4): 341–8.

Enloe, Cynthia 1990, *Bananas, beaches and bases: making feminist sense of international politics*, Berkeley: University of California Press.

Eriksen, Stein Sundstol 2009, 'The liberal peace is neither: peacebuilding, statebuilding and the reproduction of conflict in the Democratic Republic of Congo', *International Peacekeeping*, 16(5): 652–66.

Esposito, John L. 1999, *The Islamic threat: myth or reality?*, 3rd edition, New York: Oxford University Press.

Esty, D. C. 2002, 'The World Trade Organization's legitimacy crisis', *World Trade Review* 1(1): 7–22.

Evans, Gareth 2008, *The responsibility to protect: ending mass atrocity crimes once and for all*. Washington, DC: Brookings.

Evans, Gareth and Grant, Bruce 1995, *Australia's foreign relations: in the world of the 1990s*, 2nd edition, Melbourne: Melbourne University Press.

Evans, Gareth and Sahnoun, Mohamed 2002, 'Responsibility to protect', *Foreign Affairs* 81(6): 99–110.

Evans, Martin 2005, *Conflict in Afghanistan: studies in asymmetric warfare*, London and New York: Routledge.

Falk, Richard 1995, *On humane governance*, Cambridge: Polity Press.

Falk, Richard 1999, *Predatory globalization: a critique*, Cambridge: Polity Press.

Falk, Richard 2000, 'Global civil society' in R. Falk (ed.), *Predatory globalisation*, Cambridge: Polity Press.

Falk, Richard 2001, *Religion and humane global governance*, London: Palgrave.

Falkner, Robert 2005, 'American hegemony and the global environment', *International Studies Review*, 7(4): 585–99.

Ferguson, Kathy 1993, *The man question: visions of subjectivity in feminist theory*, Berkeley: University of California Press.

Fierke, Karin 2007, *Critical approaches to international security*, Oxford: Polity Press.

Fitzpatrick, K. 2007, 'Advancing the new public diplomacy: a public relations perspective', *The Hague Journal of Diplomacy* 2 (3): 187–211.

Flax, Jane 1990, *Thinking fragments: psychoanalysis, feminism, and postmodernism in the contemporary West*, Berkeley: University of California Press.

Forsythe, David 2000, *Human rights in international relations*, Cambridge: Cambridge University Press, 2000.

Foucault, Michel [1973] 1983, *This is not a pipe*, trans. James Harkness, Berkeley: University of California Press.

Foucault, Michel 1984, 'What is enlightenment?', trans. C. Porter in Paul Rabinow (ed.), *The Foucault reader*, New York: Pantheon Books.

Frank, Andre Gunder 1967, *Capitalism and underdevelopment in Latin America: historical studies of Chile and Brazil*, New York: Monthly Review Press.

Freedman, Lawrence 1998, *The revolution in strategic affairs*, Adelphi Paper 318, Oxford: Oxford University Press for the Institute for Strategic Studies.

Freedman, Lawrence 2004, *Deterrence*, Oxford: Polity Press.

Friedman, Thomas 1999, *The Lexus and the olive tree*, New York: HarperCollins.

Fry, Greg E. 1997, 'Framing the islands: knowledge and power in changing Australian images of "the South Pacific"', *The Contemporary Pacific* 9(7): 305–44.

Fry, Greg and O'Hagan, Jacinta 2000, *Contending images of world politics*, London: Palgrave.

Fukada-Parr, Sakiko 2004, 'Millennium Development Goals: why they matter', *Global Governance* 10(4): 395–402.

Fukuyama, Francis 1989, 'The end of history?' *National Interest* 16: 3–18.

Fukuyama, Francis 2004, *State-building: governance and world order in the 21st century*, Ithaca NY: Cornell University Press.

G20, 2009a, *Leaders Statement – The global plan for recovery and reform* (2 April) available at www.g20.org/Documents/final-communique.pdf.

G20, 2009b, *Declaration on Strengthening the Financial System* (2 April) Available at www.g20.org/Documents/Fin_Deps_Fin_Reg_Annex_020409_-_1615_final.pdf.

G20, 2009c, *Communiqué – Meeting of Finance Ministers and Central Bank Governors, London* (4–5 September) Available at http://g20.org/Documents/FM__CBG_Comm_-_Final.pdf.

Gaddis, J. L. 1986, 'The long peace: elements of stability in the post-war international system', *International Security* 10(4): 99–142.

Gaddis, J. L. 1990, *Russia, the Soviet Union and the United States: an interpretive history*, 2nd edition, New York: McGraw Hill.

Gaddis, J. L. 2005, *The Cold War: a new history*, New York: Penguin.

Gale, F. 1998, '"Cave, Cave! Hic dragones": a neo-Gramscian deconstruction and reconstruction of international regime theory', *Review of International Political Economy*, 5(2): 252–84.

Gal-Or, N. 2005, 'NAFTA Chapter eleven and the implications for the FTAA: the institutionalisation of investor status in public international law', *Transnational Corporations* 124(2): 121–59.

Ganguly, Šumit 2001, *Conflict unending: India–Pakistan tensions since 1947*, New York: Columbia University Press.

Garthoff, R. L. 1994, *The great transition: American-Soviet relations and the end of the Cold War*, Washington DC: Brookings Institution Press.

Gat, Azar 1989, *The origins of military thought from the Enlightenment to Clausewitz*, Oxford: Clarendon Press.

Geertz, Clifford 1963, 'The integrative revolution: primordial sentiments and civil politics in the new states', in Clifford Gertz (ed.), *Old societies and new states*, New York: Free Press.

Gelb, Leslie H. 2009, *Power rules: how common sense can rescue American foreign policy,* New York: HarperCollins.

Gellner, Ernest 1983, *Nations and nationalism*, Ithaca: Cornell University Press.

General Assembly, United Nations 2009, 'General Assembly Debate on the Responsibility to Protect', 97th – 100th plenary meetings, General Assembly Hall, available at www.un.org/webcast.

George, Jim 1994, *Discourses of global politics: a critical (re)introduction to international relations*, Boulder: Lynne Rienner Publishers.

George, Jim and Campbell, David 1990, 'Patterns of dissent and the celebration of difference: critical social theory and international relations', *International Studies Quarterly*, Special Issue 34(3): 269–93.

George, Nicole 2010, '"Just like your mother?" the politics of feminism and maternity in the Pacific Islands', *The Australian Feminist Law Journal*, 32.

George, Susan 2004, *Another world is possible if …*, London: Verso.

Germain, Randall D. 1997, *The international organization of credit*, Cambridge and New York: Cambridge University Press.

Germain, Randall D. 2010, *Global politics and financial governance,* New York: Palgrave.

Ghandi, Leila 1998, *Postcolonial theory: a critical introduction*, Sydney: Allen & Unwin.

Ghani, Asraf and Lockhart, Clare 2008, *Fixing failed states; a framework for rebuilding a fractured world*, Oxford: Oxford University Press.

Gibney, Matthew J. 2004, *The ethics and politics of asylum: liberal democracy and the response to refugees*, Cambridge: Cambridge University Press.

Giddens, Anthony 1984, *The constitution of society*, Cambridge: Polity Press.

Giddens, Anthony 1990, *The consequences of modernity*, Stanford: Stanford University Press.

Giddens, Anthony 1999, *Runaway world: how globalization is reshaping our lives*, London: Profile.

Gill, Stephen 1990, *American hegemony and the Trilateral Commission*, Cambridge: Cambridge University Press.

Gill, Stephen (ed.) 1993, *Gramsci, historical materialism and international relations*, Cambridge: Cambridge University Press.

Gill, Stephen 1995, 'Globalisation, market civilisation, and disciplinary neoliberalism', *Millennium*, 24(3): 399–424.

Gill, Stephen 1998, 'New constitutionalism, democratisation and global political economy', *Pacifica Review*, 10(1): 23–39.

Gill, Stephen 2000, 'Toward a postmodern prince? the battle in Seattle as a moment in the new politics of globalisation', *Millennium*, 29(1): 131–40.

Gill, Stephen 2002, 'Constitutionalizing inequality and the clash of globalizations', *International Studies Review*, 4(2): 47–65.

Gilpin, Robert 1981, *War and change in world politics*, Cambridge: Cambridge University Press.

Gilpin, Robert 1988, 'The theory of hegemonic war', *Journal of Interdisciplinary History*, 18(4): 591–613.

Gilpin, Robert 2001, *Global political economy: understanding the international economic order*, Princeton: Princeton University Press.

Glenn, J. 2008, 'Global governance and the democratic deficit: stifling the voice of the south', *The Third World Quarterly* 29(2): 217–38.

Glenn, Russell 2007, *Counterinsurgency in a test tube; analyzing the success of the Regional Assistance Mission to the Solomon Islands (RAMSI)*, Santa Monica: RAND.

Global Humanitarian Assistance. 2009, *Global humanitarian assistance 2009*, available at www.globalhumanitarianassistance.org/analyses-and-reports/gha-reports/gha-reports-2009.

Goede, Marieke de 2005, *Virtue, fortune and faith: a geneology of finance*, Minneapolis: Minnesota University Press.

Goede, Marieke de 2006, *International political economy and poststructural politics*, Houndmills: Palgrave.

Goldstein, Joshua 2001, *Gender and war: how gender shapes the war system and vice-versa*, Cambridge: Cambridge University Press.

Goldstone, Richard and Smith, Adam 2008, *International justice pursuit: the architecture of international justice at home and abroad,* London: Routledge.

Golinksi, Jan 2005, *Making natural knowledge: constructivism and the history of science*, Cambridge: Cambridge University Press.

Gong, Gerrit W. 1984, *The standard of civilization in international society*, Oxford: Clarendon Press.

Goodman, James 2007, 'Reflexive solidarities: between nationalism and globalism' in J. Goodman and P. James (eds), *Nationalism and global solidarities*, London: Routledge.

Goodman, James and Ranald, P. (eds) 1999, *Stopping the juggernaut: public interest versus the multilateral agreement on investment*, Annandale: Pluto Press.

Goodman, Martin 2007, *Rome and Jerusalem: the clash of ancient civilizations*, London: Allen Lane.

Gourevitch, Peter A. and Shinn, James 2005, *Political power and corporate control*, Princeton: Princeton University Press.

Gramsci, Antonio 1971, *Selections from the prison notebooks*, ed. and trans. Quintin Hoare and Geoffrey Nowell Smith, New York: International Publishers.

Grant, R. and Newland, K. 1991, *Gender and international relations*, Bloomington: Indiana University Press.

Gray, Colin 1998, *Modern strategy*, Oxford: Oxford University Press.

Gray, Colin 1999, 'Clausewitz rules, OK', *Review of International Studies* 25: 161–82.

Gray, Colin 2000, *International law and the use of force*, Oxford: Oxford University Press.

Gray, John 1995, *Liberalism*, 2nd edition, Minneapolis: University of Minnesota Press.

Graz, Jean-Christophe 2004, 'Transnational mercantilism and the emergent global trading order', *Review of International Political Economy* 11(3): 597–617.

Greenfeld, Liah 1992, *Nationalism: five roads to modernity*, Cambridge MA: Harvard University Press.

Greenfeld, Liah 2006, *Nationalism and the mind: essays on modern culture*, Oxford: Oneworld.

Grewe, Wilhelm 2000, *The epochs of international law*, trans. Michael Byers, Berlin: Walter de Gruyter.

Grieco, Joseph M. 1990, *Cooperation among nations: Europe, America, and non-tariff barriers to trade*, Ithaca, Cornell University Press.

Griffiths, Martin (ed.) 2005, *Encyclopedia of international relations and global politics*, London: Routledge.

Griffiths, Martin and O'Callaghan, Terry 2002, *International relations: the key concepts*, London: Routledge.

Grillo, Ralph, Ballard, Roger, Ferrari, Alessandro, Hoekema, André J., Maussen, Marcel and Shah, Prakash (eds) 2009, *Legal practice and cultural diversity*. London: Ashgate.

Grotius, Hugo [1625] 2005, *The rights of war and peace*, Richard Tuck (ed.), Indianapolis: Liberty Fund.

Grundig, Frank 2006, 'Patterns of international cooperation and the explanatory power of relative gains: an analysis of cooperation on global climate change, ozone depletion, and international trade', *International Studies Quarterly*, 50(4): 781–801.

Grygiel, Jakub J. 2006, *Great powers and geopolitical change*, Baltimore: The Johns Hopkins University Press.

Guelke, Adrian 2006, *Terrorism and global disorder*, London: I. B. Tauris.

Gurr, Ted R. 2000, *Peoples versus states: minorities at risk in the new century*, Washington DC: United States Institute of Peace Press.

Haas, Peter 1990, 'Obtaining international environmental protection through epistemic consensus', *Millennium*, 19(3): 347–63.

Haas, Peter 2002, 'UN conferences and constructivist governance of the environment', *Global Governance* 8(1).

Haas, P., Keohane, R. and Levy, M. 1993, *Institutions for the earth: sources of effective environmental protection*, Cambridge, MA: MIT Press.

Habermas, Jürgen 1972, *Knowledge and human interests*, trans. Jeremy Shapiro, Cambridge: Polity Press.

Habermas, Jürgen 1987, *The philosophical discourse of modernity,* Cambridge: Polity Press.

Habermas, Jürgen 1998, *The inclusion of the other: studies in political theory*, trans. Ciaran Cronin and Pablo De Greiff, Cambridge: Polity Press.

Hacking, Ian 1999, *The social construction of what?*, Cambridge, MA: Harvard University Press.

Haddad, Emma 2008, *The refugee in international society: between sovereigns*, Cambridge: Cambridge University Press.

Hagmann, Tobias and Hoehne, Markus V. 2007, 'Failed state or failed debate? Multiple Somali political orders within and beyond the nation-state', *Politorbis* 42: 20–26.

Hajer, M. 1997, *The politics of environmental discourse: ecological modernization and the policy process*. Oxford, UK: Oxford University Press.

Hall, John and Ikenberry, G. John 1989, *The state*, Milton Keynes: Open University Press.

Hall, Rodney Bruce 1999, *National collective identity: social constructs and international systems*, New York: Columbia University Press.

Halliday, Fred 1986, *The making of the second Cold War*, London: Verso.

Halliday, Fred 1988, 'Hidden from international relations: women in the international arena' *Millennium: Journal of International Studies* 17(3): 419–28.

Halliday, Fred 1994, *Rethinking international relations*, Houndmills: Macmillan.

Halliday, Fred 2001, 'The romance of non-state actors' in W. Wallace (ed.), *Non-state actors in world politics*, London: Palgrave Macmillan.

Halverson, K. 2001, 'Protection and humanitarian assistance in the refugee camps in Zaire: the problem of security' in Howard Adelman and Astri Suhrke (eds), *The path of a genocide: the Rwanda crisis from Uganda to Zaire*, Piscataway: Transaction Publishers.

Hamieri, Shahar 2009, 'Capacity and its facilities: international state building as state transformation', *Millennium: Journal of International Studies*, 38(1): 55–81.

Hamilton, Keith and Langhorne, Richard 2011, *The practice of diplomacy: its evolution, theory and administration*, 2nd edition, London: Routledge.

Hanson, Marianne 2002, 'Nuclear weapons as obstacles to international security', *International Relations* 16(3): 361–80.

Hanson, Marianne 2005, 'Regulating the possession and use of nuclear weapons: ideas, commission and agency in international security politics' in Ramesh Thakur, Andrew F. Cooper and John English (eds), *International commissions and the power of ideas*, New York: United Nations University Press.

Hanson, Marianne 2010, 'The advocacy of states: their normative role before and after the U.S. call for nuclear zero', *The Nonproliferation Review*, 17(1): 71–93.

Harvey, David 1989, *The condition of postmodernity*, Cambridge: Blackwell.

Harvey, David 1997, *Justice, nature and the geography of difference*, Oxford: Basil Blackwell.

Hasenclever, A., Mayer, P. and Rittberger, V. 1997, *Theories of international regimes*, Cambridge: Cambridge University Press.

Haslam, Jonathan 2002, *No virtue like necessity: realist thought in international relations since Machiavelli*, New Haven: Yale University Press.

Hastings, Adrian 1997, *The construction of nationhood: ethnicity, religion and nationalism*, Cambridge: Cambridge University Press.

Hathaway, James C. 2007, 'Forced migration studies: could we agree just to "date"?', *Journal of Refugee Studies*, 20(3): 349–69.

Hawkins, Darren G. et al. (eds) 2006, *Delegation and agency in international organisations*, Cambridge: Cambridge University Press.

Hayek, Friedrich 1976, *Law, legislation and liberty, Vol. 2: the mirage of social justice*, London: Routledge and Kegan Paul.

Hayes, Carlton J. H. 1960, *Nationalism: a religion*, New York: Macmillan.

Hayter, Teresa 2004, *Open borders: the case against immigration controls*, London: Pluto Books.

Heinemann-Gruder, Andreas and Grebenschikov, Igor 2006 'Security governance by internationals: the case of Kosovo', *International Peacekeeping*, 13(1): 43–59.

Heisenberg, Werner 1961, 'Planck's discovery and the philosophical problems of atomic physics' in Werner Heisenberg, Gerd W. Buschhorn and Julius Wess, *On modern physics*, New York: Clarkson Potter.

Held, David 1980, *Introduction to critical theory*, Berkeley: University of California Press.

Held, David 1995, *Democracy and the global order: from the modern state to cosmopolitan governance*, Cambridge: Polity Press.

Held, David 1997, 'Cosmopolitan democracy and the global order' in J. Bohman and M. Lutz-Bachman (eds), *Perpetual peace*, Cambridge: MIT Press.

Held, David 1998, 'Democracy and globalization' in D. Archibugi, David Held and Martin Köhler (eds), *Re-imagining political community: studies in cosmopolitan democracy*, Cambridge: Polity Press.

Held, David 2006, 'Reframing global governance: apocalypse soon or reform!' *New Political Economy* 11(2):157–76.

Held, David, Kaldor, Mary and Quah, Danny 2010, 'The hydra-headed crisis,' *Global Policy Journal*, 1(1), available at www.globalpolicyjournal.com/articles/global-governance/hydra-headed-crisis.

Held, David, McGrew, Anthony G., Goldblatt, David and Perraton, Jonathon 1999, *Global transformations*, Cambridge: Polity Press.

Helleiner, Eric 1994, *States and the reemergence of global finance*, Ithaca: Cornell University Press.

Helleiner, Eric and Pagliari, Stefano 2009, 'Towards a new Bretton Woods? The first G20 Leaders Summit and the regulation of global finance', *New Political Economy* 14(2): 275–87.

Helleiner, Eric, Pagliari, Stefano and Zimmermann, Hubert (eds) 2010, *Global finance in crisis*, London: Routledge.

Henrikson, Alan K. 2006, 'Diplomacy's possible futures', *The Hague Journal of Diplomacy* 1(1): 3–27.

Herz, John 1950, 'Idealist internationalism and the security dilemma', *World Politics* 2(2).

Herz, John 1962, *International politics in the atomic age*, New York, Columbia University Press.

Higgott, Richard and Phillips, Nicola 2000, 'Challenging triumphalism and convergence: the limits of global liberalization in Asia and Latin America', *Review of International Studies* 26: 359–79.

Higgott, Richard and Weber, Heloise 2005, 'GATS in context: development, an evolving lex mercatoria and the Doha Agenda', *Review of International Political Economy* 12(3): 434–55.

High Level Panel on Threats, Challenges and Change, 2004, *A more secure world: our shared responsibility*, New York: United Nations, available at www.un.org/secureworld.

Hindess, Barry 2001, 'The liberal government of unfreedom', *Alternatives* 26(2): 93–111.

Hinsley, F. H. 1963, *Power and the pursuit of peace: theory and practice in the history of relations between states*, Cambridge: Cambridge University Press.

Hinsley, F. H. 1973, *Nationalism and the international system*, London: Hodder & Stoughton.

Hinsley, F. H. 1986, *Sovereignty*, Cambridge: Cambridge University Press.

Hirsch, J. 2003, 'The state's new clothes: NGOs and the internationalization of states', *Rethinking Marxism* 15(2): 237–62.

Hirst, Paul and Thompson, Grahame 1996, *Globalization in question: the international economy and the possibilities of governance*, Cambridge: Polity Press.

Hobbes, Thomas [1651] 1968, *Leviathan*, London: Penguin Books.

Hobsbawm, Eric J. 1997, *Nations and nationalism since 1780: programme, myth, reality*, revised edition, Cambridge: Cambridge University Press.

Hobson, J. A. 1968, *Imperialism: a study*, London: George Allen & Unwin.

Hobson, John 2004, *The Eastern origins of Western civilization*, Cambridge: Cambridge University Press.

Hocking, Brian (ed.) 1999, *Foreign ministries: change and adaption*, Basingstoke: UK, Macmillan.

Hoffman, Mark 1987, 'Critical theory and the inter-paradigm debate', *Millennium* 16(3): 231–56.

Hoffman, Peter J. and Weiss, Thomas G. 2006, *Sword & salve: confronting new wars and humanitarian crises*, Lanham, MD.: Rowman & Littlefield.

Holbraad, Carsten 1970, *The Concert of Europe: a study in German and British international theory, 1815–1914*, London: Longman.

Holsti, K. J. 1985, *The dividing discipline: hegemony and diversity in international theory*, Boston: Allen & Unwin.

Holzgrefe, J. L. and Keohane, Robert O. (eds) 2003, *Humanitarian intervention: ethical, legal and political dilemmas*, Cambridge: Cambridge University Press.

Holzscheiter, A. 2005, 'Discourse as capability: non-state actors' capital in global governance', *Millennium: Journal of International Studies* 33(3): 723–46.

hooks, bell 1981, *Ain't I a woman? Black women and feminism*, Boston: South End Press.

Horgan, John 2005, *The psychology of terrorism*, London: Routledge.

Horgan, John and Taylor, Max 2006, 'A conceptual framework for addressing psychological process in the development of the terrorist', *Terrorism and Political Violence* 18(4).

Horkheimer, Max [1937] 1972, 'Traditional and critical theory', in Horkheimer, *Critical theory: selected essays*, trans M. J. O'Connell et al., New York: Herder and Herder.

Horsley, Richard A. 1979, 'The Sicarii: ancient Jewish "terrorists"', *The Journal of Religion* 59(4): 435–58.

Hoselitz, Bert, F. 1952, 'Non-economic barriers to economic development', *Economic Development and Cultural Change* 1(1): 8–21.

Hough, Richard Lee 2003, *The nation-state: concert or chaos*, Lanham: University Press of America.

Houtart, F. and Polet, F. 2001, *The other Davos: the globalization of resistance to the world economic system*, New York: Zed Books.

Howard, LiseMorjé 2008, *UN peacekeeping in civil wars*, Cambridge: Cambridge University Press.

Howard, Michael 1978, *War and the liberal conscience*, London: Temple Smith.

Howard, Michael 2001, *The invention of peace: reflections on war and international order*, London: Profile Books.

Hudson, A. 2001, 'NGOs transnational advocacy networks: from "legitimacy" to political responsibility?', *Global Networks* 1(4).

Hulsman, John and Lieven, Anatol 2005, 'The ethics of realism', *National interest* 80(1): 37–43.

Human Rights Watch 2001, 'Cluster bombs in Afghanistan', backgrounder, October, available at www.hrw.org/en/reports/2001/10/31/cluster-bombs-afghanistan.

Human Rights Watch 2002, 'Fatally flawed: cluster bombs and their use by the United States in Afghanistan', *Human rights watch report*, 14(7)(G), December.

Human Security Report 2005, *War and peace in the 21st century*, Human Security Centre, University of British Columbia, Oxford: Oxford University Press.

Huntington, F. A. 1989, 'Animals fight, but do not make war' in J. Groebel and R.H. Hinde (eds), *Aggression and war: their biological and social bases*, Cambridge: Cambridge University Press.

Huntington, Samuel 1993, 'The clash of civilizations', *Foreign Affairs* 72(3): 22–49.

Huntington, Samuel P. 1999, 'The lonely superpower', *Foreign Affairs*, 78(2): 35–49.

Hurd, Elizabeth Shakman 2007, 'Theorizing religious resurgence,' *International politics* 44(6): 647–65.

Hurd, Elizabeth Shakman 2008, *The politics of secularism in international relations*, Princeton: Princeton University Press.

Hurd, Elizabeth Shakman 2011, 'A suspension of (dis)belief: the secular-religious binary and the study of international relations,' in Calhoun, Juergensmeyer and VanAntwerpen (eds), *Rethinking secularism*, Oxford: Oxford University Press.

Hurd, Ian 2011, *International organizations: politics, law, practice*. Cambridge: Cambridge University Press.

Hurrell, Andrew 1995, 'International society and the study of regimes: a reflective approach', in Volker Rittberger (ed.), *Regime theory and international relations*, Oxford: Clarendon Press.

Hurrell, Andrew 2005, 'Pax Americana or the empire of insecurity?', *International Relations of the Asia-Pacific*, 5(2): 153–76.

Hutchings, Kimberly 2005, 'Speaking and hearing: Habermasian discourse ethics, feminism and IR', *Review of International Studies*, 31(1): 155–65.

Hutchinson, John and Smith, Anthony (eds) 1994, *Nationalism*, Oxford: Oxford University Press.

Hutchinson, John and Smith, Anthony (eds) 1996, *Ethnicity*, Oxford: Oxford University Press.

Huyssen, Andreas 1984, 'Mapping the postmodern', *New German Critique* 33: 8.

ICISS 2001, *The responsibility to protect: report of the International Commission on Intervention and State Sovereignty*, Ottawa: International Development Research Centre.

Ignatieff, Michael 1994, *Blood and belonging: journeys into the new nationalism*, London: Vintage.

Ikenberry, G. John 2001, *After victory: institutions, strategic restraint, and the rebuilding of order after major wars*, Princeton, NJ: Princeton University Press.

Ikenberry, G. John 2002, *America unrivaled: the future of the balance of power*, Ithaca: Cornell University Press.

IISS (International Institute for Strategic Studies) 2011, *The military balance*, vol. III, London: Routledge.

Inayatullah, Naeem and Blaney, David 2004, *International relations and the problem of difference*, New York and London: Routledge.

The Independent Commission on Disarmament and Security Issues 1982, *Common security: a blueprint for survival* (The Palme Report), New York: Simon and Schuster.

Intergovernmental Panel on Climate Change 2001, *Climate change 2001 – synthesis report: summary for policymakers*, available at www.ipcc.ch/publications_and_data/publications_and_data_reports.shtml.

International Commission on Nuclear Non-Proliferation and Disarmament (ICNND) 2009, *Eliminating nuclear threats: a practical agenda for global policymakers*, Report of the International Commission on Nuclear Nonproliferation and Disarmament, available at www.icnnd.org/Reference/reports/ent/default.htm.

International Labour Organization 2004, *Report of the World Commission on the social dimensions of globalization,* Geneva: ILO.

International Monetary Fund 2006, *Global financial stability report: market developments and issues*, Washington DC: IMF.

International Monetary Fund 2010, *Factsheet: IMF standing borrowing arrangements*, available at www.imf.org/external/np/exr/facts/gabnab.htm.

IPPNW 2005, *International Physicians for the Prevention of Nuclear War: international campaign to prevent small arms violence*, www.ippnw.org.

Jackson, J. H. 2008, 'The case of the World Trade Organization', *International Affairs* 84(3): 437–54.

Jackson, Patrick Thaddeus 2005, 'Relational constructivism: the NATO bombing campaign as a war of words', in Jennifer Sterling-Folker (ed.), *Making sense of IR theory*, Boulder, CO: Lynne Rienner.

Jackson, Patrick Thaddeus 2010, *The conduct of inquiry in International Relations: philosophy of science and its implications for the study of world politics*, London: Routledge.

Jackson, Richard et.al. 2011, *Terrorism: a critical introduction*, Basingstoke: Palgrave Macmillan.

Jacobsen, Karen 2006, 'Refugees and asylum seekers in urban areas: a livelihoods perspective', *Journal of Refugee Studies*, 19(3): 273–86.

Jakobsen, Janet and Pellegrini, Ann (eds) 2008, *Secularisms*, Durham: Duke University Press.

James, Alan 1986, *Sovereign statehood: the basis of international society*, St Leonards: Allen & Unwin.

James, C. L. R. [1938] (2001) *The Black Jacobins*, Harmondsworth: Penguin.

James, Jeffrey 2006, 'Misguided investments in meeting Millennium Development Goals: a reconsideration using ends-based targets', *Third World Quarterly*, 27(3): 443–58.

Jameson, Fredric 1984, 'Postmodernism or the cultural logic of late capitalism', *New Left Review* 146.

Jarvis, Darryl S. L. 2000, *International relations and the challenge of postmodernism: defending the discipline*, Columbia: University of South Carolina Press.

Jarvis, Darryl S. L. (ed.) 2002, *International relations and the 'third debate': postmodernism and its critics*, Westport: Praeger.

Jay, Martin 1973, *The dialectical imagination: a history of the Frankfurt School and the Institute of Social Research, 1923–1950*, London: Heinemann.

Jeffery, Renée 2005, 'Tradition as invention: the "traditions tradition" and the history of ideas in international relations', *Millennium: Journal of International Studies* 34(1): 57–84.

Jennings, Francis, Fenton, William, Druke, Mary and Miller, D. (eds) 1985, *The history and culture of Iroquois diplomacy: an interdisciplinary guide to the treaties of The Six Nations and their league*, Syracuse University Press: Syracuse.

Jensen, Kenneth (ed.) 1993, *The origins of the Cold War: the Novikov, Kennan, and Roberts 'Long Telegrams' of 1946*, revised edition, Washington: US Institute of Peace Press.

Jervis, Robert 1976, *Perception and misperception in international politics*, Princeton: Princeton University Press.

Jervis, Robert 1979, 'Deterrence theory revisited', *World Politics*, January 31(2).

Joachim, J. 2003, 'Framing issues and seizing opportunities: the UN, NGOs and women's rights', *International Studies Quarterly* 47(2).

Joffe, Josef 1995, 'Bismarck or Britain? Toward an American grand strategy after bipolarity', *International Security*, 19(4): 94–117.

Joffe, Josef 1998, *The great powers*, London: Phoenix.

Johnson, Chalmers 2000, *Blowback: the costs and consequences of American empire*, New York: Henry Holt.

Johnson, J. T. 1999, *Morality and contemporary warfare*, New Haven: Yale University Press.

Jones, James 2008, *Blood that cries out from the earth: the psychology of religious terrorism*, Oxford: Oxford University Press.

Jones, Roy E. 1981, 'The English School of international relations: a case for closure', *Review of International Studies* 7: 1–13.

Jönsson, Christer and Hall, Martin 2005, *Essence of diplomacy*, Basingstoke UK: Palgrave Macmillan.

Josselin, D. and Wallace W. 2001, 'Non-state actors in world politics: a framework' in W. Wallace (ed.), *Non-state actors in world politics*, London: Palgrave Macmillan.

Juergensmeyer, Mark 1993, *The new Cold War? religious nationalism confronts the secular state*, Berkeley: University of California Press.

Kacowicz, A. 2007, 'Globalization, poverty and the North-South divide', *International Studies Review* 9(4): 565–80.

Kaempf, Sebastian 2008, 'Waging war in the new media age: images as strategic weapons and the ethics of contemporary warfare', in Glen Creeber and Royston D. Martin (eds), *Digital cultures: understanding new media*, Maidenhead, UK: Open University Press.

Kaldor, Mary 1990, *The imaginary war: understanding East–West conflict*, Oxford: Blackwell.

Kaldor, Mary 1999, *New and old wars: organised violence in a global era*, Stanford: Stanford University Press.

Kaldor, Mary 2006, *New and old wars: organized violance in a global era*, 2nd edition, Cambridge: Cambridge Polity Press.

Kaldor, Mary, Anheier, Helmut and Glasius, Marlies 2003, *Global civil society 2003*, London: Centre for the Study of Global Governance.

Kamat, S. 2004, 'The privatization of public interest: theorizing INGO discourse in a neoliberal era', *Review of International Political Economy* 5(4): 585–615.

Kamenka, Eugene (ed.) 1975, *Nationalism: the nature and evolution of an idea*, Canberra: ANU Press.

Kant, Immanuel [1795] 1970, 'Perpetual peace: a philosophical sketch', in *Kant's political writings*, ed. Hans Reiss, trans. H. B. Nisbet, Cambridge: Cambridge University Press.

Kant, Immanuel [1785] 1987, *Fundamental principles of the metaphysic of morals*, trans. T. K. Abbott, Buffalo NY: Prometheus Books.

Karnow, Stanley 1994, *Vietnam: a history*, revised and updated edition, London: Pimlico.

Karns, M. P. and Mingst, K. A. 2010, *International organizations: the politics and processes of global governance*, 2nd edition, Boulder: Lynne Rienner Publishers.

Katzenstein, Peter J. (ed.) 1996, *The culture of national security: norms and identity in world politics*, New York: Columbia University Press.

Katzenstein, Peter J. 2006, 'Multiple modernities as limits to secular Europeanization?' in Timothy A. Bynes and Peter J. Katzenstein (eds.), *Religion in an expanding Europe*, Cambridge: Cambridge University Press.

Katzenstein, Peter J. and Byrnes, Timothy A. (eds.) 2006. *Religion in an expanding Europe*. Cambridge: Cambridge University Press.

Katzenstein, Peter J. and Sil, R. 2004, 'Rethinking Asian security: the case for analytical eclecticism' in J. J. Suh, P. J. Katzenstein, and P. Carlson (eds), *Rethinking security in East Asia: identity, power and efficiency*, Stanford: Stanford University Press.

Keal, Paul 1984, *Unspoken rules and superpower dominance*, Houndmills: Macmillan.

Keal, Paul 2003, *European conquest and the rights of indigenous peoples: the moral backwardness of international society*, Cambridge: Cambridge University Press.

Keane, John 2000, 'Secularism?' in David Marquand and Ronald L. Nettler (eds), *Religion and democracy*, Oxford: Blackwell Publishers.

Keck, Margaret and Sikkink, Kathryn 1998, *Activists beyond borders: advocacy networks in international politics*, Ithaca: Cornell University Press.

Keene, Edward 2002, *Beyond the anarchical society: Grotius, colonialism and order in world politics*, Cambridge: Cambridge University Press.

Keene, Edward 2005, *International political thought: a historical introduction*, Cambridge: Polity Press.

Keeton, George W. 1939, *National sovereignty and international order: an essay upon the international community and international order*, London: Peace Book Company.

Kegley, Charles W. Jr. 1993, 'The neoidealist moment in international studies? Realist myths and the new international realities', *International Studies Quarterly* 37: 131–46.

Kegley, Charles W. Jr. (ed.) 1995, *Controversies in international relations theory; realism and the neoliberal challenge*, New York: St Martin's Press.

Kellow, A. 2002, 'Comparing business and public interest associability at the international level', *International Political Science Review*, 23(2).

Kennan, George ['X'] 1946, 'The sources of Soviet conduct', *Foreign Affairs* 25: 566–82.

Kennan, George 1951, *American diplomacy 1900–1950*, Chicago: University of Chicago Press.

Kennan, George 1958, *The Reith lectures*, London: British Broadcasting Corporation.

Kennan, George 1996, 'Morality and foreign policy', in *At a century's ending: reflections 1982–1995*, New York: W. W. Norton.

Kennedy, Paul 1994, 'Conclusions', in Geir Lundestad (ed.), *The fall of great powers: peace, stability, and legitimacy*, Oxford: Oxford University Press.

Keohane, Robert O. 1984, *After hegemony: cooperation and discord in the world political economy*, Princeton, NJ: Princeton University Press.

Keohane, Robert O. 1986, *Neorealism and its critics*, New York: Columbia University Press.

Keohane, Robert O. 1989, *International institutions and state power; essays in international relations theory*, Boulder: Westview.

Keohane, Robert O. 2002, 'The globalization of informal violence' in Craig J. Calhoun, Paul Price and Ashley Timmer (eds), *Understanding September 11*, New York: W. W. Norton & Co.

Keohane, Robert O. and Nye, Joseph S. [1977] 1989, *Power and interdependence: world politics in transition*, Boston: Little, Brown.

Keohane, Robert O. and Nye, Joseph S. 2001, *The club model of multilateral cooperation and the World Trade Organization: problems of democratic legitimacy*, John F. Kennedy School of Government, Harvard University, Visions of Governance in the 21st Century Working Paper 4, available at www.ksg.harvard.edu/visions/publication/keohane_nye.pdf.

Kerr, William A. 2005, 'Vested interests in queuing and the loss of the WTO's Club Good; the long-run costs of US bilateralism', *The Estey Centre Journal of International Law and Trade Policy* 6(1): 1–10.

Khatchadourian, Raffi 2007, 'Azzam the American: the making of an Al Qaeda homegrown', *The New Yorker*, 22 January.

Kiely, R. 2005, 'The changing face of anti-globalization politics', *Globalizations* 2(1): 134–50.

Kirschner, Jonathan (ed.) 2003, *Monetary orders*, Ithaca: Cornell University Press.

Kissinger, Henry 1964, *A world restored*, New York: Grosset and Dunlap.

Kissinger, Henry 1994, *Diplomacy*, New York: Touchstone.

Klein, Naomi 2001, 'Reclaiming the commons', *New Left Review* 9, May/Jun.

Kohn, Hans [1944] 1967, *The idea of nationalism*, London: Collier.

Krasner, Stephen D. (ed.) 1983, *International regimes*, Ithaca: Cornell University Press.

Krasner, Stephen D. 1999, *Sovereignty: organized hypocrisy*, Princeton: Princeton University Press.

Kratochwil, Friedrich 1989, *Rules, norms and decisions*, Cambridge: Cambridge University Press.

Kubálková, Vendulka and Cruickshank, Albert 1985, *Marxism and international relations*, Oxford: Clarendon Press.

Kwa, A. 2003, *Power politics in the WTO*, Bangkok: Focus on the Global South.

Kymlicka, Will 2007, *Multicultural odysseys: navigating the new international politics of diversity*, Oxford: Oxford University Press.

Laffey, Mark and Weldes, Jutta 1997, 'Beyond belief: ideas and symbolic technologies in the study of international relations', *European Journal of International Relations* 3(2): 193–237.

Lake, David A. 1996, 'Anarchy, hierarchy, and the variety of international relations', *International organization* 50(1): 1–33.

Lambourne, Wendy and Herro, Annie 2008, 'Peacebuilding theory and the United Nations Peacebuilding Commission: implications for non-UN interventions', *Global Change, Peace and Security*, 20 (3): 275–89.

Lamy, S. 2005, 'Contemporary mainstream approaches: neorealism and neoliberalism' in John Baylis and Steve Smith (eds), *The globalization of world politics*, 3rd edition, Oxford: Oxford University Press.

Langhorne, Richard 1992, 'The regulation of diplomatic practice: the beginnings to the Vienna Convention on Diplomatic Relations, 1961', *Review of International Studies* 18(1):3–17.

Langlois, Anthony 2001, *The politics of justice and human rights: Southeast Asia and universalist theory*, Cambridge: Cambridge University Press.

Lanoszka, A. 2009, *The World Trade Organization: changing dynamics in the global political economy*, Boulder and London: Lynne Rienner.

Lapid, Yosef 1989a, '*Quo vadis* international relations? Further reflections on the "next stage" of international theory', *Millennium: Journal of International Studies* 18(1): 77–88.

Lapid, Yosef 1989b, 'The third debate: on the prospects of international theory in a post-positivist era', *International Studies Quarterly* 33(3): 235–54.

Larsen, Jeffrey A. (ed.) 2002, *Arms control: cooperative security in a changing environment*, Boulder: Lynne Rienner Publishers.

Larsen, Jeffrey A. and Wirtz, James J. (eds) 2009, *Arms control and cooperative security*, Boulder: Lynne Rienner Publishers.

Larson, D. W. 1985, *The origins of containment: a psychological explanation*, Princeton: Princeton University Press.

Lawrence, T. J. 1919, *The society of nations: its past, present and possible future*, New York, Oxford University Press.

Lebow, R. N. 2003, *The tragic vision of politics: ethics, interests and orders*, Cambridge: Cambridge University Press.

Lebow, R. N. 2008, *A cultural theory of international relations*, Cambridge: Cambridge University Press.

Lebow, R. N. 2010, *Forbidden fruit: counterfactuals and international relations*, Princeton: Princeton University Press.

Lee-Koo, Katrina 2002, 'Confronting a disciplinary blindness: women, war and rape in the international politics of security', *Australian Journal of Political Science* 37: 525–36.

Lee-Koo, Katrina 2007, 'Security as enslavement, security as emancipation: gendered legacies and feminist futures in the Asia-Pacific' in Anthony Burke and Matt McDonald (eds), *Critical security in the Asia-Pacific*, Manchester: Manchester University Press.

Lee-Koo, Katrina 2008, '"War on Terror"/"War on Women"', in R. Bleiker, A. Bellamy, R. Devetak and S. Davies (eds), *Security and the 'war on terror'*, London: Routledge.

Leguey-Feilleux, Jean-Robert 2009, *The dynamics of diplomacy*, Boulder, CO: Lynne Rienner.

Leonard, Vidhya and Alakeson, Leonard 2000, *Going public: diplomacy for the information society*, Foreign Policy Centre, London.

Levy, David and Newell, Peter 2002 'Business strategy and international environmental governance: toward a neo-Gramscian synthesis' *Global Environmental Politics* 2(4): 84–101.

Levy, David and Newell, Peter (eds.) 2005 *The business of global environmental governance*, Cambridge MA: MIT Press.

Levy, Jack S. 1983, *War in the modern great power system, 1495–1975*, Lexington: University Press of Kentucky.

Levy, Jack. S. 1986, 'Organizational routines and the causes of war', *International Studies Quarterly*, 30:193–222.

Levy, Jack S. 1998, 'The causes of war and the conditions of peace', *Annual Review of Political Science* 1: 139–65.

Levy, Jack S. and Thompson, William R. 2010, *Causes of war*, Chichester: Wiley-Blackwell.

Linklater, Andrew 1982, *Men and citizens in the theory of international relations*, London: Macmillan.

Linklater, Andrew 1990, *Beyond Realism and Marxism: critical theory and international relations*, London: Palgrave Macmillan.

Linklater, Andrew 1996, 'The achievements of critical theory' in Steve Smith, Ken Booth, Marysia Zalewski (eds), *International theory: positivism and beyond*, Cambridge: Cambridge University Press.

Linklater, Andrew 1997, 'The transformation of political community: E.H. Carr, critical theory and international relations', *Review of International Studies*, 23, pp. 321–338

Linklater, Andrew 1998, *The transformation of political community: ethical foundations of the post-Westphalian era*, Cambridge: Polity Press.

Linklater, Andrew 2007, 'Distant suffering and cosmopolitan obligations', *International Politics*, 44(1): 19–36.

Linklater, Andrew, and Suganami, Hidemi, 2006, *The English School of international relations: a contemporary reassessment*, Cambridge: Cambridge University Press.

Lipson, Charles 1985, *Standing guard*, Berkeley: University of California Press.

Litfin, Karen 1994, *Ozone discourses*, New York: Columbia University Press.

Locke, John [1690] 1988, *Two treatises of government*, Peter Laslett (ed.), Cambridge: Cambridge University Press.

Loescher, Gil, Milner, James, Newman, Edward and Troeller, Gary (eds) 2008, *Protracted refugee situations: political, human rights and security implications*, Tokyo: United Nations University Press. An edited volume that explores the causes of protracted refugee situations, the roles of different actors in seeking to remedy these situations, and specific cases of refugees living in these situations, i.e. Afghan, Palestininan, Somali, Sudanese, Bhutanese and Burmese populations.

Low, Nicholas and Gleeson, Brendan 1998, *Justice, society and nature: an exploration of political ecology*, London: Routledge.

Lowe, Vaughan, Roberts, Adam, Welsh, Jennifer and Zaum, Dominik 2008, *The United Nations Security Council and war: the evolution of thought and practice since 1945*, Oxford: Oxford University Press.

Luard, Evan, 1986, *War in international society*, London: I. B. Tauris.

Luttwak, E. N. 1987, *Strategy: the logic of war and peace*, Cambridge: Harvard University Press.

Lyotard, Jean-François 1979, *La condition postmoderne*, Paris: Les Editions de Minuit.

Lyotard, Jean-François 1984, *The postmodern condition: a report on knowledge*, trans. Geoffrey Bennington and Brian Massumi, Minneapolis: University of Minnesota Press.

Lyotard, Jean-François [1988] 1991, 'Rewriting modernity' in *The inhuman: reflections on time*, trans. Geoffrey Bennington and Rachel Bowlby, Stanford: Stanford University Press.

Machiavelli, Niccolò [1513] 1998, *The prince*, trans. Peter Bondanella and Mark Musa, Oxford: Oxford University Press.

Mahmood, Saba 2005, *Politics of piety: the Islamic revival and the feminist subject*, Princeton: Princeton University Press.

Make Poverty History campaign 2005, Make Poverty History website, www.makepovertyhistory. org.

Mallaby, Sebastian 2002, 'The reluctant imperialist: terrorism, failed states and the case for American empire', *Foreign Affairs*, 81(2): 2–7.

Maloney, Suzanne 2002, 'Identity and change in Iran's foreign policy,' in Shibley Telhami and Michael Barnett (eds), *Identity and foreign policy in the Middle East*, Ithaca: Cornell University Press.

Mann, Michael 1986, *The sources of social power*, Vol. 1, Cambridge: Cambridge University Press.

Marr, David and Wilkinson, Marian 2003, *Dark victory*, Sydney: Allen and Unwin.

Martens, K. 2006, 'Professionalised representation of human rights NGOs to the United Nations', *The International Journal of Human Rights* 10(1).

Marx, Karl [1848] 1977, 'Communist manifesto', in *Karl Marx: selected writings*, ed. David McLellan, Oxford: Oxford University Press.

Marx, Karl and Engels, Friedrich 1977, *Karl Marx: selected writings*, ed. David McLellan, Oxford: Oxford University Press.

Mattingly, Garret 1955, *Renaissance diplomacy*, London: Jonathan Cape.

Mayall, James 1990, *Nationalism and international society*, Cambridge: Cambridge University Press.

Mazower, Mark 2009, *No enchanted palace: the end of empire and the ideological origins of the United Nations*, Princeton, NJ: Princeton University Press.

McCauley, Clark 2007, 'Psychological issues in understanding terrorism and the response to terrorism' in Bruce Bongar, Lisa M. Brown, Larry E. Beutler, James N. Breckenridge and Philip G. Zimbardo (eds), *Psychology of terrorism*, New York: Oxford University Press.

McCauley, Clark and Moskalenko, Sophia 2008, 'Mechanisms of political radicalization: pathways toward terrorism', *Terrorism and Political Violence*, 20(3): 415–33.

McCleary, Rachel 2009, *Global compassion: private voluntary organizations and U.S. foreign policy since 1939*, Oxford: Oxford University Press.

McChesney, R. 2001, 'Global media, neoliberalism and imperialism', *Monthly Review*, March.

McDonald, H., Ball, D., Dunn, J., Van Klinken, G., Bourchier, D., Kammen, D. and Tanter, R. 2002, *Masters of terror: Indonesia's military and violence in East Timor in 1999*, Canberra Papers on Strategy and Defence No. 145, Canberra: Strategic and Defence Studies Centre, ANU.

McDonald, Matt 2005, 'Be alarmed? Australia's anti-terrorism kit and the politics of security', *Global Change, Peace & Security* June 17(2).

McDonough, D.S. 2006, 'Nuclear superiority: the "new triad" and the evolution of nuclear strategy', *Adelphi Paper*, 383, London: IISS and Routledge.

McGrane, Bernard 1989, *Beyond anthropology: society and the other*, New York: Columbia University Press.

McGrew, Anthony 2007, 'Globalization in hard times: contention in the academy and beyond' in G. Ritzer (ed.), *Blackwell research handbook on globalization*, Oxford: Blackwell.

McGuire, P. and Tarashev, N. 2006, 'Tracking international bank flows', *BIS Quarterly Review*, 11 December.

McKeogh, C. 2002, *Innocent civilians: the morality of killing in war*, London: Palgrave.

McMichael, Philip 2006, 'Peasant prospects in the neoliberal age', *New Political Economy*, 11(3): 407–18.

McMichael, Philip 2008, *Development and social change: a global perspective*, 3rd edition, Thousand Oaks: Pine Forge Press.

McMichael, Philip (ed.) 2010, *Contesting development: critical struggles for social change*, London and New York: Routledge.

McNamara, R. S. and Blight, J. G. 2003, *Wilson's ghost*, New York: PublicAffairs.

Meadows, Donella H., Meadows, Dennis L., Randers, Jorgen, Behrens III, William H. (eds) 1972, *The limits to growth*, New York: Universe Books.

Mearsheimer, John J. 2001, *The tragedy of great power politics*, New York: W. W. Norton & Co.

Mearsheimer, John J. 2005, 'Hans Morgenthau and the Iraq War: realism versus neo-conservatism', *Open Democracy*, available at www.opendemocracy.net/democracy-americanpower/morgenthau_2522.jsp.

Mearsheimer, John J. 2007, 'Structural realism' in Tim Dunne, Milja Kurki and Steve Smith (eds), *International relations theories*, Oxford: Oxford University Press.

Mearsheimer, John J. and Walt, Stephen 2003, 'Iraq: an unnecessary war', *Foreign Policy* 134: 50–9.

Meinecke, Friedrich 1962, *Machiavellism: the doctrine of raison d'état and its place in modern history*, trans. D. Scott, New Haven: Yale University Press.

Migdal, Joel 2001, *State in society: studying how states and societies transform and constitute one another*, Cambridge: Cambridge University Press.

Mill, John Stuart [1859] 1983, *On liberty*, Harmondsworth: Penguin Books.

Miller, David 1999, 'Bounded citizenship' in K. Hutchings and R. Dannreuther (eds), *Cosmopolitan citizenship*, Houndmills: Macmillan.

Miller, David and Dinan, William 2003, 'Global public relations and global capitalism', in David Demers (ed.), *Terrorism, globalization and mass communication*, Spokane, WA: Marquette Books.

Miller, J. D. B. 1981, *A world of states*, London: Croom Helm.

Minear, Larry 2002, *The humanitarian enterprise: dilemmas and discoveries*, West Hartford, Conn.: Kumarian.

Mirsepassi, Ali 2000, *Intellectual discourse and the politics of modernization: negotiating modernity in Iran*, Cambridge: Cambridge University Press.

Modelski, George 1987, *Long cycles in world politics*, London: Macmillan.

Moghaddan, Fathi 2005, 'The staircase to terrorism: a psychological exploration', *American Psychologist*, 60(2): 161–9.

Mohanty, Chandra 1984, 'Under Western eyes: feminist scholarship and colonial discourses', *boundary 2*, 12/13(1): 333–58.

Moon, Parker Thomas 1925, *Syllabus on international relations*, New York, MacMillan.

Montesquieu, Charles-Louis de Secondat [1748] 2000, *The spirit of laws*, A. M. Cohler, B. C. Miller and H. S. Stone (eds), Cambridge: Cambridge University Press.

Montevideo Convention on the Rights and Duties of States, 26 December 1933, available at www.cfr.org/sovereignty/montevideo-convention-rights-duties-states/p15897.

Morgenthau, Hans J. 1946, *Scientific man versus power politics*, Chicago: University of Chicago Press.

Morgenthau, Hans J. 1972, 'From great powers to superpowers', in B. Porter (ed.), *The Aberystwyth papers: international politics, 1919–1969*, London: Oxford University Press.

Morgenthau, Hans J. [1948] 1973, *Politics among nations: the struggle for power and peace*, 5th edition, New York: Alfred Knopf.

Morgenthau, Hans J. 2010, *Il concetto del politico. Contra Schmitt*, ed. Alessandro Campi, Soveria Mannelli: Rubbettino.

Morton, Adam 2002, '"La Resurrección del Maíz": globalisation, resistance and the Zapatistas', *Millennium*, 31(1): 27–54.

Mosley, Layna 2003, *Global capital and national governments*, New York: Cambridge University Press.

Mosley, P. 2004, 'The IMF after the Asian crisis: merits and limitations of the "lender of last resort" role', *The World Economy* 24(5): 597–629.

Mount, Gavin 2000, 'A world of tribes?' in Greg Fry and Jacinta O'Hagan (eds), *Contending images of world politics*, Macmillan.

Mount, Gavin 2010, *The problem of peoples: global politics, ethnicity and the struggle for legitimacy*, LAP Lambert.

Munck, Ronaldo and O'Hearn, Denis (eds) 1999, *Critical development theory – contributions to a new paradigm*, London: Zed Books.

Münkler, Herfried 2006, *Vom Krieg zum Terror*, Zurich: VonTobel Stiftung.

Murray, Al 1997, *Reconstructing realism: between power politics and cosmopolitan ethics*, Edinburgh: Keele University Press.

Muthu, S. 2003, *Enlightenment against empire*, Princeton: Princeton University Press.

Najmabadi, Afsaneh 2008, '(Un)veiling feminism', in *Secularisms*, Janet R. Jakobsen and Ann Pellegrini (eds), Duke University Press.

Nandy, Ashis 1987, *Traditions, tyranny and utopias: essays in the politics of awareness*, Oxford and New Delhi: Oxford University Press.

Nandy, Ashis 2002, 'The beautiful, expanding future of poverty: popular economics as a psychological defense', *International Studies Review*, 4(2): 107–121.

Nash, Manning 1989, *The cauldron of ethnicity in the modern world*, Chicago: Chicago University Press.

National Commission on Terrorist Attacks Against the United States 2004, *The 9/11 commission report*, New York and London: W. W. Norton & Co.

Neufeld, Mark 1995, *The restructuring of international relations theory*, Cambridge: Cambridge University Press.

Neumann, Iver B. 1999, *Uses of the other*, Minneapolis: University of Minnesota Press.

Neumann, Iver B. and Welsh, Jennifer 1991, 'The other in European self-definition: an addendum to the literature on international society', *Review of International Studies* 17: 327–48.

Newell, Peter 2000, *Climate for change: non-state actors and the global politics of the greenhouse*, Cambridge: Cambridge University Press.

Newell, Peter 2008, 'The marketisation of global environmental governance: manifestations and implications' in Parks, J. Conca, K. and Finger, M. (eds.) *The crisis of global environmental governance: towards a new political economy of sustainability*, London: Routledge

Newell, Peter and Paterson, Matthew 1998, 'Climate for business: global warming, the state and capital', *Review of International Political Economy*, 5(4).

Newell, Peter and Paterson, Matthew 2010, *Climate capitalism: global warming and the transformation of the global economy,* Cambridge: Cambridge University Press.

Newfang, Oscar 1924, *The road to world peace: a federation of nations*, New York, Putnam.

Newman, Edward 2006, 'Exploring the "root causes" of terrorism', *Studies in Conflict and Terrorism* 29(8): 749–51.

Nicolson, Harold 1954, *The evolution of the diplomatic method*, London: Macmillan.

Nicolson, Harold [1939] 1969, *Diplomacy*, London: Oxford University Press.

Niebuhr, Reinhold 1953, *Moral man and immoral society: a study in ethics and politics*, New York: Charles Scribner's Sons.

Nietzsche, Friedrich [1882] 1974, *The gay science*, trans. Walter Kaufmann, New York: Random House.

Nolan, P., Sutherland, D. and Zhang J. 2002, 'The challenge of the global business revolution', *Contributions to Political Economy* 21: 91–110.

Numelin, Ragnar 1950, *The beginnings of diplomacy: a sociological study of intertribal and international relations*, London and Copenhagen: Oxford University Press and Ejnar Munksgaard.

Nussbaum, M. (ed.) 1996, *For love of country; debating the limits of patriotism*, revised edition, Boston: Beacon Press.

Nye, Joseph S. 1988, 'Neorealism and neoliberalism', *World Politics* 40(2): 235–251.

Nye, Joseph S. 1990, *Bound to lead*, New York: Basic Books.

Obama, Barack 2009, 'Protecting our security and our values', speech delivered at National Archives Museum, Washington DC, 19 May.

Oberdorfer, Don 1998, *From the Cold War to a new era*, Baltimore: Johns Hopkins University Press.

O'Brien, R., Goetz, Anne Marie, Scholte, Jan Aart and Williams, Marc 2000, *Contesting global governance*, Cambridge: Cambridge University Press.

O'Brien, R. and Williams, M. 2004, *Global political economy: evolution and dynamics*, Basingstoke: Palgrave Macmillan.

O'Brien, Robert and Williams, Marc 2010, *Global political economy: evolution and dynamics*, London: Palgrave.

OECD 2007, *Principles for good international engagement in fragile states and situations*, available at www.oecd.org/dataoecd/61/45/38368714.pdf.

OECD 2008, *Statebuilding in times of fragility*, Paris: OECD.

Ohmae, K. 1995, *The end of the nation state: the rise of regional economies*, London: Harper Collins.

Olson, William, 1972, 'The growth of a discipline' in Brian Porter (ed.), *The Aberystwyth papers: international politics 1919–1969*, London: Oxford University Press.

Öniş, Z. and Şenses, F. 2005, 'Rethinking the emerging post-Washington consensus' *Development and Change* 36 (2): 263–90.

Onuf, Nicholas 1989, *World of our making*, Columbia: University of South Carolina Press.

Onuf, Nicholas 1998, 'Constructivism: a user's manual', in Vendulka Kubálková, Nicholas Onuf, and Paul Klowert (eds), *International relations in a constructed world*, Armonk, NY: M. E. Sharpe.

Orford, Anne 1999, 'Muscular humanitarianism: reading the narratives of the new interventionism', *European Journal of International Law*, 10(4): 679–711.

Organski, A. F. K. and Kugler, Jacek 1980, *The war ledger*, Chicago: The University of Chicago Press.

Orwell, George 1945, 'Notes on nationalism', *Polemic*, London, May, available at http://orwell.ru/library/essays/nationalism/english/e_nat.

Østerud, Øyvind 1996, 'Antinomies of postmodernism in international studies', *Journal of Peace Research* 33(4): 385–90.

Ottaway, M. 2001, 'Corporatism goes global: international organizations, non-governmental organization networks and transnational business', *Global Governance* 7(3).

Pagden, Anthony 1993, *European encounters with the new world: from renaissance to romanticism*, New Haven: Yale University Press.

Palme Commission 1982, *Common security – a programme for disarmament: the report of the Independent Commission on Disarmament and Security Issues*, London and Sydney: Pan.

Paris, Roland 2003, 'Peacekeeping and the constraints of global culture', *European Journal of International Relations*, 9(3): 441–73.

Paris, Roland 2004, *At war's end: building peace after civil conflict*, Cambridge: Cambridge University Press.

Parsons, Craig 2006, *A certain idea of Europe*, Ithaca, NY: Cornell University Press.

Pastor, Robert A. and Hoffmann, Stanley H. (eds) 1999, *A century's journey: how the great powers shape the world*, New York: Basic Books.

Patel, Raj 2008, *Stuffed and starved: the hidden battle for the world food system*, Brooklyn, NJ: Melville House.

Paterson, Matthew 1996, *Global warming, global politics,* London: Routledge.

Paterson, Matthew 2009, 'Post-hegemonic climate change?' *British Journal of Politics and International Relations* 11(1), 140–58.

Paterson, Matthew and Grubb, Michael 1992 'The international politics of climate change', *International Affairs* 68(2): 293–310.

Paterson, Matthew, Humphreys, D. and Pettiford, L. 2003, 'Conceptualizing global environmental governance: from interstate regimes to counter-hegemonic struggles', *Global Environmental Politics* 3(2): 1–7.

Pease, K. K. 2006, *International organizations: perspectives on governance in the twenty-first century*, third edition, Upper Saddle River, NJ: Prentice Hall.

Perkovich, George 2005, *Faulty promises: the US–India nuclear deal*, Carnegie Endowment for International Peace, Policy Outlook, September.

Perez de Cuellar, Javier, 1997, *Pilgrimage for peace: a Secretary General's memoir*, London: St. Martin's Press.

Perlez, Jane 2001, 'Arms control nominee defends shifting view', *New York Times*, 30 March.

Petito, Fabio and Hatzopoulos, Pavlos (eds) 2003, *Religion and international relations: the return from exile*. New York: Palgrave Macmillan.

Pettman, Jan Jindy 1996, *Worlding women: a feminist international politics*, Sydney: Allen & Unwin.

Pettman, Jan Jindy 1998, 'Nationalism and after', *Review of International Studies* 24: 149–64.

Philpott, Daniel 2001, *Revolutions in sovereignty: how ideas shaped modern international relations*, Princeton: Princeton University Press.

Picciotto, R. 2003, 'A new World Bank for a new century', in C. R. Goddard, P. Cronin and K. C. Dash (eds), *International political economy: state-market relations in a changing global order*, 2nd edition, Boulder: Lynne Rienner Publishers.

Pieterse, J. 2004, *Globalization or empire?*, London: Routledge.

Pincus, J. R. and Winters, J. A. (eds) 2002, *Reinventing the World Bank*, Ithaca: Cornell University Press.

Pisani-Ferry, J. and Santos, I. 2009, 'Reshaping the global economy', *Finance and Development* 46(1): 8–12.

Pitts, Jennifer 2005, *A turn to empire: the rise of imperial liberalism in Britain and France*, Princeton, NJ: Princeton University Press.

Pogge, Thomas 1989, *Realising Rawls*, Ithaca: Cornell University Press.

Pogge, Thomas 1994, 'Cosmopolitanism and sovereignty' in C. Brown (ed.), *Political restructuring in Europe: ethical perspectives*, London: Routledge.

Pogge, Thomas 2002, *World poverty and human rights: cosmopolitan responsibilities and reforms*, Cambridge: Polity Press.

Pogge, Thomas 2004, 'The first United Nations Millennium Development Goal: a cause for celebration?' *Journal of Human Development* 5(3): 377–97.

Potter, Pitman B. 1929, *This world of nations: foundations, institutions, practices,* New York, Macmillan.

Powaski, R. E. 1998, *The Cold War: the United States and the Soviet Union, 1917–1991*, New York: Oxford University Press.

Powell, Colin 1992–93, 'U. S. forces: challenges ahead', *Foreign Affairs* 71(5): 32–45.

Preece, Jennifer Jackson 1997, 'Minority rights in Europe: from Westphalia to Helsinki', *Review of International Studies* 23: 90–1.

Preece, Jennifer Jackson 2005, *Minority rights: between diversity and community*, Cambridge, Polity.

Price, Matthew E. 2009, *Rethinking asylum: history, purpose, and limits*, Cambridge: Cambridge University Press.

Price, Richard 2003, 'Transnational civil society and advocacy in world politics', *World Politics* 55(4).

Price, Richard and Reus-Smit, Christian 1998, 'Dangerous liaisons? Critical international theory and constructivism', *European Journal of International Relations* 4(3): 259–94.

Quigley, Anita 2006, 'Image better left than right', *The Daily Telegraph*, 5 December.

Rahnema, Majid with Bawtree, Victoria (eds) 1997, *The post-development reader*, London: Zed Books.

Ramsey, P. 1961, *War and the Christian conscience: how shall modern war be conducted justly?*, Durham: Duke University Press.

Ranke, Leopold von [1833] 1950, 'Die grossen Mächte', *Historisch-politische Zeitschrift*, 2(1833): 1–51, English translation 'The Great Powers', in Theodore von Laue, *Leopold Ranke: The formative years*, Princeton: Princeton University Press.

Rasler, Karen A. and Thompson, William R. 1994, *The great powers and global struggle, 1490–1990*, Lexington: The University Press of Kentucky.

Rawls, John 1971, *A theory of justice*, Cambridge: Harvard University Press.

Rawls, John 1999, *The law of peoples*, Cambridge: Harvard University Press.

Reilly, Benjamin 2006, 'Political engineering and party politics in conflict-prone society', *Democratization*, 13 (5): 811–27.

Reimann, K. 2006, 'A view from the top: international politics, norms and the worldwide growth of NGOs', *International Studies Quarterly* 50(1).

Renan, Ernest [1882] 1995, 'What is a nation?' in M. Chabour and M. R. Ishray (eds), *The nationalist reader*, London: The Humanities Press.

Reus-Smit, Christian 1999, *The moral purpose of the state: culture, social identity, and institutional rationality in international relations*, Princeton: Princeton University Press.

Reus-Smit, Christian 2002, 'Imagining international society: constructivism and the English School', *British Journal of Politics and International Relations*, 4(3):487–509.

Reus-Smit, Christian 2004a, *American power and world order*, Cambridge: Polity Press.

Reus-Smit, Christian 2004b, *The politics of international law*, Cambridge: Cambridge University Press.

Reus-Smit, Christian and Snidal, Duncan (eds) 2008, *The Oxford handbook of international relations*, Oxford: Oxford University Press.

Reychler, Luc 1996, 'Beyond traditional diplomacy', *DSP Discussion Papers* 17, Leicester: Centre for the Study of Diplomacy.

Reynolds, Henry 1987, *Frontier*, Sydney: Allen & Unwin.

Ricardo, David [1817] 1973, *The principles of political economy and taxation*, London: Dent.

Rice, Condoleeza 2007, Secretary of State Condoleezza Rice on transformational diplomacy, 8 February, available at http://newdelhi.usembassy.gov/pr022607.html (US Embassy New Delhi).

Richardson, James L. 2001, *Contending liberalisms in world politics: ideology and power*, Boulder: Lynne Rienner Publishers.

Richardson, James L. 2008, 'The ethics of neoliberal institutionalism', in C. Reus-Smit and D. Snidal (eds), *The Oxford handbook of international relations*, Oxford: Oxford University Press.

Richardson, Louise 2006, *What terrorists want: understanding the terrorist threat*, London: John Murray Publishers.

Rid, Thomas and Hecker, Mark 2009, *War 2.0: irregular warfare in the information age*, London: Praeger.

Riedel, Bruce 2010, *The search for al Qaeda: its leadership, ideology, and future*, revised edition, Washington DC: Brookings Institution.

Rieff, David 2002, *A bed for the night*, London: Vintage.

Rieff, David 2008, 'A false compatibility: humanitarian action and human rights', in Jean-Marc Biquet (ed.), *Humanitarian stakes No 1: MSF Switzerland's review on humanitarian stakes and practices*, Geneva: MSF.

Ringmar, Erik 1996, *Identity, interest and action*, Cambridge: Cambridge University Press.

Rittberger, V. and Zangl, B. 2006, *International organization: polity, politics, policies*, New York: Palgrave.

Roach, Steven C. (ed.) 2008, *Critical theory and international relations: a reader*, London: Routledge.

Roach, Steven C. 2010, *Critical theory of international politics*, London: Routledge.

Roberts, Adam 2003, 'Law and the use of force in Iraq', *Survival* 45(2): 31–56.

Roberts, G. 1999, 'The counterproliferation self-help paradigm: a legal regime for enforcing the norm prohibiting the proliferation of weapons of mass destruction', *Denver Journal of International Law and Policy*, 27(3).

Roberts, T. and Parks, B. 2007, *Climate of injustice: global inequality, North-South politics and climate policy*, Cambridge, Mass: MIT Press.

Robinson, W. and Harris, J. 2000, 'Towards a global ruling class? Globalization and the transnational capitalist class', *Science and Society* 64(1): 11–54.

Robison, Richard, Beeson, Mark, Jayasuriya, Kanishka, Kim and Hyuk-Rae 2000, *Politics and markets in the wake of the Asian Crisis*, London: Routledge.

Rodrik, Dani 1999, *The new global economy and developing countries*, Washington: ODC.

Roesad, K. 2000, 'Managing globalisation and human security in Indonesia', *The Indonesian Quarterly* 28(4).

Roht-Arriaza, Naomi 2006, *The Pinochet effect: transnational justice in the age of human rights*, University of Pennsylvannia Press.

Rosecrance, Richard 1986, *The rise of the trading state: commerce and conquest in the modern world*, New York: Basic Books.

Rosenau, James 1992, 'Governance, order, and change in world politics' in James Rosenau and Ernst-Otto Czempiel (eds), *Governance without government: order and change in world politics*, Lexington: Lexington Books.

Rosenau, James and Czempiel, Ernst-Otto 1992, *Governance without government: order and change in world politics*, Cambridge: Cambridge University Press.

Rosenberg, Justin 1994, *The empire of civil society: a critique of the realist theory of international relations*, London: Verso.

Rosenberg, Justin 2000, *Follies of globalisation theory*, London: Verso.

Rostow, Walt 1960, *The stages of economic growth: a non-communist manifesto*, London: Cambridge University Press.

Rotberg, Robert I. 2003, 'Failed states, collapsed states, weak states: causes and indicators', in Robert Rotberg (ed.), *State failure and state weakness in a time of terror*, Washington DC: World Peace Foundation and Brookings Institute Press.

Rousseau, Jean Jacques [c1756] 1917, 'Statement of St. Pierre's project', in *A lasting peace through the federation of Europe and the state of war*, trans. and ed. C. E. Vaughan, London: Constable and Co.

Rowse, Tim 1993, 'Mabo and moral anxiety', *Meanjin* 2: 229–52.

Ruddick, Sara 1989, *Maternal thinking: toward a politics of peace*, Boston: Beacon Press.

Ruggie, John G. 1982, 'International regimes, transactions, and change: embedded liberalism in the postwar economic order', *International Organisation* 36: 379–415.

Ruggie, John G. 1983, 'Continuity and transformation in the world polity: toward a neorealist synthesis', *World Politics*, 35(2): 261–85.

Ruggie, John G. 1998, *Constructing the world polity: essays on international institutionalization*, London: Routledge.

Rupert, Mark 1995, *Producing hegemony: the politics of mass production and American global power*, Cambridge: Cambridge University Press.

Rupert, Mark 2003, 'Globalising common sense: a Marxian-Gramscian (re-)vision of the politics of governance/resistance', *Review of International Studies* 29: 181–98.

Rupert, Mark 2007, 'Marxism and Critical Theory' in T. Dunne, M. Kurki and S. Smith (eds), *International relations theories: discipline and diversity*, Oxford: Oxford University Press.

Rupert, Mark and Solomon, Scott 2006, *Globalization and international political economy*, Lanham: Rowman and Littlefield.

Russell, Ruth B. 1958, *A history of the United Nations Charter: the role of the United States 1940–1945*, Washington DC: The Brookings Institution.

Russett, Bruce 1993, *Grasping the democratic peace: principles for a post-Cold War world*, Princeton: Princeton University Press.

Russett, Bruce 2005, 'Bushwhacking the democratic peace', *International Studies Perspectives* 6: 395–408.

Ruzicka, J. and Wheeler, N.J. 2010, 'The puzzle of trusting relationships in the Nuclear Non-Proliferation Treaty', *International Affairs*, 86(1):69–85.

Sagan, Scott 1989, 'The origins of the Pacific War', in R. I. Rotberg and T. K. Rabb (eds), *The origins and prevention of major wars*, Cambridge: Cambridge University Press.

Sageman, Marc 2004, *Understanding terror networks*, Philadelphia: University of Pennsylvania Press.

Said, Edward 1979, *Orientalism*, New York: Vintage Books.

Santiago, Jose, 2009. 'From "civil religion" to nationalism as the religion of modern times: rethinking a complex relationship', *Journal for the Scientific Study of Religion*, 48(2): 394–401.

Sarkees, Meredith, Reid, Frank, Whelon, Wayman and Singer, David J. 2003, 'Inter-state, intra-state, and extra-state wars: a comprehensive look at their distribution over time, 1816–1997', *International Studies Quarterly* 47(1): 49–70.

Satow, Ernest [1917] 1979, *A guide to diplomatic practice*, 5th edition, London: Longman.

Saurin, Julian 1995, 'The end of international relations? The state and international theory in the age of globalization', in John Macmillan and Andrew Linklater (eds), *Boundaries in question*, London: Pinter.

Saurin, Julian 1996, 'Globalisation, poverty and the promises of modernity', *Millennium: Journal of International Studies*, 25(3): 657–80.

Schaefer, Brett D. 2006, 'A progress report on the U.N.', *Backgrounder* 1937, Washington DC: The Heritage Foundation.

Schaefer, Peter J. 2008, 'Postwar nation-building', *Stability operations and state-building: continuities and contingencies*, Kaufmann, G. (ed.), Carlisle Barracks: Strategic Studies Institute.

Schell, Jonathan 2001, *The unfinished twentieth century: the crisis of weapons of mass destruction*, New York: Verso.

Schelling, Thomas 1960, *The strategy of conflict*, Cambridge: Harvard University Press.

Schelling, Thomas 1966, *Arms and influence*, New Haven: Yale University Press.

Schelling, Thomas C. and Halperin, Morton H. [1961] 1985, *Strategy and arms control*, London: Pergamon-Brassey's.

Schlesinger, Stephen 2003, *Act of creation: the founding of the United Nations*, Boulder, CO: Westview Press.

Schlesinger, Stephen 2008, 'Bush's stealth United Nations policy', *World Policy Journal* 15(2):1–9.

Schmidt, Brian 1998, *The political discourse of anarchy: a disciplinary history of international relations*, Albany: State University of New York Press.

Schmitt, Carl 1976, *The concept of the political*, trans. George Schwab, New Brunswick: Rutgers University Press.

Scholte, Jan Aart 2005, *Globalisation: a critical introduction*, 2nd edition, Basingstoke: Palgrave Macmillan.

Schultz, G., Kissinger, H., Nunn, S. and Perry, W. 2008, 'Toward a nuclear free world', *The Wall Street Journal*, 15 January

Schwartz, Herman M. 2009, *Subprime nation*, Ithaca: Cornell University Press.

Schwartz, Herman M. and Seabrooke, Leonard (eds), 2009, *The politics of property booms*, New York: Palgrave.

Schwartzenberger, Georg 1964, *Power politics: a study of world society*, London: Stevens.

Schweller, Randall L. 1998, *Deadly imbalances: tripolarity and Hitler's strategy of world conquest*, New York: Columbia University Press.

Schweller, Randall L. 2006, *Unanswered threats: political constraints on the balance of power*, Princeton: Princeton University Press.

Scott, Shirley V. 2004a, *International law in world politics: an introduction*, Boulder, CO: Lynne Rienner.

Scott, Shirley V. 2004b, *The political interpretation of multilateral treaties*, Leiden: Martinus Nijhoff.

Seabrooke, Leonard 2001, *US power in international finance: the victory of dividends*, London: Palgrave.

Seabrooke, Leonard 2006a, *The social sources of financial power*, Ithaca: Cornell University Press.

Seabrooke, Leonard 2006b, 'Civilizing global capital markets: room to groove?' in Brett Bowden and Leonard Seabrooke (eds), *Global standards of market civilization*, London: Routledge/ RIPE Series in Global Political Economy.

Searle, John 1995, *The construction of social reality*, Harmondsworth: Penguin Books.

Seib, Philip (ed.) 2009, *Toward a new public diplomacy: redirecting U.S. foreign policy*, Basingstoke, UK: Palgrave Macmillan.

Sen, Amartya 2009, *The idea of justice*, London: Allen Lane.

Senese, P. D. and Vasquez, J. A. 2008, *The steps to war: an empirical study*, Princeton: Princeton University Press.

Seton-Watson, H. 1977, *Nations and states: an enquiry into the origins and the politics of nationalism*, London: Methuen.

Shapcott, Richard 2000, 'Solidarism and after: global governance, international society and the normative "turn" in international relations', *Pacifica Review* 12: 147–65.

Shapcott, Richard 2009, 'Dialogue and International Ethics: Religion, Cultural Diversity and Universalism', in Patrick Hayden (ed.), *The Ashgate Research Companion to Ethics and International Relations*, Surrey: Ashgate.

Shapcott, Richard 2010, *International ethics: a critical introduction*, Cambridge: Polity Press.

Shapiro, Michael J. 1988, 'The constitution of the Central American Other: the case of Guatamala' *The politics of representation*, Madison: University of Wisconsin.

Sharman, J. C. 2006, *Havens in a storm*, Ithaca: Cornell University Press.

Sharp, Paul 2001, 'Making sense of citizen diplomats: the people of Duluth, Minnesota, as international actors', *International Studies Perspectives* 2:131–50.

Sharp, Paul 2009, *Diplomatic theory of international relations*, Cambridge: Cambridge University Press.

Sharp, Paul and Wiseman, Geoffrey (eds) 2007, *The diplomatic corps as an institution of international society,* Basingstoke: Palgrave Macmillan.

Shaw, Malcolm N. 2008, *International law*, 6th edition, Cambridge: Cambridge University Press.

Sheehan, Cindy 2006, 'Matriotism', www.huffingtonpost.com/cindy-sheehan/ matriotism_b_14283.html, 8 March.

Shepherd, Laura (ed.) 2010, *Gender matters in global politics: a feminist introduction to international relations*, London: Routledge.

Shotter, John 1993, *The cultural politics of everyday life*, Milton Keynes: Open University Press.

Shue, Henry 1980, *Basic rights*, Princeton: Princeton University Press.

Shue, Henry 1983, 'The burdens of justice', *The Journal of Philosophy*: 600–8.

Shultz, George, Perry, William, Kissinger, Henry and Nunn, Sam 2007, 'A world free of nuclear weapons', *The Wall Street Journal*, Op-Ed, 4 January.

Silke, Andrew 2003, 'Becoming a terrorist' in Andrew Silke (ed.), *Terrorists, victims and society: psychological perspectives on terrorism and its consequences*, Chichester: John Wiley & Sons Ltd.

Silke, Andrew 2004, 'Courage in dark places: reflections on terrorist psychology', *Social Research* 71(1): 178.

Sinclair, Timothy J. 2005, *The new masters of capital*, Ithaca: Cornell University Press.

Singer, David Andrew 2007, *Regulating capital*, Ithaca: Cornell University Press.

Singer, Peter 2002, *One world: the ethics of globalisation*, Melbourne: Text Publishing.

Singer, Peter and Gregg, Tom 2004, *How ethical is Australia*, Melbourne: Schwartz Publishing.

SIPRI *see* Stockholm International Peace Research Institute.

Sisk, Timothy D. (ed.) 2011, *Between terror and tolerance: religious leaders, conflict and peacemaking*, Washington, DC: Georgetown University Press.

Skinner, Quentin 1989, 'The state' in T. Ball, J. Farr and R. Hanson (eds), *Political innovation and conceptual change*, Cambridge: Cambridge University Press.

Skinner, Quentin 2009, 'A genealogy of the modern state', *Proceedings of the British Academy*, 162: 325–70.

Sklair, Leslie 1997, 'Social movements for global capitalism: the transnational capitalist class in action', *Review of International Political Economy* 4(3): 514–38.

Sklair, Leslie 2001, *The transnational capitalist class*, Oxford: Blackwell.

Skocpol, Theda 1979, *States and social revolutions*, Cambridge: Cambridge University Press.

Slaughter, Amy and Crisp, Jeff 2010, 'A surrogate state? The role of UNHCR in protracted refugee situations', *New issues in refugee research*, Research Paper No. 168, Geneva: United Nations High Commissioner for Refugees.

Slaughter, Steven 2005, *Liberty beyond neoliberalism: a republican critique of liberal governance in a globalising age*, Houndmills: Palgrave.

Sluga, Glenda 1998, 'Identity, gender, and the history of European nations and nationalisms', *Nations and Nationalism* 4(1): 87–111.

Small Arms Survey, 2010, available at www.smallarmssurvey.org/weapons-and-markets.html.

Smillie, Ian and Minear, Larry 2004, *The charity of nations: humanitarian action in a calculating world*, West Hartford, Conn.: Kumarian.

Smith, Adam [1776] 1998, *An inquiry into the nature and causes of the wealth of nations: a selected edition*, Kathryn Sutherland (ed.), Oxford: Oxford University Press.

Smith, Anthony D. 1983, 'Nationalism and classical social theory', *British Journal of Sociology*, 34(1), March.

Smith, Anthony D. 1986, *The ethnic origins of nations*, London: Basil Blackwell.

Smith, Anthony D. 1991, *National identity*, London: Penguin.

Smith, Anthony D. 2000, 'The "sacred" dimension of nationalism', *Millennium*, 29(3): 791–814.

Smith, Anthony D. 2010, *Nationalism: theory, ideology, history*, London: Polity.

Smith, J. and Wiest, D. 2005, 'The uneven geography of global civil society: national and global influences on transnational association', *Social Forces* 84(2).

Smith, Michael J. 1986, *Realist thought from Weber to Kissinger*, Baton Rouge, Louisiana State University Press.

Smith, Michael J. 1992, 'Liberalism and international reform' in Terry Nardin and David R. Mapel (eds), *Traditions of international ethics*, Cambridge: Cambridge University Press.

Smith, Steve 1996, 'Positivism and beyond' in Steve Smith, Ken Booth and Marysia Zalewski (eds), *International theory: positivism and beyond*, Cambridge: Cambridge University Press.

Smith, Steve 2004, 'Singing our world into existence: international relations theory and September 11', *International Studies Quarterly* 48(3): 499–515.

Smith, Steve 2005, 'The contested concept of security' in K. Booth (ed.), *Critical security studies and world politics*, Boulder: Lynne Rienner Publishers.

Smith, Steve, Booth, Ken and Zalewski, Marysia (eds) 1996, *International theory: positivism and beyond*, Cambridge: Cambridge University Press.

Snape, Richard H., Gropp, Lisa and Luttrell, Tas 1998, *Australian trade policy 1965–1997: a documentary history*, Sydney: Allen & Unwin in association with DFAT.

Snyder, Jack 2000, *From voting to violence: democratization and nationalist conflict*, New York, W.W. Norton.

Snyder, Jack (ed.) 2011, *Religion and international relations theory*, New York: Columbia University Press.

Soeane, J. and Taddei, E. 2002, 'From Seattle to Porto Alegre: the anti-neo-liberal globalization movement', *Current Sociology* 50(1): 99–122.

Soroush, Abdolkarim 2002, *Reason, freedom, and democracy in Islam: essential writings of Abdolkarim Soroush*, New York: Oxford University Press.

Spivak, Gayatri 1987, *In other worlds: essays in cultural politics*, New York: Routledge.

Sprinz, Detlef F. and Vaahtoranta, Tapani 1994, 'The interest-based explanation of international environmental policy', *International Organization*, 48 (1): 77–105.

Spruyt, Hendrik 1994, *The sovereign state and its competitors*, Princeton: Princeton University Press.

Stanger, Allison 2009, *One nation under contract*, New Haven, CT: Yale University Press.

Stapleton, Augustus 1866, *Intervention and non-intervention or the foreign policy of Great Britain from 1790 to 1865*. London: Murray.

Steans, Jill 2006, *Gender and international relations: issues, debates and future directions*, second edition, Cambridge: Polity Press.

Stein, Arthur 2008, 'Neoliberal institutionalism' in C. Reus-Smit and D. Snidal (eds), *The Oxford handbook of international relations*, Oxford: Oxford University Press.

Stepan, Alfred, Toft, Monica and Shah, Timothy (eds) 2011, *Rethinking religion and world affairs*, Oxford: Oxford University Press.

Sterba, J. P. 1996, 'Understanding evil: American slavery, the Holocaust, and the conquest of the American Indians', *Ethics* 106(2): 424–48.

Stiglitz, Joseph 2006, *Making globalization work*, London: Norton.

Stockholm International Peace Research Institute 2006, *The SIPRI yearbook 2006: armaments, disarmaments and international security*, Oxford: Oxford University Press.

Stockholm International Peace Research Institute, 2010, *Yearbook*, Chapter 8: 'World Nuclear Forces', Oxford: Oxford University Press, available at www.sipri.org/yearbook/2010/08.

Stowell, Ellery 1921, *Intervention in international law*, Washington, DC: J. Bryne.

Strange, Susan 1988, *States and markets*, London: Pinter Publishers.

Strange, Susan 1992, 'States, firms and diplomacy', *International Affairs* 68(1): 1–15.

Strayer, Joseph, 1965, *Feudalism*, Princeton: Van Nostrand.

Struyk, R. 2002, 'Transnational think-tank networks: purpose, membership and cohesion', *Global Networks* 2(1): 83–90.

Suganami, Hidemi 1978, 'A note on the origin of the word international', *British Journal of International Studies* 4: 226–32.

Suganami, Hidemi 1989, *The domestic analogy and world order proposals*, Cambridge: Cambridge University Press.

Suganami, Hidemi 1996, *On the causes of war*, Oxford: Oxford University Press.

Suhrke, Astri 2007, 'Reconstruction as modernization: the "post-conflict" project in Afghanistan', *Third World Quarterly* 28(7): 1291–308

Sydney Morning Herald 2010, 'Canada takes hard line on Tamil migrants', 18 August.

Sylvester, C. 2002, *Feminist international relations: an unfinished journey*, Cambridge: Cambridge University Press.

Tamimi, Azzam 2000, 'The origins of Arab secularism,' in *Islam and secularism in the Middle East*, John L. Esposito and Azzam Tamimi (eds), New York: New York University Press.

Tannenwald, Nina 1999, 'The nuclear taboo: the United States and the normative basis of the nuclear non-use', *International Organisation* (53)3: 433–68.

Taylor, Charles 2007, *A secular age*, Cambridge, Mass.: Belknap Press.

Taylor, P. 2004, 'The new geography of global civil society: NGOs in the world city network', *Globalizations* 1(2): 265–77.

Tchsirgi, N. 2004, *Post-conflict peacebuilding revisited: achievements, limitations, challenges*, New York: International Peace Academy.

Teschke, Benno 2003, *The myth of 1648: class, geopolitics and the making of modern international relations*, London: Verso.

Teschke, Benno 2004, 'The origins and evolution of the European states-system' in W. Brown, S. Bromley and S. Athreye (eds), *Ordering the international*, London: Pluto Press.

Teubner, G. (ed.) 1997, *Global law without a state*, Aldershot: Ashgate.

Thakur, Ramesh 2001, 'Global norms and international humanitarian law: an Asian perspective', *International Review of the Red Cross* 83 (841): 19–43

Thakur, Ramesh 2002, 'Security in the new millennium', in Andrew Cooper, John English and Ramesh Thakur (eds), *Enhancing global governance: towards a new diplomacy?*, Tokyo: United Nations University Press.

Thakur, Ramesh 2006, *The United Nations, peace and security*, Cambridge: Cambridge University Press.

Thomas, Caroline 2000, *Global governance, development and human security*, London: Pluto Press.

Thomas, N. 1994, *Colonialisms culture: anthropology, travel and government*, Cambridge: Polity Press.

Thomas, N. and Tow, W. 2002, 'The utility of human security: sovereignty and humanitarian intervention', *Security Dialogue* 33(2): 177–92.

Thomas, Scott M. 2005, *The global resurgence of religion and the transformation of international relations: the struggle for the soul of the twenty-first century*. New York: Palgrave Macmillan.

Thomson, Janice 1994, *Mercenaries, pirates, and sovereigns*, Princeton: Princeton University Press.

Thucydides [c. 431 BC] 1972, *History of the Peloponnesian War*, trans. Rex Warner, Harmondsworth: Penguin.

Tickner, J. Ann 1992, *Gender in international relations: feminist perspectives on achieving global security*, New York: Columbia University Press.

Tickner, J. Ann 2001, *Gendering world politics: issues and approaches in the post-Cold War era*, New York: Columbia University Press.

Tickner, J. Ann 2005, 'What is your research program? some feminist answers to international relations methodological questions', *International Studies Quarterly*, 49(1): 1–21.

Tickner, J. Ann and Sjoberg, L. 2007, 'Feminism' in Tim Dunne, Milja Kurki and Steve Smith (eds), *International relations theories*, Oxford: Oxford University Press.

Tilly, Charles 1975, 'Reflections on the history of European state-making' in C. Tilly (ed.), *The formation of national states in Europe*, Princeton: Princeton University Press.

Tilly, Charles 1978, *From mobilisation to revolution*, New York: Random House.

Tilly, Charles 1985, 'War making and state making as organised crime' in P. Evans, D. Rueschemeyer and T. Skocpol (eds), *Bringing the state back in*, Cambridge: Cambridge University Press.

Tilly, Charles 1992, *Coercion, capital and European states*, Cambridge: Basil Blackwell.

Todorov, Tzvetan 1993, *On human diversity: nationalism, racism and exoticism in French thought*, trans. Catherine Porter, Cambridge: Harvard University Press.

Toft, Monica Duffy, Philpott, Daniel and Shah, Timothy Samuel 2011, *God's century: resurgent religion and global politics*, New York: W.W. Norton & Co.

Tonkin, Elizabeth, McDonald, Maryon and Chapman, Malcolm (eds) 1989, *History and ethnicity*, London: Routledge.

Toynbee, Arnold J. 1934, *A study of history*, vol. III: *The growth of civilizations*, Oxford: Oxford University Press.

Toynbee, Arnold J. 1939, *A study of history*, vol. IV: *The breakdown of civilizations*, Oxford: Oxford University Press.

Triggs, Gillian 2006, *International law: contemporary principles and practices*, Chatswood: LexisNexis Butterworths.

Tucker, David 2001, 'What is new about the new terrorism and how dangerous is it?', *Terrorism and Political Violence* 13(3): 1–14.

UK Cabinet Office 2008, *National security strategy of the United Kingdom: security in an interdependent world*, CM 7291, March (London), available at www.official-documents.gov.uk/document/cm72/7291/7291.asp.

Underhill, Geoffrey R. D., Blom, Jasper and Mügge, Daniel (eds) 2010, *Global financial integraton thirty years on,* Cambridge: Cambridge University Press.

UNIFEM 2009, 'Together we must … end violence against women and girls and HIV & AIDS', available at www.unifem.org/attachments/products/TogetherWeMust_en.pdf.

UNIFEM 2010, 'Rapid gender needs assessment of flood affected communities', available at www.unifem.org/attachments/products/PakistanFloods2010_RapidGenderNeeds Assessment_en.pdf.

United Nations 2004, *A more secure world: our shared responsibility*, report of the High-level Panel on Threats, Challenges and Change, New York: UN.

United Nations 2005, *World summit outcome document*, UN document A/60/1, 24 October.

United Nations 2009, *Implementing the responsibility to protect*, report from the Secretary-General, Ban Ki-moon, UN document A/63/677.

United Nations Conference on Trade and Development (UNCTAD) 1991–, *World investment report*, New York: United Nations, www.unctad.org, heading 'Main publications'.

UNCTAD 2005, *World investment report: TNCs and the internationalization of R&D*, New York: United Nations.

UNCTAD 2006, *World investment report: FDI from developing and transition economies, implications for development*, New York: United Nations.

UNCTAD 2009, *World investment report: transnational corporations, agricultural production and development,* New York: United Nations.

United Nations Development Programme (UNDP) 1990–, *Human development report,* New York: United Nations, available at http://hdr.undp.org/reports.

UNDP 2002, *Human development report 2002: deepening democracy in a fragmented world*, New York: United Nations.

UNDP 2005, *Human development report 2005: international cooperation at a crossroads: aid, trade and security in an unequal world*, New York: Oxford University Press.

United Nations Educational Scientific and Cultural Organization (UNESCO) 2010, *Commission on the status of women, 54th session*, February, available at www.un.org/womenwatch/daw/beijing15/index.html.

United Nations Environment Programme 2005, 'Conclusion: main findings', *Millennium ecosystem assessment*, available at www.greenfacts.org/ecosystems/#99.

United Nations High Commissioner for Refugees (UNHCR) 2005, *2004 global refugee trends: overview of refugee populations, new arrivals, durable solutions, asylum-seekers, stateless and other persons of concern to UNHCR*, Geneva: UNHCR, available at www.unhcr.org/statistics/STATISTICS/42b283744.pdf.

UNHCR 2006, *Refugees by numbers, 2005 edition*, available at www.unhcr.org/464062f52.html.

UNHCR 2010, *2009 Global trends: refugees, asylum-seekers, returnees, internally displaced, and stateless persons*, Geneva: United Nations High Commissioner for Refugees.

United Nations Population Fund (UNFPA) 2005, *Gender and changes in tsunami-affected villages in Nanggroe Aceh Darussalam province*, available at www.oxfam.co.uk/what_we_do/issues/conflict_disasters/gender_tsunami.htm.

University of Warwick 2009, *The Warwick Commission on international financial reform*, Coventry: University of Warwick.

US 2002, *The national security strategy of the United States of America*, Washington, DC, September.

Vasquez, J. 1998, *The power of power politics*, 2nd edition, Cambridge: Cambridge University Press.

Vattel, Emer de [1758] 2008, *The law of nations, or, principles of the law of nature, applied to the conduct and affairs of nations and sovereigns*, Béla Kapossy and Richard Whitmore (eds), Indianapolis, Ind: Liberty Fund.

Vattimo, Gianni 1988, *The end of modernity: nihilism and hermeneutics in post-modern culture*, trans. Jon R. Snyder, Cambridge: Polity Press.

Vattimo, Gianni 1992, *The transparent society*, trans. David Webb, Baltimore: Johns Hopkins University Press.

Vickers, R. 2004, 'The new public diplomacy: Britain and Canada compared', *The British Journal of Political and International Relations* 6(2).

Vincent, R. J. 1974, *Non-intervention and the international order*, Princeton: Princeton University Press.

Vincent, R. J. 1986, *Human rights and international relations*, Cambridge: Cambridge University Press.

Vinci, Anthony 2005, 'The strategic use of fear by the Lord's Resistance Army', *Small Wars and Insurgencies* 16(3): 360–81.

Virilio, Paul 1986, *Speed and politics*, trans. Mark Polizzotti, New York: Columbia University Press.

Virilio, Paul 2002, *Desert screen: war at the speed of light*, London: Continuum.

Vitoria, Francisco de 1991, 'On the laws of war' in A. Pagden and J. Lawrence (eds), *Vitoria: political writings*, Cambridge: Cambridge University Press.

Vogler, J. 1995, *The global commons: a regime analysis*, Sussex: Wiley.

Vreeland, J. R. 2003, *The IMF and economic development*, Cambridge: Cambridge University Press.

Wæver, Ole 1998, 'Insecurity, security, and asecurity in the west European non-war community', in Emanuel Adler and Michael Barnett (eds), *Security communities*, Cambridge: Cambridge University Press.

Walker, Martin 1993, *The Cold War and the making of the modern world*, London: Fourth Estate.

Walker, R. B. J. 1987, 'Realism, change and international political theory', *International Studies Quarterly*, 31(1):65–86.

Walker, R. B. J. 1993, *Inside/outside: international relations as political theory*, Cambridge: Cambridge University Press.

Walker, R. B. J. 1994, 'Social movements/world politics', *Millennium: Journal of International Studies* 23(3): 669–700.

Walker, R. B. J. 1995, 'From international relations to world politics', in Joseph Camilleri, Anthony Jarvis, and Albert Paolini (eds), *The state in transition: reimagining political space*, Boulder: Lynne Rienner.

Wallach, L. and Woodall, P. 2004, *Whose trade organization? A comprehensive guide to the WTO*, New York: The New Press.

Wallerstein, Immanuel 1974, 'The rise and future demise of the world capitalist system: concepts for comparative analysis', *Comparative Studies in Society and History*, 16(4): 387–415.

Wallerstein, Immanuel 1979, *The capitalist world-economy: essays*, Cambridge: Cambridge University Press.

Wallerstein, Immanuel 1996, 'The inter-state structure of the modern world-system', in Steve Smith, Ken Booth and Marysia Zalewski (eds), *International theory: positivism and beyond*, Cambridge: Cambridge University Press.

Walt, Stephen M. 1987, *The origins of alliances*, Ithaca: Cornell University Press.

Walt, Stephen M. 1991, 'The renaissance of security studies', *International Studies Quarterly* 35: 211–39.

Walt, Stephen M. 1998, 'International relations: one world, many theories', *Foreign Policy* 110: 29–46.

Waltz, Kenneth N. 1959, *Man, the state and war*, New York: Columbia University Press.

Waltz, Kenneth N. 1979, *Theory of international politics*, New York: Random House.

Waltz, Kenneth N. 1993, 'The emerging structure of international politics', *International Security*, 18(2): 44–79.

Waltz, Kenneth N. 1999, 'Globalization and governance', *PS: Political Science and Politics*, 32: 693–700.

Waltz, Kenneth N. 2000, 'Structural realism after the Cold War', *International Security* 25(1): 5–41.

Walzer, Michael 1977, *Just and unjust wars: a philosophical argument with historical illustrations*, New York: Basic Books.

Webb, Michael C. 1995, *The political economy of policy coordination*, Ithaca: Cornell University Press.

Webb, M. 2004, 'Defining the boundaries of legitimate state practice: norms, transnational actors and the OECD's project on harmful tax competition', *Review of International Political Economy* 11(4): 787–827.

Weber, Cynthia 1995, *Simulating sovereignty: intervention, the state and symbolic exchange*, Cambridge: Cambridge University Press.

Weber, Eugen 1976, *Peasants into Frenchmen: the modernization of rural France, 1880–1914*, Stanford: Stanford University Press.

Weber, Heloise 2004, 'The "new economy" and social risk: banking on the poor', *Review of International Political Economy*, 11(2): 356–86.

Weber, Heloise 2006, 'A political analysis of the PRSP initiative: social struggles and the organization of persistent relations of inequality', *Globalizations*, 3(2):187–206.

Weber, Heloise and Berger, Mark T. (eds) 2009, *Recognition and redistribution: beyond international development*, London: Routledge.

Weber, Martin 2005, 'The critical social theory of the Frankfurt School and the "social turn" in IR', *Review of International Studies* 31(1): 195–209.

Weber, Max 1948, 'Politics as vocation' in H. H. Gerth and C. Wright Mills (eds), *From Max Weber*, New York: Routledge and Kegan Paul.

Weber, Max 1996, 'The origins of ethnic groups' in John Hutchinson and Anthony Smith (eds), *Ethnicity*, Oxford: Oxford University Press.

Weiss, Linda 1998, *The myth of the powerless state*, Ithaca: Cornell University Press.

Weiss, Thomas G. 2004, 'The humanitarian impulse' in David Malone (ed.), *The UN Security Council: from the Cold War to the 21st century*, Boulder, Co.: Lynne Reinner.

Weiss, Thomas G. 2005a, *Military-civilian interactions: humanitarian crises and the responsibility to protect,* 2nd edition, Lanham, MD: Rowman & Littlefield.

Weiss, Thomas G. 2005b, *Overcoming the Security Council reform impasse: the implausible versus the plausible*, Berlin: Friedrich Ebert Stiftung, Occasional Paper 14.

Weiss, Thomas G. 2007, *Humanitarian intervention: ideas in action*, Cambridge: Polity Press.

Weiss, Thomas G. 2010, 'Kenya, acting sooner rather than later', *Great decisions 2010,* New York: Foreign Policy Association: 17–30.

Weiss, Thomas G. and Hubert, Don 2001, *The responsibility to protect: research, bibliography, background*, supplementary volume to the Report of the International Commission on Intervention and State Sovereignty, Ottawa: International Development Research Centre.

Weiss, Thomas G. and Korn. David A. 2006, *Internal displacement: conceptualization and its consequences*, London: Routledge.

Weiss, Thomas G., Cortright, D., Lopez, G.A. and Minear, Larry (eds) 1997, *Political gain and civilian pain: humanitarian impacts of economic sanctions*. Lanham, MD: Rowman & Littlefield.

Wellman, D. J. 2004, *Sustainable diplomacy: religion and ethics in Muslim-Christian relations*, Basingstoke: Palgrave.

Welsch, Wolfgang 1988, 'Postmoderne: Genealogie und Bedeutung eines umstrittenen Begriffes' in Peter Kemper (ed.), *Postmoderne oder der Kampf um die Zukunft*, Frankfurt: Fischer.

Wendt, Alexander 1987, 'The agent-structure problem in international relations theory', *International Organizations* 41, No. 3: 335–70.

Wendt, Alexander 1992, 'Anarchy is what states make of it: the social construction of power politics', *International Organisation* 46(2): 391–425.

Wendt, Alexander 1999, *Social theory of international politics*, Cambridge: Cambridge University Press.

Westad, O. A. 2005, *The global Cold War: Third World interventions and the making of our times*, Cambridge: Cambridge University Press.

Whaites, Alan 2008, *States in development: understanding statebuilding*, DFID Working Paper, London: Department for International Development.

Wheeler, Nicholas J. 1992, 'Pluralist or solidarist conceptions of humanitarian intervention: Bull and Vincent on humanitarian intervention', *Millennium: Journal of International Studies* 21(2).

Wheeler, Nicholas J. 2000, *Saving strangers: humanitarian intervention in international society*, Oxford: Oxford University Press.

White, Brian 2005, 'Diplomacy' in John Baylis and Steve Smith (eds), *The globalization of world politics*, 3rd edition, Oxford University Press.

White House, The 2002, *The national security strategy of the United States of America*, The White House.

Wieviorka, Michel 2004, 'The making of difference', *International Sociology* 19(3).

Wight, Martin 1966, 'Why is there no international theory?' in Herbert Butterfield and Martin Wight (eds), *Diplomatic investigations: essays in the theory of international politcs*, Sydney: Allen & Unwin.

Wight, Martin 1977, *Systems of states*, Leicester: Leicester University Press.

Wight, Martin 1978, *Power Politics*, 2nd edition, Hedley Bull and Carsten Holbraad (eds), Harmondsworth: Penguin Books.

Wight, Martin 1991, *International theory: the three traditions*, Gabriele Wight and Brian Porter (eds), Leicester: Leicester University Press.

Wiktorowicz, Quintan 2005, 'A genealogy of radical Islam', *Studies in Conflict and Terrorism*, 28(2): 75–97.

Williams, Marc 1994, *International economic organisations and the Third World*, London: Harvester Wheatsheaf.

Williams, Marc 1999, 'The World Trade Organisation, social movements and "democracy"' in A. Taylor and C. Thomas (eds), *Global trade and global social issues*, London: Routledge.

Williams, Marc 2005, 'Civil society and the world trading system', in D. Kelly and W. Grant (eds), *The politics of international trade: actors, issues, and regional dynamics*, London: Palgrave.

Williams, Michael C. 2005, *The realist tradition and the limits of international relations*, Cambridge: Cambridge University Press.

Williams, William Appleman 1962, *The tragedy of American diplomacy*, New York: Delta.

Wilson, Erin K. 2010, 'Beyond dualism: expanded understandings of religion and global justice,' *International studies quarterly* 54(3): 733–754.

Wilson, Peter 1998, 'The myth of the "first great debate"', *Review of International Studies*, Special Issue 24: 1–16.

Wilson, Woodrow 1918, 'Fourteen points speech', US Department of State, International Information Programs, available at http://usinfo.org/docs/democracy/51.htm.

Wiseman, Geoffrey 2004, 'Polylateralism' and new modes of global dialogue,' in Christer Jönsson and Richard Langhorne (eds), *Diplomacy vol. III: Problems and issues in contemporary diplomacy*, London: Sage.

Wiseman, Geoffrey 2005, 'Pax Americana: bumping into diplomatic culture', *International Studies Perspectives* 6 (4): 409–30.

Wiseman, Geoffrey 2011, 'Norms and diplomacy: the diplomatic underpinnings of multilateralism', in James P. Muldoon Jr et al., *The new dynamics of multilateralism: diplomacy, international organizations, and global governance*, Boulder, CO: Westview Press.

Wiuff Moe, Louise 2009 'Negotiating political legitimacy: the case of state formation in post conflict Somaliland', *Issues Paper 10 Centre for International Governance and Justice*, Camberra: ANU.

Wohlforth, W. C. 1993, *The elusive balance: power and perceptions during the Cold War*, Ithaca: Cornell University Press.

Wollstonecraft, Mary [1792] 1992, *A vindication of the rights of woman*, London: Penguin.

Woods, Ngaire 1999, 'Order, globalization and world politics', in A. Hurrell and N. Woods (eds), *Inequality, globalization and world politics*, Oxford: Oxford University Press.

Woods, Ngaire 2001, 'Making the IMF and the World Bank more accountable', *International Affairs* 77(1): 83–100.

Woods, Ngaire 2003, 'Order, justice, the IMF and the World Bank' in R. Foot, J. Gaddis and A. Hurrell (eds), *Order and justice in international relations*, Oxford: Oxford University Press.

Woods, Ngaire 2006, *The globalizers: the IMF, the World Bank and their borrowers*, Ithaca: Cornell University Press.

Woods, Ngaire and Lombardi, D. 2006' 'Uneven patterns of governance: how developing countries are represented in the IMF', *Review of International Political Economy* 13(3): 480–515.

World Bank 2009, *Annual report 2009*, Washington D.C.: World Bank.

World Bank 2010, *Global economic prospects 2010: crisis, finance, and growth*, Washington D.C.: World Bank.

World Commission on Environment and Development 1987, *Our common future*, Oxford: Oxford University Press.

World Economic Forum, 'Knowledge navigator', available at www.weforum.org.

World Resources Institute 2001, 'CO$_2$ emissions: CO$_2$ emissions per capita', *Earth trends: environmental information*, available at http://earthtrends.wri.org/searchable_db/index.php?theme=3&variable_ID=666&action=select_ countries.

World Social Forum 2002, World Social Forum Charter of Principles, available at www.forumsocialmundial.org.br/main.php?id_menu=4&cd_language=2.

World Trade Organization 2005, *World trade report 2005: trade, standards and the WTO*, available at www.wto.org/english/res_e/publications_e/wtr05_e.htm.

World Trade Organization 2010a, *International trade statistics 2010*, Geneva: WTO.

World Trade Organization 2010b, *World trade report 2010: trade in natural resources*, Geneva, available at www.wto.org/english/res_e/booksp_e/anrep_e/world_trade_report10_e.pdf.

World Watch Institute, 'Online feature: climate change: climate change resources', available at www.worldwatch.org/features/climate/resources/#7.

World Watch Institute, *State of the world 2005: redefining global security*, Washington: World Watch Institute.

Wynne, B. 1994, 'Scientific knowledge and the global environment' in M. Redclift and T. Benton (eds), *Social theory and the global environment*, London: Routledge.

Yanacopulosi, H. 2005, 'The strategies that bind: NGO coalitions and their influence', *Global Networks* 5(1).

Yergin, Daniel 1978, *Shattered peace: the origins of the Cold War and the national security state*, London: Andre Deutsch.

Young, Mitchell, Zuelow, Eric and Sturm, Andreas (eds) 2007, *Nationalism in a global era: the persistence of nations*, London: Routledge.

Young, Oran 1998, *Global governance: learning lessons from the environmental experience*. Cambridge, MA: MIT Press.

Zakaria, Fareed 2003, *The future of freedom: illiberal democracy at home and abroad*, New York: Norton Publishers.

Zalewski, Marysia and Parpart, Jane (eds) 1998, *The 'man question' in international relations*, Boulder: Westview Press.

Zalewski, Marysia and Parpart, Jane (eds), 2008, *Rethinking the man question: sex, gender and violence in international relations*, London: Zed Books.

Zaum, David 2007, *The sovereignty paradox: the norms and politics of international statebuilding*, Oxford: Oxford University Press.

Zolo, Danilo 2002, *Invoking humanity: war, law and global order*, trans. Federico and Gordon Poole, London: Continuum.

Zweifel, T. D. 2006, *International organizations and democracy*, Boulder: Lynne Rienner Publishers.

INDEX

11 September 2001 attacks, 162, 209, 248, 292, 394

Acharya, Amitav, 168
Adler, Emmanuel, 168
Adorno, Theodor, 68, 95
Afghanistan, 422
Albright, Madeline, 89
alliance building, 28
Alliance of Small Island States, 481
al-Qaeda, 209, 402–3, 407
    disaggregation of, 403
    origins and evolution of, 292, 403
Amin, Samir, 383
Amnesty International, 115
anarchy, 3, 4, 14, 37, 196
    and constructivism, 106–7
    cultures of, 107
    international anarchy, 39–41
    realist conception of, 44
    thick, 107
Anderson, Benedict, 153
Angell, Sir Norman, 11, 57, 155
Annan, Kofi, 381, 403–34, 437
Anti-Ballistic Missile Treaty, 174
anti-capitalist movement, 392
    chronology of, 393
    goals and tactics, 394
    significance of, 395
ANZUS, 286
APEC, 354
Archibugi, Daniele, 130
Aristotle, 110
Armitage, David, 144
arms control, 14, 56, 172–88
    and the Cold War, 288
    during the Cold War, 174–5
    cooperation on, 181
    definition, 173
    and disarmament, 176, 179
    export-control measures, 176
    and human rights, 180
    and IR theory, 181–2
    and nuclear weapons, 182–6
    in the post-Cold War, 175–9
    rationale for, 174
    small arms and conventional weapons,
        179–81
    treaties, 178–6
arms trade, 180

Aron, Raymond, 40, 269, 270, 271
Asad, Talal, 324
ASEAN Regional Forum, 167, 306
Ashley, Richard, 4, 31, 70, 96
Ashworth, Lucian, 11
assessments of creditworthiness, 362, 368
Australia
    Aboriginal peoples, 251, 253
    human rights, 448
    Immigration Restriction Act 1901, 452
    White Australia Policy, 452
Australia Group, 176
authority, 396
    and control, 145
    and culture, 252
    and power, 138
Ayson, Robert, 199–215

balance of power, 11, 36, 40, 108, 271
Ban Ki-moon, 437
Bank for International Settlements, 365, 366
banks, capital adequacy ratios, 365
Barnett, Michael, 168, 308
barriers to trade, 344, 352, 356
Basel Accord II, 368
Basel Committee on Banking Supervision, 366,
    369
Baudelaire, Charles, 94
Baudrillard, Jean, 92, 93
Beitz, Charles, 123, 124, 126
Bellah, Robert, 153
Bellamy, Alex, 168, 218–30
Ben Ali, Zine El Abidine, 331
Bentham, Jeremy, 3, 51, 443
Benton, Lauren, 252
Berger, Mark T., 372–84
Berlin Mandate, 479
Biddle, Stephen, 200
bin Laden, Osama, 209
Biological and Toxin Weapons Convention,
    175, 179
biological weapons, 179, 185
bipolar systems, 42, 260, 274
Bisley, Nick, 281–93
Bleiker, Roland, 91–101
Bodin, Jean, 138–9, 141
Boege, Volker, 423
Bolton, John, 306
Booth, Ken, 163, 168

Bourguiba, Habib, 330
Boutros-Ghali, Boutros, 262
Brahimi, Lakhdar, 418
Bretton Woods system, 28, 337, 351, 363–4
Brezhnev doctrine, 289
Brodie, Bernard, 164
Brown, Anne, 423
Brown, Chris, 3, 12, 248, 254
Brownlie, Ian, 431
Brundtland, Gro Harlem, 467
Brundtland Report, 465–6
Bull, Hedley, 11, 28, 120
    anarchy, 8, 247–8
    arms control, 173
    great powers, 274
    international society/system, 247
    methods of acquiring knowledge in IR, 11
Burke, Anthony, 98, 160–70
Burke, Edmund, 258–63
Bush, George H., 157
Bush, George W., 55, 186, 207, 227, 262, 411
Business Council on Sustainable
        Development, 315
Butterfield, Herbert, 9, 38
Buzan, Barry, 163

Caedel, Martin, 191
Cairns Group, 355
Calhoun, Craig, 326
Campbell, David, 93, 98, 146
Canberra Commission, 186
capital, movement of, 350, 363, 366
capitalism
    and climate change, 483
    critique of, 63–5
    and efficiency, 63
    liberal, 53
    popular, 314, 364
    rise of, 63
Caroline affair, 226–7
Carpenter, R. Charlie, 84
Carr, E.H., 11, 26
    Marxism, 67
    nationalism, 156
    realism, 7, 38, 39
Casanova, José, 326, 329
categorical imperative, 71, 122–5, 130
Centre for Global Governance, 316
Cesa, Marco, 268–79
Chandler, David, 418
change, 16
    constructivist understanding of, 111–18
    and great powers, 275–6
    and warfare, 212

chemical weapons, 179, 185
Chemical Weapons Convention, 165, 179
Chiaruzzi, Michele, 35–47
China, civil war, 284
Christianity, 137, 328
citizenship, 146
civil society, 318
civilisation, 251
Clark, Ian, 3, 248
class conflict, 65, 66
Clausewitz, Carl von, 164, 204, 205, 206, 208, 271
Clements, Kevin, 423
Climate Action Network, 319
climate change, 128, 475–85
    and Critical Theory, 483
    definition, 476
    and environmental justice, 468
    global politics of, 477–84
    marketisation of climate governance, 484
    and Marxism, 483
    organisation of negotiations on, 481
    role of knowledge and interests in, 483
    scientific consensus on, 476, 478
Club of Rome, 464
cluster munitions, 179, 227–9
    collateral damage, 228
    indiscriminate effects of, 227, 228
coercion, 139
Cohen, Robert, 434
Cohn, Carol, 169
Cold War, 281–93
    from 1945–53, 282–6
    from 1953–69, 286–7
    from 1969–85, 287–8
    from 1985–91, 288–9
    arms control, 174–5, 288
    arms race, 287
    and the avoidance of military
        conflict, 291
    and capitalist international relations, 291
    causes of, 290–1
    and the Chinese civil war, 284
    containment, 283–4
    definition, 282
    détente, 287–8
    diplomacy and, 260
    great powers after, 276–8
    ideological antagonism in, 282
    and IR, 290–1
    and Korea, 286
    legacy of, 292
    nuclear weapons and, 291
    and security, 282
    status of Berlin, 284, 286

colonialism, 383, 400
  see also European colonisation
Commission for Sustainable Development, 470
Communist Manifesto, 65, 66
communitarianism, 122, 396
communities
  epistemic, 483
  legal and cultural, 156
  and populations, 150
  security, 116–18, 168, 192
community, 31
comparative advantage, 351
Comprehensive (Nuclear) Test Ban Treaty, 165
Concert of Europe, 260, 272, 273, 274
conflict, 192
  ethnic conflict, 155
  management of, 181
  see also violence, war
conflict resolution, 117
Connolly, William, 94, 101, 325
Connor, Walker, 152
Constant, Benjamin, 53
constitutionalism, 383
constructivism, 13, 32, 33, 103–18
  'alter-casting', 114
  and arms control, 182
  balance of power, 108
  change in the international system, 111–18
  and the Cold War, 290
  and diplomacy, 266
  and global economic institutions, 340
  and global finance, 369
  and identity, 104–11, 114–16
  international conflict and security
      communities, 116–18
  making meaning, 105
  methodology, 104
  rules and norms, 106
  security, 168
  war, 108
containment, 283–4
control, and authority, 145
Convention against Torture, 224
Convention on Biological Diversity, 466
Convention on Cluster Munitions, 179, 227
Convention on Conventional Weapons,
    principle of discrimination, 224
Convention on the Elimination of
    All Forms of discrimination against
    Women, 442
Convention on the Protection of Civilians, 223
Convention Relating to the Status of Refugees,
    453–5, 459
conventional weapons, 173

cooperation, international, 55, 389–90, 469
  and climate change, 477
  and globalisation, 395
  and justice, 126
  regional economic, 56
Coordinating Committee for Multilateral Export
    Controls, 176
Copenhagen Accord, 468
Corporation for Foreign Bondholders, 362
Correlates of War Project, 214
cosmopolitanism, 71, 123, 396–7
  criticism of, 396
  and humanitarianism, 429
  and justice, 121
  and social contract theory, 130
  and sovereignty, 146
counter-hegemonic political movements,
    73, 74
Cox, Robert, 13, 8, 30, 69, 71, 73–4, 470
  mutually assured destruction, 174
Crawford, Neta C., 109–10
credit ratings agencies, 314, 368
Creveld, Martin van, 207, 209
critical theory, 13, 8, 13, 15, 62–75
  and climate change, 483
  Frankfurt School of Critical Theory,
      68–71
  and global economic institutions, 340
  and global environmental politics, global,
      470–1
  nationalism, 156
  security, 168–70
  and state-building, 420
Cuban missile crisis, 162, 164, 286
culture, 73
  and legal authority, 252
  and nationalism, 150
  patriarchal, 81
current affairs, 2
customary international law, 236–7
  binding nature of, 237
  and humanitarian intervention, 431
  and the UN General Assembly, 304

Davies, David, 5
Davies, Sara E., 450–61
Davis, Mike, 373
death of God, 94, 95
decolonisation, 154, 253, 286
  diplomacy and, 261
  effect of, 261
  and refugees, 456
deconstruction, 98–9, 169
democracies, foreign relations among, 193

democracy
  consumer, 93
  cosmopolitan, 28, 129–30, 317, 396–7
  democratic peace theory, 54–5
  global, 396
  spread of, 13, 419
democratic peace theory, 54–5, 193
  influence on US foreign policy, 55
Deng, Francis, 434
dependency theory, 380
deregulation, 389–90, 392
Derrida, Jacques, 99
d'Escoto Brockmann, Father Miguel, 437
deterrence, 164, 207, 260
  see also nuclear deterrence
Deutsch, Karl, 168
developing countries, 374–9, 392–6
  and climate change negotiations, 468
  and environmental justice, 468
  refugees in, 456
development, 372–84
  concept of, 378
  definition, 382
  evaluation of, 378
  and inequality, 376–5, 377, 382
  neoliberal conception of, 381
  policy formation for, 380
  and poverty, 375, 377, 382
  and power, 376
  purpose and targets of, 382
  relational approach to, 375
development assistance, 58
Devetak, Richard, 1–19, 62–75, 98, 134–47
Dickinson, G. Lowes, 39
difference, 31
Dinnen, Sinclair, 420
diplomacy, 14, 41, 256–67
  bilateral, 259
  and capacity-building, 264
  definitions of, 257
  diplomacy of violence, 208
  diplomatic immunity, 262–3
  evolution of, 258–63
  future of, 263
  of the great powers, 260
  and the Gulf War, 158
  hyphenated diplomats, 265
  modern, 259, 264
  multilateral, 259
  and nationalism, 154
  and power, 270
  pre-modern diplomacy, 258–9
  public, 266
  and representation and lobbying, 264

  resident ambassadors, 259
  and the study of IR, 265–6
  transformational, 264–5
  trends in, 264–5
  Vienna Convention on Diplomatic Relations, 262
disarmament, 143–4, 166, 183
  and arms control, 176, 179
  and security, 183–5
discrimination, 77, 78
disintermediation, 366, 367
domestic politics, 15
double effect, doctrine of, 224–5
Doyle, Michael, 54–5
Drago Doctrine, 363
Drago, Luis, 363
Duarte, Sergio, 183–5
Dunant, Henry, 428
Dunn, John, 135
Dunne, Tim, 245
Dupont, Alan, 165

Earth Summit, 466
East Timor, 161
Eckersley, Robyn, 462–74
economic growth and environmental quality, 465
economic rationalism, 390
economic sanctions, humanitarian consequences of, 433
economics
  Keynesian, 363, 365
  laissez-faire, 351
  neoliberal, 73
Elshtain, Jean Bethke, 88
emancipation, 13, 97, 154
embedded journalism, 202
Emergency Committee for Humanitarian Response, 430
empiricism, 69, 324
Engels, Friedrich, 64
English School of IR, 8, 28, 244–6
Enlightenment, 10, 49, 94, 251, 443
Enloe, Cynthia, 80
environment movement, 464
environmental legislation, 464
environmental politics, global, 462–74
  actors in, 463
  and critical theory, 470–1
  and ecological security, 466–7
  environmental efficiency of production, 466
  and environmental justice, 467–8
  and neoliberal institutionalism, 469
  in the post-Cold War context, 466–8

environmental politics, global (*cont.*)
   and realism, 469
   research on, 464
   rise of the environment as a global political
      issues, 464–6
   and sustainable development, 464–6
   theories of, 469–71
environmental regulation, 466
environmental treaties or regimes, 469
epistemic communities, 483
epistemology, 24, 97
equality, 122–5
equity, intra- and inter-generational, 465
Erikson, Stein Sundstol, 420
ethics, 31, 447
   of conviction, 45
   of war, 218–30
   global, 127–9
   of responsibility, 36, 44–6
ethnic cleansing, 156, 434
Euromarkets, 364
Europe, medieval, 137
Europe, 'velvet' revolutions in, 289
European colonisation, 243–55
   and development of law, 251
   impact of, 245
   racial hierarchy and, 251
   'standard of civilisation', 251
European Community Humanitarian Aid Office,
   430
European Union, 114, 117, 277
   Common Agricultural Policy, 352
   External Action Service, 266
Evans, Gareth, 434

failed states, 145, 207, 415, 416–17
Falk, Richard, 57, 396
Falkner, Robert, 473
feminism, 13, 32, 76–90
   challenge to masculine bias, 79–80
   critical, 88–9
   critique of, 87–8
   differences between sex and gender, 81–4
   goals of feminist IR theory, 79
   identity-based, 87
   IR agenda, 77–9
   and the language of international
      politics, 82
   liberal, 86–8
   maternal and cultural, 88
   postmodern, 88–9
   security, 168–70
   theories of IR, 86–9
   war, 169–70

feudalism, 137–8
Financial Stability Board, 369
Financial Stability Forum, 368
fixed exchange rate, 364
foreign aid, 58
Forsberg, Randall, 110
Foucault, Michel, 94, 99
Foundation for International Environmental
   Law and Development, 481
foundationalism, 31–2
Framework Convention on Climate Change,
   466, 478, 481
   Ad Hoc Working Groups, 481
   Alliance of Small Island States, 481
   Conference of the Parties, 481
   negotiation of, 481
   participation of non-state actors, 482
   Secretariat, 481
   Subsidiary Body on Implementation, 481
   Subsidiary Body on Science and Technology,
      481
France
   Declaration of the Rights of Man, 50, 153, 443
   Revolution, 50, 204
Frankfurt School of Critical Theory, 68–71
free trade, 50, 350–2
free trade agreements, 239, 354
freedom, 53
Fukuyama, Francis, 60, 420

'G' forums, 391
G8, 390
G20, 341, 358, 369, 391
G77 + China, 481
game theory, 211
Gandhi, Mahatma, 110
Gat, Azar, 208
Geertz, Clifford, 152
Gellner, Ernest, 152
gender
   inequality, 77, 78, 84–5
   roles, 84
   and sex, 81–4
genealogy, 98–9
General Agreement on Tariffs and Trade, 239,
   338
Geneva Conventions, 109, 165, 232, 305, 428
   as customary law, 223
   gaps in, 223
   and insurgency, 224
   jus in bello, 222, 223
   principle of discrimination, 224
   principle of proportionality, 224
   protection of non-combatants, 224

Genocide Convention, 224
George, Jim, 9, 22–34, 62–75, 96
Germany, 472
Ghani, Asraf, 420
Ghannoushi, Rashid, 330
Giddens, Anthony, 388
Gill, Stephen, 73, 383
Gillard, Prime Minister Julia, 81
Gilpin, Robert, 276
Global Climate Coalition, 315
global economic institutions, 15, 115, 336–47, 390
    conditionalities imposed by, 314
    and constructivism, 340
    and critical theory, 340
    democratic deficit in, 346
    and the global economy, 340–5
    legitimacy and democratic credentials of,
       345–7
    and liberalism, 340
    membership, 345
    and national authorities, 346
    perspectives on, 339–40
    rationales for, 380
    and realism, 340
    transparency, 346
    voting mechanisms in, 345, 346
global economy
    and global economic institutions, 340–5
    and global governance, 337–40
    politicisation of, 395
global finance, 360–70
    from 1900–45, 362–3
    from 1946–71, 363–4
    from 1972–81, 364–5
    from 1982–92, 365–6
    from 1993–2000, 366–8
    from 2001, 368–9
    architecture of the system, 362, 364, 366–8
    and constructivism, 369
    credit booms and liquidity busts, 368–9
    credit ratings agencies, 368
    data-sharing and surveillance and, 368
    debt crises, 365–6
    and financial socialisation, 363
    and Gramscian critical theory, 369
    international regimes for, 361–2
    international regulation of, 363
    in IR, 361
    'over-lending', 364–5
    privatisation of, 365
    and realism, 369
    risk management models, 369
    self-regulation, 368
    study of, 369–70

Global Financial Crisis, 57, 337, 339, 346, 389, 392
    explanations for, 357
    and the G20, 341, 358
    government stimulus packages, 357, 358
    impact on developing countries, 343
    and protectionism, 344
    recovery from, 357–8
    and trade, 356–7
global governance, 14–17, 29, 114, 247
    and climate change, 477–8
    and the global economy, 337–40
    and non-state actors, 115
    and the WTO, 344
global justice
    in practice, 129
    theories of, 119–31
    see also justice
global trade, 348–59
    agricultural trade, 355
    deficiencies in the system, 352–4
    definitions of terms, 349–50
    and free trade, 350–2
    and the Global Financial Crisis, 356–7
    most favoured nation status, 351
    national treatment rules, 351
    in natural resources, 358
    opposition to a regime of, 350
    preferential trade arrangements, 354–5
    and protectionism, 352
    reform of the system, 355–6, 358–9
    rules of origin arrangements, 356
    see also trade
globalisation, 14–17, 43, 338, 386–97
    actors in, 388–9
    and the anti-capitalist movement, 392, 393, 394
    breadth of the connections and ramifications
       of, 389
    critique of, 396–7
    definition, 15, 387–92
    and diplomacy, 264
    economic, 470
    effects on states, 145
    explanations of, 387
    and foreign and domestic policy, 389
    hyperglobalisationism, 145, 311, 387, 390
    and justice, 124–5
    and neoliberalism, 74, 339
    political implications of, 388
    and postmodernity, 93
    sceptical explanation of, 387–8
    and sovereignty, 145
    and terrorism, 407
    theory of international politics, 311
    transformationalism, 388–7

'gold-dollar' standard, 364
Goldblatt, David, 15
Goodman, James, 310–21
Gorbachev, Mikhail, 175, 289
Gore, Vice President Al, 467
governance
    authoritarian, 399, 446
    and globalisation, 396
    and identity, 114–16
    see also global governance
Gramsci, Antonio, 30, 66, 72–3
Gramscian critical theory, 30, 71–4, 369
    see also critical theory
Gray, Colin, 164
great powers, 14, 42, 268–79
    after the Cold War, 276–8
    attributes of, 277
    current situation, 277
    definition, 269–71
    historical perspective, 271–3
    importance of non-material resources, 277
    and international change, 275–6
    and international order, 274–5
    in IR theory, 273–6
    and nuclear proliferation, 277
    spheres of influence, 273, 274
    superpowers, 273
Greeks, 258
Greenfeld, Liah, 152
Gregg, Tom, 129
Grotius, Hugo, 6, 8, 232
Group of 77, 261
groupthink syndrome, 196
guerilla warfare, 213

Habermas, Jürgen, 69–70, 71, 94, 125
Hagmann, Tobias, 423
Hague Conferences, 428
Halliday, Fred, 254, 317, 321
HALO, 228
Halperin, Morton, 174
Hanson, Marianne, 172–88
Harper, Stephen, 451
Harvey, David, 92
Hayek, Friedrich, 59
Hegel, G. W. F., 66, 94
hegemony, 30, 36, 72, 73, 248, 351
    and climate change, 482
    and environmental politics, global, 469
hegemonic stability theory, 351
hegemonic war theory, 275
Held, David, 15, 130, 146, 396
Helsinki Final Act, 287
Herz, John, 164

hierarchy, 3
history, progressivist concept of, 65
Hobbes, Thomas, 7, 38, 141
    Leviathan, 139–40
    state of nature, 7, 38, 139
    state of war, 140
    state system, 467
Hobsbawm, Eric, 151
Hobson, J. A., 53
Hoehne, Markus V., 423
Hoffman, Mark, 5
Holsti, K. J., 5
hooks, bell, 87
Horkheimer, Max, 68
Howard, Prime Minister John, 451
human rights, 154, 440–9
    current conception of, 444
    focus on the individual, 445
    future of, 447–9
    historical development of the idea, 442–3
    and international law, 239
    and natural law, 443
    nature of, 446, 448
    promotion of, 448
    rules and norms, 249
    and security, 162
    and state sovereignty, 434
    and the UN Charter, 441
    UN human rights instruments, 442
humanitarian intervention, 213, 416, 426–39
    history of, 431–3
    rationale for, 431
    and the responsibility to protect, 433–8
humanitarianism, 16, 182, 431
    and arms control, 180
    and cosmopolitanism, 429
    magnitude of, 429–30
    origins of, 427–30
Hurd, Elizabeth Shakman, 322–34
Hurd, Ian, 296–309
Huyssen, Andreas, 92
hyperglobalisationism, 145, 387, 390

idealism, 66
identity, 30–1
    changing, 114
    and constructivism, 104–11
    and governance, 114–16
    group identity, 113, 326
    inter-subjective, 105
    national identity, 113, 152, 153
    and the Other, 105
    state identity, 113, 114
    and terrorism, 407

ideology, 73
Ignatieff, Michael, 158
Ikenberry, G. John, 56
imperialism, 250–3, 363, 376
    critique of, 53
    rise of, 63
independence, declarations of, 144–5
indigenous peoples, 155, 251, 253
Industrial Revolution, 63
inequality, 372–84
    and development, 376–5, 377, 382
    relational approach to, 375
    scale and character of, 373–5, 378
information, and state-building, 142
Infrastructure Recovery and Assets Platform, 343
institutionalism, 8, 55–6
institutions, gendered, 89
insurgencies, 400
intellectual property rights, 354
InterAction, 430
interdependence, 42, 290, 410
    economic, 339, 350
    and justice, 124–5
interests
    and identity, 105
    and knowledge, 69–70
    and power, 40
    see also national interests
Intergovernmental Panel on Climate Change, 468, 470
Intermediate Nuclear Forces Treaty, 174, 179
International Arms Trade Treaty, 180
International Atomic Energy Agency, 182, 234
International Bank for Reconstruction and Development: see World Bank
International Chamber of Commerce, 314
International Code of Conduct against Missile Proliferation, 176
International Commission on Intervention and State Sovereignty, 433
International Commission on Nuclear Non-proliferation and Disarmament, 167, 182, 187
International Committee of the Red Cross/ Crescent, 111, 222, 428
    mission statement, 429
International Council for Voluntary Action, 430
International Court of Justice, 26, 233, 234, 235, 300
    Legality of Nuclear Weapons case, 224
    North Sea Continental Shelf case, 237
    Reparations for Injuries Suffered in the Service of the United Nations, 304
International Covenant on Civil and Political Rights, 239, 445

International Covenant on Economic, Social and Cultural Rights, 239, 441, 446
International Covenant on the Rights of the Child, 442
International Criminal Court, 222, 234, 305, 433
    Nicaragua v. The United States of America case, 226
International Development Association, 342
international environmental law, 240
International Finance Corporation, 342
international human rights law, 233, 444
international human rights regime, 318, 444
    moral foundations of, 328
international humanitarian law, 109, 181, 239, 428
    documents of, 223
international institutions, 56
    and constructivism, 104–11
    participation in, 130
International Labor Organization, 305
international law, 43, 164, 191, 231–41, 328
    during the 19th century, 251
    controversies in, 240–1
    and customary international law, 236–7
    definitions of a refugee, 453
    development of, 233
    enforcement mechanisms, 233
    and general principles of law, 237
    and human rights, 239
    institutions of, 233–4
    and international environmental law, 240
    and international humanitarian law, 239
    and international trade law, 239
    and judicial decisions and teachings, 237–8
    law of the sea, 239
    major areas of, 238
    non-binding instruments, 238
    and non-state actors, 240
    and soft law, 238
    sources of, 234–8
    and sovereignty, 142
    treaties, 235–6
    and use of force, 238–9, 240
International Law Commission, 234
International Monetary Fund, 314, 338, 341–2
    Articles of Agreement, 363
    assessments of creditworthiness, 115
    Compensatory Financing Facility, 341
    contested policies of, 392
    Extended Fund Facilities, 341
    and global environmental politics, global, 470
    impact on recipient countries, 341
    Poverty Reduction Strategy Paper, 380, 383
    Special Drawing Rights, 115, 365
    stabilising role of, 342

International Monetary Fund (*cont.*)
    Stand-by Arrangements, 341
    structural adjustment programs, 341, 366
    Supplemental Reserve Facility, 341
    voting mechanisms in, 367
international networks, 117
international non-government organisations,
        316–20
    advocacy groups, 317, 318
    agenda-setting function, 318–19
    autonomy of, 320
    expansion of, 316
    and human rights, 318
    influence of, 317–20
    international agency of, 317–18
    political status of, 318–20
    relations with corporations and
            intergovernmental institutions, 319
    role in international relations, 320
    transnationalisation, 316–17
    see also non-government organisations
international order, 39
    global, 396
    great powers' contribution to, 244, 274–5, 278
international organisations, 15, 43, 114
    cooperation among, 367
    independence of, 308
    limits on their power, 306, 308
international political economy, 361
international politics, 3
    definition, 2–4
    freedom from ethical prescriptions, 38
    language of, 82
international regimes, 56
International Relations, 1–12
    changing issues in, 14–17
    and the Cold War, 290–1
    'critical turn' in, 12–14, 16, 32
    definition, 1–4
    English School, 8, 28
    'first great debate' in, 11, 25
    'Great Divide' in, 3–4, 12–14
    journals, 6
    mainstream theory, 26–9
    origins and agendas of the discipline, 1–19
    professional associations, 6
    relevance of, 100
    'second great debate' in, 11–12
    teaching and research in, 6
    theory and practice of, 12–17
    'third great debate' in, 12, 97–9
    traditions of thought in, 6, 7–9
international relations, 22–34
    and arms, 181–2

critical theories, 33, 68–74
    and diplomacy, 265–6
    era of critical diversity in, 29–33
    and feminism, 77
    Frankfurt School of Critical Theory, 68–71
    Gramscian critical theory, 30, 71–4, 369
    and justice, 120–1
    Marx and Marxism in, 67–8
    nations and nationalism in, 155–7
    need for, 23–4
    ontology, epistemology and science in, 24
    and religion, 323–5, 326
    in the US, 57
    and war, 181–2, 190
international society, 28, 155, 182, 243–55
    concept of, 244–6
    European origins of, 250
    and the global economic institutions, 345
    institutions of, 248
    limits of, 249–50
    mutual expectations and reciprocity, 247
    mutual recognition, 246
    and nationalism, 152–5
    nature of, 246–9
    non-governmental organisations, 248, 249
    norms of, 249
    rules and norms, 247, 248
international system, 13, 67, 247
    anarchical, 196
    change in, 111–18
    crisis of legitimacy, 441
    Hobbesian, 467
    and sovereignty, 144
international trade law, 129, 239, 350–2
International Tribunal for the Law of the Sea,
        234
International Women's Year, 83
intersubjectivity, 247
investment protection, 315–16
Iran, 331–2
Iraq, 422
Italy, Renaissance diplomacy, 258, 259

Jackson, Patrick Thaddeus, 103–18
James, Alan, 141
James, Jeffrey, 381
Jameson, Fredric, 92
Japan, post-war state-building in, 415–16
Jarvis, Darryl, 99
Jeffrey, Renée, 9
Johnson, J. T., 220
Jones, Joshua S., 103–18
Jones, Roy, 245
jus ad bellum, 165, 219–22

criteria for, 221
preemptive self-defence, 225–7
right intention, 220
jus in bello, 165, 222–5
and cluster bombs, 227–9
doctrine of double effect, 224–5
just war, 219–22
for a just cause, 220–1
last resort, 221
procedural requirements, 221–2
proportionality of ends, 221, 224
prudential criteria, 221
justice
and cosmopolitan democracy, 129–30
cross-border obligations, 125
and the 'difference principle', 126
distributive justice, 58, 130
domestic, 125
environmental justice, 467–8
and equality, 122–5
global justice, 119–31
and interdependence, 124–5
and international relations, 120–1
and legitimacy of a war, 220
liberal justice, 126–9
objective justice, 220
procedural justice, 10, 120
requirements of, 123–4
social justice, 59
subjective justice, 220
substantive justice, 120
see also global justice

Kaempf, Sebastian, 202–3
Kaldor, Mary, 16, 209
Kant, Immanuel, 8, 10, 24–5, 50, 71, 122–5, 130
Kantian liberalism, 58
Katzenstein, Peter, 168, 328
Keal, Paul, 243–55
Keene, Edward, 250, 251
Kelton, Maryanne, 348–59
Kennan, George, 45, 260, 261, 276, 283–4
Kennedy, Paul, 275
Keohane, Robert, 55, 56, 406–7
Khan, A. Q., 183
Khomeini, Ayatollah, 332
Kilcullen, David, 212–14
Kissinger, Henry, 186, 287
knowledge
gendered, 89
kinds of, 70
knowledge constitutive interests, 69–70
and power, 30, 31, 96, 483
sources of, 80

Kohn, Hans, 156
Korean War, 286
Kosovo, post-conflict state-building in, 416
Kratochwil, Friedrich, 104
Kymkicka, Will, 254
Kyoto Protocol, 315, 319, 468, 479
Buenos Aires Plan of Action, 480
Clean Development Mechanism, 484
commitments, 479
common but differentiated responsibilities,
468, 471
implementation and enforcement, 480
instruments, 479
Marrakesh Accords, 480
the US and, 471, 480

Lake, David, 55
landmines, 179, 180, 224
Langlois, Anthony J., 440–9
Lapid, Yosef, 5, 12
law of the sea, 239
laws of war, 108, 222, 428
League of Nations, 10, 26, 53, 154, 260
Lee-Koo, Katrina, 76–90
Lenin, V. I., 66, 67
Levy, Jack S., 196, 204, 208, 214
liberal internationalism, 29, 36, 49, 181
liberalism, 7–8, 11, 48–61
classical, 52, 58
and the Cold War, 291
commercial, 56–7
contemporary theory, 54–9
critiques of, 28, 60
democratic peace theory, 54–5
economic, 350
embedded, 57, 338, 351, 355, 363
empirical theory, 54–8
and global economic institutions, 340
historical–political context of, 49–54
and human rights, 441
institutionalism, 55–6
and international non-government
organisations, 318
Kantian liberalism, 24–5
Keynesian, 390
and law, 13
and nationalism, 155
normative theory, 58–9
political economy, 63
and realism, 7
security concepts, 167
social, 52
and war, 13, 26–7, 208
limits to growth, 464–6

Linklater, Andrew, 8, 71, 125, 130, 245
  ethics, 254
  globalisation, 30–1, 146
  nationalism, 156
  sovereignty, 146
Lippman, Walter, 163
List, Friedrich, 353
Locke, John, 8, 49, 50
Lockhart, Clare, 420
Luttwak, Edward, 164
Lyotard, Jean-François, 92, 93

Machiavelli, Niccolò, 6, 7, 37–8, 45, 259
Magritte, René, 97
Maine, Sir Henry, 10
Mann, Michael, 143
Marcuse, Herbert, 68
market civilisation, 73, 74
markets, 66
  access to, 129, 314, 350, 356
  emerging, 367
  free, 50, 52
Marshall Plan, 284
Marx, Karl, 63–5
Marxism, 8, 13, 29, 53, 62–75
  and climate change, 483
  historical and intellectual context,
    63–5
  as historical materialism, 65–7
  in IR, 67–8
  justification of war, 158
  nature of the state and states-system, 67
  and state-building, 143
  theoretical framework of, 65
McDonald, Matt, 169
McGrew, Anthony, 15, 396
McNamara, Robert, 162, 164
Mearsheimer, John, 42, 44, 46, 164
medieval Europe, 137, 138
mercantilism, 63, 352
Mexico
  debt crisis, 367
  Zapatista movement, 392
Middle East, Western interference in, 407
Migdal, Joel, 418
migrants
  definition, 452
  illegal migrants, 452
migration, 450–61
  causes of, 452
  control of, 451–3
  definition, 452
military technology, 200, 205, 212
  digital media, 202–3

Mill, John Stuart, 8, 52
  On Liberty, 52
Millennium Development Goals, 343, 377,
    379–81, 468
  advocates of, 382–3
  criticism of, 383
  goals of, 383
  and poverty, 381–3
  rationale for, 380–1
Millennium Ecosystem Assessment, 468
Miller, David, 122
Miller, J. D. B., 135
minority peoples, protection of, 155
Missile Technology Control Regime, 176
modernisation theory, 376–7
Moe, Wiuff, 423
Moellendorf, Darrell, 126
Mohanty, Chandra, 87
Monroe Doctrine, 363
Montesquieu, 44
Montreal Protocol, 478
Morada, Noel, 435–6
moral standards, universal, 445
Morgenthau, Hans, 27–8, 37, 39–40
  national security, 163
  political morality, 45
  principles of political realism, 40
  prudence, 45
  Vietnam War, 46
Mount, Gavin, 148–59
Multilateral Agreement on Investment, 319, 392
multilateral economic institutions: *see* global
    economic institutions
Multilateral Investment Guarantee Agency, 342
multilateralism, 10, 354, 395
multinational corporations, 311–16, 463
  autonomy of, 320, 341
  credit ratings agencies, 314
  dominance of, 392
  finance multinationals, 312, 314
  influence of, 314–16
  international agency of, 313
  manufacturing multinationals, 312–13
  political status of, 314–16
  power of, 311, 313–14
  rationale for and motivation of, 312
  research and development funding, 312
  role in international relations, 320
  strategic lawsuits against public participation,
    315
  and tax avoidance, 313, 314
  as transnational actors, 316
  transnationalisation, 312–13
multipolar system, 42, 274

mutually assured destruction, 174
Myrdal, Alva, 183

Naijmabadi, Afsaneh, 333
Nandy, Ashis, 375
Narmada Valley, India, 376, 377
national identity
    and civil religion, 153
    language and, 154
national interests, 7, 149
    and war, 191, 208
nationalism, 14, 122, 148–59, 289
    civic, 156
    critique of, 123
    definition, 149–51
    economic, 350
    ethnic, 15, 156
    formal expression of, 150
    ideology of, 143
    in IR, 155–7
    and modern states, 152–5
    and modernity, 152
    schools of, 152–3
nationality, definition, 149–51
nations, 148–59
    definition, 149–51
    in IR, 155–7
    and states, 150, 156, 157
    subjective qualities of, 151
natural law, 443
neo-Gramscianism, 30, 71–4
neo-Marxism, 30
neoliberal institutionalism, 55–6, 420
    and climate change, 482
    and global environmental politics,
        global, 469
neoliberalism, 12, 28, 70, 390
    and development, 381
    disciplinary, 383
    and globalisaion, 339, 390, 397
    institutionalisation of, 395
    and sovereignty, 145
neorealism, 12, 28, 30, 41–2, 43
    and diplomacy, 265
    and neoliberalism, 53, 55–6, 70
    and religion, 324
New START agreement, 183
New World Order, 157–8
Newell, Peter, 475–85
Niebuhr, Reinhold, 38
Nietzche, Friedrich, 31, 94, 95, 99
Nixon, President Richard, 353
Nolan, Anna, 423
Non-Aligned Movement, 261

non-governmental organisations, 15, 310–21,
        392–6, 463
    and global governance, 115
    and globalisation, 395
    humanitarian work, 430
    international, 316–20
    power of, 470
    women's, 83
Non-Proliferation of Nuclear Weapons Treaty,
        165, 166
non-state actors, 15, 143, 310–21
    and multilateralism, 395
    role of culture and ideology, 396
North American Free Trade Agreement, 392
    investment protection provisions, 315
North Atlantic Treaty Organization, 284
North Korean nuclear weapons program, 298
North–South divide, 355, 383, 458
nuclear deterrence, 162, 174, 183, 184
nuclear non-proliferation regime, 186–7
Nuclear Non-Proliferation Treaty, 175, 179,
        182–3, 185
    Review Conference, 187
Nuclear Suppliers Group, 176
nuclear weapons, 182–6
    and the Cold War, 291
    disarmament, 185
number of, 176
Nussbaum, Martha, 122

Obama, President Barack, 166, 183, 411
    and the Kyoto Protocol, 471
    multilateral diplomacy, 262
OECD Principles for Good International
        Engagement in Fragile States, 423–4
Ohmae, Kenichi, 387
Olson, William, 11
ontology, 24, 71
Onuf, Nicholas, 104, 106
Organization for Security and Co-operation in
        Europe, 167
Organization of the Petroleum Exporting
        Countries, 365, 481
orientalism, 252
Orwell, George, 151
Ottawa Convention, 165, 179, 180
ozone regime, 478

pacta sunt servanda principle, 236
Paine, Thomas, 50
Paris, Roland, 415, 421, 423
Partial Nuclear Test Ban Treaty, 174
Peace of Westphalia, 142, 250, 272
peacebuilding organisations, 117

Permanent Court of International Justice, 10
Perraton, Jonathon, 15
Pettman, Jan Jindy, 79
philosophy of science, 24
Pinochet, Augusto, 113
piracy, 240
Pogge, Thomas, 123, 124, 125, 126, 129
    Millennium Development Goals, 381
political communities, inclusionary, 13
political ecology, global, 470–1, 472, 473
political economy, 63
political obligation, theory of, 139
politics
    autonomy of, 37
    and religion, 328
    and war, 208–10
positivism, 12, 25, 69, 95, 220
    legal, 444
    and religion, 324
    and scientific IR, 25
postmodernism, 15, 31, 71, 91–101
    debates about, 99–100
    definition, 92
    as a new historical period, 92–3
    and representation, 158
    and sovereignty, 146
    as a way of understanding modernity, 93–7
poststructuralism, 98
poverty, 372–84
    alleviation of, 343
    definition, 375
    and development, 375, 377, 382
    and environmental justice, 468
    'Make Poverty History' campaign, 394
    and Millennium Development Goals, 381–3
    relational approach to, 375
    representation of, 380
    scale and character of, 373–5, 378
    in slum or squatter communities, 373
Poverty Reduction Strategy Paper, 380, 383
Powell, Colin, 211
power, 4, 39, 418
    and authority, 138
    and the capacity to wage war, 204
    components of, 269
    and development, 376
    distribution of, 269
    hegemonic war theory, 275
    and interests, 40
    and knowledge, 30, 31, 96, 483
    long cycle theory, 275
    military power, 270
    a morality of, 38
    multidimensional nature of, 270

power cycle theory, 275
power politics, 7, 37
    power transition theory, 275
    and security, 163
    soft power, 73, 278
    and terrorism, 401, 406
    Western economic and cultural power, 407
powers
    revisionist, 39, 42
    status quo, 39
    see also great powers
preemptive self-defence, 225–7
privatisation, 390
'problem-solving' theory, 13, 30, 69
Program of Action to Prevent, Combat and
        Eradicate the Illicit Trade in Small Arms
        and Light Weapons, 180
protectionism, 344, 352
    see also barriers to trade
prudence, 44–6, 221
public goods, 352, 382

raison d'état, 36, 45, 139
Ranke, Leopold von, 272
rationalism, 8, 69, 79
Rawls, John, 58, 59, 124
    justice, 121, 126
    social contract, 124
Reagan, President Ronald, 288
realism, 7, 8, 35–47
    anarchy, 44
    classical, 27, 37–9, 43, 208
    and the Cold War, 290
    critiques of, 28
    emphasis on history, 37
    and global economic institutions, 340
    and global environmental politics, global,
        469, 472
    and global finance, 369
    and international anarchy, 39–41
    international use of violence, 43
    and the Iraq War, 46
    justification of war, 157
    and law, 13
    and liberalism, 7
    and mercantilism, 352
    offensive, 44
    ontology and epistemology of, 24
    origin of the tradition, 37–42
    political morality, 45
    prudence and responsibility, 44–6
    security, 163, 181
    the state, 43–4
    structural, 27, 41–2, 43, 324

theory and practice of, 43
use of violence, 26–7
and war, 13
reason of state, 36, 45, 139
refugee law
origins of, 453–4
purposes of, 454–5
rights of, 454
refugees, 450–61
access to education and health care, 459
causes of, 454
current situation, 458–60
definition, 452, 456, 459
distribution of, 455–8
fear of political persecution, 453, 455
forcibly displaced persons, 455–6, 457
need for political solutions, 460
numbers of, 456
and people smuggling, 460
procedures for the recognition of refugee
status, 454
protection complementary to that of the
Convention, 459
in 'protracted situations', 455, 459
resettlement of, 453, 460
rights of, 454
regime theory, 482, 483
regional trade agreements, 354
Reilly, Benjamin, 421
religion, 105, 139, 322–34
assumptions about, 324, 328
fundamentalist interpretations of, 15, 409
and human rights, 447
and international relations, 323–5
marginalisation of, 326
and politics, 325, 326, 327, 328
and secularism, 327, 332–3
and terrorism, 401, 409–10
and war, 209
representation, politics of, 97–8, 158, 170
responsibility to protect, 213, 263, 427, 433–8
pillars for implementation of, 437
Reus-Smit, Chris, 10
revolution, 154, 206
American, 50, 144, 153, 443
French, 50, 153, 204
in the Middle East, 333
military, 142, 143
Russian, 453
'velvet' revolutions, 289
revolutionalism, 8
Ricardo, David, 63, 351
Rice, Condoleezza, 88, 89
Richardson, J. L., 48–61

Richardson, Louise, 407
Richelieu, Cardinal, 259
rights, 445–6
civil and political rights, 239, 441, 445
economic, social and cultural rights, 239, 441, 446
group rights, 446
see also human rights
Rio Declaration on Environment and
Development, 240, 465
Rodrik, Dani, 353
rogue states, 162
Roman hegemony, 258, 271, 402, 410
Romanticism, and the Enlightenment, 94
Rosecrance, Richard, 56
Rosenau, James, 15
Rosenberg, Justin, 68
Rothwell, Donald R., 231–41
Rousseau, Jean-Jacques, 14, 38
Ruddick, Sara, 88
Ruggie, John, 57
rule of law, 246
rules and norms, 247, 248
constitutive, 106
regulative, 106
Rupert, Mark, 74
Russia
debt crisis, 367
Revolution, 453
see also Soviet Union

Said, Edward, 32, 252
Saint Pierre, Abbé, 10
SALT agreements, 174
Scheaefer, Peter, 420
Schelling, Thomas, 174, 208, 210, 211
Schmitt, Carl, 37
Schwarzenberger, Georg, 270
science, 24
Scott, Shirley V., 236
Seabrooke, Leonard, 360–70
Searle, John R., 112
SEATO, 286
secularism, 322–34
definition, 325
and European history, 329
foundation principle of modern politics, 323
history of, 325–6
politics of in the Middle East and North
Africa, 329–33
power and authority of, 323
and religion, 327, 332–3
secularist settlement, 325, 327, 333
varieties of, 327, 328, 332
and world politics, 326–9

securitisation, 366
security, 14, 160–70
  and climate change, 476
  collective security, 11, 164, 167
  common security, 167, 181
  comprehensive security, 161, 167
  constructivist approaches, 168
  contested nature of, 161
  cooperative security, 167
  crises, 161–3
  critical approaches, 168–70
  definition, 163
  and development, 377
  and disarmament, 183–5
  ecological security, 466–7
  economic security, 162
  extended security, 165
  feminist approaches, 168–70
  food security, 353, 373
  human security, 161, 167
  liberal approaches, 165–8
  national security, 163, 406
  and nuclear weapons, 166–7
  and power, 163
  realist approaches, 164–5, 181
  security dilemma, 4, 44, 164, 174
  theories and concepts of, 163–70
security communities, 116–18, 168, 192
  security dilemma, 4, 44, 164, 174
Selden, John, 232
self-determination, 74, 144, 151, 245, 292
  in Eastern Europe, 283
  of indigenous peoples, 253
  a universal right, 154
self-radicalisation, 409
Sen, Amartya, 381
Senese, Paul, 194
Seven Nation Initiative, 187
sex and gender, 81–4
Shapcott, Richard, 119–31
Sharp, Paul, 256–67
Sheehan, Cindy, 88
Shue, Henry, 125
Sil, Rudra, 168
Singer, Peter, 124, 127–9
Skinner, Quentin, 137
Sklair, Leslie, 312
Skocpol, Theda, 143
Slaughter, Steven, 386–97
small arms and light weapons, 179–81
Smith, Adam, 50, 63, 351
Smith, Anthony, 152
Smith, Steve, 12, 95
sociability, 191–3

social systems, stability in, 112
soft law, 238
soft power, 73, 278
Solomon Islands, Regional Assistance Mission
    to, 419, 420, 422
Solomon, Scott, 74
Soroush, Abdulkarim, 333
Southeast Asia, debt crisis, 367
sovereignty, 43, 113, 135, 139
  abuse of, 431
  concept of, 138–42
  contingent nature of, 434
  critique of, 123
  and freedom to resort to war, 191
  and the global economic institutions, 346
  and globalisation, 145
  and international law, 142
  and international society, 249
  and justice, 125
  meaning of, 138–41
  origins of the idea of, 141–2
  popular, 153
  principle of, 141, 144
  and war, 191–3
  and weapons, 173
Soviet Union, 53
  collapse of, 276, 290
  foreign policy reform, 288
  support for independence movements, 286, 288
  and the US, 174
  see also Russia
'Spaceship Earth', 465
Spruyt, Hendrik, 144
St Augustine, 38
stagflation, 364–5
'standard of civilisation', 251
START agreements, 174
state-building, post-conflict, 414–24
  agenda of, 418–19
  assumptions about, 417, 421
  criticism of, 420–2
  future of, 422–4
  hybrid approaches to, 423
  impacts of, 422
  OECD principles for international
      engagement in fragile states, 423–4
  and peacebuilding, 421
  politics of, 419–20, 421
  and war-making, 142–5
states
  administrative capabilities, 143
  definition, 135–6
  disarming competitors, 143–4
  distribution of capabilities across, 42

evolution of the system, 271
failed states, 145, 207, 415, 416–17
freedom to resort to war, 191, 192
functions of, 43, 72, 98, 136, 191, 418
future of the sovereign state, 145–6
and globalisation, 390
as international citizens, 129
and identity, 451
and immigrants, 451
interactions among, 116
legitimacy of, 136, 248, 470
modern, 134–47
monopoly over the use of force, 16, 43, 135,
    206, 406
monopoly rights of, 145
and nationalism, 152–5
and nations, 150, 156, 157
nature of, 41, 67
as political societies, 136
proliferation of, 261
radicalisation of, 261
realist conception of, 43–4
right to self-defence, 220, 238, 240
right to conduct its internal affairs without
    interference, 244
rise of the modern, 142–3
rogue states, 162, 211
role of culture and ideology, 72
socialisation of, 261
solidarism among, 249
state-building as war making, 142–5
territoriality, 43
treaties between, 235
use of terrorism, 400
stereotypes, 252
Stiglitz, Joseph, 355
stock markets, participation in, 364
Strategic Arms Limitation Treaty, 287
Strategic Offensive Reductions Treaty, 179
strategic studies, 164
Strayer, Joseph, 137–8
structural adjustment programs, 341, 342, 366, 380
Suganami, Hidemi, 189–98, 245
sustainable development, 343, 464–6

tax havens, 368
taxation, and state-building, 143
Taylor, Charles, 329
terrorism, 16, 162, 206, 209, 227, 248, 398–412
    complexity of, 405
    contemporary, 404–5, 406
    and conventional military forces, 406
    definition, 399–401
    and dominance of external powers, 407

emotive nature of the issue, 401
features of, 400–1, 405–6
globalisation of, 402, 406–9
growth of, 405
history of, 402
and insurgency, 400
Islamist, 43
misperceptions about, 409–10
motivation of, 400, 403, 410
and power, 401
psychology of, 410
and religion, 401, 409–10
roots in society, 401, 405
and self-radicalisation, 409
study of, 401–3
war on, 185
Teschke, Benno, 68, 137, 138, 143
Thakur, Ramesh, 433
Thatcher, Margaret, 89
theory, need for, 23–4
think tanks, 6, 314
Third World, 374
Thompson, William R., 196
Thomson, Janice, 143
Thucydides, 6, 7, 9, 37, 275
Tickner, J. Ann, 79, 82–4, 89, 168
    security, 163
Tilly, Charles, 136, 142, 143
Todorov, Tzvetan, 151
trade
    barriers to, 344, 352, 356
    comparative advantage, 351
    free trade agreements, 354
    preferential trade arrangements, 354–5
    regional trade agreements, 354
    and security, 350
    see also global trade
tragedy of the commons, 469
transnational actors, 16
transnational corporations: see multinational
    corporations
transnational networks, 16
transnational organisations, 43
transparency, 93, 346
treaties, 165, 174, 178–6, 233, 235–6
    declarations, 236
    negotiation of, 236
    principle of pacta sunt servanda, 236
    ratification of, 236
    registration with the UN Secretariat, 236
    reservations, 236
    titles of, 236
Treaty of Westphalia, 232, 259, 326
Truman Doctrine, 284

Truman, President Harry S, 283, 379
Tschirgi, Necla, 421
Tunisia, 330–1
    Islamic Association, 331
    Islamic Tendency Movement, 330, 331

unilateralism, 211, 213
unipolarity, 44, 262, 276
United Nations, 53, 165, 233, 260, 286, 296–309
    as an actor in world politics, 304–5
    Advisory Committee on Administrative and
        Budgetary Questions, 303
    allocation of costs among members, 303
    Charter: see United Nations Charter
    Children's Fund, 429
    Climate Change Convention, 315, 319
    Commission on the Status of Women, 78
    Conference on Environment and
        Development, 315, 465, 478
    Conference on the Human Environment, 465
    Conference on the Illicit Traffic in SALW, 180
    conferences, 305
    Declaration on the rights of Indigenous
        Peoples, 155
    definition of terrorism, 399
    deliberative functions, 305
    Development Programme, 167, 318–19, 430
    distribution of powers in, 300
    Economic and Social Council, 83, 299, 316
    Environment Programme, 465, 468, 470
    Environmental Security Council (proposed),
        467
    foreign policy, 105
    as a forum, 305
    Framework Convention on Climate Change,
        466, 478, 481
    functions of, 304–8
    General Assembly, 301, 302–4, 305
    Global Compact, 315
    High Commissioner for Refugees, 429, 453
    High Level Panel on Threats, Challenges and
        Change, 162, 437
    Human Development Programme, 83
    human rights instruments, 442
    Inter-Agency Standing Committee, 430
    limitations on its activities, 298
    Mine Action Programme, 228
    Monetary and Financial Conference, 338
    obligations arising from membership, 298
    Office for the Coordination of Humanitarian
        Affairs, 429, 430
    organs of, 299–304
    peacekeeping operations, 56, 115, 302, 303,
        306, 416
    resolutions of, 233, 304
    as a resource, 306–7
    responsibility to protect, 437
    the Secretariat, 307
    Security Council: see United Nations Security
        Council
    Trusteeship Council, 300
    Universal Declaration of Human Rights, 304,
        441, 444
    World Food Programme, 430
United Nations Charter, 297–8, 432
    human rights and, 441
    international law of war, 219, 225–6, 232
    Preamble, 156, 165–6
    status of, 297
    types of clauses in, 297
United Nations Convention on the Law of the
    Sea, 239
United Nations Security Council, 83, 184, 301,
    307, 432–3
    authority to intervene, 220, 239, 300, 307
    and Iraq, 302
    membership, 302
    responsibility of, 233, 301–2
Universal Declaration of Human Rights, 304,
    441, 444
universalism, 126–30, 445–7, 449
US
    alliances in the Asia-Pacific region, 287
    Declaration of Independence, 50, 144, 153,
        443
    economic and military strength, 472
    and environmental treaties, 471
    Export Enhancement Programme, 353
    financial crisis, 356
    financial socialisation, 366, 368
    fixed exchange rate, 353, 364
    foreign aid policy, 379
    foreign policy, 28, 55
    and global environmental politics, global,
        471–3
    hegemonic power, 56
    hegemony, 211, 262, 279, 351, 361
    invasion of Iraq, 219, 240
    justification for the Gulf War, 157
    and the Kyoto Protocol, 471, 480
    legitimation crisis, 73
    Marshall Plan, 284
    military power, 276
    military technology, 205
    Monroe Doctrine, 363
    multilateralism, 354
    National Security Strategy, 225
    political system, 472

private voluntary humanitarian agencies, 429

protectionism, 353

role in international organisations, 367

shareholder protection legislation, 369

and the Soviet Union, 174

'subprime' markets, 369

trans-Pacific partnership agreement, 354

Truman Doctrine, 284

unilateralism, 56, 213, 240, 262, 353

use of cluster munitions, 227, 229

value of the dollar, 367

and Vietnam, 287

and the WTO, 354

utilitarianism, 51, 58, 124

utopianism, 11

values

'Asian' values, 447

and justice, 120

liberal values, 445

moral value, 45

Vasquez, John, 194

Vattel, Emer de, 8, 141

Vattimo, Gianni, 92

Vienna Convention, 478

Vienna Convention on Diplomatic Relations, 261, 262–3

Vienna Convention on the Law of Treaties, 235

Vincent, R. J., 246

Vinci, Anthony, 210

violence

against civilian targets, 400

and norms, 109–10

for political aims, 400

purpose of for terrorists, 400

as a tool of statecraft, 164

against women, 78

see also conflict, war

Virilio, Paul, 93

Vitoria, Francisco de, 220, 221

Voluntary Organisations in Cooperation in Emergencies, 430

Vulnerability Finance Facility, 343

Waldock, Sir Humphrey, 226

Walesa, Lech, 289

Walker, R. B. J., 9, 146

Wallerstein, Immanuel, 67–8

Walt, Stephen, 46, 162, 164

Walter, Benjamin, 68

Waltz, Kenneth, 3, 36

Marxism, 67

multipolar systems, 274–5

neorealism, 41–2

theory of international politics, 41–2

war, 7

Walzer, Michael, 122, 225

war, 1–2, 14, 37

actions and inactions leading to, 197

asymmetric, 211

capacity to wage, 204

causes of, 189–98

chance occurrences as causes of, 195

changing character of, 199–215

civil war, 200, 204, 206, 215

as a clash of wills, 210–11

and constructivism, 108

contributory causes, 190, 194–7

contributory negligence leading to, 197

control of media during, 202–3

'costless' war, 202, 203

development of military technology, 200

diversity of, 200–4

and embedded journalism, 202

ethics and laws of, 218–30

in European history, 142

fog of war, 205

gendered politics of, 86

guerilla warfare, 16, 213

hegemonic war, 276

identity as a cause of, 209

impact of, 190

insensitive acts leading to, 197

inside sovereign states, 192

insurgencies, 200, 206, 211, 224

'just war', 219–22

justification of, 157, 219

large-scale, 211–15

laws of, 108, 152, 165, 222–5, 428

military and economic costs of, 174

moral restriction on the use of force, 224

necessary causes, 190, 193–4

new international norms for, 213

and non-state actors, 209

and organised social groups, 192

as organised violence, 206–7

and politics, 208–10

preemptive, 192, 225–7

prevention of, 11, 18, 197, 220

preventive, 192

reasons for limited nature of, 109

reckless acts leading to, 197

regular causal paths to, 190, 194

revolutionary, 206

self-defence, 192, 225–7

and sociability, 191–3

and social and political change, 212

war (*cont.*)
    and sovereignty, 191–3
    and state-building, 142–5
    symmetrical, 210
    technology in contemporary war, 212
    unintended consequences of, 205
    as violence, 204–6
    war-conducive mechanisms of, 195–6
war on terror, 185, 203, 212, 403, 411
Warsaw Pact, 284, 353
Washington Consensus, 339, 379–81, 391
    criticism of, 380
Wassenaar Arrangement on Export Controls for
        Conventional Arms and Dual-Use Goods,
        176
weapons of mass destruction, 93, 173, 201, 213,
        240
Weber, Eugen, 154
Weber, Heloise, 372–84
Weber, Martin, 62–75
Weber, Max, 45, 135, 136, 151
Weiss, Thomas G., 426–39
Wendt, Alexander, 14, 33, 104, 106
Whaites, Alan, 418
White Australia Policy, 452
Wight, Martin, 7, 37, 254
    great powers, 270
    international politics, 3
    international society, 248
    Marxism, 67
    revolutionism, 191
    traditions of thought in IR, 8
Williams, Marc, 336–47
Williamson, John, 339
Wilson, Peter, 11, 26
Wilson, President Woodrow, 11, 53, 154, 208
Wiseman, Geoffrey, 256–67
Wolfers, Arnold, 163
Wollstonecraft, Mary, 51, 86
women
    discrimination, 77
    disadvantage in international politics, 77
impact of global challenges on, 78–9
issues disproportionately affecting, 78
subjects of IR study, 80
World Bank, 338, 342–4
    approach to development, 342
    Basic Needs strategy, 342
    and global environmental politics, global, 470
    humanitarian work, 430
    Infrastructure Recovery and Assets Platform,
        343
    Poverty Reduction Strategy Paper,
        380, 383
    Vulnerability Finance Facility, 343
World Commission on Environment and
        Development, 465–6
World Economic Forum, 314, 393
world order
    just, 126–30
    neoliberal, 93
world politics, 3
World Social Forum, 319–20, 381, 393, 394
world-system, 68
World Trade Organization, 56, 234, 239, 305,
        314, 344–5, 358
    contribution to global governance, 344
    Development Round, 319
    Dispute Settlement Understanding, 344
    Doha Round, 380
    as a forum, 344
    and global environmental politics, global,
        470
    Millennium Round, 319, 349
    Seattle meeting, 353, 392, 395
World War I
    diplomacy and, 260
    and IR theory, 10
    reasons for, 26

Yalta Conference, 283

Zangger Committee, 176